AF348724

MOTIVATING SELF AND OTHERS

This book describes the essential nature of human motivation by integrating the best ideas and evidence from motivational and evolutionary science. In doing so, the authors explain how the cultivation of goal–life alignment and "thriving with social purpose" motivational patterns can inspire optimal functioning and enhance life meaning. Readers are provided with a comprehensive framework for guiding research and intervention efforts along with motivational principles designed to summarize the major themes in effective efforts to motivate yourself and those you wish to help or encourage. Special emphasis is placed on the importance of life meaning in empowering our motivational systems and protecting us from downward spirals of disappointment and suffering. Compelling evidence is provided to support the view that social purpose is as fundamental as self-interest in human motivational systems. The authors also focus on the catalytic role of social purpose in enabling humans to soar above all other species.

MARTIN E. FORD is Professor and Senior Associate Dean in the College of Education and Human Development at George Mason University. During his thirteen years at Stanford he received early career awards from two APA divisions (7 and 15) and created Motivational Systems Theory, an offshoot of his father's Living Systems Framework and the foundation for his work as an organizational leader.

PEYTON R. SMITH developed and delivered leadership training worldwide for a decade prior to his retirement and after more than thirty years of engineering and sales management, primarily at Digital Equipment Corporation and Microsoft Corporation. His evidence-based leadership and executive coaching programs have been recognized with numerous awards.

MOTIVATING SELF AND OTHERS

Thriving with Social Purpose, Life Meaning, and the Pursuit of Core Personal Goals

MARTIN E. FORD

George Mason University

PEYTON R. SMITH

CAMBRIDGE
UNIVERSITY PRESS

CAMBRIDGE
UNIVERSITY PRESS

University Printing House, Cambridge CB2 8BS, United Kingdom

One Liberty Plaza, 20th Floor, New York, NY 10006, USA

477 Williamstown Road, Port Melbourne, VIC 3207, Australia

314–321, 3rd Floor, Plot 3, Splendor Forum, Jasola District Centre,
New Delhi – 110025, India

79 Anson Road, #06–04/06, Singapore 079906

Cambridge University Press is part of the University of Cambridge.

It furthers the University's mission by disseminating knowledge in the pursuit of
education, learning, and research at the highest international levels of excellence.

www.cambridge.org
Information on this title: www.cambridge.org/9781108491655
DOI: 10.1017/9781108869164

© Martin E. Ford and Peyton R. Smith 2021

This publication is in copyright. Subject to statutory exception
and to the provisions of relevant collective licensing agreements,
no reproduction of any part may take place without the written
permission of Cambridge University Press.

First published 2021

A catalogue record for this publication is available from the British Library.

ISBN 978-1-108-49165-5 Hardback
ISBN 978-1-108-79878-5 Paperback

Cambridge University Press has no responsibility for the persistence or accuracy of
URLs for external or third-party internet websites referred to in this publication
and does not guarantee that any content on such websites is, or will remain,
accurate or appropriate.

*To our wives, children, and grandchildren, who bring social purpose
and abundant life meaning to our lives each and every day*

Contents

Tables

Preface

Our motivation for writing this book was to share with the world what we have learned in our scholarly and professional lives about the nature of humanity and how each of us can become a better person. For the past decade we have immersed ourselves in the latest scientific advances in psychology and human development in an effort to construct a practical, evidence-based understanding of how to help people increase their capacity for self-direction and develop patterns of optimal functioning. Our ongoing quest is based on a strategy that we call the "Big Bet" – a term often used by budding entrepreneurial teams to caption their proposition to potential investors. Our Big Bet is the hypothesis that

Scientific understanding of what makes humans naturally successful, coupled with	+	*Self-understanding* of your core personal goals and learned motivational patterns, can provide you with	→	The insights and tools needed to increase your *effectiveness, well-being, and life meaning*.

Essentially, our bet is that if you make an effort to learn the fundamental science underlying motivation and optimal functioning, and then apply that knowledge to your own personal goals and life circumstances, you will increase your capacity for self-direction as well as your ability to lead – and to help others lead – a more successful and meaningful life.

The Big Bet comes with a big payoff. As you begin to look at life through the lens of your core personal goals, you will see how you can better align your daily activities with what really matters to you. And like an expert physician, your ability to diagnose and find solutions to complex motivational problems will become enriched and more intuitive as you learn about all the human qualities that make successful goal pursuit possible. That in turn will make extraordinary achievements seem more attainable.

xiii

Adversity and uncertainty will seem less overwhelming because you will always be able to find a way to restore a sense of direction and a resilient belief in your capacity to overcome obstacles and challenges.

And that's not the only payoff. Our work is also guided by the observation that when people invest themselves in activities that are aligned with their core personal goals, and those goals are infused with *social purpose* and pursued with a *thriving* motivational orientation, they experience greater effectiveness, an enhanced sense of life meaning, and improved health outcomes. The evidence for these positive outcomes is provocative and compelling, with far-reaching implications not only for individuals striving to improve their own lives but also for leaders and helping professionals.

In short, *goal–life alignment* and *thriving with social purpose* are the keys to leading a productive and fulfilling life. The positive thoughts and feelings those motivational achievements spark are good for us in so many ways. The energy and creativity they unleash fuel our ability to accomplish great things, grow in response to new challenges, and change for the better.

Merging Science, Practice, and Big Ideas

Our immersion experience has been rather unique in that it has involved an intellectually intense partnership between a professor and a corporate executive. By teaming up, we have been able to accomplish things that we would never have been able to achieve acting alone, including the development of the Thriving with Social Purpose (TSP) Theory of Motivation and Optimal Functioning that is at the heart of this book (M. Ford & Smith, 2007), along with the "spin-off" TSP Theory of Life Meaning that we introduce in Chapter 7.

Our collaborative effort to bridge science and practice has focused on the ambitious task of synthesizing the best theoretical and empirical work available across a broad range of specializations related to motivation and optimal functioning. Our aspirations thus go beyond describing the next "big idea" for enhancing human motivation. We are more like puzzle enthusiasts trying to identify the best ideas (and evidence) that science has to offer so that we can, slowly but surely, connect the puzzle pieces related to motivation and optimal functioning in a unified way. In short, ours is a *systems* approach that is based on a strong belief that, regardless of how exciting a particular "big idea" might be, it will have limited value if it is not embedded within an accessible framework that encompasses the natural unity of the whole person-in-context.

Throughout *Motivating Self and Others*, we have adopted a strategy in which we move rather quickly in each chapter to the "bottom line" of what contemporary science has to offer and to our integration of those ideas and evidence. Along the way we point to some of the scholarly contributions that provide the best in-depth coverage of each topic so that our sources are clear and readers can dig deeper into areas that seem particularly intriguing. By "standing on the shoulders of giants," we hope that the scientific underpinnings for our ideas are evident, while also putting us in a position to scan across the independent contributions of scholars working on related topics. This vantage point has enabled us to work on the critical but previously neglected task of integrating those contributions (and some of our own!) into a clear overall picture.

The Value of Integrative Science

Emphasizing synthesis (in addition to analysis) is generally not a winning strategy for basic researchers, most of whom are required to publish (or perish) in journals where scientific advancement is associated with specialized knowledge and expertise. The value of integrative science becomes more evident when efforts are made to communicate scientific knowledge to broader audiences who are primarily concerned with solving complex, real-world problems. For example, back in the early 1980s, one of us (Ford) was assigned to teach a course on Motivational Processes in Education at a leading research university (Stanford). In his first attempt at covering the relevant territory, Ford followed a standard survey of theories approach. Students learned about goal setting, self-efficacy, learned helplessness, self-determination, and a variety of other "big ideas" in the field of human motivation. But it was clear that they were not getting a sense of how these ideas fit together, even though the leading scholars in these areas were all true "giants."

This experience inspired Ford to try to synthesize the core substantive themes in more than thirty different motivation theories in psychology, education, and business into an accessible, unified framework. This led to the creation of Motivational Systems Theory (M. Ford, 1992), an overarching framework guided not only by the best theory and research available on human motivation but also by a comprehensive model of human behavior and development developed by his father called the Living Systems Framework (D. Ford, 1987/2019; M. Ford & D. Ford, 1987/ 2019). The availability of this integrative resource paid immediate dividends not only on the research front but also in class, as students could now see the "forest for the trees." They were better equipped to appreciate the significance of the advances they were reading about in scientific journals and the potential interconnections between different specialized topics in the field. They were also better able to apply the relevant science to practical motivational problems they were dealing with in their jobs and in their personal lives.

What You Will Learn

By grounding *Motivating Self and Others* in a broad systems framework, we believe that we can provide you with these same kinds of insights and practical wisdom. We start our journey into the science of human motivation by explaining how nature has equipped you with several mechanisms that make self-direction possible. These mechanisms evolved because they helped us survive and thrive in challenging life circumstances, not only by strengthening our individual capabilities but also by enhancing our capacity to live and work in cooperative groups with shared interests.

We then help you discover the "leaders within you" – your *core personal goals* that represent the strongest and most authentic motivational forces in your repertoire of "possible selves" (Markus & Nurius, 1986). Our basic premise is that life is all about the ongoing process of imagining goal possibilities and then selectively pursuing those opportunities most likely to enhance our *survival with well-being* (Damasio, 2003).

> *The first secret to success, happiness, and life meaning is to know your core personal goals and to make life choices that ensure you will be able to pursue those goals on a regular basis.*

To help you appreciate this insight, we provide you with the most recent thinking from evolutionary biology and motivational psychology while also introducing you to the Assessment of Personal Goals (APG), an online tool designed to help you identify your most important sources of motivation and life meaning (https://apg.gmu.edu).

In the next chapter of *Motivating Self and Others*, we explain how personal goals naturally work together with emotions and personal agency beliefs as a leadership team. In doing so, we emphasize how thoughts and feelings that are grounded in current realities but also filled with hope for the future create a fertile psychological climate for imagining possible goal options while also providing sound advice about which goal thoughts should be "in the driver's seat" at any given point in time. We also clarify that goal attainment requires not only strong leadership from *motivational headquarters* but also a responsive environment and effective support from the *instrumental troops* (e.g., goal-relevant knowledge and skills) responsible for carrying out the leaders' directives.

We then use Motivational Systems Theory as a foundation for constructing the TSP Theory of Motivation and Optimal Functioning. TSP is what results when each of the elements in motivational headquarters is effectively "amplified" while also incorporating concerns that go beyond ourselves, thereby increasing our capacity for personal growth, teamwork, and effective leadership of others. Of particular interest is the fact that *life meaning* naturally flows from the qualities associated with thriving motivational patterns that have been infused with social purpose. These qualities include active engagement in goal pursuit, resilience in the face of obstacles and setbacks, and a genuine interest in helping others attain *their* core personal goals. These insights led us to construct the TSP Theory of Life Meaning, which is intended to both illuminate and demystify one of the most important yet least understood aspects of optimal human functioning.

Although TSP represents human motivation at its best, it is within the grasp of every reader. That is because *we are wired for TSP*, with an evolved infrastructure of prosocial motives and social-cognitive skills that support a wide variety of impressive – and at times inspirational – human achievements. Although our self-enhancing goal pursuits can be quite compelling, we are also naturally designed to formulate and pursue goals focused on helping others, and doing so often makes us feel good – sometimes to our surprise! That is a profoundly important dynamic from a motivational perspective. It means that, absent pathology, social purpose is something we are born with. That is why we spend so much time engaging in culturally and developmentally enriching activities, such as connecting with friends and family, sharing knowledge and expertise, serving in supportive leadership roles, and relieving others' distress and suffering. Indeed, social purpose is what caused humans to soar above all other species.

> *TSP thus represents a second secret to success, happiness, and life meaning – a life-affirming pathway for simultaneously promoting the well-being of self and others.*

In the final two chapters, we shift our focus from the task of constructing a framework of ideas and evidence to the practical question of how you can apply insights from the science of human motivation and optimal functioning to increase goal–life alignment and TSP in self and others. To accomplish this objective, we offer seven broad principles for motivating self and others and explain how they can be used to address the kinds of motivational questions and dilemmas that people often face in their daily lives.

We also provide readers with a concise "toolbox" of figures, formulas, and frameworks designed to help readers remember the key ideas in our book and envision how they might be used for their practical purposes.

It is our Big Bet that by helping readers gain a working understanding of what it takes to motivate self and others, we can empower people to make a difference in their own lives and in the lives of others. The odds are now in our favor, as progress has accelerated on many fronts, including

- a deeper understanding of the evolutionary roots underlying the human capacity for *self-direction* and behavior change
- increased awareness that it is difficult to sustain motivation and life meaning unless *core personal goals* are aligned with life circumstances
- greater appreciation of the powerful and ubiquitous role that *emotions* play in activating goals, guiding our decisions, and energizing our thoughts and actions
- major advances in understanding the nature and coordination of *conscious and nonconscious thought processes* in the pursuit of personal goals
- groundbreaking research on *brain plasticity*, revealing that, under the proper conditions, significant changes in brain and behavioral functioning are far more common and achievable than previously imagined
- progress in identifying the evolutionary, neural, and biochemical processes underlying *survival with well-being* (Damasio, 2003), with many of those processes oriented toward cooperation, helping, and social bonding
- growing awareness that *social purpose* and *social intelligence* are central to virtually all forms of human activity, and thus "a life well lived" results from effective efforts to motivate self *and* others

Our ideas and conclusions have also been significantly influenced by the burgeoning fields of positive psychology (Seligman & Csikszentmihalyi, 2000; Snyder & Lopez, 2002, 2009) and positive organizational scholarship (e.g., Cameron et al., 2003) – two domains in which the scientific study of optimal functioning is flourishing. In each of these fields, the human capacity for self-direction and self-renewal and the benefits of developing that capacity are central organizing themes – just as they are in our TSP frameworks. However, rather than focusing on qualities that are assumed to be "positive" regardless of an individual's circumstances, we offer a more *contextual* view that recognizes that "psychological traits and processes are not inherently positive or negative; instead, whether psychological characteristics promote or undermine well-being depends on the context in which they operate" (McNulty & Fincham, 2012, p. 101).

As part of this contextual view, we introduce a new concept in this book called *equipoise*, which captures the idea that effective goal pursuit is a dynamic process that requires not only doing the "right things" but also an appropriate degree of psychological and behavioral flexibility so that ongoing adjustments can be made when there is a need to adapt to changing circumstances. Equipoise helps explain, for example, why, across many different categories of occupational success, a "giving" motivational orientation (what we will call "social purpose") is characteristic of both the best performers and – when equipoise is lost – the worst performers (Grant, 2013).

We invite you to join us as we share what we have learned about the science of motivation and optimal functioning. Our Big Bet is that by doing so, you will enhance both your own and others' ability to lead a life filled with meaningful accomplishments and an enduring sense of well-being.

CHAPTER I

Motivation and Optimal Functioning
Making the Most of Our Natural Gifts

> There's so much to discover about being human. The more we know,
> the better equipped we are to build the lives we want.
>
> – Barbara L. Fredrickson, *Positivity*

> Fish gotta' swim, birds gotta' fly.
>
> – lyricist Oscar Hammerstein

When we see fish swim and birds fly, it seems perfectly natural. After all, that's what they are designed to do. So, what comes naturally to members of our species? Although there are many answers to this question, they all boil down to a fundamental, overarching design principle (Damasio, 2003; Klinger & Cox, 2004):

Humans evolved to formulate and selectively pursue goals that, when accomplished, would enhance their survival and well-being, both individually and collectively.

That design principle has made it possible for humanity to accumulate cultural solutions and innovations at a breathtaking pace. As a result, we can live virtually anywhere on the planet. We can imagine possibilities that do not yet exist and adapt to unfamiliar circumstances. We can invent new capabilities (like flying!) and share what we have learned with others.

Like all species, we are creatures of habit. Yet we are also capable of profound change. Indeed, because of the way we are designed, it is possible for *every individual person* to envision a better future for themselves and to take action to try to make those goal thoughts a reality. In other words, we are all designed to be *self-directed*. Within each and every one of us is the power to improve – or even transform – our own lives and the lives of those around us.

Surprisingly, during much of the twentieth century, scientists studying motivation were not particularly interested in what makes us self-directed or how to strengthen that natural capability. Instead, mainstream theory and research focused on how our actions are influenced by external forces (like rewards and punishments) and biological mandates (like drives and impulses). Goal images and ideas were not only ignored as potential targets of research; they were regarded as unimportant and "unscientific" (D. Ford, 1987/2019; Seligman et al., 2013).

This mechanistic (machine-like) view of humans inhibited progress in understanding the natural gifts that enable us to be self-directed. Fortunately, things gradually began to change mid-century as *systems* models focused on goal pursuit began to emerge (e.g., G. Miller et al., 1960) and *humanistic* scholars introduced compelling theories emphasizing concepts like "self-actualization" and the "fully functioning person" (Maslow, 1954, 1962; Rogers, 1961). Eventually, by the 1980s, all mainstream theories of motivation were using terms that acknowledged the central role of self-direction in human behavior and development – terms like *goal setting, self-efficacy, self-determination, internal locus of control,* and *personal striving,* to name just a few (M. Ford, 1992).

Nevertheless, it has been challenging for both psychologists and the general public to escape the historical vestiges of a way of thinking that emphasized external direction over self-direction. It is easy, for example, to think of goal setting as something that bosses and parents and teachers do for us. Emotions can be dismissed as transient and unsystematic motivational forces. Even beliefs about personal control and competence can be treated as little more than a psychological facade, with the external influences that shape those beliefs still regarded as the underlying causes of our actions.

In short, it is not enough to superficially acknowledge that thoughts and feelings are part of the motivational landscape. Each of us must have genuine respect for self-direction as a basic, unifying design principle to truly understand our potential for motivating self and others. Yes, we are of course all influenced a great deal by forces outside of our control. That too is part of how we are designed. But when we look at the way our species evolved over the eons, it is clear that life is all about *imagining goal possibilities* and then *selectively pursuing those opportunities most likely to enhance our "survival with well-being"* (Damasio, 2003). That is the central organizing force in human behavior and development (Klinger & Cox, 2004; Seligman et al., 2013).

The Difference between Functioning and Optimal Functioning

There are many things we can do to strengthen and enrich motivation. That is the key to transforming ordinary lives into extraordinary lives. Yet, when we look at the basics of human functioning, it is clear that motivational processes are always active at some level. We can't stop our minds from generating goal images and ideas. We can't stop ourselves from having thoughts and feelings that influence what goals we pursue. Even when our minds are wandering and we are not actively pursuing any particular goal, motivationally relevant thoughts and feelings continue to flow (as when we are daydreaming, reflecting on recent events, or worrying about life's uncertainties). The most we can do is to try to calm down the mind's natural inclination to evaluate and emotionally respond to things we perceive and think about. Indeed, that is the key skill that "mindfulness meditation" experts seek to cultivate in themselves and their students (Goyal et al., 2014). By diminishing the strength of the "spark before the flame" (an apt metaphor from traditional Buddhist literature), those who have mastered this skill can quickly dismiss evaluative thoughts that might otherwise lead to mental commotion and worry.

The example of the "motivated meditator" makes it clear that, when we consider how the human mind is naturally designed, the question isn't how to turn someone's motivation "on" or "off." Rather, the question is, among all of the possibilities that cross our minds, why we choose to pursue some goals (with varying degrees of frequency, effort, and persistence) and not others. And can we use our capacity for self-direction to make different choices – *better* choices, with better outcomes for ourselves and others? In other words, can we go beyond ordinary functioning to something closer to *optimal functioning*? Or, to use the lingo we will introduce later in this book, can we go from merely "getting by" to *thriving with social purpose*?

Motivation is, of course, not the only pathway to self-improvement or for helping others with their goal pursuits. As we will explain in some detail in Chapter 5, optimal human functioning can also be promoted by developing knowledge and skills, by enhancing biological health and fitness, and by increasing available opportunities and resources. Nevertheless, because motivation plays a leadership role in directing, organizing, and regulating goal-directed activity, it is often the most powerful and efficient pathway for developing human potential. Indeed, studies of world-class experts and performers have repeatedly shown that the highest levels of achievement and creativity are most closely associated not with precocious talent or extraordinary intelligence but with motivational qualities such as passionate interest, a sense of personal mission or life purpose, high levels of energy and persistence, and a strong and resilient sense of self-confidence and courage (Bronk, 2014; Damon, 2008; Dweck, 2006; Snyder & Lopez, 2002, 2009). Without the invigorating and sustaining power of these personal leadership qualities, cultivation of other elements of the person–environment system may be of little consequence. Imagine, for example, spending years developing the knowledge and skills needed to succeed in a career that doesn't really interest you or devoting much of your adult life to trying to fit in with a social network that ultimately leaves you feeling empty and unfulfilled.

In contrast, increased motivation for a particular kind of goal pursuit encourages us to take action to create the conditions needed to attain those goals – like seeking out new capabilities or searching for the right "fit" in our personal and professional relationships. Motivation focuses our attention, energizes our thoughts and actions, and keeps us going when obstacles and shortcomings get in the way. In simple terms, if motivation is sufficiently strong, it can transform the entire system. That is why this book highlights the challenge of "motivating self and others." Motivation is the key to making your life a *better* life – a life filled with purpose, fulfillment, and meaning.

What Is Motivation?

In this book you will learn about motivation from three different perspectives. At the core of *Motivating Self and Others* is an integrative, evidence-based theoretical framework – the Thriving with Social Purpose Theory of Motivation and Optimal Functioning – that is focused on the *psychological* processes within the person-system, with a special emphasis on motivational processes and their leadership functions. However, to the extent possible within an arena where scientific consensus on many details has not yet been reached, we also try to explain how basic motivational mechanisms work at a *neurological* level. That helps anchor our psychological concepts in the physical reality of the human body while also affirming that those concepts are not just arbitrary mental constructions that sound good yet fail to represent how our minds and bodies actually function. Finally, we offer an *evolutionary* perspective focused on the quest to understand the origins of what is unique to human motivation (and human nature in general) as it was shaped over many millennia by "gene–culture coevolution" (Lumsden & Wilson, 1981; Richerson & Boyd, 2005; E. O. Wilson, 2012). Of particular interest is a growing consensus that, while most of our physical and instrumental capabilities (e.g., bipedalism, sweat glands, opposable thumbs) evolved as a result of ecological selection pressures, our *humanity*, or essential human nature, evolved mostly as a result of social selection pressures that put goals related to *social purpose* at the center of our collective experiences. As we will see, insights into how we evolved can help us become more self-directed and more capable of helping others achieve their personal and professional goals.

As you immerse yourself in the layered chapters of this book, you will learn that motivation is a complex, multifaceted phenomenon. However, because motivational processes work in part by controlling what thoughts, feelings, and perceptions capture our attention, you probably already have a pretty good intuitive sense of what motivation is all about. To test this hypothesis, try the following thought experiment:

> Think of the most motivating activity or experience you engaged in during the past few weeks. What were you trying to do? How did you feel? Were there particular thoughts and feelings that stood out in your mind during that experience?

Over the years we have collected hundreds of anecdotes in response to such questions. The stories people tell are both informative and inspiring. Some focus on extraordinary events, such as overcoming a major obstacle, helping someone in crisis, or birthing a baby. Others focus on everyday events that are reliable sources of life meaning, such as spending time with loved ones, earning respect through hard work, or becoming immersed in a favorite activity.

Although such stories vary widely in content, nearly all of them share common themes – themes that are at the heart of what motivation is all about. See if these themes apply to your experience.

1. A Strong Sense of Purpose (Goal Theme)
When people are highly motivated, they *feel* self-directed. They have personally compelling goal thoughts in their minds (e.g., "This is really important to me"; "I am on a mission") and a sense that these ideas and images are self-chosen. Usually these goal thoughts involve clearly conceived outcomes ("I know what I want"; "This is what I need to do") or vivid images that exemplify an extraordinarily meaningful part of their lives (e.g., images of loved ones; images of tranquil locations). The most powerful goal thoughts typically encompass multiple sources of motivation and are accompanied by feelings of authenticity and personal identity (e.g., "This is the real me"; "I am doing what I was meant to do").

2. Emotional Experiences That Are Powerful and Memorable (Emotion Theme)
Strong motivational patterns are virtually always infused with strong emotions. These emotions are not uniformly positive (e.g., emotions like

fear, anger, and guilt and related affective states like pain and fatigue can be highly motivating), but positive emotions (e.g., excitement, happiness, affection) usually predominate in the stories people tell us about their most motivating life experiences. These experiences are highly memorable because events that are emotionally intense are almost always easier to recall than experiences that are emotionally bland or neutral (Bower, 1981).

3.   Feeling Self-Confident and Supported (Personal Agency Belief Theme)
When people are highly motivated, they feel empowered and believe that they can overcome problems and obstacles. One source of empowerment is confidence in your personal capabilities, which is the dominant focus of many motivation theories. However, an equally important source of motivational power is a fundamental belief that the world around you (e.g., the social, material, and informational resources in your environment) will be supportive of your goal pursuits. When we have faith both in ourselves *and* in the resources and opportunities available to us, our thinking about what is possible becomes robust and expansive ("The sky's the limit!").

You can also get an intuitive feel for these three motivational themes by running the opposite thought experiment – that is, by thinking of a time when you were decidedly *un*motivated with respect to some challenge or opportunity (e.g., a request to do an onerous chore; an invitation to attend an event that did not appeal to you). In all probability, one or more of the elements described above was clearly deficient. It might be the lack of a strong or personally meaningful goal (e.g., "That's not my thing"), or the goal may lack sufficient clarity to be motivationally compelling (e.g., "I'm not sure what's in it for me"). There would almost certainly be a lack of any strong supporting emotion (e.g., "I just don't feel like it"), which may reflect a more general state of energy depletion (e.g., "I'm just not up to it right now"). Even if you have positive goals and emotions activated, you might dismiss the opportunity based on a belief that you do not have the necessary skills (e.g., "I'm intrigued but wouldn't have a clue what to do") or the necessary resources to take advantage of the opportunity (e.g., "Sounds great, but I can't afford it").

It's Good to Have a Goal!

We frequently use this phrase to affirm that rewarding life journeys begin with personal goals that are powerful and meaningful. The phrase is a bit deceptive, because in reality, our neurons are continuously firing in ways that cause goal-related thoughts and feelings to pop into our heads – as evidenced, for example, by neuroimaging studies and eye-gaze experiments that link brain-based activity with goal-directed thoughts and actions. So, to be more precise, what we are really trying to emphasize when we say "It's good to have a goal!" is that you can optimize your goal pursuits if you can (a) increase your *awareness* of the personal goals that are the most compelling and meaningful for you and (b) enhance the *clarity* of those goal thoughts so that they can direct and organize your behavior with strength and precision.

Do you have a good feel for what kinds of challenges and opportunities are most likely to capture your attention and "rev your motor"? Do you know what your *core personal goals* are – that is, the goals that, when activated and fulfilled, provide you with the greatest emotional rewards? Do you have any sense of whether your core personal goals are aligned with your current life circumstances? And do you have any idea how you might "rethink" your goals or change your circumstances to improve your goal–life alignment? These are some of the questions that we will be addressing throughout this book as we work through the implications of what it means to be *self-directed*, with personal responsibility to take that natural design principle and make the most of it.

Motivational Systems Theory

Consistent with the thought experiment we invited you to carry out to tap into your intuitive understanding of motivation, scientists have focused on three sets of psychological processes – personal goals, emotions, and personal agency beliefs – in their efforts to understand the key factors involved in motivating self and others. These processes work closely together as a *motivational system* (M. Ford, 1992) and therefore cannot be understood in isolation.

Personal goals provide direction (i.e., self-direction) by mentally representing the future outcomes you hope to achieve and by preparing your mind and body to pursue those outcomes. Among your overall repertoire of personal goals, *core personal goals* are the strongest sources of direction and energy – which is why we metaphorically refer to them as "the leaders within you."

Consistent with the integrative concept of *possible selves* (Markus & Nurius, 1986), different "leaders" may come to the forefront as you take on different roles and explore different ways of fulfilling the desired outcomes that you have envisioned. The most effective goal thoughts will be those that not only can arouse your passions but are also capable of efficiently organizing your thoughts and actions around coherent purposes and targeted objectives.

Emotions and personal agency beliefs (aka PABs) are also essential contributors to the leadership team in *motivational headquarters* – our metaphor for the dynamic convergence and integrated processing of personal goals, emotions, and personal agency beliefs. The unique role of emotions and PABs is to provide helpful guidance, sound advice, and, when necessary, compelling demands about what goals should be pursued at what level of effort and persistence.

Fans of the Star Trek franchise can picture how motivational headquarters operates by imagining the ship's captain (the directive function) being peppered with urgent reports about the ship's condition and impending threats (and opportunities), coupled with advice (offered with a combination of logic and emotion) about what actions need to be taken.

As we will see, in providing such advice, emotions and PABs influence the leader in different ways. When emotions are triggered, they activate particular kinds of goal thoughts. Imagine, for example, not seeing your wallet or smartphone where you expected it to be. That would immediately trigger emotions like surprise and consternation (if not panic!), which in turn would activate a goal to see the missing item and have it in your possession. Emotions also influence – through feelings that range from gentle nudges to irresistible urges – which mentally activated goals get selected for actual goal pursuit. Emotions help us prioritize goal options by energizing certain thought patterns over others ("I won't be able to think about anything else until I find my wallet") and by preparing the body for particular kinds of action ("I can't just sit here and do nothing!").

Personal agency beliefs also participate in this "here and now" decision-making process ("OK, calm down, I'm good at finding things"). However, their unique strength is in situations where there is a need to reflect on available capabilities and resources before making a decision about whether to pursue (or to continue pursuing) a goal. Indeed, the primary role of PAB thinking is to provide the leader with a realistic assessment of what outcomes might be anticipated if a particular goal is pursued. It is important to maintain hope and persistence when a goal is in fact attainable ("I'm sure I can find my wallet if I carefully retrace my steps"). However, if goal pursuit would likely be a waste of time and energy – or perhaps even counterproductive – the leader needs to be advised accordingly ("I'm probably not going to be able to find my wallet, so I better start calling my credit card companies ASAP!").

Motivational science took on a fresh new look when it began to recognize the central role that these self-directive and self-regulatory influences play in human behavior and development. However, the tendency has been for motivational scholars to focus on one particular facet of motivation rather than looking at the integrated functioning of personal goals, emotions, and personal agency beliefs. This "one at a time" approach can help provide specialized knowledge about particular aspects of motivation, but it leaves a significant gap in terms of understanding how motivation naturally operates in the real world, where goals, emotions, and personal agency beliefs always work together as a leadership *team*.

> To date, our field is characterized by theoretical fragmentation, with a multitude of constructs denoting similar phenomena ... and theories that are largely complementary but lack integration. Fragmentation hinders not only the development of a cumulative science of motivation and emotion but also our communication with policy-makers and practitioners. (Pekrun & Marsh, 2018, p. 20)

To address the need to not only "zoom in" on specific motivational elements, but also to "zoom out" to see broader motivational patterns, co-author Martin Ford developed *Motivational Systems Theory* (MST) during his professorial career at Stanford University. MST is grounded in a comprehensive, evidence-based theory of human behavior and development called the *Living Systems Framework* (LSF), which was developed in the 1980s by Donald Ford (Martin's father) to help guide human development scholars and practitioners in interdisciplinary fields of research and practice. That is not to say that Motivational Systems Theory was developed primarily as an academic exercise. Indeed, the initial impetus for developing MST was more practical than theoretical. Due to a new teaching assignment, Ford found himself struggling to help his doctoral students make sense of the hodge-podge of motivation theories that had suddenly sprung up in the 1970s and 1980s, after it had become acceptable to take mental phenomena such as goal thoughts, emotional triggers, and self-evaluations seriously. What was clearly needed was some way to think about motivation that was simultaneously simpler yet more comprehensive – in other words, more *systematic*.

MST's ability to respectfully "stand on the shoulders of giants" and to consolidate their scientific contributions within a coherent framework paved the way for efforts to use MST to guide research and intervention in a variety of applied fields of study. For example, during his executive training directorship at a large Fortune 50 corporation, co-author Peyton

Smith was impressed with the inclusive nature of MST and its applicability to real-world problems, and subsequently used it as the foundation for an international leadership program he developed and implemented on five different continents.

When You Stand on the Shoulders of Giants, You See More

There are a number of advantages to using an integrative systems model to understand motivation and optimal functioning. Perhaps the most obvious is the capacity of such models to be thorough and complete in their coverage of relevant phenomena. For example, while some motivation theories focus on just one or two categories of goal content (e.g., equity theory, self-worth theory, achievement motivation theory), MST includes a comprehensive goal taxonomy that covers *twenty-four* fundamentally distinct goal themes. Even Maslow's (1954) popular needs hierarchy only covers a fraction of this motivational "road map."

MST is also unique with respect to its emphasis on the ubiquitous importance of emotions in motivational patterns. Although respect for the role that emotion-regulation processes play in motivation and optimal functioning is growing (e.g., Gross, 2015; Harley et al., 2019; Pekrun, 2018; Thompson, 2011), emotions are still regarded by many scholars as hard to pin down in a scientific way. Although they are generally not left out of motivation theories completely – emotions are hard to ignore when trying to understand why people do what they do! – it is evident that there has been less emphasis on emotions than on expectancies, beliefs, goals, and values in mainstream motivational theorizing.

In short, there has been a fundamental imbalance in the scientific literature when it comes to understanding the role and significance of thoughts and emotions in human motivation. MST helps restore the proper balance.

Similarly, MST is one of the few scientific theories that places as much weight on context beliefs (beliefs about environmental responsiveness) as on capability beliefs (beliefs about personal competence) when trying to understand the choices people make. That is a direct result of the emphasis in systems models on seeing the environment as an infused element within a person's functioning. This *contextual* orientation helps combat the tendency to look at motivation in overly narrow or individualistic terms. The MST approach to self-direction is a genuinely "systems" way of thinking in which the person is embedded in the environment and the environment is embedded within the person (D. Ford, 1987/2019; D. Ford & Lerner, 1992; McNulty & Fincham, 2012; Vondracek et al., 2014).

> The dynamics of motivation do not rest solely within the organism. Nor do they live solely in the situations that may trigger them. Instead, motivations work within the interplay between organism and situation . . .. The unit of analysis, the "thing" to pay attention to directly, is the human-environment system, the dynamic that arises as organism and situation "play" or influence one another to create what comes next. (Dunning, 2016, pp. 27–28)

Motivation and Leadership

Although our motivational thoughts and feelings are anchored in human biology, both at the neurological level and through gene–culture coevolution, motivation is fundamentally a psychological phenomenon. It is therefore only natural that we would focus much of this book on the internal workings of the human mind (including the vast amount of mental activity that occurs outside of awareness). However, because our ultimate purpose is to better understand how motivation can promote optimal functioning – both at the everyday level and in terms of broader developmental pathways – we take the *Motivating Others* part of our book title very seriously. Humans are social animals who are designed to live and work in groups and in collaboration with other individuals. In many of these settings there is a need for people to carry out, at an interpersonal or collective level, the same leadership functions fulfilled by personal goals, emotions, and personal agency beliefs at the individual level. What that means conceptually is that, with just a little bit of tweaking and translating, Motivational Systems Theory can also serve as a theory of effective leadership – especially when viewed through the lens of the *Thriving with Social Purpose* (TSP) framework we designed to represent "motivation at its best." In simple terms, *leadership is fundamentally about motivating others.*

Consistent with this way of thinking, our view of leadership is much broader than the stereotypical image of a CEO or elected official. In effect, a leader is anyone in a role that includes motivating others as a systematic part of what they must do to succeed. That of course includes chief executives, commanding officers, and others at the top of an organization chart. But our concept of leadership also includes parents, teachers, counselors, coaches, managers, and supervisors. It includes advocates, opinion leaders, and people who "market" ideas and products designed to improve people's lives. Essentially, a leader is anyone who is committed to producing positive, enduring change in how other people function. And the best leaders are those who are effective in helping others progress toward optimal functioning in their own lives.

Another Thought Experiment

Now that we have clarified the rationale for the *Motivating Others* part of our book title, we can move to a second thought experiment. This one focuses on how you have impacted someone else's motivation:

> Imagine a time when you successfully motivated someone to make a significant change in their behavior – for example, investing more time and energy in an important activity or behaving in a more responsible or appropriate way. How did you approach this challenge? What did you say or do that was effective? How did you know the change was meaningful and lasting?

This thought experiment is a bit more complex than the first in that it asks for information not only about your own motives, but also about someone else's internal thoughts and feelings, which can only be known through inference (e.g., based on how they act and the choices they make, or on what they say about their experience). Nevertheless, when people describe how they know that "real" change has occurred, they focus primarily on motivational themes, as follows.

1. The Individual's Words and Actions (Especially Actions!) Clearly Demonstrate a Commitment to Change (Goal Theme)

The key to meaningful change is alignment of the desired behavior pattern with the individual's personal goals. You cannot effectively motivate someone if you do not have some sense of what goals are important to them and how you might connect with those natural sources of direction and energy. In particular, you cannot motivate people by simply telling them what their personal goals *should* be (e.g., "I want you to be the best student in the class"; "I want you to stop taking me for granted"). By definition, a goal is not personal until it becomes psychologically "owned." The individual does not have to share *your* reasons for wanting change to occur, but there does need to be *some* reason for accepting (and ultimately embracing) the change and maintaining it in your absence. That is why one essential element in motivating others is being able to skillfully and creatively connect valued behavior patterns (e.g., driving safely, practicing the piano, meeting a higher standard) to an individual's existing repertoire of core personal goals. Recognizing the fundamental importance of making such connections, in Chapter 3 we will talk about methods and tools for identifying core personal goals in self and others.

2. The Individual's Expressed Feelings Suggest That the Behavior Change Is Likely to Be Self-Sustaining (Emotion Theme)

As noted earlier, strong motivational patterns are virtually always infused with strong emotions. If someone makes a desired change but the effort is halfhearted (e.g., randomly ordering a low-calorie meal from time to time; offering to pitch in but then not actually contributing much work), meaningful change has probably not yet occurred. Conversely, if the energy level remains strong while behavior change efforts are being made, you can be confident that something good is happening. Positive emotions like enthusiasm and pride are particularly diagnostic when looking for indicators of self-sustaining behavior change, as we are naturally motivated to continue doing things that produce such emotions.

3. The Individual Appears to Feel Self-Confident and Supported in Their Efforts to Change (Personal Agency Belief Theme)

Change can be hard. It takes a strong commitment and a lot of energy to disrupt an established pattern, replace it with something new, and then make it stick. So, when you have been able to remove self-doubts or help someone feel at ease with a change, that is a very good sign. Yet, to be able to do this, you will first need to establish a sense of trust by showing that you have the person's best interests at heart. Being able to trust that someone trying to influence you will be responsive and helpful (e.g., by providing effective coaching, social-emotional support, or essential resources) removes a potentially huge motivational barrier.

Now let's back up a step to the other part of our second thought experiment. How did you approach the challenge of trying to motivate someone to make a significant change in their behavior?

When people are asked to address this question in the context of long-term success (i.e., when sustainable improvement has occurred rather than just an expedient, temporary change), their responses are highly congruent with MST principles for motivating others (M. Ford, 1992; M. Ford & Smith, 2007). Prominent themes include:

1. Visioning of a Better Future and a Strong Belief in the Attainability of That Desired Outcome

These goal-defining and goal-strengthening qualities are often at the heart of successful efforts to motivate others. In effect, the person functioning as the change agent, or "leader" of the change process, is seeking to facilitate optimal functioning in others by engaging in the same kind of positive, approach-oriented thinking that is characteristic of effective efforts to improve the leader's own functioning. There is a clear, compelling goal that the leader effectively communicates by finding some way to "attach" that goal to others' personal goals. The leader also inspires persistence and creativity by encouraging others to believe that they have the ability and opportunity to be successful. In many cases it appears that much of a leader's success is attributable to the infectious nature of the leader's own motivational characteristics.

2.   Emphasizing Facilitation Rather than Direct Control
There is no doubt that motivation by fear (e.g., through intimidation, threats, or coercive contingencies) can influence behavior in the moment. However, such tactics are not only notoriously ineffective in producing sustainable change; they can also backfire by reducing trust, undermining commitment to change, and redirecting available energy to avoidance goals. Consequently, the more reliable pathway to meaningful change is to try to create circumstances that are emotionally inviting and clearly aligned with the personal goals of those you seek to influence. In other words, you need to respect the fact that people are naturally self-directed. If, for example, you tell someone "this is for your own good" without explanation, that message will probably feel inauthentic and uncaring. Even worse, the person is likely to feel that you are trying to control them and react in a defensive or oppositional way (e.g., "What you mean is that it's good for YOU!"). Rather than emphasizing the outcomes you want, it is far more effective to focus – in an informative rather than controlling way (Deci & Ryan, 1985; Ryan & Deci, 2018) – on outcomes that are meaningful to the person you seek to influence. Even if those outcomes are negative (e.g., loss of privileges or possible reputational damage), people will generally be much more receptive to suggestions and honest explanations than to threats and manipulations.

Sometimes it is hard to explain the personal relevance of a motivational message because of the young age of the recipient or because of the novelty or complexity of the desired outcome (e.g., try explaining the need for people to reduce their "carbon footprint" to someone unfamiliar with that concept). In cases where goal alignment is not readily apparent or cannot be easily understood, trust in the individual delivering the message is paramount. That is why parenting experts, coaching professionals, and political strategists place so much emphasis on relationships as a foundation for motivating others. If you feel that someone is just telling you what to do for their own purposes, your response is likely to be quite different than if you believe that person is sincerely trying to help you achieve what is important to you and to others you care about (Grant, 2013).

3. *Establishing an Emotional Connection*

Attempts to motivate others tend not to proceed efficiently when individuals are treated impersonally (i.e., as if they were objects rather than people). That is why concepts like emotional climate, social-emotional support, and empathy have received so much attention in the behavior change literature, and why they are frequently mentioned as factors contributing to successful efforts to motivate others. Empathy is a particularly powerful concept because it combines concern for others with efforts to understand others' perspectives and feelings (including their motivational states). That is an empowering combination for those seeking to motivate others.

4. *Focusing on Helping Goals*

When people tell us about their most successful attempts to motivate others, they naturally gravitate to examples where, in terms of their own personal goals, they felt a strong desire or obligation to help others. Such goals are not necessarily the only motives guiding their change efforts, but they do tend to be among the most salient themes in their goal descriptions. Evidently there is something uniquely powerful about intentionally and effectively promoting the welfare of others in meaningful ways, whether those "others" are your children, your students, your clients, or humanity in general. And the motivational impact is not just within the leader. People respond most favorably to leaders whose intentions are perceived to be centered on helping their followers. When we believe that our leaders are genuinely inclined to put the interests of others above their own self-interest, we gravitate to them emotionally, feel a sense of trust and security, and want to align our own goal pursuits with the goals they are advocating.

Thriving with Social Purpose

The growing repository of stories about "motivation at its best" encouraged us to create an elaboration on Motivational Systems Theory that focused specifically on motivation and optimal functioning. We had come to realize that these rich descriptions of real-life triumphs were helping us understand the natural processes underlying efforts to motivate self and others. We were also guided by MST-inspired research studies that focused on motivational profiles of people widely regarded by their peers as being unusually competent, caring, or responsible (M. Ford, 1996; M. Ford et al., 1989). In addition, we were informed by a parallel stream of theory and research organized under the label "positive psychology" that gained substantial momentum during the late 1990s and 2000s (Seligman & Csikszentmihalyi, 2000; Snyder & Lopez, 2002, 2009). Positive psychology has focused much of its attention on motivation-related themes, including hope, optimism, resilience, positive emotions, and the high-functioning experience of "flow" (Csikszentmihalyi, 1991, 2003). We liberally cite the work of several of positive psychology's intellectual leaders in this book.

Thriving with Social Purpose (TSP) is the phrase we have selected to summarize the broad motivational approach to life that seems to be most reliably associated with optimal functioning in humans. It is difficult to summarize all of the concepts and evidence that went into building the TSP framework without first describing the foundation for that framework, which we lay out in the next three chapters. However, we can highlight here why we think this integrative theory of motivation and optimal functioning is important for anyone concerned with the challenge of motivating self and others. Here are some of the key features and outcomes associated with a TSP motivational pattern:

1. *TSP Is a Natural Way of Being*

Humans, like so many other animals, are a social species. We innately seek relationships, not only for their own rewards, but also because they facilitate other goal pursuits. Researchers studying motivation in infants, for example, have converged on the conclusion that humans are born with a natural desire to explore, learn, and bond with others. Newborns look, reach, listen, and cry as they try to acquire informational and material resources and influence their social environment. They do not need to be taught to pursue goals in an active, self-directed way (as every new parent soon learns!). They do not need to be taught to be concerned about others or to have inclinations to help and cooperate with others (Hrdy, 2009; Keltner, 2009; Tomasello, 2009). These innate motivational qualities of course need to be nurtured and cultivated, just as our physical and intellectual capabilities need to be developed and refined in the course of our daily lives. But it is not necessary to go against basic human nature to motivate yourself or others to pursue a goal, or to have some sense of social purpose. You just need to take the natural gifts you were born with and make the most of them, while also remaining alert to those who might undermine your TSP qualities. As Mae Jemison, the first African American woman to travel in space wisely advised: *"I was born motivated, like you all were . . . [but beware] – people try to demotivate you."*

2. *TSP Enables Imagination and Creativity to Flourish*

Life is filled with ups and downs and bumps and bruises. Sometimes it is quite adaptive to be cautious and detached. Nor is it possible to effectively pursue every goal we might envision. We have limited energy resources that can be easily depleted under conditions of uncertainty and challenge, especially when we are not sleeping or eating well or when there are too many stressful events going on in our lives at the same time. Nevertheless, when our natural inclination – or what we like to call our "home page" motivational orientation – is to actively pursue the goals that capture our attention and imagination with confidence, tenacity, and productive energy, our capacity for creativity and positive change is maximized. Moreover, when we focus not just on ourselves but also on the broader impact of our actions for others, our thinking is more open-minded and innovative.

3. *TSP Contributes to Health, Well-Being, and Longevity*

It makes sense that if we live our lives in ways that are consistent with how we are naturally designed to function, we will feel better and live longer. And indeed, there is ample and growing evidence to support this hypothesis. One source of evidence is the vast scientific literature on stress, which pushes people toward non-TSP modes of functioning (e.g., avoidance, defensiveness, self-absorption). Chronic, energy-depleting stress is consistently associated with a wide variety of emotional and physical health problems (Thoits, 2010). Conversely, there is growing evidence that stress reduction and enhanced life meaning are associated with many health benefits (Czekierda et al., 2017; Grossman et al., 2004; Khoury et al., 2015). There is also considerable evidence that dispositional optimism and interpersonal trust are associated with good health outcomes (Barefoot et al., 1998; Scheier & Carver, 2018). Another source of evidence for the hypothesis that "TSP is good for you" is research linking altruism and social bonding to a wide spectrum of indicators related to well-being, including longevity (Post, 2005, 2007; Ryff & Singer, 2001). Evidently, adopting habits of living and working that are at odds with our evolutionary heritage is not a winning strategy when it comes to long-term health and survival.

4.   Life Meaning Flows Naturally from TSP Experiences

Thriving with Social Purpose is a way of approaching life's opportunities and challenges that yields many benefits. It helps people progress effectively toward the goals that matter most to them. It enables people to pursue goals in ways that support rather than jeopardize their emotional and physical health. It also increases people's ability to help others lead better lives. However, there is another impact of TSP that, in effect, takes all of these benefits to another level – a level that is an integral part of our concept of optimal functioning. As we will explain in Chapter 7 when we introduce the *Thriving with Social Purpose Theory of Life Meaning*, TSP contributes directly to a sense that "life is worth living." This psychological experience is difficult to engineer, and yet it is a natural consequence of TSP modes of functioning. That is an important benefit not only for individuals with respect to their own goal pursuits, but also for leaders who may sometimes wonder if the rigors and responsibilities associated with their leadership roles (e.g., as parents, teachers, supervisors, or executives) are really "worth it." For those guided by a TSP motivational orientation, the nearly universal response is "absolutely!"

5.   Followers Respond Best to Leaders with TSP Qualities

Those used to thinking of "leaders" as people who can easily make things happen because they have a lot of power (due to money, position, or weapons) may find it hard to associate TSP motivational patterns (especially the social purpose component) with images of commanding officers and ruthless chief executives. But from our broader perspective of leadership, where leaders generally must first earn the trust and respect of followers before they can have much long-term impact, TSP is an indispensable foundation for effective leadership. This is consistent with the idea that the individuals most likely to be able to make good things happen in leadership roles are those with strong, clear goals; robust personal agency beliefs; a positive and balanced emotional outlook; and authentic concern for others' well-being. We are hardwired to want to respond cooperatively and enthusiastically to people who display these kinds of qualities.

Equipoise

As we will explain in Chapter 2, humans evolved in variable, changing environments. As a result, a "one size fits all" solution is not adaptive, nor is that the way we are designed. To function effectively, we need to be versatile. We need a diverse repertoire of strategies and possibilities. Like a sailor setting and resetting her sails to match the shifting winds, we need to be able to balance and flexibly adjust our decisions and actions to the multiple forces involved in the ever-shifting milieu of goal pursuit.

This design principle, which we call *equipoise* (as explained in Chapter 4), is an essential part of our TSP conceptual framework, as it helps clarify the nature of our hypothesized connection between TSP and optimal functioning. Specifically, we are *not* proposing that TSP is appropriate for all circumstances or the only pathway to success in any given situation. Flexibility is essential for optimal functioning! In some circumstances it may make perfect sense, for example, to be avoidant, pessimistic, or mistrustful. Rather, we are proposing that, with few exceptions, TSP provides the most natural – and thus the most reliably productive – "home page" motivational orientation over the long haul. Indeed, when you later read about the specific components composing the TSP motivational pattern, you will see that the concept of equipoise is deeply embedded within each element in the TSP framework.

Let the Journey Begin!

Motivation is a complex but inherently intriguing topic. Our objective is to share with you what we have learned about motivation over the years and to prepare you to apply that knowledge to the opportunities and challenges you face in your personal and professional goal pursuits. When you finish reading and reflecting on the contents of this book, you will appreciate the significance of motivation in people's lives and the many benefits of striving for goal–life alignment and TSP patterns of functioning. You will have new conceptual and practical tools for strengthening motivation, enhancing effectiveness, and increasing life meaning in yourself and others. And you will understand why TSP leaders are so effective in attracting followers and motivating them to align their goals around a shared purpose.

First, though, we must acquaint you with the scientific foundation that makes these insights possible. Let's start our journey by looking at how self-direction evolved from its simple beginnings in early life forms to its most elaborated expression (to date) in human motivational systems.

CHAPTER 2

Self-Direction
How Nature Has Equipped You to Survive,
with Well-Being

> Successful pursuit of goals is not just the most important thing in the life of humans and other animals; it is ultimately the only thing that counts toward survival, life's bottom line.
>
> — Eric Klinger and W. Miles Cox, "Motivation and the Theory of Current Concerns"

> You have brains in your head. You have feet in your shoes. You can steer yourself in any direction you choose.
>
> — children's author Dr. Seuss, *Oh, the Places You'll Go*

Imagine that you are a high-powered automobile with all the latest technology. Oh, the amazing things you can do! You can communicate with satellites. You can simultaneously monitor dozens of variables and report on potential problems. You can even steer yourself through traffic and park in tight spaces without any help from your owner!

There is one big limitation, however. No matter how powerful and sophisticated you might be, you do not have any capacity for self-direction. Someone else has to decide what destination you will head toward. Someone else has to decide where to park and for how long. Someone else has to decide what future adventures you will experience. You may have some impressive *instrumental* capabilities, but you are sorely lacking in *leadership* qualities.

People also have some pretty amazing instrumental capabilities. We can talk and write in complex sentences – sometimes in more than one language. We can compose songs, and then play those songs on a variety of instruments. We can build fancy machines (like cars and satellites!) to help us do things we could never do on our own. But *what really makes us special is our remarkable capacity for directing our own thoughts and action.* We can imagine possibilities, choose alternative pathways and destinations, and direct our mind and body to work toward accomplishing the goals that we have envisioned for ourselves. We have the capacity to take charge of our lives and to create not only new opportunities, but also new capabilities.

These leadership qualities must be cultivated, however. There is good news and bad news in this regard. The good news is that you do not need to do anything to be self-directed in a fundamental sense. Throughout each day, as we move from one life episode to the next, we naturally size up opportunities and challenges – often with little awareness of what motivates us – and then selectively seek to accomplish the *personal goals* that seem most compelling to us among the available options. That is the essence of self-direction. As we will see, our minds and bodies evolved to enable us to control aspects of our world, ourselves, and others that are important to us, thereby ensuring our individual and collective vitality. As a result, the basic processes involved in motivating self and others come naturally to us. *We are goal-directed, socially connected, continuously learning creatures.* That is how we are designed.

Consistent with this premise, we generally *feel* most alive when we are keenly aware of the thoughts and emotions involved in the self-directed pursuit of compelling personal goals. Dreaming about the future, making meaningful choices, immersing ourselves in planning and problem solving, striving to make things better, connecting with other people – these are the things that are at the heart of the human experience. Conversely, when we do not have a sense of direction and purpose, we tend to feel "lifeless" – bored, depressed, or otherwise dispirited. Even when we don't know why we feel this way, we intuitively know that we *shouldn't* feel this way.

Now for the bad news: although we have a natural capacity to imagine and feel and anticipate and choose, few of us know how to make the most of our motivational assets. Perhaps that is to be expected given that, until recently, self-direction has not been a major theme in either education or the human sciences. Nevertheless, a rapidly accumulating body of theory and research suggests that we can now begin to answer key questions about the origins of human motivation and how motivation works in our daily lives. Self-direction evolved from our natural striving for *survival with well-being* (Damasio, 2003), which is an outgrowth of the relentless effort for self-preservation reflected in all life forms. That in turn led to the elaboration of a variety of motivational systems designed to enhance not only our own lives but also the lives of others with whom we are socially and emotionally connected.

Following this logic, our journey within these pages starts by tracing the evolution of the remarkable capabilities most closely associated with the capacity for self-direction. The more you know about these capabilities and how they evolved, the better prepared you will be to learn how to motivate self and others and thereby enhance your ability to lead – and to help others lead – a productive and meaningful life.

The Mind and the Brain

Our fundamental premise is that *efforts to motivate self and others are more likely to succeed if they are consistent with basic human nature.* People will naturally respond to efforts to strengthen motivation when those efforts are fashioned from the same evolved mechanisms that enabled our primordial ancestors to become self-directed and capable of adaptive behavior change. From this perspective, it is evident that virtually everyone has the tools to motivate self and others. You just need to know how those tools work and how you can put them to good use.

The Continuity Assumption

Understanding how the mind organizes and directs behavior may appear like a near-impossible undertaking given the enormous complexity of human life. However, because we share many attributes with our evolutionary ancestors, we can gain valuable insights by looking at very simple life and extrapolating up the evolutionary ladder.

Darwin suggested that the human brain evolved from the basic structures found in other mammals and that many of its features are continuous with those of other species (D. S. Wilson, 2007). Following the basic logic of *natural selection,* structures that enhanced reproductive fitness and the survival of genetically related organisms not only became more prevalent in subsequent generations of a particular species, they also served as a foundation for the development of new adaptations and (ultimately) new species (Wagner, 2014). As a result, in many important respects human brains differ from those of other mammalian species as a matter of degree, not kind (Geary, 2005).

This *continuity assumption* may seem like a stretch given that the ratio of brain tissue to overall body tissue is significantly greater in humans than in any other animal. Indeed, the brain size expansion associated with the evolution of our neocortex and forebrain structures was massive compared to other animals (Semendeferi & Damasio, 2000). Yet the way that brain development occurred as it evolved into human form helps illustrate the validity of the continuity assumption. The new information processing and control capabilities associated with these evolving brain structures did not replace or push aside the subcortical systems beneath them. Instead, they were integrated with the existing structures, analogous to adding modern microprocessors to the tried-and-true mechanical systems of an automobile (Berridge 2003). As a result, older brain mechanisms that once governed behavior in a dictatorial manner were now organized into a shared governance structure with a coordinated system of checks and balances.

The motivational significance of this integration of newer and older brain components is profound. For example, the brain regions associated with fear responses are ancient compared to more recent layers involved with higher level reasoning (e.g., the prefrontal cortex). Nevertheless, because the newer layers have some ability to override, or at least mitigate, the more automatic older layers, we can "think our way out" of frightening experiences, such as those caused by a scary but objectively harmless person or object. You may not be able to prevent the emotion from being triggered, but you can "put it in its place" by questioning its validity, reinterpreting its meaning, or minimizing its impact. Such *reappraisal* techniques are at the core of many systems of psychotherapy (e.g., D. Ford & Urban, 1963, 1998; Prochaska & Norcross, 2019).

Our bigger, newer brains thus reflect elaborations in complexity and sophistication within a common framework involving "layers" of functionality rather than a totally new evolutionary invention (Geary, 2005). The results that those elaborations make possible – for example, consciousness, self-awareness, creative problem solving, mental time travel (i.e., thinking about the past or future), and cultural learning (i.e., learning from others, innovating, and passing on those innovations, so that each generation does not have to "start from scratch") – may make it seem like we have little in common with other creatures. But when it comes to the basics of how the mind works, it is clear that we can learn a lot by looking at our evolutionary heritage (Bernard et al., 2005).

What the Brain Does

Following Denton (2005) and most other neuroscientists studying mental functioning, we begin with the simple premise that, essentially, the "mind is what the brain does. Dualism [i.e., the view that mental activity does not have a physical basis] is out" (p. 29).

Because being "brainy" is typically associated with academic intelligence, the mind is often thought of as a powerful information processing and computing system. However, recent advances in the behavioral and brain sciences have shown that this view of the mind is too limited

(Damasio, 1994; Doidge, 2007). Although our brains do process massive amounts of information, the main function of the brain is to cause behaviors to occur that will produce favorable consequences for ourselves and others we care about. Damasio (2003) refers to these favorable consequences as *survival with well-being* – the prime directive around which all goal pursuit is organized. Even today it is evident that "our brains still bear evidence of their original purpose: to manage our bodies and minds in the service of living, and living happily, in the world with other people" (Immordino-Yang & Damasio, 2007, p. 4).

Consistent with this conclusion, the most dramatic period of brain growth occurred when our ancestors began to live in cooperative, egalitarian groups capable of innovating and sharing their improvements in everyday living conditions (Geary, 2005). As a result, the *collective intelligence* of human groups has played a much more impactful role in the evolution of our species than has the intelligence of individual "experts" (Malone et al., 2010; Woolley et al., 2010). We may feature high-achieving individuals in our history books, documentaries, and award ceremonies, but most of the consequential advances in the lives of humans have resulted from the collective brainpower of collaborative, innovative groups.

Over evolutionary time the brain has become increasingly important in coordinating the mental and physical activity needed to survive and thrive. That is because most organisms with brains live in highly variable environments. Under such circumstances brains need to be malleable, or "plastic" – that is, capable of adapting to new challenges. This does not mean that plasticity is unlimited, or that infinite plasticity would be desirable (or even viable). Nevertheless, brains are by far the most malleable organs in the body, even in relatively primitive organisms that have been around for eons. As Doidge (2007) explains,

> the brain ... is not an inanimate vessel that we fill; rather it is more like a living creature with an appetite, one that can grow and change itself with proper nourishment and exercise .... As neurons are trained and become more efficient, they can process *faster*. This means that the speed at which we think is itself plastic. (pp. 47, 67)

So the mind is not just about "brainpower" in the sense of accumulated knowledge or computational speed. It is also about motivation, self-governance, and social integration. Perhaps most fundamentally, it is about *self-directed decision-making and action designed to produce desired consequences for self and others.*

Why Self-Direction Became a Necessity

The first forms of life survived or perished at the whim of their environment. Similar to membership in an exclusive club, the simple rule was "have exactly the right characteristics or you're out." The rule was inflexible because those pioneering organisms couldn't change either the environment or their own characteristics. For example, when ambient temperatures increased by a degree or two, the life forms in that habitat were likely to die because they no longer fit in with that environment. Perhaps a few "mutants" with slightly higher heat tolerances would live to have offspring who were also more likely to survive the warmer weather. But members of this new "club" would only be fine until temperatures changed again, and then the exclusionary process would repeat itself. This meant that most species were ultimately doomed to extinction, as, with few exceptions, the natural selection process could not keep up with rapid, large-scale environmental change. It is estimated that approximately 99 percent of all the species that have ever existed on this planet are now extinct (Shih, 2015).

This somewhat cruel reality continued for eons. However, over time most surviving life forms evolved, by necessity, mechanisms that enabled them to adjust (within limits) to environmental changes that might threaten their existence. Consider, for example, the Arctic cod:

> a perfectly unremarkable occupant of the world's oceans. Except for one thing: The Arctic cod – *Boreogadus saida* – lives and thrives within six degrees of the North Pole, nine hundred meters below the surface, in waters that regularly chill below zero degrees Celsius. At that temperature, the internal fluids of most organisms turn into ice crystals with edges as beautiful as well-forged swords, and just as deadly, for they carve up living tissue like butter. Warm-blooded animals have a built-in thermostat that allows them to survive in subfreezing weather. Fish don't. And yet, there's the Arctic cod. *B. saida* survives by producing antifreeze proteins that lower the freezing temperature of its body fluids, much like the antifreeze in a car's engine coolant. These proteins are prototypical examples of nature's innovative powers. Change the amino acid sequence needed to produce a particular protein, and presto, huge areas of the earth's oceans become livable. (Wagner, 2014, pp. 107–108)

The evolution of self-directive properties escalated further as species developed methods for dealing with predators in their environment. That is when organisms started to take charge of their lives, with natural selection helping to preserve the most effective of those innovations. As a result, survival and extinction were no longer fully dictated by the organism's environmental masters. This shift in the balance of power was only miniscule at first, and even with humans it is evident that environmental conditions continue to play a huge role in the life options we have available to us (as illustrated by the effects of poverty, global warming, air pollution, and pandemics). Nevertheless, with the emergence of mechanisms that enabled some semblance of self-direction, species were no longer completely at the mercy of the environment. Organisms could now influence or at least partially control some of their environment's effects on them.

Our journey through evolutionary time starts with the advent of self-direction. We use this term to refer to a set of progressively evolving capabilities in everything from very primitive life forms to humans, while recognizing that very simple organisms are "self-directed" only at a rudimentary level. Such organisms (e.g., microbes and plants) cannot invent new responses or new strategies; they can only follow biologically preprogrammed instructions on what to do within a range of circumstances prototypical for that species. Most people would not characterize this as "self" direction since we are used to thinking of the self as we experience it – as a conscious, creative mental force. Nevertheless, even very simple organisms are self-directed in the sense that they have mechanisms that enable them to fend off threats and seek out life-sustaining resources. For example, many plants have survival mechanisms that are nothing short of astonishing.

> Plants "forage" for resources like light and soil nutrients and "anticipate" rough spots and opportunities. By analyzing the ratio of red light and far red light falling on their leaves, for example, they can sense the presence of other chlorophyllated competitors nearby and try to grow the other way .... Plants can't run away from a threat but they can stand their ground .... At the smallest nip to its leaves, specialized cells on the plant's surface release chemicals to irritate the predator or sticky goo to entrap it. Genes in the plant's DNA are activated to wage systemwide chemical warfare, the plant's version of an immune response.... Some of the compounds that plants generate in response to insect mastication – their feedback, you might say – are volatile chemicals that serve as cries for help. Such airborne alarm calls have been shown to attract both large predatory insects like dragon flies, which delight in caterpillar meat, and tiny parasitic insects, which can infect a caterpillar and destroy it from within. (Angier, 2009, p. D2)

Functionally similar mechanisms enabling organisms to exercise control over their fate (with varying degrees of success) can be found in organisms all the way up to the top of the evolutionary ladder.

For organisms that rely solely on biological preprogramming, innovative adaptations to changing conditions can only occur across generations through natural selection of novel genetic solutions that arise from dynamic "genotype networks" (Wagner, 2014). That is not to say that such organisms had a fatal design flaw or that they were necessarily more vulnerable than other species. As Wagner (2014) explains,

> everywhere on this planet, a relentless shuffling and mixing and recombining of genes takes place. Wherever microbial life occurs, in the depths of the oceans and on arid mountaintops, in scalding hot springs and on frigid glaciers, in fertile soils and desiccated deserts, inside and around our bodies, life is experimenting with every conceivable combination of new genes, rereading, editing and rejuggling its metabolic texts without pause, yielding an enormous and still growing diversity of metabolisms. (p. 83)

Moreover, preprogrammed biological arrangements can work just fine if the organism's environment is relatively stable and their genetic makeup allows for some flexibility. A stately tree, for example, may last for centuries within a broad range of environmental circumstances. Indeed, it appears that many species can adapt to changes in the environment using mechanisms that cause DNA material surrounding a set of genes to switch those genes on or off – or somewhere in between, like a dimmer switch (Wagner, 2014). But what if the range of environmental conditions exceeds normal boundaries? What if, for example, necessary nutrients disappear altogether from the immediate environment? Or a new predator (e.g., a deadly tree fungus) suddenly shows up?

Some organisms evolved capabilities that enabled them to avoid such threats by transporting themselves into less hostile circumstances. But even that adaptation assumes that agreeable circumstances exist in some reasonable proximity. What if things are bad all around and there's no apparent escape? Unless the organism gets a helping hand from some outside source (e.g., via an endangered species designation), survival of the species may be impossible without capabilities that enable organisms to actively *create* better living conditions as threats and opportunities arise. That is the situation that early life forms on our planet faced and that continues to be the central challenge in the lives of all animals, including humans.

Our Approach to Understanding How Self-Direction Evolved

To understand the motivational systems underlying the capacity for self-direction, we must start by understanding goals. That is the most straightforward approach given our focus on the natural mechanisms underlying human motivation. As Klinger and Cox (2004) explain in their *Handbook of Motivational Counseling*:

> If animals evolved with a motile strategy to go after the substances and conditions they need, the most basic requirement for their survival is successful goal-striving. In that case, all animal evolution, right up to humans, must have centered on natural selection of whatever facilitated attaining goals. This must mean that everything about humans evolved in the service of successful goal-striving – including human anatomy, physiology, cognition, and emotion. (p. 5)

Following this principle, the lens through which we will view motivation is the *goal*. Ever since early life forms had to "go from here to there" to get what they needed to survive (Denton, 2005), goal images – mental representations of desired outcomes – served as the rudder of their actions. Self-direction, which we consider to be the sine qua non of motivation, is ultimately all about imagining goal possibilities and then selectively pursuing those opportunities most likely to enhance our survival with well-being (Damasio, 2003).

As we will see, both the infrastructure to support goal striving and goals themselves have undergone spectacular changes over the course of evolutionary history, leaving humans with several unique and remarkable capabilities – for example, the ability to envision future possibilities that are quite different from our current realities. These advances were accomplished, however, by building on a foundation of already existing mechanisms designed to facilitate effective goal pursuit – a foundation that remains an intrinsically important part of human nature.

The Evolution of Self-Direction

The Emergence of Goals and Sensors to Activate Them

It is not surprising that the blood plasma chemical composition (e.g., levels of sodium, potassium, and calcium magnesium) of the first creatures to emerge from the ancient oceans and swamps closely matched the chemical mix in the waters that sustained them. These creatures, when their home was always in the water, didn't have to worry about getting sufficient levels of these ubiquitous chemical nutrients. Organisms swimming around in the primordial soup had pretty much everything they needed right there. Survival was made possible "just by showing up."

Things changed when creatures left their natural nutrient bath. Once on dry land, organisms could only survive if they were "hardwired" with systems that motivated them to seek out and ingest those same vital chemical nutrients that were once only a membrane away – and to begin doing so before their biological systems started shutting down. Organisms without these motivational systems failed to survive and reproduce. For such organisms, nature's "rule number one" was simple: pursue the right goals in a timely manner or perish.

Even before organisms crawled out onto dry land, selection pressures produced genotypes that supported the functional capabilities (phenotypes) that land-based creatures would need to effectively pursue the "right" goals, such as maintaining energy and chemical balance, repairing wear and tear, and evading injury. Metaphorically, the *primordial goals* directing these hardwired motivational systems can be thought of as being "preinstalled," analogous to the computer industry practice of prepackaging hardware and software. When your new smartphone arrives, for example, it has a basic level of functionality preinstalled (e.g., to take a picture or video; to access a nearby Wi-Fi network), which it always retains even after other applications are added. Similarly, the primordial goals that kept these early organisms alive were retained when, eons later, additional goals became possible. For example, we've retained the urge to eat – among the most ancient of primordial goals – even though today many of us wish that this goal was a bit less compelling!

Consistent with nature's "rule number one," our primordial organisms not only needed the right "preinstalled" goals to survive, they also needed a way to activate those goals promptly when specific threats arose. In the field of biology, *homeostasis* is a term often used to describe the "physiological processes that keep the conditions within the body constant" (Denton, 2005, p. 8). Homeostatic systems are capable of activating timely and appropriate action to achieve the primordial goals that are critical to the survival of the organism. Activation of these primordial goals in the pursuit of homeostasis is among the simplest and most ancient form of *self-directed motivational systems*.

The homeostatic processes regulating our biological systems are analogous to the homeostatic mechanisms in the thermostat that regulates your home's heating and cooling systems. There are very fancy thermostats available, but in their simplest form, only three components are actually required. The first is a way for you to set the desired temperature (i.e., the goal). The second is a sensor that can detect conditions that are inconsistent with the preset goal. Finally, some mechanism for triggering a corrective response is needed when current conditions do not resemble the desired conditions (i.e., turn on the heater or air conditioner until the desired temperature is reached).

The earliest primordial goals included homeostatic set points essential to the organism's survival – for example, proper levels of internal oxygen, water, salt, glucose, or temperature. Internal sensors (sometimes called *interoceptors*) evolved within the nervous system to detect change with respect to these set points. These sensors provided the necessary infrastructure for homeostatic motivational systems to flourish. In such systems, the instant a change is sensed that goes beyond the organism's normal range of functioning, a warning signal (i.e., sensor alarm) is produced. This in turn "fires up" the system components responsible for ensuring that this warning is heeded. The result: a simple yet effective demonstration of self-directed goal pursuit.

How do these early evolving motivational systems resemble motivational systems in humans? The warning signals produced by these sensors are perhaps the earliest traces of what we today would call *emotions*. The basic mechanism was simple: sensors would trigger a "primal emotion" (Denton, 2005) when something needed to happen to maintain homeostasis (e.g., cool down, drink water, escape from a predator). The triggered emotion would then activate goal pursuit by causing "change and commotion" in the biological and behavioral life of the organism (Damasio, 2003). Organisms with the genes supporting these mechanisms survived and reproduced, while those without them became extinct.

The earliest alarm signals triggering the primal emotions that were "causing all the commotion" were probably limited to *nociceptive* signals (i.e., signals of pain). Moreover, at this early point in the evolutionary sequence, "pain" was almost certainly a purely neurochemical phenomenon, not a conscious experience. As Denton (2005) explains, "invertebrates, which have no brain, show reactivity to noxious stimuli, *per se,* indicating this reactivity can occur in the absence of awareness of such stimuli" (p. 62). Pain was thus one of the earliest design features in motivational systems. Pain was the messenger – even before it could be consciously felt – and its message was clear and compelling: "something's wrong – better make it right!"

Nature's initial approach to facilitating self-direction may have been limited to pain; however, as Damasio (2003) tells us, nature had a nice afterthought. With the passage of evolutionary time, pain inhibitors (e.g., endorphins) and associated receptors evolved to provide "a better than neutral life" or what we today call *well-being*. It seems that almost from the very beginning, the repertoire of mechanisms supporting self-direction involved much more than avoiding pain and surviving. Our motivational systems compel us to seek not only life, but also a *better* life. Experiencing well-being is highly motivating!

The experience of actually *feeling* pain and *feeling* well-being did not develop until the next phase in the evolution of self-direction – namely, the phase following the advent of consciousness. Nevertheless, it is enlightening to realize that many of the most powerful and reliable principles of human motivation are based on mechanisms that evolved in some of the simplest life forms on the planet.

> There is abundant evidence of "emotional" reactions in simple organisms. Think of a lone paramecium, a simple unicellular organism, all body, no brain, no mind .... This simple organism is designed to detect certain signs of danger – steep variations in temperature, excessive vibrations, or the contact of a piercing object that might rupture its membrane – and react by proceeding to a safer, more temperate, quieter place. Likewise, it will swim in the trail toward greener water pastures after detecting the presence of chemical molecules it needs for energy supply and chemical balance. The events I am describing in a brainless creature already contain the essence of the process of emotion that we humans have – detection of the presence of an object or event that recommends avoidance and evasion or endorsement and approach. The ability to react in this manner was not taught – there is not much pedagogy going on in paramecium school .... This shows that nature has long been concerned with providing living organisms with the means to regulate and maintain their lives automatically, no questions asked, no thoughts needed. (Damasio, 2003, pp. 40–41)

The Birth of Consciousness – a Fleeting Glimpse

Homeostatic systems made it possible for organisms to pursue simple primordial goals at an automatic level, without any mechanism for consciously influencing what they were doing. This basic arrangement served many organisms well for eons. In fact, such mechanisms are so efficient and dependable that to this day, even in humans, goal pursuit continues to be mostly a nonconscious endeavor. (Note that we'll be using the term "nonconscious" rather than "unconscious" because the latter term usually implies a lack of consciousness – as when people are asleep or in a comatose state – whereas we will be emphasizing mental activity that occurs beneath awareness during the normal course of our daily activities.)

The fact that all but a sliver of ongoing mental activity occurs outside consciousness is not well known outside the scientific community. Yet this is an essential design feature of human motivational systems. Consistent with our continuity assumption, nature has maintained the same general strategy of organizing as many capabilities as possible into nonconscious predispositions and habits, thus making it possible to pursue most goals quickly and reliably with minimal investments of mental energy (Bargh & Barndollar, 1996). Ensuring that energy resources remain available "when the going gets tough" is an essential requirement for successful goal pursuit (Baumeister & Tierney, 2011).

There was a point in evolutionary history, however, when reliance on the automatic, nonconscious pursuit of primordial goals was no longer sufficient. As organisms that had begun to explore life out of the water began to venture further inland, with no nutrient-rich "primordial soup" nearby to nourish them, survival now depended on being able to find and effectively use resources in the environment. And as resources became scarce, selection pressures increased for adaptive self-direction capabilities. In particular, the *time gap between goal activation and goal fulfillment* became a critical factor in the survival of the organism.

One way in which time was important had to do with the need to maintain motivation when a life-threatening problem could not be quickly resolved (e.g., due to the animal's lack of proximity to food or water). Some mechanism was needed to ensure that urgent biological needs remained the organism's top priority until those needs were addressed. The mechanism that emerged was the earliest manifestation of *consciousness*, a property of brain-based mental functioning that reflects the selective energizing of high-priority information (e.g., goal-relevant information). Being able to keep critical information in awareness during goal pursuit was the key to surviving high-stakes biological and environmental challenges. As Denton (2005) explains,

> the evolutionary origin of consciousness came from primal emotions arising from chemical sensors and receptors, internal and some surface ... which signalled the immediate existence of the organism was threatened .... Examples of primal emotion include thirst arising from desiccation of the organism, or breathlessness or "hunger for air," which occurs with choking or any other cause that cuts off the air supply. Such overwhelming sensations that commandeer the whole stream of consciousness are choreographed from the lower or basal areas of the brain. (pp. 107, 7)

As an increasing number of primarily aquatic creatures evolved into primarily nonaquatic organisms, major new environmental hazards (e.g., scarcity of water, glucose, and salt) threatened survival. Imagine, for example, an evolutionarily ancient creature crawling around on dry land and running low on water. The now proven biological sensor alarm mechanism could be relied on to initiate goal-directed activity, but some enhancement was needed to ensure that the "get water" goal remained a priority over time while the thirsty creature searched for water. Otherwise our little lizard might simply abandon the search after an initial, unsuccessful flurry of activity. The biological sensor alarms could perhaps be reactivated as electrochemical signals renewed the call for action, but without some kind of goal maintenance mechanism there would be no coherence to the resulting activity. The lizard would simply zig-zag around until its biological systems shut down from dehydration.

The need for a goal maintenance or *persistence* mechanism created selection pressures that resulted in a very rudimentary form of consciousness characterized by an awareness of *feelings* unique to each emotion pattern (e.g., the feeling of thirst). Because this newly evolved mechanism could only be energized for a relatively short period, we call it a "fleeting glimpse" of consciousness. This brief glimmer of subjective awareness – which remains all that many creatures today can experience – is analogous to the feature on modern automobiles that produces an audible warning if the vehicle is too near an obstacle. When the driver hears the warning, attention immediately shifts to the obstacle and corrective action is taken with almost 100 percent reliability. A strong emotion works the same way – based on a continuous and automatic assessment of bodily or environmental conditions, there is a moment when the "alarm bell" (or opportunity bell) goes off. That virtually ensures a timely response because, until the conscious feeling subsides, it is hard to focus on anything other than the goal activated by the triggered emotion (e.g., get water).

This early manifestation of consciousness was enabled by the advent of increasingly sophisticated brain-based "body maps" – essentially, an elaboration on the mechanism of sensor alarms that made it possible for the brain to organize signals from multiple, related sources from within the body into a unified neural representation (Damasio, 2003). The term *body map* refers to an organized cluster of neurons in the brain that is collectively responsible for representing the status of another part or region of the organism's body. A tickle to the foot, for example, will cause a specific set of brain-based neurons associated with the "mapping" of that foot to fire.

Body maps initially evolved to make the homeostatic processes discussed earlier more efficient. This was accomplished by ensuring that the brain-based neurons controlling a particular homeostatic process were in close proximity to the neurons representing the state of a relatively distant part of the body, thus further speeding up the organism's ability to "read and react" when opportunities and threats arose. For motivation at this basic biological level, nature's premise was clear: the race does indeed go to the swiftest.

Body maps began developing before the emergence of consciousness, but it was evidently not long (in evolutionary time) before the confluence of neurons organized around a common purpose made the mentally energized state we call consciousness possible. The mechanism was a straightforward elaboration on the triggering component of the homeostatic motivational system. Specifically, when the brain's representation of what was going on in the body suggested the presence of a dangerous deviation from a biological "set point," a conscious awareness of the affected body part – a *feeling* – would arise. Each such feeling involved two aspects: *valence* (i.e., some variation on pain or pleasure), and *content* (i.e., the unique qualities of the feeling that made it identifiable as thirst vs. hunger vs. breathlessness, etc.). As Damasio (2003) explains,

> the essential content of feelings is the mapping of a particular body state . . . . For example, the micro- and macrostructure of tensed muscles are a different content than relaxed muscles . . . . Another example, and perhaps the most important one, is the composition of the blood relative to some chemical molecules on which our life depends, and whose concentration is represented, moment by moment, in specific brain regions . . . . the substrate of feelings is the set of neural patterns that map the body state and from which a mental image of the body state can emerge. A feeling in essence is an idea – an idea of the body and, even more particularly, an idea of a certain aspect of the body, its interior, in certain circumstances. A feeling of emotion is an idea of the body when it is perturbed by the emoting process. (pp. 87–88)

For example, in the thirst system, the brain continuously maps hydration signals from various parts of the body. When the neural mapping of these body states indicates insufficient hydration, adjacent neurons governing the homeostatic systems associated with thirst reduction are provoked. This gives rise to an unpleasant and distinctive feeling recognizable as thirst. That persistent thirst feeling causes the thirst reduction neurons associated with the "get water" goal to keep firing until some thirst-quenching action is taken.

Feelings are thus motivating in both an informational way (because they have unique content) and in an energizing way (because they inspire action when they reach a certain magnitude). But feelings do not start the motivational response – that is what emotions do. The process starts at a nonconscious, automatic level with the triggering of an emotion, and then feelings arise as the relevant body maps are updated to reflect the "change and commotion" caused by the emotion. In other words, *triggered emotions activate the pursuit of a goal, while feelings sustain that pursuit.* Goal pursuit is thus typically well under way before we have any conscious awareness that a goal has been activated (LeDoux, 1998).

It is important to understand that the body mapping process is continuous and occurs even in the absence of emotional turbulence. Emotions are motivational specialists that are triggered when there is a need for appropriate action to facilitate the attainment of a specific kind of goal (e.g., getting nourishment, avoiding predators). Feelings, on the other hand, can arise at any time. The most salient feelings are those associated with strong emotions, but feelings may also reflect more general properties of the body's functioning (e.g., a general feeling of fatigue or relaxation). Analogous to the information on a weather map, the most attention-grabbing features will be those associated with lots of "change and commotion" (imagine the emotional equivalent of a thunderstorm or blizzard). However, general summary information may also be useful in guiding behavioral choices during relatively calm periods ("I should go for a walk while I still have enough energy to enjoy it").

In sum, "fleeting glimpses" of conscious feelings evolved as a powerful mechanism for sustaining self-directed activity, especially in circumstances where goal attainment required a coordinated investment of energy over an extended period of time. In effect, this was the first, primitive version of the "stick with it" capability that, in humans, we call willpower (Baumeister & Tierney, 2011; Inzlicht & Schmeichel, 2012). The feelings associated with primal emotions also conveyed information about how immediate and vigorous the goal pursuit needed to be – the stronger the feeling, the greater the degree of urgency. Indeed, when the conscious experience of an emotion reaches a certain threshold, it is virtually impossible to ignore (Frijda, 1988). What begins as a suggestive emotional humming in the background (e.g., a vague sensation that you need to go to the bathroom) can quickly turn into a persistent nagging sensation and ultimately into an urgent demand for your undivided attention ("I need to go RIGHT NOW!"). Feelings are thus able to "amplify" what may begin as a faint motivational response, thus making motivation stronger and more effective in facilitating both survival and well-being. As we will discuss later (in Chapter 5), this evolutionary ancient strategy of motivational amplification is a cornerstone of our *Thriving with Social Purpose Theory of Motivation and Optimal Functioning.*

From a Fleeting Glimpse to a Coherent Image

The emergence of consciousness in the context of primal emotions was a "big deal" in the evolution of self-direction (Denton uses the term "masterpiece"). The most immediate impact was to provide a mechanism for prolonging the influence of existing motivational systems directed by primordial goals. However, this development also initiated the transformation of emotions from *inflexible, single-purpose tools focused on the maintenance of biological steady states* into what ultimately would become a set of *highly flexible motivational mechanisms that help guide us in virtually every situation we encounter.*

The increasing versatility of emotions was made possible as organisms developed capabilities enabling them to integrate information about *internal conditions* provided by their interoceptors and proprioceptors (i.e., the sensory receptors responsible for monitoring the body's internal conditions and position in space) with information about *external conditions* provided by their exteroceptors (i.e., the sensory receptors responsible for mapping the external environment, such as those in the eyes, ears, nose, and skin). As a result, not only was pursuit of a goal such as "get water" more likely to continue long enough to ensure goal attainment, but that ambition could now be mentally connected to relevant visual, auditory, or olfactory cues (e.g., the sound of a nearby creek) and associated actions (e.g., moving in a particular direction toward the sound of the creek).

One product of that integration of internal and external information was the ability to bring mental images of the environment into consciousness. That enabled organisms to sustain not only the feeling that they needed to take some action, but also a coherent image of the physical places such action would need to occur. Perceptions were thus fused with feelings into a single unit of understanding. That in turn made it virtually impossible to perceive something without triggering some kind of emotion.

> Even the simplest animal must make decisions at every moment. Left or right? Go or stop? Eat or don't eat? . . .. These decisions [are made] effortlessly and automatically by having what is sometimes called a "like-o-meter" running in their heads at all times . . .. There's no need for a weighing of pros and cons, or for a reasoning system. Just flashes of pleasure and displeasure.

We humans have a like-o-meter, too, and it's always running. Its influence is subtle, but careful experiments show that you have a like-dislike reaction to everything you are experiencing, even if you're not aware of the experience. (Haidt, 2006, pp. 26–27)

This newly elaborated form of consciousness was the catalyst for a transformational change in what organisms were capable of in terms of self-direction. Organisms could now associate feelings of pleasure and displeasure with images of their world that initially had no significance (e.g., a nearby watering hole). Through this mechanism some of these images could then become goals in their own right. In other words, organisms were no longer limited to pursuing only those goals that had been genetically "preinstalled." Now they could also pursue *neuroimaged goals* that they constructed from their ongoing life experiences. What an amazing and important development! This was the beginning of a new era in the evolution of Earth's species – the era of *self-constructing living systems* (D. Ford, 1987/2019).

The transformative evolutionary events that enabled organisms to mentally construct goal images (neuroimaged goals) resolved a "bottleneck" that emerged when organisms began to face adaptational challenges in increasingly variable environments. Having a primordial goal and the underlying mechanisms needed to support its successful pursuit for every possible challenge that the environment might throw at an organism became too "expensive." It literally would take up too much brain tissue – analogous to carrying around one device to play your music, another device to get your email, another for GPS guided navigation, and another to make phone calls. Wouldn't it be easier to carry just one device that does all of these things plus handle future needs as they might arise with the download of new applications?

To understand how motivational systems directed by neuroimaged goals developed and why such systems were so effective in terms of conferring a survival advantage, it is necessary to say a bit more about the essential nature of consciousness. First, it is important to understand that *consciousness is not a thought process; it is an energizing process* (D. Ford, 1987/ 2019). Specifically, consciousness is a form of energy that selectively highlights information available to the brain, analogous to a music producer using an audio mixer to highlight certain sounds that may otherwise be experienced as "background noise," with little resulting impact. The information that may be highlighted includes everything from perceptions of the surrounding environment to simple internal sensations (e.g., hunger, pain, micturition) to complex goals, plans, and memories. Logically, then, any thought process that we are capable of doing consciously can also be done outside of consciousness (Hassin, 2013). As we will see, selectively energizing our thoughts often helps us think more effectively, especially when multiple sources of information need to be integrated and solutions require a high level of precision (e.g., it is hard to solve complex equations and crossword puzzles in an "autopilot" mode). Yet most of our thinking happens outside of consciousness.

Although consciousness has often been mistakenly regarded as a binary capability in the evolution of species – either they have it or they don't – it is better understood in terms of a continuum. At one end of the evolutionary scale are the fleeting glimpses of conscious awareness that we have been discussing, which many animals are capable of. Further along the continuum are species that are able to integrate information from a variety of sources (e.g., sensations, observations, memories) into coherent images that allow them to pursue goals over extended periods of time. This ongoing process of highlighting mental activity of greatest current relevance is what we usually think of as consciousness. The ability to energize goal-relevant thoughts and feelings on a continuous basis is an essential requirement in species that need more than automatic instinctual reactions to survive. As evolutionary biologist Richard Dawkins concludes, "Consciousness has to be there . . .. It's an evolved, emergent quality of brains. It's very likely that most mammals have consciousness, and probably birds, too" (Powell, 2011, p. D1).

At the other end of the continuum is fully developed human self-awareness, which is widely regarded as the highest form of consciousness (Leary, 2004). That is not to say that self-awareness is totally lacking in other animals. Yet there is a big difference between having a fleeting glimpse of self-awareness and possessing the full repertoire of capabilities that humans are able to employ. As Leary (2004) explains,

> evidence strongly suggests that most other animals do not have a self at all and that those species that do possess a self have only a very rudimentary one compared with human beings .... Only animals with a self – those with the cognitive ability to focus their attention on and think consciously about themselves – can think deliberatively about themselves, form images of what they are like (a self-concept), evaluate themselves (and react emotionally to their self-evaluations), talk to themselves in their own minds, and purposefully control their own behavior with some conscious goal in mind .... Although an animal without a self thinks, feels, and behaves, it cannot think about thinking, feeling, and behaving .... [Or] imagine the world

from other ... perspectives, including the ability to imagine how one is perceived and evaluated by others. (pp. 4–5, 10–11)

Functionally, consciousness is nature's tool for mentally highlighting key patterns of information that need to be kept in awareness for a period of time while a goal is being pursued. When goal pursuit only involves automatic responses to primordial goals, there is no need for such a mechanism. For example, we don't need to be conscious of our internal temperature for our body's cooling and heating systems to work (e.g., sweating and shivering, respectively). But when goal attainment depends on the coherent orchestration of a complex pattern of activity over time, there needs to be some way of energizing the right neurons at the right time and sustaining goal pursuit in the face of distractions, temptations, and fatigue.

This ability to selectively energize mental activity has produced some spectacular benefits, as we will see. However, these benefits did not come without a cost (Leary, 2004). Paradoxically, consciousness in its highest form – human self-awareness – can also cause unintended side effects. One common side effect is the disruption of reliable habits and routines (which explains why football coaches often call a time out to force the opposing team's kicker to think about an upcoming field goal attempt). Another is the tendency to keep energizing information that is no longer useful, as illustrated by habits of mental rumination often found in people suffering from depression, insomnia, and social anxiety (e.g., "I can't stop reliving that experience"; "I can't stop wondering what they're thinking about me"). Motivation scholars have repeatedly found that people who are able to stay focused on the *actions* needed to make goal progress are generally more effective in their goal pursuits than those who constantly worry about their internal mental *states* (as illustrated by those who focus more on their feelings of distress than on what it would take to alter those feelings) (Dweck & Leggett, 1988; Kuhl & Beckmann, 1994).

When consciousness first emerged as an evolutionary solution, it was primarily an adaptation designed to highlight *body state* information. The powerful feelings associated with breathlessness, hunger, thirst, salt depletion, and other biological states virtually guaranteed that the right goals would be prioritized when survival was threatened.

That same mechanism was then used to highlight information about potentially relevant events in the *environment* using structures within the body responsible for sensing what was going on outside the body. This made it possible to focus mental energy on potentially goal-relevant *perceptions* – for example, on sights, sounds, and smells associated with food or predators. Heightened awareness of potential threats and opportunities of this sort had obvious survival value.

Once organisms developed the ability to selectively energize perceptions, they could also use that capability to bring *memories* into consciousness. In effect, any perception that left an enduring mental impression could be mentally reinstated and become an object of conscious awareness. What made a perception memorable? To a large extent it was the magnitude of the feelings attached to it. Indeed, it has been well established that emotionally salient memories are much more vivid and enduring than emotionally bland memories (Bower, 1981; Damasio, 1994; Vaillant, 2002). Conversely, experiences tend to become less memorable when the clarity or potency of the connection between perceptions and feelings is reduced. For example, recent research suggests that morphine taken promptly after a war-time injury may significantly reduce the probability that wounded troops will develop posttraumatic stress disorder (Holbrook et al., 2010). Morphine not only reduces the feelings of pain and fear associated with a traumatic experience for some patients, it also interferes with memory processing (i.e., both the perceptual and feeling components of what is remembered may be weakened).

So far we have discussed how consciousness can energize information related to your present functioning (feelings, perceptions) and to your past functioning (memories). But from a motivational perspective what really makes consciousness a powerful tool for enhancing self-direction is its ability to energize thoughts and feeling about the *future*. Once this capability evolved, opportunities and threats could not only be sensed, they could now be *anticipated*. At least in a primitive sort of way, organisms now had the ability to engage in *forethought* (i.e., awareness of expected future circumstances in relation to a goal).

The result of this evolutionary advance was an enhanced ability to connect current circumstances with past and anticipated future experiences. Imagine, for example, a fully land-based descendant of our primordial lizard waking up to hunger pangs via the now well-proven emotional "alarm signal." The hunger feeling effectively provides the initial motivation to solve the problem, but what if there is no food in the immediate area? A solution would then have to be mentally constructed, with consciousness facilitating that process. Specifically, our starving creature would need to anticipate where food might be located based on clues in the current situation (e.g., scents from relevant food sources) and past experience (e.g., memories associated with successful hunger reduction), and then link those mental images to appropriate action. With just a tiny dose of consciousness, the hungry lizard could mentally connect all of those elements into a coordinated image.

This milestone in the elaboration of consciousness represented a huge leap forward. Although behavior was still more reactive than creative, self-direction could now be based (at least to a limited degree) on life experience rather than being limited to built-in instincts and reflexes. That new capability in turn created additional selection pressures favoring brain plasticity.

From Coherent Images to Simple Planning

Over the eons, as the number and complexity of neurons in the brain continued to rise, the range and amount of information that could be selectively energized and brought into consciousness increased. Eventually, the continued elaboration of consciousness made it possible for some higher animals to go beyond the construction of simple mental associations. In these animals, consciousness evolved further to become a tool for helping them plan for the future (Mulcahy & Call, 2006).

It was once thought that only humans could engage in planning for future needs. However, it is becoming increasingly clear that this ability has roots more ancient than previously thought (Suddendorf, 2006). For example, Correia et al. (2007) recently concluded that "food-caching Western scrub-jays (*Aphelocoma californica*) can relate their previous experience as thieves to the possibility of future cache theft by another bird, are sensitive to the state of their caches at recovery, and can plan for tomorrow's breakfast" (p. 856). This is evidence that, over time, the ability to mentally connect images of the past, present, and future played an increasingly important role in the evolution of consciousness as a tool for facilitating survival and well-being.

The progression from images to plans was not just a quantitative achievement reflecting the ability to think farther into the past or future. There was also a qualitative transformation as consciousness evolved into a capability for *mentally manipulating* images and ideas, thus adding an important degree of flexibility to animal instincts and habits. Consciousness was no longer just a tool for getting useful information onto the mind's "front-burner." It was also a tool for shaping mental images, thereby making them more useful for self-direction. That development placed an even higher premium on brain malleability.

Imagine, for example, a fox seeking to capture a rabbit for food. If the fox simply ran to where the rabbit was first seen, the food would be gone by the time the fox got there. Skillful hunting requires a more flexible kind of mental calculation that enables the fox to imagine likely scenarios that have not yet happened, as well as possible variations on those scenarios. As a result of these kinds of selection pressures, consciousness evolved to enable more of a future orientation. Reactive thinking only works in unchanging or slowly changing environments. Anticipatory thinking, on the other hand, makes it possible to organize and guide behavior not just in terms of *current* events in a specific time and place, but also in terms of *hypothetical* events in imagined future times and places. That in turn makes it possible to prepare more effectively for upcoming challenges – for example, by conserving energy or obtaining help from others.

Of course, planning capabilities in humans have advanced far beyond the simple demonstrations of cleverness that evolutionary biologists have observed in other animals. Indeed, Roberts (2002) has concluded that most animals are able to project no more than twenty minutes into the future. Nevertheless, the evolved ability to go beyond "snapshots" to "episodes" connecting past, present, and future escalated self-direction to a new level. As motivation became increasingly future oriented, goal possibilities expanded and more advanced forms of creative problem solving began to emerge. Creativity was further fueled by the emergence of new emotion patterns that were far more flexible than the primal emotions supporting the operation of primordial homeostatic mechanisms.

The Development of "Emotions-Proper"

Most people (including many emotion scholars) do not think of primal emotions like thirst and craving for salt as "true" emotions in the traditional sense of that word. That is because our culture has learned to use the word "emotion" for responses to life experiences that are personally meaningful rather than biologically mandated (e.g., while thirst is essentially the same experience for all humans, I might be emotionally indifferent to some things that may frighten you, like a large dog or a clown face). In these personalized instances the emotion pattern itself does not need to be learned (e.g., the biological and expressive elements of a basic fear response are innate), but the thoughts, perceptions, and memories that emotions get connected to are highly dependent on personal experience. In contrast, primal emotions are inflexibly (and thus reliably) associated with primordial goals. Thirst, for example, is automatically triggered when dehydration occurs. That connection does not need to be learned, nor can it be "unlearned."

Because of our interest in understanding the origins and fundamental nature of human motivation, we have adopted the view that it is useful to think of primal emotions as being functionally related to what Damasio (2003) calls *emotions-proper* (i.e., emotions like surprise, fear, joy, anger, and disgust). There is no doubt that this latter set of emotions is more advanced (evolutionarily speaking) than primal emotions. Nevertheless, "emotions-proper," rather than emerging as brand new motivational systems, appear to involve the same evolved mechanisms governing primal emotions – specifically:

> Sensors → internal alarm signals → "change and commotion" → updated body maps → feelings → conscious awareness of the circumstances causing the alarm.

Understanding that "emotions-proper" function in much the same way as primal emotions clarifies why some emotional connections are so easy to learn. Once organisms developed the ability to create mental images of the environment, there was natural selection pressure to develop capabilities for "tagging" the images of the environment they were moving around in with goal-relevant information. Emotions provided a reliable and efficient mechanism for this purpose. Some images were positive and associated with opportunity (e.g., the scent of prey). Other images were negative and associated with danger (e.g., the scent of a predator). In this way, things that were not a hardwired part of the organism's motivational systems could become *emotionally competent stimuli* in their own right (Damasio, 2003). That in turn made it possible to make quick decisions about possible opportunities and threats rather than wasting precious time redundantly reevaluating familiar elements of the environment.

Our earlier reference to Haidt's (2006) metaphorical "like-o-meter" is a useful way to think about how this tagging process works. Recall that, as consciousness evolved, emotions and perceptions became part of a unitary experience. As a result, when something was perceived in relation to a goal, it would acquire a degree of emotional salience – the more important the goal and the relevance of the perception to that goal, the stronger the emotion. Through this associative process, goal-relevant perceptions – like the sight or smell of food or a predator – would acquire the ability to trigger an emotion. That in turn led to a conscious feeling along the lines of the "flashes of pleasure or displeasure" that Haidt described. Positive feelings motivated approach behavior, whereas negative feelings motivated avoidance behavior.

The specific content of the positive or negative feeling also mattered a great deal. For example, an awareness of leaves rustling nearby might trigger surprise, an emotion that effectively stops activity while current conditions are assessed for possible threats. Or, the sound of leaf rustling might trigger fear, an emotion that motivates avoidance and escape. Alternatively, if leaf rustling was associated with the idea that fellow tribe members might be moving through the woods toward food or water, that sound might instead trigger excitement, an emotion that motivates vigorous goal pursuit.

As brains became bigger and more complex, and more things could be perceived and remembered, the range of environmental objects and circumstances that could acquire a degree of emotional salience increased dramatically. For example, in the everyday life of a dog, the repertoire of emotionally salient perceptions might include the smell of an opened can of dog food, the sight of a chew toy lying on the ground, the sound of a door opening or a leash being handled by the owner, and various tactile expressions of affection from the dog's owners. The range of emotionally competent stimuli (i.e., objects and/or situations capable of arousing emotions) would be far greater for the dog than, say, a lizard. And yet, the emotional life of a dog looks quite impoverished when compared to adult humans, who seem to attach some level of emotional meaning to almost everything they experience (Damasio, 2003; Haidt, 2006; Leary, 2004).

With the advent of *emotional learning* – the ability to "tag" observations and perceptions with emotional content – rapid adaptation to changing circumstances became possible. This was another giant step forward in the evolutionary progression of motivational systems. In theory, almost anything could become an object of interest, or fear, or pleasure depending on its relationship (e.g., a help or a hindrance) to a primordial or neuroimaged goal. Moreover, once an image had acquired the properties of a strong and reliable emotional "marker," it could then become paired with other images, thus creating an amplified *network* of emotionally competent stimuli (as illustrated by a dog owner's varied repertoire of vocalizations and facial expressions) (Damasio, 2003).

Understanding how an emotionally competent stimulus works is essential for understanding how to motivate self and others. When a stimulus becomes emotionally competent, it functions like a "key" for a particular emotional "lock." When the stimulus key fits the neural structures responsible for triggering a particular emotion (i.e., the stimulus is "competent"), the emotion-triggering lock (e.g., the amygdala) activates the brain's emotion-execution sites (e.g., the hypothalamus), and a characteristic pattern of "change and commotion" ensues in the body and brain. Typical changes, for example, might include an increase or decrease in heart rate, blood pressure, and electrochemical activity; the release of emotion-specific hormones; and the stimulation of appropriate muscle movements (e.g., approach, withdrawal, or defensive activity). Consistent with the highly social nature of motivational systems in many species (especially humans), also typical are changes that communicate to others the nature of the emotional state that is being experienced (e.g., changes in facial expressions, body language, and voice pitch or frequency).

These changes are usually initiated before there is any awareness that an emotionally competent stimulus has been encountered and the emotion-triggering process has started. It is not until feelings arise that we have a sense of how our body and mind have begun to respond. That is a profoundly important feature of human motivation. *If a stimulus is "emotionally competent," you can't stop it from triggering the emotion.* All you can do is manage the emotional response once you become aware of it – usually, for example, upon feeling your heart rate increase, or your muscles tense up, or your face flush.

That does not mean that these emotional responses are "fixed and final." The same flexibility that makes emotional learning possible also makes it possible to learn *new* emotional associations. Such "relearning" is commonplace, for example, when you develop new capabilities or when your life circumstances change, especially if the new experiences are salient and convincing (e.g., when you master a previously scary task like riding a bike for the first time). However, developing new emotional associations may be extremely difficult if the initial learning experience is very negative and it occurred under painful or traumatic conditions (Pitman, 2011). Our brains evolved during a time when survival depended on remembering to be afraid upon reencountering something capable of producing significant pain or damage. This is why, for example, many war veterans and crime victims struggle with posttraumatic stress disorder.

Understanding the differences between emotions and feelings can be very empowering. For example, if you are anticipating speaking in public and that triggers a fear response, you can acknowledge and accept that this response is a normal consequence of your innate emotional learning mechanisms (as opposed to being seen as a personal failing). Then, you can take deliberate steps to learn how to manage that fear response (as opposed to assuming "there's nothing I can do about it"). Effective emotional management (e.g., using breathing exercises, cognitive reinterpretation techniques, or exceptionally diligent preparation) can then lead to success experiences that yield new (additional) emotional associations with the fear-inducing stimulus. Of course, you could also simply try to avoid public speaking, but if that is your chosen path, be forewarned that this will provide little opportunity for change in the learned fear response.

It doesn't take long for an initially nonconscious emotional response to generate consciously experienced feelings characteristic of that emotional state – typically less than a second or so (Damasio, 2003). This happens as a result of our brain's body maps being quickly updated by internal sensors monitoring the bodily changes associated with the emotional response (e.g., changes in heart rate and hormonal activity). It is interesting to consider circumstances in which a strong feeling (e.g., of a pounding heart) was no longer useful by the time you felt it (e.g., feeling fear only after a scary experience has ended – like when you swerve to avoid a car that unexpectedly pulls out in front of you). Such situations vividly illustrate the fact that feelings arise from emotions "after the fact" rather than being an intrinsic part of the initial emotional response. Emotions initially evolved to support immediate action (e.g., your swerve). We then developed feelings (e.g., realizing your heart was pounding) to help us maintain a state of readiness for further action.

It is important to reiterate that none of these basic mechanisms for triggering and sustaining emotional responses began with the emergence of "emotions-proper." The mechanisms we have been describing are essentially the same ones that govern our primal emotions and the primordial goals they serve. What really makes this phase in the evolution of self-direction distinctive and important is the capacity for emotional learning. Being able to connect innate emotion "templates" to specific aspects of the environment makes it possible to quickly convert salient objects and experiences into emotionally competent stimuli. That is why, unlike skill learning (especially complex skills like calculus and golf!), most emotional learning is effortless, automatic, and persistent. Once infant chimps see their mother scream and jump when a poisonous snake crawls nearby, for example, those little chimps are likely to forever do likewise whenever they encounter a snake. Even more intriguing, we do not always have to be consciously aware that a learned emotionally competent stimulus is nearby in order for the paired emotion to trigger (Damasio, 2003). It's as if we had a personal bodyguard ready to take action to protect us from dangerous elements (like snakes in the grass) while we focus our attention on the task at hand (e.g., hiking toward a destination).

Natural selection favors rapid reactions. To that end, brains are constantly "jumping to conclusions" (Koch, 2004, p. 23) and filling-in missing details automatically and nonconsciously. Consider that our open eyes, each with an estimated 100 million photoreceptors, produce an average of 10 million bits of information every second (Koch, 2004, p. 63). Thankfully, only a small fraction of the massive amount of data that are continuously striking the visual cortex ever makes it to awareness. But that is what makes the concept of an emotionally competent stimulus so important. Such stimuli are able to have an immediate impact, without analysis and judgment, even in the face of many potential distractions. That is important in a world full of danger and opportunity.

The evolution of empathy provides a particularly compelling example of the importance of minimizing the time delay between perceiving and acting on an emotionally competent stimulus. As de Waal (2009) explains, "empathy is part of a heritage as ancient as the mammalian line. Empathy engages brain areas that are more than a hundred million years old" (p. 208). Rudimentary forms of empathy emerged when mammals began to evolve from reptiles and survival increasingly became a shared problem (i.e., most mammals are social species [meaning that they can only survive in groups]). That is when the adaptive value of being able to instantaneously coordinate action with others in similar circumstances – for example, through emotional contagion and motor mimicry – became especially evident. Such adaptations are vividly illustrated by "a flock of birds taking off all at once because one among them is startled by a predator . . .. The selection pressure on paying attention to others must have been enormous. The bird that fails to take off at the same instant as the rest of the flock may be lunch" (de Waal, 2006, p. 25). Paying close attention to others' emotional states also became increasingly important to the survival of one's offspring, as mammalian parents who were insensitive to their infants' needs were at much higher risk of failing to have their offspring reach reproductive age compared to parents who responded reliably and effectively to events threatening their children's survival (Hrdy, 2009).

How do these emotion-triggered, rapid-response motivational systems work? What are the mechanisms that enable us to react "without thinking" (i.e., with little or no conscious deliberation) in the face of urgent threats and opportunities? What Damasio (2003) calls the "presentation stage" (p. 58) occurs when we happen to encounter an emotionally competent stimulus. Out of the oceans of sensory data, a vague "quick and dirty" resemblance of some aspect of the environment that has been previously paired with, say, danger can trigger fear and its ensuing string of physiological events (e.g., blood rushing to the large muscles, hormonal and steroidal releases, digestion shut down, pupil dilation). All of this happens within milliseconds and often before we become consciously aware of the fear-inducing stimulus. And the process is remarkably reliable – otherwise, we would have become extinct long ago!

Furthermore, our close encounter with the emotionally competent stimulus can be imaginary and produce precisely the same response. In other words, mere thoughts and memories of emotionally provocative objects or people can trigger the paired emotion. Undoubtedly, this was highly adaptive during life on the savanna 40,000 years ago, as it is in most cases in today's world. However, that may be of small comfort to those of us who get a pounding heart just by thinking about an upcoming speech or an especially irritating co-worker!

The evolutionary significance of emotional learning becomes even more apparent when this advance is linked to the previously discussed capacity for constructing ad hoc solutions to novel problems via neuroimaged goals. Indeed, these enhancements logically go together as there wouldn't be any need for "tagging" new objects and experiences with emotional content if there was no mechanism for adding goals beyond those that had been "preinstalled" (keeping in mind that emotions exist to motivate selective goal pursuit). What was evolving, then, was not just a separate set of capabilities, but rather a unitary *motivational system* governed by the integrated functioning of goals and emotions.

For most creatures, the addition of motivational systems directed by neuroimaged goals represented the "end of the line" with respect to the evolution of self-direction. But not for our hominid ancestors. Self-direction in humans includes several elaborations beyond those discussed thus far. These elaborations are reflected in our brain structures, in our motivation-related thought processes, and in our social and emotional life.

Self-Direction in Humans

Self-Awareness and Mental Time Travel

Self-awareness exists in humans and, at a very rudimentary level, in a few other species – as evidenced, for example, by their ability to recognize themselves in a mirror (Leary, 2004). Following the classic evolutionary strategy of "building on what works" through innovative elaborations on existing systems (Wagner, 2014), the same basic mechanism used to provide an emotional wake-up call for food and water was applied to an increasing range of mental phenomena – feelings, perceptions, memories, thoughts about the future, and, finally, thoughts and feelings about the self. As a result, more and more of the mind's functions became accessible to consciousness.

Denton (2005) has described self-awareness as the highest form of consciousness. And why not – consider the obvious evolutionary advantages of being able to shine the bright light of consciousness not only on information related to your interactions with the environment, but also on the "self" responsible for governing those interactions. When the self became an object of awareness, self-direction was no longer just something you did; it was also something you could explore and understand and influence. For example, you could evaluate your goals and plans in light of your capabilities and shortcomings and consider possible alternatives. You could assess your habits and whether they were contributing to goal progress or causing unintended negative consequences. You could reflect on your feelings and beliefs and question their validity. In short, you could continuously monitor the mental activity associated with self-direction, and then use that information to become more effective in your goal pursuits.

The common theme in all these new possibilities conferred by the conscious self is *self-directed innovation*. We no longer had to rely solely on biologically based innovations arising from dynamic genotype networks and natural selection (Wagner, 2014). We could now learn from ourselves and others in ways that profoundly transcended simple mechanisms of associative learning. Self-direction had evolved into a fundamental agent of self-change. *Motivation and creative thought and action had become inextricably linked.*

The emergence of self-awareness was associated with the development of a special kind of memory called *episodic memory* that allows people to think about themselves not only as actors in the present, but also as actors in past life episodes (Tulving, 1985). The ability to mentally reconstruct events and experiences from the past also made it possible to mentally construct hypothetical *future* episodes containing the same kind of information as found in episodic memories (e.g., time, place, and goal-relevant information). The resulting ability to engage in mental simulations, or *mental time travel* (Suddendorf & Corballis, 1997), is perhaps the most far-reaching consequence of the development of self-awareness. Once we were aware that there was a future in which we and our offspring would continue to live, and that our success and survival in the future was related to our experiences in the present, life changed dramatically. "Live for the moment" was no longer the only option. We were now, by design, living for the future as well.

The emergence of mental time travel capabilities was a crucial step in the evolution of humanity (Suddendorf & Corballis, 2007). As T. D. Wilson (2002) explains,

> an organism that has a concept of the future and past, and is able to reflect on these time periods at will, is in a better position to make effective long-term plans than one that does not – providing a tremendous survival advantage .... Imagine the advantage of having a more flexible mental system that can muse, reflect, ponder, and contemplate alternative futures and connect those scenarios to the past. The practice of agriculture, for example, requires knowledge of the past and thinking about the future; why bother putting seeds in the ground now if we cannot envision what will happen to them over the next few weeks? (p. 51)

The ability to connect past, present, and future within a perspective of self-awareness helped fuel some of humankind's most impressive achievements, including "cultural, religious, and scientific concepts about origins, destiny, and time itself" (Suddendorf & Corballis, 1997, p. 133). As Seligman et al. (2013) explain,

> humans are extraordinary among animals in their capacity for the prospection necessary for long-term, shared, stable enterprises such as government, law, schools, commerce, collective bargaining, and retirement planning. Commitments, relationships, values, and convictions, even "the self" as a persisting entity, are a matter not just of how one has acted or is acting but of how one thinks about the future and how one will or would act in various futures. (p. 129)

Such achievements were made possible in part by the fact that mental time travel created a need for symbolic communication that could transcend time and place. And this is precisely what linguistic and mathematical systems do by connecting arbitrary, but culturally agreed upon, symbols with conscious manifestations of our perceptions, feelings, and thoughts (e.g., *I love you, je t'aime, te amo*, and *jeg elsker deg* all have precisely the same meaning). We can then use those symbols to help us think about and elaborate on our perceptions, feelings, and thoughts – and to share them with others. Words and phrases that represent broad concepts (like honesty, fairness, and social purpose) and clarifying propositions (e.g., "Good things come to those who wait") are particularly useful tools for bringing nonconscious mental activity into consciousness and for enabling us to use our conscious mind to help direct, control, and regulate our behavior (D. Ford, 1987/2019).

Another particularly useful property of mental time travel is the ability to simulate goal pursuit and its possible consequences in our imagination before engaging in any real-world activity. That capability makes it possible to "prime" the mind and body for the upcoming experience and to make mental adjustments as needed. The more vivid the simulation, the greater the impact. That is why mental imagery, when properly harnessed, can be so effective in managing emotions, coordinating action, exercising self-control, and facilitating learning and behavior change (Guillot & Collet, 2010; Knauper et al., 2009). *When mental imagery incorporates self-awareness and mental time travel, you can literally see yourself changing as a result of your (simulated) actions.*

Perhaps it is not surprising that something as powerful as self-awareness might have a downside as well. As Leary (2004) warns, the ability to think self-consciously can be both a blessing and a curse. On the one hand, self-awareness facilitates innovation and personal growth by enabling us to imagine how the future might be better than the present. On the other hand, it can also cause us to become self-absorbed, as illustrated by habits such as ruminating about imagined failures and shortcomings, worrying excessively about things that might go wrong, and obsessing about what others might think of us. Indeed, self-conscious thoughts and emotions are contributing factors in a wide range of psychological problems, including depression, narcissism, hypochondria, ego-defensiveness, and social anxiety.

It thus appears that consciousness in its highest form is associated with many distinctly human qualities – both good and bad. It enables the self to function as a potent change agent while also creating a need to quiet the self when it becomes our "personal tormentor" (Haidt, 2006, p. 207).

When Goals Became Personal

Self-awareness transformed the nature of motivation in a truly fundamental way. Prior to self-awareness, neuroimaged goals were simply mental images of perceived or remembered solutions that were activated each time an emotionally tagged object was encountered. This was of course a tremendous advance compared to motivational systems that relied exclusively on primordial goals. However, the process was still rather mechanistic in the sense that any organism within the same species and with the same history of emotional learning would be likely to produce the same kind of goal image and respond in the same way in similar circumstances (which explains why theories of human behavior should not be based solely on research with rats and pigeons and the like). In contrast, when goal images began to include the self as the actor pursuing that goal, they were no longer just a "generic" mental picture of a desired outcome or event. They were now *personalized* goal thoughts!

To review the evolution of self-direction: in its initial, most simple form, triggered primal emotions reliably activated *primordial* goals – that is, goals which directed "standard" solutions. Next, we see how some creatures evolved "fleeting" consciousness capabilities which supported goal maintenance over time (albeit for a very brief period). Such capabilities made it possible to imagine "custom" desired outcomes – thus adding *neuroimaged* goals to that species' goal repertoire. Over eons of evolution, those fleeting glimpses of awareness encompassed an increasing range of mental activity and became much longer in duration. Eventually, the self became an object of awareness, and self-awareness, or "self-consciousness" emerged. With the addition of this capability, *personal* goals – goals that imagined outcomes *in the context of the self* – were added in layered fashion to our ancient repertoire of primordial and neuroimaged goals.

When the environment is highly variable and rapidly changing, only creatures capable of activating personal goals can consistently adapt. Consistent with that observation, humans are the only species that can live almost anywhere on the planet.

The difference between neuroimaged goals and personal goals might be compared to watching a movie versus making your own movie. In the former (neuroimaging) scenario, you may be able to learn a lot about the plot and the setting, and make good predictions about what actions are likely to lead to good and bad outcomes, but your perspective would be limited to what you actually observed and experienced in the past. In contrast, with self-awareness, you are the producer, director, and main actor in your life movie. In that scenario, you have the ability to imagine yourself performing in different ways and in different settings. You can't redo what has already been filmed, but you can imagine doing things differently in the future (e.g., by rewriting the script or changing the other characters). You can imagine new plot lines and alternative endings. Perhaps most importantly, you can imagine yourself changing what you set out to accomplish, since after all, the goals you are pursuing are your *personal* goals.

Sternberg and Spear-Swerling (1998) use the term "personal navigation" (PN) to refer to this uniquely human aspect of self-direction. They define personal navigation as

> a person's control of his or her voyage through life . . .. PN involves finding a direction in life; maintaining this direction when appropriate and changing it when appropriate; moving in the direction that is appropriate for the circumstances; using navigational aids in order to maintain the desired direction; and overcoming the obstacles that inevitably present themselves in any voyage. One's PN is enhanced to the extent that one is self-aware with respect to needs, desires, and goals. (pp. 221–222)

Seligman et al. (2013) also use the metaphor of "navigating into the future" to describe the human capacity for imagining possibilities and then drawing upon past experience "to update a branching array of evaluative prospects that fan out before them . . .. These prospects can include not only possibilities that have occurred before but also possibilities that have never occurred – and these new possibilities often play a decisive role in the selection of action" (p. 119).

Of course, even as the producer/director of your "life story," you will have constraints on what you can do as you think about how you will pursue your personal goals. Your "equipment" (e.g., biological and intellectual capabilities) will limit what you can do to some extent. Navigating in demanding conditions or in "troubled waters" on a regular basis can deplete energy resources and leave you vulnerable to making poor decisions. Financial constraints and political realities may keep you from fulfilling some of your more ambitious aspirations. And you may have to deal with some "cast members" (e.g., certain family members or co-workers) who are uncooperative, egocentric, or just not that good a fit in terms of the parts you would like them to play (metaphorically speaking).

Yet, even when we feel burdened by many constraints in the course of our daily lives, there remains a fundamental sense that goal pursuit originates from our own emotions, thoughts, and actions. In other words, we *feel* self-directed. That feeling of *personal agency* is one of the key features distinguishing motivation in humans from motivation in other species. Indeed, the experience of having no sense of personal agency – as connoted by terms such as hopelessness, futility, and loss of control – is one of the most disorganizing and motivationally debilitating things that can happen to a human being (Baumeister, 1990; Clark & Kissane, 2002).

Personal Agency Beliefs

One of the most important developments in the evolution of self-direction in humans was the expansion of our motivational systems to include appraisals related to personal agency, or as they are known in Motivational Systems Theory, *personal agency beliefs*. Previously, before the capacity for self-awareness and mental time travel evolved, only two kinds of motivational processes were needed: goals and emotions. Goals provided direction and organizational coherence, consistent with their leadership role in mental activity. Emotions provided goal-activating energy and motivational advice focused on prototypical life challenges and opportunities. Yet emotions have limitations when the decisions to be made involve consequences beyond a short-term time frame. Emotions are focused more on energizing and regulating action in the present than on guiding investments in the future. Analogous to a push that gets a flywheel spinning, emotions are often at their peak when they are initially triggered, with the feelings responsible for sustaining the emotion's impact tending to fade rather quickly unless we do something mentally or behaviorally to reignite or strengthen them (e.g., vividly imagining success or failure outcomes; repeating the actions that triggered the emotion in the first place).

The development of the "self" and its associated long-term visioning and planning capabilities created both a need and an opportunity for an additional, more general motivational advising mechanism – one that could help provide a "reality check" by ensuring that information about personal capabilities and environmental resources were incorporated more systematically into important decisions. The solution was the development of a third member of the motivational leadership team: *personal agency beliefs*, or expectancies about the consequences of personal goal seeking (M. Ford, 1992). In tandem with emotions, personal agency beliefs help people decide which goals to pursue at what level of effort and persistence. For example, self-confidence and trust encourage active engagement, risk-taking, and investment of resources. In contrast, self-doubt and suspicion tend to have a de-motivating effect.

The presence of personal agency beliefs in our ongoing stream of mental activity helps us make wise decisions and stay on track in our goal pursuits. For the most part, this is a nonconscious process involving ongoing comparisons between personal goal thoughts (i.e., the *desired* and *undesired* consequences of goal seeking) and thoughts about personal agency (i.e., the *expected* consequences of goal seeking). For example, when you engage in conversation, you are constantly generating sentences and facial movements based, in part, on how you expect others to respond. Occasionally those expectations prove to be very wrong (e.g., you unintentionally say something insulting or offensive), and suddenly a natural process requiring very little attentional energy can turn into a difficult struggle to maintain one's reputation – and perhaps a valued relationship – that extends well beyond a single conversational episode. That is consistent with the idea that personal agency beliefs evolved in conjunction with self-awareness and mental time travel to help guide complex decision-making over extended time periods.

That is not to say that emotions lack potency or validity when it comes to more complex decisions. But as decision-making became increasingly future oriented, additional help was needed to ensure that decisions requiring deliberative forethought and analysis would not be made on the basis of feelings alone. As explained in more detail in Chapter 4, personal agency beliefs provide that extra layer of guidance by mentally representing the anticipated results of pursuing a goal.

The evolutionary significance of personal agency beliefs may also be related to their impact when they intrude into consciousness and serve as an antidote to feelings of despair and hopelessness. "Life's bottom line" is protected when we maintain a fundamental belief that the future can be better than the past, even when the going gets tough.

Such beliefs can also help us sustain goal pursuit when extraordinary amounts of time or effort are required – as is so often the case when pursuing long-term goals or when our energy resources are being rapidly depleted. For example, the science of "willpower" suggests that the natural motivational consequences of energy depletion (e.g., becoming less patient with others or less able to resist the temptation to procrastinate or "behave badly") can be forestalled, at least for a while, if you believe that your willpower capabilities are essentially limitless (Job et al., 2010). Although such a belief is not fully accurate – motivation is always dependent on biology and context (Baumeister & Tierney, 2011; Inzlicht & Schmeichel, 2012) – the fact that such beliefs can help sustain motivation beyond typical limits illustrates the important role that personal agency beliefs play in helping us get the most out of the resources we do have.

Human Emotions

Most of the basic emotion patterns that inform and inspire our lives today evolved prior to the emergence of self-awareness. Nevertheless, the scope and richness of human emotions is far greater than in other animals. Because of the increased number and complexity of neurons in our bigger brains, we can acquire more information about the emotional salience of the world around us. Indeed, we seem to have a virtually limitless capacity to mentally "tag" the objects, people, and experiences we encounter in our daily lives with emotional information (Haidt, 2006). As result, "few if any objects in the world are emotionally neutral" (Damasio, 2003, p. 56).

It is hard to underestimate the importance of this evolutionary development, as it means that context-relevant goals can be activated by triggered emotions with lightning speed across a broad array of situations, including those we have not yet encountered, with emotions then helping to regulate goal progress as events unfold. Indeed, when brain damage disrupts people's automatic emotion-tagging and emotion-triggering capabilities, the results can be quite shocking. Such damage causes exemplary employees and citizens to suddenly become unconcerned about their social relationships and incapable of pursuing the personal goals associated with daily living (Damasio, 2003).

> Why? Because they could not adequately incorporate emotion into their thinking. Instead of becoming more rational and logical when their decisions were free from emotion, these patients did not care what other people thought of their behavior, were unable to learn from their past mistakes, and did not stop and change course when it became clear that their current actions were leading them astray. Critically, these patients had intact knowledge but had no sense of risk or morality and so would plow ahead into decisions that any "rational" person would find, at best, short-sighted or a waste of time and, at worst, dangerous, stupid, or immoral. (Immordino-Yang, 2016, p. 27)

Human emotions are also unique with respect to the richness and complexity of the thematic thoughts we associate with the feelings that arise from our emotional experience. With self-awareness and mental time travel, the implications of feeling an emotion can extend far beyond the circumstances that triggered the emotion. We can wonder what the feelings mean and construct explanations that add substance and generality to the emotional experience (e.g., "If it bothers me this much, it must be really important to me"). Thematic thoughts can also amplify feelings and thus perpetuate or even intensify the emotional response (e.g., "This guilt is driving me crazy, I can't stop thinking about what I did"). Alternatively, thematic thoughts can persuade us to discount the significance of a particular feeling and cause it to shrivel up and vanish (e.g., "Why am I feeling jealous? I don't even want what they have").

Finally, human emotions are unique with respect to the range and complexity of social emotions we experience. Although social emotions supporting social bonding and group cohesion are commonplace in many species (de Waal, 2006, 2009), those that depend on self-awareness are seen almost exclusively in humans. Included among these "self-conscious" emotions are some of the most compelling in our motivational repertoire – for example, guilt, shame, embarrassment, and pride. In addition, as selection pressures placed increasing emphasis on social interdependence and cooperative childrearing, the capacity for empathy grew from simple state matching to sophisticated "mind reading" (de Waal, 2006). As a result, emotions such as sympathy and compassion emerged as powerful sources of motivational "glue" for families, communities, and other meaningful social groups (Hauser, 2006; Keltner, 2009; Post, 2007).

It would therefore be a big mistake to assume that social emotions are just some minor evolutionary elaboration on our "primary" emotions (D. Ford, 1987/2019). Humans need highly developed social emotions to survive and to thrive. Indeed, as we will see in Chapter 6, social emotions are at the heart of the evolutionary transformation that took place during the Middle Pleistocene period and ultimately led to the development of human life as we know it. The personal goals that fueled this transformation – what we will refer to as *social purpose* goals – could only be effective if there were emotions in place that would reliably activate those goals. That is why the capacity for experiencing these emotions is "preinstalled" – as evidenced, for example, by the fact that infants are capable of empathy (at the level of emotional state matching) within a few hours of birth (Eisenberg et al., 2003; Hauser, 2006).

Although social emotions need to be cultivated (i.e., efforts need to be made to connect them to "emotionally competent stimuli" that are adaptive in a particular individual's life circumstances), the capacity for experiencing them does not need to be learned (absent pathology). That would be too risky given the caregiving circumstances of human infants as our species evolved. As Hrdy (2009) has explained, human infants needed empathic abilities as well as ways to express their emotions to others to ensure that they would be well fed and cared for in the context of increasingly "alloparental" circumstances (i.e., circumstances involving multiple caregivers in addition to the mother). Infants who were unable to distinguish between caring and uncaring adults, and to evoke responsive caregiving from those who could be motivated to provide it (e.g., through emotionally competent stimuli such as crying and gesturing), were likely to quickly perish on the savanna.

Social Purpose and Social Intelligence

The motivational developments described in the preceding paragraphs were accompanied by transformational increases in brain size. As explained in Chapter 6, this increase in "brainpower" was fueled by selection pressures for cooperative living that required advanced motivational resources as well as greatly enhanced social-cognitive and social self-control knowledge and skills – what we will refer to as *social intelligence*. Over time this more egalitarian way of functioning – which yielded "such a better way of life" than the prevailing mode of hierarchical social organization dominated by alpha males (e.g., as seen in extant African gorillas) – led to increases in societal complexity and in opportunities for cultural learning. That in turn placed further demands on what the mind and brain needed to be able to do to keep up with the requirements for cooperative living.

This cascade of evolving selection pressures ultimately produced the kind of "threshold effect" that living systems theorists point to when seeking to understand rapid, transformational change in an organism's structure and functions (D. Ford, 1987/2019; Wheatley, 1999). D. S. Wilson (2007) has called this transformation (aka "tipping point") in human evolution the *Cooperation Divide*. He chose that phrase because the evolution of advanced capabilities for pursuing social purpose goals was the catalyst for significant elaborations on many of the attributes regarded as uniquely human – for example, widespread symbolic communication and sharing of resources, routine reliance on division of labor and other teamwork arrangements, and the biggest brains on the planet (in EQ – encephalization quotient – terms). These developments were part of an emergent, highly social, and relatively fast-paced kind of evolution known as *cumulative cultural evolution,* which greatly accelerated what humanity was capable of achieving (Richerson & Boyd, 2005; E. O. Wilson, 2012). All other species had to basically "start from scratch" each generation when learning how to respond to everyday problems and opportunities. That is why the characteristic behaviors of (for example) birds, bears, and baboons are about the same now as they were eons ago. In contrast, humans became teachers and learners who could not only mentally store solutions across generations; they could also innovate on those solutions as well as innovate on top of others' innovations – and then share that accumulating knowledge with others!

This ratcheting up of accumulated knowledge and skills, which remains on an accelerating trajectory, has yielded achievements that are immensely greater than any one person could possibly invent in their lifetime. For example, through cumulative cultural evolution, humans have learned how to live productively in climates ranging from deserts to forests to tropical islands. Our ancestors and contemporaries built shelters ranging all the way from thatched roofs to skyscrapers to space stations. Our communications capabilities evolved to include smoke signals, the telegraph, and smartphones. None of these advances would have been possible without some mechanism to allow our knowledge and skills to break out of their "genetic cage." Prior to cumulative cultural evolution, knowledge and skills could only survive from one generation to the next by being passed on through genetic coding.

As part of this transformation, our hominid ancestors developed extensive capabilities for communicating information about their goals, emotions, and personal agency beliefs to others. Our facial anatomy evolved more muscles (thus enabling more elaborate facial expressions) and more flexible structures for producing vocalizations (Keltner, 2009). And, to ensure that these enhancements did not go to waste, we became far more skilled at interpreting facial expressions and vocalizations to infer what others are thinking and feeling. Over time we also developed the capacity for advanced language capabilities, thus providing us with a powerful new way to share thoughts, feelings, and intentions.

> We do not know how the snowball of language and culture first began to roll. But perhaps it grew so dramatically and quickly because consciousness and communication enabled humans to bring the processes and products of prospection [i.e., future-oriented thought and action] into the light. Language and culture are multipliers of the effectiveness of prospection given that many minds are so often better than one – creating a wider pool of evidence, sharing imagination and examination of alternatives, functional specialization, and coordinated responses. (Seligman et al., 2013, p. 130)

These social-cognitive capabilities are innate and do not require learning (absent pathology). Infants, for example, are capable of recognizing facial expressions and responding empathically to others' distress (Hauser, 2006; Hrdy, 2009). In addition, we are far more attuned than other primates to problems such as figuring out who we can trust and who is likely to be unresponsive or hurtful. We also have special skills related to collaborative activities that require interdependent individuals to make unique, coordinated contributions toward shared goals.

Tomasello (2009) succinctly summarizes the key qualities associated with the emergence of human forms of social intelligence:

> To get from ape group activities to human collaboration, we need three basic sets of processes. First and most importantly, early humans had to evolve some serious social-cognitive skills and motivations for coordinating and communicating with others in complex ways involving joint goals and coordinated division of labor among the various roles – what I will call skills and motivations for shared intentionality. Second, to even begin these complex collaborative activities, early humans had first to become more tolerant and trusting of one another than are modern apes . . .. And third, these more tolerant and collaborative humans had to develop some group-level, institutional practices involving public social norms and the assignment of deontic status to institutional roles. (pp. 54–55)

Why did humans develop these advanced forms of social intelligence? Or as Hrdy (2009) asks, "How on Darwin's earth did the stage for such cooperation get set?" Her simple answer: "to care and to share is to survive. . . . [That is] how mind reading, empathy, and the other underpinnings for higher levels of cooperation became so well developed" (p. 11). Immordino-Yang (2016) offers a similar explanation: "human nature is to nurture and be nurtured" (p. 71).

Early interpretations of Darwin's theory tended to emphasize the role of competition ("survival of the fittest") and Machiavellian types of social intelligence. This was supplemented by a welcome emphasis on dyadic attachment relationships (primarily between mothers and their offspring) that facilitated social bonding and social learning (Ainsworth et al., 1978; Bowlby, 1969). Yet Hrdy (2009) gets at the heart of the transformational developments in social purpose and social intelligence by emphasizing *the critical survival advantages associated with shared, cooperative child rearing and interdependent roles in cohesive social groups.* As a result, we are "wired" to cooperate, or as Keltner (2009) puts it, "born to be good."

Of course, like all primates, humans are also quite capable of being selfish and competitive when it comes to resources, status, and power. That makes sense given that "all viable organisms must have a selfish streak; they must be concerned about their own survival and well-being or they will not be leaving many offspring" (Tomasello, 2009, pp. 4–5). And humans are obviously not the only species capable of cooperative or altruistic behavior. Most primates also have a meaningful repertoire of other-oriented goals that can be activated from time to time. However, what enabled humans to cross the Cooperation Divide was the evolution of *longer-term, relationship-oriented social purpose goals* related to collaboration, helping, and social responsibility. The emergence of these "modern" social purpose goals increased the probability that offspring (and other genetically related individuals) would survive and reach reproductive age (Sober & Wilson, 1998).

Earlier we emphasized Damasio's observation that *survival with well-being,* rather than survival alone, appears to better describe the fundamental unifying principle organizing evolutionary progress. From that perspective, an equally important consideration is the ways in which altruism and collaboration have facilitated well-being in human development. And have they ever! As Tomasello (2009) explains, "To an unprecedented degree, *homo sapiens* are adapted for acting and thinking cooperatively in cultural groups, and indeed all of humans' most impressive achievements — from complex technologies to linguistic and mathematical symbols to intricate social institutions — are the products not of individuals acting alone, but of individuals interacting" (pp. xv–xvi).

In short, the evolution of *modern social purpose* was the fundamental catalyst for the development of many uniquely human aspects of self-direction. Social purpose enabled humans to soar — together!

Accelerated Learning and Behavior Change

Consciousness evolved — and continued to evolve — for one simple reason: to facilitate goal-directed behavior change, and thus survival with well-being. When consciousness first emerged as a fleeting glimpse of attentional energy, its role was to get the organism to change what it was doing *right now* (e.g., "Need water, go get it") (Denton, 2005). At each step along the way, further elaborations of consciousness evolved in response to a need to support goal pursuit over longer and longer periods of time in environments filled with increasing levels of complexity and unpredictability.

At its highest level, consciousness provides a mechanism for actually engineering behavior change. That is why understanding consciousness — especially as it relates to what you choose to pay attention to — is so important for understanding the processes involved in motivating self and others.

The Mind's Division of Labor

Although we have emphasized the advances in self-direction made possible by the evolution of consciousness, it is vitally important to understand that all animals, including humans, still rely primarily on nonconscious processes to govern their behavior. Although the focused energy provided by consciousness is essential when novel or unexpected challenges arise, much of life is lived at a more routine level. We develop comfortable patterns that work well for us most of the time, and like someone on a sled looking for the fastest route down a snowy hill (Doidge, 2007, crediting Alvaro Pascual Leone), we naturally return again and again to the well-worn tracks representing our strongest predispositions and habits. This *self-organizing* property of living systems (D. Ford, 1987/2019) is extraordinarily efficient. Conscious mental activity consumes far more energy (e.g., calories) and moves at a snail's pace compared to nonconscious mental activity, which is amazingly fast (Bargh, 2017).

Surprisingly, psychological science has only recently begun to grasp the full implications of this arrangement. When information-processing models became prominent in the 1960s and 1970s, there was a clear understanding that the amount of information that could be attended to and held in "working memory" at any one time was quite limited (Cowan, 2001; G. Miller, 1956). That is why it is virtually impossible to concentrate effectively on more than one complex activity at a time – as evidenced, for example, by research on distracted driving (e.g., Drews et al., 2008). However, there was also an implicit assumption in many theories of learning and cognition that not much interesting was going on outside of consciousness.

A growing body of research has taken dead aim at that assumption and blown it out of the water. You would probably be amazed (and perhaps alarmed!) at what you can do with little or no awareness. Underneath the surface your mind is constantly observing, evaluating, and running "subroutines" as it carries out its governing responsibilities (Bargh, 2017; Bargh & Barndollar, 1996). Almost every adult has had the experience of driving a few miles – which obviously takes a great deal of precise mental activity – and not being able to recall doing it. As you type on a keyboard you may hear the words in your head but be barely aware of all the little moves your fingers are making (and if you do start to think about your fingers, your typing will likely be disrupted). In a conversation you may consciously think about a couple of main ideas in advance, but then utter a sequence of appropriate words and sentences with no awareness of what you are about to say until you've said it. Somehow, we say the right things (more or less) even though, at least at a conscious level, we don't need to think about each word we say. Otherwise our conversations would take a very long time!

And that's just scratching the surface. Research psychologists and neuroscientists have convincingly demonstrated that almost everything we do involves powerful nonconscious thought processing. We mimic the mannerisms and facial expressions of people we interact with and have no idea we're doing it (Lakin et al., 2003). We think we're immune to political ads and other manipulative images in the media, but the evidence strongly suggests otherwise (Bargh, 2002; Dijksterhuis et al., 2005). We don't think we judge people until we know something about them, but beneath awareness our "like-o-meter" is evaluating and comparing and classifying from the very first glimpse (Haidt, 2006). As T. D. Wilson (2002) explains,

> there is more agreement than ever before about the importance of non-conscious thinking, feeling, and motivation . . .. The mind operates most efficiently by relegating a good deal of high-level, sophisticated thinking to the unconscious, just as a modern jumbo jetliner is able to fly on automatic pilot with little or no input from the human, "conscious" pilot . . .. We take in 11,000,000 pieces of information a second, but can process only 40 of them consciously . . .. The ability to size up our environments, disambiguate them, interpret them, and initiate behavior quickly and nonconsciously confers a survival advantage and thus was selected for. (pp. 5–6, 23–24)

All of this has led some psychologists to conclude that conscious mental processing is rather overrated in terms of its impact on our behavior and decision-making relative to nonconscious mental activity (Wegner, 2002). However, the overall body of evidence suggests that *both* are essential for effective self-direction, and they must work together in coordinated fashion if good things are going to happen (e.g., Mamede et al., 2010). This does not mean that there are actually two minds battling each other for control over what you think and do. There is just one mind, with one set of cognitive functions. What varies from moment to moment is the level of conscious energy applied to different thoughts that are going on in your mind.

This energy-efficient arrangement is analogous to shining a flashlight in a dark room filled with furniture and other objects, some in plain sight and others stored away in drawers and closets. All the "stuff" in the room is there whether you pay attention to it or not. But energizing certain elements in the room by shining the flashlight on it can help you remain coherent in your thoughts and actions as you move about the room (as opposed to being "unenlightened" about possible obstacles to goal progress). That energy can also make it possible to change or rearrange the contents of the room (analogous to learning and conceptual change). Of course, some thoughts may require extra effort to bring them into awareness, analogous to having to open a closet to recall what's inside. And if your mental "room" is too cluttered, you may not be able to find some things at all.

To clarify further: when we talk about the conscious mind and the nonconscious mind, we are using a verbal shortcut that really refers to thinking at different levels of energy activation within a unified mind. The vast majority of our mental activity occurs completely outside of consciousness. That activity represents what we have been calling the nonconscious mind. But there is also a tiny sliver of cognitive activity that is sufficiently energized to bring it into awareness. That activity is what we have been calling the conscious mind. Within the conscious mind, there is a continuum of energy levels that may be applied to a thought or perception. It is as if our "mental flashlight" comes with the equivalent of a bezel that can be turned to yield a brighter, narrower focus or a somewhat broader, more diffuse awareness. That enables us to devote laser-like attention to an urgently important goal when necessary, or to conserve energy when all that is needed is a vague awareness of what is going on around us.

With this understanding, it is now possible to consider in more depth how conscious and nonconscious mental processes work together as a unit to help ensure adaptive self-direction in the face of different kinds of challenges. The nonconscious mind has to be firmly in control of a vast array of operations while also remaining open to directives and suggestions for change from the conscious mind. Conversely, the conscious mind has to be respectful of the powerful routines and habits of the nonconscious mind, while also being assertive and timely in its investment of limited energy resources to promote innovation and self-improvement.

The Rider and the Elephant

We have found Haidt's (2006) metaphor of a "rider on an elephant" to be particularly useful in understanding how people need to approach the task of trying to develop their capacity for motivating self and others. One key aspect of this metaphor is that it vividly conveys the essential notion that consciousness (the rider) is usually more of a passenger than a driver for our immense, nonconscious mind (the elephant), which is what causes most of our actions to occur. We tend to repeat our daily routines without much conscious thought until something unexpected happens. Indeed, trying to steer or regain control of an elephant can be exceedingly tricky. Often the rider has the *illusion* of being in control, but in reality, the elephant was just doing what the nonconscious mind wanted to do anyway (e.g., enjoying a high-calorie dessert while the rider tries to provide after-the-fact justifications, like "I won't eat all the frosting" or "I'll exercise tomorrow"). At other times the elephant lumbers along while the rider helplessly watches, like a golfer desperately trying to correct a bad swing habit ("Doggone it, why do I keep lifting my head?").

From time to time a skilled rider can actually gain some control over the elephant and steer it onto a new pathway or toward a new outcome. This is often seen when someone is making progress on learning a new skill or developing a new relationship. Yet transformational change of *existing* behavior patterns – especially when they are ingrained over a long period of time – is notoriously difficult (as illustrated by the poor success rate of New Year's resolutions).

The motivational challenge, then, is to slowly but surely build new habits in the (nonconscious) elephant by applying available "steering" (conscious) energy in a tenacious and balanced way (Gallagher, 2009). If you don't steer enough, or you keep letting up, you probably won't accomplish much (as many chronic dieters can attest). You'll just keep repeating the same old habits. But if you steer too much your "elephant" is likely to get confused and disorganized. Imagine the golfer who steps up to address the ball while consciously thinking "head down, elbow in, hands forward, anchor left heel, swing slow." The result of this oversteering is usually "paralysis by analysis" (and perhaps a few lost golf balls!).

The metaphor of a rider on an elephant is perfect for illustrating the roles that conscious and nonconscious experience play in successful goal pursuit in different kinds of circumstances. In situations where the elephant "fits in" and knows what to do, all that is needed is a light touch from the rider, with a little tug here and a little adjustment there. In situations where the elephant needs to learn a new skill, the rider will need to take charge, but in more of a motivating and teaching capacity than in a confrontational role. In contrast, when existing habits need to be replaced with new behaviors (and ultimately with new habits), the rider will need to find some way to prevent the elephant from doing what it normally does, while also steering the elephant to less comfortable options. That is why effective pursuit of an ambitious behavior change goal may require enormous investments of conscious energy – and lots of practice! Indeed, significant behavior change can be so demanding that it may be impossible to sustain progress without support from a network of caring individuals who can help you maintain your commitment to change.

In short, scientists across a wide range of disciplines are discovering that the adept use of conscious energy – or what MacCoon et al. (2004) call "context-appropriate balanced attention" – is the key to translating motivation into effective efforts to learn and improve. There is both an art and a science to mastering this evolved mechanism for facilitating the pursuit of personal goals. In particular, the rider is essential for helping the elephant make sure that the most important things are being prioritized, and for encouraging the elephant to explore new opportunities and expand capabilities for pursuing new and existing goals. Of course, staying focused on what you need to do to achieve the outcomes that matter most to you can be very difficult when your conscious mind is filled with uncertainties and worries (Kuhl & Beckmann, 1994; Leary, 2004). Sometimes even just changing direction can be a struggle. But as we will emphasize throughout this book, if you understand how consciousness works and why it emerged as an important tool in our evolutionary past, you can use that understanding to steer both yourself and others toward a more productive and meaningful future.

CHAPTER 3

Core Personal Goals
The Leaders within You

If one does not know to which port one is sailing, no wind is favorable.

    – philosopher Lucius Annaeus Seneca, *Letters from a Stoic*

The thought that life could be better is woven indelibly into our hearts and our brains.

    – songwriter Paul Simon, "Train in the Distance"

In the preceding chapter we saw how the earliest motivational systems were led by *primordial goals* such as the need for oxygen and energy. With the emergence of consciousness, motivational systems directed by *neuroimaged goals* became possible. Organisms with this capability could use mental images of past experiences and future possibilities to guide their behavior. These "masterpieces" of evolutionary innovation (Denton, 2005) remain a central part of our heritage. And finally, with the emergence of self-awareness, the highest form of consciousness (Leary, 2004), motivational systems led by self-constructed *personal goals* evolved. At this level goal images and ideas could not only be perceived and remembered; they could also be invented and transformed.

If Klinger and Cox (2004) are correct in concluding that the "successful pursuit of goals is . . . the most important thing in the life of humans and other animals" (p. 3), then it is evident that the next logical step in our "big bet" strategy is to explore the science of personal goals and its implications for motivating self and others. Our approach is consistent with a general understanding that has emerged in both the research literature and the popular press that self-awareness of your most personal and deeply felt motives is an essential prerequisite for effective decision-making and personal growth (Csikszentmihalyi, 2003; T. D. Wilson, 2009). When you look beneath the surface features of your everyday life, who do you see? What matters to you most? What are the things that fascinate you and capture your attention? What are you passionate about? When you look at the choices you make, what feels particularly satisfying and authentic?

A variety of terms have been used to identify basic human motives, including needs, wants, values, and various phrases incorporating the word "goal" (Klinger & Cox, 2004; Locke, 2002). For reasons that will become clearer as we guide you through this chapter, we have elected to use the phrase *core personal goals* to describe the most emotionally powerful of these self-directive influences (M. Ford & Nichols, 1991; Nichols, 1994). Throughout life, our core personal goals are shaped by a wide variety of influences, including (but not limited to) our biological heritage, family upbringing, culture, educational opportunities, and unique personal experiences. As they are formed and strengthened (i.e., thought about more often, both consciously and beneath awareness), our core personal goals increasingly provide the framework of ideas, images, and feelings that organize and guide what we choose to do and who we choose to be. That is why they are so influential in shaping our basic identity and personality. And yet, paradoxically, we are often unaware of these influences and the powerful role they play in our lives.

Self-awareness of your core personal goals is thus the first and perhaps the most important step in learning how to become more self-directed. Such awareness can enable you to identify the underlying sources of satisfaction and dissatisfaction in your work, in your relationships, and in your leisure pursuits. That in turn can empower you to make wise choices about how to invest your time and energy. Conscious affirmation of your core personal goals can also help you maintain confidence, hope, and a sense of self-integrity under conditions of stress and adversity (Brady et al., 2016). Over time this continuous reinforcement of the alignment between your core personal goals and consequential decisions and actions can help you achieve a profound sense of purpose and life meaning.

In addition, knowledge of your core personal goals can help you see how all of the chapters in your life story and the many different "possible selves" (Markus & Nurius, 1986) that you have developed fit together into an organized, coherent whole. That is the kind of self-knowledge that enhances inner strengths while also causing others to see you as a person of *integrity* – someone who can be trusted to live their life according to consistent priorities and principles. Learning how to foster this kind of *goal–life alignment* can also improve your ability to help others achieve these same insights in their lives.

Discovering your "true self" (motivationally speaking) is by no means an easy task. Recall that, by evolutionary design, our personal goals operate largely outside of awareness. Moreover, when we are aware of our personal goals, it often tends to be at a relatively shallow level. For example, you might have a long to-do list without feeling that any of those items belong on your "things I really care about" list. You might be able to enumerate many different reasons you need to complete a task but not understand why it is so hard to make it a priority. You might perceive that you are doing all of the things you are supposed to be doing but still experience a sense of emptiness or a feeling that something is missing.

The challenge, then, is that the personal goals that define the core of our underlying identity and personality are primarily in the domain of the nonconscious "elephant" (Haidt, 2006; see Chapter 2). In contrast, our conscious "rider" tends to be more focused on surface-level challenges and opportunities (e.g., meeting deadlines; conforming to social expectations). As a result, we tend to focus our attention on the day-to-day objectives that we want to accomplish without necessarily understanding the broader meaning and implications of those goal thoughts. But that is precisely what each individual needs to do to energize and strengthen "the leaders within you." Being able to identify the core personal goals that direct and organize your most consequential thoughts and actions is the key that will unlock your potential for motivating self and others.

> To be happy for life, you must first try to know yourself . . .. Yet while everyone assumes that his or her identity is transparent, there are, in fact few things so covered with veils as one's own nature. (Csikszentmihalyi, 2003, pp. 19, 167)

At the end of this chapter we describe two useful tools for identifying the personal goal themes that are the most compelling and meaningful for you across a broad range of circumstances: the *Taxonomy of Human Goals* (M. Ford & Nichols, 1987/2019) and the *Assessment of Personal Goals* (M. Ford & Nichols, 1991, 2005). First, though, we provide an overview of what personal goals are and why they are so important to your success and well-being.

Essential Qualities of Personal Goals

Up to now, we've told a story about self-directed motivational systems that is heavy on plot and setting but rather thin on descriptions of our "leading" characters – our *core personal goals*. In this section we transition from a discussion of why and how motivational systems led by personal goals evolved to a direct focus on what personal goals are. A clearer understanding of your goal thoughts and what they are designed to do for you will enable you to harness and strengthen your most important motivational assets.

Definition of a Personal Goal

Before defining what a *personal* goal is, it is useful to understand the more general concept of a goal.

> *A goal is a positively valued end point in a sequence of activity.*

That end point might be something desirable that you try to achieve, or it might be something undesirable that you try to avoid. For example, a soccer player might have a goal of kicking (or heading) a soccer ball into a net. Conversely, for the player guarding the net, the "positively valued end point" would be not allowing the soccer ball to go into the net. In life, we have many goals in both the "go for it" and "stop it" categories.

People often think of a goal as something external to themselves – something that is defined and valued by an employer or teacher or some other authoritative source. But our focus is on the kind of goals that are in your mind, not in the outside world.

> *Personal goals are thoughts – your thoughts – about desired (or undesired) future states and outcomes.*

Personal goals are *ideas* about what you want, what you need, and how you hope things will turn out.

This internal–external distinction is not always easy to maintain, since goal representations suggested by the general culture, the media, and the people we live and work with often have a substantial impact on our own goal thoughts. And since most of this influence happens outside awareness, it is often difficult to pinpoint the origin of a particular goal thought or when an idea has been transformed into a personal goal. Nevertheless, the distinction between what others think *should* be important to you and what actually *is* important to you is critical.

> *Personal goals are saturated with emotion and meaning.*

Externally defined goals remain motivationally irrelevant until we assess them (emotionally and cognitively) as having some personal significance. That is why we use the term "personal" to refer to goals that are mental representations of your desired and undesired outcomes. To avoid repetition, we will sometimes drop the modifier, but in doing so we will try to ensure that the context of the discussion makes it clear that when we say "goal" with no modifier, we are referring to a *personal* goal.

Personal goals generally take the form of an image or concept of what a good (or bad) outcome would look like or feel like. That outcome may be specified with a high level of clarity (analogous to a high-definition television signal), or it may be kind of fuzzy, with few defined details (analogous to an out-of-focus photograph). For example, you might have a vague notion that you want to feel healthier and have more energy. Or you might have a more specific goal to lose ten pounds and exercise vigorously each day for thirty minutes.

There is no requirement that your goal thoughts take any particular form in terms of conceptual clarity. They are what they are, just like other thoughts that may be activated in your mind (e.g., vivid and not-so-vivid memories). However, one of the most well-established findings in motivational science is that *clearly conceived goals are more likely to lead to successful outcomes than goals conceptualized in vague or imprecise terms* (Locke & Latham, 1984, 2019). This does not mean that personal goals have to be behavioral and quantifiable to be effective. Goals can be big and expansive and still be effective as long as they provide you with a meaningful image or concept of what significant progress or a successful outcome might look or feel like.

One way to enhance the clarity of high-level goals is to link them to subgoals in aligned *goal networks* (see Figure 3.1). Our mind naturally organizes our personal goals and their associated subgoals in patterns that

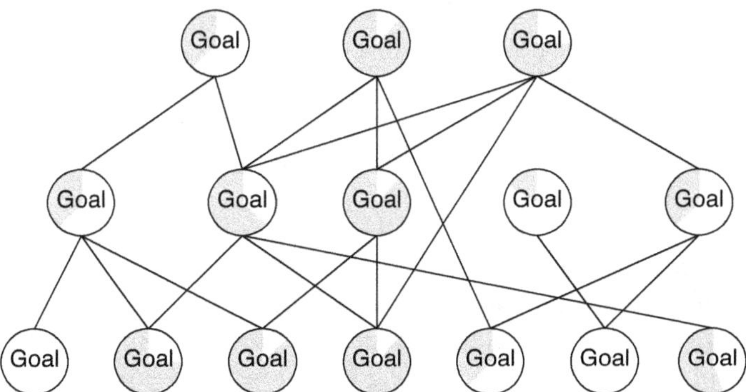

Figure 3.1 Illustrative network of personal goals.
Note: The networked personal goals are shown with subgoal relationships (represented by lines) and importance or strength (represented by shading).

progressively lead in a unified direction toward a larger goal. For example, the concrete logistical goal of finding an appropriate place to live can facilitate larger, more abstract goals related to community, safety, social status, and emotional well-being.

The linkages between subgoals and high-level goals also help us maintain motivation by infusing the entire sequence with coherence and meaning. Consider, for example, the goal of earning a college degree – which you can easily picture in the form of a diploma or a graduation ceremony. Progress toward this goal will almost certainly be facilitated if the specific steps needed to attain that degree are clear and motivating in their own right (R. Miller & Brickman, 2004; R. Miller et al., 1999). With the right subgoals, you can naturally progress toward high-level goals without losing focus on what you need to do next to get where you want to go.

In short, while goal progress requires contributions from many different system components, it is the leadership team in motivational headquarters that is responsible for ensuring that sound decisions are made about what goals and subgoals should be prioritized. Personal goal thoughts set the stage by providing direction at multiple levels with varying degrees of automatic and conscious control and varying amounts of cross-goal communication (see Figure 3.1). Emotions and personal agency beliefs contribute to the decision-making process by helping us sort through our goal options and by ensuring that we prioritize the right goals at the right times (as we saw in Chapter 2 and will discuss in more detail in Chapter 4).

Some Related Terms

There are several different terms that are commonly used to refer to personal goals. We have found it helpful to use *personal goal* as a general label for all kinds of motivational content, with other related words reserved for subsets of personal goals that share certain qualities. The most familiar words along these lines are needs, wants, and values.

Needs. The term *need* tends to be used for high-level goals that have a strong biological or emotional basis (see Figure 3.1). For example, primordial goals such as thirst for water and air are typically included in this category. Some psychological theories of motivation have also focused on this subset of personal goals (e.g., Maslow's physiological and safety needs; Murray's harm avoidance and succorance needs; Deci and Ryan's autonomy, competence, and relatedness needs) (Maslow, 1954; Murray, 1938; Ryan & Deci, 2018). Needs are generally assumed to be deep (i.e., ingrained within the nonconscious elephant), enduring, and resistant to change. Needs may or may not be highly prioritized in the sense of being a frequent object of attention. However, having an activated personal goal within the "need" category generally implies a sense of emotional urgency and a strong bias to mentally focus on that goal to the exclusion of other goals until it is satisfied, or some other need takes precedence.

Wants. The term *want*, on the other hand, tends to be used for lower level personal goals that emerge from our ongoing learning experiences and that are more context-specific. Consistent with this description, there is a tendency to reserve the term "want" for things that are (relatively) easy for the conscious rider to identify and that can be imaged or described in concrete terms. For example, hunger pangs signal a "need" to eat, but then when you imagine fulfilling that goal in a specific way you might think "I want seafood" (as opposed to "I need seafood," which sounds like an inauthentic exaggeration). Similarly, you might be bored and "need" some excitement but "want" to achieve that goal by watching a football game or going to a casino.

In short, although we can learn to want something very much, wants are generally perceived to be more voluntary or discretionary than needs. This perception is consistent with the principle of *equifinality* (Simon, 1967), which suggests that one important aspect of goal pursuit is being able to creatively conceptualize a variety of different ways to satisfy the same high-level goal (e.g., "I wish I could figure out some good alternatives for those tasty but unhealthy snacks I've been eating").

The difference between needs and wants (as those terms are commonly used) is perhaps best illustrated by personal goals associated with addictions or other instances where people find themselves on a rapidly accelerating "hedonic treadmill" (Brickman & Campbell, 1971; Galak & Redden, 2018). This metaphor summarizes the idea that for certain kinds of experiences, we quickly *habituate* to (get used to) what satisfies a "want," which may then prompt a greater future want (i.e., in terms of the amount, frequency, or intensity of whatever satisfied you originally). This escalation can ultimately cause us to say that we "need" what we originally just wanted. This transition is typically associated with a perceived reduction in willpower in the face of temptation to succumb to the addictive activity or substance, as illustrated by the use of terms that suggest a biologically based need (like "hunger" or "craving") to describe the motivational experience. That is why it is so important for people who are trying to combat addiction to maintain a firm belief that, even under duress, willpower can effectively defend against temptations and impulses (Job et al., 2010).

Fortunately, not all experiences that bring us happiness and satisfaction are subject to the hedonic treadmill phenomenon. Indeed, as we will see later (in Chapter 7), the most reliable sources of life meaning tend to be quite resistant to such adaptations (Diener et al., 2006; O'Brien & Kassirer, 2019; Y. Yang & Galak, 2015). They "never get old" or lose their motivational impact. That in turn implies that happiness is more under our control than hedonic treadmill theory would lead us to believe – assuming, of course, that we take the time to learn what those reliable pathways to life meaning are and how best to follow them.

> Many things make people happy, from eating foods to cashing checks. Alas, these sources are united by a sadder fate: The more we experience some dosage of pleasure, the less pleasurable the dosage . . .. [Yet] people are slow to adapt to the warm glow of giving. The happiness we get from giving appears to sustain itself. (O'Brien & Kassirer, 2019, p. 193)

Values. Like needs, *values* are a subset of high-level personal goals (i.e., among the top level "bubbles" in Figure 3.1). However, in contrast to needs, which are typically viewed as having their roots in biology or emotion, values are generally assumed to have originated within the ideals and customs of social groups (e.g., families, communities, and cultures). We gradually learn the values that are consistently communicated to us through socialization processes such as teaching, modeling, and contingent reinforcement (e.g., values related to gender roles, religious and political beliefs, and cultural traditions). Some of these values may seem rather arbitrary or peculiar (e.g., local customs). Others may seem outdated or no longer appropriate (e.g., social conventions related to gender differentiation or old technologies). However, when these values reflect themes related to morality (e.g., distributive justice, compassion for people in need), such learning occurs naturally and, for the most part, automatically. That is because, as we will document in more detail in Chapter 6, *moral* values have a strong biological basis (Hauser, 2006).

Consistent with this observation, recent scientific advances in psychology, anthropology, and social neuroscience make it clear that we are "wired" for social interdependence, both in terms of motivation – what we have been calling *social purpose* – and the fundamentals of social intelligence (Hauser, 2006; Hrdy, 2009; Keltner, 2009; Keltner et al., 2010). We do not have to learn how to develop emotional attachments (Bowlby, 1969), nor does anyone need to teach us that "harm to the other is harm to the self" (Damasio, 2003, p. 172). These universal human values are a natural result of our evolutionary heritage. Newborn infants cry when they hear others cry (Eisenberg et al., 2003). Altruistic motivation is evident in very young children (Hrdy, 2009; Tomasello, 2009; Warneken, 2015; Warneken & Tomasello, 2006). Brain reward systems are activated by cooperative behavior (Rilling et al., 2002). People are reliably attracted to those who exhibit generosity, kindness, and concern for others (Barclay, 2010; Boehm, 2012). Although prosocial goals and feelings vary in strength across individuals, they are an important part of every human's motivational repertoire (absent pathology) (Batson, 2011; M. Ford & Nichols, 1991). As Brewer (2004) explains,

> human beings are adapted for social living . . .. We are not suited for survival as lone individuals, or even as small family units. Many of the evolved characteristics that have permitted humans to adapt to a wide range of physical environments, such as omnivorousness and tool making, create dependence on collective knowledge and cooperative information sharing. As a consequence, human beings are characterized by *obligatory interdependence* . . .. Our evolutionary history is a story of co-evolution of genetic endowment, social structure, and culture. (p. 107)

Values that do not have a strong moral dimension – such as those reflecting etiquette rules, dress codes, and other group-specific "protocols" and social conventions – may or may not be "internalized" and become personal goals (Arsenio & Ford, 1985; Tisak & Ford, 1986). Some of these values may feel like a good fit and ultimately become part of your personal identity. Indeed, some may rival moral values in motivational strength through the power of social influence (e.g., via peer group norms or "tried-and-true" cultural traditions). Others, however, may seem old-fashioned, inauthentic, or incompatible with your core personal goals (although you may pretend otherwise in certain social settings for expedient reasons). The value internalization process may also be highly selective (as illustrated by the mostly nonshaded circles in Figure 3.1). Politicians, for example, often seem to have private lives that are at odds with their public statements about core values (Sternberg, 2003).

In the same way that goal–life alignment is vital for well-functioning individuals, *value alignment* is the motivational foundation on which strong groups and organizations are built. Many leaders understand this principle but only think about it as it applies to followers. Most corporate "cultures," for example, espouse certain values. The question then becomes, are those corporate values really shared by everyone – especially those responsible for leading the organization? Or is there a "counterculture" set of different, perhaps unspoken, values that are the true priorities (e.g., "Quality is job one" vs. "Shipments are all that count"; "Everyone must sacrifice" vs. "Everyone must sacrifice except the bosses")?

Reflecting on such considerations is an important part of the self-discovery process. Are you confident that your core personal goals are in fact well aligned with the values you think you have? You may believe that you have certain core values as a result of having been immersed in social and cultural groups that espouse those values. But have you actually internalized those values? In other words, are they *personal*? Keep in mind that the conscious rider is often mistaken about what motivates the nonconscious elephant (T. D. Wilson, 2002). Indeed, the vast majority of people believe they consistently act with integrity (Strohminger et al., 2017), even when it is obvious to others that a person's words and deeds are inconsistent. An objective assessment of your core personal goals and the degree to which they are consistently aligned with the choices you make can help protect you against this kind of unintended hypocrisy.

What Personal Goals Do

Personal goals organize and direct our lives toward outcomes that will benefit us in ways that are consistent with the overarching design principle of striving for survival with well-being (Damasio, 2003). In other words, their job is to *lead*. For the most part this is a quiet, implicit kind of leadership that operates beneath awareness (Bargh, 2017). Energizing our goal thoughts by bringing them into consciousness from time to time helps us stay on track and maintain efficiency, but even this is more of an oversight kind of leadership than something that requires a lot of sustained attention and effort. Significant investments of energy are most likely to be required when unexpected obstacles or goal conflicts arise or when there is a need for significant behavior change. That is when leadership capabilities are put to the test.

The essence of leadership is defining a vision and motivating self and others to help make that vision a reality. Consistent with those concepts, personal goals are *future-oriented* thoughts. The unique role of personal goals is to mentally represent outcomes that do not yet exist and to help prepare us to try to produce (or avoid) those outcomes.

Although you may not be aware of it, the neurons associated with goal thoughts are firing away on a continuous basis as you move from one life episode to the next. This makes sense given that (as explained in Chapter 2) almost everything we perceive and think about is emotionally "tagged" in some way, and those triggered emotions are the primary mechanism through which goals are activated. Even when we try to quiet the mind through relaxation or meditation techniques, there is no "off" switch when it comes to our personal goal thoughts.

Now, that does not mean that we are constantly acting on those goal thoughts (thank goodness!). Goal pursuit is selective and punctuated by frequent (and often rather extended) interludes of "mind wandering" that are often disconnected from our immediate context – as illustrated by phenomena such as daydreaming, fantasizing, reminiscing, and speculating about hypothetical future problems and opportunities (Christoff et al., 2009; Mason et al., 2007). Yet personal goals are the main organizing force for most of these mental interludes as well. Indeed, it appears that the main function of this mind-wandering activity is to enable the mind to carry out "flexible mental explorations – simulations – that provide a means to prepare for upcoming, self-relevant events before they happen" (Buckner et al., 2008, p. 30). This is consistent with our earlier discussion (in Chapter 2) of the adaptive value of our evolved capabilities for mental time travel.

> As any normal human being can attest, when a person disengages from externally oriented goal-directed behavior, her mind is not idle – instead, she can become absorbed in a dynamic stream of free-form thought that is associated with mind wandering, spontaneous recollection of previous memories, production of hypothetical scenarios and future plans, and other personal and social thoughts and imaginings .... Emerging conceptions of brain functioning reveal that neural networks responsible for maintaining and focusing attention into the environment appear to toggle with a so-called default mode of brain function (DM) that is spontaneously induced during rest, daydreaming, and other nonattentive but awake mental states. (Immordino-Yang, 2016, pp. 44, 50)

Regardless of whether your brain is in active goal pursuit mode or in mental simulation (default) mode, once activated, your personal goals carry out three distinct but interrelated leadership functions. Each function can be linked to a different phase of goal processing: goal evaluation, goal commitment, and goal maintenance.

Goal evaluation phase. Initial activation of a goal focuses your attention on information of potential relevance to the pursuit of that goal. This often creates a Darwinian competition for your attention among a variety of subgoals that have the potential to satisfy the activated goal. Consider, for example, the experience of walking through an outdoor marketplace. If you are hungry or planning a meal, there may be many intriguing alternatives from which you will then need to make choices aligned with your goal evaluation criteria (e.g., in terms of cost, anticipated satisfaction, and health consequences). Much of this evaluative processing occurs outside of consciousness as a result of "priming" from emotionally evocative words and images (Bargh, 2017). This is evidenced by the fact that we often find it hard to articulate why we have certain feelings or preferences about things or people we might choose to interact with. For example, it may be hard to explain why you chose one food vendor over another ("I just felt like it" – or, in the words of the rider, "You'd have to ask the elephant").

As the science of the "new unconscious" has revealed, goal evaluation processing can be extremely rapid – within a few hundred milliseconds according to the experts (Ferguson & Zayas, 2009). Speedy goal processing that can occur without conscious reflection is highly adaptive in many situations. Imagine, for example, a child running out in front of your car. Being able to take immediate action before you are aware of what you are thinking could save a life. However, when goal choices are more complex and there are a lot of relevant factors to be sorted out, goal evaluations will tend to move to the forefront of consciousness and become increasingly deliberative. As Damasio (1994) explains, evaluative thoughts and feelings "point us in the proper direction, take us to the appropriate place in a decision-making space, where we may put the instruments of logic to good use" (p. xiii). It is thus the *combination* of emotion and logic that enables us to make sound decisions.

> Scientific understanding of the influence of emotions on thinking and learning has undergone a major transformation in recent years. In particular, a revolution in neuroscience over the past two decades has overturned early notions that emotions interfere with learning, revealing instead that emotion and cognition are supported by interdependent neural processes. It is literally neurobiologically impossible to build memories, engage complex thoughts, or make meaningful decisions without emotion. (Immordino-Yang, 2016, p. 18)

Goal commitment phase. After a specific goal representation has been judged to meet the necessary "conditions of satisfaction" (Searle, 1981) – often in less than the blink of an eye – processing moves to the *goal commitment* phase. That goal thought can now be regarded as an *intention* (e.g., "I know what I want – a piece of pizza"). Internal (mental) communication, which initially was centered within the leadership team in "motivational headquarters" (i.e., the team of personal goals, emotions, and personal agency beliefs), now shifts to the function of organizing the "instrumental troops" for action (M. Ford, 1992). In this phase, goal thoughts direct your planning and problem-solving systems to go figure out what to do, while also preparing your biological and behavioral systems for action. In some cases, this may simply require the activation of an already well-organized mental "schema" (e.g., a pizza-buying habit) that can enable you to pursue a goal with the same efficiency as someone on a sled following a well-worn track in the snow (Doidge, 2007). In other cases, a substantial amount of problem solving and reflective thought may be required before you can effectively act on an intention (e.g., "I really want a piece of pizza but I have to make sure all the ingredients are OK for me to eat"). The strength of a goal commitment can quickly wane if subsequent feedback raises concerns about the challenges associated with pursuing the goal, or if it suggests that your expectations would not be met.

Goal maintenance phase. The third function of personal goals is to sustain ongoing goal pursuit in the face of obstacles, distractions, and setbacks – both external (as when people are trying to pull you in different directions or "life throws you a curve") and internal (as when you experience goal conflicts or emotional turbulence). In this *goal maintenance* phase, goal thoughts serve as a reminder that a desired outcome remains unfulfilled (e.g., "They ran out of pizza, but I'm still hungry"). This in turn mobilizes self-regulatory processes focused on helping you stay on track toward your goal. These processes have the challenging job of facilitating goal progress by making necessary adjustments, removing obstacles and distractions, and taking strategic actions that help you stay organized and focused on the task at hand until the goal is achieved or replaced by another goal. Such efforts can rapidly deplete available energy resources (Muraven & Baumeister, 2000), which is why it is important to find ways to "reenergize" the motivational system from time to time when attainment of a goal requires a high level of effort and persistence (e.g., rewarding yourself when certain milestones are reached).

An extensive body of research illustrates how important these self-regulatory managers are for optimal human functioning in every avenue of life, from school to work to athletics to all aspects of mental and physical well-being (Bembenutty et al., 2013; Boekaerts et al., 2000; Vohs & Baumeister, 2016). Self-regulation – which is also studied under the umbrella concept of "self-control" – has become one of the most widely studied aspects of human behavior not only because of its critical role in helping people make progress toward particularly challenging goals (e.g., losing weight or quitting smoking), but also because self-regulatory skills are remarkably important for developing competent, resilient children and adolescents (Block & Block, 1980; Mischel et al., 1988). For example, Moffitt et al. (2011) have demonstrated the developmental benefits of being able to stay "on track" in the pursuit of personally and culturally valued goals in a longitudinal research program involving a cohort of more than 1,000 New Zealand children. Based on multiple measures of self-control from ages three to eleven (from researcher-observers, teachers, parents, and the children themselves), this research team found that children manifesting low levels of self-control were more likely to experience poor physical health outcomes, substance dependence, personal finance problems, and criminal offenses in young adulthood than those manifesting high levels of self-control. This same research group also found that, in a British cohort of over 500 sibling-pairs, the sibling with lower self-control consistently had poorer outcomes on a variety of indicators of school performance and antisocial behavior despite their shared family background. Consistent with these data, Daly et al. (2015) found in two large British samples (N=16,780) that self-control deficits in childhood predicted the emergence and persistence of patterns of unemployment in adulthood.

The ability to maintain goal commitments under duress continues to contribute to optimal functioning throughout middle and later adulthood. That is particularly true for those who face unrelenting life challenges. Adults with strong self-regulatory capabilities are

> exceptionally good at forming and maintaining secure, satisfying attachments to other people . . .. [They are] more stable emotionally and less prone to anxiety, depression, paranoia, psychoticism, obsessive-compulsive behavior, eating disorders, drinking problems, and other maladies . . .. The results couldn't be clearer: Self-control is a vital strength and key to success in life. (Baumeister & Tierney, 2011, pp. 12–13)

In sum, there are three different leadership functions performed by personal goals: (a) *goal evaluation* – envisioning goal options and deciding which ones to pursue; (b) *goal commitment* – forming intentions and preparing mind and body to organize around a targeted objective; and (c) *goal maintenance* – motivating the instrumental functions engaged in pursuing the goal to keep working until the goal (or some acceptable transformation of the goal) has been accomplished. In theory these functions will tend to unfold in this sequence for any particular goal. However, in reality things are not always that linear, especially when our brain is in "default mode" and mentally exploring possible scenarios and options. We usually have a mix of different goals competing for our attention, and like a pack of runners in a marathon, these goals are constantly shifting positions in terms of "who's out in front." This requires us to recalibrate and reevaluate our goal choices and commitments on an ongoing basis in terms of importance, situational appropriateness, time urgency, and other "real-time" considerations (Heckhausen & Kuhl, 1985).

Indeed, in our daily lives there is a constant Darwinian competition going on beneath awareness among a vast array of personal goals (Gallagher, 2009). For example, this morning I found myself trying to mentally sort through many different goals that were vying for my conscious rider's attention. I realized that the deadline for filing a tax return was drawing near and I needed to prioritize that goal. However, I also needed to complete a writing assignment for this book and help my wife with some logistical tasks associated with an upcoming trip. It also crossed my mind that I hadn't called my parents for quite a while and I still needed to prepare for a major presentation at work. And these were just the goals that I was consciously aware of – who knows how many others were lurking just beneath the surface, and how long I could go before changing circumstances would further expand the roster of goal candidates! Is it any wonder that most people find it difficult to juggle their family, work, and personal commitments on an everyday basis?

Now imagine throwing some kind of disruption into that goal mix, like a health scare or a relationship crisis. Then imagine that the disruption is a chronic source of turmoil rather than a temporary disturbance. That is when even those with an extensive repertoire of motivational strengths may need extra support or professional help.

Short-, Medium-, and Long-Term Goals

Our evolutionary heritage has made the process of activating short-term personal goals a breeze. We see something novel or unexpected, and the impact on our goal thoughts is immediate (within milliseconds). We encounter (or recall) a familiar situation, and the impact on our goal thoughts is immediate. People say things to us (or we imagine what they will say to us), and the impact on our goal thoughts is immediate.

In all of these situations, it is triggered emotions – even those that give us just a little nudge beneath awareness – that activate goal thoughts. Because some degree of emotional content is associated with almost everything we experience (Damasio, 2003; Haidt, 2006), goals of one type or another are being activated virtually all the time (mostly at a nonconscious level). We can try to empty our mind of goal thoughts, but since we have limited conscious control over the goal activation process, this is ultimately a near-impossible task. What is somewhat more under our control are skills that can be used to regulate the mental "change and commotion" (Damasio, 2003) caused by triggered emotions – skills such as those used in meditation or deep relaxation, where the focus is on quieting the mind's natural tendency to classify, judge, and ruminate. Being able to control the amplitude of emotional responses and the interpretations we assign to the feelings that arise from those responses is a key part of what we will later call (in Chapter 5) *emotional wisdom*.

Our evolved cognitive capabilities also make medium-term personal goals – i.e., goals that represent desired outcomes that are hours or days into the future rather than seconds or minutes – reasonably easy to formulate. This is particularly evident in the context of emotional attachments with family and close friends and in recurring relationships with mentors, business partners, and the like. We have evolved to develop enduring social bonds that transcend time and space and to discover personal goals around those important relationships. Medium-term goals also tend to flow naturally around hobbies and special interests – essentially, anything we find emotionally engaging and memorable. This is true even among young children (DeLoache et al., 2007).

Long-term personal goals, on the other hand, do not come to us quite as naturally. Being able to imagine and plan events relatively far into the future is a critical skill for the world we live in today, but it is not something for which our evolutionary heritage has provided much help.

> Whereas prehistoric peoples looked only a few days ahead, we spend a great deal of time thinking about and waiting for paychecks, educational degrees, promotions, retirement, and other distant goals . . . . In short, we are living today with a mental apparatus for self-reflection that evolved because it had adaptive value for intelligent, bipedal animals living in Africa tens of thousands of years ago. (Leary, 2004, p. 23)

Perhaps our inherent limitations with respect to long-term thinking should not be surprising given that other members of the animal kingdom rely almost exclusively on motivational mechanisms designed for short-term goal pursuit (e.g., emotions and feelings linked to neuroimaged goals), and these mechanisms are still prominent in human motivational systems. Moreover, the intellectual capabilities required to formulate and successfully pursue long-term goals (e.g., abstract thinking, hypothetical reasoning, and sophisticated self-control strategies) do not mature in human development until adolescence and early adulthood (L. Steinberg, 2005). Cultural factors can also play an inhibiting role. It may be hard to stay focused on long-term goals when popular media and expedient work cultures tend to promote instant gratification or equate self-sacrifice with foolishness.

Long-term thinking about hypothetical futures can also become a source of emotional distress if it is allowed to dominate our thinking. As Leary (2004) points out, the invention of agriculture over 10,000 years ago created a new reality in which survival with well-being was now tied to uncertain conditions in the distant future. The biological and cultural gains associated with the agricultural revolution were astounding; however, it was not without a psychological cost, as from that point forward humans spent far more time worrying about the future. That in turn made humans more vulnerable to excessive anxiety and other emotional disorders associated with a persistent focus on "worst case scenarios." From that perspective, it is perhaps not surprising that many politicians (and voters!) choose to ignore information about the dangers of phenomena like deficit spending and global warning.

Despite these limitations and potential pitfalls, cultivating the capacity for adaptive long-term thinking is well worth the effort, assuming that "the curse of the self" (Leary, 2004) is kept in check. An orientation to think about short- and medium-term accomplishments in the context of long-term goals is one of the key features associated with successful goal pursuit and life meaning (Baumeister, 1991; Emmons, 2003). That is because the connection between proximal and distal goals adds motivational strength in both directions. Thinking about distal goals (e.g., writing a book or losing thirty pounds) has been shown to be an ineffective motivational technique unless such goals are linked to proximal subgoals that energize activity and yield (mostly!) encouraging feedback (e.g., writing ten pages a day or losing a pound a week). Conversely, linking short and medium-term goals to longer-term goals helps bring an emotionally fulfilling sense of purpose and meaning to daily activities. As Baumeister (1991) explains,

> goals often come in nested hierarchies . . .. It is usually possible to derive a set of short-term goals from a long-term goal. But the reverse does not necessarily hold true. Having a set of short-term, low-level goals does not guarantee that they will add up to a meaningful long-term goal. It is quite possible to grope one's way through life always looking only a few days or weeks ahead . . . keeping up with the press of obligations and demands, the children's needs, the repairs and maintenance on one's possessions, meeting deadlines, paying

the endless bills, doing the endless chores, and so forth. People who live entirely that way may eventually come to feel that their lives are lacking something, for all the proximal goals do not add up to a suitably high-level purpose in life. (p. 35)

Approach and Avoidance Goals

Earlier we defined personal goals as thoughts about desired *or* undesired future outcomes. When those thoughts focus on a positive future state (e.g., hitting my tee shot in the middle of the fairway), they are often called *approach goals* because to succeed we must progress toward the outcome being envisioned. Conversely, when those thoughts specify a negative future state (e.g., not hitting my tee shot into the nearby water hazard), they are typically called *avoidance goals* because to succeed we must prevent or steer clear of the outcome being envisioned.

Although it is sometimes possible to reframe avoidance goals in approach terms and vice versa (e.g., staying healthy vs. avoiding illness), the two perspectives are not simply different ways to say the same thing. There is a big motivational difference between trying to advance toward a good outcome and trying to prevent something bad from happening. Even "maintenance" goals (i.e., those focused on maintaining stability or preventing change) can be pursued with a focus on success or a concern about failure. Imagine, for example, enthusiastically rooting for your favorite team to keep a winning streak alive versus watching the game in misery because you fear that the streak might come to an end.

Avoidance goals may of course be quite appropriate for circumstances involving clear threats and vulnerabilities. Nevertheless, a predisposition to think in terms of avoidance goals puts people at risk for debilitating motivational patterns characterized by energy depletion and persistent pessimism and anxiety (Roskes et al., 2014). In contrast, a general orientation to conceptualize goals in approach terms is associated with increased motivation, creativity, and life meaning (Parker et al., 2010).

These findings made us wonder why so many people fall into a habitual pattern of prioritizing avoidance goals. Perhaps this is a consequence of the fact that there are far more pain receptors than pain inhibitors in the biological infrastructure underlying our motivational systems (Damasio, 2003). (Recall that primordial goals were originally activated by pain receptors, with "well-being" mechanisms evolving later.) For example, a telling study in which high school students were asked to recall recent emotionally salient episodes found that, out of twenty-seven emotions studied, sadness lasted the longest – up to 240 times longer than emotions of the shortest duration, like surprise and feeling relief (Verduyn & Lavrijsen, 2015). In the words of Fredrickson (2009), "bad always trumps good" when these feelings are salient and in direct competition with one another. This means that when people experience painful feelings of one sort or another on a chronic basis (e.g., due to social anxiety, physical stress, or persistent loneliness), it may be hard to cheer up or to find the energy needed to focus on much of anything other than avoiding those feelings. And that's not all:

> To make matters worse, the psychological systems that monitor the world for potential threats are biased toward false positives. All animals are far more likely to react to a benign stimulus as if it is a threat than to react to a threat as if it is benign. From an evolutionary standpoint, a bias toward false positives makes adaptive sense . . .. But with their ability to dwell on future events in their minds, people can conjure up and dwell for long periods of time on bad things that might happen in the future. (Leary, 2004, p. 85)

Intrinsic and Extrinsic Motivation

Earlier the term "goal" was described as a valued end point in a sequence of activity. But many personal goals also serve as intermediate points, or subgoals, for larger or more distant outcomes (see Figure 3.1). For example, striving for a good grade on a test, although a potentially important goal in its own right, is also a necessary step in passing courses and getting an academic degree. Getting a degree may in turn be a prerequisite goal for qualifying for certain kinds of jobs that are of interest to you – a longer-term goal. Getting a good job may also be a means of financing a variety of other personal goal pursuits.

When we are motivated to do something for its own sake – that is, the goal being pursued is an end point that seems important and emotionally compelling to us – the motivation is typically characterized as *intrinsic*. Conversely, when we are motivated to do something solely for its instrumental value in helping us progress toward some other desired outcome, the motivation is typically classified as *extrinsic*. For example, "fun" activities are generally regarded as being intrinsically motivated. On the other hand, "chores" are usually assumed to be extrinsically motivated.

The distinction between intrinsic and extrinsic motivation has been useful in a general way because it has generated research showing that personal goals really matter. If you and I are doing the same thing but for different reasons, both the activity and the results of that activity will tend to play out very differently. For example, students with personal goals focused on understanding and mastery are more likely to retain what they have learned – and an interest in what they have learned – than students whose goals are oriented more toward performance evaluation outcomes (Midgley et al., 2001). People whose helping behavior is motivated by an authentic concern for others are generally viewed much more positively than those who are equally generous but are seen as helping for expedient or manipulative reasons (Grant, 2013).

The contrast between intrinsic and extrinsic motivation has also been useful in terms of differentiating what happens when personal goals are activated by emotions associated with an individual's internal thought processes rather than in response to emotions triggered by external pressures and incentives (Deci, 1980; Deci & Ryan, 1985). Motivation that flows from our spontaneous interests and concerns tends to be more enduring and reliable than motivation that is initiated by an environmental influence such as a promised reward or a threatened punishment. That is because when the environmental contingencies are removed, your behavior will naturally gravitate back to the goal pursuits that are the most compelling and meaningful to you.

Extrinsic motivation (alone) thus lacks authenticity and durability. That is a key reason why "facilitation, not control, should be the guiding idea in attempts to motivate humans" (M. Ford, 1992, p. 202). This advice is supported by a wealth of empirical research showing that productivity is inhibited and creativity is stifled when intrusive efforts are made to control people's thoughts and actions (Amabile, 1996; Deci & Ryan, 1985). Even valued rewards such as praise and money can sometimes backfire as motivational tools if they are perceived as inauthentic, coercive, or manipulative, with "strings attached" in terms of future performance or compliance expectations (Brophy, 1981; Brummelman et al., 2017; Deci et al., 1999).

Although the terms "intrinsic" and "extrinsic" continue to be fairly prominent in both the scientific and popular literature, we have elected not to use them in our conceptual framework because they seem to invite people to reduce motivational patterns to two categories and to adopt a simplistic "either-or" perspective on motivation. Such thinking is inconsistent with the equipoised way that motivational systems work. An extrinsically motivated act is typically part of a string of subgoals that eventually connects to an intrinsically motivated outcome (e.g., you might be highly motivated by a monetary reward because you are intrinsically motivated to enjoy the rewards that money can buy). Most goal pursuits, therefore, will involve a combination of intrinsic and extrinsic motivation. Moreover, it is not uncommon for things that initially are extrinsically motivating to become intrinsically motivating. That sometimes occurs, for example, when some interesting or likable quality is discovered in an initially boring task or person. It can also occur as part of a natural progression from something that at first seems really difficult (like riding a bike or playing the piano) but eventually starts to feel rather effortless. That is why

> it is a mistake to equate – as some current writers appear to do – intrinsic motivation with desirable motivation and extrinsic with undesirable. Both are important and necessary .... What may very well be more important than whether particular goals are intrinsically or extrinsically motivated is whether the intrinsically motivated goal at the end of the chain is appetitive [approach] ... or aversive [avoidance] .... People with more aversive goals are generally less satisfied with life and work than those with fewer aversive goals. (Klinger & Cox, 2004, pp. 7–8)

Personal Goals as Leaders of a Control System

Maintaining goal progress in the face of a constant stream of internal and external distractions and challenges is no easy task. It requires not only sound leadership and a reliable energy source, but also a coordinated effort from "followers" (e.g., knowledge and skill-related processes) who can effectively work as a team under the direction of the leaders. Understanding how these followers translate directives and other goal-relevant information into effective action is therefore an important part of getting to know "the leaders within you."

What are the essential characteristics of this teamwork arrangement?

One of the catalysts for the transformative events associated with the emergence of early life forms was the evolution of simple homeostatic *control systems* designed to ensure that the conditions needed for survival (e.g., appropriate water, salt, and temperature levels) were maintained under variable environmental conditions. As explained in the previous chapter, these homeostatic systems worked much like the familiar thermostat, with a "preinstalled" (primordial) goal and two primary functional components: a *comparator* responsible for detecting discrepancies between an active goal and current conditions, and an *output function* responsible for causing corrective action to occur when the discrepancy becomes larger than some tolerable margin (Carver & Scheier, 1998; G. Miller et al., 1960). Essentially these same mechanisms are involved not only in motivational systems directed by primordial goals, but also, with some elaborations, in motivational systems directed by personal goals. Consequently, even though the comparator function in humans typically involves a complex goal matrix with many inputs, understanding the fundamental mechanisms involved in simple homeostatic control systems can nevertheless tell us a lot about how our mind's leadership functions operate.

Figure 3.2 portrays the various sources of information that are inputs to the comparator in the context of human goal pursuit. These include personal goals – information about *desired* and *undesired* outcomes – and a mental stew of perceptions, expectancies, and feelings representing information about *current* outcomes (flowing along the *feedback* pathway) and *anticipated future* outcomes (flowing along the *feedforward* pathway). Like most illustrations of "cybernetic" (i.e., control system) operations, arrows are drawn to show the

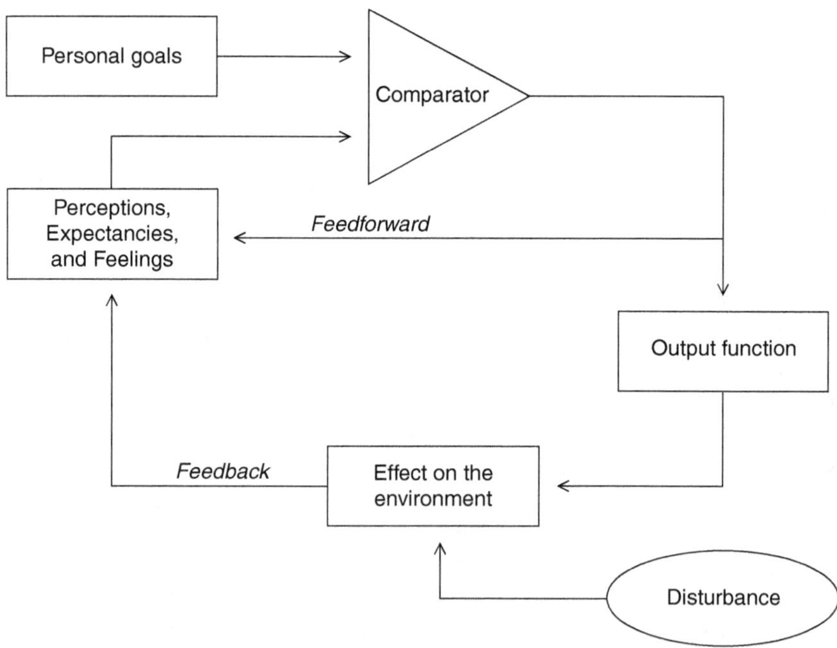

Figure 3.2 Diagram of the basic cybernetic control functions.

progression of events within a particular episode of goal pursuit. However, it is vitally important to understand that "the functioning of a control system is a continuous process in which all functions are always occurring" (D. Ford & M. Ford, 1987/2019, p. 7). In addition, for simplicity this picture omits information about the mental and physical infrastructure underlying the key processes in control system functioning (e.g., energy production from biological processes; information flow from memory processes). Omitting these enabling structures and functions does not mean they are unimportant; it is simply a way of highlighting certain essential self-leadership and teamwork processes involved in the pursuit of personal goals.

How Personal Goals Are Activated

If we could somehow carve up the continuous flow of life's ongoing journey into discrete segments, we would see that our daily lives comprise "episodes" of goal-directed activity (D. Ford, 1987/2019), each beginning with an energy source capable of activating a personal goal. That energy source, just as we have seen with life forms far less evolved than humans, is one or more triggered emotions. What triggers a particular kind of emotion at a given magnitude depends on an individual's unique history of emotional learning (in combination with some innate, species-typical emotional associations).

How do thoughts and emotions interact in motivational headquarters? Keep in mind that activation of a personal goal does not necessarily mean that it will be prioritized and actively pursued. It simply means that the goal is now in the mix of thoughts competing (metaphorically speaking) for a priority position in the comparator box of the control system – what we earlier referred to as the *goal evaluation* phase of goal processing. This is an important point because some goals that make it into this competition have a far better chance of being selected and pursued than others. How do we choose among the many possibilities that come to mind as we navigate our way through life? Triggered emotions get the motivational ball rolling by activating personal goal thoughts, but then what? How does your brain decide which personal goals to pursue among all the options that have been activated? Should you act on that impulse, or inhibit it? Is it time to work, or play? Play it safe, or go for it? Go it alone, or ask for help?

From Goal Activation to Goal Selection and Pursuit

While the *activation* of a personal goal is closely linked to triggered emotions, the *selection* of a personal goal – referred to earlier as the *goal commitment* phase of goal processing – is influenced by a variety of factors. Specifically, a personal goal may emerge as a "winning intention" in the ongoing competition among goal thoughts through four different pathways. All four pathways can (and often do) function outside awareness.

Goal profile. The most straightforward pathway leading to goal selection is through your existing self-constructed *goal profile* – the repertoire of especially meaningful personal goals you have built up over your lifetime as a result of your biological heritage, cultural environment, developmental upbringing, and learning opportunities. Throughout our lives each of us develops a unique configuration of ideas about what kinds of experiences and outcomes are the most engaging and fulfilling, and the best indicators of our "authentic self." For example, you might see yourself as a highly organized person who enjoys making things orderly or more efficient. Or you might see yourself as someone who thrives when striving for excellence, or pursuing justice, or helping others in need. Our natural tendency is to seek out and pay special attention to opportunities and challenges that are aligned with these ideas.

Some themes in your goal profile will be particularly strong, as evidenced, for example, by the magnitude of the emotions associated with those ideas and images. Keep in mind the fact that goal thoughts are generated on a near-continuous basis as part of the ongoing flow of life events. What thoughts will naturally and spontaneously come to your mind most frequently, or with the highest priority? Analogous to the list of "favorite" websites you have saved in your browser, thoughts aligned with your *core personal goals* are the ones most likely to capture your imagination (M. Ford & Nichols, 2005; Nichols, 1994). Because these emotionally compelling goal themes tend to come to the forefront in many different situations, they can be thought of as representing the "core" of your identity and personality (M. Ford, 1992).

Context information. Personal goals are also commonly prioritized as a result of *context information* suggesting what goals are relevant and appropriate for a particular situation. Indeed, one of the least studied but most important achievements in the development of young people is learning to identify what goals make sense in different contexts (Chevalier, 2015). The phrase "when in Rome, do as the Romans do" captures the simple logic of this selection pathway. You size up what goals are afforded by a particular context – often within milliseconds, with little or no conscious effort – and rule out goals that don't make sense for that situation. In cases where you have sought out a particular setting because of its relevance to a goal that is important to you (e.g., going to a fitness center to enhance well-being, or going to the library to study for an important exam), situational cues simply reinforce the choices you have initiated. However, in situations where you are following someone else's lead, you may pursue goals other than those you would normally choose on your own. Information about what is expected in a particular context may even cause you to behave in ways that are novel or "out of character" with your usual actions. That is not necessarily a bad thing. Although situational pressures and constraints can funnel people toward choices that feel inauthentic, such forces can also be used constructively to encourage people to explore new roles and experiences that are "out of their comfort zone."

Periodic selection and pursuit of new goals in new contexts may also play an essential role in maintaining mental flexibility and a healthy brain. That is why a lifelong learning orientation is such a valuable habit to cultivate. As Doidge (2007) explains,

> postmortem examinations have shown that education increases the number of branches among neurons. An increased number of branches drives the neurons farther apart, leading to an increase in the volume and thickness of the brain. The idea that the brain is like a muscle that grows with exercise is not just a metaphor. (p. 43)

Emotions. Decisions about whether to prioritize a goal are also influenced by the continuing impact of the *emotions* that originally activated the goal, and by additional emotions that arise as goals are being evaluated and compared to one another. This can happen even before we are consciously aware of the feelings produced by an emotion. Indeed, some emotional responses are so closely associated with goal-directed action that it is as if the emotion and goal are wedded together (imagine your response to seeing a scary spider or eating rotten-tasting food). Nevertheless, despite the essential role of emotions in activating personal goals, they generally function as advisors, not as leaders in the goal pursuit process. Feeling afraid or disgusted or angry or guilty does not automatically mean that you will act on those emotions or judge them to be appropriate. Still, emotions can make an extremely compelling case to the leaders about what personal goals should be prioritized if they are sufficiently intense or persistent.

Emotions can be especially influential when the cognitive advisors responsible for anticipating likely outcomes (i.e., personal agency beliefs) are weakened or confused, as is often the case when people are fatigued, under the influence of alcohol or drugs, or stuck in circumstances they did not seek out.

To use a sailing metaphor, emotions are like the puff of wind that powers the sails and gets the sailboat moving. Once in motion, it is mostly the tiller (personal goal) that steers the boat. However, the wind can make it a lot easier to steer in some directions than others, just as emotions can influence us to favor some goals over others. The two motivational forces operate as a team. When there is no enabling wind, the tiller is irrelevant (no goal activation). Conversely, when it is purely the wind (emotions) driving the boat, a condition described by sailors as "out of control" exists.

Emotions are not just informative, however, when they are (metaphorically speaking) "huffing and puffing." Because we encounter very few things in our daily lives that are truly emotionally neutral (Damasio, 2003), our emotions are constantly "nudging" us to prioritize certain kinds of choices over others (e.g., our favorite snack over others on the grocery shelf that we know would be healthier; a polite response rather than all of the confrontational things we wish we could say) (Thaler & Sunstein, 2008). This more subtle kind of emotional influence is what helps people navigate through complex situations that could otherwise leave us paralyzed with uncertainty or information overload. Like a trusted executive assistant who makes timely suggestions about what you need to focus on and prioritize *right now*, emotions can help the leaders maintain smooth, efficient functioning despite facing an ongoing stream of goal choices and a complex terrain filled with obstacles, doubts, and distractions.

Personal agency beliefs. Goal choices can also be influenced by the *personal agency beliefs* we associate with particular activities and experiences. These motivational advisors provide the leaders with two kinds of assessments, each focused on goal attainability. *Capability beliefs* are expectations about whether you personally "have what it takes" to reach a goal (M. Ford, 1992) – for instance, completing a marathon or cooking a great meal for your family. Such beliefs are often referred to by terms such as self-confidence or self-efficacy (Bandura, 1977, 1982, 1997). *Context beliefs* are expectations about whether your environment has the resources and support needed to attain a goal (M. Ford, 1992). For example, you might be quite certain you could cook a great meal but doubt whether you have all the necessary ingredients or expect that your family would prefer to go out for dinner.

Beliefs about what we can accomplish are not the only kind of self-oriented beliefs we develop. As we will see in the next chapter, we also develop beliefs about *who we are,* as illustrated by terms like "identity," "self-image," and "personality." However, because the motivational impact of these descriptive self-concepts flows through their influence on our directive and regulatory functions (i.e., our personal goals, emotions, and personal agency beliefs), our focus will be primarily on beliefs that are directly linked to goal striving.

When a goal is activated, and capability and context beliefs are both strong, the resulting message is "go for it." The emotion advisors pick up on these "positive vibes" and add motivational energy to the decision-making process. Positive personal agency beliefs thus function like a magnet, pulling people in the direction of their perceived strengths and resources. This not only leads us to prioritize things that we already feel good about, it also serves as a mechanism for developing new personal goals around novel experiences that turn out well for us. For example, you might halfheartedly try out a new activity (e.g., such as cooking or gardening), but then become increasingly interested in it as you discover not only that you have a hidden talent for such things, but also that others are supportive of your efforts to cultivate that talent.

Common "disconnects" between goal activation and goal pursuit for potentially onerous activities like dieting and exercise provide additional insight into how capability and context beliefs can not only inhibit motivation, but can also help rejuvenate motivation that has dissipated over time. The pursuit of challenging goals related to weight loss and healthier lifestyles can be especially discouraging, as the hoped-for result may not be immediately evident, and many competing goals can get in the way. Yet a "stop, then restart" intervention can strengthen motivation by allowing capability and context beliefs to be "reset" on a new timetable.

> People's motivation to begin pursuing their aspirations fluctuates and can fail them entirely .... [Yet] new beginnings can open new "mental accounts" and alter self-evaluations .... By psychologically separating people from their past selves and failures, temporal landmarks that open new time periods can help people relegate their missteps to the past and elevate their self-image and confidence. (Dai et al., 2015, pp. 1928, 1934)

How Personal Goals Lead

Once a commitment – or at least a tentative commitment – to pursue a goal has been made, the selected personal goal is compared with perceptions, expectancies, and feelings that help clarify where you stand with respect to the goal. If these comparisons make it clear that you are not yet close to your target, your goal thoughts will direct your mind and body to search for possible methods for progressing toward the desired outcome. If this search suggests that the goal is probably unattainable, the commitment may be withdrawn.

Imagine, for example, seeing an ad for a fantastic online sale that is about to expire. You look at the time (current condition) and try to judge whether you could complete the transaction before the sale ends (future condition). As you are making this judgment you might also consider whether you can afford the sale item, the probability that the item will meet your expectations, whether you could get a better deal somewhere else, or any number of other goal-relevant factors.

In systems terms, goal-related inputs representing current and anticipated future conditions are called *feedback* and *feedforward,* respectively (see Figure 3.2). The meaning of the perceptions, expectancies, and feelings that convey the feedback and feedforward information flowing into and through the system will of course depend heavily on our personal histories, so information about the past (memory) also plays a key role in goal pursuit. That is not to say that lots of experience will automatically make the challenge of integrating feedback and feedforward information an easy task. Memories and beliefs can undermine goal pursuit if they cause us to only perceive what we want (or expect) to perceive rather than what's actually being communicated to us (Nisbett & Ross, 1980). Indeed, *there are few barriers to effective functioning more common than having inaccurate or incomplete perceptions and expectations about goal progress.*

From a motivational perspective, the perceptions, expectancies, and feelings of greatest consequence are those associated with goal-relevant emotions and personal agency beliefs (see Figure 3.3). These are the processes responsible for integrating feedback and feedforward information into summary thoughts and feelings that offer useful information and sound advice to the directive (personal goal) function in motivational headquarters. Figure 3.3 also highlights the role of emotions in activating personal goals (as depicted by the vertical arrow in the upper left part of the diagram).

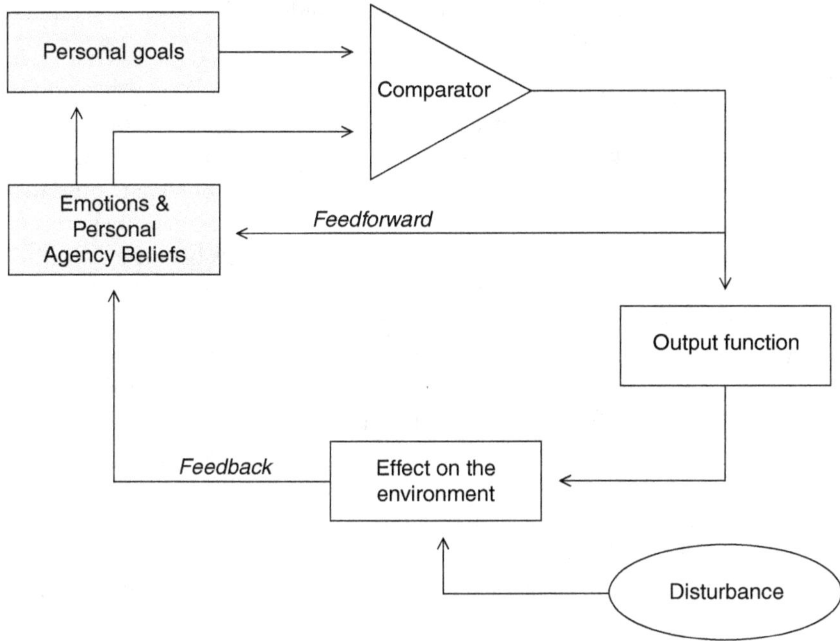

Figure 3.3 Diagram of the basic cybernetic control functions featuring the leadership team in "motivational headquarters."

The extent to which you can make informed decisions about goal options and goal progress depends in large part on the quality of the information and counsel provided by your "advisors" in motivational headquarters. Beliefs about personal agency must be realistic but also resilient. Pollyannaish thinking does not make for effective leadership, but nor does assuming that the future can be no better than the present. Similarly, emotions must be grounded in reality yet also capable of capturing our attention (e.g., "If I don't prepare well for this exam I could really be in serious trouble"). The key is to maintain *equipoise* across a wide variety of challenges and opportunities as the motivational milieu is updated and transformed. As Carver (2004) explains,

> for biological entities, being able to respond quickly yet accurately confers a clear adaptive advantage . . .. A person with very reactive emotions is prone to overreact and to oscillate behaviorally. A person who is emotionally nonreactive is slow to respond even to urgent events. A person whose

reactions are between the two extremes responds quickly but without undue overreaction and oscillation. (pp. 18–19)

When the input from your motivational advisors leads to a decision to initiate or continue pursuit of a goal, that decision can be thought of as a *commitment* to pursue a goal. Commitment is of course more of a continuum than an "on-off" phenomenon. Clear, consistent guidance and persuasion from your emotions and personal agency beliefs can strengthen commitment, especially as gentle reminders become amplified to the level of persistent nagging or even coercive urging. On the other hand, confusion or disagreement among the advisors can make it hard to form or stick with a commitment. This is a common outcome when we feel conflicting beliefs and emotions (e.g., "I'm scared even though there is no logical reason to be afraid"; "I know it's wrong but I'm not sure I can resist the temptation"). Commitment can also be elusive when we are uncertain about how rocky the pathway to success will be (e.g., "I'd like to apply for that job but I don't know if I'm ready for it").

Difficulty in making commitments can also occur when too many different goals are vying for attention and priority, thus creating a mental "traffic jam" in the comparator. Although it is normal to have a mix of different goals directing our actions – a phenomenon known as *motivational pluralism* (U. Kaplan & Tivnan, 2014) – there are limits to the degree of complexity and incongruity that can be effectively managed. People who chronically experience "goal overload" often spend too much time worrying about their choices rather than progressing toward their goals (Kuhl & Beckmann, 1994). Failure to resolve ongoing goal conflicts can in turn negatively impact mental and physical health (Emmons & King, 1988).

Of course, as most everyone who has made a New Year's resolution knows all too well, goal commitment does not ensure that we will actually follow through on that commitment. An appropriate plan of action (e.g., a weight loss plan) still needs to be developed and carried out effectively. Your commitment may waver as the initial emotional energy that led to the commitment subsides, or as feedback suggests that you underestimated the difficulty of maintaining goal progress. Often a well-intentioned commitment to change simply gets overpowered by stability-maintaining habits – or, metaphorically speaking (Haidt, 2006), by the "elephant in the room" (e.g., "I tried to stick to that diet but I just couldn't get into it").

Maintaining goal commitments can be especially challenging when energy resources have been depleted – for example, due to illness, fatigue, chronic pain, extended mental duress, or simply a lack of food. As

Baumeister and Tierney (2011) explain, motivation and self-regulation are not just the result of a computer-like brain calculating cost-benefit analyses. "In their eagerness to chart the human equivalent of the computer's chips and circuits, most psychologists neglected one mundane but essential part of the machine: the power cord" (p. 42).

The term "output" reflects the fact that this is the action-oriented part of the process responsible for actually changing your current circumstances. If all goes well, your actions will produce changes that match the "conditions of satisfaction" specified by your personal goal (Searle, 1981). Feedback indicating that you have successfully achieved your goal, or that you are making good progress toward your goal, will trigger positive emotions and affirming personal agency beliefs. That in turn provides encouragement to continue the process of goal pursuit. Conversely, feedback indicating that your actions are ineffective will tend to discourage goal-seeking efforts.

Now imagine that you are pursuing not just one goal, but multiple goals with several alternative action plans associated with each goal. Imagine "disturbances" coming at you from all different angles. Imagine trying to process and integrate multiple feedback and feedforward inputs from many different sources. That is a more accurate picture of what control system processing looks like in humans than a simple linear chain of events. Fortunately, most of these events occur beneath awareness where, as we've seen, processing is fast and effortless. Nevertheless, *the ability to select the most accurate and informative inputs with which to make good decisions* is a particularly valuable skill (Endsley, 1985; Gallagher, 2009).

This brief journey through the control system model reveals that one of the most useful aspects of this model is how it simultaneously emphasizes not only the powerful influence of personal goals as psychological leaders, but also the complex web of interdependencies between leaders and followers, any of whom can facilitate or undermine progress. Analogous to a troubleshooting guide in a repair manual, the control system model can help you diagnose strengths and weaknesses and identify where breakdowns in decision-making and execution may have occurred. It can also help us recognize how important it is to keep our attention clearly focused on what our control system is trying to control (Gallagher, 2009; Kuhl & Beckmann, 1994).

What a Control System Controls

Understanding that humans pursue goals in ways that are consistent with the properties of adaptive control systems raises the question: just what is it that we are trying to control? During much of the twentieth century, few would have thought to ask the question in this way, as mainstream theories of human behavior generally assumed that it was the environment rather than the person doing most of the controlling (e.g., Hull, 1943; B. Skinner, 1974; J. Watson, 1930). Such theories are no longer in favor because it is now evident that the basic operating principle is the reverse:

We do things because we are trying to control our environment – or, more precisely, the consequences we get from the environment.

This profound insight (D. Ford, 1987/2019; Powers, 1973) underlines how important it is for individuals to achieve clarity with respect to the content of their personal goals. Essentially, it means that the primary reason we do things is to transform thoughts about desired and undesired consequences (personal goals) into actual results consistent with those thoughts.

Specifically, the consequences we are trying to control are of two types. At a *cognitive-perceptual* level, we try to align anticipated consequences (feedforward) and perceived consequences (feedback) with our desired consequences (personal goal). For example, when I push "Start" or turn the key in my car's ignition, I want to hear the engine running. When I open the refrigerator door, I want to see something good to eat. When I meet with a potential employer, I want to get a job offer. To facilitate success in controlling these inputs, humans have many information-processing and behavioral tools at their disposal. We can explore, learn, invent, experiment, remember, and discard all kinds of ideas and strategies. We can also use these capabilities to change our goals, plans, and beliefs when circumstances warrant. These informational and behavioral "self-construction" capabilities (D. Ford, 1987/2019) are analogous to the growth and self-repair activities that routinely occur in biological systems.

We also try to control *affective* consequences (i.e., feelings) associated with our goal pursuits. We want to feel happy. We want to feel competent and proud. We want to feel hopeful and empowered. We want to feel loved and respected. We want to feel that life is meaningful and worth living. Indeed, it is when such feelings arise that new personal goals are most likely to develop (Fredrickson, 2009). We are attracted to things that make us feel capable or special. We want to be around people who make us feel respected and secure. Conversely, we tend to avoid circumstances that make us feel distressed or inadequate.

In Chapter 5 we will continue to emphasize the importance of attention as a key tool for facilitating goal progress, not only with respect to producing real-world results, but also in terms of controlling our emotional experience. There is an art to this process, as goal progress can be undermined if our experience is either overly constrained by past experience or, conversely, not well grounded in reality. In other words, equipoise with respect to the interplay between imagination and reality must be maintained. Nevertheless, one of the great contributions of psychological science has been to show how we can change the way we experience life – and ultimately how our brains function – by training our conscious rider to willfully control the thoughts and feelings we attend to as we pursue goals and respond to environmental disturbances (Begley, 2007; Doidge, 2007; Fredrickson, 2009; Kashdan, 2009; Lyubomirsky, 2008; Seligman, 1991; Snyder & Lopez, 2002). It is now clear that when it comes to this aspect of motivation and optimal functioning, "learning to shift your attention away from unhelpful thoughts and emotions and recast negative events in the most productive light possible is one of the most important of all 'health habits' to cultivate" (Gallagher, 2009, p. 201).

Attention is also a critical element in managing goal conflicts. That is why students, job seekers, and politicians are often told by their advisors to "keep your eyes on the prize." This sound advice may often fall into the category of "easier said than done" given the difficulty of fending off compelling distractions and temptations (Baumeister & Tierney, 2011; Harley et al., 2019). Nevertheless, controlling *attention* is a powerful way to maintain control over what *intentions* take precedence when goal conflicts arise.

Identifying Your Core Personal Goals

Earlier in this chapter we identified self-awareness of your core personal goals as an essential element in learning how to motivate self and others. Without this fundamental self-knowledge, decision-making will tend to be superficial and shortsighted rather than coherent and anchored in a stable set of guiding principles. Responses to work and relationship problems will tend to be impulsive and misguided rather than constructive and satisfying. Achievements will tend to be ephemeral rather than cumulative and meaningful. Integrity may be hard to maintain, in reality and as perceived by others.

Unfortunately, most people have little experience with any of the steps involved in bringing implicit personal goal thoughts into consciousness. Even the fact that such thoughts are often not immediately accessible to the conscious mind is not well known. As a result, the need for shared words and concepts that can help people label and categorize personal goal themes is rarely addressed in educational and work settings. Developing measurement tools that can identify the content and strength of an individual's personal goals has generally not been a priority for basic or applied scientists, despite some notable exceptions (Emmons, 1989; M. Ford & Nichols, 1991, 2005; Henderson, 2009; Little, 1983; Markus & Nurius, 1986; Nichols, 1994). Evidence-based guidelines for helping people apply self-knowledge of their personal goals to practical concerns have been virtually nonexistent.

We have devoted a significant part of our professional lives to addressing these very issues. In the remainder of this chapter we share what we have learned and identify key resources for readers interested in applying the science of personal goals to their own lives.

The Taxonomy of Human Goals

All science starts with a good classification system for the kinds of phenomena involved, whether those phenomena are chemical elements, celestial bodies, or, as in our case, personal goals. Such classification schemes are the cornerstone of all theory construction (D. Ford, 1987/2019).

In the early days of psychology, it was taken for granted that identifying a person's underlying motives was an essential prerequisite for anyone seeking to understand, impact, or improve human behavior. As a result, several pioneering scholars developed wide-ranging motivational taxonomies to help address this concern. For example, McDougall (1933) proposed a taxonomy of "instincts" that covered over a dozen major behavior domains (e.g., eating, mating, parenting, combat, escape). Murray (1938) proposed a taxonomy of twenty-eight needs encompassing the full range of behaviors most commonly seen in humans (e.g., aggression, acquisition, nurturance, play, sex). Maslow (1943) famously constructed a shorter list of needs organized in hierarchical fashion, with Physiological and Safety needs at the bottom of the hierarchy and Belongingness-Love, Esteem, and "Self-Actualization" needs at the upper levels of the hierarchy. In later iterations Maslow also proposed the less familiar categories of Aesthetic and Cognitive needs, while also introducing the concept of "self-transcendence" as a motivational step beyond self-actualization (Koltko-Rivera, 2006; Maslow, 1969).

Interest in goal content among psychological scientists quickly faded during the latter half of the twentieth century as powerful new conceptual frameworks were developed that focused more on external influences on behavior or on the acquisition of knowledge and skills. In addition, there was increasing recognition that goal categories that merely describe what people do are not very useful. Such descriptions are like medical diagnoses that simply relabel symptoms (e.g., "gastritis") rather than point to underlying causes. For example, saying that we have sex because we have a "need" for sex does not account for the wide variety of reasons that people engage in sexual activity (e.g., to make a baby or to make money). The thoughts directing such activity could be anywhere from highly self-focused (e.g., physical pleasure, sexual conquest) to highly other-focused (e.g., give pleasure to your partner, fulfill a relationship obligation).

Although early motivational taxonomies proved to be of limited utility, there was still an urgent need for this kind of tool. Having meaningful concepts and a rich vocabulary for thinking about and discussing personal goals can greatly facilitate successful goal pursuit. In that spirit, M. Ford and Nichols (1987/2019, 1991) developed a comprehensive *Taxonomy of Human Goals* during their intensive collaboration at Stanford University in an effort to facilitate the scientific study of personal goals and to help practitioners assist clients with motivation-related challenges. The taxonomy was constructed by taking the best ideas that motivational science had to offer and integrating that information with clinical evidence illuminating the nature of people's thoughts about desired and undesired outcomes. Care was taken to make sure each goal category represented thoughts about the *outcomes* of behavior and not the behaviors themselves. Consistent with the notion that *personal* goal profiles are unique to each individual, primordial goals related to homeostatic biological functions (e.g., eating, sleeping, temperature maintenance) are omitted from the Taxonomy of Human Goals.

Constructing a concise taxonomy of all the different kinds of personal goal thoughts that humans may have is a challenging task. From one perspective the possibilities are endless, as everyone constructs their own unique mix of perceptions, feelings, and memories, and every situation brings with it some new elements and nuances. However, if the focus is on goal *themes* rather than on individual goal thoughts, it is possible to organize personal goals into a finite number of categories. Ford and Nichols accomplished this by following an iterative process of testing and refining candidate goal categories until informants were no longer able to describe goal thoughts that could not be easily classified somewhere in the taxonomy. The result: twenty-four highly durable personal goal categories, as displayed in Table 3.1 along with descriptions representing both the approach and avoidance manifestations of each goal theme.

Table 3.1 *The Ford and Nichols Taxonomy of Human Goals*

Integrative social relationship goals	
Belongingness	Building or maintaining attachments, friendships, intimacy, or a sense of community; avoiding social isolation or separateness
Social Responsibility	Keeping interpersonal commitments, meeting social role obligations, and conforming to social and moral rules; avoiding social transgressions and unethical or illegal conduct
Equity	Promoting fairness, justice, or equality; avoiding unfair actions
Resource Provision	Giving approval, support, assistance, advice, or validation to others; avoiding selfish or uncaring behavior
Self-assertive social relationship goals	
Individuality	Being unique, special, or different; avoiding similarity or conformity
Self-Determination	Being free to act or make choices; avoiding social pressure, constraints, or coercion
Superiority	Comparing favorably to others in terms of winning, status, or success; avoiding unfavorable comparisons with others
Resource Acquisition	Obtaining approval, support, assistance, advice, or validation from others; avoiding social disapproval or rejection
Affective feeling goals	
Entertainment	Experiencing feelings of excitement or heightened arousal; avoiding boredom or stressful inactivity
Tranquility	Feeling relaxed and at ease; avoiding stressful overarousal
Happiness	Experiencing feelings of joy, satisfaction, or well-being; avoiding feelings of emotional distress or dissatisfaction
Bodily Sensations	Experiencing feelings of pleasure associated with physical sensations, physical movement, or bodily contact; avoiding unpleasant or uncomfortable bodily sensations
Physical Well-Being	Feeling healthy, energetic, or physically robust; avoiding feelings of lethargy, weakness, or ill health
Cognitive goals	
Exploration	Satisfying one's curiosity about personally meaningful events; avoiding a sense of being uninformed or not knowing what's going on
Understanding	Gaining knowledge or making sense out of something; avoiding misconceptions, erroneous beliefs, or confusion
Intellectual Creativity	Engaging in activities involving original thinking or novel or interesting ideas; avoiding mindless or familiar ways of thinking
Positive Self-Evaluations	Maintaining a sense of self-confidence, pride, or self-worth; avoiding a sense of failure, guilt, or incompetence

Table 3.1 (*cont.*)

Task goals	
Mastery	Meeting a challenging standard of achievement or improvement; avoiding incompetence, mediocrity, or decrements in performance
Task Creativity	Engaging in activities involving artistic expression or creativity; avoiding tasks that do not provide opportunities for creative action
Management	Maintaining order, organization, or productivity in daily life tasks; avoiding sloppiness, inefficiency, or disorganization
Material Gain	Increasing the amount of money or tangible goods one has; avoiding the loss of money or material possessions
Safety	Being unharmed, physically secure, and free from risk; avoiding threatening, depriving, or harmful circumstances
Subjective organization goals	
Unity	Experiencing a profound or spiritual sense of connectedness, harmony, or oneness with people, nature, or a greater power; avoiding feelings of psychological disunity or disorganization
Transcendence	Experiencing optimal or extraordinary states of functioning; avoiding feeling trapped within the boundaries of ordinary experience

Although the categories in the Ford and Nichols taxonomy are not as "personalized" as the actual, momentary goal thoughts people may have in a particular situation, they provide a way of describing goals that highlights their most distinctive property, namely, *goal content*. As an analogy, imagine someone asking you what kind of car you own. You might say "Ford Explorer" knowing that in most cases this will convey the essential information the listener is looking for. For some purposes you may need to add other properties of the vehicle to your description (e.g., color, model year, engine size), just as you might note other properties of a personal goal beyond its core content (e.g., intensity, setting, connections to other goals). And occasionally you may need to provide a description that is truly unique to your individual car (e.g., its Vehicle Identification Number), just as you might do when you need to describe a goal in "idiographic" (one-of-a-kind) terms (e.g., imagine a counseling psychologist seeking to develop a therapeutic plan for a particular client). Nevertheless, our experience is that, when it comes to looking at goal *patterns* over time and across settings, the Taxonomy of Human Goals is a particularly informative tool. The utility of a comprehensive goal taxonomy is even more apparent when there is a need to identify compatible or complementary patterns of personal goals between individuals (e.g., potential marital partners) or among the members of a social group (e.g., a leadership team or self-managed work unit).

There are two overarching divisions in the taxonomy. One subset of personal goals refers to desired outcomes within your mind and body (i.e., thoughts, feelings, and other subjective experiences). The other refers to desired outcomes of your interactions with the environment. Logically, all personal goals must fall into one of these two broad divisions.

There are three different sets of goals representing "within-person" desired outcomes. *Affective feeling goals* are thoughts about particular kinds of feelings or emotions that you may want to experience. *Cognitive goals* refer to different kinds of mental representations that you may be motivated to construct or maintain – for example, accurate thoughts, meaningful thoughts, novel thoughts, or positive thoughts about the self. Finally, *subjective organization goals* represent special "whole-person" experiences (combining affect, perception, and cognition) that you may be motivated to pursue in the context of your social, educational, recreational, or spiritual activities.

There are also three different sets of personal goals representing desired "person–environment" outcomes. *Self-assertive social relationship goals* are thoughts focused on promoting your own interests in the context of other people. Conversely, *integrative social relationship goals* – which we will later refer to as "social purpose" goals – are thoughts focused on helping others and promoting the well-being of the social groups and relationships in which you have a personal investment. (See Koestler [1967, 1978] for an extended discussion of human self-assertive and integrative tendencies and the importance of balancing these motivational systems in an equipoised way.) While *task goals* may also involve people, the main focus of this set of personal goals is on how you relate to nonsocial aspects of the environment or to practical (as opposed to relationship-oriented) aspects of social interactions (e.g., managing people's work assignments or engaging in commerce).

Table 3.1 provides a conceptual overview of each category in the Taxonomy of Human Goals. We invite you to study the words in this table and the extent to which they feel congruent or incongruent with your personal goals, as they have been carefully chosen to capture not only the essential substance of each goal theme, but also the qualities that make each goal theme unique. For example, people who have strong Intellectual Creativity goals often do not have any particular investment in Task Creativity (and vice versa) despite the obvious semantic connection between those categories. Similarly, distinguishing between Mastery and

Superiority is critical for understanding achievement motivation, as it reveals whether the primary concern is "getting ahead" in comparison with previous personal achievements (self-improvement) or in comparison to others' achievements (winning).

Most of the thematic categories in the Taxonomy of Human Goals are familiar and straightforward, consistent with the fact that they were derived in large part from the statements of "ordinary folks" about what outcomes are of greatest importance to them. For example, many people say they want to feel safe and experience good physical health (Safety, Physical Well-Being). It is also common for people to say in various ways that they want to feel good about themselves and be happy and stress free (Positive Self-Evaluations, Happiness, Bodily Sensations, Tranquility). In addition, spontaneous goal statements often emphasize the importance of having opportunities to explore, learn, grow, and be creative (Exploration, Understanding, Mastery, Intellectual Creativity, Task Creativity). Goal thoughts related to having fun and having nice things are also familiar themes (Entertainment, Material Gain).

Of particular importance for our *Thriving with Social Purpose Theory of Motivation and Optimal Functioning* is the subset of goal themes listed under the heading of "integrative" social relationship goals. In contrast to "self-assertive" social relationship goals, which focus on gains for the individual, integrative goal themes reflect a concern for social interdependence and the welfare of others, each in a different way.

Belongingness goals focus on creating, maintaining, or enhancing social bonds (e.g., in families, friendships, communities, work organizations, or cultural groups). Consistent with our evolutionary history, such bonds are a central concern for most people, as they provide a primary context for the mutual exchange of valued emotional, informational, and material resources. Themes related to belongingness include caring, intimacy, loyalty, and group identity.

Social Responsibility goals represent a desire to maintain cooperative relationships and good social standing by behaving in accordance with social rules, expectations, and obligations. People who resonate to qualities such as reliability, conscientiousness, and trustworthiness are especially likely to make such goals a high priority.

Equity goals center on social comparison concerns, and are especially relevant in peer relationships (e.g., with friends, spouses, co-workers, or juries). Such goals are particularly prominent among people who are bothered by social injustice, unequal sharing of resources, or the victimization of helpless or disadvantaged individuals.

Finally, *Resource Provision* goals reflect a desire to enhance other people's lives by altruistically offering resources such as material aid, informational support, emotional validation, or task assistance to people who are in need of such resources. Such goals are particularly likely to be activated in the context of asymmetrical social roles in which one person is responsible for providing resources to another (e.g., parent-child or teacher-student relationships). Resource provision is also a common theme in close relationships where the mutual exchange of such resources is one of the organizing principles for that relationship (e.g., friendship or spousal relationships).

Although other goal taxonomies have been proposed (e.g., Chulef et al., 2001), the Ford and Nichols Taxonomy of Human Goals has proven to be a particularly useful tool for classifying the full range of personal goal content found in motivational systems, and for providing verbal "handles" that empower people to engage in conscious reflection and shared discussion of goal themes and variations (e.g., Austin & Vancouver, 1996; D. Bergin, 1989; Boekaerts et al., 2006; Boekaerts et al., 2012; Doest et al., 2006; Henderson, 2009; Mansfield et al., 2012). We now turn to the measurement tool that Ford and Nichols designed to assess the strength of each of the twenty-four goal categories represented in this taxonomy.

The Assessment of Personal Goals

One of our guiding assumptions in this book is that self-awareness of core personal goals is an essential prerequisite for motivating self and others. That leads to the question of whether there are valid and reliable methods for helping people acquire that self-awareness. Although several motivationally relevant psychological assessments have become quite popular in recent decades – for example, Holland's Self-Directed Search, the Strong Interest Inventory, the Myers-Briggs Type Indicator, and the CliftonStrengths assessment – it is often difficult to translate the surface-level descriptions they offer into useful explanations or predictions. Suppose, for example, that you received a high score on the "Social" dimension in the widely used Self-Directed Search assessment (also used in the Strong Interest Inventory). Inspection of the goal categories in the Taxonomy of Human Goals reveals that there are many different types of social goal content. If I am attracted to "social" work contexts, does that mean Equity or Superiority? Resource Acquisition or Resource Provision? Belongingness or Social Responsibility?

Similarly, suppose your most distinctive score on the Myers-Briggs Type Indicator was on the "Thinking" dimension. Does that imply that you are particularly attracted to Understanding goals? Intellectual Creativity goals? Exploration goals? Or perhaps other goals for which "thinking" is a commonly used means for making goal progress (e.g., Mastery and Management)?

And what is one to make of the list of thirty-four "talent themes" in the CliftonStrengths assessment? While several of those categories appear to reflect personal goal themes such as those included in the Taxonomy of Human Goals (e.g., "competition" $\rightarrow$ superiority; "maximizer" $\rightarrow$ mastery; "consistency/fairness" $\rightarrow$ equity), many other strengths are simply a descriptive relabeling of broad skill sets (e.g., "People strong in the Communication theme generally find it easy to put their thoughts into words"; "People strong in the Intellection theme are characterized by their intellectual activity"). Still others reflect themes more closely associated with the emotion and personal agency belief components of motivation (e.g., Empathy, Self-Assurance, Positivity). While many find great intuitive value in this kind of assessment, the lack of an organizing conceptual framework limits the potential utility of the resulting list of strengths.

On a much smaller scale, several idiographic (i.e., case-specific) motivational assessments have been developed that are more closely aligned with contemporary theory and research on personal goals (e.g., Emmons, 1989; Little, 1983; Markus & Nurius, 1986). And yet, although these methods may be quite useful in counseling and mentoring settings, they are not based on a unifying taxonomy with shared terms that can make it possible to compare and contrast personal goals within and across individuals. Consequently, there is still a need for an assessment designed to identify, at an individualized level but within a common classification scheme, the powerful underlying sources of motivation that constitute "the leaders within" each of us.

Following this logic, M. Ford and Nichols (1991, 2005), after completing the Taxonomy of Human Goals, focused on the task of developing and refining a specialized measurement tool designed to help people access their *core personal goals* using a common set of goal themes. The resulting assessment capitalized on the fact that strong feelings usually signal the presence of strong goals (Nichols, 1994) – just as they did early in our evolutionary history. The underlying rationale for their work was straightforward:

1. It is important to identify your core personal goals, as such knowledge makes it possible to pinpoint sources of motivational opportunity and engagement, satisfaction and dissatisfaction, and life meaning.

2. Personal goals generally function outside of consciousness, so goal identification requires some method for bringing goal thoughts into consciousness.
3. Since we can only be conscious of things that we can perceive (D. Ford, 1987/2019; Haidt, 2006), techniques for bringing goal thoughts into consciousness need to evoke powerful images and feelings.

Goal thoughts are often brought into consciousness by having people talk or write about their goals (Locke & Latham, 2019). However, such techniques are more effective for context-specific goals than for underlying core personal goals. Capitalizing on the fact that strong goals are typically accompanied by strong emotions, the techniques used by Ford and Nichols involve mentally inserting yourself into a broad range of everyday life episodes and then reflecting on your emotional reaction to those experiences (e.g., "A person you work with has been unjustly criticized by one of your superiors. Would it bother you if you didn't try to correct this injustice?"). Answers to such questions make it possible to "connect the dots" across seemingly disparate situations, with the result being the identification of a small set of *personal goal themes* representing your most powerful sources of satisfaction (when you advance toward your core goals) and dissatisfaction (when your core goals are thwarted or disrespected). This goal profile can then be used as an "executive summary" of the motivational factors most likely to determine whether you will find future opportunities and experiences to be engaging and fulfilling.

Being able to consciously access your personal goal profile is essential for consequential tasks such as those involved in career decision-making and relationship choices. Imagine, for example, being conflicted about a job offer that would require you to move away from your family and familiar surroundings. Being able to assess whether the new job was well aligned with your identity and core goals could help you avoid a very serious mistake. This quality of *goal–life alignment*, or alignment of life circumstances and personal goals, is also the key issue in helping you achieve a sense of balance and integrity in your daily life. A clear understanding of your personal goal profile can help you align everyday tasks with high-level goals and ensure that you reserve time and energy for the activities and interests that are the most meaningful to you.

This same logic can be extended to efforts to motivate others. For example, if you understand and consciously think about the things that are most important to your spouse or romantic partner, you will be in a much better position to anticipate what kind of actions (or reactions) are likely to support or violate your partner's core personal goals. Even if these core personal goals are not particularly important to you (e.g., you might not care much about punctuality or social protocol), you can ensure that you do not inadvertently disrespect your partner – who presumably *is* important to you – by aligning your behavior with the outcomes your partner cares about the most. Failure to do so will naturally lead your partner to conclude "you must not care about me if that's how you to choose to behave."

Similarly, by attending to the core personal goals of employees, employers can more effectively create work contexts that employees will reliably experience as satisfying and meaningful, thus facilitating high levels of morale, productivity, and retention. That is a key indicator that goal alignment has been achieved. In contrast, organizational leaders who are unaware of or unconcerned about the motivational priorities of their followers are likely to repeatedly violate their followers' core personal goals – for example, by creating feelings of inequity, raising safety concerns, or failing to respect needs for privacy and autonomy. Followers who experience such violations will in turn feel disrespected and will assume that their leaders are uncaring, clueless, or worse. Inevitably, motivation will become increasingly vulnerable and both commitment and productivity will suffer.

These kinds of concerns led Ford and Nichols to create and validate the *Assessment of Personal Goals* (APG), which can be accessed at https://apg.gmu.edu. The APG is a science-based tool that, in combination with the *APG Personal Application Guide* (M. Ford & Smith, 2013), can yield powerful practical results for those who want to identify their most compelling personal goal themes and then apply that knowledge to enhance their motivation, decision-making, and life meaning. The APG is grounded in an integrative theory of human motivation called *Motivational Systems Theory* (M. Ford, 1992; M. Ford & Smith, 2007) that explains how personal goals, emotions, and personal agency beliefs work together as a leadership team (see Chapter 4). Motivational Systems Theory is in turn based on a comprehensive theory of human behavior and development called the *Living Systems Framework* (D. Ford, 1987/2019).

From the perspective of Motivational Systems Theory, the key to leading a happy and productive life is *successfully aligning your core personal goals with consequential life choices and ongoing investments of time and energy*. Creating this essential goal–life alignment requires a clear understanding of the personal goal profile you have developed throughout your life. This is a more difficult task than one might imagine given the frequency of goal-related talk in everyday conversation. The problem is that such talk is often focused on organizational or societal goals, not personal goals. Moreover, our conscious "rider" can easily become captivated by low-level goals in the immediate situation at the expense of high-level goals that infuse goal pursuits with meaning. So, while it may not be difficult for you to identify operational or surface-level goals, we all need help making our "implicit self" – our deep, enduring profile of core personal goals – accessible in a meaningful way. That is the kind of self-knowledge that can inspire visionary thinking and reveal new pathways to personal and professional fulfillment.

Consistent with this perspective, the APG was designed to help people improve their lives by providing a method for identifying deeply felt motives within a standardized framework (i.e., the Taxonomy of Human Goals; see Table 3.1). Using a common vocabulary makes it possible for people to share thoughts and feelings about the personal goals that matter most to them.

The APG provides estimates of goal strength for each category represented in the Taxonomy of Human Goals. "Highly compelling" scores point to goal themes likely to be centrally involved in your core personal goals. For example, a very high score on the *Equity* scale suggests that you would likely find a wide variety of situations involving fairness and justice concerns to be emotionally compelling. That is not to say that your version of an Equity goal and my version of an Equity goal would necessarily look the same at a surface level. You and I may have different kinds of lower level (context-specific) goals connected to that same high-level goal theme (e.g., seeking justice in the workplace vs. ensuring fair treatment of family members). Nevertheless, when different people have core personal goals within the same category, it is generally easy to identify those goals as variations on the same theme, like different kinds of birds or different versions of the same model car.

APG goal category scores just below the "highly compelling" level are of special interest as well. That is because scores in this range point to goal themes that may also serve as reliable sources of satisfaction and life meaning in certain kinds of circumstances. For example, you might have a positive orientation toward *Understanding* or *Mastery* goals but only experience them as highly compelling within a specific field of expertise. Being able to see such interests as part of a more general goal theme can help you think about whether you might find other activities that afford attainment of the same type of goal more attractive than you might have anticipated.

The APG also points to goal categories that are not consistent priorities for you, but that from time to time may capture your attention due to situation-specific interests or instrumental connections to core personal goals in other categories. For example, a teenager who is not generally concerned about *Material Gain* may become preoccupied with saving money because buying a car is seen as an essential vehicle (no pun intended) for achieving *Self-Determination*.

In addition, the APG identifies goal categories that are clearly not a priority for you (i.e., you would rarely have a strong personal goal oriented toward those themes), as well as goal categories that you are likely to actively avoid because they have negative emotional associations for you. For example, older adults often have very low scores in the goal category of *Entertainment* because they tend to find emotionally arousing experiences like roller coasters and loud parties to be stressful rather than enjoyable.

The APG has been used in at least ten different countries on four different continents: North America, Asia (Japan), Europe (France, Germany) and South America (Argentina, Brazil, Colombia, Peru). In a review published in the scientific journal *Measurement and Evaluation in Counseling and Development*, the APG was characterized as

> a unique online tool that can facilitate efforts to help people understand the sources of their discontent, predict how they might respond emotionally in particular situations, and evaluate opportunities in terms of their potential for satisfying core personal goals .... The APG Web site has undergone extensive technical and user testing ... [and] also makes it possible for respondents to view their goal profile immediately after completing the assessment. (Henderson, 2009, pp. 248, 246)

The APG makes it possible to identify thematic categories in which your most compelling personal goals are likely to be found. Based on that foundation, the *APG Personal Application Guide* (M. Ford & Smith, 2013) then helps you connect these goal themes to your unique, "real-life" choices and circumstances, with those connections ultimately culminating in a personalized, context-specific mapping of actions likely to increase your *goal–life alignment*. As we have emphasized throughout this chapter, that is one of the keys to enhancing motivation and life meaning in self and others. Conversely, failing to recognize serious "core goal violations" may be damaging not only to your own emotional and physical health, but also to the well-being of those you live and work with. As T. D. Wilson (2009) warns, there are consequences to failing to understand ourselves. People who exhibit discrepancies between implicit and explicit measures of their self-concepts or motives have been found to be especially low in emotional well-being and especially high in physiological reactivity, anxiety, self-doubt, defensiveness, and narcissism . . .. It thus seems to be to people's advantage to discover what is under their mental hoods. (p. 387)

Realizing that chronic feelings of distress and dissatisfaction may be resolvable through deliberate efforts to create goal–life alignment can be a joyful and rejuvenating part of a successful healing process. The APG (and companion Personal Application Guide) can also help people who are feeling unfulfilled discover pathways to a more meaningful life – one in which *thriving* outweighs *coping* as a mindset for dealing with life's opportunities and challenges (Winell, 1987/2019). Often, the emptiness can best be filled by seeking out circumstances that allow personal goals associated with *social purpose* to move to the forefront of our thinking. Thriving and social purpose are the themes that are at the heart of the motivational framework we will describe in Chapters 5, 6, and 7.

It is recommended that you complete the *Assessment of Personal Goals* at https://apg.gmu.edu before moving on to the next chapter. That will provide you with a richer appreciation of *Motivational Systems Theory* (presented in Chapter 4) and how the qualities associated with a *Thriving with Social Purpose* motivational pattern (Chapters 5 and 6) can yield abundant life meaning (Chapter 7). It will also give you a comprehensive mapping of your own core personal goals – an important first step in empowering you to effectively motivate self and others.

Motivational Systems Theory
The Leadership Team in Motivational Headquarters

> We have more than enough theories of motivation and more than
> enough data on motivational phenomena .... We need to be more
> clever with what we already have.
>
> – Frank J. Landy and Wendy S. Becker,
> "Motivation Theory Reconsidered"

> The strength of the team is each individual member. The strength of
> each member is the team.
>
> – professional basketball coach Phil Jackson

Throughout this book we have been metaphorically referring to the leadership team responsible for envisioning, evaluating, and energizing the pursuit of personal goals as "motivational headquarters." A brief overview of how goals, emotions, and personal agency beliefs carry out their leadership functions was outlined in the discussion of control systems in Chapter 3 (see Figure 3.3). We will now consider in more depth, using a conceptual framework called *Motivational Systems Theory* (M. Ford, 1992), how these motivational processes work together as an organized unit. Understanding how this collaborative leadership arrangement operates – and the conditions under which it can become disrupted – is an essential foundation for learning how to motivate self and others.

Essential Qualities of Motivational Systems

All systems can be understood from two vantage points (Koestler, 1978). From one perspective, there is the unitary functioning of the system as a whole. From another perspective, we can look at the functioning of the individual parts or components of the system. For example, in human motivational systems, we can focus on personal goals, emotions, or personal agency beliefs as separate contributing processes, or we can focus on their collective influence on the person-system. Until recently, psychological science has focused more on specialized components than on the integrated functioning of motivational systems (Baumeister, 2016; Dweck, 2017; M. Ford, 1992; McCombs, 1991; Pintrich, 1994).

In Chapter 2 we focused on the question of how each element involved in human motivational systems evolved as a way of clarifying some of the essential qualities of "basic human nature." We then provided (in Chapter 3) a more detailed discussion of the nature and functioning of the personal goal component of motivational systems. In this chapter we will elaborate on the emotion and personal agency belief components of motivational systems and how they interact with each other and with personal goal thoughts. However, such interactions also need to be understood from the vantage point of how the system functions as a whole. The two most important system properties from this perspective are *organization* and *equipoise.*

Organization

Organization exists when various components are combined into a unit in such a way that the whole is markedly different than the sum of the parts – like the picture produced when a jigsaw puzzle has been completed. Consistent with this metaphor, Wheatley (1999) emphasizes that "systems reveal themselves as patterns, not as isolated incidents or data points" (p. 125). Unfortunately, much of what we know (or at least think we know!) about human functioning and development is based on "snapshots" focused on one or two isolated components in a narrow range of circumstances. And yet, when it comes to complexly organized systems like humans, it is hard to get a meaningful picture of an individual's current functioning or future potential unless you can "get the big picture" across a panorama of life episodes.

Although organization can sometimes emerge out of chaos (Hilpert & Marchand, 2018; A. Kaplan & Garner, 2017; A. Kaplan et al., 2019; Wheatley, 1999), it is not an arbitrary phenomenon. As D. Ford (1987/ 2019) explains, the value of organizing parts into a system

> is to produce possibilities the parts do not have separately. If different organizations of parts produced no new possibilities there would be no reason for new organizations to occur or continue. That is a central premise underlying evolutionary theory. New organismic organizations evolved because they provided characteristics of greater survival and reproductive value in a particular environmental niche than did other organismic organizations. (p. 37)

Organizing component parts into a unified system involves both gains and losses. For example, a marriage can enhance intimacy and security, but it may also restrict personal freedom. Similarly, although the evolution of the capacity for self-awareness was the catalyst for many of humanity's greatest achievements, it also enabled people to ruminate about their fears and failures in motivationally self-defeating ways (Leary, 2004). The net result may be positive or negative depending on what outcomes are emphasized. But the key to organization is that something new – something *innovative* – is created. Indeed, the primary mechanism for creating innovations is through organization (or "reorganization").

The brain, with multiple layers that evolved at different times, is a perfect example of this strategy of constructing new capabilities on an existing foundation. The "robustness" that resulted from brain evolution produced some astonishing gains, but that robustness came at a price. As Wagner (2014) explains,

> valuable things are usually not free, and robustness is no exception. Its price – a high one – is complexity …. Why doesn't ruthlessly efficient nature get rid of all this complexity? The answer is "the environment" – or rather, "the environments." [Complexity] is actually the secret to survival *in more than one environment.* (pp. 186, 188)

A good example of how the system property of organization works can be seen in the human body's response to dieting. It turns out that the simple idea of losing weight by eating less is not so simple. Indeed, reducing caloric intake is unlikely to help most people lose weight over time (Benton & Young, 2017). That is because our evolved biological and motivational systems developed a variety of methods to help balance the intake and expenditure of energy. Recall that in the lives of early humans, the availability of food was somewhat unpredictable and erratic. As a result, a number of compensatory mechanisms naturally "kick in" when we start dieting. Those mechanisms include, for example, hormonal changes to stimulate appetite, increased craving for high-caloric foods, and a reduction in overall metabolic rate to match food intake.

One way that motivational psychologists have studied organization is through research on what Ryan and his colleagues call the *integrative process* (Ryan & Deci, 2018; Weinstein et al., 2013). Integration is promoted by "mindful awareness" of the goals, emotions, and personal agency beliefs governing our decisions and actions. Consistent with our earlier emphasis on how awareness of core personal goals can contribute to optimal functioning, research on this topic has revealed that

> integrative processing of experience is conducive to wellness and effective functioning …. When functioning in an integrative manner, a person has enhanced access to the motives, emotions, and meanings underpinning his or her actions, which better enables him or her to selectively identify behaviors that fit with personal values and life goals and to be authentic and wholeheartedly engaged. For these reasons, integration enhances vitality and wellness. (Weinstein et al., 2013, p. 69)

These same scholars also concluded that integration "encourages prosocial and responsive behavior, as well as low levels of prejudice and high levels of empathy and closeness in relationships" (p. 73). As we will see (in Chapter 5), this synergistic combination of psychological vitality and social responsivity – or what we call *Thriving with Social Purpose* – exemplifies motivation at its (human) best.

We have many mechanisms designed to help us maintain organized functioning (Ecker & Gilead, 2018). For example, self-awareness evolved largely for this purpose. Yet the more complex the system the harder it can be to maintain organization (Wagner, 2014). Indeed, many common types of human dysfunction reflect the difficulty of maintaining integrated functioning in the face of vexing goal conflicts (such as those that test our integrity or willpower), internal emotional turmoil (as illustrated by a panic attack or a guilty conscience), or incompatible "possible selves" (imagine a soldier trying to adjust to life back home after many years in overseas combat). Such challenges provide compelling evidence for the importance of organization in human functioning. Indeed, there are few things as motivating as wanting to avoid feelings of psychological disorganization ("I want to but I'm afraid I'll lose control"; "I wish I could stop feeling so torn up inside").

Equipoise

As we have seen, the story of how motivational systems evolved has as its central theme the emergence of new and increasingly sophisticated mechanisms for pursuing goals related to survival with well-being. However, the more capable and multifaceted a system becomes, the greater the need for coordinating and balancing mechanisms that can keep the many components of the system working in harmony. That brings us to the second key property of overall system functioning.

Imagine a sailor navigating a small sailboat on the open sea. The experienced sailor will understand the need to monitor the ever-changing environment (e.g., wind speed and direction, sea swell, weather conditions) and to make appropriate adjustments to the tiller, sail, and body weight distribution to harmonize with these conditions and thus maintain optimal hull speed performance. If the sailor steers too much into the wind, or pulls in the sail too much, the boat will stall. Similarly, if the sail is too full or body weight is positioned incorrectly, the boat may swamp.

When all of the proper adjustments are continuously fine-tuned, the sailboat moves efficiently through the water and the sailor experiences a sense of harmony with the sailboat and the sea. We have selected the term *equipoise* as the best available description of this dynamic pattern.

> *Equipoise refers to the ongoing effective balancing and counterbalancing of the multiple forces involved in goal pursuit.*

Equipoise results not when a fixed, "right" amount of a given attribute has been achieved (like the "right" amount of salt in a recipe), but rather when each element in a dynamic system functions in unison toward a common purpose. As Wheatley (1999) succinctly puts it, "stasis, balance, equilibrium, these are temporary states. What endures is process – dynamic, adaptive, creative" (p. 90).

The concept of equipoise suggests that there may be many different "right" ways for each component of the system to function depending on external conditions and the status of other system components. That is why, for example, it is impossible to distill good parenting or effective leadership into a simple behavioral formula. Indeed, the assumption that certain kinds of strategies or tactics will be uniformly good or bad – also known as the *fallacy of uniform efficacy* (Bonanno & Burton, 2013) – is one of the biggest obstacles to understanding optimal system functioning. Responses that were perfect for navigating one kind of challenge (e.g., forgiving someone when a bad outcome is not their fault) may be cata-strophic under other conditions (e.g., forgiving someone when a bad outcome reflects their persistent inclination to make irresponsible choices). Moreover, the "right" configuration of responses in any given set of circumstances may be quite different for different people. For example, while a young person may respond well to "big brother" or "big sister" coaching from someone a few years their senior, a thirty-year veteran taking that approach would likely be viewed as inauthentic and better suited for the role of a wise elder.

As with the system property of organization, equipoise is particularly hard to sustain when strong emotions are in play. Consider, for example, the challenge of maintaining equipoise when speaking in front of a group.

For those who rarely engage in self-conscious reflection, this may be a relatively easy task. But many people list public speaking among their most dreaded fears. What was easy to say to a few friends over coffee can become a nightmare when saying it in front of a large audience. Accomplished speakers know, however, that a small amount of fear (which most would refer to as anxiety) can actually be beneficial at the outset. It gives them energy and helps maintain a certain level of animation that is picked up by their audience. Anxiety can then turn into excitement as you see the audience reacting favorably and you hear yourself successfully getting on with the speech (or at least averting any imagined disasters!).

Along these same lines, actors often report that their rehearsals (without an audience) are "flat" compared to their opening night performances. So the actor's ideal response – an *equipoised* response – requires an understanding of the ebb and flow of different emotions under different conditions (e.g., rehearsal vs. "the real thing") and the ability to manage those emotions to optimal effect. Too much anxiety and the performance may be ruined; too little anxiety and they may lose their edge. What is "too much" or "too little" will vary by individual, but what will not vary is the need to make ongoing adjustments as factors that may influence their performance ebb and flow – just as the sailor must do when facing the challenges of the open sea.

Equipoise applies to nearly every aspect of person-system functioning. However, it is a particularly important quality of motivational systems because it is virtually impossible to maintain equipoise without relying heavily on *anticipatory thoughts and feelings*, which is the "modus operandi" of all motivational processes. In simple homeostatic systems (analogous to a thermostat), it may be possible to function effectively by simply reacting to ongoing feedback. However, as we have seen, self-direction in humans requires not only the capacity to respond effectively to feedback, but also a proactive, future-oriented approach to goal pursuit (Parker et al., 2010). Changes in the environment and in biological states need to be anticipated before it is too late to make adjustments (imagine planning a big holiday meal or an international business trip). We also need to be able to predict how best to respond to challenging conditions for which we have little or no prior feedback (e.g., steering a car on an icy road; helping a family member in crisis).

The importance of future-oriented thinking that combines "fixed rules and flexible strategies" (Koestler, 1967) is well illustrated by the challenge of sailing on the open sea. For example, our experienced sailor will attentively watch for ripples in the water that signify an approaching gust of wind. As conditions become more volatile, vivid mental simulations will play out in the sailor's mind as different scenarios are contemplated (e.g., anticipating that currents will be stronger closer to shore). Specific goals, contingency plans, and preparatory actions will shift in priority not only as circumstances change, but also as *potential* circumstances become more or less salient in the sailor's conscious and nonconscious thoughts.

Now imagine trying to navigate a life predicament and, rather than focusing on how to resolve it, you instead become preoccupied with things that happened in the past (like who is to blame for your predicament). Or perhaps all you can think about is the mental activity you are experiencing *right now* (e.g., relentless feelings of anger or guilt). Getting stuck in an aversive "mental soup" of evaluative thoughts and feelings rather than maintaining action-oriented goal progress can quickly lead to a loss of equipoise and increased motivation to escape from difficult circumstances, even those that are well within our capacity to resolve (Kuhl & Beckmann, 1994).

Equipoise is also a key concept for understanding motivational systems because the interdependencies among goals, emotions, and personal agency beliefs are, by design, very strong. For example, although we need to vigorously pursue goals to survive and thrive, pursuing too many goals at once can be emotionally disruptive. Emotions need to have sufficient strength (i.e., feeling) to energize behavior, but not so much as to cause disorganized thinking. Self-confidence can sustain motivation during rough times, but overconfidence can also cause people to fail to prepare for circumstances they are not yet ready to handle.

In sum, equipoise is an essential concept for understanding human functioning and development, and especially important for understanding motivational systems (Kashdan & Rottenberg, 2010). Moreover, its importance is closely related to the degree of complexity involved in a particular motivational challenge. Equipoise is relatively easy to maintain in familiar, predictable circumstances and under conditions of low stress. Even a novice may be able to manage the multiple forces involved in steering a small sailboat on a clear day with a light breeze and a good mentor nearby. The true test of a system's ability to maintain equipoise is how it responds when, metaphorically speaking, a storm is brewing and mental, physical, and emotional resources are being tested (as evidenced by strong feelings of "pressure" or stress).

It is also important to reiterate that equipoise should not be confused with the concept of equilibrium, or even the more flexible concept of dynamic equilibrium. *Equipoise is not evidenced by behavioral stability, but by behavioral versatility.* This versatility is what enables the best sailors to handle a wide range of challenges – just as evolution favors the most versatile creatures who can adapt to the widest range of environmental conditions.

Motivational Systems Theory

The decade between the mid-1970s and mid-1980s was a particularly exciting period for psychologists interested in the role that motivational processes play in learning, achievement, and personal development. During this period Seligman (1975) – who later became one of the "founding fathers" of positive psychology – published his highly influential theory of *learned helplessness* in animals and humans. Bandura's (1977, 1982) concept of *self-efficacy* became a big hit among those looking for a more systematic and practical way to study the impact of personal agency beliefs on learning and behavior change. Several theories organized around the concept of *intrinsic motivation* also emerged during this period, including optimal experience theory (Csikszentmihalyi, 1975, 1991), which introduced the popular concept of *flow*, and self-determination theory (Deci, 1980; Deci & Ryan, 1985). In addition, leading scholars proposed various control system models (Carver & Scheier, 1981; Powers, 1973), differential emotion frameworks (Ekman, 1972; Izard, 1977; Plutchik, 1980), and goal-based approaches to human motivation (e.g., Emmons, 1986; Locke & Latham, 1984; Markus & Nurius, 1986).

As with many scientific advances, most of these innovative efforts proceeded independently from one another. That made it difficult for those trying to use these theories in applied settings to grasp the "big picture" of human motivation and to identify common ground. That in turn has limited the development of scientifically credible tools and resources for those interested in motivating self and others.

In an attempt to unify the best available ideas and evidence in this field and make them more accessible to scholars and practitioners, M. Ford (1992) created an integrative theory of motivation called Motivational Systems Theory (MST). This framework is not only among the most comprehensive theories of motivation currently available, it is also the only one explicitly grounded in a *living systems* approach to human behavior and development (D. Ford, 1987/2019; D. Ford & Lerner, 1992; M. Ford & D. Ford, 1987/2019), which is increasingly recognized as the most viable pathway for advancing basic and applied knowledge in the human sciences (e.g., Buckley, 1967; Dunning, 2016; Jantsch, 1980; J. Miller, 1978; Powers, 1989; Prigogine & Stengers, 1984; von Bertalanffy, 1975; Vondracek et al., 2014).

MST does not contradict any of the popular contemporary theories noted throughout this book. Indeed, its stated intent is to advance science by "standing on the shoulders of giants." Nevertheless, one should not underestimate either the theoretical or practical value of adopting an integrative perspective. When a theory only focuses on a single component of a motivational system, there is a tendency to see that component as *the* central influence in the system rather than as a "team player" that is heavily influenced by other components (Hirschi, 2009). That limits the scope – and sometimes the validity – of a promising "big idea." Indeed, as a result of ongoing empirical work, many of the theories that emerged during the fertile period between the mid-1970s and mid-1980s have found it necessary to broaden the range of motivational phenomena included in their conceptual frameworks (e.g., Dweck, 2017; Ryan, 2012, 2019; Ryan & Deci, 2018).

Narrow theoretical approaches to human motivation can also make it difficult to appreciate the critical role that larger system qualities like organization and equipoise play in determining the impact of individual components. Consider, for example, an Olympic basketball team filled with top professionals who are more interested in demonstrating their talents than in coordinating their talents. Knowing how the team plays together will probably be a better predictor of outcomes in competitive games than knowing how skilled each player is.

Along these same lines, simply having "more" of a given motivational quality isn't necessarily going to produce a better result. As we saw with the adjustments a sailor needs to make to keep a boat afloat and moving forward, "too much of a good thing" at the component level (e.g., a strong emotional response) can turn out to be a very bad thing at the system level (as when "emotional flooding" occurs).

Motivational Systems Theory also extends the reach of motivation theories by virtue of the fact that it is embedded in a comprehensive, evidence-based, intervention-oriented theory of human behavior and development called the *Living Systems Framework* (D. Ford, 1987/2019). As a result, MST not only recognizes the individual and collective contributions of personal goals, emotions, and personal agency beliefs to human motivation, it also respects the influential role played by other parts of the person-system. Indeed, we will spend considerable time in Chapter 5 discussing the critical role that biological functioning, knowledge and skills, and environmental circumstances play in efforts to motivate self and others.

> A successful theory of motivation will be one that places the interactions of all these causal agents front and center in its concerns, and also likely dismisses trying to highlight one cause or set of causes as the primary ones from which all else is secondary. (Dunning, 2016, p. 28)

Formula for Human Functioning

Motivational System Theory begins by emphasizing the need to understand that motivational processes operate in collaboration with other system components. In a nutshell, the *effective pursuit of personal goals* (aka human functioning) requires four essential elements:

1. The person must have the *motivation* needed to initiate and maintain goal pursuit until the desired outcome is attained.
2. The person must have the *knowledge and skills* needed to construct and execute actions that will produce the desired outcomes.
3. The person's *biological structure and functioning* must be able to support the motivation and knowledge and skills elements required for successful goal pursuit.
4. The person's *environment* must facilitate, or at least not excessively impede, progress toward the desired outcome.

These ideas are summarized in MST using the formula shown in Figure 4.1.

It is important to note that the multiplication and division symbols used in this formula do not represent formal mathematical statements about the relationships among component processes. They are simply intended to

$$\text{Human Functioning} = \frac{\text{M} \times \text{K\&S}}{1/\text{Biology}} \times \text{Env}$$

Figure 4.1 The *Motivational Systems Theory* Formula for Human Functioning.
Note: The large-scale components of human systems and the relationships among them can be represented using a heuristic formula that emphasizes the dynamic interactions among motivational processes (M), knowledge and skills (K&S), biological subsystems, and the environment (Env). The formula shows biology as a denominator to emphasize that its primary role is to support the M and K&S components. Biology is represented in reciprocal form since its role is to nourish and strengthen (rather than weaken) the impact of the other components on human functioning.

convey the notion of interdependency that is at the heart of a systems approach. Such interdependencies may be straightforward (as when functioning is improved by additional resources), or they may be complex and nonlinear (as when stress levels must escalate beyond a certain threshold before a significant impact on functioning is evident).

Along these same lines, a particularly important implication of a systems approach is that enhanced functioning in one system component can often enhance the functioning of the whole system. That is a principle that helping professionals often use to their advantage (e.g., dysfunctional emotion patterns can often be altered by strengthening a client's capability and context beliefs). On the other hand, sometimes the "system is only as strong as its weakest link." For example, it may be difficult to accomplish even simple everyday tasks if you are hit hard by a flu bug or are feeling an overwhelming sense of fatigue. Other "show stoppers" might include apathy, panic, ignorance, political obstacles, or a lack of essential resources.

The benefits of a systems view are particularly well illustrated by high-stakes performance contexts where positive outcomes are highly dependent on the effective and coordinated functioning of each component. Imagine, for example, that you are investigating the possible cause of a fatal one-car automobile accident. If the driver is very young, you might assume that inexperience (deficit in knowledge and skills) was probably a significant factor. If the driver appears to have been drinking, you might guess that biological impairments played a major role. If the weather conditions were dangerous at the time of the crash, that fact would no doubt be at the forefront of your thinking. And if a smartphone was lying on the floor of the damaged car, you might suspect that the driver's attention was focused on goals other than those associated with the driving task at hand.

Formula for Human Motivation

In MST human motivation is defined as an organized system focused on self-direction. Specifically:

> *Motivation is the organized patterning of the mind's leadership and advising functions:*
>
> *personal goals* (directive thoughts about desired and undesired potential future states),
>
> *emotions* (mechanisms that activate goal thoughts and energize and regulate goal pursuit), and
>
> *personal agency beliefs* (thoughts about the anticipated consequences of pursuing a goal).

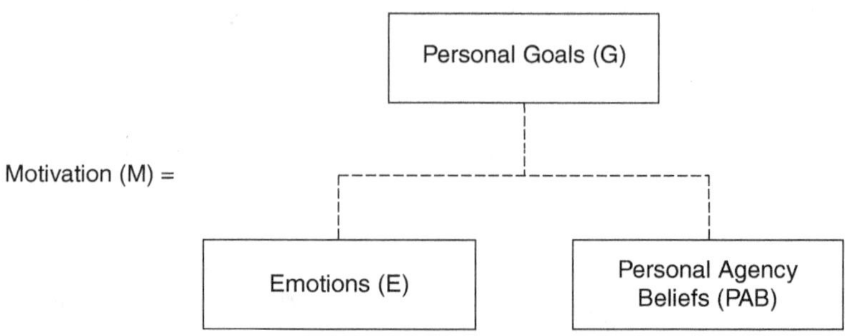

Figure 4.2 The *Motivational Systems Theory* Formula for Human Motivation with an associated diagram.
Note: The components of motivational systems and the relationships among them can be represented using a heuristic formula or a graphical representation. The formula emphasizes the dynamic interactions among personal goals, emotions, and personal agency beliefs. The diagram emphasizes the leadership role played by personal goals in motivational systems, with emotions and personal agency beliefs serving primarily in an advisory capacity.

The collaborative nature of the work these processes carry out can be represented using a simple formula similar to the one used for human functioning in general. As illustrated in Figure 4.2, we have also found it useful to portray the concept of a motivational system using a graphic that emphasizes the leadership role played by personal goals.

Together, these closely allied processes enable people to imagine future possibilities while also guiding their decision-making about which alternatives to pursue at what level of effort and persistence. The team in motivational headquarters consists of a leader (the personal goal component) and two sets of advisors (emotion and personal agency belief components) that work closely with the leader and with each other. For example, assessing the attractiveness of a job opportunity will involve not only weighing the pros and cons (personal goals) associated with the opportunity, but also sorting out evaluative thoughts and feelings such as excitement (am I attracted to this opportunity only because it's new?), self-doubt (do I have what it takes to succeed in this job?), and guilt (what will happen to my co-workers if I leave?).

It is also important to reiterate that the multiplication symbols used in the MST Formula for Human Motivation are not intended to convey a simple linear relationship among motivational components. Indeed, there is a tendency for relationships between motivational processes and motivational "outputs" (e.g., effort, persistence, performance) to be curvilinear (as represented graphically by a bell-shaped function). Such relationships reflect the dynamic system properties of organization and equipoise. More of a given motivational element is generally better up to a point, but beyond some threshold equipoise is lost, and functional losses begin to outweigh gains. In extreme cases disorganization of the whole system can result, as evidenced by disorders such as paranoid thinking, uncontrolled anxiety, and obsessive-compulsive behavior.

A simple illustration of this general phenomenon is the classic "Yerkes–Dodson law" from the early days of psychology (see Figure 4.3) (Yerkes & Dodson, 1908). In the context of human motivation this law asserts that performance will tend to increase as emotional arousal increases, but only up to a threshold level, after which performance will tend to decrease due to excessive (as opposed to beneficial) stress, loss of self-control, or other outcomes related to a loss of equipoise.

This scientific principle has stood the test of time, as illustrated by the fact that a variety of motivation theories have been organized around concepts such as *optimal arousal* or *optimal challenge* (e.g., Berlyne, 1971; Csikszentmihalyi, 1991; Farley, 1991). These theories have generally focused

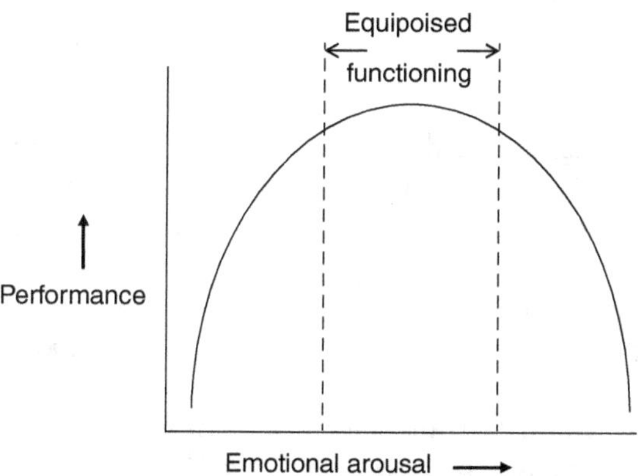

Figure 4.3 Relationship between level of emotional arousal and performance.
Note: This figure illustrates the importance of equipoise in relationships between motivational processes and performance. Emotional arousal contributes to performance up to a threshold level, beyond which increases in emotional arousal predict decreases in performance. The optimal level of emotional arousal has been shown to vary with the motor complexity of the performance (Yerkes & Dodson, 1908). We refer to the functioning within the vertical lines as being equipoised.

on contextual factors – for example, circumstances that are distressing because they lack sufficient stimulation (thus resulting in emotions like boredom or loneliness) or because they exceed a threshold of manageable stimulation (thus leading to feelings like panic or dread). However, the concept of optimal arousal is also useful for understanding biologically based differences in approach-avoidance motivation. For example, Farley (1991) has suggested that "thrill seekers" (aka Type T personality) have an unusually low baseline level of internal arousal and thus need a steady diet of externally generated excitement to maintain an optimal level of arousal. Conversely, those with an unusually high baseline level of internal arousal (aka "little t" personality) are likely to be wary, shy, and much more comfortable with familiar people and routines than with novelty and risk.

Personal Goals

Personal goals have two basic properties: they mentally represent outcomes to be pursued and achieved (or avoided), and they direct the other components of the person-system to try to produce those outcomes (or prevent them from occurring) (Austin & Vancouver, 1996; D. Ford, 1987/ 2019). The first property is typically referred to as the *content* of a goal. The second property (directing) is typically referred to as the *function* of a goal. Both properties operate outside of consciousness most of the time.

Goal Content

Goal content is the imagined version of something you hope to turn into a reality (or to avoid having become a reality). That image serves not only as a target for goal pursuit, but also as a criterion for assessing your progress. The Ford and Nichols *Taxonomy of Human Goals* (see Chapter 3) provides a comprehensive accounting of the thematic categories of personal goal content that people may experience in their thinking about desired future outcomes.

Whereas Ford and Nichols have been primarily concerned with how high-level goal themes organize our everyday thoughts, feelings, and actions, several other motivation theories have focused on methods for identifying mid-level patterns of goal content. The terms used to describe these mid-level goals – for example, personal strivings (Emmons, 1986), personal projects (Little, 1983), life tasks (Cantor & Fleeson, 1991), and possible selves (Markus & Nurius, 1986) – suggest their potential utility for framing discussions about motivation in clinical and counseling settings.

However, mid-level goal content is more meaningful when it is connected to high-level goal themes (see Figure 3.1 in Chapter 3). That is how you can best tell if a particular project or ambition is likely to be a "passing fancy" or an enduring source of satisfaction.

Directive Function of Personal Goals

Many motivation theories ignore goal content and focus instead on the mechanisms through which personal goals carry out their leadership functions. Some of these theories emphasize the powerful directive influence of nonconscious goal thoughts. For example, research by Bargh and his colleagues (Bargh, 2017) has been tremendously influential in showing that goals operating beneath awareness routinely have potent effects on motivation. As we have emphasized all along, the ability to direct much of our behavior at a nonconscious, "energy-efficient" level is one of the key design principles organizing human motivational systems.

Yet, most theories pertaining to the directive properties of personal goals focus on conscious manifestations of personal goals. For example, there is a vast literature on *goal setting* that explains how directive thoughts across a wide range of content areas can be deliberately shaped to maximize their influence on motivation and achievement. This research has been effectively summarized by Locke and Latham, who are among the acknowledged leaders in this field (Locke & Latham, 1984, 2019). The essential findings are compelling and fully consistent with our earlier discussion of control systems (see Figure 3.3 in Chapter 3), where we emphasized the importance of getting high-clarity, action-oriented information into the comparator (decision-making) process. It's hard to make good decisions or to assess your progress effectively if you're not sure what target you're aiming for.

Many hundreds of studies have been designed to test the efficacy of goal-setting interventions and techniques. These studies have consistently demonstrated that clearly conceived personal goals – that is, goals that provide precise guidance about relevant actions, timelines, and standards for progress or success – are more likely to have the intended motivational impact than goals conceptualized in vague or overly general terms. That is why we have included *intentional goal setting* as one of the key "amplifiers" of the K&S (knowledge and skills) component of human functioning (see Chapter 5).

For instance, a goal of taking a brisk walk for thirty minutes each day after dinner will direct behavior more reliably than a well-intentioned but amorphous vow to get more exercise, or a visual image of yourself looking fit and buff (even if that image is really vivid, like being surrounded by admirers on the beach). By itself, an image provides a target but no clear direction (i.e., what to do to reach the target). A vague intention suggests a direction (start exercising), but no clear target (e.g., in terms of where, when, and how much to exercise).

As illustrated by this example, clearly formulated goals work because they "nail down" both *content* (by translating high-level goal thoughts into more concrete ideas and images) and *direction* (by pointing to specific pathways to success). When personal goals are conceptualized in this way, they connect goal thoughts to critical situations that afford attainment of the goal, thereby increasing the probability that intentions will lead to action.

A simple and effective way to take advantage of this principle is illustrated by Gollwitzer's research on *implementation intentions* (Gollwitzer, 1999; Gollwitzer & Sheeran, 2006). This technique, which we will discuss in more detail in Chapter 5, involves prescribing specific self-statements for people trying to build new habits using the format, "When I encounter circumstance 'X,' I will do action 'Y'" (e.g., "When I brush my teeth, I will take my pills"; "When I go to a fast food restaurant, I will order water as my drink"). Such goal thoughts can be further strengthened by generalizing them to a broad range of similar circumstances (e.g., "When I am ordering a meal, I will have water as my drink").

Directives from motivational headquarters also tend to be more potent if they incorporate challenging but realistic standards for goal attainment. If a future state is conceptualized that is not much different than the current state, that image may not be very motivating (e.g., imagine yourself striving to lose one pound in three months). On the other hand, if what is envisioned is too discrepant from current conditions, the advisors in motivational headquarters (i.e., your emotions and personal agency beliefs) are likely to raise "red flags" (e.g., anxiety and self-doubt) that slow down or even shut down goal pursuit. For example, a commitment to lose ten pounds in three months will likely be more sustainable than a goal to lose ten pounds in one week.

Personal goals that incorporate unrealistic standards are more likely to undermine than increase motivation, not only because they invite "infighting" in motivational headquarters, but also because success is in fact so unlikely. That creates a circumstance where both feedforward (expected outcomes) and feedback (actual outcomes) are negative – a surefire recipe for reducing commitment to a goal. That is why *flexible standards* – that is, goal thoughts you are prepared to revise upward or downward as circumstances change – are so important in efforts to motivate self and others (M. Ford, 1992). Equipoise is impossible to maintain when standards are adopted that are rigid and insensitive to new information – as illustrated, for example, by people who are unable to forgive themselves (or others) for minor transgressions, or who try to plan out every element of a business or romantic encounter. Life is filled with ups and downs and unexpected twists and turns. Being able to "roll with the punches" and do a little improvising from time to time is an essential part of successful goal pursuit.

Somewhat counterintuitively, most people find it easier to *raise* goal standards than to lower them (Bandura & Cervone, 1986), perhaps due to "'wishful thinking" or because lowering one's standards can feel like an admission of weakness or failure (to self or others). But in many cases "flexing" the criteria for progress or success down a bit is exactly what is needed to avoid unrealistic standards and their demotivating consequences. Indeed, learning when it is OK to "give yourself a break" is an important part of maintaining a positive outlook on the future when progress is stalled or slower than anticipated. That is why, for example, golf courses have several different tees (starting points) for each hole. The game of golf is much more enjoyable when the length of each hole is aligned with the golfer's capabilities.

Consistent with the general concept of self-direction, the goal-setting literature has also documented the fact that goals that originate from other's directives are generally less compelling than *self-set goals* that originate from our own thinking (Deci & Ryan, 1985; Locke & Latham, 1984). This is especially true when no effort has been made to align external mandates with the personal goals of those receiving those mandates. This fundamental error tends to make people feel unappreciated, or even worse, disrespected. That is why one of the most important skills that parents, teachers, and organizational leaders can develop is to learn how to connect their directives with the personal goals of those they are trying to influence. This can be accomplished either indirectly, through means–ends connections (e.g., by ensuring that cooperation and compliance result in personally valued consequences), or even better, in a more direct way by involving the person receiving the directive in the goal-setting process itself. Simple actions along these lines can have surprisingly beneficial effects by setting into motion the key processes associated with sustained commitment to a goal.

Motivational scientists have also emphasized the striking differences between personal goals formulated in *approach* terms versus those

Goal Orientation

	Approach	Avoidance
Progressing well	Happy	Relieved
Progressing poorly	Sad	Anxious

Figure 4.4 Emotional consequences of approach versus avoidance goal orientations. *Note:* In general, the emotions experienced as a result of positive or negative goal progress will differ, as shown above, depending on goal orientation.

conceptualized in *avoidance* terms. Although both orientations are essential for real-world adaptation, self-direction will tend to be stronger and more reliable when your mental "home page" (i.e., your naturally preferred way of thinking about goals) is approach oriented (Parker et al., 2010). That is because thinking about future challenges in terms of gains that might be acquired (approach goals) creates a very different *mindset* compared to a focus on losses that might be suffered (avoidance goals). An approach goal orientation is generally associated with productive action, openness to change, and personal growth. In contrast, an avoidance goal orientation is typically associated with hesitance, resistance to change, and a reluctance to explore opportunities (Dweck, 2006; Elliot, 1999). The emotional tone is also completely different. As shown in Figure 4.4, those who regularly pursue goals from an approach orientation tend to experience the normal ups and downs of everyday living, while those who pursue goals from an avoidance orientation tend to lead a dreary existence dominated by fears about the future.

The difference between directive thoughts conceptualized in approach versus avoidance terms is particularly evident when these contrasting goal orientations are applied to essentially the same goal content. For example, extensive research on achievement motivation (McClelland, 1985) has consistently shown that people focused on attaining success in vocational settings behave very differently than those focused on avoiding failure. That is a key reason why organizational cultures and communications from leaders that highlight job insecurity tend to inhibit creativity (Amabile, 1996).

Along these same lines, educational psychologists have found that a student's motivation to get good grades will play out very differently if the goal is to earn good grades versus avoid bad grades (Ames, 1992; Elliot,

1999). In the former case, the student tends to be action oriented and focused on learning. Anxiety about grades may exist but it tends to be the constructive kind of anxiety that gets channeled into increased effort (the ascending part of the Yerkes–Dodson curve; see Figure 4.3). In contrast, when performance-avoidance goals are dominant, a great deal of attention tends to be diverted from working to worrying. Disconcertingly, it appears that many well-intentioned teachers are inadvertently demotivating their students by placing too much emphasis on performance norms (relative to fixed, externally defined standards or other students' performance) rather than focusing on developmentally appropriate standards and the ability of each student to improve with effort (Dweck, 2006; D. Park et al., 2016).

Goal–Life Alignment

One of the core concepts in Motivational Systems Theory is the idea that particular configurations of goals, emotions, and personal agency beliefs are not intrinsically good or bad; rather, the question is whether they are a good fit for a specific person in a particular set of circumstances. That does not mean "anything goes" – there are in fact important boundary conditions on each motivational process (e.g., emotions that are relentlessly disorganizing; personal agency beliefs that are wildly unrealistic), and equipoise must be maintained at the system level. Nevertheless, MST places greater emphasis on the "goodness of fit" between motivational patterns and the environments in which they operate than on having the "right" goals, emotions, or personal agency beliefs in some absolute sense. As Bandura (2019) warns, "it is of limited value to motivate people for change if they lack the resources and environmental supports to realize those changes" (p. 14).

A particularly important instance of this general principle is MST's emphasis on the concept of *goal–life alignment*. This concept was discussed earlier (in Chapter 3) in the context of using your APG results and the *APG Personal Application Guide* to help you make consequential life decisions (e.g., with respect to a job opportunity or a new relationship). Goal–life alignment is also a central concept in the integrative theory of life meaning described in Chapter 7. Decisions that place you in environments that repeatedly thwart or disrespect your core personal goals will leave you chronically stressed and emotionally drained, which in turn can lead to physical health problems and impaired immune system functioning (Aldwin, 2007; Thoits, 2010). In contrast:

Decisions that place you in environments that support and encourage the pursuit of your core personal goals will make it possible for you to thrive developmentally and to experience abundant life meaning.

Personal Agency Beliefs

In Chapter 2 we explained how the evolved capacity for "mental time travel" made it possible for humans (and a few other advanced species) to play out goal-seeking scenarios in their mind before initiating action. Since mental simulations do not provide any feedback about the *actual* consequences of the actions one imagines taking, it is necessary to substitute thoughts about *expected* consequences (a type of feedforward information) in such scenarios. In MST expectancies about the consequences of personal goal seeking are called *personal agency beliefs*, or PABs (M. Ford, 1992). PABs help provide a "reality check" by ensuring that information about personal capabilities and environmental opportunities and resources are incorporated into decisions about what goals to pursue. PABs assess whether personal goals are realistic and attainable, and for those goals that are being actively pursued, the likelihood that further progress can be made.

Although many expectancies are based on direct past experience with a particular activity or individual (e.g., "I can easily calculate my share of a restaurant bill" or "That person has always been really nice to me"), PABs – like all thoughts – can become generalized into broader concepts (e.g., "I'm good at math" or "I know I can trust that person"). As a result, the motivational role of PABs goes far beyond simply remembering events that transpired in the past. PABs also provide educated guesses and broad advice about what goals to prioritize under what circumstances, and how much effort and persistence should be expended in pursuing those goals.

Following this logic, over the past several decades motivation scholars have focused much of their attention on the PAB component of motivational systems. For example, self-efficacy is the central motivational concept in Bandura's (1986) social-cognitive theory. Deci and Ryan's self-determination theory was built on the assumption that people are motivated to do things that make them feel competent and autonomous (Deci & Ryan, 1985). Seligman's concepts of learned helplessness and learned optimism are based on the idea that it is motivationally essential for us to perceive contingency between actions and future outcomes (i.e., we must believe our contexts will be responsive to our goal-seeking efforts) (Seligman, 1975, 1991). The consequences of experiencing (or losing) a fundamental sense of personal agency has also been highlighted in theories of effectance motivation (Harter, 1978; R. White, 1959), personal causation (deCharms, 1968), self-worth (Covington, 1992), reactance (Brehm, 1972), causal attributions (Weiner, 1986), and optimal experience (Csikszentmihalyi, 1975, 1991).

The basic premise underlying all of these theories – for which there is now extensive empirical evidence – is that to develop and maintain strong motivational patterns it is necessary to have a fundamental belief that *the future can be better than the present* (Snyder, 1994; Snyder et al., 2002). This requires a belief that there are pathways that can lead to a better future as well as a belief that you have the capabilities and support needed to successfully follow those pathways. In other words, motivation requires faith in yourself as well as faith in the people and resources you depend upon.

Consistent with this conclusion, Motivational Systems Theory affirms that there are two distinct types of personal agency beliefs. *Capability beliefs* reflect judgments about whether you have the knowledge, skills and biological capabilities needed to attain a goal. In contrast, *context beliefs* focus on whether the environment will support your efforts to pursue a goal. PABs thus make it possible to bring all of the major components of human functioning into the decision-making process in motivational headquarters, as shown in Figure 4.5.

Most scientific theories focused on the PAB component of human motivation include both capability and context beliefs to some degree (e.g., Bandura, 1982; Eccles et al., 1998; McClelland, 1985; Rotter, 1966;

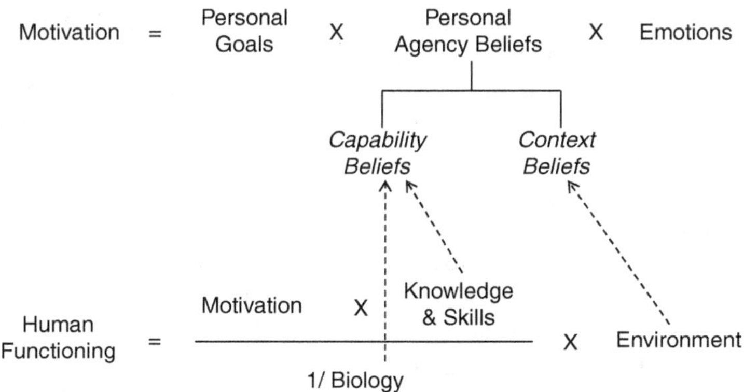

Figure 4.5 Illustration of how appraisals of biological functioning, knowledge and skills, and the environment are represented in "motivational headquarters."

Ryan & Deci, 2018; Snyder, 1994; Weisz & Stipek, 1982). However, much more research has been conducted on capability beliefs than on context beliefs.

PABs work collaboratively with emotions as advisors to the leaders in motivational headquarters. PABs and emotions thus have similar functions but work in very different ways, thereby providing checks and balances that safeguard the system from relying too much on intellect or too much on emotion. That is a key way that equipoise is maintained in the overall motivational system.

During the early years of modern motivational theorizing there was a rather one-sided emphasis on PABs relative to the emotion advisors. That imbalance reflected a general misunderstanding about the essential role of emotions in motivational patterns. PABs were widely understood to be moderately stable and continuously active, like a reliable aide who quietly follows you around wherever you go. Emotions, on the other hand, were often portrayed as transient, fleeting influences on behavior that didn't contribute much to consequential decisions and actions. As neuroscientist Richard Davidson explains (in Winerman, 2012):

> In the mid-1970s, there was hardly any research on emotion – it was hardly considered a field .... The cognitive psychologists who were beginning to hold sway at that time regarded emotion as just something that interrupts cognition. The idea that emotions are adaptive – that they can play an important role in decision-making and behavior – emerged considerably later .... The idea that the cortex was involved in emotion was really heresy .... Emotion was very much regarded as a primitive kind of psychological process. (p. 30)

Yet it is now evident that, in addition to the ancient danger alarm systems that get triggered from time to time to help us deal with immediate threats to our survival and well-being (Denton, 2005), almost everything we encounter has some degree of emotional salience (and valence) – as evidenced, for example, by our ongoing mental chatter (self-talk), which routinely labels objects and experiences as good or bad (Damasio, 2003; Haidt, 2006; Leary, 2004). Nichols (co-creator of the Ford and Nichols goal taxonomy) has expanded on this notion by proposing the concept of a "valence field" to describe the emotional milieu that people must operate within at any given moment (personal communication, January 6, 2013). This image of being enveloped by a dynamic field of many emotional plusses and minuses is congruent with Haidt's (2006) "like-o-meter" metaphor and with Damasio's (2003) description of the brain-based body mapping process that is the basis for our conscious feelings.

In short, it is now clear that our motivation-related thoughts (i.e., our goals and personal agency beliefs) are always embedded within an "emotional soup" that greatly influences their meaning and impact.

Capability Beliefs

This component of motivational functioning is similar in many respects to Bandura's (1995) popular concept of *self-efficacy*, which he defines as "the belief in one's capabilities to organize and execute the courses of action required to manage prospective situations" (p. 2). However, in MST, such judgments may reflect not only beliefs focused on specific courses of action, but also broad evaluations about whether you "have what it takes" to successfully accomplish a particular goal. Yet, consistent with Bandura's emphasis on "prospective situations," the key in both theories is that such thoughts focus on the future – that is, on the *anticipated* consequences of exercising your mental and physical resources.

This raises an important point about PABs that is often not explicitly recognized – namely, that *memories* about your past successes and failures may or may not be incorporated into your personal agency beliefs. Memories often influence beliefs about the future, but remembering what you were capable of in the past is not the same thing as anticipating what outcomes you might expect to be able to accomplish in the future. For example, you may feel highly vulnerable when the time comes to go to the dentist, or to speak in public, even though you've always had good outcomes in the past. Conversely, you may have a history of repeated failures on some task (e.g., passing a driving test; playing poker for money) and still feel supremely confident that "this time things will be different."

Moreover, capability beliefs only matter (in a motivational sense) if they are linked to an activated personal goal. For example, you may recall a time when you tried to ride a horse and you just couldn't do it no matter how hard you tried. That episode may have left you with a negative enduring memory about your horse-riding capabilities. But assuming nothing new comes up where you would need to consider the possibility of trying to ride a horse in the future, that memory is not going to be a demotivating factor in your daily life – unless, of course, it causes you to develop a more generalized belief about personal incompetence (e.g., "whenever I try something new, I fail"). Even if you do encounter a new horse-riding situation, there is no guarantee that your discouraging memory will be connected to that situation. You might think "that was a long time ago and it doesn't really mean anything for my current circumstances."

As this example suggests, capability beliefs can vary tremendously in terms of content and level of generality. Such beliefs may focus on a specific skill or attribute in a particular context (e.g., "I am capable of making pancakes"), or on a multifaceted set of skills related to a particular context (e.g., "I am capable of making breakfast for my family"), or on a broad range of capabilities that apply to a wide variety of contexts (e.g., "I am a good cook"). Moreover, as illustrated by the arrows in Figure 4.5, capability beliefs can reflect self-confidence or self-doubt about virtually any aspect of the person-system. For example, you may believe that you have short-comings related to visual acuity, muscle strength, memory, or communication skills. You may have concerns about your capacity for self-control, sustained attention, or dealing with emotional stress. You may feel incapable of pursuing a goal without more logistical, technical, or "tacit" knowledge. Indeed, many efforts to motivate self and others fall short because they have not adequately pinpointed the specific nature of the capability beliefs that are inhibiting goal progress. That is an important prerequisite for determining whether such beliefs are unfounded (i.e., the beliefs need to be more accurate) or there are reality-based deficits in knowledge, skills, or biological capabilities that need to be addressed.

Context Beliefs

Thoughts about the attainability of a personal goal may also reflect judgments about whether elements of the context are likely to facilitate or constrain efforts to make progress toward that goal. Such judgments may focus on social elements (e.g., a supportive boss or a difficult co-worker), emotional elements (e.g., a cheerful or depressing emotional climate), informational elements (e.g., the presence of a helpful teacher or mentor), or resource elements (e.g., the availability of necessary tools, materials, and funding). For example, an avid golfer might abandon an outing despite being eager to get back on the course due to an expectation of unplayable weather conditions or negative spousal reactions. A politician might cancel a speech designed to attract critical votes if there is an expectation that the event will be disrupted by protesters or ignored by the media. A manager who feels overworked and underpaid might be more likely to seek equitable treatment if she trusts that people in authority will feel obligated to correct any documentable injustice with "no hard feelings."

At a broader level, both real and imagined environmental conditions can play a huge role in human development through their motivational impact on context beliefs. That is especially evident when comparing supportive, resource-rich environments that create upward spirals of motivational engagement and competence development with impoverished environments that tend to "flat line" efforts to grow and develop. Consider, for example, a young child growing up in a home where the parents constantly support and encourage exploration, learning, and creativity. Now imagine that same child being raised by caregivers who are harsh, arbitrary, or neglectful. Attachment theory predicts that social and emotional development will progress very differently in these two scenarios, with context beliefs heavily implicated in these differences (M. Ford & Thompson, 1985).

Consistent with this theory, attachment researchers have documented in both primates and humans that the "mental models" children develop about what they can expect from significant adults in their lives do indeed have pervasive and enduring effects on their well-being and future developmental potential (Ainsworth et al., 1978; Bowlby, 1969; Sroufe & Waters, 1977). Mental models that incorporate positive context beliefs provide the motivational foundation needed to develop secure attachment relationships, which in turn predict positive developmental outcomes such as cooperation, social competence with peers, the ability to form trusting relationships, and the capacity for effective parenting (Raby et al., 2015; Sroufe, 1983, 2005). In contrast, when infants experience chronically unresponsive caregiving, they develop mental models infused with negative context beliefs, as illustrated by anxious and avoidant attachment relationships. These insecure attachment patterns are associated with apathy, lack of curiosity, and inability to trust others (Ainsworth et al., 1978; M. Ford & Thompson, 1985; Sroufe, 1983). As Hrdy (2009) warns (citing a personal conversation with evolutionary psychiatrist Randy Nesse), "as soon as we become convinced that love is impossible, love becomes impossible. The same is true of trust" (p. 133).

Starting life with a view of the world filtered through negative context beliefs can also compromise the development of positive capability beliefs and the natural emergence of social purpose goals – not only in childhood, but on into adolescence and adulthood (Simpson, 2007). Simply put, it is hard to view yourself in a positive light if important others don't, or to develop authentic concern for significant people in your life if you believe they don't care about you. As many counselors and therapists can attest, the developmental impact of these downward spirals of insecurity and mistrust can be widespread and enduring, affecting virtually every meaningful relationship in an individual's life (e.g., "I'm not a good person and don't deserve to be happy"; "People can't be trusted so it's best not to connect with others").

The motivational power of context beliefs can also be seen in adult working relationships. For example, research on motivation in employment settings clearly demonstrates the importance of organizational culture in generating upward and downward spirals of engagement and productivity (Cameron et al., 2003). When trust is high and people feel supported, that facilitates effort, commitment, and creativity, and organizations flourish (Jones & George, 1998; Luthans & Avolio, 2003; Zand, 1972). Conversely, when people feel that they don't have the support and respect of their bosses or co-workers, those beliefs can erode organizational loyalty and motivate employees to do the minimum needed to get by (Farnham, 1989).

One useful way to categorize context beliefs is by function (i.e., how they support goal pursuit). There are four different dimensions in this regard (M. Ford, 1992). First, *the environment must be congruent with an individual's profile of core personal goals.* That is what we have been referring to as *goal–life alignment.* Alignment is present when the context is a good "fit" for what you are trying to do. It is highly likely, for example, that someone with core personal goals focused on superiority and material gain will experience the good fit conferred by goal–life alignment if they take a job in a high-powered sales firm. Conversely, consider the plight of an individual with a core goal of equity taking a job where the work culture encourages favoritism and discrimination. Such misalignment is a recipe for motivational disaster. Misalignment can also occur when the environment is perceived as highly controlling rather than affording some degree of personal choice (Deci & Ryan, 1985; Ryan & Deci, 2018). Motivation is often diminished when people do not feel any "ownership" of the goals they are told they should prioritize.

Positive context beliefs also depend on having *an environment that is congruent with the person's cognitive, behavioral, and biological capabilities.* The fit has to be right not only in motivational headquarters, but also in terms of the "instrumental troops" responsible for carrying out goal directives. Imagine, for example, trying to work in an office where your allergies are continuously triggered by excess dust and mold. Or trying to learn in a classroom where you do not understand the words the teacher is saying. The goals may be fine for the context in general – trying to learn is certainly appropriate in a classroom – but success also requires a Darwinian kind of fit between what the environment requires and what you are capable of doing. If you are, metaphorically speaking, a really capable fish but you are a "fish out of water," you may flounder (so to speak) until you learn to adapt to that unfamiliar environment.

In some cases the objective fit between a person's capabilities and what is required to succeed in a prospective environment is just fine, but a persistent (inaccurate) belief that "I don't fit in there" discourages the person from pursuing vital learning and growth opportunities. For example, first-generation college students and applicants from underrepresented groups may wonder if they belong at elite universities or in academically competitive fields of study. Cultivating a "belonging mindset" (Rattan et al., 2015) can serve as a powerful antidote to this kind of motivational barrier.

Positive context beliefs may also be at risk when the environment lacks the *material and informational resources* needed to facilitate goal progress. Imagine being excited about preparing a special dinner and then realizing you're out of a key ingredient. You have the right goals and capabilities for the situation, but without ready access to necessary resources you may lose interest in cooking your own meal and decide to go out to eat instead. Similar demotivating effects may be felt when you are seeking sound advice or guidance on how to overcome an obstacle (e.g., through a friend or an online search) but no solution is in sight. At just about every step of the way, we depend on resources like money, technology, and knowledgeable others to help us get where we want to go.

Finally, positive context beliefs depend on having an environment with an *emotional climate* that suggests that significant people in your life are with you, not against you. That is the primary source of "motivational glue" in child-caregiver attachment bonds, intimate friendships, close teaching and coaching relationships, and strong professional alliances. Research has linked qualities such as emotional warmth, social support, and trust to enhanced motivation and positive developmental and health outcomes in a wide variety of home, work, school, and clinical settings (e.g., Balliet & Van Lange, 2013; Barefoot et al., 1998; Baumrind, 1978; C. Bergin, 1987/2019; Cohen & Wills, 1985; Ryff & Singer, 2001; Simpson, 2007). Such qualities also promote upward spirals of positive affect and achievement in situations where goal progress depends on collaboration and teamwork (Fredrickson, 2009).

> Trust is often described as a "social glue" in relationships, groups, and societies, in that it connects people and facilitates thoughts, motives, and behaviors that promote collective goals. It is a powerful construct, as there is growing evidence that individuals with high (vs. low) trust in other people are more likely to behave cooperatively in the face of uncertainty and

conflicting interests, are more likely to sustain volunteering activities, report greater life satisfaction, exhibit greater physical health, and even live longer. (Van Lange, 2015, p. 71)

These same sorts of outcomes are characteristic of individuals who are immersed in supportive social environments (Cohen & Wills, 1985; Ryff & Singer, 2001). That is because such environments are fertile breeding grounds for trust and emotional positivity. Simply put, responsive social contexts and positive context beliefs go hand in hand. When we feel like the world is with us and we can depend on others to be there when we need them, our motivational and physiological systems become stronger and more resilient.

Personal Agency Belief Patterns

As we have seen, capability and context beliefs are quite distinctive in terms of their focus (within the self vs. outside the self) and content (type of influence on goal pursuit). So why do we lump them together under the heading of "personal agency beliefs"? The reason is that they operate as a unitary system, like an advisory board. While it is possible to look at each advisor separately, the motivational outcome remains rather unpredictable until you get a joint perspective. This important principle is illustrated by the personal agency belief patterns shown in Figure 4.6.

		Context Beliefs		
Capability Beliefs Expectations about your knowledge and skills and biological resources	*Strong*	A1/A2 Antagonistic or Accepting	T Tenacious	R Robust
	Moderate or Variable	D Discouraged	C Cautious	E Encouraged
	Negative	H Hopeless	I Insecure	F Fragile
		Negative	*Moderate or Variable*	*Positive*

Context Beliefs
Expectations about the responsiveness of your environment

Figure 4.6 The *Motivational Systems Theory* taxonomy of personal agency belief patterns.

As you review each of the ten PAB patterns (noting that the upper left cell contains two alternative patterns), keep in mind that all of them can be adaptive when the beliefs are objectively accurate. Indeed, *beliefs that are out of touch with reality are a barrier to equipoise and a major source of human dysfunction.*

For example, it is considered normal and adaptive for people mourning the loss of a family member to experience a sense of *Hopelessness* and deep sorrow while they cope with the implications of their irreversible loss. *Insecurity* may be the optimal motivational pattern in situations where you are in fact woefully unprepared for an important obligation (e.g., a high-stakes test or business meeting). *Antagonism* may be perfectly rational in circumstances where goal progress is being thwarted by prejudice or abuse.

It is also evident, however, that success and well-being depend in no small amount on whether the "home page" setting for your PABs is generally positive. For example, if you tend to be insecure or antagonistic in most situations, even when the circumstances do not warrant that response, happiness will be elusive, and many opportunities will be lost. Your physical health will also likely suffer (Ryff & Singer, 2001; Scheier & Carver, 2018; Van Lange, 2015). Conversely, if your predisposition is to wake up and feel hope and optimism about the day ahead, your PABs will be a source of motivational vitality that will help you deal with life's inevitable setbacks and failures (Bandura, 1982, 1997; Carver & Scheier, 2014; Seligman, 1991).

As can be seen by looking at the upper right portion of Figure 4.6, there are three PAB patterns that are particularly adaptive in the sense of striving for a motivationally strong baseline (i.e., home page) setting. The *Robust* pattern is particularly adaptive in situations where effective independent performance is essential (e.g., taking an exam, interacting with a client, participating in an athletic event). The R pattern reflects confidence that personal goals can be accomplished even when success requires substantial effort, persistence, and creativity. From this vantage point, obstacles are simply an intrinsic part of the challenge. Negative feedback is seen as an informative measure of how far you have to go rather than as a preview of future outcomes. Positive results are not just hoped for, they are expected (e.g., "I am ready for this challenge – let's go!"; "I know I can accomplish my goal if I keep working at it").

Robust PABs are not optimal for every situation, however. Indeed, they can result in unwarranted self-assurance or misplaced faith in others when there are capability or context limitations that need to be addressed. For example, the *Encouraged* pattern is more appropriate when you are trying to improve (rather than simply implement) your capabilities. From this perspective the self is understood to be somewhat fallible, but the context is seen as a reliably helpful partner in goal striving. Such beliefs can help prevent overconfidence in learning and skill development situations while also encouraging openness to seeking constructive input from others.

When studying capability beliefs, scholars and helping professionals have tended to focus primarily on low self-confidence as a barrier to learning and optimal performance. However, PAB appraisals that are arrogant or exaggerated can also lead to disappointing results. That is because overconfident people generally do not feel a need to prepare for upcoming challenges or to reflect on negative outcomes (since they are "not my fault"). Encouraged PABs are also a good fit for tasks requiring cooperation among people with different kinds of expertise. In such situations people must balance self-confidence with a healthy respect for others' capabilities and their own personal limitations (e.g., "We make a great team – I couldn't have done this on my own"; "I know I'm not where I need to be yet, but with the resources available to me I'm confident I'll get there").

In contrast to the E pattern, *Tenacious* PABs are particularly well suited for circumstances in which people must maintain persistence and courage in the face of significant challenges from physical, social, or economic elements of the environment. In this mindset some degree of environmental unresponsiveness is seen as natural and predictable. This expectation enables people to prepare in advance for anticipated sources of difficulty and stress (e.g., unrelenting bosses, irritable family members, unresponsive service providers, hostile opponents). In addition, strong capability beliefs promote determination and fortitude in the face of conditions that might otherwise seem overwhelming (e.g., I'm not going to let a few setbacks get me down"; "These people are tough but so am I!").

The remaining PAB patterns may also be adaptive when they match the reality of what you are experiencing. However, if one of these patterns is your customary outlook on life, watch out! Having chronic doubts about both your personal capabilities *and* your environmental support systems is like trying to drive a car with your foot on the brake. You may be able to make some progress, but the pace will be slow and inefficient. And if you keep "driving" like that on a continuous basis, the chronic stress may cause internal damage (i.e., your emotional and physical health may suffer).

Consistent with this metaphor, the *Cautious* pattern is characterized by uncertainty and tentativeness in goal striving. This is a natural consequence of the PAB advisory team providing "mixed messages" to the personal goal leaders in motivational headquarters. Imagine driving through a town where all the traffic lights are flashing yellow. The caution lights are not sufficient to stop goal progress; however, they create a mindset where the focus is more on worrying about what might be "around the corner" than on working toward the destination you are trying to reach (e.g., "I'm not sure if I can handle this situation, a lot of things could go wrong"; "I'm hoping for the best but fearing the worst").

The *Antagonistic* and *Accepting* PAB patterns both reflect a belief that goal progress is being thwarted by some major obstacle or threat. This does not mean those beliefs are necessarily accurate. In some cases, blaming others or outside circumstances for negative outcomes may simply be a defensive method for maintaining positive self-evaluations – a powerful motive for many individuals (e.g., Covington, 1992; Harter, 1990; Tesser, 1986). However, in many situations it is quite appropriate to attribute negative outcomes to unsupportive or hostile environmental conditions (as when someone is being victimized by discrimination or an abusive family member). In such circumstances an antagonistic mindset can provide the necessary energy and determination to try to overcome the obstacle (e.g., "I'll show them what happens when you treat people that way"; "I'm not quitting until I get this %@?*#&! thing to work!"). Alternatively, one can try to minimize the adverse impact of the hostile environment by trying to better understand what is happening or by learning to predict the circumstances under which victimization is most likely to occur (e.g., "All I can do for now is accept reality and try to keep it from getting to me"; "I know I can't stop it, but that doesn't mean I have to dwell on it") (Markman et al., 2013; Rothbaum et al., 1982).

In contrast to the A1 and A2 patterns, people with *Fragile* PABs generally blame themselves for problems and failures. In this mindset, the self is seen as inadequate and therefore highly reliant on others for help and support. Motivation may not be visibly impaired when good outcomes are occurring, but like a flower that needs a lot of water and sunshine to keep on growing, it doesn't take much for things to start deteriorating. Even just a little bit of adversity can trigger withdrawal or excessive help seeking (e.g., "I feel like an imposter – I don't think I can keep up this charade"; "You're going to have to help me – there's no way I can do this on my own").

Like those with Fragile PABs, people experiencing *Insecure* PABs suffer from a fundamental lack of confidence in their personal capabilities in their current situation. However, motivation is even more vulnerable in the *I* pattern because the environment is less likely to be seen as a reliable source of comfort or assistance. As a result, any inclination to keep pursuing a goal may rest on the thinnest of hopes (e.g., "I feel defenseless and don't know who I can turn to"; "The only thing that can save me now is a miracle").

The *Discouraged* PAB pattern is also associated with vulnerability and weakness; however, in this case the primary source of any remaining hope for a good outcome is the self, not the environment. Consequently, Discouraged individuals tend to look to their own devices when trying to identify, sometimes with increasing desperation, a way to make something good happen (e.g., "This is just not working – now what I am going to do?"; "I can't deal with these people – I wish there was some other option").

Last, and clearly least in terms of baseline PAB patterns, is the *Hopeless* pattern. This is generally the most motivationally debilitating pattern because neither the self nor the environment is seen as a potential source of help or improvement. As a result, goal progress is considered impossible, bad outcomes are regarded as inevitable, and no course of action can be imagined that would change those expectations. Persistent feelings of hopelessness have been linked not only with depression, but also with premature death (Seligman, 1975) (e.g., "I'm ruined and there's nothing anyone can do about it"; "It's no use – I give up").

It is worth reiterating that, although we do tend to develop PAB habits (thus our "home page" metaphor), capability and context beliefs need to be highly dynamic to remain appropriately aligned with changing circumstances in an equipoised way. Indeed, inflexible expectations (whether positive or negative) are often a symptom of being out of touch with reality. Sometimes we receive feedback that contradicts our expectations, and we need to be able to make sense of that. We eventually learn to trust some people we weren't sure about at first, while at the same time we lose faith in others. We become more confident as we gain experience in a situation, but we may also see our capabilities become "outdated" as circumstances change or become more challenging.

In short, the science of personal agency beliefs is well established, empirically sound, and extremely useful for those seeking guidance about how to motivate self and others. The positive impact of believing in self and others (within appropriate boundaries of accuracy) has been established in every major life domain (e.g., Bandura, 1982, 1986, 1995, 1997; Carver & Scheier, 2014; Dweck, 2006; Elliot & Dweck, 2005; Pajares & Urdan, 2006; Ryan & Deci, 2018; Scheier & Carver, 2018; Seligman, 1991; Snyder, 1994; Snyder & Lopez, 2002, 2009). PABs not only function (along with emotions) as powerful motivational advisors, they also help shape the agenda and priorities of the "leader" through their impact on personal goal thoughts. Influencing PABs can thus have reverberating effects on the entire motivational system.

What is your home page motivational orientation with regard to personal agency beliefs? We have designed the *Assessment of Personal Agency Belief Patterns* (APP; available at https://apg.gmu.edu) to help you identify the capability and context beliefs that most readily come to your mind when you encounter new challenges and opportunities (M. Ford & Smith, 2010). We invite you to take a few minutes to complete that assessment and see what PAB pattern (as shown in Figure 4.6) has the strongest "gravitational pull" for you.

Personal Goals and Personal Agency Beliefs

We have described personal goals and personal agency beliefs as being in the functional roles of leader and advisor, respectively. In this capacity, PABs can exert tremendous influence on motivation by boosting confidence or raising significant doubts about an envisioned course of action. Keep in mind, though, that personal agency beliefs only matter if they are linked to a personal goal thought. Metaphorically speaking, the advisor can't have any impact on the leader if the leader isn't focused on what the advisor is thinking about.

A look back at the control system model displayed in Chapter 3 (Figure 3.3) illustrates how personal goals and PABs rely on one another. Recall that PABs are evaluative thoughts involving a comparison between a desired consequence (personal goal) and an anticipated consequence (i.e., what you expect to happen if you were to pursue that goal). If there is no relevant personal goal thought funneling into the "comparator," a capability or context belief will be essentially meaningless – just another passing thought with no practical value (at that point in time). For example, you may think you are incapable of eating insects like you saw someone do on a television show, but if you are not in a position of having to contemplate eating insects (e.g., while stranded in the wilderness without food), that negative capability belief probably won't have any motivational impact. Speculations about the responsiveness of people we never expect to interact with (e.g., a sports hero or celebrity heartthrob) would be similarly inconsequential.

PABs that are irrelevant for currently activated goals may nevertheless have an impact on the selection and pursuit of future goals. That is because capability and context beliefs with no current connection to personal goals can nevertheless draw our attention toward particular targets, which then gives our emotional "like-o-meter" (Haidt, 2006) a chance to size things up. That can lead to a desire to approach or avoid things we don't know much about. For example, we tend to be attracted to novel challenges that we see as a good fit to our talents. We feel comfortable around new acquaintances who express interest in our concerns and beliefs. We resonate to new experiences that make us feel competent and in control (sometimes to our surprise!) and tend to gravitate back to such experiences when given the opportunity to do so. Conversely, we tend to avoid circumstances that make us feel helpless or inept. Through all of these mechanisms, PABs, in partnership with our emotion advisors, play a fundamental role in determining which personal goals we will choose to pursue.

Emotions

Personal goals lay dormant in our mind's repertoire of potential thoughts until they are energized by the "change and commotion" associated with triggered emotions. Activated goals then compete for a priority position in motivational headquarters based on a dynamically shifting landscape of internal and external considerations that our PAB and emotion advisors are constantly monitoring and evaluating.

Emotions play a highly influential role in this Darwinian competition among activated personal goals. Yet not all decisions require a lot of emotional energy. As explained in Chapter 3, goals may be selected from the activated options through the use of learned "scripts" that automatically specify, with little emotional fanfare, what to do in particular circumstances (as illustrated by repetitive morning routines, carefully orchestrated meeting protocols, and ingrained relationship habits).

Nevertheless, the most common scenarios in modern life are those that can be "framed" but not fully scripted, as illustrated by the wide range of conversations we have throughout the day. In such scenarios there are many ongoing choices that need to be made and not a whole lot of time to make them. As we have seen, emotions are particularly well suited for such circumstances, as they evolved to help us quickly adapt to changing circumstances. Emotions can nudge (or push) the decision-making process in a particular direction and prepare the mind and body for appropriate action within milliseconds, even before we are conscious of this initial motivational reaction (Damasio, 2003; Ferguson & Zayas, 2009). Conscious feelings, which reliably arise as the body maps associated with the triggered emotions are updated, can then help sustain goal pursuit or suggest an alternative course of action (as when an argument that overheats leads to conciliatory apologies).

A useful metaphor for illustrating the importance of emotions in goal selection and pursuit is that of driving a car ("down the highway of life" one might say). On each trip, certain decisions will be scripted by the selected route and the "rules of the road" (e.g., if I see a red light, I must stop). However, many unscripted choices must also be made, including those suggested by emotions that "won't go away" until some appropriate action is taken – for example, feeling scared enough to pull over and let a tailgating truck go by, or feeling sufficiently annoyed to aggressively maneuver around a slow-moving vehicle being driven by a distracted driver. Personal agency beliefs may take the lead in the motivational advising process when there is more time for reflection and reasoning (e.g., when planning which route to take), but during the drive itself, the chief motivational navigators helping you stay on track toward your target are likely to be your emotions (in tandem with attentional processes that highlight relevant "emotionally competent stimuli" such as potentially reckless drivers).

As portrayed in Figure 4.2 (at the beginning of this chapter), emotions are one of three major components of human motivational systems. Emotions, in turn, are composed of three subcomponents integrated into a functional unit (D. Ford, 1987/2019). At the heart of each emotion pattern is a *biological* component that supports the energy production and action requirements associated with the pursuit of an activated goal in a particular set of circumstances (e.g., increased or decreased heart rate; accelerated breathing). Fundamentally, emotions evolved to facilitate action. New emotions emerged over evolutionary time as changing conditions of living produced new action requirements for survival, reproduction, and well-being.

In addition, emotions include an *expressive* element, as evidenced by the fact that there are characteristic facial and vocal expressions, gestures, and body language associated with different emotion patterns. These expressive features help communicate what is being felt to others, which is an important way that people influence how others respond to them. Scientists now understand how this expressive element of emotions helps fire *mirror neurons* in the observer's brain that in turn can trigger that same emotion in the observer (Keltner, 2009; Rizzolatti & Craighero, 2004). This "tightly coupled" emotional communication – which is found in many social animals, not just humans – is highly adaptive, as it helps alert group members to circumstances they too should attend to (e.g., the presence of a significant opportunity, obstacle, or danger). In that manner, the communication function of emotion can trigger the motivational function of emotion in others. *Emotional contagion,* the underlying process supporting empathy, is a term often used to describe this mechanism for sharing emotions (de Waal, 2009; Hatfield et al., 1994).

Each emotion pattern also includes an *affective* element. That is the conscious "feeling" part of the emotion that evolved to help sustain its motivational impact. Feelings are conscious perceptions that arise from the brain's mapping of the bodily changes caused by the triggering of an emotion. Consistent with the biochemistry of these bodily changes, each feeling typically has a valence – some variation on pleasure or pain. That is why we tend to think of emotions as being positive or negative even though the feelings associated with each emotion pattern are qualitatively unique.

> *Emotions play out in the theatre of the body. Feelings play out in the theatre of the mind. (Damasio, 2003, p. 28)*

At the core of each feeling is an "idea of the body being in a certain way" (Damasio, 2003, p. 85) – a reference to the biological and expressive components of the emotion pattern. However, as we explained in Chapter 2, feelings tend to get linked to thoughts and perceptions in learned associative networks rather than existing in some "pure" state. That is why Damasio defines a feeling as *"the perception of a certain state of the body along with the perception of a certain mode of thinking and of thoughts with certain themes"* (p. 86, italics added).

That definition may sound rather complex to those not used to thinking in systems terms, but it helps explain how emotions can play such a pervasive motivational role in our daily lives. Feelings arise from emotions, but they are not just conscious manifestations of an emotional state. Feelings are closely linked to a variety of context-specific thoughts and perceptions (e.g., just ask someone what makes them feel particularly angry or fearful and you'll see what we mean). Moreover, feelings can make certain kinds of thoughts and perceptions more accessible even if they are not directly related to that particular feeling. For example, when we feel good about some accomplishment or good fortune, we tend to focus on pleasant experiences, have an optimistic mindset, and think more broadly and creatively (though not necessarily more accurately!). In contrast, when negative feelings cannot be resolved in a timely manner, we tend to focus on troubling experiences and adopt a pessimistic mindset (Fredrickson, 2009).

Emotions evolved as short-term motivational advisors, and even with the ability of feelings to sustain the motivational impact of emotions beyond an initial impulse, that remains the primary role they play in human motivation (M. Ford, 1992). Analogous to a push that gets a flywheel spinning (D. Ford, 1987/2019), emotions are immediately salient when they first get triggered, but then they tend to fade rather quickly unless you do something mentally to keep reactivating them (e.g., through rumination or reflection). Of course, the same emotion can be repeatedly activated if the circumstances that triggered the emotion do not change (as in the case of a chronically abusive parent or boss). However, change is what most emotions are specifically designed to produce. For example, if you experience fear, you will be motivated to escape whatever frightened you, thus changing the circumstances that triggered your fear response in the first place. If you feel a strong sense of guilt, you will be motivated to change your behavior and make amends to those who suffered as a result of your wrongdoing.

The idea that there are triggers – or in Damasio's (2003) terms, *emotionally competent stimuli* – that reliably cause our emotional "flywheel" to spin is a useful concept for understanding emotions. That understanding can help us prepare for future situations and make good decisions about how to conduct ourselves in those situations. For example, you might plan your work schedule to minimize interactions with a hostile co-worker, or ask a friend to accompany you to a predictably stressful social gathering.

The image of a flywheel that needs some kind of push to make it spin can also assist people in determining whether unwanted emotions are an adaptive response to authentically unfavorable circumstances, or a maladaptive response triggered (or sustained) by mental distortions, exaggerations, or excessive rumination. To extinguish unwanted emotions, sometimes the circumstances need to change (e.g., "I need to get out of this unrewarding marriage"), and sometimes unrealistic thinking needs to change (e.g., "I need to quit expecting my spouse to see everything the way I do"). These are of course not mutually exclusive alternatives. The most traumatic cases of chronic distress often involve a combination of objectively horrible conditions and distorted thinking. In such cases experienced professional help is often needed to sort things out and develop pathways for more adaptive functioning.

As is the case for PAB patterns, *all emotions are adaptive with respect to the general circumstances for which they evolved.* This does not mean, however, that they will be adaptive in all of the specific situations that reliably trigger those emotions. Culture, technology, population growth, and other major changes in human history have dramatically altered our circumstances compared to those our ancestors experienced. Our bodies are adapted for life on the African savanna some 150,000 years ago, yet today we live in a much different world. As a result, we have many built-in emotional triggers that make sense in terms of our biological heritage but not necessarily in terms of our current cultural circumstances. That is another way that knowledge of how emotions work can help us avoid maladaptive behavior. For example,

> reactions that lead to racial or cultural prejudices are based in part on the automatic deployment of social emotions evolutionarily meant to detect *difference* in others because difference may signal risk or danger, and promote withdrawal or aggression. That sort of reaction probably achieved useful goals in a tribal society but is no longer useful, let alone appropriate, to ours. We can be wise to the fact that our brain still carries the machinery to react in the way it did in a very different context ages ago. And we can learn to disregard such reactions and persuade others to do the same. (Damasio, 2003, p. 40)

Different Emotions Have Unique Motivational Functions

We have found it useful to organize our thinking about emotions in three groupings that are roughly associated with the three "eras" in the development of motivational systems that we identified in Chapter 2. When motivational systems directed by primordial goals first appeared on the scene, *primal emotions* (Denton, 2005; see Chapter 2) evolved to help keep homeostatic set points within boundaries. Much later, the ability to construct mental images fueled the development of motivational systems directed by "neuroimaged" goals. That in turn created a need for *instrumental emotions* (e.g., fear, anger, joy, interest) that could be flexibly associated not only with a narrow set of innate triggering conditions, but also with new experiences through emotional learning. Finally, the evolved capacity for self-awareness, which ushered in the modern era of motivational systems directed by "personal" goals, made *social emotions* organized around themes related to social interdependence possible.

Many theories focused on motivation and emotion are known as "differential emotion" theories because they focus, at least in part, on identifying different kinds of emotion patterns and their unique characteristics. These theories are extremely useful because they help us understand the evolutionary origins and motivational functions of fundamentally distinct emotion patterns. That in turn contributes to our understanding of how the power of emotions can be constructively harnessed to help people accomplish their personal goals.

Yet to date there is no fully agreed upon list of basic emotions. There are many highly credible scholars who have published such lists (e.g., Ekman, 1972; D. Ford, 1987/2019; Izard, 1977; Plutchik, 1980); however, no two lists are identical, and there is considerable variability among even the most well researched lists. That is largely because scientists disagree about whether some emotions are truly "basic" or simply a noteworthy variation on, or derivation from, an archetypal theme. Yet it is evident that "ordinary folk" perceive and experience many more distinct emotion categories than those proposed in classic differential emotion theories (Cowen & Keltner, 2017), and that within any "basic" emotion theme there are many variations, including those that blend different themes together in organized, recognizable patterns (Cowen et al., 2019).

Another obstacle to the creation of a consensus list is the extensive and nuanced terminology that has been culturally developed to describe emotions. Nor do different cultures fully agree on what terminology should be used, or even what categories are relevant (Cordaro et al., 2018; Russell, 1991; Wierzbicka, 1995). Terms vary not only with respect to emotional content, but also with regard to context, intensity and "purity" (i.e., the extent to which only one type of emotional response is implicated). Some terms also merge emotion and PAB information, which is natural since emotions and PABs are designed to work together in a unified way (as connoted by some of the terms used to describe the PAB patterns in Figure 4.6, e.g., antagonistic and hopeless). It would seem, then, that we should heed Damasio's (2003) warning that although "there is a venerable tradition of classifying emotions in varied categories .... The classifications and labels are manifestly inadequate .... The borders between categories are porous" (p. 43). As Cowen et al. (2019) explain,

> the two most commonly studied models of emotion – the basic six and the affective circumplex (comprising valence and arousal) – provide an incomplete representation of emotional experience and expression .... Each of those models captures at most 30% of the variance in the emotional experiences people reliably report and in the distinct expressions people reliably recognize. That leaves 70% or more of the variability in our emotional experience and expression uncharted .... A full understanding of emotional expression and experience requires an appreciation of a wide degree of variability in display behavior, subjective experience, patterns of appraisal, and physiological response, both within and across emotion categories. (p. 70)

Based on this wisdom, we abandoned our effort to construct a definitive taxonomy of emotion patterns after several years of diligent but ultimately inconclusive selecting, elaborating, and fine tuning. Instead, we offer a list that simply aspires to include a broad range of examples of different kinds of emotion patterns (see Table 4.1). This table is based in large part on the emotion taxonomy described in the Living Systems Framework (D. Ford, 1987/2019), as the LSF incorporates one of the most comprehensive differential emotions theories available in the scientific literature. However, not all of the LSF emotion categories are represented in this table. Moreover, we also included one emotion, *elevation*, not included in the LSF taxonomy to illustrate the kind of work currently being conducted by positive psychology

Table 4.1 *The motivational functions of selected emotions*

Emotion pattern	Associated motivational function
Examples of emotions that evolved to facilitate the activation, continuation, or inhibition of behavior	
Happiness	Encourages continuation of effective/rewarding behavior *"YES, we're making progress. This is terrific! I'd like to try that again."*
Sadness	Encourages termination of ineffective/unrewarding behavior *"NO, this just isn't working out. It's bad and I can't do anything about it. I give up."*
Interest	Promotes exploration and information acquisition *"Hey, check this out. I may need to know this. I wonder what would happen if … ?"*
Boredom	Delays or terminates exploration and information acquisition *"This is so irrelevant. I'm just wasting my time. We've been over this a million times."*
Examples of emotions that evolved to help people cope with potentially disruptive or damaging circumstances	
Surprise	Interrupts and refocuses attention *"What's going on here? What in the world … ? You're kidding!"*
Anger	Urges surmounting or removing of obstacles or actions in response to perceived injustice, insult, or encroachment *"This has got to stop. I can't take this anymore! That is totally unfair!"*
Fear	Elicits caution or threat avoidance *"Something bad is about to happen to me. I've got to escape. I'm in danger!"*
Disgust	Urges avoidance of contaminated environments *"This is repulsive. I've never experienced anything so revolting. I can't stand it."*

Table 4.1 *(cont.)*

Emotion pattern	Associated motivational function

Examples of emotions that evolved to help facilitate interpersonal bonding and promote cooperation

Affection/love	Fosters caretaking and the development of committed relationships *"I care about you. We're all in this together. You're part of me."*
Loneliness	Fosters social contact and reunion with significant others *"I miss him/her. I need someone to be with me. I feel alone and isolated."*
Shame/Guilt	Encourages conformity with social norms, values, and rules *"I feel so humiliated. I'll never do that again. I need to make amends."*
Contempt	Urges rejection of or efforts to influence transgressors *"You're not like us. You don't belong here. Shape up or ship out!"*
Elevation	Encourages virtuous conduct on behalf of others *"That is inspiring – humanity at its best. I want to follow that example."*

emotion scholars, who have encouraged emotion theorists to broaden their conceptualization of human emotions to include motivationally consequential self-transcendent experiences such as compassion, gratitude, contentment, awe, and ecstasy (e.g., Haidt, 2006; Stellar et al., 2017).

Consistent with the view that the successful pursuit of goals is "life's bottom line" (Klinger & Cox, 2004), the first cluster of emotions represented in Table 4.1 evolved to motivate us to start, stop, or continue pursuing outcomes of potential personal relevance. Feelings associated with *happiness* (e.g., satisfaction, pleasure, joy) are particularly important because they motivate us to "keep at it" when things seem to be going well in our goal pursuits. Such feelings are associated with accomplishment and the desire to repeat or surpass previous experiences of goal fulfillment. They also inform us more generally about how our life is currently going. *Sadness*, in contrast, encourages us to withdraw when things aren't going so well or when we realize that we can no longer pursue certain goals (e.g., when coping with the loss of a loved one). Downhearted feelings also help prevent people from "banging their head against a wall" when continued effort is likely to simply produce continued disappointment.

Interest evolved to fuel exploration of the environment for information of potential relevance to current and future goal pursuits. Such information is vital because it can increase both the range of alternative actions we can envision as well as the effectiveness of those actions. Interest is typically triggered by goal-relevant perceptions and memories (as is evident from the words and images that advertisers use to try to capture our attention). However, interest can also be activated by external sources of novelty that are not clearly related to our personal goals (e.g., "I wonder what that's all about"). The related emotion of *boredom*, on the other hand, keeps us from wasting time on irrelevant information or information that is already familiar to us. Boredom motivates a desire to "move on" to more important goals or to more useful sources of information.

The second cluster of emotion examples shown in Table 4.1 evolved to help us deal with threats and obstacles that have the potential to disrupt goal progress or cause personal harm. *Surprise* is an effective means of interrupting ongoing activity so that sudden, unexpected events can be evaluated for their potential personal significance. *Disgust* helps us avoid contaminated environments that might make us physically sick or kill us. *Anger* is an adaptive response in circumstances where there are significant obstacles to goal attainment that must be overcome or removed. In contrast, *fear* motivates avoidance and escape not only from situations that we know to be threatening or dangerous, but also from circumstances that are so unfamiliar or overwhelming that we feel "out of control."

The examples included under the third heading in Table 4.1 are all social emotions. Humans, like many animals, evolved as social beings, meaning our ancestors lived in groups and depended on one another to attain essential personal goals (such as predator avoidance and hunting for food). Our species could not survive alone in the ancestral environment for very long. Indeed, most people find it aversive to live alone (which is why solitary confinement is considered one of the most severe forms of punishment). As a result, early humans with evolved capabilities for cooperation and social intelligence survived to reproduce, whereas individuals with more contentious inclinations were not so successful (Boehm, 2012; Hrdy, 2009; D. S. Wilson, 2007).

Social emotions evolved to encourage interpersonal bonding and cooperative living (Damasio, 2003; D. Ford, 1987/2019). For example, feelings of *affection* and *love* motivate us to pursue integrative social relationship goals and to strengthen interpersonal attachments and commitments. Such feelings are particularly important in the context of caring relationships (e.g., parental and spousal relationships, long-term friendships). In a similar vein, *loneliness* motivates us to reach out for social contact. Love and loneliness go hand in hand to support social bonding, which evolved "to promote reliable, high-cost altruism among individuals who depend on one another for survival and reproduction" (Brown & Brown, 2006, p. 1).

Other social emotions evolved to facilitate efforts to live and work together in cooperative groups that could only exist by ensuring a high level of compliance with shared values and norms. For example, *shame* and *guilt* evolved to encourage people to conform to social rules and expectations. Guilt can be triggered even in the absence of direct social feedback as we anticipate the impact of our actions on others. That is why those who lack empathic capabilities (e.g., sociopaths) rarely feel guilty. Shame, on the other hand, is more likely to be triggered when we actually experience negative social feedback, like a disapproving look, verbal disparagement, or group ostracism. Shame is associated with social rejection and fear that one's reputation will be damaged – outcomes that most people are particularly eager to avoid. We inherited these concerns from our ancient ancestors, when rejection from the group was often equivalent to a death sentence. Conversely, the emotion of *contempt* motivates us to reject those who act in irresponsible or disrespectful ways.

The last emotion listed in Table 4.1, *elevation*, is a promising new candidate for "basic emotion" status and an example of the variety of social emotion patterns that have captured the attention of scholars in the field of positive psychology (along with emotions such as gratitude, admiration, and forgiveness). Most emotion taxonomies that include social emotions place much more emphasis on negative emotions (e.g., guilt, shame, embarrassment, loneliness, resentment, jealousy, contempt) than on positive emotions. But in recent years there has been increasing interest in additional emotions that may have evolved to fuel efforts to actively promote helping, sharing, and cooperative group living.

Haidt (2006), in his efforts to explore such emotions, was wondering what the opposite of moral disgust might look like when he came across a collection of letters composed by Thomas Jefferson (the founder of Haidt's employer at that time, the University of Virginia) that included "a full and perfect description of the emotion I had just begun thinking about" (p. 194). This description included information about all of the major components of an emotion pattern, with special emphasis on the motivational impact of "elevated" feelings and sensations:

> When any ... act of charity or of gratitude, for instance, is presented either to our sight or imagination, we are deeply impressed with its beauty and feel a strong desire in ourselves of doing charitable and grateful acts also .... Every emotion of this kind is an exercise of our virtuous dispositions, and dispositions of the mind, like limbs of the body, acquire strength by exercise. (Jefferson, as quoted in Haidt, 2006, p. 195)

Research related to this emotion (e.g., Algoe & Haidt, 2009; Silvers & Haidt, 2008) suggests that elevation does indeed reinforce cooperative behavior and bonding with others, both within and beyond existing social networks. It apparently does so not only by energizing integrative social relationship goals such as belongingness and resource provision, but also by producing experiences that fall within the unity and transcendence categories in the goal taxonomy presented in Chapter 3.

What about Empathy?

It may seem curious that we have omitted empathy from Table 4.1 given our relatively heavy emphasis (compared to other emotion taxonomies) on social emotions. However, empathy is not a particular emotional state. Rather, it is a complex, layered process designed to ensure that contextually appropriate emotions are activated based on social information. Empathy is thus an essential part of what we call *emotional wisdom*, one of the key components of the *Thriving with Social Purpose Theory of Motivation and Optimal Functioning* described in Chapters 5 and 6.

Perhaps the simplest way to understand empathy is to focus on the result of this process rather than the various steps that may be involved in producing that result. That is why we define human empathy as *catching another's feelings*, where the idea of "catching" includes both emotional activation and efforts to understand (to varying degrees) the other's circumstances and motivation. Empathy thus helps to promote effective functioning by helping us size up "what's going on" while also providing the motivational fuel (triggered emotions) for contextually appropriate action. For example, absent severe pathology, humans are strongly inclined to feel some degree of empathic concern and compassion when someone important to them is in distress (Batson, 2011; Batson et al., 2002). Empathy is also a key mechanism for assessing the trustworthiness of caregivers and potential social partners (Hrdy, 2009).

The emotional activation component of empathy is sometimes called *emotional contagion* (de Waal, 2006; Hatfield et al., 1994) because, absent any complex interpretive process, this phase of an empathic response can produce an automatic and virtually instantaneous triggering of a matching or contextually appropriate emotional state. Emotional activation from social stimuli typically arises from a combination of auditory and visual cues (e.g., a startled bird cries out and causes an entire flock to simultaneously take flight; a victimized person expresses outrage and observers respond with angry calls for justice). This state matching process – which is supported in part by "mirror" neurons that fire not only when acting but also when observing the same action (Keltner, 2009; Rizzolatti & Craighero, 2004) – existed long before hominids came on the scene. Indeed, emotions are involved in virtually every communication not only between humans, but throughout the animal kingdom (de Waal, 2006). "I feel, therefore I am" (Eakin, 2003) would seem to be the best way to summarize the motivational experience of social creatures (keeping in mind that personal goals are activated via triggered emotions). Perhaps that is why "people with immobile or paralyzed faces feel deeply alone, and tend to become depressive, sometimes to the point of suicide" (de Waal, 2009, p. 83).

The contextual awareness/understanding component of empathy, which is sometimes called *perspective taking*, requires (a) self-awareness (e.g., young infants' empathic abilities are limited to emotional contagion until they pass this developmental milestone) (de Waal, 2009), (b) an awareness that others have thoughts and feelings of their own, and (c) the ability to infer others' psychological states from physical clues (also known as "Theory of Mind" abilities, e.g., Cacioppo et al., 2006). In humans, the most informative clues in this regard are facial expressions and sounds related to facial expressions, as evidenced by the fact that "at birth, an enormous amount of brain tissue, especially in the neocortex, is already allocated to processing faces, facial expressions, gestures, and vocalizations of others" (Hrdy, 2009, p. 40).

Clearly, we are born with the infrastructure needed to connect with others through shared emotional experience. However, these "innate potentials for empathy, mind reading, and collaboration" do not just blossom automatically; they need to be "switched on" by responsive caregivers who possess these same qualities (Hrdy, 2009, p. 286). Infants and young children who experience this kind of responsiveness are significantly more likely than those in insecure attachment relationships to go on to develop cooperative relationships with peers and other adults (Raby et al., 2015; Sroufe, 1983, 2005) and to manifest motivational patterns saturated with emotional "positivity" (M. Ford & Thompson, 1985; Thompson, 1991).

Positivity: The Cumulative Power of Positive Emotions

Some emotion theorists focus less on the unique motivational functions of different emotions and more on whether those emotions have a positive or negative valence (e.g., Lazarus, 1991). However, from the integrative perspective of MST, both function and valence are essential qualities of emotions. That is because, although each emotion pattern has a distinct motivational function, positive and negative emotions collectively function in very different ways. Negative emotions (like disgust, fear, and anger) tend to narrow our focus of attention to a particular "problem at hand" so that we will be motivated to do what is specifically required to avoid harm or overcome obstacles. In contrast, positive emotions tend to "broaden people's ideas about possible actions, opening our awareness to a wider range of thoughts and actions than is typical" (Fredrickson, 2009, p. 21).

Using the flashlight metaphor we introduced in Chapter 2, activation of a negative emotion is functionally equivalent to twisting the bezel to produce a narrow "beam" of attention focused on a specific problem or threat. It is easy to imagine how that kind of mechanism would have survival value. Consider, for example, the life-and-death consequences of eating rotten food but not reacting to that food until it had already been ingested. Or encountering a predator but being distracted by hunger pangs during the few seconds when escape was still possible.

In contrast, activation of a positive emotion is functionally more like twisting the flashlight bezel in the opposite direction, thus producing a broader field of awareness of current circumstances and possibilities. This more expansive perspective on the world facilitates learning and creativity. It also promotes personal growth and self-discovery. By enlarging the focus of attention to encompass others as well as self, positive emotions also encourage people to connect with one another and appreciate the qualities that unify them (Fredrickson, 2009).

That does not mean that the effects of positive emotions are always beneficial. Twisting the bezel to expand awareness can lead to bad outcomes if the highlighted thoughts are clearly maladaptive (e.g., unwarranted stereotypical thinking; hubristic pride) (Gruber et al., 2011). Nevertheless, the broadening effect of positive emotions has clear survival value, as Fredrickson (2009) emphasizes in her well-regarded "broaden-and-build" theory of positive emotions:

> positive and negative emotions mattered on different time scales. Whereas the narrowed mindsets sparked by negative emotions were valuable in instances that threatened our ancestors' survival in some way, the broadened mindsets sparked by positive emotions were valuable ... because – over time – such expansive awareness served to *build* our human ancestors' resources, spurring on their development of assets, abilities and useful traits. These new resources functioned as reserves, better equipping our ancestors to handle later threats to survival. (p. 22)

Consistent with the hypothesis that positive emotions have survival value, there is growing evidence that people whose daily experience trends more toward positive emotions, or *positivity*, live longer than those whose lives are filled with negativity – perhaps as much as a full decade longer (Chida & Steptoe, 2008; Howell et al., 2007). A preponderance of positive emotions is also associated with healthy sleep patterns, improved immune system functioning, less damaging responses to stress, and lower risk of chronic disease. As Fredrickson (2009) explains, "with positivity, you are literally steeped in a different biochemical stew .... Negativity prompts cell decay. Positivity promotes cell growth. At a very basic biological level, then, positivity is life-giving" (pp. 75, 94).

Psychologists focused on the scientific study of happiness have reached similar conclusions (e.g., Lyubomirsky et al., 2005), especially when happiness is defined not only in the narrow sense of frequently experiencing a particular emotional state, but also in the broader sense of experiencing feelings of satisfaction about goal progress. From this perspective,

> becoming happier doesn't just make you *feel good*. It turns out that happiness brings with it multiple fringe benefits. Compared with their less happy peers, happier people are more sociable and energetic, more charitable and cooperative, and better liked by others. Not surprisingly, then, happier people are more likely to get married and to stay married and to have richer networks of friends and social support .... [They] show more flexibility and ingenuity in their thinking and are more productive in their jobs. They are better leaders and negotiators and earn more money. They are more resilient in the face of hardship, have stronger immune systems, and are physically healthier. Happy people even live longer. (Lyubomirsky, 2008, pp. 24–25)

As we will see in subsequent chapters of this book, positive emotions are closely related to the quality of our social relationships and to our sense of social purpose. Indeed, one of the primary mechanisms fueling upward spirals of positivity and physical health is the perceived quality of our social connections (Kok et al., 2013).

Personal Goals and Emotions

Because emotions can be so powerful in terms of dominating our consciousness and influencing our behavior, we often think of them as having "a life of their own." After all, emotions are organized systems in their own right, each with "its own special rules of operation" (Lazarus, 1991, p. 822). Nevertheless, emotions serve as advisors in motivational headquarters, not as leaders. Their role is to activate relevant personal goals – each of which functions like a "suggestion" to the leader – and then to help energize the pursuit of goals that merit priority consideration in the current situation, thus "crowding out" competing goals that lack emotional salience and urgency (Frijda, 1988).

This is not a process over which we have much conscious control. Sensory inputs (e.g., sights, sounds, smells, tactile sensations) routinely trigger emotions with the metaphorical equivalent of just a few "pixels" of information, before we have any awareness that an emotional response has taken place. Emotions can also be triggered outside awareness by certain kinds of biochemical processes such as hormonal activity or nociceptive (pain causing) chemicals released from cells. In addition, emotions are contagious. They can be triggered, via mirror neuron mechanisms, by emotions in others. Emotions thus carry out their motivational function of reporting on potential threats and opportunities quickly, effortlessly, and, to a remarkable extent, beneath awareness – at least until the conscious feelings associated with those emotions "catch up" through the ongoing process of updating body maps (as discussed in Chapter 2).

The process of energizing some goal pathways over others not only facilitates decision-making (Damasio, 2003), it also creates a state of action readiness. What kinds of action? Some emotions (e.g., interest, joy, affection, elevation) encourage exploration and further investment in promising goal options. Others (e.g., guilt, disgust) inhibit the pursuit of goals associated with unproductive, inappropriate, or dangerous behavior patterns. Still other emotions (e.g., anger, fear, loneliness) help people deal with obstacles and threats to core personal goals. In each case, though, emotions only have meaning in relation to some personal goal that you are at least actively considering, if not actually pursuing.

This means that whenever you see someone experiencing a strong emotion (including yourself!), you can reliably infer that there must be one or more strong goals "in play." Stated differently, we rarely get emotional about something that we don't care about (Immordino-Yang, 2016). That is a key guiding principle used by parents, spouses, and others seeking to understand the concerns of people they feel close to (especially when self-awareness or verbal communication abilities are limited). It is also an important diagnostic tool for counselors and helping professionals seeking to understand their clients' core personal goals and the obstacles inhibiting progress toward those goals.

Emotions and feelings provide a window into motivational headquarters.

Look deeply enough into the mental activity associated with your strongest emotions – what you attend to, what you remember, what choices you make – and you will begin to see recurring goal themes that are at the heart of your most meaningful and consequential thoughts and actions.

As we saw with personal agency beliefs, the "like-o-meter" mechanism that is such an important part of our emotional heritage makes it possible for emotions to provide advice not only about existing goal thoughts, but also about goals that have not yet been imagined. Indeed, one of the reasons emotions are so powerful is that they can become "attached" to almost anything if the circumstances are right (D. Ford, 1987/2019). You can see something interesting in an advertisement and think "I'd like to learn more about that." A pleasant encounter with a stranger might lead you to think "I'd like to get to know that person better." Conversely, we can quickly develop avoidance goals if our "gut reaction" to something (or somebody) is fear or disgust.

People who are responsible for developing human potential and helping people overcome difficult challenges (e.g., parents, teachers, health care professionals) often develop considerable skill in orchestrating circumstances so as to avoid negative "like-o-meter" responses to things that are perceived as boring or unpleasant or potentially frightening. Imagine, for example, trying to convince a reluctant child to engage in an unfamiliar activity, or trying to persuade a patient to comply with an onerous medical regimen. You can't prevent the initial negative reaction, but you can try to engineer a different reaction by "reframing" the challenge, thus effectively changing it into a different situation (e.g., "This is a lot like that thing you did so well the other day"; "Before you know it this will just be a natural part of your daily routine"). Learning how to harness the natural power of positive and negative emotions to help people make adaptive choices is an essential prerequisite for motivating self and others.

Personal Agency Beliefs and Emotions

In the previous section we emphasized the automatic triggering of emotions via sensory and biochemical inputs. But because emotional learning is so natural and ubiquitous, emotions can also be triggered by mental events (i.e., just by thinking). The triggering process is essentially the same – beneath awareness and often with just the tiniest bit of goal-relevant information. Indeed, such information may simply be a memory of an *emotionally competent stimulus* (Damasio, 2003), as when something exciting or frightening comes to mind (as illustrated, for example, by a scary memory). In principle, however, most any kind of goal-relevant thought could become capable of triggering an emotional response. Prominent among such thoughts are personal agency beliefs. PABs become associated with emotions very early in life as we develop mental models of our caregivers and of ourselves as actors exploring and interacting with the environment. The memories and expectations embedded in those mental models then become elaborated into enduring motivational patterns that help govern our decisions and actions in a wide variety of settings (M. Ford, 1986a; M. Ford & Thompson, 1985).

The interplay between emotions and PABs is thus an iterative process in which each informs and influences the other – just as you would expect from a team of advisors who work collaboratively to provide the leader with the best overall advice possible. Sometimes everyone is "on the same page" and decisions can be made quickly and easily. For example, you might encounter an exciting opportunity, reflect for a moment about possible obstacles, feel further energized when you can't think of any reason not to proceed, and then have your motivational advisors deliver a message, in unison, to "go for it." Conversely, something that initially frightens you may, upon further review, be confirmed as a dangerous and uncontrollable threat, thus resulting in a strong, unambiguous message to take evasive action. Spectacularly, in situations where emotional learning has already occurred, all of this can happen automatically and effortlessly, within a few milliseconds.

Yet, our thoughts and emotions do not always see things in such a harmonious way. Indeed, many types of human dysfunction can be attributed to the ease with which nonconscious emotional influences can "hijack" decision-making authority in motivational headquarters (or, as Haidt might say, the ease with which the elephant can overpower the rider). Syndromes such as agoraphobia and posttraumatic stress disorder illustrate how emotions can disrupt the normal "advising" process by flooding our motivational systems. Even when we are able to keep our emotions in an equipoised state, many of our most difficult decisions involve conflicts between what our head and our "gut" are telling us. That is not a sign of weakness or poor design, however. Having two different kinds of evaluation systems working together from different vantage points makes perfect sense given the need to take into account different kinds of short-term and longer-term issues and concerns when making important life decisions.

In short, emotions are terrific "first responders," but they are not necessarily the best advisors when it comes to more complex, prolonged goal pursuits. PABs are thus an essential part of the process of sizing up challenges and opportunities. And yet the quality of the advice that capability and context appraisals can provide is likely to be limited – or even self-defeating – if those appraisals are inaccurate.

What about "M"?

In the first part of this chapter we emphasized the integrated functioning of goals, emotions, and personal agency beliefs, including a "formula for human motivation" and corresponding graphic designed to encourage readers to always consider all three sets of component processes when running "motivational diagnostics" on a particular problem or opportunity (see Figure 4.2). In doing so we also reminded readers that although motivation plays a leadership role in human functioning and development, it is only one part of the broader "formula for human functioning," which also includes knowledge and skills (K&S), biological subsystems, and the environment (see Figure 4.1).

However, we then spent much of the rest of this chapter looking at the individual components of "M" along with interactions between pairs of those components. That of course is a necessary prerequisite for understanding how those components fit together as part of a motivational system. But please do not be misled by this effort to analyze motivational components that, in reality, are *always* integrated. Emotions will just be inconsequential blips on the motivational radar screen if they do not activate coherent personal goal thoughts supported by aligned PABs. Desires and aspirations will end up being nothing more than "wishful thinking" if the emotions and PABs in motivational headquarters fail to affirm their viability.

The fact that goals, emotions, and PABs always work together as a team is easiest to appreciate when dealing with a specific motivational puzzle. Take, for example, the fact that while one of the motivational "experts" writing this book has little difficulty maintaining an ideal body weight, the other constantly struggles to keep his weight in check. Of course, some of that difference may be attributable to factors other than motivation (e.g., genetic predispositions). Nevertheless, our emotional experiences in situations related to weight gain are drastically different. For the "right-sized" co-author, healthy and unhealthy food choices are similarly attractive, so it is relatively easy to make sensible choices. For the other, due to the presence of extra taste sensitivity – a form of the so-called supertaster pattern (Duffy & Bartoshuk, 2000) – many vegetables are aversively bitter. Physical exercise is also a less emotionally compelling choice for the overweight co-author, despite this goal having a constant presence in his "mental soup" of potential goals that might be pursued. With a sedentary job and favorite activities that involve relatively low levels of physical activity (e.g., reading, piano, spectator sports), it is challenging to find emotional triggers that will elevate physical exercise to a higher priority level than other competing goals. While the ideal-weight co-author enjoys hiking and other outdoor activities (independent of any weight loss concern) and has a spouse with aligned interests (e.g., she is a master gardener and Hip Hop dancer), the overweight co-author has an aversion to most outdoor activities (with the exception of the not so vigorous game of golf) and a spouse whose allergies make it difficult for her to be outdoors for an extended period of time.

Taken together, these circumstances make it difficult for the overweight co-author to maintain faith in his ability to achieve weight loss goals or to see his day-to-day environment as being conducive to losing weight. On the other hand, he has been able to "exercise" sufficient willpower to avoid any weight *gain* for many years. Moreover, after a major health scare, the motivation to make lifestyle changes became sufficiently escalated to fuel a sustainable weight loss of fifteen pounds. Key to that effort was the use of Gollwitzer's (1999) concept of "implementation intentions" (as outlined earlier in this chapter) (e.g., "When the morning news come on TV, I will only watch from my exercise bike").

We invite you to enrich your understanding of Motivational Systems Theory by applying its two basic formulas – the *Formula for Human Functioning* and *Formula for Human Motivation* – to some of your own life choices that you find motivationally puzzling, just as we have tried to do in the preceding paragraphs. Perhaps you are feeling "stuck" in an unsatisfying job or relationship and need to diagnose the specific goals, emotions, and capability and context beliefs that are holding you back from exploring other options. Perhaps you constantly find yourself wishing you had more time for the "best things in life" but have never tried to analyze why your life choices rarely include those personal favorites. As "creatures of habit" we may implicitly assume that we are powerless to motivate ourselves (or others) to change for the better. Yet, sometimes all it takes is one strategic "tweak" to some part of the system to create a new developmental trajectory.

One of the benefits of mapping out the "whole system" of factors involved in motivational challenges is that the resulting profile can be used to help guide a "what if" exercise in which the impact of altering one or more system components is simulated (via a thought experiment or through discussion with knowledgeable others). For example, a seriously injured athlete facing an "identity crisis" might decide to pursue sports-related goals in a different context, like coaching or sport management. A discouraged job seeker might take a step back and look at K&S deficits that are inhibiting career progress. Some relationship problems might be alleviated by trying to break out of unproductive motivational habits, like being overcontrolling or chronically antagonistic. In other cases, all that may be needed is a new mindset that motivates productive change by questioning the validity of inaccurate PABs or unwarranted emotions.

How Is MST Related to Other Theories of Motivation?

Although throughout this book we liberally cite many of the scholarly "giants" on whose shoulders we have stood as we progressed with our theoretical construction work, it is beyond the scope of this book to provide a conceptual mapping of how Motivational Systems Theory concepts align with each of the more than thirty major categories of motivation theories that have been proposed since the beginning of the twentieth century, starting with Freud's (1920/1948, 1923/1947) psychoanalytic theory. However, such a mapping can be found in Chapter 6 of *Motivating Humans* (M. Ford, 1992, Table 6.1). This twenty-seven-page table includes theories that are largely of historical interest (e.g., instinct theories, need theories, drive theories, field theory); theories that arose primarily in the domains of work and achievement motivation (e.g., two-factor theory, equity theory, expectancy-value theories); theories that were centered (at least initially) on the human desire to feel competent and in control (e.g., effectance motivation theories, reactance theory, personal causation theory, learned helplessness/optimism theory, self-determination theory); theories organized around various kinds of goal concepts (e.g., goal-setting theory, goal orientation theories, idiographic theories of goal content) – and more!

Now, one might assume that a mapping like this circa 1992 would be quite out of date. Yet for the most part that is not the case, as most of the theoretical advances that have occurred over the past 25+ years have been incremental elaborations on existing frameworks. So, while the table lacks some of the more contemporary references for those theories that are still on a "continuous improvement" trajectory, it remains a useful starting point for mapping out the territory that MST was designed to cover. For example, Dweck's (2006, 2017) highly visible research program featuring growth versus fixed motivational mindsets was well under way in the 1980s, though under somewhat different concept labels (e.g., mastery vs. helpless goal orientations). Once you see that Deci and Ryan are the originators and main architects of self-determination theory (e.g., Deci, 1980; Deci & Ryan, 1985) – a theory that is closely aligned with MST's human development/optimal functioning orientation – it is easy to search for more recent elaborations on that conceptual framework (e.g., Ryan & Deci, 2018). That search would reveal that self-determination theory now comprises six mini-theories (cognitive evaluation theory, organismic integration theory, causality orientations theory, basic psychological needs theory, goal contents theory, and relationships motivation theory). That set of theoretical elaborations illustrates the need for even the most sophisticated motivation scholars to be increasingly expansive with respect to the scope of their theorizing, while also illustrating the challenges associated with integrating the broad range of relevant content within a unified conceptual framework.

Group Motivational Systems Theory

One of the advantages of a living systems approach to understanding human motivation is that the same underlying concepts can be used to understand motivation at the level of individuals and groups (J. Miller, 1978). In humans, which are widely regarded as among the most "ultra-social" of all creatures (Richerson & Boyd, 2005; D. S. Wilson, 2007; E. O. Wilson, 2012), there is a strong, natural propensity to join groups and to follow group leaders with certain kinds of qualities – namely, those associated with what we will define in the next chapter as a *Thriving with Social Purpose* (TSP) motivational pattern (M. Ford & Smith, 2007). Our TSP framework, when applied to individuals, is an elaboration on Motivational Systems Theory that focuses on optimal functioning. Yet when the *TSP Theory of Motivation and Optimal Functioning* is applied to groups (e.g., families, teams, or organizations), it is perhaps better thought of as an elaboration on what we call *Group Motivational Systems Theory*, or GMST.

Although goals, emotions, and PABs are intrinsically psychological phenomena, they can function in coherent, unified ways across individuals, thus serving to organize and guide the behavior of social groups. Consistent with this premise, the key concepts in GMST are (a) *shared personal goals*,

(b) *shared emotions*, and (c) *shared personal agency beliefs*, especially as they are manifested within the context of a group that is authentically functioning as a collective. What would such a group look like? A "group" can include social units of any size, from dyads (e.g., marital or business partners) to small teams and working groups to large-scale political movements to cultures and whole nations. Yet the tighter the social interdependencies, the more useful the GMST framework is likely to be.

> Highly interdependent individuals, whether in dyads or larger groups, function not as separate goal pursuers, but as one self-regulating unit – a *transactive goal system* .... Relationship partners (e.g., romantic partners, coworkers, parents and children, teachers and students) can have such strong interdependence among their goals, goal pursuits, and goal outcomes that they become inextricably linked subparts of one self-regulating system. This system's goal outcomes depend on how well the subparts integrate their actions to form an efficient whole .... It is clear that any satisfactory under-standing of real-world goal outcomes requires a sophisticated theoretical analysis of individuals' social embeddedness. And yet the dominant theories of goal pursuit adopt an individual level of analysis, depicting people as self-regulators who enact self-control in pursuit of self-oriented goals. (Fitzsimons & Finkel, 2018, pp. 332–333, 336)

The concept of "sharing" can be a bit tricky to operationalize, as the term refers to the *content* of what different individuals are thinking and feeling, not the *process* through which they might have come to experience aligned goals, emotions, and PABs. For example, employees in a large agency or business might share some of the same core values and priorities due to a common leader or organizational culture, not because they have directly communicated with one another. Conversely, a special interest group might come into existence precisely because of frequent conversations and correspondence among like-minded individuals.

Shared Emotions

It is commonplace in theory and research on organizations to talk about the importance of shared goals, as illustrated by phrases like "team player," "shared vision," and "win-win" thinking (e.g., Covey, 1989; Gittell, 2003). However, consistent with the premise that goals are activated by triggered emotions, shared emotions were the first and remain the most fundamental mechanism for transforming individual organisms into collectives. Effective group leadership is therefore not just a matter of clarifying what the group should try to accomplish; it also requires that prospective group members be *collectively energized* to pursue those outcomes. Indeed, the most obvious factor differentiating groups that function in unison from those where group members are "doing their own thing" is the presence of shared emotional energy.

Put another way, you know that people are functioning as a group when the triggering of an emotion in one individual has a contagious influence on the emotional life of other group members. The experience of seeing others respond in similar ways to a particular problem or opportunity helps create a collective orientation, and ultimately a shared identity that motivates people to think and act in ways that are aligned with the actions of other group members. That is why, for example, it is generally easier to become emotionally connected to a local sports team than to other teams you might admire – especially if you attend or watch games with others who already feel that connection.

The powerful unifying effects of emotional contagion can perhaps be seen most easily in creatures that rely primarily on "hardwired" primordial goals (such as those associated with predator avoidance) and associated neuroimaged (learned) goals that link those primordial goals with specific environmental conditions. For example, a flock of birds will reliably respond as a collective to a loud noise or sudden disturbance. The motivational impact of that emotionally competent stimulus (Damasio, 2003) is amplified through the emotional responses of multiple birds in the flock, which in turn strengthens the activated safety goal and corresponding collective action (i.e., flying away together in a remarkably synchronized fashion).

However, with few exceptions (e.g., innate attachment mechanisms designed to keep infants and young children who are incapable of surviving on their own near their caregivers), the emotional processes that predispose humans to become members of a particular group are generally more suggestive than imperative. That is consistent with our earlier characterization of emotions as motivational advisors. We tend to gravitate toward groups that family members and others in our immediate life space have joined, but other choices are possible (in contrast to "birds of a feather" that can only "flock together"). Moreover, patterns of group identification and commitment can change significantly over time as our horizons expand and new opportunities arise. Still, as is evident with other socially oriented creatures, the most salient predictors of group cohesion and strength are the depth and intensity of the emotions tied to the group's purposes and activities.

Consider, for example, the remarkable power and unity of a mob whose collective passions have been aroused by a perceived injustice. Initially the mob just consists of individuals with diverse goal profiles. But with the proper emotional catalyst, those individuals can be transformed into a robust collective organized around a common goal. A group leader might, for example, direct the mob's attention to some emotionally competent stimulus that inflames their passions (e.g., a physical symbol of the transgressors' unjust actions, or some emotionally evocative "fighting words"). Emotional contagion can then amplify motivation even further, until the group's energy level reaches a fevered pitch and the group becomes increasingly likely to take on "a life of its own." Indeed, the actions of the collective may be contrary to how group members would normally act on their own (especially if they do things to hide their individuality, like wearing a mask).

The power of emotions in activating group goals can be seen in many other circumstances involving disruptive emotional experiences. For example, family members living their separate lives will quickly come together when a medical crisis arises. Bickering government leaders can quickly become a unified national force when threatened by an outside enemy. Victims of the same disease or oppressor often develop friendships that are profoundly deeper than those emerging out of proximity or convenience.

Positive group emotions can function in precisely the same way. For example, the joy of a championship sports team can bring an entire city together around a common point of pride. Fraternal organizations use emotionally saturated symbols and emotionally provocative initiation rituals to encourage group bonding and mutual advocacy and assistance. Social media networking groups often emerge around a topic that group members are passionate about, like their favorite hobby, band, or area of special expertise. The common thread in each of these examples is how triggered emotions can be strengthened and become catalysts for group formation when they are shared with others.

In short, shared emotions that have been "turbocharged" under conditions of great urgency, threat, or opportunity are among the strongest sources of motivational glue within a group. This is perhaps best illustrated by the powerful bonding experience of serving with others in combat.

Shared Goals

Once the emotions activating group goals are strong enough to motivate collective action, the key to optimal group functioning is channeling that energy toward shared goals that define the identity and purpose of the group. To maximize efficient use of group members' knowledge and skills, groups often function according to *division of labor* principles that, by definition, mean that different group members may be focused on rather different operational goals at the level of individual tasks or assignments. However, motivational strength is gained when people understand that their different contributions are all designed to facilitate progress toward shared objectives within a unified enterprise, like preventing criminal activity, or contributing to a multidisciplinary diagnostic team, or trying to get someone elected to political office (e.g., "We may be doing different things but we're all in this together"; "We make a great team because we each bring something unique to the table"). Conversely, the absence of authentically shared goals often leads to group dissonance and dysfunction – or, in extreme cases, group dissolution.

This transformation of individual goal thoughts into collective goal thoughts is the group-level manifestation of the principle of *goal alignment* (M. Ford, 1992) that is so critical to the effective pursuit of personal goals. At an individual level goal alignment occurs when priorities are unambiguous (absence of goal conflicts) and connections between immediate objectives and high-level goals are clear. Similarly, goal alignment at the group level is evidenced by

- agreement about what objectives to pursue ("Our basketball team needs to play relentless defense and only take high-percentage shots to beat this team");
- a personal commitment from each group member to embrace those objectives – in other words, the agreed upon objectives are *internalized* and thus actually function as personal goals ("I'm totally sold on the coach's plan"); and
- an ability to actually put aside individual concerns in favor of the concerns of the group ("I'm going to pass the ball to the player with the best chance to score rather than worry about how many points I'm scoring").

Taken together, these elements are the essence of effective teamwork, as illustrated by high-functioning work groups (Grant, 2008, 2013) and by the way championship sport teams create a "whole that is greater than the sum of the parts."

Group goal alignment is facilitated when group members share an overarching shared identity goal. Such goals fall within the *belongingness* category in the Taxonomy of Human Goals (see Table 3.1). When people identify with a group and a corresponding belongingness goal occupies a high-level position in their personal goal hierarchies, the group itself functions as an emotionally competent stimulus. The group can be global in scope (e.g., "I am a cancer survivor, just like all of you") or more community-based ("Hey, the Seahawks are my favorite football team as well – Go Hawks!"). And once that belongingness goal is activated, it can in turn trigger and sustain emotions related to connecting and caring. The ultimate marker for group goal alignment is when just *thinking* about the group reliably triggers positive emotions and associated feelings (as when people think about their alma mater or hometown). The result is a strong sense of loyalty that pulls group members together even when doing so might be detrimental to the self (e.g., sacrificing free time or personal recognition to help ensure that organizational goals are achieved). Identification with a group also makes other integrative social relationship goals more salient as potential concerns within the context of that group (i.e., concerns related to equity, social responsibility, and resource provision). It is easy to see why belongingness goals were so adaptive for our hominid forebears, whose welfare depended on being able to cooperate with tribe members and contribute to the group's survival and well-being.

In GMST, the principle of *multiple goals* (M. Ford, 1992) also applies in analogous fashion to motivation at the individual level. Earlier we described the "Darwinian competition" among goal thoughts that routinely characterizes our everyday decision-making (much of which occurs outside awareness). When you have more than one reason to select a particular goal to pursue over other activated goal options, the odds that you will prioritize that goal escalate. For example, suppose that you have a goal to lose weight and it crosses your mind (perhaps because of the emotions triggered when you looked at yourself in a mirror) that you should do some exercise. If you have a looming work deadline and you are behind on your chores and a family member is asking you to do something else, the probability that you will take time out to exercise may be rather slim (no pun intended). In contrast, if you are thinking about the image you saw in the mirror and the lecture your doctor gave you last week and the fact that your high school reunion is just a month away, the odds of exercise progressing from an activated goal to a selected goal are likely to rise significantly even in the face of competing alternatives. Similarly, the probability of maintaining a commitment to exercise over time will escalate when you have more than one activated goal "defending" that commitment.

The motivational power of multiple goals can also be seen across individuals at the GMST level. When each member of the collective shares the same highly prioritized goal, it is analogous to everyone turning their eyes to look at the same target. Individual egos and personal agendas fade, and the success of the group becomes the dominant focus. As efforts to pursue the group goal get under way, the diverse talents of individual group members all get channeled along the same pathway. Motivation can then be further strengthened if each individual has multiple reasons to continue to prioritize the group goal (i.e., each group member has a variety of subgoals that are "attached" to the organizational goal). For example, using the terminology in the Taxonomy of Human Goals, coaches love to recruit college athletes whose motivational profile includes a rich combination of personal goal thoughts like "I thrive on the excitement of competing (entertainment, superiority) and seeing myself get better (mastery)," "I can't let my teammates or my coaches down (social responsibility, equity)," "I couldn't live with myself if I brought shame to this team (positive self-evaluations)," and perhaps most importantly, at an overarching level, "I treasure being part of this team (belongingness) and I really want to help it succeed (resource provision)."

This same example can be used to illustrate the essence of effective leadership from the perspective of GMST. When universities seek to hire a head coach, or when coaches seek to identify or cultivate leaders from among their players, the number one thing they are looking for is someone who can promote goal alignment at the group level and harness the power of multiple goals toward team objectives. As outlined above, that includes skills such as being able to get everyone on the same page, keeping people focused on team priorities and values, promoting a strong sense of loyalty and responsibility to teammates, and understanding how to work individually with each player to align their individual goals with team goals. Experience and expertise are of course important considerations in selecting potential leaders. However, once those "baseline" criteria have been achieved, the selection process is mostly focused on who can help team members thrive within the context and culture of the team by instilling in each individual group member shared objectives organized around high-level social purpose goals.

Earlier we discussed the importance of emotions in *activating* group goals, thus transforming individual motivation into collective motivation. But emotions also help *sustain* group motivation after goal pursuit has been initiated, just as they do when people are pursuing their individual goals. Some emotions (e.g., anger, scorn, and contempt) require bursts of energy to be functionally effective and thus are hard to sustain over an extended period of time. Other emotions are more suited to the role of "keeping the flywheel spinning," with lots of opportunities to give a little push here and a little push there – along with the occasional big spin!

What kinds of emotions do group leaders typically use on a day-to-day basis to sustain and strengthen loyalty and commitment to group objectives? Some effectively use positive emotions like affection and pride, but far too often people rely first and foremost on emotions like fear and guilt because of their psychologically coercive impact. Fear in particular is often used to control group members because its evolved function is to influence behavior "right now." But relying solely on fear-based emotions comes with a price – namely, the stifling of creativity, growth, and "cooperative spirit" (Amabile, 1996). If you are OK with innovation and collaboration being temporarily disabled, and compliance is your only goal, that may be an effective way to achieve the results you seek "right now." For example, advertising designed to motivate people to vote for a particular candidate tends to become increasingly negative as Election Day approaches because triggering fear about what the opposing candidate might do has proven to be one of the most effective way to energize voters to go to the polls. Similarly, highlighting the actions of a feared enemy capable of threatening a group's integrity and viability (e.g., a business competitor or hostile nation) is a tried-and-true technique for motivating people to make personal sacrifices. Parents often use "scare tactics" (e.g., threatened punishment; frightening emotional displays) to try to ensure that young children won't run out into a street, or new teenage drivers won't make a fatal error in judgment.

However, when it comes to optimal group functioning, the goal of the moment is rarely the only consideration. Leaders and followers typically have *relationships* that help determine the ongoing success of the group, thus making it necessary to consider whether the use of coercive motivational techniques will damage that relationship. Bosses and employees have to continue working together after that urgent deadline has passed. Coaches and players have to keep trying to improve after the big game is over. Parents and children have to continue living together after the fights over homework and house rules are over. If not balanced by healthy doses of emotional warmth and encouragement, fear-based techniques can ultimately "shut down" motivation by sapping energy and by creating context beliefs that are so emotionally aversive that followers just want to escape that context (at least mentally, if physical escape is not an option).

In contrast, when leaders rely more on emotions like pride in belonging to a group and genuine affection for other group members, group motivation tends to be both strong and enduring. Those are not the only emotions that can effectively energize group activity, but they are the "emotional ties that bind" enduring groups together. That is why, for example, effective military leaders systematically promote these emotions ("The Few. The Proud. The Marines"). Great coaches often speak of their love for players and trying to promote players' love of each other. Successful parenting is typically associated not only with setting and enforcing standards of conduct, but also with frequent displays of emotional warmth (Baumrind, 1978; C. Bergin, 1987/2019). This clearly identifiable emphasis on "group positivity" is, just as we saw for individuals, the key to creating upward spirals of collective effort, creativity, and accomplishment (Fredrickson, 2003, 2009).

Importantly, effective leaders are careful not to promote group identity at the expense of individual identity. As we will discuss in the next chapter, optimal functioning requires an equipoised balance between other-enhancing and self-enhancing personal goals. Leaders cannot reliably motivate group members "over the long haul" if they do not respect the fact that each group member will have core personal goals that go beyond those that happen to be consistent with the needs of the group. Indeed, the most effective leaders try to use group membership as a way to connect with – rather than compete with – an individual's existing core personal goals. That in turn makes it easy for people to internalize group goals as "their very own."

Shared Personal Agency Beliefs

In the same way that PABs can strengthen individual motivation, shared capability and context beliefs can empower group motivation by reinforcing group confidence and resolve across individuals pursuing shared goals. The significance of shared capability beliefs in group motivation has been highlighted in the extensive body of research on *collective efficacy*. Studies contrasting collective and individual efficacy clearly demonstrate that collective efficacy is more than the sum of the strength of individual capability beliefs (Goddard et al., 2004; C. Watson et al., 2001). Beliefs about whether a particular group is capable of accomplishing a shared goal are functionally distinct from beliefs about whether you are generally capable of contributing to a group's success. For example, you might lack confidence in your ability to sustain close relationships but have great faith in the strength of a particular relationship that has "stood the test of time." Or you might think of yourself as a versatile and resilient teacher but have significant doubts about whether you can teach effectively in the context of colleagues and administrators who are jaded and cynical.

A shared belief in the group's capabilities for attaining shared goals does not necessarily mean that, from the perspective of the *social* system, context beliefs will be positive. While faith in others' support of your goal pursuits is the essence of context beliefs for an individual person, that faith is a *capability* of the social system (i.e., it is a manifestation of collective efficacy within the system rather than being part of the context of the system). *Group* context beliefs refer to expectations about forces outside that social system that may facilitate or constrain the group's functioning. For example, does the group have access to outside financial resources that can help sustain its vitality? For many small businesses and nonprofit agencies, that is the key to collective survival with well-being. Is the group perceived as legitimate by the surrounding cultural context? For a company under investigation, or for a couple like Romeo and Juliet, the answer is likely to be "not so much."

In general, positive group context beliefs are motivating and negative group context beliefs are demotivating. However, just as we saw when looking at individual PABs, it is the *integrated patterning* of capability and context beliefs that determines how group goal pursuit will be impacted. Up to a point, circumstances that make life difficult for, say, a minority group or underdog team or start-up company may actually *intensify* motivation (assuming that shared capability beliefs are strong), consistent with the Tenacious PAB pattern outlined earlier in this chapter (see Figure 4.6). However, when the context seems relentlessly unfair, unsupportive, or hostile, it may be difficult for a group that feels victimized to remain hopeful and encouraged.

What Would an Optimally Functioning Motivational System Look Like?

In this chapter we have provided you with an overview of how the human motivational system works. Understanding what each component of this unified system is designed to do and how personal goals, emotions, and personal agency beliefs work together as a team is an essential prerequisite for learning how to motivate self and others. Such knowledge has been rapidly accumulating over the past several decades, but integrating that knowledge into a coherent and comprehensive framework has been a challenge due to the complex, multicomponent nature of human motivation. Motivational Systems Theory was designed to address that challenge. MST unifies the "big ideas" in motivational science and sets the stage for practical applications of those ideas.

Thinking about how to motivate self and others from a more applied perspective logically leads to the question, "what are the qualities associated with an optimally functioning motivational system?" In the next chapter we will attempt to answer that question. In doing so, we will use the concept of *amplification* to describe the processes that can help us move from adequate to optimal functioning. What would your overall motivational system look like if all of its components were effectively "amplified" in an equipoised way, and then infused with social purpose? And can motivation be further strengthened by enhancing our knowledge and skills, biological capacity, and environmental resources – that is, by improving the functioning of the person-system as a whole?

Read on to learn more about human motivation at its best.

CHAPTER 5

Thriving with Social Purpose
Human Motivation at Its Best

> People appear to thrive when they can successfully achieve, through their own actions, the goals that they have chosen …. The idea of deliberately choosing and developing one's own life course is an exciting prospect to consider.
> — Marlene Winell, "Personal Goals: The Key to Self-Direction in Adulthood"

> We achieve for ourselves only as we appreciate the problems and concerns of others – and only as we see our own lives as part of a much greater social purpose.
> — Manning Marable, *Black Liberation in Conservative America*

In this chapter we will provide you with science-based descriptions of how people can transform their lives for the better by learning how to "amplify" motivation in an equipoised way – thus producing a *thriving* motivational pattern – and by making *social purpose* a fluid but persistent priority in their overall profile of personal goals. It is the combination of *thriving with social purpose* (TSP) and *goal–life alignment* that makes it possible for people to "make the world a better place" while also experiencing enhanced motivation and optimal functioning. That in turn leads to feelings of *life meaning,* which will be our focus in Chapter 7.

First, though, we need to acquaint you with the nature, origins, and impact of the elements associated with thriving and social purpose so that you can understand why we have come to view TSP as representing *human motivation at its best* – not in every situation, but as an overall way of life that you can rely on to frame how you approach everyday challenges and opportunities. When you make TSP your "home page" motivational orientation, you are taking the evolved gifts that nature gave you – and that enabled humans to soar beyond the capabilities of all other species – and cultivating them to maximize their effectiveness in your own personal ecology. That in turn is a pathway for enhancing *survival with well-being* for both you and those who are influenced by your TSP qualities.

Analogous to our earlier discussion (in Chapter 4) about the need to align personal agency belief patterns with the realities of changing life circumstances, a TSP home page orientation does not mean that you must always be in a thriving mode or that you should always prioritize social purpose goals. It just means that TSP is your typical and most comfortable starting point – that is, you are naturally forward-thinking, with both self-awareness and awareness of others; you are generally inclined to be optimistic and tenacious in your goal pursuits; and social purpose is infused into your thinking whenever it is appropriate for the circumstances at hand. In circumstances where a TSP motivational pattern is less of a fit, or when your energy resources are depleted (and it is thus difficult to amplify much of anything), or when you just need some time for yourself, other motivational responses may be more adaptive.

Developing strong TSP predispositions can have profound benefits. When TSP becomes your motivational home page rather than just an occasional peak experience, you will begin to generate the kind of upward spirals that lead to extended periods of optimal functioning across many life domains (Fredrickson, 2003; Kok et al., 2013; Vondracek et al., 2010). You will find yourself activating goals with increased clarity and pursuing them with greater confidence and commitment. Your aspirations and achievements will become both richer and broader. And gratifyingly, you will know these things are happening because your mind and body will generate positive emotions and feelings of life meaning at increasingly greater levels of depth and frequency.

Developing a Model of Optimal Functioning Based on Motivational Systems Theory

Motivation is an ever-present, naturally occurring aspect of human functioning. However, just as our biological functions may not always operate at peak levels of efficiency and effectiveness, our goals, emotions, and personal agency beliefs can also operate in ways that are less than optimal. For example, the thoughts and feelings that guide our decisions may lead to dysfunctional choices that create vulnerabilities in our lives. Or they may only be strong enough to enable us to get by in a stagnant, dreary kind of way – what Damasio might call surviving *without* well-being. Yet it seems evident that we are not designed to pursue life priorities in a self-defeating or halfhearted manner. Optimal functioning is characterized by frequent and persistent efforts to pursue the goals that bring you and others the greatest satisfaction, and to do so with the energy and commitment needed to make meaningful progress toward those goals.

Earlier we emphasized that motivation is intrinsically future oriented. Thus, from a motivational perspective optimal functioning is "more about the journey than the destination." Results are important, but the primary focus is on the *process* of goal striving. When we feel like "all systems are go" and we're "hitting on all cylinders" we experience joy and a heightened sense of productivity. Athletes often strive for such experiences as they know that peak performance is most likely to occur when they can enter "the zone" – a state in which the overall mind/body system is functioning in an optimal way. In the zone, hard work and persistence feel uncomplicated and effortless.

The popular concept of *flow* (which is part of a broader theory of optimal experience) is also commonly used to describe the qualities associated with optimal functioning (Csikszentmihalyi, 1991, 2003). Notably, flow qualities are largely motivational in nature – for example, experiencing goal clarity and a sense of optimal challenge, becoming immersed in an activity without any self-consciousness, having a sense of personal control and effectiveness, and experiencing feelings of enjoyment and life meaning. Indeed, there is a good chance that "flowlike" experiences were among those that came to mind when you considered our thought experiment in Chapter 1 ("think of the most motivating activity or experience you engaged in during the past few weeks").

Motivational Systems Theory was designed to capture all of the different facets of motivation within a single, integrated model. However, it is primarily a model of *functioning* (i.e., here's how we are designed; here's how things work) rather than a model for *improving* functioning. Therefore, to make MST more useful as a framework for personal development and professional intervention, another layer needs to be added that focuses specifically on the nature of *optimal functioning* – not only at the level of individual components, but also within the overall person-system.

Building a useful framework for understanding how motivation contributes to optimal functioning is a challenging enterprise – one that has occupied us for many years (e.g., M. Ford & Smith, 2007). Such a framework not only needs to address current functioning, it also needs to maintain a strong developmental perspective – that is, it cannot just focus on the results of the moment. For example, an immediate "payoff" obtained through shortcuts or social manipulation may turn out to be rather shortsighted if one also considers the "strings attached" to that achievement, such as loss of trust or closing off of future opportunities.

Moreover, what is optimal at any given moment may be subject to much debate depending on what specific personal goals are prioritized. Therefore, a more useful approach to understanding motivation and optimal functioning is to focus on broad patterns of functioning related to Damasio's *survival with well-being* paradigm. The primary objectives from this perspective are to look for evidence of success and impact over time and across goal pursuits (rather than focusing on specific episodes), while also maintaining a strong focus on "system" qualities such as organization and equipoise.

In this chapter we describe an approach to the challenge of motivating self and others that is aligned with this broad developmental perspective. The *Thriving with Social Purpose (TSP)* model is built directly and firmly on the foundation provided by Motivational Systems Theory (and its "parent" theory, the Living Systems Framework), and is consistent with MST's philosophy that science and practice can best be advanced by "standing on the shoulders of giants." In other words, *TSP is a theory-guided, evidence-based, integrative model* designed to consolidate and leverage accumulated scientific wisdom about aspects of motivation that seem to be consistently associated with meaningful accomplishments and positive developmental outcomes.

In the TSP model we wed together concepts related to motivational *processes* – collectively referred to as "thriving" – with concepts related to motivational *content* – collectively referred to as "social purpose" (i.e., integrative social relationship goals). Although each of the elements in this model can be considered separately – and that will be how we initially present the concepts – what truly makes the TSP motivational pattern "optimal" is their combined impact. As we will see in the next chapter when we discuss how selection pressures for cooperative group living led to the development of bigger, more "socially intelligent" brains, the capacity for thriving is closely related to the evolutionary developments that made social purpose a basic design feature of the human species. Thriving and social purpose are also functionally connected through their impact on life meaning – a neglected topic that will be our primary focus in Chapter 7.

The Concept of Amplification in System Functioning

We have elected to use the concept of *amplification* to convey both the meaning and spirit of the processes involved in "optimizing" motivation. Amplification implies an *increase in potency* (e.g., louder volume, stronger signal, expanded description) as well as a *gain in effectiveness* (e.g., greater clarity, dependability, or impact). Amplification of our natural capabilities greatly increases the odds for successful outcomes. In essence, amplification is what takes us from merely living our lives to experiencing *quality of life* – or, in Damasio's terms, survival *with well-being*.

Consistent with the twin themes of potency and effectiveness, the concept of amplification as it applies to human motivation refers to "the development of dynamic, mutually reinforcing patterns of goal, PAB, and emotional functioning that motivate people to invest themselves in new challenges and opportunities rather than adopt a stagnant or defensive posture" (M. Ford & Smith, 2007, p. 160). Amplification is thus associated with goal striving that seeks to improve on current capabilities, methods, and results. The impact of these motivation-sustaining, growth-oriented patterns of goal pursuit is felt throughout the entire person-system, with the positive effects escalating as goals, emotions, and PABs reinforce one another. Evidence of amplified motivation might include, for example, functional changes such as sharpened attentional focus and clarity of purpose, heightened feelings of energy and personal empowerment, increased efficiency and productivity, accelerated learning and competence development, and enhanced health and well-being.

Put another way, when goals, emotions, and personal agency beliefs are jointly amplified, that fuels what can be thought of as the polar opposite of a "vicious cycle" – that is, a cycle of *cascading vitality* (M. Feldman & Khademian, 2003) in which things tend to get better and better when circumstances are favorable, while also tending to go "from bad to better" rather than "from bad to worse" when circumstances are unfavorable. Although it is difficult to engineer this kind of cyclical process, TSP seems to be a particularly reliable source of cascading vitality.

Accelerated growth of the kind that TSP motivational patterns encourage requires some sort of energizing catalyst to initiate the process (Prigogine & Stengers, 1984). In the case of TSP, the primary catalytic element appears to be *positive emotions* and associated feelings of *life meaning* (as explained in Chapter 7). Fredrickson (2003) has described how positive emotions transform the way we think and act by enhancing self-awareness, creativity, problem solving, and openness to change. Such emotions generate "upward spirals" toward optimal functioning and enhanced emotional well-being ... by broadening individuals' habitual modes of thinking and action and building lasting resources that promote future experiences of positive emotions. As this cycle continues, positive emotions transform individuals into more resilient, socially integrated, and capable versions of themselves. (p. 169)

Using the Concept of Amplification to Transform the Formula for Human Functioning into a Formula for Optimal Human Functioning

In Chapter 4 we introduced the *Motivational Systems Theory* Formula for Human Functioning (see Figure 5.1) as a heuristic tool for summarizing the four major subsystems involved in the pursuit of personal goals ("what life is all about").

$$\text{Human Functioning} = \frac{M \times KS}{1/\text{Biology}} \times \text{Env}$$

Figure 5.1 The *Motivational Systems Theory* Formula for Human Functioning.
Note: The large-scale components of human systems and the relationships among them can be represented using a heuristic formula that emphasizes the dynamic interactions among motivational processes (M), knowledge and skills (K&S), biological subsystems, and the environment (Env). The formula shows biology as a denominator to emphasize that its primary role is to support the M and K&S components. Biology is represented in reciprocal form since its role is to nourish and strengthen (rather than weaken) the impact of the other components on human functioning.

To transform this formula into one that represents *optimal* human functioning, it is necessary to add an appropriate set of "amplifiers" not only to the M subsystem (aka motivational headquarters), but also to each of the other three subsystems. We accomplished this objective through extensive reviews of relevant theory and research, with an emphasis on outcome-oriented, evidence-based empirical work. Although the resulting formulas are neither comprehensive (i.e., incorporating all possible amplifiers) nor the only way to organize the relevant evidence, we are confident that we have assembled many of the best available examples of "potent and effective" amplifiers for all aspects of human functioning. Summary labels for each of the four sets of amplifiers are incorporated into the *Formula for Optimal Human Functioning*:

$$\text{Optimal Human Functioning} = \left[\frac{[\text{TSP}]\text{M} \times [\text{GSS}]\text{K\&S}}{1/[\text{PHR}]\text{Biology}} \times [\text{R}]\text{Env}\right]\text{Equipoise}$$

Key:

      M = Motivation

  TSP = Thriving with Social Purpose (amplified M infused with Social Purpose [SP] Goals)

  K&S = Knowledge and Skills

  GSS = Goal-Striving Skills (a set of K&S amplifiers)

Biology = Biological Systems

  PHR = Personal Health Responsibility (a set of Biology amplifiers)

  Env = Environment

[R]Env = Responsive Environment (amplification through contextual influences)

Equipoise = Dynamic, System–Wide Adaptation to Changing Conditions

The elements composing the M amplifier (i.e., Thriving motivational processes, further strengthened by the infusion of Social Purpose goals) will be described in the first half of this chapter and in each of the book's remaining chapters. However, in the latter half of the current chapter we will also be systematically considering some of the key amplifying elements involved in each of the other components of human functioning (i.e., Goal-Striving Skills, Personal Health Responsibility, and a Responsive Environment). Our decision to incorporate these elements into the *TSP Theory of Motivation and Optimal Functioning* reflects the fact that the primary function of motivation is to cause us to take actions that will enhance survival with well-being, including efforts to strengthen and sustain our knowledge and skills, our physical health and capacity, and the responsiveness of the environments in which we pursue our personal goals. Motivation also plays a leadership role in promoting optimal functioning by orchestrating the dynamic changes required to maintain equipoise – that is, the effective, context-appropriate balancing and counter-balancing of the multiple forces involved in goal pursuit.

Amplifying Your Motivational Functioning: Thriving with Social Purpose (TSP)

$$\text{Optimal Human Functioning} = \left[\frac{[\textbf{TSP}]\textbf{M} \times [\text{GSS}]\text{K\&S}}{1/[\text{PHR}]\text{Biology}} \times [\text{R}]\text{Env}\right]\text{Equipoise}$$

After years of research, analysis, and "putting the puzzle pieces together," we have become convinced that, as a general orientation to life's opportunities and challenges, *Thriving with Social Purpose (TSP)* is indeed "motivation at its (human) best." We reached this conclusion through two rather different scientific story lines. From a psychological perspective, the directive and regulatory processes that contribute to TSP motivational functioning have repeatedly been identified as reliable contributors to life success (and life meaning!) in virtually every domain of human endeavor. In the pages that follow we will summarize the research that supports this conclusion and that has been most influential in our thinking about motivation and optimal functioning.

Somewhat to our surprise, another story line – one focused on the evolution of motivational systems – led us along a very different scientific pathway to precisely the same conclusion. We did not initiate this part of our "big bet" strategy with the idea of trying to verify or corroborate the research being conducted by motivational psychologists. We were simply trying to organize our thinking around the guiding premise that efforts to motivate self and others are most likely to succeed when they are based on how we are naturally designed.

And yet, the more we explored the emerging consensus among evolutionary scholars about the qualities that caused humans to flourish as a species, the more we realized that both thriving and social purpose were at the heart of that success story. Indeed, it appears that TSP was the driving force behind the emergence of a host of social-cognitive and interpersonal skills supporting *cumulative cultural evolution* – for example, skills related to "mind reading" (inferring others' intentions, beliefs, and emotional states) and sharing information (e.g., through direct instruction, observational learning, and guided mentoring). This ratcheting up of K&S demands and capabilities ultimately led to the development of cultural and technological achievements far beyond what could have been accomplished through genetic evolution alone or through individual experiential learning (Tomasello, 2009). Thanks to TSP, activities such as teaching, teamwork, and improving on the achievements of others became second nature to humans on the other side of the "Cooperation Divide" (D. S. Wilson, 2007). Suddenly (in evolutionary time), a species was not just trying to survive in the world, it was trying to "make the world a better place."

A groundbreaking study by Dean et al. (2012) illustrates the importance of TSP qualities in human evolution. In this comparative problem-solving study, groups of capuchin monkeys, chimpanzees, and 3–4-year-old children were given a "cumulative culture puzzlebox" which could be solved at three sequential stages, each building on the previous stage. Solutions at each level yielded increasingly attractive rewards (carrot, then apple, then grapes for chimpanzees and capuchins; stickers of increasing size and attractiveness for children). The results showed dramatic differences between human and nonhuman problem solving. Whereas nearly half of the children made it all the way to level three, very few chimpanzees or capuchins were able to go beyond even the first level of the puzzlebox (despite having substantially more time than the children to try to do so). Why were the children so successful? They routinely and repeatedly engaged in teaching through verbal instruction, imitation of others' effective actions, and spontaneous helping behavior, with the most successful children displaying these patterns at the highest levels of frequency. In contrast, the chimpanzees and capuchins virtually never engaged in any form of teaching, collaboration, or prosocial activity.

The implications of this remarkable study are clear and consistent with many other converging lines of evidence. Humans are naturally designed to work in teams and to directly help others attain valued rewards through direct help and instruction. We are not just cooperators; we are also teachers and innovators and communicators that spread useful knowledge and skills to others, near and far.

In the pages that follow we will first describe the qualities associated with *thriving* (aka amplified motivation), and then discuss the positive consequences of infusing *social purpose* goals into a thriving motivational pattern. But make no mistake – what transformed our species was the combination of thriving *with* social purpose. As life became more collaborative and egalitarian, those with a strong sense of social purpose were in the best position to lead. And yet, to lead effectively, there also needed to be strong support for innovation. Those most likely to do the innovating were – you guessed it – those with a thriving motivational orientation. In the context of social purpose, thriving was a powerful engine for "making the world a better place." In contrast, without social purpose, the benefits of thriving are attenuated. As the famous saying goes, "no one cares what you know until they know you care."

Thriving

In Chapter 4 we introduced the *Motivational Systems Theory* Formula for Human Motivation as a heuristic tool for representing the three subsystems involved in motivating self and others. As summarized in

Motivation (M) = G X PAB X E

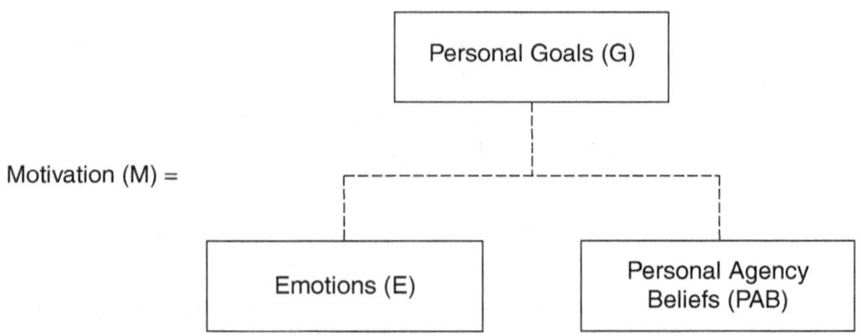

Figure 5.2 The *Motivational Systems Theory* Formula for Human Motivation with an associated diagram.
Note: The components of motivational systems and the relationships among them can be represented using a heuristic formula or a graphical representation. The formula emphasizes the dynamic interactions among personal goals, emotions, and personal agency beliefs. The diagram emphasizes the leadership role played by personal goals in motivational systems, with emotions and personal agency beliefs serving primarily in an advisory capacity.

Figure 5.2, personal goals are the leaders of our motivational systems. Emotions evolved as a mechanism for activating goals and energizing and regulating goal-directed activity. Later, personal agency beliefs developed as another kind of motivational advisor, with a focus on assessing whether the K&S and Biology components of human functioning were capable of producing the outcomes envisioned by the leader (capability beliefs), and whether the Environment would be supportive of such efforts (context beliefs).

Now, imagine each element in the motivational system operating at its highest level of potency and effectiveness (the two themes associated with the concept of amplification). The leader would be dynamic and action oriented. The emotion advisors would be attentive, savvy, and capable of providing disciplined guidance. The PAB advisors would be confident and hopeful but also grounded in reality.

We have organized these ideas into four integrative concepts that summarize the amplifying qualities associated with "human motivation at its best." An *active approach* goal orientation is what results when the directive function of personal goals is amplified. *Personal optimism* and *mindful tenacity* enable us to maintain effort and persistence under a wide array of circumstances, consistent with the Robust, Encouraged, and Tenacious PAB patterns described in Chapter 4 (see

Figure 4.6). Finally, the concept of *emotional wisdom* integrates the themes associated with an astute, trusted advisor, such as experience, social insight, and prudence.

We have selected the term *thriving* to refer to what happens when all of the elements in motivational headquarters are collectively amplified while also operating in an equipoised manner. The concept of thriving incorporates all of the themes described in the preceding paragraphs, while also suggesting the presence of (or potential for) strength and reliability in the supporting K&S, Biology, and Environment components of human functioning. That is an important consideration because, as we will see, thriving motivational patterns are nourished and supported by goal-striving skills, personal health responsibility, and a responsive environment. Some compensation is possible when "the going gets rough" in one part of the system (e.g., a thriving motivational orientation can help people overcome physical and social challenges; a responsive environment can help people overcome knowledge and skill deficits), but over time optimal functioning is difficult to sustain if *any* element in the overall system is chronically weak or unreliable:

Amplified Motivation (Thriving) = [[AA]G × [PO][MT]PAB × [EW]E]Equipoise

Key:
>G = Personal Goal
>AA = Active Approach (goal amplifier)
>PAB = Personal Agency Beliefs
>PO = Personal Optimism (capability belief amplifier)
>MT = Mindful Tenacity (context belief amplifier)
>E = Emotions
>EW = Emotional Wisdom (emotion amplifier)

Equipoise = Dynamic, System–Wide Adaptation to Changing Conditions

In the paragraphs that follow, the qualities associated with a thriving motivational pattern are described for each component in the MST framework. When all of these qualities are integrated within an equipoised motivational system, we experience feelings of vitality and positivity. We feel self-directed and courageous but also grounded and authentic. We expect to make continuous progress toward meaningful personal goals through productive engagement with life challenges and opportunities. In short, when we are motivationally thriving, optimal functioning becomes a possibility.

Active Approach: Amplifying Motivation through Strong Self-Leadership

> Twenty years from now you will be more disappointed by the things you didn't do than by the ones you did do. So throw off the bowlines. Sail away from safe harbor. Catch the tradewinds in your sails. Explore, Dream, Discover.
>
> – H. Jackson Brown Jr., *P.S. I Love You*

The key to establishing a thriving motivational pattern is, first and foremost, the cultivation of strong, forward-looking leadership qualities in the personal goal component of system functioning (Lopez, 2013; Winell, 1987/2019). As we emphasized in Chapter 3, these qualities include a clear understanding of our core personal goals and the ability to stay actively focused on those goals. However, the mindset that we adopt when thinking about goal pursuit is also important – as illustrated, for example, by the fact that the Ford and Nichols Taxonomy of Human Goals (Chapter 3) describes each category of goal content in both approach terms (i.e., the outcome thought of as *what you want*) and avoidance terms (i.e., the outcome thought of as *what you don't want*). Although an avoidance goal orientation can be highly adaptive in certain circumstances (e.g., when danger is present), optimal functioning at a more general level is associated with an approach goal orientation.

Strong self-leadership requires a willingness to explore alternatives and take psychological risks – not indiscriminately, but in an equipoised manner. Consistent with Reeve's (2013) concept of "agentic engagement," high-functioning individuals try to *create* the conditions that will facilitate goal progress rather than to *wait* for those conditions to arise. Motivationally, the essence of that mindset is a persistent bias toward initiating action when considering whether to pursue a desired outcome.

In our TSP framework we call this persistent bias an *active approach* goal orientation. This amplifier concept is a combination of two closely related themes: an active (as opposed to passive or reactive) goal orientation that favors action over inaction, and an approach (as opposed to avoidance) goal orientation that favors moving toward positive outcomes rather than away from negative outcomes.

Different orientations to goal pursuit lead to very different thought processes. An active approach goal orientation facilitates creative thinking, an open mind, and personal growth. In contrast, a reactive, avoidance-oriented mindset is associated with narrow-minded thinking and mental rigidity. Now, that is not always a bad thing. When people are focused on trying to avoid a bad outcome, they may become more vigilant and attentive to detail, more systematic in their thinking, and more careful and accurate in their responses.

> However, a growing body of empirical research portrays a less rosy picture of avoidance motivation. First, avoidance motivation has negative implications for performance on tasks that require flexible cognition, mental manipulation, and holistic thinking (e.g., creative tasks) .... Second, the negative consequences of avoidance motivation reach far beyond performance on specific types of tasks, as avoidance regulation has been shown to deplete energy, induce negative affect, decrease subjective well-being, and undermine performance in the long run .... In short, avoidance regulation appears to be designed for surviving rather than thriving; it can help people avoid negative psychological experiences that could be harmful, but it cannot yield the type of positive psychological experiences that are needed for one to develop to one's full capacity. (Roskes et al., 2014, pp. 133–134)

As explained in Chapter 4 (Figure 4.4), the emotional implications of these contrasting ways of thinking are also very different. Indeed, the amplifying power of an active approach orientation is largely a result of its emotional content. Positive emotions like satisfaction and pride are commonplace when goals are pursued in a proactive, approach-oriented way because it is apparent that successes flow, in large part, from your own initiatives. Of course, that also means taking personal responsibility for poor performance, but since those with an active approach orientation generally see "failure" as a temporary setback rather than as evidence of some personal defect, negative emotions tend to be transient. In contrast, those who pursue goals with an avoidance orientation tend to experience chronic anxiety and little joy in life. Positive outcomes are more a temporary relief than a source of enduring happiness ("Whew, I dodged another bullet").

You might be wondering (as we did), if the emotional lives of those with an active approach orientation are so much more favorable, why do so many people cling to avoidance motivational habits? At a species level, the answer appears to be simple: nature's "better safe than sorry" principle was a top priority in evolution (i.e., although well-being is important, survival is paramount) (Damasio, 2003). As a result, "painful" emotions like fear and sadness generally have more immediacy in terms of how we allocate and focus our attention (Frijda, 1988). Yet, while negative emotions help ensure our biological and social survival, *it is the mind-opening power of positive emotions that serves as the primary catalyst for heightened creativity, problem solving, and well-being* (Fredrickson, 2009; Halvorson & Higgins, 2013).

What this means is that, while it may be relatively easy to maintain an active approach orientation to goal pursuit in routine, familiar situations, that mindset can be hard to sustain in circumstances that are outside our "comfort zone." This is especially likely to be true for those who are dispositionally wary of change or who have a history of emotional learning that has taught them that it is "safer" to react to others' initiatives. For example, all it takes is a few experiences with social rejection and exclusion to learn that "putting yourself out there" can create significant vulnerabilities (imagine keeping a great idea to yourself because you are apprehensive about how others will react to you). It is also easy to become passive and avoidant if your tendency is to get stuck in a mental soup of worry and uncertainty whenever you think about moving forward toward challenging goals.

An active approach orientation also requires effort and persistence (i.e., energy) and an equipoised deployment of available energy resources. Optimal functioning is therefore difficult to sustain for those who are chronically fatigued or overwhelmed with responsibilities. There are also those who have learned to associate inaction with physical comfort and low psychological stress (note that we are trying hard to avoid the term "lazy" since not taking action is often a motivational choice!). For example, children with indifferent or overly permissive parents may learn that that they can stall or whine their way out of physically demanding chores without suffering any negative consequences. Similarly, workers who are not held accountable by their supervisors may learn that minimal effort often has positive consequences (such as being able to deflect uninteresting work to others). Conversely, those who have learned the opposite lesson – namely, that good things happen to those who participate and contribute – are more likely to develop a habit of responding with constructive action when a demanding task or challenging opportunity presents itself ("let's do this thing"). Such habits can have profound long-term consequences:

> Over the last several decades, classroom engagement, which refers to students' constructive, enthusiastic, cognitively focused participation in learning activities, has been established as an anchor central to students' academic experience and performance …. This kind of engagement, which is considered a key marker of academic motivation … seems to serve both as a gateway to learning and as a protective factor against negative academic outcomes all across students' educational careers. (E. Skinner et al., 2016, pp. 2100–2101)

An active approach orientation is also more natural for those whose life experiences have exposed them to a wide variety of activities and opportunities. The odds of finding new interests and cultivating new relationships can be significantly enhanced by adopting an "explorer" orientation in our daily lives. This is a major responsibility of parents and teachers, many of whom may not realize how easily the natural curiosity of a young child can succumb to the habits of a lifestyle dominated by externally imposed routines and passive goal pursuits.

> Children are born with boundless curiosity. In the beginning, infants get excited by brightly colored objects, slight changes in the sound of their mother's voice, and anything within their small field of vision …. As their senses become more developed with age, their wonder and excitement expands, and they venture out a bit further. Every cupboard and drawer hides a mystery worthy of investigation …. But something happens to this innocent and courageous exploration. Society gets in the way. We are given an endless series of rules and obligations that keeps our curiosity in check …. Instead of learning about history, science, and great literature, we are taught how to do well on standardized tests …. Rather than being encouraged to learn about ourselves and our interests, we are more often taught how to make decisions about what to do with our lives as early as possible so we won't waste time achieving our goals. (Kashdan, 2009, pp. 7–8)

In sum, an active approach goal orientation will help you make the most of your capacity for self-direction. This mindset promotes engagement with a wide variety of social, cultural, educational, and vocational opportunities while also creating the motivational foundation for continuous self-improvement and feelings of life meaning. When you amplify your goal seeking in this way, you take control of your life rather than passively letting others dictate your options and opportunities.

Decades of research provide strong support for the critical role that an active approach goal orientation plays in optimal functioning. Notably, this work has been conducted within the context of many different motivation theories. Of particular interest for the TSP Theory of Motivation and Optimal Functioning is Winell's (1987/2019) distinction between a *coping* (reactive, avoidant, stability-maintaining) orientation and a *thriving* (active, positive, improvement-seeking) orientation. Winell's research, which was inspired by the Living Systems Framework, emphasizes the fact that, although coping responses can help us "get it together" when our lives are disrupted, long-term benefits come to those whose approach to life challenges and opportunities is to think more like a pilot than a passenger. Sternberg and Spear-Swerling (1998) refer to this process of taking control of your life voyage as "personal navigation," or PN. In doing so, they highlight the importance of equipoise in effective navigation, much as we did in Chapter 4 with our sailing metaphor:

> We believe that navigation is an apt metaphor for what people actually need to do in order to gain, maintain, and, at times, reestablish control over their lives …. PN involves finding a direction in life; maintaining this direction when appropriate and changing it when appropriate; moving in the direction at a velocity that is appropriate for the circumstances; using navigational aids in order to maintain the desired direction; and overcoming the obstacles that inevitably present themselves in any voyage …. These are the things that, for many people, give meaning to their lives. (pp. 221–222, 241)

Several other motivation theories – including some of the most impactful lines of inquiry in this field over the past fifty years – have emphasized the benefits of an active approach orientation that guides goal pursuit in an equipoised way. For example, McClelland's (1985) research on achievement motivation has consistently revealed that outcomes are more favorable for those focused on a *motive for success* versus those oriented toward a *motive to avoid failure*. Kuhl and Beckmann's (1994) work comparing *action* and *state* goal orientations also provides compelling evidence of the power of an active approach orientation to problem solving. Whereas action-oriented people under stress maintain an outward focus that targets possible solutions ("What are my alternatives?"), state-oriented individuals tend to turn inward and adopt a more passive stance ("I don't like feeling this way").

Dweck's (1986) well-researched contrast between *helpless* and *mastery* goal orientations further illustrates the link between active approach thinking and optimal functioning. Whereas those with a mastery orientation generally believe their capabilities are malleable (i.e., they can get better at most anything they put their mind to), those with a helpless orientation don't see much benefit to hard work. Indeed, they tend to avoid challenges that might yield learning and self-improvement for fear that such efforts will simply reveal inherent weaknesses that can't be changed ("Why bother, I'm no good at math"; "I've tried dieting, but nothing works for me").

In recent years Dweck and her colleagues (Dweck, 2006, 2017; Rattan et al., 2015) have elaborated on this distinction by comparing a generative motivational orientation she calls a *growth mindset* with the more motivationally limiting alternative known as a *fixed mindset*. Those with a fixed mindset tend to give up "when the going gets tough." Even worse, they tend to ignore or reject constructive criticism and feel threatened by others' successes. Such thinking further strengthens the durability of their belief that "I'm stuck with the way things are," along with associated feelings of helplessness and depression (Miu & Yeager, 2015). In contrast, those with a growth mindset are more likely to embrace a challenge and "give it their best shot," because effort, patience, and persistence are believed to reliably result in desired self-improvement (Yeager & Dweck, 2012). That makes learning "cool" and failure "no big deal." In addition, rather than taking negative feedback personally (which is perhaps an understandable response when you think someone is criticizing an unalterable part of who you are), growth-oriented individuals appreciate having information that might help them improve. One consequence of this mindset is that, rather than seeing the world through a competitive, social comparison lens, they are more likely to be inspired by the successes of others ("If they can do it, then so can I!").

The common theme in all of these theories is the notion that, when people think about the uncertainties and challenges of the future as something positive to be embraced rather than something negative to be feared (and avoided!), they are more likely to actively explore and learn from their environments. That in turn tends to produce not only actual improvement but also feelings of empowerment and satisfaction likely to fuel further progress toward optimal functioning. In contrast, those who go through life feeling like there is little to gain and much to lose will be motivated to "play defense," focusing first and foremost on stability maintenance (Halvorson & Higgins, 2013). Yet, when we look at how humans are naturally designed and what makes them successful, it is clear that "the best defense is a good offense."

Personal Optimism: Amplifying Motivation through Confident Self-Assurance

> Believe you can and you're halfway there.
> — US president Theodore Roosevelt

Recall that personal agency beliefs are thoughts that connect motivational headquarters with the rest of the person-system ("Do I have the capabilities and environmental supports necessary for successful pursuit of this goal?"). When the message from your PABs is "all systems are go," that can significantly amplify motivation by encouraging active goal pursuit. It can also further strengthen the inclination to seek out and explore opportunities and challenges (thus fueling the active approach amplifier). Conversely, PABs can quickly "put on the brakes" if fundamental doubts arise about personal capabilities or environmental resources.

Before reviewing the outpouring of evidence documenting the role of strong capability beliefs in optimal functioning, we will first summarize what the notion of *personal optimism* means in the context of our TSP framework. While the phrase *capability belief* is applicable to a particular goal or set of related goals (e.g., "I believe I can do this job"), the term *optimism* suggests more of a disposition or habit to "accentuate the positive" when sizing up what you might be capable of doing. That is why we have been using the metaphor of a home page when characterizing the motivational impact of PAB patterns (see Figure 4.6 in Chapter 4). Because PABs and emotions operate in tandem as motivational advisors, positive thoughts about what you can accomplish in the future (with appropriate effort and persistence) naturally cultivate a mindset infused with positive emotions. Those emotions (e.g., interest, excitement, and pride) then become a catalyst for upward spirals of creative thought and effective problem solving (Fredrickson, 2003, 2009). That is how motivation and skill development can synergistically push each other to accomplishments far beyond what you initially thought you would be capable of achieving.

It is important to emphasize that "accentuating the positive" does *not* mean blindly thinking (or saying to yourself) "I can do anything I set out to accomplish!" An overgeneralized, Pollyannaish belief like this is likely to backfire (i.e., make people feel *less* capable) because it obviously cannot be completely true, and thus any such belief will increasingly feel inauthentic and discouraging. So, for us, personal optimism is more of a "persistent bias," much like the concept of an active approach goal orientation. It means that, within the boundaries of what is realistic, with some possible outcomes being negative and others being positive, we would generally expect outcomes toward the more positive end of the continuum, yet below the level of mere "wishful thinking" (e.g., "the rejection rate for that elite scientific journal is over 95 percent, but I'll bet I can get this article accepted in one of these other Tier 1 journals if I keep trying").

While there is a vigorous debate in the scientific literature over whether a bias toward positive self-perceptions is healthy and productive (Taylor & Brown, 1994), we are convinced that, if manifested in an equipoised way that balances *realism about current circumstances* with *optimism about future possibilities*, having a bias toward optimistic capability beliefs is far more likely to serve as an amplifier of motivational patterns than as a source of danger or foolishness. While it is generally unwise to distort the facts about yourself as they currently exist, future outcomes are not "facts." There is a big difference between believing you can do something (now) that you can't, and believing that *in the future*, given appropriate investments of time and energy, you could do it (e.g., "I've never done that before but I'm sure I can learn").

Our cybernetic model, which shows how feedback information about current outcomes is integrated with feedforward information about anticipated future outcomes, provides a straightforward way of understanding how to combine optimism and realism in an optimal manner (see Figure 3.3 in Chapter 3). For the inputs into motivational headquarters labeled "feedforward," an optimistic bias is almost always better, assuming that this bias operates within equipoised boundaries (i.e., in the range of feasible possibilities).

In contrast, for the inputs labeled "feedback," accuracy is the key. Indeed, except in rare circumstances (e.g., persistently horrific conditions), the guiding principle is "the more accurate the better" as long as equipoise is not lost in the process. That may mean dealing with negative feedback in manageable "chunks" – perhaps starting with the highest priority issue – rather than all at once (so that it does not become emotionally overwhelming). Yet, it is generally not helpful to "sugar coat" feedback when limitations in fact exist (assuming that you are an appropriate person to provide such feedback).

Accuracy also entails making sure that feedback is not overgeneralized beyond the specific circumstances in which failure occurred (e.g., "Evidently I'm not as good at this sort of thing as I thought" vs. "I can't do anything right"). As Leary (2004) explains, many psychological problems result from perceptions that are either overly positive or overly negative distortions of the actual situation or circumstance (e.g., being blind to areas where improvement is needed; obsessing over minor flaws or vulnerabilities).

To further clarify the conditions under which motivational amplification is likely to occur, we have added the modifier "personal" to the concept of optimism. This is important because there is little evidence to support the notion that optimism in general is associated with optimal functioning, either in terms of performance accomplishments or overall well-being (Bandura, 1997; Seligman, 1991). That is why it is so important to understand motivation in terms of *personal agency*. An optimistic world view reflects positive expectations about the outcomes that people in general may experience, but it has little to do with your own specific goal pursuits. What motivates people is when they think about a desired outcome and they can see themselves attaining it *through their own actions* (either alone or as part of a broader group process within which they see themselves making significant contributions). That is the key to getting your positive emotions flowing and inspiring your thinking.

In sum, what makes personal optimism an amplifying force is having positive, yet realistic expectations about the results your actions may be able to produce. It is this coupling of encouraging feedforward (expectancy) information and accurate feedback information that makes it possible for people to ensure that the challenges they seek out are motivationally optimal (i.e., at just the right level for an individual's experience and circumstances).

Now, let's return to that "outpouring" of theory and research on the topic of capability beliefs that we mentioned earlier, which collectively points to the benefits of amplifying this facet of motivation as a pathway to optimal functioning. Where do we start?! Even if you have only followed popularized versions of this body of work, you have probably encountered several of the "giants" who have made this one of the most dynamic and intriguing areas of scientific inquiry during the past 40+ years. Rotter (1966) was among the first to kick things off with his simple but powerful distinction between an *internal* versus *external locus of control*. People with a predominantly internal locus of control believe that desired outcomes result primarily from their own actions – as opposed to the actions of powerful others, or even worse, as a result of chance factors (i.e., when no one is in control).

In 1975 Seligman published his enormously influential book on *learned helplessness*, which summarized a research program that established the critical role that personal control expectancies play in motivation, even in animals. The practical value of this approach became even more apparent when he and his colleagues expanded the learned helplessness model to encompass thinking habits – especially those reflecting *causal attributions* (Weiner, 1986) – that tend to trigger and sustain feelings of helplessness (Abramson et al., 1978). Later, Seligman (1991) expanded the scope of his theory to focus more on the positive end of the PAB continuum, using the phrase *learned optimism* to characterize the processes associated with the development of positive expectations about personal control.

In 1977 Bandura published one of the most widely cited journal articles in the history of psychology on the topic of *self-efficacy*, which subsequently led to many hundreds of studies organized around this concept. Bandura's work was a much needed antidote to the tendency to look at capability beliefs only in terms of (over)generalized personality traits (like "self-esteem"). As explained in Chapter 4, it is important to operationally define capability beliefs in tandem with the personal goals they are advising. Those goals can of course be at many different levels of a person's network of goals and subgoals (as shown in Figure 3.1 in Chapter 3). The concept of self-efficacy has been particularly useful for scenarios in which the relevant goals are at a very context-specific level (e.g., "I believe I can make this free throw" or "I am confident I can sell this product"). Yet Bandura's approach has also helped motivation scholars understand that even when higher level goals are involved, it is important to define capability beliefs in ways that are dynamic and context-sensitive.

Another "big idea" that incorporated concepts related to capability beliefs was the notion of *intrinsic* versus *extrinsic motivation* (see Chapter 3), which Deci and Ryan later developed into a broader theory of *self-determination* (Deci, 1980; Deci & Ryan, 1980). Their approach was unique because it viewed personal agency beliefs in the context of basic human needs for autonomy, competence, and relatedness. Other influential theories in this domain proposed related concepts such as *effectance motivation* (Harter, 1978; R. White, 1959), *personal causation* (deCharms, 1968), *perceived competence* (Weisz & Stipek, 1982), *self-worth* (Covington, 1992), and *dispositional optimism* (Scheier & Carver, 2018).

What was implied in many of these theories, but not always made explicit, was the fact that beliefs about personal competence and control necessarily rest as much on context beliefs as on capability beliefs. In our TSP Theory of Motivation and Optimal Functioning, this partnership between self- and environment-focused PABs is not only highlighted, it is a featured part of our thinking. We turn next to the question of how to amplify the context belief element of this PAB partnership.

Mindful Tenacity: Amplifying Motivation through Creative Persistence

> When we tackle obstacles, we find hidden reserves of courage and resilience we did not know we had.
>
> – Indian president A. P. J. Abdul Kalam

The compelling motivational messages flowing from an active approach goal orientation and a genuine sense of personal optimism are necessary but not sufficient to maintain an overall thriving pattern. To ensure that functioning is optimal, there must also be a "secure connection" between motivational headquarters and the external environment. If that connection is weak we can "lose touch" with what is really going on around us and fail to see possibilities and pathways that will lead to goal progress.

What this means in concrete terms is that, just as we saw with capability beliefs, context beliefs have the greatest positive impact when they are grounded in reality but generally upbeat about the future. That makes it possible to feel discouraged or frustrated about the obstacles you are facing now, yet still maintain a high level of motivation as you think about how to overcome those obstacles. The key is to focus on future options and opportunities rather than assume that the conditions currently inhibiting or thwarting goal progress cannot be changed (Lopez, 2013; Snyder, 1994). Motivation is amplified when you maintain a fundamental belief that at least some parts of the environment are likely to be supportive of the goals you hope to achieve, and you use that as a starting point for making thoughtful, equipoised distinctions between what is possible and what is impossible. The challenge is to find the "pockets of responsiveness" that are within most environments (e.g., who can you trust and what pathways for goal progress are available to you).

This contrast between perceived obstacles and perceived opportunities gets to the heart of what it takes to amplify context beliefs – a process that we summarize using the phrase *mindful tenacity*. We used the concept of tenacity earlier in our classifications of PAB patterns (see Chapter 4, Figure 4.6), with the "T" (Tenacious) pattern being associated with contexts that are moderately or inconsistently responsive (as opposed to being consistently responsive or consistently unresponsive). When you think of the environment in this way, you are primed to "see things as they really are" when it comes to potential obstacles to progress. Recognizing *both* opportunities and obstacles makes it possible to move forward without losing faith that you will ultimately be able to find ways to overcome current obstacles (other than those that really are "show stoppers"). That ability to see both the "half empty" and "half full" qualities of the environment, and then to use that information in an equipoised way to guide goal striving, is the essence of mindful tenacity (Carlson, 2013; Ntoumanis & Sedikides, 2018).

In contrast, when equipoise is lost, people can give up prematurely or persist in ways that are foolishly misguided (what one might call "mindless tenacity"). Indeed, there is growing evidence that motivational patterns dominated by unwavering effort and persistence in the face of obstacles can result in motivational and even biological damage (Bennett et al., 2004). Yet, perhaps the greatest vulnerability from a mental health perspective is when people are overwhelmed by the challenges in their lives and are no longer motivated to persist toward meaningful personal goals (Zainal & Newman, 2019).

As we saw earlier with our active approach and personal optimism amplifiers, there are powerful motivational benefits that naturally flow from a mindful tenacity pattern of goal seeking, with positive emotions again playing a catalytic role. Consider, for example, the different ways that people respond to a hostile working environment, such as a boss who constantly humiliates you in front of others. If you experienced this sort of treatment, would you tend to feel resignation or some other "shutting down" feeling? Would you be fuming inside and yet feel helplessly over-powered by the barriers standing between you and a resolution (e.g., the perceived risks of speaking out, or the difficulty of finding a new job)? Or perhaps your anger would lead you to strike out in "thoughtless" (as opposed to mindful) ways, ignoring others' advice and failing to consider the consequences of your actions?

There is a more constructive way to deal with this kind of challenge, one that naturally flows from mindful tenacity and the positive emotions associated with this way of "framing the problem." Imagine feeling resolute about what you have experienced ("I don't have to put up with this"), hopeful that things could get better with the right strategy ("I just need to figure out the best way to make it stop"), and confident that you could find allies (aka "pockets of responsiveness") to help you fight back. That is the "high-hope" mindset (Lopez, 2013; Snyder, 1994) that can lead to creative problem solving and courageous actions. Constructive responses might include, for example, asking for a private meeting to make your boss aware of your feelings, seeking help from a high-status colleague who can speak to your boss (or perhaps your boss's boss) on your behalf, or filing a formal complaint with someone in your HR department who has a strong reputation for effective advocacy.

Of course, there is no guarantee that being resolute and tenacious will lead to favorable outcomes in circumstances like this. Sometimes it is indeed better to "accept reality" and move on to a more responsive environment ("I really just need to get out of this place"). That is part of what it means to be "mindful." Yet, for challenges where escape is not your only or best option, seeking a resolution from an active approach mindset infused with personal optimism and mindful tenacity is the pathway that will give you the best chance to succeed (assuming that you proceed with emotional wisdom, as we will explain shortly). Otherwise you are unlikely to have the amplified level of motivation needed to persevere and endure when, inevitably, the going gets rough.

Earlier in this book we explained our fondness for golf-related examples by noting that golf is often seen as a metaphor for life. We embark on a journey that has many phases and challenges (analogous to the eighteen different holes in a round of golf), with our successes determined as much by the mental approach we take as by the skills we bring to each challenge. And in both the game of life and the game of golf, the approach to environmental obstacles that is clearly the most effective over the long haul is mindful tenacity. Imagine, for example, hitting a golf shot into a sand trap or into the woods. Many golfers are so demotivated by these hazards that they essentially give up before they even get to their ball. Instead of feeling determined and upbeat about the good outcomes that might still be possible, they halfheartedly swipe at the ball and hit another poor shot. That feedback confirms their expectations, thus strengthening their "doom and gloom" PAB mindset for circumstances involving adversity.

Now contrast that way of thinking with the mindful tenacity of professional golfer Chip Beck, whose mantra when he hits a wayward shot is to say "You gotta' love it!" (Rotella, 1995). That is his way of ensuring that, instead of feeling resignation, or helplessness, or anger – emotions that can threaten equipoise for the entire round – he will look at the challenge as an enjoyable test of his resourcefulness. The positive emotions flowing from that mental approach in turn help inspire the golfer's curiosity and creative thought. And, as many professional athletes can attest, those emotions are often highly contagious. Indeed, mindful tenacity can be an incredibly powerful motivational resource in groups as diverse as sports teams, political activists, and cancer survivors.

It is important to note that, although maintaining some level of trust in the opportunities and resources available to you is a critical element in all motivational patterns, it is particularly important in circumstances that are relatively new or unusual (e.g., novel learning situations or contexts involving unexpected events, like a medical emergency). Generally, there isn't much need to be especially mindful or tenacious in circumstances that are routine and habitual. Yet, when a new challenge or unexpected aberration arises, you can't just rely on your past experiences and existing habits. You will need guidance and support from knowledgeable others (e.g., technical experts, wise elders, or others who have encountered similar challenges). You will also need to attend more carefully to relevant information (feedback) and be more imaginative about possible solutions and pathways to goal attainment (feedforward). Using Haidt's (2006) metaphor, adaptation to these kinds of situations requires an active rider to help ensure your mindfulness and tenacity.

Earlier we cited some of the scholarly giants who made the scientific study of personal agency beliefs one of the hottest topics in psychology during the past fifty years. In many cases they offered theories that implicated not only capability beliefs but also context beliefs. For example, the concept of learned helplessness focuses on beliefs about environmental contingencies, with helplessness resulting when the individual anticipates that "If I try, nothing good will happen."

Some of the more notable scientific enterprises influencing our thinking about context beliefs include research on *trust* (Barefoot et al., 1998; Jones & George, 1998; Luthans & Avolio, 2003; Simpson, 2007; Van Lange, 2015; Zand, 1972), *reactance* (Brehm, 1972), *hope* (Lopez, 2013; Snyder, 1994), and *flexibly tenacious goal striving* (Gollwitzer et al., 2008; Legrand et al., 2017). We have been particularly influenced by Snyder's concept of *pathway thinking*, which connotes not only a positive outlook on future possibilities, but also the creative problem-solving element that is such an essential part of mindful tenacity. In addition, we have (of course!) been influenced by Langer's (1989) catalytic conceptualization of *mindfulness*, which has increasingly focused on what she so compellingly refers to as the "psychology of possibility":

> *knowing what is and knowing what can be are not the same thing* …. The psychology of possibility first requires that we begin with the assumption that we do not know what we can do or become. Rather than starting from the status quo, it argues for a starting point of what we would like to be. From that beginning, we can ask how we might reach that goal or make progress toward it. It's a subtle change in thinking, although not difficult to make once we realize how stuck we are in culture, language, and modes of thought that limit our potential. (Langer, 2009, p. 15)

This prospective way of looking at the world encourages motivation and creativity because it is more consistent with the way we are designed as self-directed living systems capable of mentally exploring and envisioning alternative futures.

Emotional Wisdom: Amplifying Motivation through Attractive Adaptability

I've learned that people will forget what you said, people will forget what you did, but people will never forget how you made them feel.

– author and poet Maya Angelou

As we have seen, emotions play a number of very special roles in human life. They activate personal goals. They energize our motivational systems. They give us a quick read on preferences, opportunities and threats. They regulate thoughts and actions. They help us remember important things. And while negative emotions focus our attention on potentially harmful threats and prepare our bodies for fast action, positive emotions serve as catalysts that unleash our creative potential and capacity to thrive. What an invention!

It is perhaps no surprise that something this powerful can be a source of not only tremendous vitality and profound life meaning, but also devastating pathology and extreme mental disorganization. Consequently, the process of "amplifying" the emotion component of human motivation is more about harnessing this power so as to optimize its impact than simply seeking to increase the amount of it. The image of a powerful elephant being harnessed by a savvy rider who understands and respects the elephant's emotional life is particularly apt for this aspect of motivational thriving. That is why we call this process *emotional wisdom*.

Emotional wisdom is complex because it involves both a self-oriented and a social-oriented set of capabilities, with the former being necessary but not sufficient for effective goal pursuit. The self-oriented part of emotional wisdom requires authentic self-awareness and fluent emotional understanding, as well as the ability to "ratchet up" and "ratchet down" emotions to meet situational demands and opportunities. The social part involves detecting (and catching!) emotions of others and then acting on those emotions in contextually appropriate ways. These four "facets" of emotional wisdom are summarized in Figure 5.3.

Our use of the phrase *attractive adaptability* is intended to summarize how the various themes that collectively constitute emotional wisdom work together to amplify motivation and support optimal functioning. "Adaptability" emphasizes the need to adjust or reconcile emotions as circumstances change, and is thus an essential capability for maintaining

	Self	Social
Perception and understanding	Emotional Self-Awareness	Empathy
Control over actions and emotions	Emotional Self-Regulation	Social-Emotional Competence

Figure 5.3 Four facets of emotional wisdom.

equipoise, especially in situations involving emotional turmoil or emotion-triggering surprises (e.g., experiencing betrayal or humiliation; receiving a scary medical diagnosis). Adaptability requires a rich understanding of what stimuli are "emotionally competent" for you and those you interact with (e.g., "She really pushes my buttons"; "I think he feels threatened by me"). Adaptability also requires self-awareness of the implications of triggered emotions as they ebb and flow (e.g., "I better change the subject before I say something I'll regret later"). Adaptability is thus highly dependent on your sensitivity to ongoing emotional signals, both internal (e.g., your "like-o-meter" responses) and external (e.g., from others' facial expressions, body language, and verbal cues), and on your ability to differentiate among various kinds of emotional experiences.

> Emotion differentiation is a skill that is relevant to a wide range of psychological problems and disorders. Those more adept in constructing granular, precise experiences will be better able to deal with them, no matter their intensity. Those experiencing less granularity in their negative experiences are easily overwhelmed by stress and are susceptible to unhealthy emotion-regulation strategies such as binge drinking and eating, aggression, and self-injurious behavior. Knowing whether someone is experiencing frequent, intense negative affect is insufficient for predicting whether they are going to be healthy and functional. These psychological outcomes depend on whether a person is also effective at differentiating those experiences. Results from psychological experiments suggest that people can be trained to become better at constructing more granular experiences. At the heart of these interventions is the expansion of a person's emotion vocabulary. (Kashdan et al., 2015, p. 14)

Adaptability also requires emotional self-regulation capabilities that are appropriate for the circumstances at hand. Some situations require "up-regulation" relative to your current state – for example, getting yourself focused and ready for a performance situation by visualizing images of goal progress or engaging in rituals that trigger positive emotions. Other situations, such as those involving high levels of animosity or worry, require "down-regulation" strategies such as relaxation, deep breathing, and cognitive reinterpretation. Down-regulation is a particularly challenging aspect of emotional wisdom because the "two-way street" between the brain components controlling our emotion-triggering mechanisms (e.g., the amygdala) and our conscious thought processes (e.g., prefrontal cortex) runs like a super-highway in one direction and a foot path in the other. As LeDoux (1998) explains, it is well known that the connections from the cortical areas to the amygdala are far weaker than the connections from the amygdala to the cortex. This may explain why it is so easy for emotional information to invade our conscious thoughts, but so hard for us to gain conscious control over our emotions. (p. 265)

A useful metaphor for understanding the adaptability aspect of emotional wisdom is the use of the channel and volume settings on a TV remote control to optimize your viewing experience. It is of course not possible to literally control emotional experience in this technically precise way, especially when those experiences are traumatic and irreversible. Yet for most emotions in everyday life it is useful to understand emotional wisdom as a developed ability to intentionally control both the "emotional channel" you are tuned to (e.g., interest vs. anxiety when a new person joins a group that is important to you) and the "volume" (up or down) to the optimal level for that particular situation. Too much emotion, too little emotion, or simply the wrong kind of emotion for the circumstances, and things could go very badly (imagine shouting, or yawning, or giggling while being reprimanded by your boss). In contrast, when your life experiences and observations have helped you understand the optimal channel and volume for a wide variety of different circumstances, and you are skilled at managing these emotional settings, you can consistently act – and interact with others – in an equipoised, emotionally wise manner.

This metaphor can be extended to broad patterns of emotional life, consistent with our concept of thriving as something that transcends specific situations. Recall that, like all motivational processes, emotions operate on a continuous basis. To facilitate optimal functioning, the "preset" emotion channels that are generally on throughout the day should be positive emotions such as interest, affection, and gratitude (i.e., assuming they are contextually appropriate) rather than those associated with chronic stress, such as anxiety, anger, and depression. An important first step in progressing toward this goal is to align daily activities with core personal goals, thus ensuring that goal pursuits are, for the most part, emotionally engaging and meaningful. Understanding the emotionally beneficial consequences of goal–life alignment is therefore an important part of emotional wisdom.

The concept of emotional wisdom also suggests that you possess at least an intuitive understanding of how positive emotions can help you "be at your best." As we have seen, positive emotions facilitate an active approach goal orientation and broaden the range of information, ideas, and actions that people are open to considering, thus facilitating the creative thinking and behavioral flexibility associated with mindful tenacity. In addition, positive emotions facilitate enduring growth in personal and social resources, including motivational and contextual resources such as personal optimism and social support. Through these natural *broaden-and-build* mechanisms (Fredrickson, 2009), emotional wisdom can help you cope with unavoidable stress and improve your health, well-being, and longevity. That is why many "tried-and-true" techniques used by psychotherapists target qualities associated with emotional wisdom, such as emotional self-awareness, understanding the origins and consequences of emotions, and regulation of emotional states (D. Ford & Urban, 1998; Prochaska & Norcross, 2019).

In the context of emotional wisdom, the meaning of "attractive" in the phrase "attractive adaptability" relates to the social consequences of how you manage your emotions and respond to others' emotions. You are much more likely to be viewed by others as responsive, trustworthy, and enjoyable to be around if you can effectively "read" and adapt to the emotional signals people convey (both consciously and nonconsciously). As we will see (in Chapter 6), successful goal pursuit for members of our ultrasocial species is highly dependent on being able to develop and maintain a positive social reputation. People who are insensitive to others' emotions or disinterested in other people's feelings are unattractive to others and highly vulnerable to social rejection ("What a jerk, it's always all about him").

Fortunately, one of the most powerful legacies of our evolutionary forebears is a remarkable capacity for inferring (from emotional, behavioral, and context information) what is going on in another's person's mind (Cacioppo et al., 2006). Humans are by far the best at inferring the thoughts and feelings of others. Of particular importance from a motivational perspective is the ability to size up another person's concerns (i.e., what personal goals are activated or have the potential to be activated) and the emotions and personal agency beliefs associated with those concerns. Even just a glimpse of what is going on in another person's "motivational headquarters" can be enough to promote *shared intentionality* – the interpersonal version of goal alignment and the core dynamic of cooperative goal pursuit (Tomasello, 2009).

What are some of the evolved tools that made "mind reading" so natural for members of our species? We can look at facial expressions and body movements and make quick inferences about the underlying emotions that likely produced a smile or a grimace. We can also ask questions about people's goals, emotions, and personal agency beliefs to test the accuracy of our mind-reading efforts. Even when a conversation isn't feasible, we can look at a person's eyes and body positioning and infer what is capturing their attention. That is because at some point following the primate ape/hominid evolutionary split, hominids evolved white sclera – an enormously useful adaptation that helps us see what people are actually looking at! Of course, people often try to hide their true feelings and intentions (e.g., it is usually harder to figure out the object of someone's attention if they are wearing dark glasses), which is why emotionally wise individuals "focus on what people do, not on what they say."

Another aspect of emotional wisdom that helps make you attractive to others is knowing how to use your motivational mind-reading skills to enhance your social interactions and relationships. It is particularly important to show context-appropriate interest and empathic concern, and to respond to people in ways that indicate you are on the same "emotional wavelength." Such responses often trigger positive emotions in others and cause them to feel an emotional connection with you.

Achieving a high level of social-emotional competence (and therefore social attractiveness) can be challenging because it relies on all of the capabilities associated with adaptability. For example, it is hard to show appropriate sympathy and offer the right kind of help if you don't sense that someone is distressed or understand something about why they are feeling that way. It is also hard to show the kind of personal interest and concern that elicits favorable reactions from others if you are preoccupied with your own emotions. Yet even those who are emotionally adaptable may be seen as "unattractive" if they do not find certain kinds of interactions emotionally engaging (e.g., those outside of a narrow range of interests) or if their social relationship goals are focused mainly on self-enhancement (i.e., they have the capacity for emotional insight but lack social purpose goals). It is hard to like people who don't seem to care about you or respect the things you care about.

The notion of "wisdom" also suggests that experience plays a large role in people's ability to function optimally, especially in social settings. For example, people who are naive when it comes to social manipulation strategies may fall prey to charming individuals with selfish or malicious intentions (Grant, 2013). Because of their lack of experience with adult roles, responsibilities, and cultural expectations, teenagers are (as a group) notoriously deficient in emotional wisdom (M. Ford & Smith, 2011). Indeed, this age group is often seen as uniquely vulnerable because they are susceptible to making unwise decisions in emotionally charged situations that call for self-restraint (e.g., in sexual encounters, parties with alcohol and drug use, or driving with friends). Yet some adolescents are more skilled than others with respect to the building blocks of emotional wisdom, including self-awareness, emotional regulation skills, and empathic concern. These are the young people who are recognized by adults as "maturing quickly" and having the best chance to move successfully into leadership roles (i.e., because they are viewed as being both self-regulated and socially attractive). Conversely, adolescents with limited emotional awareness and emotional regulation skills are more likely to experience adjustment and behavior problems (Silk et al., 2003). Indeed, it has been estimated that between 40 percent and 75 percent of all psychiatric disorders are characterized by problems associated with emotional reactivity and emotional regulation (Gross & Jazaieri, 2014).

Our concept of emotional wisdom may, on the surface, sound rather similar to the popular concept of *emotional intelligence* (aka "EI"). After all, research in that domain has generally focused on the same kinds of phenomena (e.g., Bar-On, 2006; Goleman, 1995; Mayer & Salovey, 1997). Yet the EI concept has been essentially abandoned by most psychological scientists because of a lack of conceptual precision with regard to what EI is and what it is not (Mayer et al., 2008). Ironically, this limitation has overshadowed the essence of what made EI such an exciting concept in the first place. Specifically, the idea of being "emotionally intelligent" pointed to a neglected source of success and resilience – namely, certain elements associated with the thriving with social purpose pattern of motivation and optimal functioning. Yet powerful ideas can quickly fade if they lack clarity and precision. For example, descriptions of EI often highlight personal agency belief concepts like self-confidence and optimism – which, as we have seen, represent a fundamentally different part of motivational headquarters. It is also common for EI descriptions to include qualities associated with an active approach goal orientation (e.g., personal initiative, change orientation). This tendency to "overreach" is also seen in EI descriptions that have expanded to encompass social purpose goals. Although empathic feelings and emotion management skills can facilitate the pursuit of social purpose goals, these are distinct features of human motivational systems.

So, while we were inspired by the efforts of EI researchers and their respect for the power of human emotions, the theoretical giants in this field who had the greatest influence on our thinking about motivational amplification were a diverse group of scholars focused specifically on the composition and motivational functions of emotion patterns. Earlier we noted the foundational role that D. Ford's (1987/2019) Living Systems

Framework played in our thinking about the complexly organized nature of emotion patterns, the different types of emotional content that evolved over time, and the specific functions that emotions play in motivational patterns. Scholars at the forefront of rapidly advancing research on the regulatory functions of emotions further shaped our thinking about the ubiquitous presence and influence of emotions in multilevel biobehavioral and developmental systems (e.g., Gross, 1998, 2015; Thompson, 1991, 2011; Thompson et al., 2008). Ekman (1972) helped us understand how emotions influence behavior outside of consciousness (e.g., through facial expressions linked to triggered emotions), and how the evolved role of emotions can be clarified by looking at emotional response patterns. Bargh's (2017) revealing research on the automaticity of emotional functioning further advanced our thinking about how much of our emotional life takes place at a nonconscious level. Yet, at the same time Haidt (2006) and other emotion scholars (e.g., Algoe & Haidt, 2009; Cowen et al., 2019) opened our thinking to the possibility that standard emotion taxonomies may be deficient in their consideration of emotions that uplift the human spirit, both individually and collectively.

In addition to these eminent psychologists, several neuroscientists had a significant impact on our understanding of emotions and how they contribute to optimal functioning. LeDoux's (1998, 2002) work on the "emotional brain" provided us with new insights about the mechanisms through which emotions are triggered and then embedded in our memories through emotional learning. De Waal's (2009) theorizing about the evolutionary origins and neural mechanisms involved in empathy was particularly helpful in facilitating our understanding of the interpersonal aspects of emotional wisdom.

An outpouring of recent work on social-emotional learning (SEL) has also provided compelling ideas and evidence related to emotional wisdom and the impact of emotion-focused learning on the development of social competence (Durlak et al., 2015; Weissberg, 2019; Wentzel, 2019). Evidence-based SEL interventions have demonstrated that, through direct instruction and through changes in school climate and culture, children (and adults!) can "acquire and apply the knowledge, skills, and attitudes necessary to understand and manage emotions, set and achieve positive goals, feel and show empathy for others, establish and maintain positive relationships, and make responsible decisions" (Weissberg, 2019, p. 65).

Yet, the single most powerful influence in our thinking about the role of emotions in motivational systems was Damasio's (1994, 2003) work on the relationship between emotions and feelings and the biological bases for these psychological phenomena. Indeed, understanding the fundamental difference between nonconsciously triggered emotions and the conscious feelings that flow from those emotions (through a "body mapping" process that incorporates associated thoughts and perceptions) is a fruitful starting point not only for understanding emotional wisdom, but for promoting it.

As we will see in the next chapter, the qualities associated with emotional wisdom provided an essential part of the motivational infrastructure required for the evolution of social purpose goals. Indeed, our interest in social purpose became increasingly "amplified" the more we learned about emotional wisdom and all of the other characteristics of motivational patterns most closely associated with optimal functioning. We came to realize that most of the great achievements in human history resulted from a combination of thriving *with* social purpose. Moreover, the individuals capable of sustaining the highest levels of productivity, well-being, and life meaning seemed to be those whose thriving motivational patterns were infused with social purpose.

We concluded that social purpose is as fundamental to human nature – and therefore human motivation – as self-interest. Efforts to motivate self and others that do not respect this fundamental design principle are destined to fall short of expectations.

Thriving with Social Purpose

If you want to lift yourself up, lift up someone else.
> – educator and civil rights activist Booker T. Washington

Self-Assertion, Integration, and Optimal Functioning

In Chapter 3, we explained that humans are naturally designed to seek both self-enhancing outcomes – what Koestler (1967, 1978) calls our *self-assertive* tendency – and other-enhancing outcomes, or what Koestler calls our *integrative* tendency. Agency and communion (Bakan, 1966) are similar concepts that are often used to describe these motivational tendencies. Decades of research on the personality and behavioral factors associated with broad patterns of human competence verify that optimal functioning is closely associated with simultaneous strength in *both* tendencies, and with being able to shift from self-assertion to integration (and vice versa) in an equipoised, context-appropriate way (M. Ford, 1985, 1986a, 1986b; Grant, 2013). Only those who can flexibly move from one motivational orientation to the other as needed, and who have the versatility needed to accomplish both sets of goals, can hope to achieve the highest levels of effectiveness and well-being. That is why emotional wisdom is such an important part of what it takes to maintain optimal functioning. Self-interest must be coupled with self-restraint to ensure success. Loyalty and altruism can be wonderful things, but not if they are naively or foolishly offered to those who would exploit you.

Consistent with these propositions, game theory researchers studying cooperation and competition have demonstrated that optimal results are associated with a strategy favoring cooperation (as a "home page" orientation) that can be adeptly adjusted to a competitive orientation when other players do not cooperate – and then quickly adjusted back to cooperation when forgiveness seems appropriate (a classic example of equipoise in action) (Barclay, 2010). Psychological scientists have converged on the same kind of findings with respect to more general patterns of self-assertive and integrative aspects of human functioning. For example, research on personality traits stereotypically associated with "masculinity" and "femininity" – traits that map closely onto the concepts of self-assertion and integration – has consistently shown that the highest levels of effectiveness and well-being are achieved when *both* sets of traits are cultivated, regardless of gender (Bakan, 1966; Spence & Helmreich, 1978; Wiggins & Holzmuller, 1978). Scholars seeking to identify the qualities associated with effective leadership have reached essentially the same conclusion, as followers are attracted to those who manifest a combination of personal strength (e.g., decisiveness and self-confidence) and social purpose (e.g., integrity and commitment to the common good) (Csikszentmihalyi, 2003; Hougaard & Carter, 2018).

On the other end of the competence spectrum, research on human psychopathology suggests that many diagnostic categories are characterized by major deficits in either self-assertion or integration (or both), or by a failure to balance the two motivational tendencies in an equipoised way. For example, sociopathic disorders are characterized by gross deficiencies in prosocial goals and in the capacity to experience empathy and guilt (Walsh & Wu, 2008). In contrast, "loss of self" is often implicated in serious emotional disorders and in people whose individual identities are chronically suppressed in the service of group goals (Koestler, 1978).

It appears clear that efforts to seek status, dominance, and independence are greatly enhanced, especially in the long run, when combined with respect for others and their personal goals. Similarly, efforts to nurture and help others and to promote justice and teamwork are more successful when social purpose is combined with self-assertive goals and capabilities

(Grant, 2013). It is also evident that we are naturally designed to develop both sets of capabilities and to use those capabilities in an equipoised way. As Nesse (2006) concludes, "Genes that make individuals who are indiscriminately selfish or generous are soon eliminated by natural selection" (p. 209).

Now, you may be wondering: if optimal functioning is associated with high (and equipoised) levels of *both* self-assertion and integration, why do we only include social purpose in our concept of "human motivation at its best"? What about "Thriving with Self-Assertion"? Or perhaps "Thriving with Self-Assertion and Integration"?

Needless to say, we carefully considered these logical possibilities as we designed our TSP Theory of Motivation and Optimal Functioning. Yet, as we examined empirical evidence related to the question of what motivational patterns are associated with the best *developmental* outcomes (aka optimal functioning over long time periods), we kept coming back to three extraordinarily compelling considerations associated with our guiding principle of *survival with well-being*:

1. Social integration is a key factor influencing longevity (Hawkley & Cacioppo, 2010; Holt-Lunstad et al., 2017; Ryff & Singer, 2001). Indeed, "the magnitude of the links between relationships and health is comparable to that for established biomedical and behavioral risk factors of long-standing public health concern such as smoking, high cholesterol, and physical activity" (Schetter, 2017, p. 511). Close relationships help people cope with adversity and stress and fulfill basic needs associated with emotional security, love, and belongingness. They also provide a secure base and resources "that foster exploration, personal growth, and goal strivings, all of which are essential for health and well-being" (Pietromonaco & Collins, 2017, p. 531). It thus seems clear that there are a variety of mechanisms through which TSP motivational patterns, and environments that foster such patterns, can help people lead long, healthy lives.

2. Life meaning is closely associated with the pursuit of social purpose goals. Life meaning can also flow from self-assertive pursuits, but that seems to be more a function of the *process* of goal striving (i.e., thriving). The most reliable formula for experiencing life meaning is when a thriving motivational pattern is infused with integrative social relationship goal content (see Chapter 7 for an extended discussion of TSP and life meaning).

3. As we will explain in some detail in Chapter 6, the evolution of human intelligence – as manifested, for example, by sophisticated mind-reading skills, the capacity for mental time travel, accelerated brain development, and cumulative cultural evolution – was closely associated with the emergence of social purpose goals as a central organizing force in human behavior and development. It appears that social purpose was the catalyst for many aspects of human nature that made it possible for humanity to rise to a dominant position on the planet, ultimately leading to what E. O. Wilson (2012) has described as the "social conquest of earth."

In short, while the benefits of a thriving motivational pattern can be experienced whether people focus on self-enhancing or other-enhancing goal content, the best long-term outcomes for both individuals and groups, at least with respect to survival with well-being, seem to be associated with the adoption of a *thriving with social purpose* home page motivational orientation. TSP is "motivation at its best" because, quite simply, it is the quality of people's functioning that is the most human. Indeed, *TSP is what made us human.*

This conceptualization of motivation and optimal functioning is displayed in Figure 5.4, which builds on the MST graphic by adding the four thriving amplifiers along with an "infusion" of SP goal content.

The elevation of social purpose to a special status within the broad array of personal goals that humans pursue makes sense given how humans evolved. The fundamental mechanism in the evolution of all life forms is natural selection of qualities that are the most adaptive for a species within a range of environmental circumstances. Natural selection is a process through which heritable traits that increase an individual's fitness (with respect to survival and reproduction) become more common, while those that decrease an individual's fitness become less common. Goals of a self-assertive nature evolved largely through *individual selection* (i.e., "survival of the fittest" individuals). Social purpose goals, on the other hand, evolved in large part because of *group selection* (i.e., "survival of the fittest" groups) and *social selection* (i.e., the evolution of social behavior within a group, aka gene–culture coevolution), each of which created survival struggles favoring cooperation, teamwork, and group cohesion. Group selection was a particularly powerful mechanism in human evolution, and accounts for much of what is unique about human life (E. O. Wilson, 2012). Strong individuals can accomplish some pretty impressive things, but they are no match for the sensational things that strong groups can accomplish. For

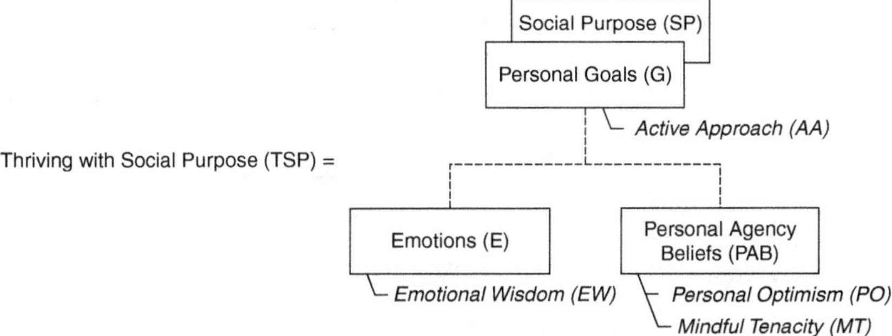

Figure 5.4 *Thriving with Social Purpose:* Formula for "motivation at its (human) best" with an associated diagram.
Note: The elements composing the motivational pattern that is most closely associated with optimal human functioning – Thriving with Social Purpose (TSP) – can be represented using a heuristic formula or diagram that encompasses the amplified motivational components constituting the Thriving pattern of human motivation along with infused Social Purpose goal content.

example, nearly all modern scientific innovations have been produced by collaborative teams (Wuchty et al., 2007).

> *If Social Purpose Goals Are "Personal" Goals, It's All Just*
> *Self-Interest — Right?*

Absolutely not!

> *The essence of social purpose is the idea of seeking to accomplish something that is larger than yourself and of benefit to others.*

Even though the content of social purpose goals is clearly distinct from self-interest, some scholars and philosophers have concluded, based on the fact that social purpose originates in the (goal) thoughts of self-directed individuals, that all altruistic actions can be boiled down to self-interest, and social purpose is just some kind of facade. But that conclusion ignores the ways in which our motivational systems are designed. Saying that we only do good things for others because it makes us feel good puts the motivational cart before the horse, so to speak. *All* successful goal pursuit, whether self-assertive or integrative, feels good "after the fact," especially for approach goals. That is a manifestation of the "well-being" part of the "survival with well-being" design principle that underlies all human functioning – our evolved mechanism for ensuring that we continue to take the steps necessary to progress toward important goals and repeat what made us successful in similar future episodes. And yet, that emotion-fueled *amplifying* process (i.e., feeling good *after* a goal is attained) is not the same as the emotion-*triggering* process that actually causes us to care about other people and want to do things that benefit others.

> If we feel a "warm glow," a pleasurable feeling, at improving the plight of others, doesn't this in fact make our assistance selfish? The problem is that if we call this "selfish," then literally everything becomes selfish, and the word loses its meaning. A truly selfish individual would have no trouble walking away from another in need. (de Waal, 2009, p. 116)

So, when it comes to assessing the authenticity of social purpose, the key question is, what causal mechanisms *preceded* the actions that led us to feel good? Recall that we are designed to do things because our personal goal "leaders" in motivational headquarters direct us to do so. As we have seen, conscious feelings that emerge from goal-directed activity can help sustain that activity, but that is not the triggering mechanism (i.e., that is not why we initiated the activity).

Like all goals, social purpose goals are activated by evolved, hardwired emotions that are triggered by some sort of "emotionally competent stimulus."

For example, most people instinctively want to help, even if only from afar (e.g., through prayer or good wishes), when they see someone in distress (a stimulus that is "emotionally competent" in a wide range of circumstances). Similarly, seeing someone being victimized or treated in an unfair manner often triggers strong emotions, especially when the target is someone you care about.

That is not to say that social purpose goals are only likely to be activated when there is emotional "drama." Far from it! For most people all it takes is a little emotional nudge to elevate helping and responsibility goals to a prominent place. For example, Grant and Hofmann (2011) found that doctors and nurses were more likely to engage in hand washing when signs reminding them to do so emphasized negative consequences to patients. Grant (2008) also found that lifeguards were willing to work longer hours and take more safety-related actions if they read stories about rescues that were performed by other lifeguards. Consistent with the idea that preexisting goal hierarchies are an important factor in what goals get activated by contextual cues, people with strong prosocial personal goals are the ones most likely to respond to emotional nudges focused on those who would benefit from their actions (Grant, 2008, 2019).

For most people, the range of emotionally competent stimuli that are naturally capable of activating social purpose goals is very broad, as might be expected given the diversity of groups and social partners we interact with, and the extensive "playbook" of cultural expectations that we learn throughout our lifetimes. Indeed, absent serious pathology, it is virtually impossible to avoid activating some kind of social purpose goal in almost every social situation you encounter.

That does not necessarily mean that you will always (or even frequently) make social purpose goals a top priority. There are vast individual differences in the goal hierarchies people develop throughout their lives – as evidenced, for example, by the wide range of scores and goal profiles represented among those who have taken the *Assessment of Personal Goals* (https://apg.gmu.edu). Yet, because of the way we are designed, with both self-assertive and integrative tendencies exerting pervasive influence on our thoughts and actions, you can count on social purpose goals being persistently "in play" in your everyday interactions and relationships even though you may often not be aware of their presence.

Of course, not all actions that benefit others are motivated by social purpose. It is certainly possible to identify instances in which such actions are motivated by self-interest (imagine, to take an extreme case, helping someone commit a crime because they have threatened to kill you if you don't). Yet it is just as easy to identify instances in which actions that benefit the self are motivated by social purpose (e.g., seeking career advancement to please a parent or spouse). In short, it is clear that social purpose goals are every bit as fundamental and authentic as the self-enhancing side of human nature (M. Ford, 1985; Koestler, 1978).

Different Types of Social Purpose Goals

To understand the benefits of social purpose goals (hereafter also referred to as SP goals), it is also useful to recall (from our presentation of the Taxonomy of Human Goals in Chapter 3) that there are actually four distinct motivational themes that reflect a concern for social interdependence and the welfare of others – namely, belongingness, social responsibility, equity, and resource provision. Although these goal categories are related to one another both conceptually and empirically (M. Ford & Nichols, 1991), it is commonplace for people to vary in terms of which themes they find the most compelling. The salience of different types of SP goals can also vary considerably across situations (e.g., equity goals are more likely to be activated when social comparison information is highlighted). Moreover, because people are simultaneously members of different groups at different levels, it is natural for people to experience conflicts among their social purpose goals from time to time. For example, you might have competing loyalties to different groups (e.g., your nuclear vs. extended family), or anticipate that helping one person might harm another (e.g., a recognition award for one employee might be perceived by another deserving employee as a snub).

Cultivating, maintaining, and celebrating your identity as a member of a group that has personal significance to you is what *belongingness* is all about. Feeling like you belong to a family or community is a fundamental aspect of being human. Belongingness is also manifested in special "bonding" relationships with parents, children, romantic partners, and close friends. This same motive causes people to identify with and invest substantial time and resources in clubs, sports teams, and online social networks (Hirsch & Clark, 2019). When the net result of all of these relationships and affiliations is a strong sense of group identity and an array of deeply felt emotional attachments, we feel that life is meaningful and fulfilling. Meaningful relationships and the social-emotional resources they provide also seem to help people live longer, healthier lives (Holt-Lunstad et al., 2017; House et al., 1988; Steptoe et al., 2013).

Social responsibility goals help define what it means to be a group member in "good standing." You can't just claim to be a loyal family member; you have to prove it. You can't just say you're somebody's friend; you have to show it. And you can't just declare that you are a contributor to a group; you have to earn that reputation. The way we do these things is by acting in accordance with agreed upon expectations and rules of conduct, thus demonstrating our commitment to the group. Those who fulfill these obligations in a competent and reliable way become accepted and trusted members of the group. Those who do not are rejected and regarded as socially irresponsible. These are the mechanisms through which social responsibility goals can facilitate survival with well-being.

The key to forming a strong group is teamwork, as reflected in an appropriate division of labor (e.g., with each person contributing to the group in some meaningful way) and appropriate sharing of resources (e.g., in accordance with need or effort). When these kinds of expectations are violated, *equity* goals are often activated. People who prioritize equity goals help strengthen the groups of which they are a part by ensuring that fairness is "front and center" as a consideration in how people are treated – for example, by alerting group leaders to patterns of favoritism and discrimination, by advocating for group members who are disadvantaged or who have suffered some sort of injustice, and by punishing cheaters (people who don't play by the rules) and "free riders" (people who don't contribute their fair share).

Equity goals are particularly relevant in social interactions among peers and "teammates" (e.g., co-workers, classmates, and community members), since that is where social comparisons focused on equity make the most sense. Yet, many relationships involve asymmetrical social roles (e.g., parent and child, teacher and student, expert and novice) that are defined by the need for experienced group members to provide less mature or less capable members of the group with material, informational and social-emotional resources. In such relationships *resource provision* goals are frequently activated. Resource provision is also a central theme in successful marriages, close friendships, and business partnerships, each of which links the mutual exchange of resources to strong belongingness goals (as manifested, for example, by high levels of trust and emotional bonding). Although context-specific emotional triggers in a particular situation can motivate people to give material aid or social support in the absence of an existing relationship (as when resources are provided to strangers), humans are designed to be particularly likely to help each other when the relationship itself is an emotion-triggering source of altruistic motivation (Brown & Brown, 2006).

How Social Purpose Contributes to Survival with Well-Being

We have found that understanding the variety of specific outcomes that SP goals are directed toward makes it easier to appreciate how they uniquely contribute to survival with well-being. Where would we be if we didn't care about belonging to the family, community, and work groups that can help nourish and inspire us? What would happen if we no longer felt any sense of duty or obligation to the people that depend on us (and vice versa)? How could we possibly sustain ourselves or accomplish anything meaningful if no one cared about things like cooperation and fairness? And what kind of life would it be if we had no motivation to help one another?

As these profound questions suggest, there are many ways in which social purpose is a life-sustaining force. Research on altruism and social bonding makes it clear that the pursuit of SP goals is good for your health and well-being (Post, 2007). People whose home page motivational orientation keeps them focused on the welfare of others – not all the time or in every situation, but as a "motivational screen" through which decisions that may impact others are naturally filtered – generally have better mental and physical health outcomes, more satisfying lives, and greater emotional stability (Brown et al., 2007; Post, 2005; Ryff & Singer, 2001). Emotions like compassion and love are a powerful source of human vitality, as are PABs associated with feelings of trust and collective optimism.

Conversely, people whose lives are organized around modes of functioning that are highly self-assertive or lacking in equipoise tend to experience less optimal work, health, and relationship outcomes – as evidenced, for example, by individuals who are chronically hostile, selfish, or hypercompetitive (Friedman, 1991; Grant, 2013). And yet, for many of these individuals, the problem is not that they lack social purpose; rather, they are markedly deficient in emotional wisdom. That is why interventions to address transgressive and dysfunctional interpersonal patterns often focus on capabilities related to self-awareness, seeing things from a different (less egocentric) perspective, and regulating self-defeating cognitive and emotional habits (D. Ford & Urban, 1998; Prochaska & Norcross, 2019).

Social purpose is not only a positive life force in its own right; it also appears to expand our awareness and interest in other aspects of human experience that go beyond the self. For example, in a study conducted by a research team at Stanford University contrasting the motivational profiles of highly caring and relatively uncaring youth (M. Ford, 1996), the adolescent exemplars of social purpose were three to five times more likely than their counterparts to endorse goals related to intellectual and task creativity, unity, and understanding. That finding supports the idea that social purpose and thriving are linked phenomena that broaden interests and perspectives beyond the self, consistent with Fredrickson's (2009) broaden-and-build theory of positive emotions. In contrast, adolescents with little investment in SP goals manifested motivational patterns that are rarely associated with optimal functioning, including a self-absorbed, hedonistic pattern; a hypermasculine pattern focused on power and control; and a pragmatic-defensive pattern oriented toward stability maintenance.

It appears that caring for and about others may be part of a larger pattern of seeking to engage life in ways that are rich in meaning.

As we will discuss in greater detail in Chapter 7, the sense that "life is worth living" naturally flows from goal pursuits that are both personally fulfilling and socially worthwhile.

It appears that the outward focus of attention and curiosity manifested by those with strong SP goals promotes an active approach goal orientation that enables imagination and creativity to flourish. When people are naturally inclined to focus not just on themselves but also on the broader impact of their actions for others, their thinking becomes more flexible and inspired. They can grasp more of what is going on around them and appreciate that they are embedded within many different social, ecological, and geopolitical systems. Consistent with that observation, adolescents who routinely engage in prosocial activities tend to do better in their academic and social lives at school (Wentzel, 1993, 1996). In contrast, those who see themselves as the motivational "center of the universe" have little reason to be interested in anything that is not directly related to the self (e.g., "Why should I care? What's in it for me?").

This different way of seeing the world helps explain why those whose thriving motivational patterns are infused with social purpose are more effective as leaders and more likely to be seen as "natural leaders" by others (Csikszentmihalyi, 2003; M. Ford & Smith, 2011; Hougaard & Carter, 2018). By definition, leaders are responsible for promoting the interests and well-being of followers. Although it is easy to imagine self-absorbed leaders who promote their own interests by adopting group goals as a "means to an end," that is not a sustainable formula for creative or inspired leadership. Such leaders are more likely to do the minimum required to maintain the loyalty of followers and to resort to coercive methods of ensuring allegiance.

Fortunately, followers are naturally attuned to evidence of inauthentic social purpose. We have an innate urge to cooperate with and follow the lead of those who are helpful – and who have a reputation for being helpful. We resonate to people who can get things done (thriving) on our behalf (social purpose). But when a leader's motives appear to be self-serving, things can fall apart very quickly. Trust can quickly dissipate, which in turn can reduce followers' motivation to cooperate and to make sacrifices for the group.

In short, adding SP goals to the "motivational equation" for optimal functioning goes beyond the more incremental processes associated with amplification. When a thriving motivational pattern is saturated with a strong sense of social purpose, we experience life differently, with transformative implications for behavior and development. The transformation is analogous to changing a black-and-white photograph into a color photograph. In one respect, what we see is the same in both photographs. Yet it is obvious that there is "something missing" in the black-and-white photograph. In contrast, the color photograph seems more complete and more authentic – just as humans do when they make SP goals a natural priority in their daily lives.

Knowledge and Skills Component of Human Functioning

Motivation is necessary but not sufficient to ensure progress toward the outcomes we desire. In addition, we must have the *knowledge and skills* needed to construct and execute actions that will produce the desired outcomes.

If we start with the premise that all human functions evolved to facilitate the effective pursuit of personal goals, and then further assume that those functions are organized along the lines of the control system model presented in Chapter 3, we can organize the K&S domain of human functioning into categories that reflect the natural design elements associated with those assumptions. The resulting categories are briefly defined in Table 5.1.

Note that each category in Table 5.1 represents the fundamental *nature* of a particular function, not the amplifying processes through which those functions might be optimized (e.g., via goal-striving skills, which are described in the next section). It is also important to note that this is by no means intended to be a complete or definitive list of human functions related to the acquisition and use of knowledge and skills. Rather, we have attempted to define *categories* of K&S functioning that will encompass nearly all of the specific functions that might be enumerated. Such

Table 5.1 *Knowledge and skill (K&S) elements of human functioning*

Specialized K&S processes	Goal representations	Translation of personal goal themes into specific ideas and images capable of guiding planning, action, and evaluation
	Observation	Mental representations of ongoing circumstances of current or potential future goal relevance
	Evaluation	Comparisons between activated goals and observed conditions, expected results, or actual results
	Means–ends thinking	Formulation of strategies/plans designed to facilitate goal progress
	Simulation	Mental rehearsal and validation of strategies/plans expected to facilitate goal progress
	Physical action	Skills enabling implementation of strategies/plans in transaction with the environment (e.g., communication and persuasion skills; social-emotional signaling skills; specialized motor and movement skills)
Infrastructure K&S processes (i.e., used by each specialized process)	Memory	Mental retrieval/reconstruction of previously encountered information of current or potential future goal relevance
	Attention allocation	Selective allocation of energy resources to internal and external sources of goal-relevant information (e.g., thoughts, feelings, perceptions)
	Emotion regulation	Capabilities that enable emotions to carry out their regulatory functions and maintain equipoised functioning (i.e., down-regulation and up-regulation of emotions and feelings as needed for effective goal pursuit)

functions can of course be categorized in a variety of different ways depending on what attributes are emphasized. Our selection of categories was guided by the basic parameters of the control system model and by the functional categories used in the Living Systems Framework (D. Ford, 1987/2019).

Infrastructure Processes Supporting the Specialized K&S Elements
of Human Functioning

Just as motivational headquarters requires a power source to fuel its activities, all K&S processes require *energy* to function. The foundational energy source is the Biology component of human functioning (with support from the environment, e.g., via eating, drinking, and interacting with life-supporting microorganisms). Some aspects of energy production and use are governed by homeostatic mechanisms directed by primordial goals (e.g., blood circulation and temperature regulation are largely automatic, self-regulated processes). However, energy is also produced and allocated in response to directives from motivational headquarters. For example, emotions have a major influence on energy use because, as noted in Chapter 4, each emotion pattern includes a biological component designed to prepare the body for goal-appropriate action (e.g., "fight or flight").

All K&S processes also require information to function. Information flows to K&S processes internally from the motivation and biology components of human functioning and externally from the environment. In addition, *memory* and memory retrieval processes provide an "infrastructure" mechanism for channeling relevant information from our past experiences to K&S processes responsible for facilitating goal pursuit in the present.

Another important K&S infrastructure process is the ability to allocate energy selectively to support the information processing needed to effectively pursue personal goals. That is the primary function of *attention.* Attention can be focused – for varying time intervals – outward, on the environment, or inward, on the self. Attention is an energizing mechanism for bringing mental processes that normally function outside consciousness into awareness. Whether that is good or bad depends on how the attentional energy is allocated and utilized.

Consistent with the "selective allocation of energy" theme, we also need another kind of K&S infrastructure process to ensure that the energy produced by triggered emotions is properly regulated. *Emotion-regulation skills* – are needed to effectively act on the impulses and guidance emanating from our emotions and associated feelings, thus helping us to function with "emotional wisdom" (Gross, 1998, 2015). Sometimes that means finding the energy to overcome apathy, lethargy, or conditions that reduce the impact of emotions needed to energize goal pursuit (e.g., due to ambiguity or distractions). That is when skills for "up-regulating" emotions come into play. At other times the opposite problem must be addressed, namely, how to keep intense emotions in check. Skills for "down-regulating" emotions are particularly important when, for example, adaptive fear turns into panic, or productive anger turns into rage. It is one thing to feel the attention-focusing impact of strong emotions; it is quite another to experience the disorganizing effects of emotional flooding.

Specialized K&S Elements of Human Functioning

Following the control system model of goal pursuit (see Figure 3.3 in Chapter 3), there are a variety of specialized K&S processes needed to translate the directives from motivational headquarters into actions designed to carry out those instructions. First, *goal representation* skills are needed to transform the directive thoughts – which may be unfocused or lacking in detail – into concrete, actionable representations of desired (or undesired) outcomes. As we saw in Chapter 3, these skills can help the leader's goal thoughts become much more impactful (Locke & Latham, 1984, 2019). For example, you might make New Year's resolutions to save money or lose weight that need to be specified in quantitative, action-oriented terms before you can make any progress toward those goals. Or, at a broader level, you might feel a strong need to achieve more balance in your life but have no idea how to make that happen until you assess in some detail how you allocate your time, how your time investments align with your core personal goals, and what kinds of activities seem to yield the greatest "return on investment" with respect to well-being and life meaning.

Second, *observation* skills are needed to monitor where things stand with respect to activated goals (and conditions in general) and to actively seek out information that may facilitate or constrain goal progress. Observations of current circumstances (from all senses, not just from visual perceptions) are a critical part of the process of "framing" or "sizing up" how to approach a challenge or opportunity. Information about current circumstances is also an essential prerequisite for evaluating goal progress. For example, ample research has shown that, without ongoing feedback, efforts to clarify goal representations will have little impact on what is actually achieved (Erez, 1977; Locke & Latham, 1984). In addition, observing what others do is an important mechanism for learning what actions are likely to produce certain kinds of results and how to competently execute those actions (Bandura, 1986).

Cognitive *evaluation* is another K&S function that is naturally involved in every episode of goal-directed activity. Evaluation skills work in collaboration with emotions to assess opportunities, threats, and goal progress. Earlier we used Haidt's "like-o-meter" metaphor to describe how emotions provide an "instant appraisal" of objects, persons, and events of potential relevance to our personal goals (which may explain why the simple "Like" function on social media sites is so popular). Cognitive evaluation skills supplement and enrich those initial reactions. Indeed, both cognitive evaluation (the K&S process) and emotional evaluation (the like-o-meter process) are so natural and automatic that they are almost impossible to "turn off." We evaluate what we see and hear and smell and touch and draw conclusions based on our emotional responses and evaluative thoughts ("This isn't quite what I was looking for"). We also evaluate memories of what we have observed and experienced in the past, which can then help guide goal seeking in the present ("Remember how much we enjoyed that restaurant across town?"). In addition, evaluation skills provide information that can be used to formulate or update capability and context beliefs ("The more I think about it, the more it seems like that job would be a better fit for my skills").

Observation skills provide information about where you are (Point A); goal representation skills help clarify where you want to go (Point B); and evaluation skills help reveal the "distance" between those two points. But none of that will help much if you do not have good ideas about how to actually get from Point A to Point B. In simple, routine situations, like getting dressed in the morning or driving home from work, the required *means–ends thinking* skills may be rudimentary (e.g., simply remembering what has worked for you in the past). But in complex or highly dynamic situations the versatility of your means–ends thinking skills may be the key to success or failure (Spivack et al., 1976). Imagine, for example, planning a wedding or preparing a game plan for a championship football game. The ultimate goal is easy to conceptualize, but there are so many steps to get there, and so many things that could go wrong! That is why wedding dates are typically set many months in advance, and why football coaches spend countless hours watching video of previous games.

Once an action plan has been conceptualized, the next step is to conduct mental *simulations* of those plans to get a better idea of whether they will actually work as intended. We can also compare multiple simulations conducted by different people or with different assumptions. Recall our earlier discussion (in Chapter 2) of the evolution of mental time travel and how human development soared after we gained this remarkable capability.

The idea that we naturally (and usually very rapidly) play out scenarios in our minds to predict results before taking action is consistent with D. Ford's (1987/2019) proposition that there are three types of goal-directed activity: *instrumental* episodes (in which we actually take steps to progress toward a goal), *observational* episodes (in which we mentally "follow along" as someone else pursues a goal), and *simulation* episodes (in which we imagine the unfolding of a sequence of goal-directed activity). These are not mutually exclusive processes; for example, we might pause in the middle of an action sequence to see what someone else is doing or to imagine ourselves taking the next step. Indeed, mental simulations are naturally built in to the process of preparing to take action (i.e., as neurons begin firing in response to means-end thinking processes). Even when we are not actively engaged in goal pursuit it appears that our brain is naturally designed to engage in fragmented mental simulations (as illustrated by mind wandering, daydreaming, and reminiscing) (Buckner et al., 2008; Christoff et al., 2009; Mason et al., 2007).

The final set of skills needed to go "from Point A to Point B" is a diverse array of *physical action* capabilities that make it possible to implement the plans that you have envisioned when the time comes to execute those plans "for real." Our dependence on these capabilities is readily appreciated when the action requirements involve highly specialized motor skills (such as those developed by proficient musicians, surgeons, or athletes). Often, though, we take our everyday body movements for granted until we experience some sort of physical injury or disability (e.g., the loss of a limb or speech production capabilities). Actions of a primarily social nature (e.g., verbal and nonverbal communication skills) are also an essential prerequisite for goal pursuit in group and interpersonal settings.

Consistent with the control system premise that we use our knowledge and skills in a recursive, nonsequential way (i.e., more like browsing websites than reading a book), perhaps the easiest way to envision the ongoing functioning of K&S processes is to consider how they operate in a specific *behavior episode* (D. Ford, 1987/2019). Imagine that you are walking in the woods on your way to a camp site where your friends have already set up camp. You have a mental map that shows where you are going (goal representation) and the pathway you are supposed to take to get there (means–ends thinking). However, you recall (memory) having taken a different path last time you were at that campground. You imagine yourself following the alternative path (simulation) and try to assess which way would be faster (evaluation). You decide to go with the pathway you took earlier (directive from motivational headquarters) and take off at a brisk pace (physical action). Everything looks familiar (observation) and you estimate it will only take a few minutes to get to the camp site (evaluation). Then you learn why you were supposed to take the other route (evaluation, means–ends thinking) as a nest of slithery snakes suddenly appears in front of you (observation). You jump out of the way (physical action) and try to stay calm (emotion regulation) as you imagine yourself trying to avoid snakebites (simulation). You desperately look for an alternative path (observation, means–ends thinking) but it is hard to focus on anything other than the snakes (attention allocation). As you feel your heart pounding (energy source), it suddenly occurs to you that the safest way to proceed would be to go back to the beginning and take the recommended pathway (means–ends thinking). You run back to your starting point (physical action), re-create your mental map (goal representation, means–ends thinking), and eventually make it to the camp site (physical action, evaluation). You breathlessly and not very coherently (emotion regulation) report what you observed (memory). That motivates everyone to search the area around camp (physical action, observation) to ensure that the camp is snake-free (goal representation, evaluation), thus making it possible for everyone to relax (emotion regulation) and enjoy spending time together.

Amplifying Your K&S Functioning: Goal-Striving Skills (GSS)

$$\text{Optimal Human Functioning} = \left[\frac{[\text{TSP}]\text{M} \times [\textbf{GSS}]\textbf{K\&S}}{1/[\text{PHR}]\text{Biology}} \times [\text{R}]\text{Env} \right] \text{Equipoise}$$

Throughout life, people continuously build upon and selectively try to improve their portfolio of knowledge and skills (K&S). This *self-construction* process is a natural part of how we are designed (D. Ford, 1987/2019). However, self-improvement can be accelerated if we "put our mind to it" – that is, if we apply *goal-striving skills* that result in the creation of new or more durable neurological pathways and associated behavioral capacities. As we emphasized in Chapter 2, by elaborating and strengthening "what the mind does" (e.g., by applying GSS) we can elaborate and strengthen "what the brain is" (e.g., its neurological architecture) (Begley, 2007; Doidge, 2007; LeDoux, 2002; Winerman, 2012). Goal-striving skills are particularly effective in this regard and are thus an important part of our theorizing about motivation and optimal functioning. Even when motivation is amplified, goal progress can be thwarted by K&S deficiencies. Goal-striving skills help us overcome these limitations by accelerating the acquisition, development, and maintenance of useful K&S.

There may be many different ways to amplify the natural functions outlined in Table 5.1, thus making them more potent and effective. However, our professional experience and careful study of the scientific literature on this topic has led us to focus on four mechanisms that share a common theme, namely, enhancing the *salience and meaningfulness* of the information being observed, processed, and communicated from one function to another. These amplifying mechanisms include

- intentional goal setting;
- creative action planning;
- deliberate practice and simulation; and
- authentic reflection.

One way to enhance the salience and meaningfulness of the information being used by our K&S functions is to strategically add informational content that is directly related to the pursuit of a particular goal – for example, information about what actions will reliably produce desired results, or factors that may facilitate or impede goal progress. The key here is to add information selectively to support goal striving, thus enriching and empowering K&S functions without overwhelming them with "information overload." Timing is thus an important aspect of K&S amplification (e.g., driving directions are most useful when you are approaching a decision point), as is the experience and maturity of the individual receiving the information (e.g., a novice driver may need information delivered in more explicit terms than would an experienced driver).

Yet, increasing the *quantity* of timely, goal-relevant information may not be sufficient to accelerate goal progress if the *quality* of the information being added is poor (e.g., the information is unreliable or imprecise). Consequently, another way to increase the salience and meaningfulness of the information being used by our K&S functions is to enhance the clarity, specificity, or vividness of the information being processed (analogous to amplifying an audio or video signal). Information that has been amplified in this way is more likely than bland or "fuzzy" information to (a) capture and hold your attention, (b) be memorable, and (c) provide useful information to the other instrumental processes involved in implementing directives from motivational headquarters.

In short, our focus in the GSS model is on amplifying basic K&S functions in such a way as to enable you to make the most of the capabilities you already have while also accelerating efforts to develop and enhance new K&S. Improving your K&S capabilities can then, in turn, strengthen your capability beliefs (see Figure 4.5 in Chapter 4). As we have seen, capability beliefs are among the key factors contributing to goal commitment and the development of new personal goals (i.e., because we are generally attracted to things we do well and know a lot about). That is how the application of goal-striving skills can reliably enhance motivation and further promote optimal functioning, both in the current time frame and moving forward.

The four goal-striving skills outlined in this section collectively represent the most potent, effective, and well documented K&S pathways to accelerated learning and performance that we could identify from the available research evidence. These skills are briefly summarized below.

Intentional goal setting. As we have seen, personal goals play a leadership role in motivational headquarters. In its most simple or primordial form, goal pursuit is initiated when internal cues or features of the environment trigger an emotion (or emotions) that activate one or more goals, which in turn direct us to take some sort of goal-appropriate actions. This goal activation/goal pursuit process is, in large part, automatic and nonconscious (Bargh, 2017; Bargh & Barndollar, 1996; Ferguson & Zayas, 2009; Wegner, 2002).

Now, suppose you could take these natural motivational mechanisms and engineer them in a way that would ensure that the right goals were reliably activated at the right time in the right place. *The key is to "take charge" of the goal activation process by intentionally pairing emotionally competent stimuli (ECS) with the goals you want to prioritize in a particular situation.* For example, you might program a daily reminder on your smartphone or place a memory-jogging object next to items you use in a morning ritual. Each ECS can then serve as a preset cue capable of giving you the emotion-triggering jolt you need to energize (and grow!) the "right" neurological pathways (i.e., those leading to situationally appropriate goal activation).

This same principle applies to goal avoidance circumstances in which self-control must be exercised. In most such situations there is an emotionally salient temptation (e.g., an entertaining activity; a delicious high-calorie food) that is hard to ignore. The most effective self-control strategies tend to be those that weaken or disrupt the pairing between these emotionally competent stimuli and unwise or socially disapproved goals (e.g., Duckworth et al., 2016). For example, you can anticipate what circumstances are most likely to create self-control problems for you and then avoid those situations (e.g., restaurants that serve unhealthy food; distracting friends and co-workers). You can also try to "defang" strong temptations through environmental engineering (e.g., by giving your smartphone to someone else in your car) or by focusing attention on alternative desired outcomes (e.g., staying safe and avoiding punishment).

Of course, there is no guarantee that your consciously intended goal will always be the "winner" in the Darwinian competition among the many goal thoughts clamoring for your attention. Humans are not machines. You may be able to push a button on a car radio screen and always get the same station, but in humans there will always be some "interference" from nonconscious impulses and desires that must be overcome (Duckworth & Steinberg, 2015). Nevertheless, the more control you can exercise over the natural process of developing neural connections between specific situations and specific goals, the more likely you are to make wise and appropriate choices that lead to the outcomes you desire. All it takes is some awareness and forethought about what cues (ECS) in your everyday life settings are paired with which goals, and what new pairings might serve you better. Being mindful in this way can help you construct and strengthen adaptive ECS-goal pairings, while also helping you resist tempting but unwise choices (Damasio, 2003; Gollwitzer, 1999; LeDoux, 1998).

This is a fundamentally different way of thinking about goal pursuit than just mindlessly "going along for the ride" and following our meta-phorical elephant wherever it wants to go from moment to moment. When you take on the role of "software engineer" with respect to how goals and external cues are paired, you can slowly but surely reprogram the elephant's impulses and behavioral routines. You may be a creature of habit, but you are a *self-directed* creature of habit capable of shaping the way your brain changes and develops. All it takes is a clever rider who knows how to (at least occasionally!) outwit the elephant at its own game.

One particularly effective method for linking environmental cues to the right goals for a particular situation is the "if-then" technique pioneered by Gollwitzer (1999; Gollwitzer & Sheeran, 2006), called *implementation intentions*. The basic idea in this technique is to create or strengthen pairings between specific environmental cues (what we have been calling ECS) and specific goals. In some cases, this may involve inventing a whole new "protocol," as is often needed in unfamiliar circumstances. Imagine, for example, driving a car for the first time, or coming home from the hospital with a new baby. Doing the right thing at the right time may be difficult without creating some new "rules to live by."

Implementation intentions are also commonly used to reengineer or bypass an existing ECS/goal pairing, so that you will do something different when a powerful cue presents itself. For example, you might have a habit of ordering dessert whenever a server entices you with a tray of tempting treats. Healthier choices could be engineered if you were to create, in advance, a clear "if-then" rule for yourself that led to a different goal being activated – for example, "if they put a dessert tray in front of me, I will immediately say 'no thanks, just the check please' ... *before* they launch into a mouth-watering speech!"

The challenges involved in trying to engineer new ECS/goal pairings are vividly illustrated by research on smoking cessation. Even the most addicted smoker does not smoke in every situation. Typically, there are specific cues that trigger the emotions associated with craving, which in turn activate a smoking goal. Indeed, there are often so many ECS for smoking that it is virtually impossible to address all of them at once (e.g., smoking after eating, drinking, or sex; smoking while in the company of like-minded friends). That is a primary reason why the success rate of even the most effective antismoking interventions is quite low (Lancaster et al., 2000).

It would thus appear that, when it comes to ingrained ECS/goal pairings, you can't just try to "douse the fire" (i.e., suppress the emotion triggered by a particular ECS). That is tantamount to trying to gain conscious control over a nonconscious process. Rather, you have to try to pair the emotionally competent stimulus with different goals. You may be able to suppress an emotion's impact for a while, but eventually it will reassert itself (probably sooner than later) if you have not altered the fundamental connection between the stimulus (ECS) and response (goal activation – with different goal connections resulting from an alternative framing of the situation). Yet, with diligent practice, implementation intentions can help you successfully resist a compelling temptation "in the heat of the moment" – not just occasionally, but time after time. Although it may be difficult to engineer perfection, you can greatly increase the odds of doing the right thing when the predictable temptation actually arises by mentally connecting a specific physical cue with the choice you know you should be making (e.g., If I lose a hundred dollars gambling, I'll get up and leave the casino even if I had planned to play longer").

As explained earlier (in Chapter 4), intentional goal setting can also facilitate goal progress by enhancing the clarity of goals once they have been activated (e.g., by adding information about subgoals, necessary timing, and/or standards for success). When we intentionally refine our goal thoughts in these ways, we can effectively increase both the salience and meaningfulness of those thoughts as "calls for action." For example, perhaps you have experienced the frustration of receiving an assignment at work that leaves you uncertain about what the desired product should look like. Or a course syllabus that doesn't make it clear what you will be tested on. Or a grocery list that leaves you staring at a shelf filled with twenty different versions of a cold medication.

Now imagine the satisfying feeling of being able to confidently jump into a challenging task, or study precisely what you need to learn, or pinpoint within seconds exactly the product you have been asked to purchase. By transforming general goal concepts into specific goal images, all the time that might have been wasted on speculating and worrying can instead be invested in actually getting things accomplished. That is another way that intentional goal setting can enhance your efficiency and effectiveness.

Over the course of the past fifty years hundreds of well-designed experiments have demonstrated the power of intentional goal setting as an amplifier of K&S functioning and pathway to optimal functioning in virtually every area of human endeavor – work, school, health, sports, and more (Locke, 2002; Locke & Latham, 1984, 2019). Virtually all of these studies demonstrate the importance of goal clarity as a primary amplifying mechanism. A quick look at our cybernetic control diagram (Figure 5.5; discussed earlier in Chapter 3) makes it obvious why goal clarity is such a potent and effective mechanism. Imagine information flowing from the "personal goals" box into the comparator. It is only logical that if you put "garbage in" you will get "garbage out" (to use a computer science metaphor). As we saw in Chapter 3, both the decision-making process (the work of the comparator) and the system's subsequent activity (output function) will be impaired when the leader's directives (i.e., personal goals) are "fuzzy" or confusing.

The acronym "SMART" is often used to summarize the qualities that can enhance the potency and effectiveness of goal thoughts and goal communications. The presumed original use of this acronym (Doran, 1981) asserted that intentional goal setting could be optimized if goals were "specific, measurable, assignable, realistic and time-related." However, most who have adopted this heuristic over the years have changed the "assignable" criterion (focused on who is responsible) to "attainable" (or "achievable") to emphasize the demotivating influence of

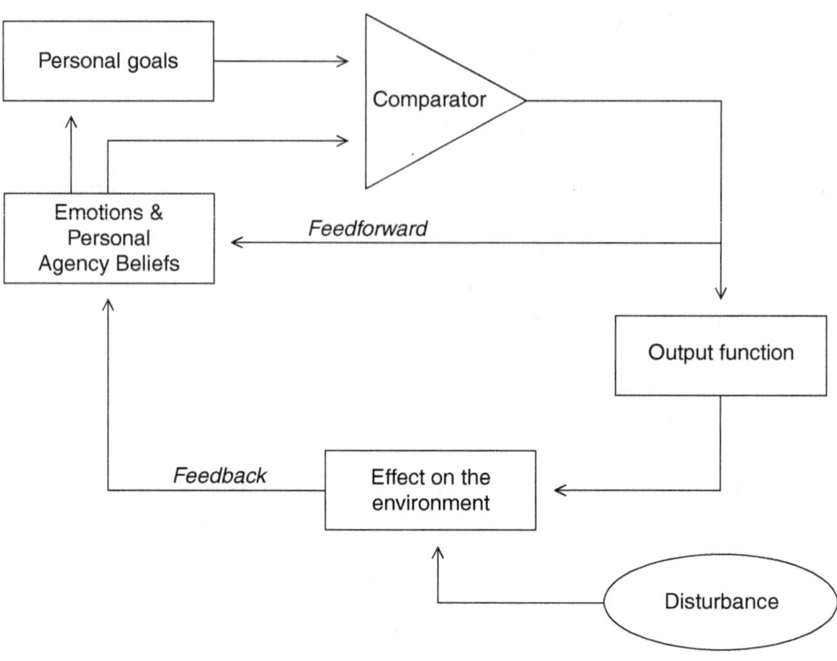

Figure 5.5 Diagram of the basic cybernetic control functions.

goals that are perceived to be too hard. That change in turn made it possible for some to convert "realistic" (which captures the same basic idea as "attainable") to "relevant," thus emphasizing the importance of taking contextual influences into account when setting "specific, measurable" goals. ("Time-bound" is also a more commonly used term than "time-related.")

Why do "smartly" defined goals work so well? Starting with a clear, practical directive empowers the rest of the instrumental troops responsible for goal progress. When you have a clear *intention*, it helps focus *attention* on goal-relevant information, thus making that information more salient and meaningful. Having a clear sense of what ideas, memories, and features of the environment are important for the task at hand can also help minimize distractions (including mental distractions, e.g., worrying). In addition, enhancing your mental focus can help you identify logical connections between actions and desired outcomes and increase your capacity for creative thought. And when both the target and the pathways to that target are clear, it is easier to assess when you are making progress and how far you still have to go.

Conversely, when a goal is conceptualized in vague or uncertain terms, it is hard to figure out what to do or to sustain the emotional energy and capability beliefs needed to maintain motivation to pursue the goal. As a result, effort and persistence tend to diminish and the goal itself becomes vulnerable to competing priorities ("I don't think I can stay awake much longer … I'm not even sure what to study").

Goal clarity can also help the advisors in motivational headquarters determine if success is a realistic expectation. That is why goal-setting guidelines typically emphasize the need to adopt standards that are both beyond current achievements but also "within reach" given relevant K&S, context, and timing parameters. It can be very demotivating to pursue a goal that is either too hard or too easy (e.g., imagine playing your favorite competitive sport with a novice or an Olympian). That is why many motivation theories emphasize the principle of "optimal challenge" (e.g.,Csikszentmihalyi, 1991; Deci & Ryan, 1985) – that is, the idea that motivation can be maximized by adopting standards that "are difficult given the person's current level of expertise, but still attainable with vigorous or persistent effort" (M. Ford, 1992, p. 256). Successes that are achieved under conditions of optimal challenge tend to be both highly satisfying and highly empowering, thus providing both an emotion and PAB mechanism for strengthening similar kinds of goal pursuits.

Creative action planning. Our goal pursuits naturally involve a lot of routine, "semiautomatic" means–ends thinking. When you go through your morning routine, or drive to the grocery store, or surf through your favorite web pages, the K&S thoughts controlling your actions don't need much conscious attention. Instead, you can rely on habits and "shortcuts" to get familiar things done reliably and efficiently. After all, why should you spend unnecessary time and energy "reinventing the wheel" when you already have a *behavior episode schema* (D. Ford, 1987/2019) for producing the desired result? Why search for a different pathway to a goal when, metaphorically speaking, you have already taken your sled up and down that snowy slope many times and created a reliable, speedy track for the next time you want to get to the bottom of the hill?

If your life is little more than one routine day after another, you may not have much need to amplify the K&S functions responsible for planning and problem solving. Your inner elephant may already have most everything it needs to get things done. But if you are like most people, from time to time you will want to try *new* things. You will encounter opportunities that you are curious about. There will be new skills you want to learn, and existing skills you want to improve. There will be life changes you want to make (e.g., to capitalize on opportunities), as well as life changes that force you to search for new solutions (e.g., due to physical or resource limitations). You may also face work or relationship challenges that make it impossible for you to always rely on your "cruise control." Those are the times when a more active and creative approach to goal pursuit is likely to be needed.

Creative action planning involves a deliberate, mindful approach to goal pursuit that is also flexible and open-minded. It integrates two distinct processes: (a) plan development skills (e.g., problem discovery, identifying obstacles, generating novel solutions, formulating contingencies) and (b) plan implementation skills, for example, Gollwitzer's (1999) implementation intentions in which anticipated future challenges and opportunities are linked to goal-directed action through concrete if-then propositions. The ultimate objective (at least in recurring situations) is to transform your best creative action plans – which initially required a great deal of conscious effort – into automatic implementation pathways that are reliable and effective.

Although a reliance on "tried-and-true" methods evolved as a preferred pathway for dealing with life circumstances, the capacity for creative thought was also essential to the survival of our early forebears. Moreover, it is evident that creativity is becoming an increasingly valuable asset in modern society. Learning how to learn and adapt and change has become a primary objective in the education of young people given the rapid pace at which knowledge is evolving in many disciplines. Formulaic approaches to success in corporations, universities, and government organizations can no longer be solely relied upon given the dynamic and unpredictable circumstances in which those organizations must function. Career development can no longer be seen as a linear process of matching personalities to work settings or socializing workers into organizational norms (Vondracek et al., 2014). As C. Ford and Gioia (1995) explain,

> in the new world of work and organization, creativity is paramount to project success and to career mobility .... Rewards will go not to those with the ability to make "rational" choices in the face of uncertainty, but to those with the ability to take creative action in the face of ambiguity. (p. 5)

The need to combine creative action planning with reliable and productive habits can be illustrated by the game of golf. Although that little white ball is just sitting there on the ground in front of you, it takes enormous skill to execute an effective golf swing. That is why, once you have developed a capable swing, the main goal is to figure out how to automatically repeat that swing time after time – just like the sled "locking in" to the well-worn tracks on the way down the snowy hill. And yet, like life, golf is filled with unexpected obstacles and circumstances that require strategic and flexible thinking. Sometimes the ball ends up in places you rarely encounter, and the only way to recover is to use your ingenuity. Sometimes your normal swing won't work because of high winds or wet grass, and you have to figure out what is likely to work better under those conditions. It is no wonder that golf is so often used as a metaphor for "the game of life." Each round of golf is simultaneously a test of your ability to execute what you already know how to do *and* your ability to come up with innovative solutions to novel problems. Adding to the challenge is the fact that negative emotions tend to stifle creativity (Amabile, 1996; Fredrickson, 2009), thus making it essential to maintain control over emotions like frustration, discouragement, and self-condemnation, all of which are commonly experienced on the golf course – and in our daily lives!

Deliberate practice and simulation. Goal-striving skills increase the potency and effectiveness of our natural K&S functions by accelerating the acquisition, development, and maintenance of useful K&S. Deliberate practice and simulation are particularly effective ways to strengthen the neurological pathways underlying the desired K&S. However, because this particular GSS component is focused on action execution, there is a premium on creating tightly organized neural patterns that will produce highly reliable results. As Hebb (1949) famously summarized, "Neurons that fire together wire together."

The amplifying role of deliberate practice in skill development and execution is well known ("practice makes perfect"). Young drivers are required by law to invest many hours in guided practice of their emerging skills before they are issued a license. Football coaches design practices to produce as many "reps" (repetitions) of key formations and plays as possible. Musicians rehearse songs over and over again until all the notes and phrases are mentally encoded and all the accompanying motor movements are reliably connected to those images at a nonconscious level. In each case, the goal is to orchestrate and sustain a pattern of brain and body activity that can be reliably executed at the appropriate time, automatically and with little conscious thought.

What is less well known is the effectiveness of vivid mental simulations in preparing the mind and body for effective action (Gawain, 2008; Martin et al., 1999). For example, golf outcomes can be significantly improved by visually imaging the perfect swing for that situation (Macy & Wilding-White, 2009). Business meetings can be executed more efficiently if you mentally rehearse what you plan to say and how much time can be allocated for each agenda item. Stressful encounters with difficult people can be managed with greater poise and effectiveness if you imagine in advance how you might respond to predictable emotional triggers.

While behavioral rehearsal (practice) is typically focused on reducing or eliminating errors and automating the execution process, mental rehearsal (simulation) is best suited for occasions when you have already developed an effective behavior pattern and you want to make sure that you optimize performance when the time comes to "deliver the goods." It is one thing to simply need more time and experience to develop the necessary expertise. It is quite another to have the ability to perform at a high level but not live up to that potential. The regret and loss of confidence associated with that kind of result can be particularly demotivating.

We have combined deliberate practice and simulation into a single amplifier concept because research in this arena suggests that a combination of physically enacting a desired performance to the best of your ability *and* imagining (mentally simulating) that performance in its "perfected" state is more effective than either technique alone (Doidge, 2007). Whether you are preparing for an athletic event, musical performance, or a stressful presentation, each technique reinforces the other. For example, whereas behavioral practice is particularly helpful in terms of decreasing variability in performance (i.e., practice increases the odds that you will do precisely what you intended to do), mental simulation is particularly helpful in terms of preparing for increasing variability in environmental conditions (e.g., imagining how you would deal with a hostile question from a client or audience member).

Authentic reflection. Earlier we noted that goal setting seems to be of little help in the absence of informative feedback about progress or results. Why this is so can be seen by examining the feedback arrow in the cybernetic model (Figure 5.5). If you remove that arrow, you no longer have a control system. Actions can still be taken (output function), but there won't be any mechanism to adjust them if they are inadequate or circumstances change (imagine a golfer hitting dozens of balls into a net and not realizing that a swing flaw was just becoming more and more ingrained). Perhaps even worse, if the feedback you receive is an inaccurate representation of what is actually happening, actions may be taken that are foolish or self-defeating (as often happens when leaders are only told what they want to hear). That is why accurate, reliable information about goal progress is so important. Sometimes feedforward (information about *anticipated* results) can help us keep progressing in the absence of feedback, but ultimately there is no substitute for an honest "reality check" when it comes to providing motivational headquarters with the information needed to make sound decisions.

We also need to pay close attention to the feedback we receive and the implications of that information for future action. Comparing the goals we are seeking with observations and expectations about goal progress is a natural process that happens automatically on an ongoing basis. That is how we are designed, both cognitively and emotionally. But if we want to make the most of this natural function, we may need to go beyond these automatic impressions, especially when we are assessing progress with regard to complex goals that require a substantial amount of time to accomplish. Imagine a political candidate skimming over some polling results or a manager glancing at a recent sales report. Will they study the figures long enough for *all* of them to "sink in," or just pick out a couple of numbers that confirm their expectations? Will they dismiss the data with some glib rationalizations and continue doing what they've always done, or will they seriously consider what the feedback means and make appropriate adjustments?

The phrase "authentic reflection" addresses these concerns with respect to how the feedback component of K&S functioning can be amplified. Since it is natural to interpret our evaluations of goal progress from the perspective of the results we are hoping for (i.e., our personal goals), it is inevitable that we will be predisposed to having a *confirmatory bias* as we search for evidence about progress and results (Nisbett & Ross, 1980). That is why science education and research training programs make a "big deal" about guarding against such biases. The same principle holds in the marketplace, where wishful thinking about customer preferences can be devastating to a business or service provider (Rabin & Schrag, 1999). Yet we can safeguard against such biases by deliberately seeking out accurate and informative feedback, even if it is not what we had planned for or envisioned.

Feedback is of course not always self-evident or self-explanatory. Just as the impact of *goal* representations can be improved by enhancing the salience or meaningfulness of those thoughts, the impact of *outcome* representations (feedback) can be improved by making that information more salient or meaningful. Often we get off track because we assess feedback superficially and expediently rather than taking the time to refine, validate, or consider the implications of the outcome information available to us. The term "reflection" suggests a more deliberate, thoughtful approach to seeking and using feedback that is based on enriched, systematic measurements of progress and critical thinking about the discrepancies between desired and current outcomes. Ellis et al. (2014) use the phrase "systematic reflection" to emphasize the importance of being comprehensive rather than selective in the process of seeking and evaluating feedback information.

Adopting this more "mindful" approach to the assessment of goal progress helps protect us against predictable evaluative biases. For example, our access to accurate feedback is often challenged by a positive self-evaluation bias that may be good for our mental health but not so good for self-improvement (Taylor & Brown, 1994). The concept of *authentic* reflection emphasizes the need to not just "believe what you want to believe" after "going through the motions" of evaluating outcomes. Rather, you must deliberately and persistently seek to improve the accuracy, salience, and meaningfulness of the feedback you receive, thus enhancing its potency and effectiveness.

The process of authentic reflection also amplifies our motivation to make needed adjustments. Serious thinking about the consequences of our actions can increase confidence in the things that work while also highlighting the need for change when outcomes are unfavorable (a process that can be amplified through creative action planning). For example, a head football coach whose favorite plays have been "figured out" by opposing coaches may need to make some significant changes if he wants to keep his job. A teacher may realize after conducting a longitudinal comparison of test scores that a lesson plan that worked well in the past is no longer a good fit for a new cohort of students.

In addition, authentic reflection can lead us to question whether the goals themselves need to be redefined (a process that can be amplified through intentional goal setting). What made great sense at one point in time may seem quite irrational under other circumstances (e.g., giving students a lot of practice writing essays when the exams that will determine whether they graduate are all multiple-choice tests). What was highly motivating when you first started pursuing a goal may seem rather ho-hum after the novelty has worn off or your skill level has increased. That is why it is so important to have *flexible standards* (M. Ford, 1992) when pursuing ongoing learning and performance goals.

What makes a standard – that is, a contextually defined goal representation – "flexible"? The key is to imagine a range of outcomes (rather than one fixed target) that represent varying levels of success, and then select the goal representation that represents an "optimal challenge" (for you). That might mean setting more challenging goals as you master new material or reach defined performance thresholds. Or, conversely, it might mean reducing investment goals when market conditions are poor, or adjusting salary aspirations when a job search is taking longer than anticipated. Developmentally, it might mean being dissatisfied with achievements that used to be celebrated (e.g., like those of a piano student who can still do little more than play a simple melody), or being thrilled with achievements that used to be routine (e.g., as when an older adult gets a clean bill of health at an annual physical). While "flexing" your performance standards can be motivationally challenging either way (e.g., raising standards can be frightening and lowering standards can be ego-deflating), people seem to be particularly reluctant to lower standards. But beware – wishful thinking can be motivationally perilous!

The consequences that follow authentic reflection (such as those involved in adjusting performance standards) illustrate how K&S processes loop back and forth in a continuous pattern, and how goal-striving skills can collectively accelerate efforts to develop and improve knowledge and skills. The principle of flexible standards also underlines the importance of keeping motivation "front and center" in efforts to improve the lives of self and others, even when the focus is on developing one of the other major components of human functioning.

Biology Component of Human Functioning

It is often said that "if you don't have your health, you don't have anything." That saying succinctly captures an inescapable design principle: we evolved as an integrated mind-body system. As a result, the motivation and K&S elements of human functioning are highly dependent on a variety of biological systems. For example, motivational headquarters cannot lead if the neural infrastructure supporting communication with the instrumental troops is damaged or "off-line" (as might occur after a concussion or serious infection). The instrumental troops cannot carry out their assigned functions if they run out of fuel (which is why many schools provide free and reduced-price meals to qualifying students). And the entire operation

Table 5.2 *Biological resources most closely associated with the pursuit of personal goals*

Threshold intelligence and brain functioning	Neurological capabilities for learning, processing information, and organizing attention and action
General health	Effectiveness and reliability of biological subsystems and overall bodily functioning
Nutrition	Availability of nourishment needed to fuel activity, growth, and vital bodily processes
Sleep	Length and regularity of periods when energy and information-processing demands are limited and bodily resources are renewed
Moderate stress	Degree to which stress levels are maintained within boundary conditions

can be disrupted if some breakdown occurs that requires "all hands on deck" (e.g., a debilitating illness or injury).

Biological processes are usually classified by subsystems that are defined by unique functions – for example, digestive, circulatory, respiratory, or neurological subsystems. For our purposes (i.e., formulating a theory of motivation and optimal functioning), it is not particularly useful to look at biological processes in terms of these traditional categories, which generally are organized around evolved primordial goals (e.g., maintaining optimal blood pressure; transporting life-sustaining substances to the cells of the body). In contrast, our classification scheme focuses on basic elements of biological functioning that are closely related to the pursuit of *personal* goals. These elements are listed in Table 5.2. Note once again that these are basic functional categories, not the amplifying processes through which those functions might be optimized.

The first category in Table 5.2 refers to the biological structures and functions primarily responsible for supporting an individual's use of *information* in the pursuit of personal goals. If there are significant deficits in, for example, the speed of information processing, or the ability to remain focused on a goal, or the ability to learn from experience, goal pursuit may be inhibited or impeded in a generalized way. Trying to find ways to accommodate such limitations is a central focus of scholars and professionals in special and remedial education (M. Ford, 1995).

Despite the popular notion that intelligence levels can somehow be summarized on a single fixed scale (like an IQ scale), intelligence is a complex construct that has a variety of meanings (M. Ford, 1985, 1986a,

1986b, 1994). Some definitions focus primarily on mental processes and their biological underpinnings, with an emphasis on K&S elements of human functioning. Others focus more on the outcomes of mental processing (i.e., goal attainment), thus combining motivation and K&S elements into a more integrated ("will and skill") view of intelligence. Still other definitions take more of a contextual or cultural view, with an emphasis on adaptation to changing environmental conditions and social circumstances. And then there are those that explicitly reject any sort of generalized definition and instead emphasize the distinctive nature of different types of intelligence. For example, there is widespread agreement that "crystallized" intelligence (the ability to effectively learn and use acquired K&S) and "fluid" intelligence (the ability to solve problems in novel circumstances) are quite distinctive, both biologically and behaviorally (Nisbett et al., 2012).

From the integrative perspective of MST, these are all potentially valid ways to think about intelligence, although we would of course propose that the most complete and useful way to define intelligence would be to meld all of these perspectives into a systems view that encompasses all of the key components of human functioning within a goal-based framework (M. Ford, 1986a, 1986b, 1994). And yet, when it comes to identifying the basic biological resources underlying "intelligent" goal pursuit, the main concern is whether an individual possesses the threshold level of intelligence and brain functioning needed to support age-appropriate learning and competence development. Once that threshold has been reached, variations in intelligence are likely to be primarily attributable to other components of human functioning (i.e., factors associated with motivation, K&S, and the environment). Below that threshold, biological factors will significantly constrain what can be accomplished (as illustrated by a child with severe disabilities or an older adult with advanced Alzheimer's disease), Nevertheless, one of the most wonderful qualities of basic human nature is the extent to which people can overcome – or at least compensate for – biological limitations by "amplifying" their motivational functions and K&S capabilities and by taking full advantage of available environmental resources (M. Ford, 1995).

The next three categories in Table 5.2 refer to the biological structures and functions primarily responsible for supporting an individual's efficient use of *energy* in the pursuit of personal goals. When we are injured or a disease process takes hold, mental and physical energy gets redirected toward those *general health* priorities. Our attention is diverted (e.g., by persistent feelings of pain or discomfort), which can make it very difficult to concentrate on other priorities. Physical energy resources may be depleted (e.g., by a flu bug or medications that cause drowsiness), thus making it difficult to sustain goal pursuit for more than a short period. Willpower becomes difficult to sustain in the face of these resource demands, as we cannot choose to reallocate energy devoted to nonconscious biological processes like fighting off infection and repairing damaged cells.

The primary source of energy for mind and body is through the intake of food substances. Thus, *nutrition* is a fundamental part of the biological infrastructure supporting goal pursuit. As is the case for many aspects of human functioning, the body operates with "fixed rules" but also has many "flexible strategies" (Koestler, 1967, 1978). The body needs calories, but it can survive within a wide range of caloric intake levels (as evidenced by the various sizes and shapes of members of the human species). At a micro level, there isn't any acceptable substitute for a wide variety of substances (e.g., certain vitamins and minerals), and yet there are typically many different kinds of food that can provide those substances. The body is remarkably capable of fighting its way back to a healthy state when we eat or drink things that aren't good for us, and yet there are limits to how much and how often we can engage in biologically disruptive behaviors like binge drinking.

The energy level needed to pursue daily goals is also difficult to sustain without a certain quantity and quality of *sleep* each day. Like an electronic device that needs to be recharged from time to time, human bodies are not designed to function continuously without periodically stopping for an extended period of limited activity. And it is not enough to simply rest for a while. Although taking a break is a helpful way to conserve energy during a busy day, the process of "recharging our batteries" requires something more akin to completely turning off a smartphone. While in "sleep mode," biological functions go into a less demanding steady state, and energy-sapping mental functions (e.g., those requiring a lot of conscious processing) effectively shut down while bodily resources are renewed.

Stress is a challenging area of research and practice that effectively illustrates the need for systems thinking in the human sciences and helping professions (A. Steinberg & Ritzmann, 1990). And yet, at its core, stress is a simple concept focused on the relationship between the demands placed on our minds and bodies and the resources available to carry out their natural functions. Like an automobile, we are designed to operate at a *moderate stress* level. It is not natural to just "sit around" for lengthy periods of time. Nor are we designed to be driven at high speeds hour after hour, day after day. Intuitively we know this to be true because we have developed the capacity to experience feelings that signal stressful inactivity (e.g., boredom, restlessness) as well as feelings that warn about excessive demands on our biological resources (e.g., disorganization, exhaustion). These feelings help motivate us to stay within biological boundaries, with lifestyles that are neither "too cold" nor "too hot," but something closer to "just right."

Amplifying Your Biological Functioning: Personal Health Responsibility (PHR)

$$\text{Optimal Human Functioning} = \left[\frac{[\text{TSP}]\text{M} \times [\text{GSS}]\text{K\&S}}{1/[\textbf{PHR}]\textbf{Biology}} \times [\text{R}]\text{Env}\right]\text{Equipoise}$$

The metaphor of operating an automobile (especially older cars) is a useful way to understand how amplification works in the context of biological functioning. Are you the kind of owner who assumes that, if the car runs, it must be fine? Do you wait for something to go wrong before doing any kind of maintenance work? Or are you the kind of owner who regularly checks your tire pressure and fluid levels and changes the oil every few thousand miles, regardless of whether there are any symptoms of dysfunction?

In general, all else being equal (e.g., quality of parts and materials), owners in the second group will have cars that perform better, last longer, and retain a higher value as they age. And so it is with people who take personal responsibility for their health habits and health outcomes. The actions associated with *personal health responsibility* (PHR) not only make our biological functions more potent and effective, they also have pervasive effects on motivation (and vice versa). That is why PHR is such an important part of our overall model of motivation and optimal functioning.

It is important to again emphasize that the biology amplifiers outlined in the next few paragraphs are not intended to be a comprehensive list of all the pathways through which biological resources might be strengthened. Rather, our objective is to identify those amplifiers that seem to be most closely associated with effective goal pursuit, as evidenced by contemporary theory and research in the biobehavioral sciences.

Equipoised diet. Our bodies are quite versatile in terms of making the most out of what we put into them. Energy can be derived from hundreds of different foods. Most life-sustaining vitamins and minerals are ubiquitously available in the substances we naturally ingest. And yet, there is a big difference between getting what you need to stay alive and optimizing the quantity, quality, timing, and impact of what you eat and drink. Many people significantly inhibit their ability to function at their best by engaging in unhealthy habits like not drinking enough water or choosing a "junk food" lifestyle over a balanced diet.

A poor diet can also impact motivation indirectly through its influence on body weight and physical appearance. That is because, for many people, there is a close relationship between body image and how we evaluate ourselves more generally (O'Dea, 2012). That in turn can lead people who become overweight (or simply perceive themselves to be overweight) to experience chronic self-doubt and self-conscious emotions that inhibit many of their goal pursuits – especially those involving other people. To make matters worse, these demotivating thoughts and feelings are often reinforced by inflexible cultural standards for weight and appearance. Cause and effect can also operate in the reverse direction, with a negative body image leading people to make unhealthy dietary choices.

Revitalizing sleep. As with diet, there is a big difference between getting an adequate amount of sleep to get by and experiencing the rejuvenating effects of a "good night's sleep" that fits your natural circadian rhythms. Unfortunately, few people consistently experience optimal sleep patterns – perhaps about 30 percent, at best (Gordon et al., 2017). That is why in modern society sleep is often described as "precious." In some cases, people have caregiving responsibilities that make this goal impossible, at least until those responsibilities recede a bit. In other cases, people simply choose to sleep less than they know they should because of the challenge of finding time to accomplish daily goals. Many such individuals have convinced themselves that they are "exempt" from nature's requirements for length and regularity of sleep. And yet, the evidence suggests that, for most of us, there are significant negative consequences associated with ignoring this ancient, natural design principle. Lack of sleep – or even just disrupted sleep – can reduce energy, willpower, and commitment to pursue important social and task goals that would otherwise be routine and relatively easy to accomplish. Sleep deprivation can also decrease our motivation to learn, perform, and interact with others at high levels of efficiency and effectiveness (Barnes & Drake, 2015; Buysse, 2014; Gordon et al., 2017).

For many people, chronic sleep deficits result not from unwise lifestyle choices but from a failure to develop capabilities for self-regulating sleep patterns. Indeed, one of the most important gifts parents can give to their children is the opportunity to learn how to go to sleep efficiently and independently, without inadvertently connecting sleep goals to goals associated with increased arousal (e.g., entertainment goals). An inability to get into "sleep mode" in a natural, reliable way can lead to a self-medicating orientation in adulthood and, ultimately, a lifetime of sleep complications.

Exercise. Given our focus on amplifying "what comes naturally" in human activity, there is perhaps no advice that one can give to those seeking to strengthen motivationally salient biological resources as straightforward as the simple mantra "use it or lose it." This profound advice applies not only to our physical movement capabilities but also to our brain functioning. Recall our earlier discussion about the brain being more like a muscle that can expand and grow than a vessel with limited capacity (Doidge, 2007). Exercise is thus a powerful amplifier that applies to all kinds of mental and physical activity. For example, numerous studies have documented the significant benefits of aerobic exercise for maintaining intellectual functioning in older adults and fending off Alzheimer's disease (Colcombe & Kramer, 2003; Erickson et al., 2015). Physical activity levels in childhood are similarly predictive of enhanced cognitive functioning across a host of tasks related to learning, memory, and executive control (Erickson et al., 2015).

On the surface the phrase "use it or lose it" may seem limited to existing functional capabilities you want to maintain (like playing a musical instrument after your high school band days are over). However, the same basic principle is just as valid when applied to opportunities to develop new capabilities or to significantly expand on existing capabilities. For example, a doctor might recommend that you seek out new hobbies that involve physical activity, or that you engage in a regimen of stretching exercises before heading out to the playing field. Failure to "exercise" these options means foregoing opportunities to strengthen the biological resources underlying successful goal pursuit.

This discussion highlights the importance of identifying your *core personal goals* when trying to engage in self-improvement that will lead to more optimal functioning. It is obvious that we will not be able to fully maintain every capability or proficiency we develop during our life's journey, or take advantage of more than a small fraction of all of the opportunities available to us. The solution to this dilemma is to engage in a strategy of *selection, optimization, and compensation* (Freund & Baltes, 1998; Marsiske et al., 1995). In the "SOC" model,

- *selection* refers to making wise choices about where to invest scarce personal resources – for example, by focusing on activities that are closely aligned with your core personal goals while allowing less useful capabilities to fade;
- *optimization* refers to efforts to amplify the capabilities and resources that reliably contribute to success in those selected goal pursuits (which may include, for example, resources resulting from a balanced diet, healthy sleep patterns, and regular exercise); and
- *compensation* reflects an understanding that you may be able to minimize the impact of age-related declines in brain and body functioning by identifying and developing compensatory areas of strength.

For example, athletes who are no longer competitive in the sports they excelled at in their youth can seek to develop compensatory skills or identify compensatory resources that enable them to continue to pursue their core personal goals in alternative ways (e.g., by coaching younger athletes or by accepting physical accommodations) or in alternative settings (e.g., by playing less physically demanding sports or seeking out a more appropriate group of competitors).

Relaxation. To a greater extent than is commonly understood, relaxation is a "tried-and-true" means of promoting general health and protecting the mind and body from high levels of stress. When properly executed, relaxation reliably produces neural and biochemical changes that sustain and strengthen available biological resources while also facilitating more efficient use of these resources. For example, as detailed in Benson's (1975) classic work documenting the benefits of meditation (and in hundreds of subsequent studies on this topic), the prototypical "relaxation response" is associated with biologically favorable changes in respiration, heart rate, blood pressure, hormonal activity, immune system functioning, and brain chemistry that are in sharp contrast to the profile of someone experiencing the dysfunctional effects of chronic stress.

There are many techniques for promoting beneficial states of relaxation, from simple breathing exercises to extended periods of meditation. Of these, one of the best validated techniques is "Mindfulness-Based Stress Reduction" (MBSR), a structured program developed by Kabat-Zinn (1994, 2012). Evidence across a broad range of studies suggests that MBSR is a potent and effective intervention for helping people cope not only with extraordinary challenges like chronic disease and life-changing disabilities, but also with the chronic hassles and problems of everyday life (Grossman et al., 2004; Khoury et al., 2015).

From the perspective of our control system model, the "secret ingredient" in MBSR and other effective relaxation techniques seems to be quieting down and letting go of the mental functions associated with worry – like thinking about what you are going to do next, or ruminating about negative experiences and possibilities. This is part of Leary's "Curse of the Self" we referenced earlier in our discussion of how the evolution of self-awareness produced certain costs along with the powerful benefits that led to its widespread emergence in humans. Referring back to Table 5.1 (the table listing basic K&S functions), the core idea in MBSR and related techniques is to allocate 100 percent of your attention to the function of Observation, and none to the function of Evaluation or any of the action-oriented functions (i.e., Means–Ends Thinking, Simulation, Physical Action). "Be in the moment" is the mantra, and control what you pay attention to by focusing on simple sensory inputs (e.g., sights, sounds, smells, and bodily sensations). If a future-oriented concern (Goal Representation) or regretful thought about the past (Memory) "invades" your stream of consciousness, their existence can be acknowledged (as an Observer might do), but they should not be dwelled upon or analyzed ("just let it go").

As these instructions suggest, relaxation of the kind associated with optimal functioning is more than an occasional state of mind and body. Rather, it is a skill that may require some diligent practice before its amplifying effects can be experienced. Nevertheless, once those beneficial effects "kick in," they are likely to be substantial and enduring. For example, a recent neuroimaging study suggests that participation in MBSR training leads to increased gray matter density in brain regions involved in self-awareness and emotional wisdom (Holzel et al., 2011a). Meditation has also been shown to lower blood pressure and improve immune functioning (Holzel et al., 2011b). In one landmark study, participants who completed a meditation program produced significantly more antibodies in response to a flu shot than those in a control group (Davidson et al., 2003). Notably, the mechanisms through which meditation has these beneficial effects are closely associated with motivation, including attention and emotion regulation, an enhanced sense of personal agency, and heightened body awareness (recall that feelings arise from integrated body mapping processes) (Holzel et al., 2011b).

In short, it appears that the ability to consciously induce biological states that combine bodily relaxation with mental alertness is a particularly effective way to enhance learning, performance, and good health outcomes. Being able to maintain a calm, coherent pattern of biological functioning under conditions that test the ability of the system to maintain organization and equipoise has both short-term benefits (e.g., facilitating optimal functioning in emergencies and high-stakes performance situations) and long-term benefits (e.g., less wear and tear on the body's life-sustaining organ systems).

Individualized care. Throughout this book we have emphasized not only the species-wide features of human motivational systems, but also the "personalized" nature of motivation and optimal functioning. For example, we have stressed how important it is to have a clear understanding of the personal goals that are particularly satisfying and meaningful to you as a unique individual (i.e., your core personal goals). We have also emphasized the personalized nature of goal–life alignment, emotional learning, and personal agency belief systems – as well as the malleability of those motivational patterns for each and every individual.

Along these same lines, many scientists and practitioners focused on human biological systems have begun to promote *personalized medicine* (sometimes called "precision medicine") as the diagnostic and therapeutic wave of the future for those seeking to promote optimal health and well-being (Agyeman & Ofori-Asenso, 2015; Schork, 2015). Personalized medicine goes beyond the fact that each of us requires a somewhat unique set of medications, treatments, and supplements to meet our health needs – although that is certainly one important manifestation of this orientation to health promotion (e.g., imagine not having access to the potent substances you have come to rely on, like allergy medications, birth control pills, and antidepressants). Rather, the more unique contribution of the personalized medicine orientation is the adoption of a systems approach that appreciates the fact that, say, a blood pressure or cholesterol reading might have very different implications depending on a person's genetic makeup, family history, diet and exercise patterns, and other biological vulnerabilities. Such an approach makes it possible for people to receive *individualized care* (analogous to ordering exactly what you want from a restaurant menu) rather than what might be called "institutionalized" care (analogous to being served the same meal as everyone else in a particular setting), thus maximizing the impact of that care while minimizing potential side effects.

A compelling example of how personalized medicine can help promote optimal functioning can be found in therapeutic applications of "proteomics" (the study of proteins) in cancer patients (Wulfkuhle et al., 2003). By profiling the molecules in a specific patient's cancer cells, susceptible areas can be identified and targeted, thus improving the potency of a therapeutic attack while minimizing any "collateral damage." Another promising application of the personalized medicine approach is the use of information about a person's genetic makeup and environmental circumstances to optimize strategies for preventing and treating chronic diseases such as diabetes, obesity, and cardiovascular disease (e.g., by relating genetic markers and dietary profiles to insulin sensitivity). This tailored approach to medical care is also being explored as a way to improve therapies for Alzheimer's and a variety of other degenerative, infectious, and autoimmune diseases.

There are also direct motivational benefits to treating people in long-term care like unique individuals (rather than interchangeable objects), thus further increasing the impact and effectiveness of the health care people receive when it is delivered in a personalized way. This philosophy of "treat them like a person, not a patient" is central to the developmental model of elder care championed by D. Ford (2013):

> The primary source of meaning in life comes from setting personal goals and accomplishing them with activities that yield pleasure and satisfaction in their achievement …. A life without goals and goal achievement yields a barren existence filled only with boredom, dissatisfaction, loneliness and feelings of anger, depression, helplessness and uselessness …. [Yet,] as limitations grow there are always options left for a person to gain satisfaction and pleasure out of life …. All you need is a basic knowledge of a person's history and behavioral activities, the genuine desire to enrich their daily life, and the imagination to create daily activity patterns based on that knowledge that will enrich that person's daily life. (pp. 485–486, 489–490)

Imagine, for example, how you might try to enrich the daily life of a parent or a nursing home resident with Alzheimer's disease. This can be a challenging task, as their capacity for mental time travel is severely limited by this disease. Yet, if you can find the right emotionally competent stimuli – like music they enjoyed throughout their life, or photographs of meaningful people and events, or action-oriented experiences (like dancing) that earlier satisfied their core personal goals – you can help them continue to experience life in ways that are meaningful and fulfilling. That is how you can help people go beyond the dreariness of merely surviving to experience what is often called *quality of life* – a property of human functioning that is closely associated with feelings of well-being and life meaning (as explained in greater detail in Chapter 7).

This more personalized approach to health care is well aligned with an understanding of humans as complexly organized, self-constructing living systems. Yet, this pathway to enhanced functioning could be further strengthened by linking it more directly to assessments of motivational patterns that may help or hinder interventions designed to enable people to make the most out of their biological resources.

Environment Component of Human Functioning

Motivational Systems Theory stresses the importance of understanding the person-system "in context," as there are so many ways that the environment can influence our thoughts, emotions, and actions. The settings in which we live our everyday lives are dynamic and complex not only in a physical sense, but also because there are many other self-directed individuals pursuing their own personal goals that must be "matrixed" into the choices we make and the actions we take. It is no exaggeration to say that every aspect of our goal pursuits is influenced by the resources available to us in our immediate and anticipated future environments.

There are many different features of the environment that can facilitate (or constrain) goal progress, and many different ways to classify those potential resources. Table 5.3 provides a concise classification scheme

Table 5.3 *Environmental resources most closely associated with the pursuit of personal goals*

Physical environment	Living conditions related to air, water, temperature, light, geography, flora and fauna, and other physical elements that influence mental and physical functioning
Tools and material resources	Instruments, appliances, substances, possessions, and other objects and entities designed to facilitate individual and collective goal striving
Informational resources and educational opportunities	Task-related and culturally shared knowledge, ideas, beliefs, and values capable of facilitating individual and collective goal striving as well as learning and competence development
Social-emotional resources	People capable of enhancing an individual's success, well-being, and integration into interpersonal and community networks through caring interactions and relationships, socialization and direct instruction, and social/political influence
Goal affordances and action opportunities	Degree to which influential properties of the physical, material, informational, and social environment are aligned with an individual's goals, beliefs, capabilities, and habits

that is useful for our purposes, as it is organized around the key requirements for goal pursuit and goal progress. After reviewing these basic requirements, we will propose several amplifying pathways that can help promote optimal functioning across a wide range of circumstances.

We often take the *physical environment* for granted, perhaps because our evolved biological functions and creative problem-solving skills have enabled us to adapt to a wide range of climates and living circumstances. Even a rather harsh environment can be tamed with the introduction of some of life's "modern conveniences" (e.g., indoor plumbing, air conditioning, convenient transportation). Yet, from time to time we are reminded how much we depend on a predictable, resource-rich physical environment (as anyone who has experienced an extended power outage or natural disaster can attest). Indeed, some of the greatest challenges to the future of humankind lie within this category (e.g., global warming, air and water pollution, energy shortages, pandemic diseases).

As the preceding discussion implies, we are also highly reliant on *tools and materials* of various kinds to accomplish individual and collective goals related to survival with well-being. Of particular importance in this regard are domesticated and manufactured food substances and the tools needed to acquire and prepare them. Other areas of human achievement for which tools and materials are particularly salient contributors include shelter, transportation, commerce, technology, and the arts.

Although the term "environment" typically evokes images related to material and energy resources, another essential way that the environment supports our goal pursuits is by providing timely and useful *informational resources*. Information is often acquired in face-to-face interactions – for example, in settings where children and young adults are being socialized and educated, or where people engaged in cooperative ventures are sharing information about objectives, plans, observations, and evaluations. However, cultural evolution has made it possible to encode information using words and images in libraries, museums, churches, universities, and many other formal and informal community settings. And of course, information is increasingly being accessed and shared through the Internet.

Given the ultrasocial nature of humans, it is not surprising that we often acquire vital informational and material resources directly from other people in our family and community networks. Yet, the resources that really make our social environment unique are those that are social-emotional in nature. We can imagine an infant receiving food and clothing from any number of people, but it is harder to see how a child's primary caregivers could effectively delegate responsibility for cultivating a basic sense of security in that child to more than a few trusted others (Ainsworth et al., 1978). It is nice to receive expressions of affirmation from acquaintances and strangers, but that is no substitute for feeling a sense of validation and acceptance from the people with whom you have a close emotional connection. A "village" of individuals who sincerely care about your survival and well-being is a powerful and precious thing. Meaningful achievements can be hard to come by in the absence of such resources.

Last but not least in our list of essential environmental resources is the notion of "fit" between person and environment, both in terms of *goal affordances* and *action opportunities*. One manifestation of fit that encompasses both of these themes is what we have been calling goal–life alignment, which is achieved when your daily activities provide you with ample opportunities to pursue your core personal goals. When the goals afforded by your everyday work, home, and leisure settings are outcomes that are important and meaningful to you, and you share those core interests and goal pursuits with others in those settings, that motivational confluence energizes thought and action and fosters a sense of identity, security, and belongingness. Goal–life alignment also strengthens context beliefs, a key component of all motivational patterns.

The opportunity to pursue goals that are well aligned with your natural profile of personal goals is a critical starting point but not the only resource needed to ensure person–environment fit. In addition, the environment must be a good fit with respect to your K&S capabilities and biological attributes. For example, you may enjoy playing tennis but be forced to choose an alternative leisure activity due to recurring knee problems. You may love to visit your grandchildren but find it difficult to do so due to an allergy to a household pet. You may find the perfect job opportunity in terms of goal affordances but fail to receive an offer due to a gap in your training or experience.

Amplifying Features of Your Environment: Responsive Environment ([R]ENV)

$$\text{Optimal Human Functioning} = \left[\frac{[\text{TSP}]\text{M} \times [\text{GSS}]\text{K\&S}}{1/[\text{PHR}]\text{Biology}} \times [\mathbf{R}]\mathbf{Env} \right] \text{Equipoise}$$

From the perspective of our control system model, we are designed to envision future outcomes that are important and meaningful to us, and then to pursue those outcomes through interactions with our physical, material, informational, and social environments. Personal goals are thoughts we have about desired outcomes. Emotions and personal agency beliefs are sources of information about current and anticipated future outcomes. Our goal thoughts, with guidance from our emotions and PABs, direct our K&S and biological subsystems (mostly at a nonconscious level) to produce the outcomes we desire through interactions with goal-relevant parts of the environment. We then use feedback from those interactions to assess progress and make any needed adjustments.

When a particular setting lacks the opportunities or resources needed to make goal progress, the environment can be described as "unresponsive." Unresponsive environments may simply be deficient in some key asset (imagine trying to navigate through an unfamiliar city late at night with no map, GPS, or friendly resident to guide you to your destination). However, if there are individuals who are actively trying to prevent you from reaching your goal, or social systems that are designed to discourage goal seeking for all but a privileged few, those circumstances may be more appropriately referred to as "hostile environments."

In contrast, optimal functioning is made possible when the environment is reliably *responsive* – that is, when it consistently facilitates (rather than constrains) your efforts to achieve the outcomes you desire. Of course, as we have seen, the environment has many facets. As a result, in most settings there are both responsive and unresponsive elements influencing your goal progress. For example, you might have strong supporters seeking to influence your boss's decision about a promotion at work, but also several rivals intent on undermining your case. You might have abundant sympathy from people who want to help you cope with an illness, but lack access to medical care that could actually remedy the illness. You might have a beautiful home with all the creature comforts you could possibly want, but no one to share it with.

Perhaps the best way to appreciate how responsive elements in the environment can amplify efforts to attain high-priority personal goals is to consider an extended example that incorporates all of the different resource categories listed in Table 5.3. Imagine that you are an employee working in a large organization. You have specific tasks and responsibilities but often work on projects with other people under managers who provide direction and oversight. You took the job because you thought, in addition to the paycheck, that it would provide you with an opportunity to do interesting work and contribute to an important enterprise.

Resource-rich physical environment. Similar to good health, we often take for granted the importance of having a *comfortable, facilitative physical environment* in which to pursue our daily goals. Yet, imagine that you arrive on your first day of work and find that your workspace is a cramped little cubicle in an uncomfortably warm, humid room. There is no window in sight and the lighting is dim and depressing. You detect a faint odor that is both irritating and persistent.

If you are like most people, your initial enthusiasm about the work you had anticipated doing would quickly be replaced by a preoccupation with goals related to physical comfort (i.e., work priorities would become secondary). Your employer might say, "Don't worry, you'll get used to it," but even if you are able to get your conscious rider to focus on work tasks, your nonconscious elephant will still be throwing its motivational weight around. For example, your work setting would likely become filled with various emotionally competent stimuli capable of triggering negative emotions each time you entered the workplace. Your context beliefs would become increasingly susceptible to demotivating influences such as those associated with Antagonistic or Discouraged PAB patterns. The chronic stress produced by an unresponsive physical environment would leave you vulnerable to health problems, both real and imagined. It's no wonder that savvy companies spend so much money on their facilities!

High-quality tools and materials. Work productivity also requires a variety of *useful tools and materials* that are "just what you need" to move forward on daily tasks. Imagine the frustration of having slow or erratic internet access, or having to use outdated hardware and software when you know how much better and faster you could perform with more versatile technology tools. As your frustration grows, you decide to take a break, yet the only food and drink available in any reasonable proximity is stagnant coffee and junk food from a vending machine. You return to your workspace and sit down in your cheap office chair and feel a twinge in your back. Protecting your back from a debilitating injury that could easily be prevented with an ergonomic chair becomes your new preoccupation.

Informative feedback and abundant learning opportunities.
Throughout this book we have emphasized how motivation and optimal functioning are enhanced when we have the best information possible to guide our thinking about goals, plans, and current circumstances. The need for *learning opportunities* and *clear, accurate information* is particularly strong in information-based work environments that rely on timely feedback from, for example, field-based employees, clients and consumers, or the financial markets. Workers also depend on their managers to provide

them with well-defined objectives and priorities and precise instructions (when needed) on how to pursue those goals. Yet, the evidence suggests that a majority of workers do not believe that management provides them with clear goals and direction, nor do managers appear to be generally aware of the poor job that many of them are doing in this regard (Farnham, 1989). Even worse, imagine going to your superiors and asking for guidance on what tasks you should prioritize, only to find that they too lack clear direction from *their* bosses!

Occasionally employees are blessed with a well-informed supervisor who works closely with the employee in a coaching role. Yet, in many work environments, encounters with superiors are infrequent and the most important source of information comes from *helpful guidance and mentoring* from experienced co-workers. The motivational impact of not having access to this kind of tacit knowledge can be enormous (Sternberg & Horvath, 1999). Imagine feeling "out of the loop" on important work matters, without anyone you can rely on to "clue you in." Or suppose you are having difficulty with some aspect of your job, but there is no one "safe" you can call upon to help you correct problems and improve your skills. Environments that are unresponsive in this way can give rise to Cautious or Insecure PAB patterns.

Nourishing social-emotional resources. Informational "nourishment" is not the only motivationally empowering kind of sharing that occurs in the workplace. Another environmental resource associated with optimal functioning is the availability of *emotional support and validation.* Indeed, research on social support has blossomed in recent decades as evidence has accumulated regarding its substantial and enduring impact on emotional and physical health (Cohen & Wills, 1985; Taylor et al., 2002; Vaux, 1988). The special link between emotions and our perceptions of support and validation can be easily appreciated by imagining yourself surrounded by a group of co-workers who consistently reject your ideas and seem not to care about you as a person. Then imagine changing jobs and working with people who genuinely respect you and value your opinions. What a difference!

When emotional and informational sources of social environmental responsiveness are both strong, the result is a high level of *trust* in the people we live and work with. In contrast, lack of trust can cause motivation to rapidly deteriorate (Farnham, 1989; Jones & George, 1998; Simpson, 2007). Imagine, for example, trying to accept the credibility of an exorbitantly paid executive who comes to your workplace to make a plea for "shared sacrifice." Or the trustworthiness of a manager who routinely makes arbitrary, unfair, or just plain incompetent decisions. Or the sincerity of a boss who promises you opportunities that never materialize. Lack of trust can undermine motivation even when all other aspects of the environment are highly responsive.

Person–environment goodness of fit. Finally, opportunities for optimal functioning are enhanced when we experience a "perfect match" between our personal characteristics and the characteristics that fit best within the environments in which we are functioning. One manifestation of this "goodness of fit" is *alignment of personal goals and goal affordances* (aka goal–life alignment). Another is *alignment of opportunities and personal capabilities*, which helps promote not only positive context beliefs (through opportunity perceptions) but also positive capability beliefs (by highlighting strengths rather than weaknesses).

Consider how person–environment fit might play out in our example of the (initially) motivated employee. Unfortunately, most employers are much more concerned about "what you can do for me" (work productivity focus) than on "what we can do for you" (work satisfaction focus). Consistent with that assertion, an extensive body of research suggests that, for the most part, there is very little relationship between job satisfaction and job performance (Iaffaldano & Muchinsky, 1985; Judge et al., 2001). Does that mean employers should ignore work satisfaction? Not at all! That would simply exaggerate the "disconnect" between employer and employee motivation. A more motivationally strategic approach would be to assess workers' personal goal profiles and special talents and then better align those with roles and assignments that make the most of those assets (Doest et al., 2006). Have you ever had an employer ask you what aspects of your job are most satisfying to you? Or what aspects of the work environment are repeatedly "violating" your core personal goals?

> It is generally assumed that a satisfied worker should be a productive worker; however, in most research examining the association between job satisfaction and job performance, the relationship is weak or nonexistent …. Rather than simply dismissing this literature as a misguided effort to connect "naturally" independent outcomes, it should be interpreted as a warning that there may be something seriously wrong with the way that many work environments are organized. Specifically, these findings suggest a pervasive lack of alignment between the personal goals of employees and their employers …. If this interpretation is accurate, facilitating the degree of

synergy between the goals of workers and organizations may be the key to a more motivated and more productive work force. (M. Ford, 1992, p. 231)

Put yourself in the shoes of the employer and consider what concrete things you might do to enhance work satisfaction while also increasing work productivity (thus creating what should be a natural positive correlation between these two indicators of work motivation). For example, if you want employees to spend more time at work, perhaps you should try to make the workplace a more interesting and engaging setting to be in, both physically and socially. Or, if you think you already have a responsive work environment, but workers are not appreciating your efforts, you could try to communicate organizational goals differently – for example, in a way that explicitly links them to common employee goals such as those related to self-determination, mastery, material gain, and social purpose.

You might also consider how jobs and work environments could be redesigned to actually facilitate the attainment of employee goals in a "win-win" kind of way (Covey, 1989). For instance, some things an organization might do to increase efficiency and save money might also help employees feel more empowered (e.g., removing an organizational layer, forming self-managed work teams, regularly seeking employee input, providing more scheduling or benefits choices). The most successful leaders naturally think about what they can give to their employees, not just what they can take from them (Csikszentmihalyi, 2003; Grant, 2013).

Organizational structures, policies, and cultures are admittedly not that easy to change once they have become institutionalized, especially in large organizations. Yet, the most direct approach to promoting goal–life alignment may not require any major organizational changes. Specifically, one might start by simply being more intentional about hiring employees with personal goals that are compatible (i.e., aligned) with the job and type of work you need them to perform. For example, interview protocols can be designed to elicit information about core personal goals and current goal pursuits (e.g., "What kind of accomplishments bring you the greatest satisfaction?" "What are some of your current goals that you'd like to share?" and as a follow up, "What are you doing to fulfill or advance those goals?"). Applicant responses can then be mapped onto the core values and operational realities of the organization. Candidates for internal promotions might be asked to complete a goal assessment (e.g., the *Assessment of Personal Goals,* as discussed in Chapter 3) and then to discuss whether (and how) the promotion is a good fit to their goal profile. Personnel evaluations tend to focus heavily on knowledge and skill qualifications, and yet people can typically acquire the necessary knowledge and skills to do a job if they have a solid K&S foundation on which to build, along with personal goals that are congruent with the requirements of the job. Establishing this "fit" between employer and employee goals is the most critical part of the evaluation yet often the most neglected.

Person–environment goal alignment can be an elusive achievement, as both the person and the environment are constantly changing and evolving. Yet sometimes all it takes is just a little bit of a "human touch" to initiate a positive motivational trajectory with a remarkably strong impact on performance. For example, Gehlbach et al. (2016) found that a simple intervention in which teachers received feedback about their similarities with specific students resulted in those students earning higher grades over the duration of the course. Notably, the impact on academic performance was greatest for underserved students.

Equipoise: A System–Wide Requirement for Optimal Functioning

$$\text{Optimal Human Functioning} = \left[\frac{[\text{TSP}]\text{M} \times [\text{GSS}]\text{K\&S}}{1/[\text{PHR}]\text{Biology}} \times [\text{R}]\text{Env} \right] \textbf{Equipoise}$$

In this chapter we have guided you through all of the components of the person-system that are most directly tied to motivation and optimal human functioning. Collectively the various sections of this chapter provide a diagnostic guide for identifying barriers and pathways to optimal functioning. Ultimately, though, all of the different components of the person-system have to work together smoothly and effectively as a unit. Following D. Ford's (1987/2019) lead, in MST that inescapable fact is called the *Principle of Unitary Functioning* (M. Ford, 1992).

In Chapter 4 we highlighted two essential system–wide prerequisites for optimal functioning: *organization*, which refers to the creation of innovative new possibilities through the effective integration of "parts" into a "whole," *and equipoise*, which points to the need for context-appropriate balancing and counterbalancing of the multiple forces involved in goal pursuit. In the *Formula for Optimal Human Functioning*, the concept of organization is implied by the bracketing of the M, K&S, Biology, and Env components into a collective unit. However, the idea that the resulting person-system would need to adapt in a dynamic, continuous way to changing conditions – like a sailor navigating a small sailboat on the open sea – is not as self-evident. That is why we have explicitly added the concept of equipoise to our formula. As any athlete or politician or emergency responder can tell you, it's not enough to be highly motivated and highly capable and in the right place at the right time. That will put you in position to do great things, but you still have to "put it all together" and also "keep it together" as you flexibly pursue your goals in real time in dynamic and often unpredictable circumstances. Moreover, the importance of equipoise grows as the stakes get larger and the margin for error gets smaller. For the athlete a momentary lapse in concentration could mean the difference between winning and losing a championship. For the politician, a single unfortunate remark could turn a significant lead into a shocking defeat. And for the emergency responder, a few lost seconds might be the difference between life and death.

Throughout this book we have provided examples of where something good can turn into something not so good when equipoise is lost. That is a key reason why the concept of amplification is so useful in understanding motivation and optimal functioning. It is easy to imagine, for example, how turning up the volume on a hearing aid could help someone for whom hearing loss is a barrier to effective functioning. Yet if the volume is turned up too high, there may be distortion and interference that reduces rather than increases clarity. Similarly, as authors we have often discussed the extent to which we should amplify our descriptions of a key concept by, for example, offering a metaphor or contrasting the concept with other related ideas. We know that if we don't say enough the concept may not connect with the reader's experience and understanding. Yet if we say too much the impact of the concept may be diluted as the reader wades through page after page of detail and loses track of the "main point" we were trying to make.

Equipoise pertains to all aspects of human functioning. For example, "practice makes perfect," but overpractice may lead to fatigue and loss of enthusiasm. "Information is power," yet we generally feel rather powerless when experiencing "information overload." Most foods are fine in moderation but potentially harmful if consumed in large quantities or in an unbalanced diet. Excessive stress can cause serious damage, yet moderate stress can help people perform, learn, and become more resilient. Creativity and reflection are essential to innovation and improvement, but they can also disrupt the automatic execution of reliably effective behavior patterns.

Equipoise is particularly important, however, when it comes to the leadership team in motivational headquarters. That is where directives are initiated and advice is given about whether one should "do more" or "ease off" or "try something else." For example, while clarity of purpose can amplify motivation, it is also important to maintain enough peripheral vision to ensure that other priorities are not overlooked. While it is good to feel passionate about the things that matter to you the most, bad things can happen when a passion becomes an obsession. Having a wide variety of relationship and work goals can help make life interesting and enriching, but it can also cause us to feel overwhelmed and discouraged. PABs are amplified when they give us confidence and hope for the future, but only if they are reined in, when needed, by realistic thinking about the present. Emotions are most effective when they are strong enough to have an impact but not so strong as to be disorganizing. Indeed, the central idea in the concept of emotional wisdom is maintaining equipoise in the sense of adjusting or reconciling different emotional "settings" as circumstances change.

Consistent with the leadership role that motivational processes play in maintaining equipoise, we have also emphasized how self-assertive and integrative goal content must be coordinated to maximize effectiveness in either type of goal pursuit. It is not just a matter of "different strokes for different folks." In our daily lives we must be, to varying extents in different circumstances, givers and takers, competitors and teammates, independent and dependent, self-serving and other-serving. We thirst for self-determination, yet we willingly give up control to others in large segments of our lives. We strive to get ahead in the material world but, for many, the primary motivation for doing so is to benefit our loved ones. We are instinctively motivated by self-preservation, yet we also evolved goals and emotions that make us acutely aware that "harm to the other is harm to the self" (Damasio, 2003, p. 172).

Still, there is no doubt that social purpose played a special role in the evolutionary development of *Homo sapiens* and continues to be a "key ingredient" in our quest for longevity and life meaning. In the next chapter we will elaborate on these themes and in doing so explain why SP goals are as real and fundamental to human nature as the bones in our body and the brain in our head. As we shall see, nature came up with an "unbeatable combination" when social purpose was wedded together with our evolved capacity for pursuing goals with an active approach orientation, personal optimism, mindful tenacity, and emotional wisdom. That is why we have concluded that the processes associated with the thriving with social purpose motivational pattern are often your "best bet" targets in efforts to motivate self and others.

First, though, we end this chapter with a unified listing of all the amplifiers that are highlighted in the expanded version of our *TSP Theory of Motivation and Optimal Functioning*. As summarized in Table 5.4,

Table 5.4 *Summary of the TSP Theory of Motivation and Optimal Functioning*

Optimal Human Functioning $= \left[\dfrac{[\text{TSP}]\text{M} \times [\text{GSS}]\text{K\&S}}{1/[\text{PHR}]\text{Biology}} \times [\text{R}]\text{Env} \right] \text{Equipoise}$

Thriving with Social Purpose (***TSP***)	Motivation (M) amplifiers:
	• Active Approach
	• Personal Optimism
	• Mindful Tenacity
	• Emotional Wisdom
	TSP results when these motivational amplifiers are infused with Social Purpose (i.e., integrative social relationship goal content, including Belongingness, Social Responsibility, Equity, and Resource Provision)
Goal-Striving Skills (***GSS***)	Knowledge and Skill (K&S) amplifiers:
	• Intentional Goal Setting
	• Creative Action Planning
	• Deliberate Practice and Simulation
	• Authentic Reflection
Personal Health Responsibility (***PHR***)	Biology amplifiers:
	• Equipoised Diet
	• Revitalizing Sleep
	• Exercise
	• Relaxation
	• Individualized Care
Responsive Environment ([***R***]Env)	Environment (Env) amplifiers:
	• Resource-Rich Physical Environment
	• High-Quality Tools and Materials
	• Informative Feedback and Abundant Learning Opportunities
	• Nourishing Social-Emotional Resources
	• Person–Environment Goodness of Fit
Equipoise	Effective, context-appropriate balancing and counterbalancing of the multiple forces involved in goal pursuit

Note: This table summarizes the expanded version of the Thriving with Social Purpose Theory of Motivation and Optimal Functioning. Each row represents one of the five major components of human functioning: (a) motivation, (b) knowledge and skills, (c) biology, (d) environment, and (e) equipoise (a property of the overall functioning of the person-system). Reliable mechanisms for "amplifying" (i.e., enhancing the effectiveness and potency of) human functioning are listed in the right-hand column. Each group of amplifier mechanisms is organized under the heading that appears in the corresponding left-hand column.

collecting each of these contributors to optimal functioning together in one table is an effective way to highlight our essential premise that motivating self and others involves the whole person-in-context, not just the "featured cast members" in motivational headquarters.

CHAPTER 6

Evolutionary Origins of Social Purpose
Human Nature on the Other Side of the Cooperation Divide

> The primary and crucial difference between human cognition and that of other animal species ... is the ability to collaborate for the purpose of achieving shared goals and intentions .... We have become the experts at mind reading, and the world champions at inventing culture.
>
> — E. O. Wilson, *The Social Conquest of Earth*

> The danger of thinking that we are nothing but calculating opportunists is that it pushes us precisely towards such behavior.
>
> — Frans de Waal, *The Age of Empathy: Nature's Lessons for a Kinder Society*

In the previous chapter, we affirmed that it makes sense – both in scientific and practical terms – to regard the amplified pattern of functioning we call *Thriving with Social Purpose* as "motivation at its (human) best." For the *Thriving* part of the TSP pattern this conclusion follows directly from the definition of amplification offered in Chapter 5 – that is, we would of course expect functioning to be more optimal if we knew how to increase the potency and effectiveness of the mechanisms governing our decisions and actions. But what about *Social Purpose*? Among the vast array of personal goals that humans commonly pursue, why have we pointed to SP goals as meriting a special status with respect to our efforts to lead productive and meaningful lives? Why not, for example, Thriving with Self-Determination? After all, that has been a central theme in many prominent motivational theories for over a half century (e.g., Brehm, 1972; Deci & Ryan, 1985; Rotter, 1966). Or how about Thriving with Happiness? That has been a popular focus for motivation books arising out of the positive psychology movement in recent years (e.g., Gilbert, 2006; Haidt, 2006; Lyubomirsky, 2008; Seligman, 2002).

In the present chapter, we will try to answer this question by explaining the catalytic role that social purpose – empowered by a thriving motivational orientation and advanced social-cognitive skills – has played in the evolution of our species' most remarkable and uniquely human qualities. As we will see, the emergence of "modern" SP goals (Stringer, 2012) – that is, social purpose goals capable of guiding complex social relationships along an extended time horizon – set the stage for the evolutionary "tipping point" D. S. Wilson (2007) calls the *Cooperation Divide*. Analogous to the dramatically different pathways taken by rainwater falling on either side of the Continental Divide (in the western United States), human development followed a very different trajectory after the alpha male–dominated hierarchical lifestyle of early hominids was rejected in favor of a new, more egalitarian way of life. For those with the "preadaptations" necessary to successfully engage in the pursuit of shared personal goals among a trusted group of collaborators and caregivers, there was no going back. Moreover, the same TSP qualities that motivated our ancestors to boldly seek a better way of life also fueled cultural innovations leading to accelerated growth in both our mental capabilities and brain size. That in turn led to a continued upward spiral of human social and practical intelligence as culture influenced what genes were most adaptive in a population. This process of *gene–culture coevolution* further strengthened SP goals and the capabilities needed to effectively pursue them (Lumsden & Wilson, 1981; Richerson & Boyd, 2005; E. O. Wilson, 2012).

Throughout this chapter we will provide you with evidence from a variety of disciplines that, taken together, provide strong support for two major conclusions about social purpose in humans that are at the heart of our TSP theory and its practical applications. Along the way we will highlight the specific findings that we found most convincing and compelling so that you too can immerse yourself in the details of the scholarly work that led us to conclude the following:

1. *Social purpose goals are real* and cannot be reduced to "self-interest in disguise."
2. *TSP led to our humanity* – that is, the catalyst for the emergence of the capabilities most unique to humans was the escalation of social purpose goals in the personal goal hierarchies of our ancestors, in conjunction with the thriving motivational qualities and associated knowledge and skills needed to ensure their effective pursuit.

In addition, we will emphasize *why* it is so important to the future of humanity to understand and appreciate that social purpose is as genuine – and motivationally irreducible – as self-interest. *What we expect from ourselves and others is heavily influenced by our beliefs about human motivation.* If we believe that everything boils down to self-interest, we will naturally look at life circumstances in terms of "what's in it for me?" and assume that everyone else is too. Over time such thinking can cause us to significantly alter what goals we prioritize by making selfishness easy to justify as the natural or "rational" choice. This way of thinking can not only narrow the range the options that people consider, it can also lead to choices that are counterproductive – not just for others, but for the decision maker as well. Yet believing that these are always the normal or "smart" choices humans make in their daily lives is a distortion of our true nature and a major obstacle to optimal functioning, which requires an equipoised balance of self-assertive and integrative goal pursuits (Koestler, 1967, 1978).

The motivational consequences of viewing social purpose as a facade are also felt through distortions of our context beliefs, as this mindset leads to the logical conclusion that when people express good intentions toward others, those motives must be inauthentic and manipulative. Over time such assumptions can foster personal agency belief patterns dominated by wariness and hostility (see Figure 4.6 in Chapter 4). Although there are certainly contexts in which such feelings are reasonable and appropriate, if this becomes our PAB "home page" it can cause us to mistrust the very people who are in a position to best help us attain our personal goals.

Social Purpose Goals Are Motivationally Irreducible

In Chapter 1 we noted that motivation can be viewed through the lens of (at least) three different disciplines. Our primary focus in this book is on the *psychology* of motivation, with a special emphasis on the leadership functions associated with personal goals, emotions, and personal agency beliefs. However, analogous to trying to understand the machine language underlying the functions of a computing application, we can also look at the *neurological mechanics* underlying the triggering of emotions, the activation and selection of personal goals, and the regulation of goal-directed activity. Finally, we can try to understand the essential nature of motivation through the lens of *evolutionary models*. Such models try to deduce from artifacts, event timelines, and phenotypes (i.e., observable features and behaviors resulting from gene-environment interactions) how ecological and social selection pressures caused various motivation-related adaptations and innovations to "catch on." Our conclusion that SP goals are an unequivocally authentic part of human nature is based on evidence from all three perspectives.

Now, you may wonder why this evidence is so important that it merits thorough coverage in the pages of this book. The reason is simple: to a very large extent, social purpose goals made us who we are, and understanding who we are – both as individuals and as a species – is the key to motivating self and others. *Homo sapiens* would not have evolved without SP goals leading the way, nor could they have survived in their absence. Indeed, like the 99 percent of all species that ultimately disappeared off the face of the Earth (Witte et al., 1992), the human race was apparently, at one point early in its development, just a few thousand individuals away from extinction (Stringer, 2012). That is why our genetic diversity is so minimal compared to most other mammalian species (notwithstanding recent evidence suggesting that the genetic material of *Homo sapiens* includes some "bits and pieces" from other, now extinct *Homo* lines) (Stringer, 2012).

Self-interest alone would not have been sufficient to enable our species to overcome the harsh ecological conditions that created this precarious genetic "bottleneck." What ultimately kept our vulnerable ancestors going and capable of adapting to adverse circumstances was the *equipoised combination of self-interest and social purpose, amplified by thriving motivational qualities.* On one level, qualities promoting cooperation, teamwork, risk-taking, and persistence were simply needed for survival. But as these qualities evolved they also became a catalyst for cultural, technological, and educational innovations that facilitated survival *with well-being.* Over time, the outcomes resulting from our enhanced capabilities for thriving with social purpose were so effective that there are now billions of humans living in increasingly interdependent societies around the globe.

It is therefore impossible to understand human nature – and especially human motivation – if we cling to the idea that phenomena such as altruism, fairness, and cooperation are simply self-interested actions masquerading as concern for others. SP goals are not just ideas we invented to make us feel good about ourselves. They are not just clever means to achieve self-interested ends. *Social purpose is hardwired into the core of our biological and behavioral functioning.*

> Most theoretical models of prosociality share a common assumption: Humans are instinctively selfish, and prosocial behavior requires exerting reflective control over these basic instincts. However, findings from several scientific disciplines have recently contradicted this view. Rather than requiring control over instinctive selfishness, prosocial behavior appears to stem from processes that are intuitive, reflexive, and even automatic. These observations suggest that our understanding of prosociality should be revised to include the possibility that, in many cases, prosocial behavior –

instead of requiring active control over our impulses – represents an impulse of its own. (Zaki & Mitchell, 2013, p. 466)

Our affirmation of SP goals as a motivationally irreducible part of human nature does not mean that we are trying to deny the existence or power of self-serving motives. Every creature on the planet must be capable of self-preservation. Self-assertive goals can also be a source of innovation and inspiration. As a result, "selfish genes" remain as important as ever in terms of understanding basic human nature and how to motivate self and others.

Nor are we trying to argue that social purpose is "more real" than self-interest or even that it is intrinsically better than self-interest. Just as unmitigated self-interest can cause people to behave in hurtful and unkind ways toward other individuals (often with self-destructive consequences), social purpose motives that are not balanced with a concern for self can lead people to make unwise choices that result in personal damage (e.g., not taking care of personal health needs; allowing con artists and cheaters to exploit them) (Grant, 2013; Post, 2007). Self-concern and concern for others are thus interdependent motivational systems (Koestler, 1967, 1978). Self-interest can only lead to effective outcomes if it is coupled with the ability to exercise self-restraint (Boehm, 2012). Similarly, social purpose can only lead to effective outcomes if it is embedded within a motivational pattern Grant (2013, p. 158) calls *otherish* giving, where "concern for others is coupled with a healthy dose of concern for the self" (in contrast to *selfless* giving). In other words, our evolved nature places a premium on maintaining equipoise with respect to the pursuit of self-enhancing and other-enhancing personal goals, with *emotional wisdom* playing a particularly key role in that process.

Yet the fact remains that while virtually everyone readily accepts the idea that humans are intrinsically self-interested, there is still a widespread belief – especially in Western cultures – that altruistic motivation is just an illusion. That is why we will devote a large part of this chapter to explaining – based on the best information that contemporary science has to offer – that social purpose goals are not only infused into our genetic heritage, they also enabled humanity to soar beyond all other species on the planet.

Evidence from Developmental Psychology

We can learn a lot about the innate aspects of human nature by looking at how young children and infants in the first hours, weeks, and months of life behave. And what they show us is consistent with the premise that we are naturally designed to pursue both self-assertive *and* integrative goals. On the one hand, it is obvious that healthy human infants are innately "selfish" (Wynn et al., 2018). They relentlessly signal their needs to caregivers and enthusiastically seek to exercise control over their immediate environments. Yet they are also innately helpful, cooperative, and "eager to connect with others" (Hrdy, 2009, p. 23). They develop strong emotional bonds with responsive caregivers (Ainsworth et al., 1978; Bowlby, 1969). They have the basic infrastructure (e.g., mirror neurons) needed to develop empathy, as evidenced by the fact that infants often cry when they hear another infant crying (Eisenberg et al., 2003; Hauser, 2006). Within the first few months of life they can instinctively tell the difference between prosocial and antisocial behavior, while also showing a clear preference to interact with helpful individuals (Hamlin et al., 2010; Wynn et al., 2018). They can understand others' needs at an instinctual level even before they are able to offer help themselves (Koster et al., 2016). And after they develop some rudimentary motor skills, very young preverbal children will reliably offer help with simple physical problems like removing an obstacle, fetching an out-of-reach object, or correcting an adult's mistake (Tomasello, 2009; Warneken & Tomasello, 2013). Particularly notable is the fact that, unlike any other species, human infants routinely provide useful information to others through pointing and gesturing (Tomasello, 2009). They also spontaneously share food and valued objects.

Could all of this simply be evidence of early success in parents' socialization of their young children? Both the age at which generosity is evident and the ubiquity of early helping, sharing, and cooperating (i.e., across cultures and even when parents aren't actively promoting such outcomes) make such a conclusion highly implausible. As Tomasello (2009) argues:

> For these five reasons – early emergence, immunity from encouragement and undermining by rewards, deep evolutionary roots in great apes, cross-cultural robustness, and foundation in natural sympathetic emotions – we believe that children's early helping is not a behavior created by culture and/ or parental socialization practices. Rather, it is an outward expression of children's natural inclination to sympathize with others in strife. (p. 13)

It is evident from numerous independent lines of research on social motivation in infancy and early childhood that SP goals have deep-rooted evolutionary origins, as do the empathic predispositions needed to respond to a wide range of emotionally competent stimuli capable of triggering the emotions that activate these SP goals (Warneken, 2015). Of course, as is the case for most human capabilities, it takes time for these biologically based motivational mechanisms to mature (Wynn et al., 2018). Yet nearly all of the emotions that reliably activate SP goals (e.g., those associated with empathic concern) have already emerged by the end of the second year of life (Batson, 2011; Warneken & Tomasello, 2006; Zahn-Waxler et al., 1992).

An experiment by researchers from the Max Planck Institute for Evolutionary Anthropology is among a number of recent developmental studies (see Hepach, 2016) that provide compelling evidence for the innate origins of SP motivational systems:

> We found that 2-year-old children's sympathetic arousal, as measured by relative changes in pupil dilation, is similar when they themselves help a person and when they see that person being helped by a third party . . . . These results demonstrate that the intrinsic motivation for young children's helping behavior does not require that they perform the behavior themselves and thus "get credit" for it, but rather requires only that the other person be helped. Thus, from an early age, humans seem to have genuine concern for the welfare of others. (Hepach et al., 2012, p. 967)

The evolved mechanisms supporting the infant-caregiver attachment relationship – the context in which belongingness goals first appear – emerge even earlier, during an infant's first year of life (Bowlby, 1969; Hrdy, 2009). These bonding mechanisms provide a powerful demonstration of how an emotionally competent stimulus (e.g., a trusted caregiver for the infant, a helpless infant for the caregiver) can trigger emotions that will reliably activate SP goals across a broad range of circumstances. The central motivational theme for both infant and caregiver is maintaining physical proximity to a "secure base" (i.e., the caregiver), thus insuring safety and access to resources (Ainsworth et al., 1978). Secure attachments are based on – and help promote – PAB patterns characterized by trust and self-assurance (see Figure 4.6 in Chapter 4). In contrast, insecure attachments reflect negative context beliefs ("I cannot rely on people close to me to support me") that also tend to erode an infant's developing capability beliefs ("I am incapable of getting people to reliably support me") (M. Ford & Thompson, 1985).

The developmental impact of these early "mental models" of the world can be profound. Children with a history of secure attachment relationships are predisposed to "approach the world with confidence and, when faced with potentially alarming situations . . . [to] tackle them effectively or to seek help in doing so." In contrast, children with a history of insecure attachment relationships learn to view the world as "comfortless and unpredictable; and they respond either by shrinking from it or doing battle with it" (Bowlby, 1973, p. 208).

These developmentally foundational motivational patterns have enduring emotional and behavioral consequences. Securely attached young children generally manifest higher levels of enthusiasm and persistence in their play and problem-solving activities, and are more cooperative in social settings (Matas et al., 1978). They are more flexible and resourceful in their social interactions, better able to cope with stress and "bounce back" from disappointments, and more effective in peer interactions requiring shared intentionality (Arend et al., 1979; Waters et al., 1979). Overall, they are more self-reliant, more empathic, better able to regulate their emotions, and more socially competent (Sroufe, 2005) – all qualities that we have associated with TSP motivational patterns.

Secure attachment relationships thus provide not only a context for fulfilling innate belongingness goals; they also serve as a potent breeding ground for the cultivation of each of the elements that contribute to the development of thriving motivational patterns (i.e., an active approach orientation, personal optimism, mindful tenacity, and emotional wisdom). Secure attachments also encourage the development of belongingness, equity, social responsibility, and resource provision goals outside the child's interactions with caregivers.

Fortunately, longitudinal evidence suggests that the anxious and defensive motivational patterns associated with a history of insecure attachments can be modified and even transformed during the course of one's life (Fraley & Roisman, 2019). Such changes can result, for example, through the natural expansion of social settings and relationships, some of which engender trust and emotional comfort. As they mature, people can also deliberately seek to understand and alter their home page PAB and emotion patterns, perhaps with help from trusted friends or professionals. For example, adolescents and young adults can use their rapidly maturing cognitive skills and expanding life experiences to reinterpret emotionally uncomfortable events and relationship patterns from their childhood.

Nevertheless, it can be difficult to replace memories and expectations filled with apprehension and mistrust with more TSP-oriented motivational patterns. It is hard, for example, to adopt an active approach orientation when you are afraid of being rejected or mistreated. It is hard to follow through on feelings of caring and compassion when you are preoccupied with personal insecurities. Conversely, when the PABs and emotions associated with secure attachments are supported and affirmed throughout childhood, TSP motivational patterns gain strength, thus enhancing the odds of experiencing optimal functioning throughout life – for example, in school (Dindo et al., 2017), in adult romantic relationships (Sroufe, 2005), in parenting roles (Raby et al., 2015), and in settings calling for leadership qualities (e.g., Englund et al., 2000).

As infants and toddlers develop and gain more experience in cooperative and competitive settings, their simple expressions of altruism and self-interest become more contextually savvy. Indeed, much of childhood socialization can be seen as a process of learning when and where it is appropriate to prioritize integrative versus self-assertive goals (an essential quality of equipoised functioning). Young children start out with a naive form of altruistic motivation that is rather undiscriminating (Tomasello, 2009). Soon, though, they learn to be more selective about the circumstances under which helping, sharing, and cooperating make sense (e.g., taking into account need, reciprocity, and relationship history) (Dunfield & Kuhlmeier, 2010). They also learn to be more discerning about self-assertive goal pursuits. For example, as they gain experience with situations that call for sharing, cooperation, and resistance to temptation, children become increasingly capable of making sound judgments about when self-restraint is called for. Indeed, it is largely through these kinds of developmental "tests" that young people develop emotional wisdom. That is why the word "mature" is often used to describe children who are making good progress (relative to their age) in mastering these challenging tasks.

Yet, the increasing complexity of prosocial behavior during early childhood should not be interpreted as some sort of weakening of the "cooperative spirit" that is embedded in our DNA.

> Young children's helping is not only flexible, but also robust. Children often help spontaneously without solicitation . . .. They help when their parents are absent, showing that neither obedience to parental authority nor parental cues drive their helping. In fact, children younger than 5 years do not seem to be concerned by whether they are being watched or acting in private, indicating that reputational effects are not foundational for prosocial behavior. Moreover, young children help not only adults; they also help their peers. Furthermore, children seem to be genuinely motivated by the other person's goal, not by showing off their good will or by their mastery of the situation. (Warneken, 2015, p. 2)

A recent study using depth sensor imaging technology to measure postural elevation confirmed the notion that authentic social purpose is evident at a very young age. This novel study found that 2-year-old children had similar changes in postural elevation when they achieved a goal for themselves or helped someone else achieve a goal (Hepach et al., 2017).

When caregivers and other socialization agents attempt to motivate children in ways that ignore the presence and power of SP goals, the results are usually disappointing (if not disastrous). As Tomasello (2009) explains,

> adults who assume that children are not naturally helpful and cooperative and attempt to make them so through external reinforcements and punishments do not create children who internalize social norms and use them to regulate their own behavior. Much research has shown that so-called inductive parenting – in which adults communicate with children about the effects of their actions on others and about the rationality of cooperative social action – is the most effective parenting style to encourage internalization of societal norms and values. Such inductive parenting works best because it correctly assumes a child is already predisposed to make the cooperative choice. (p. 46)

Evidence from Social Psychology

Logically we would expect a species in which social purpose is essential for survival and as natural as self-interest to be very "groupish." And indeed we are. Some of the most widely cited studies in the field of social psychology focus on how readily humans form social groups and experience a sense of loyalty to those groups, even when a group is arbitrarily (even randomly) constituted. Perhaps the single most famous experiment in this regard is the so-called Robber's Cave experiment (Sherif et al., 1988) in which preadolescent boys in a summer camp were divided into two groups, each unaware of the other's existence. Members of the "Eagles" and "Rattlers" quickly formed natural hierarchies and developed a strong allegiance to their assigned group. Upon learning of the other group's existence, intergroup conflict immediately emerged, including harsh name-calling, negative stereotyping, and a series of aggressive raids and retaliatory strikes. The research team was ultimately able to reduce the hostilities between the groups, but not through mere frequency of communication or physical contact. Indeed, *shared activities* often exacerbated the warfare between the groups. Rather, the secret to overcoming the group conflict was to invent compelling *shared goals* that required the two groups to work together in cooperative fashion to achieve success (e.g., pulling a "broken down" truck back to camp that required the manpower of both groups combined; dealing with a camp-wide water shortage problem created by "outside vandals").

These natural "group-centric" qualities – that is, ease of group formation around common goals and ease of defining a group in opposition to other groups – have been observed in hundreds of experiments across a wide variety of social settings. The same basic phenomena are apparent in research programs focused on social identity formation, intergroup conflict, cultural and racial prejudice, and group discrimination (Ashmore et al., 2001). It seems evident that humans are strongly predisposed to think and act in collective terms, especially when individuals have shared goals. Moreover, a "shared goal" need not be anything more than simply identifying with and feeling personal loyalty to the same group. This suggests that belongingness goals must have been part of our ancient goal repertoire and among the most powerful motives in the human species. How else could group formation be so naturally spontaneous and so emotionally compelling?

The process of activating shared goals appears to be facilitated by motivational mechanisms that amplify the impact of whatever emotions are triggered in the context of other people. In other words, when we share our experiences with others, the emotional intensity of those experiences is amplified, even when there is no shared communication (Boothby et al., 2014). This automatic (nonconscious) amplification process is strong evidence for the motivational significance of social goals in human functioning and development.

Scholars interested in the circumstances and events that bring people together have also conducted extensive research on mating preferences, especially as it relates to long-term relationships that may lead to offspring and effective caregiving. In a particularly impressive study involving 10,047 participants from thirty-three countries located on six continents and five islands, Buss (1989) found that, universally, the most sought after qualities in romantic partners were intelligence and kindness. The priority given to kindness makes sense given the role that sexual selection plays in survival with well-being.

> There are many clear benefits to mating with caretaking individuals . . . . They are likely to devote more resources to offspring. They are more likely to provide physical care – touch, protection, play, affection – and create cooperative, caring communities vital to survival. They are more likely to raise offspring that themselves do well in the mating game when they reach the age of reproduction. (Keltner, 2009, pp. 245–246)

Although some social psychologists continue to cling to the old saying "Scratch an altruist and watch a hypocrite bleed," others have provided extensive evidence supporting the hypothesis that SP goals related to altruism, especially resource provision goals, must also be a unique and irreducible part of our innate motivational infrastructure. For example, careful experiments controlling for various forms of self-interest clearly indicate that when emotions associated with empathic concern are triggered (e.g., compassion), altruistic goals are reliably activated and helping behavior becomes much more likely (Batson, 2011; Batson et al., 2002). Such findings cannot be attributed to self-focused goals and emotions because the experiments were designed so that such motives would lead to alternative choices. Indeed, after reviewing decades of research on altruistic motivation, Batson (2011) – arguably the most respected scholar in this field of study – has concluded that "It seems impossible for any known egoistic explanation of the empathy-helping relationship – or any combination of them – to account for the research evidence we have reviewed" (p. 160).

There are of course many motives for helping behavior, including some that reflect self-interest (e.g., anticipation of a reward or punishment). Yet empathic concern is not only more likely to lead to helping behavior than these other motivational pathways, it also produces helping responses that are generally more durable and more dependable (Batson, 2011). Such observations lend further support to the view that social purpose is not just self-interest in disguise.

> Love of self does not exhaust our capacity to love; we can care deeply about the welfare of at least some others . . .. Altruism is woven tightly into the fabric of everyday life and not simply decorative fringe. It is neither exceptional nor unnatural but a central feature of the human condition . . .. The dogma of universal egoism that has dominated thinking in the behavioral and social sciences, especially in psychology and economics, must give way to a pluralism of prosocial motives that includes altruism. The self-interest-only value assumption that lay at the core of the theory of rational choice must be rejected. (Batson, 2011, pp. 228–229, 233)

Consistent with Batson's advice, several social psychologists have directly confronted the assumption that self-interest is the only motive that matters in economic settings (Dunn et al., 2014). Suppose, for example, you won a large sum of money. You would no doubt immediately begin to think about all the things you might buy with that windfall. Images of cars, trips, jewelry, and other material goods would likely come to mind. But which of these things would bring you the greatest happiness?

It appears that, for the majority of us, the correct answer is "none of the above." In a compelling experiment by Dunn et al. (2008), they found that participants felt happier when they were given money to spend on another person than when they were given money to spend on themselves. They also discovered in a national sample of Americans that, while happiness was positively correlated with increased levels of spending on gifts and charity, there was no relationship between enduring happiness and spending more on oneself.

Could these results be limited to "special cases" – or perhaps not even be replicable in other experimental and cultural settings? To address these questions, Aknin et al. (2013) examined the correlation between prosocial spending and "subjective well-being" within 136 countries around the globe using data from the Gallup World Poll. The data in this poll were collected using sophisticated random selection techniques, with an average of 1,321 individuals represented per country. The results revealed a positive relationship between prosocial spending and subjective well-being in 122 out of 136 countries, with the correlations reaching statistical significance ($p < .05$) in 80 cases. Analyses controlling for potentially confounding factors confirmed that generosity is associated with well-being in rich and poor countries alike, and suggested that, on average, the impact of donating to charity on well-being is similar to that achieved by doubling one's household income, given a threshold income above the poverty level.

Of course, even a planet full of significant correlations does not necessarily confirm the presence of a cause-effect relationship between generosity and happiness. So, to further test the hypothesized impact of prosocial spending on well-being, Aknin et al. (2013) selected three countries with vastly different economic profiles – Canada, Uganda, and India – and randomly assigned participants in each country to write about a time they had spent money on others or on themselves. Subjective well-being was then assessed directly following this cognitive reinstatement of a real-life spending episode. Both within and across these two countries, higher levels of well-being were reported for episodes in which they had spent their money on others rather than on themselves. The researchers concluded that:

> Human beings around the world derive emotional benefits from using their financial resources to help others (prosocial spending) . . .. Our findings suggest that the reward experienced from helping others may be deeply ingrained in human nature, emerging in diverse cultural and economic contexts. (Aknin et al., 2013, pp. 12–13)

Evidence from Experimental Economics

The field of experimental economics applies research methods pioneered by psychologists – rigorous methods that helped elevate the scientific stature of that discipline – to problems traditionally of interest to economists, such as how people respond to varying marketplace conditions and to alternative policy options. Although mathematical modeling has yielded robust *descriptions* of how buyers, sellers, and bidders behave, controlled experimentation has made it possible to better understand *why* they behave as they do. Identifying the motivational patterns underlying individual and group financial decisions is the key to predicting what choices people are likely to make in the future under a variety of different economic circumstances. And being able to make such predictions is often the difference between a business thriving or folding, or an entrepreneur succeeding or failing.

Before the advent of experimental economics, the idea that humans are solely motivated by self-interest was a guiding assumption rather than something to be empirically tested. If people made choices that were hard to explain in terms of self-interest, such choices were assumed to reflect some hidden self-serving motive or faulty ("irrational") reasoning. But with the introduction of clever experiments designed to test whether self-interested outcomes would in fact prevail when pitted against outcomes that were not self-enhancing, it became clear that the old assumptions were not always sustainable. As Ridley (1996) observed, "much of the innovation in economics of recent years has been based on the alarming discovery by economists that people are motivated by something other than material self-interest" (p. 132). Indeed, Nobel Prize–winning economist Joseph Stiglitz, when asked to comment on the contributions of fellow Nobel laureate Vernon Smith, a pioneer in the field of experimental economics, remarked that "Among the more amusing results that have come out of experimental economics are those concerning altruism and selfishness. It appears . . . that experimental subjects are not as selfish as economists have hypothesized, except for one group – the economists themselves" (Clift, 2003).

In other words, only those people who were explicitly trained to believe that people *should* always behave in self-interested ways actually *did* behave in self-interested ways in circumstances where people normally would make choices that, at least to some extent, benefited others. That is precisely why de Waal (2009) has characterized the single-minded embrace of self-interest motives as "dangerous."

> Economists prefer to imagine a hypothetical world driven by market forces and rational choice rooted in self-interest .... In most experiments, however, such people are in the minority. The majority is altruistic, cooperative, sensitive to fairness, and oriented toward community goals .... We obviously have a problem if assumptions are out of whack with actual human behavior .... A purely selfish outlook is, ironically, not in our own best interest .... It undermines trust in others, thus making us cautious rather than generous .... It narrows our view to the point that we're reluctant to engage in the long-term emotional commitments that have served our lineage so well for millions of years. (pp. 162–163)

Experimental economists often use games to mimic the kind of real-life motivational dilemmas people face when money and social partners are involved. In one simple game called the "ultimatum" game, two players consider how to divide a meaningful sum of money between them. The role of one player is to propose exactly how much money each person gets. The role of the second player is to accept or reject that proposal. The game ends with the proposal either being implemented or, if the offer is rejected, neither player gets any money. The recipient of the offer is not permitted to make a counterproposal, nor can the game be repeated (thus eliminating reciprocity as a basis for calibrating an offer).

From a rational self-interest perspective, the "smart" choice for the individual receiving the proposal is to take whatever is offered, as the alternative is always worse (i.e., zero). Knowing this fact, the "smart" choice for the individual making the proposal is to offer the smallest amount possible. Yet, while this is exactly what chimpanzees do (with food substituting for money) (Tomasello, 2009), humans almost never play the ultimatum game this way. Those receiving the proposal expect that equity goals will be respected and routinely reject any share below 20–30 percent. In other words, most people would rather punish a greedy player at a personal cost to themselves (a phenomenon known as "altruistic punishment") than accept a blatantly unfair outcome. Those making the proposal usually have a similar view about equity and intuitively understand that not playing by the "rules of fairness" may result in bad outcomes. As a result, most people draw upon their accumulated emotional wisdom and exercise appropriate self-restraint, typically offering something near an even split. For example, in a series of ten studies across twelve different cultures, 71 percent of all proposals were in the 40–50 percent range (Fehr & Schmidt, 1999). Evidently it is "normal" for humans to prioritize concerns related to fairness and trust in circumstances involving resource distribution.

Perhaps the most extensively studied paradigm in experimental economics is the so-called Prisoner's Dilemma game. In this game, two players who choose to cooperate can each earn a reward by doing so. However, a significantly larger reward can be earned by "defecting" while the other player is cooperating. Yet if both players defect, neither one gets anything.

From a self-interest perspective, the most compelling choice is to defect, as that is the only way to have a chance at the largest reward, and it also protects the player from being victimized by a defector. Yet nearly half of all players choose to cooperate in a "one-shot" Prisoner's Dilemma game (Hrdy, 2009). Even more impressive from an SP goal perspective is evidence showing that, when the game is allowed to continue over numerous trials (as is typical in much of economic life) and many different game-playing strategies are compared, the clear winners are strategies that "start out cooperative, assume that others have [a] good reputation until proven otherwise, give to cooperators, retaliate against defectors … and forgive defectors who start being cooperative again" (Barclay, 2010, p. 12). In other words, the best long-term strategy for maximizing gains is to engage in mutual cooperation while remaining alert to instances of misplaced trust. And that is precisely how the vulnerable species *Homo sapiens* started its remarkable upward spiral on the planet Earth. When our forebears started to behave in this fashion, their survival prospects improved markedly and they increasingly experienced well-being, which in turn reinforced their cooperative spirit and their ability to "live long and prosper."

Participants in the Prisoner's Dilemma game are typically strangers. In fact, different strategies are often compared through computer simulations. Yet "the prisoner's dilemma is a dilemma only if you have no idea whether you can trust your accomplice. In most real situations, you have a very good idea how far you can trust somebody" (Ridley, 1996, p. 138). Even strangers can size each other up rather quickly in terms of who they can trust – not because we are all trained to be expert lie detectors, but because we have natural, innate capabilities for perceiving and interpreting emotional expressions related to self-interest and authentic social purpose.

> If people are asked to play the prisoner's dilemma with each of a group of strangers in turn, but given just thirty minutes to meet the partners first, they prove remarkably good at predicting which of the strangers will defect and which will cooperate in the game . . .. Our faces and our actions seem to advertise with disarming frankness just what is going on in our heads . . .. Anger, fear, guilt, surprise, disgust, contempt, sadness, grief, happiness – all are universally recognizable, not just in one culture, but across the globe. (Ridley, 1996, pp. 138–139)

Consistent with this emphasis on the importance of sizing up opponents' intentions, it appears that players with superior "Theory of Mind" capabilities (Cacioppo et al., 2006) can effectively take advantage of opponents who only focus on their own goals and strategies – assuming that the "mind reader" is not overly aggressive about pushing for self-serving outcomes (Press & Dyson, 2012; Stewart & Plotkin, 2012). So, what are the telltale signs that give untrustworthy people away? It appears from recent research that it is actually the *patterning* of multiple gestures rather than any one clue that enables us to determine when trust might be a concern (DeSteno et al., 2012). Specifically, while none of the following body cues predicted untrustworthiness alone, taken together they were quite informative: leaning away from the observer, crossing arms as if to block the observer, touching or grasping or rubbing hands together, and touching the face or body. The importance of visual cues in assessing trustworthiness was further demonstrated by showing that face-to-face encounters yielded far more accurate predictions of whether someone could be trusted than similar online interactions.

Evidence from Social Neuroscience

Neuroscientists have capitalized on the methods of experimental economics to investigate the biology of cooperation and altruism. Findings from these "neuroeconomic" studies consistently point to the important role that social purpose goals – and the emotions that activate them – play in decision-making. Both the speed and reliability with which *emotionally competent stimuli* – such as receiving an unfair offer or an unexpected invitation to cooperate – can trigger heightened activity in neural regions associated with emotions (e.g., the anterior insula) suggest that the mechanisms activating SP goals are indeed hardwired into our brain (Rilling et al., 2008; Sanfey et al., 2003). That is why, for example, we can become so agitated when experiencing or observing an unjust action, and so tenderhearted when we encounter unexpected kindness.

Evidence supporting the importance of SP goal activation mechanisms also comes from research on brain-damaged individuals. As we have discussed in earlier chapters, people with normal brains have something akin to an emotional "like-o-meter" that helps guide moment-to-moment decision-making by influencing goal activation, goal commitment, and goal persistence (Haidt, 2006). In contrast, patients with damaged prefrontal lobes have great difficulty making even simple choices due to the lack of an informative "emotional biasing" mechanism. As a result, such individuals have trouble meeting their social and professional obligations, planning for the future, and maintaining any kind of coherent goal-directed activity, especially when it involves interactions with other people (Damasio, 1994).

One of the most compelling sources of evidence for the authenticity of social purpose is research indicating that the pursuit of SP goals is intrinsically pleasurable. For example, when participants in the Prisoner's Dilemma game engage in mutual cooperation, four brain regions associated with the processing of pleasurable rewards are typically activated (i.e., the caudate nucleus, nucleus accumbens, ventromedial frontal/orbitofrontal cortex, and rostral anterior cingulated cortex) (Rilling et al., 2002). Similar findings have also been obtained in studies of cooperation and altruism using other kinds of experimental paradigms (e.g., Harbaugh et al., 2007; Moll et al., 2006). The only individuals who show weak activation of these brain areas are those who are biologically deficient in the emotion-triggering mechanisms needed to activate SP goals (e.g., sociopaths and those showing symptoms of psychopathy) (Rilling et al., 2007).

In addition, neuroscientists have found that reward centers in the brain are activated not only when cooperating with a like-minded partner, but also when punishing a defector (de Quervain et al., 2004). It thus appears that revenge is indeed sweet for those who feel victimized by "cheaters" and "free riders" (assuming, of course, that equipoise is not lost in the process of seeking to restore justice). Even more impressive is evidence indicating that simply observing fair and unfair social encounters is often sufficient to activate these equity-based neurological responses. In a clever experiment by Singer et al. (2006), researchers found that when observers saw an unfair player receive a painful shock, that experience did not trigger the same level of empathic concern as when a cooperative player was observed to be in pain. In fact, males who observed an unfair player getting shocked expressed a desire for revenge and had brain activation patterns consistent with that motive (i.e., increased activation in reward areas).

In sum, the motivational impact of these brain-based SP goal activation mechanisms is immediate, strong, and reliable. This is compelling evidence for SP goals being directly "wired" into our brain functioning. Moreover, due to the evolution of mirror neurons (Rizzolatti & Craighero, 2004), SP goals are activated frequently and in a broad range of circumstances. Mirror neurons cause us to have the same brain regions activated whether we are an actor or merely an observer of some meaningful behavior pattern (de Vignemont & Singer, 2006). It seems clear that the human capacity for empathy is directly tied to a variety of neural structures that allow us to "resonate" emotionally with those around us (Singer, 2006; Singer & Lamm, 2009), thus further empowering our instinct to integrate with others.

Also consistent with the view that SP goals are motivationally irreducible is growing evidence directly linking the pursuit of SP goals with biochemical changes in the brain. For example, serotonin appears to promote cooperative behavior in challenging situations like the Prisoner's Dilemma game (Wood et al., 2006). Dopamine – a "well-being" neurotransmitter involved in the brain's reward centers – has also been linked with cooperation and teamwork (Walter et al., 2011). Evidently the anticipation and experience of collaborating with others in the pursuit of shared goals is an intrinsically pleasurable experience.

Because dopamine also facilitates the flow of information to other parts of the brain – thus supporting attention, problem solving, and memory – there is a biological basis for proposing a link between cooperation and learning. And indeed, evidence consistent with this hypothesis is pervasive in the hundreds of studies comparing cooperative goal structures with competitive and individualistic goal structures. Assuming that individual accountability is not lost in the process, students who learn in settings organized around group goals consistently outperform peers who learn on their own or in settings that emphasize competition or social comparison (Johnson & Johnson, 1975; Slavin, 1981, 1987). Notably, it is not sufficient to simply organize learners into group activities. As we saw with the Robber's Cave experiment, what amplifies motivation is the creation of *shared goals* that infuse tasks with social purpose. Indeed, for many tasks it is not even necessary for group members to be physically co-located – the desired effects on learning and achievement can be attained as long as participants are committed to a shared purpose.

Research on the effects of oxytocin on motivation and social behavior provide further support for the primacy and authenticity of SP goals in human functioning. Oxytocin is a hormone that also functions as a neurotransmitter, with effects that are diverse but generally focused on the facilitation of social bonding. For example, oxytocin is associated with empathy (Domes et al., 2007), trust (Baumgartner et al., 2008), and a willingness to help others (Kirsch et al., 2005). Nor are the effects of oxytocin limited to genetically related individuals (Campbell, 2010). Neuroeconomists have found that when people are administered a dose of oxytocin they are more likely to share and donate money, even with strangers (Kosfeld et al., 2005; Zak et al., 2005).

Earlier we discussed the central role that secure caregiver-infant attachments play in laying the foundation for TSP motivational patterns. When securely attached infants smile or cry, they are more likely than infants with insecure attachments to function as emotionally competent stimuli for their caregivers, as evidenced by greater activation of dopamine-associated brain reward regions and greater oxytocin response in the caregiver (Stratharn et al., 2009). Over time, the trustworthy responses of caregivers facilitate the development of strong capability and context beliefs in young children (M. Ford & Thompson, 1985). Such outcomes are consistent with recent evidence indicating that the oxytocin receptor gene is associated with the development of psychological resources such as optimism, mastery, and self-esteem (Saphire-Bernstein et al., 2011).

Variations in both oxytocin and vasopressin receptor genes also predict a wide variety of outcomes associated with generosity and cooperation, which helps explain why some people seem to be dispositionally more inclined to be altruistic and socially responsible than others. Simply put, "oxytocin and vasopressin serve to make even strangers feel like kin" (Poulin et al., 2012, p. 14).

A related mechanism through which SP goals are activated is the vagus nerve, which originates in the spinal cord and is connected to most of the body's major organs. The vagus nerve communicates information about the state of the body to the brain (recall our earlier discussion about feelings arising from brain-based body maps), while also producing a range of physical changes that we associate with compassion and concern for others.

> The vagus nerve is directly connected to rich networks of oxytocin receptors, those neuropeptides intimately involved in the experience of trust and love. As the vagus nerve fires, stimulating affiliative vocalizations and calmer cardiovascular physiology, presumably it triggers the release of oxytocin, sending signals of warmth, trust, and devotion throughout the brain and body and, ultimately, to other people .... When we sigh in soothing fashion, or reassure others in distress with our concerned gaze or oblique eyebrows, the vagus nerve is doing its work, stimulating the muscles of the throat, mouth, face, and tongue to emit soothing displays of concern and reassurance. (Keltner, 2009, pp. 229–230)

Given the unusually intensive caregiving requirements for mammals, and especially for human infants (who have one of the longest maturation periods of any animal), it makes sense that we would have evolved innate mechanisms for triggering emotions such as love and compassion. These emotions reliably activate SP goals and produce conscious feelings that help sustain those goals and escalate their importance in a caregiver's hierarchy of personal goals. Indeed, parents are often amazed at the strength and depth of the emotions they feel when their children are in danger (Bowlby, 1988). Can there be any doubt that SP goals are "for real" given the powerful and involuntary way that feelings of caring and compassion typically arise? Is there any way that self-interest can explain the physically intense feelings we experience or the things our faces and voices do when we reconnect with a loved one, or see them suffer? It is simply not credible to assert that, in the end, "it all boils down to self-interest." That sentiment ignores the fact that SP goal activation is largely a nonconscious process that is affirmed – not initially caused – by the conscious feelings we experience when pursuing SP goals. As de Waal (2009) points out, "a truly selfish individual would have no trouble walking away from another in need" (p. 116).

Summing Up the Case for Motivational Irreducibility

In the first five chapters of this book we explained the essential mechanisms involved in all motivational patterns, regardless of goal content. We described these mechanisms from the perspective of psychological functioning (aka motivational headquarters), neurological underpinnings, and evolutionary processes. Our simple position, grounded in science, is that any kind of species-wide goal-directed behavior pattern governed by these fundamental mechanisms represents an authentic motivational system at work. Although the specific goal targets and emotional triggers associated with such systems are influenced by the environment, their underlying structure and operations are innate.

As evidenced by the compelling research reviewed in the preceding pages, SP goal pursuit is universal and governed directly by our evolved mechanisms for initiating and sustaining goal-directed behavior. Manifestations of social purpose appear very early in life and across all of humanity, just like other irreducible motivational systems (e.g., those related to exploration and learning). We can see the roots of social purpose in our evolutionary ancestors, and appreciate how selection pressures favoring cooperation and social bonding elevated our species. We can also see the evolved mechanisms supporting SP goal pursuit "in action" using sophisticated experimental techniques and the tools of modern biology and neuroscience.

Perhaps most notably, it is now clear at both the psychological and neurological levels that the pursuit of social purpose goals brings us the same kind of satisfaction and joy (when things go well), and the same kind of disappointment and anguish (when things don't go so well), as the pursuit of other kinds of outcomes widely assumed to be an intrinsic part of human nature (e.g., food, sex, power, and privilege). Taking actions that enhance others' well-being can also reduce stress and lead to improved health outcomes (Brown et al., 2003; von Dawans et al., 2012). Indeed, as we will see in the next section, it was precisely when SP goal pursuit began to feel as rewarding as the pursuit of self-enhancing goals that humanity began to soar. When our experience of well-being became closely tied to actions such as cooperating with others, sharing resources, and helping our companions, we became more likely to engage in adaptive behaviors that enhanced our *collective* survival.

And that is why we have embraced Damasio's concept of *survival with well-being*. Well-being is not just a minor evolutionary embellishment on the primal theme of avoiding pain and illness (as illustrated by early evolving emotions such as fear and disgust). It is a key mechanism for ensuring that we *actively approach* goals likely to enhance our survival – like developing mutually cooperative relationships with our comrades and allies, or caring for young people who may later contribute to the betterment of society. In other words, the experience of well-being is itself a survival mechanism – one that gives us an extra advantage in our own life journey and in our interactions with others. That is why Hrdy (2009) concluded that "to care and to share is to survive" (p. 11).

How Thriving with Social Purpose Led to Our Humanity

It is difficult to appreciate how our ancestors' TSP capabilities shaped the course of human history without first considering how evolution works in general. There are three key processes involved in transformational evolutionary change at the species level:

1. **There must be an ongoing struggle for survival.** As a result of changing conditions (e.g., rapid climate change; reduced food availability; increased predator activity), current adaptations are insufficient to ensure survival.
2. **More effective adaptations must be available within the species' functional repertoire.** Those adaptations might already be present in some members of the species (as when some members of a bacterial species are resistant to antibiotics), or they may need to emerge from (a) genotype networking processes that accelerate innovative solutions through a "relentless shuffling and mixing and recombining of genes"

(Wagner, 2014, p. 83), (b) relevant cultural innovations, or (c) some combination of genetic and cultural influences.

3. **The more effective adaptations must be transmitted from one generation to the next and become more frequent as a result of natural selection** (i.e., the evolutionary process by which heritable traits that increase an individual's fitness become more common across the population, while those that decrease an individual's fitness become less common). Such transmission must be sufficiently rapid and reliable to keep up with the pace of environmental change.

It is important to note that natural selection alone is not sufficient for transformational evolutionary change. As Wagner (2014) explains,

> the power of natural selection is beyond dispute, but this power has limits. Natural selection can *preserve* innovations, but it cannot *create* them . . . . Darwin realized that natural selection allows innovations to spread, but he did not know where they came from in the first place . . . . Nature's many innovations – some uncannily perfect – call for natural principles that accelerate life's ability to innovate, its *innovability* . . . . At the core of this innovability is the self-organized multidimensional fabric of genotype networks, hidden behind life's visible splendor, but creating this splendor. It is the hidden architecture of life. (pp. 5, 14, 194)

When environmental circumstances are harsh or rapidly changing, those conditions tend to accelerate the rate at which innovative adaptations that might otherwise have been suppressed rise to the forefront. Moreover, when those innovations are highly fitness-enhancing, the improved outcomes – for example, being able to exploit new food sources or experiencing the benefits of mutual cooperation – can become a catalyst for change, thus causing the "new and improved" genomes to spread at a viral pace throughout the population.

Over time this *innovation diffusion* process can transform a vulnerable population into one capable of overcoming rather than succumbing to environmental threats. And that is where our TSP-inspired story of human evolution begins. In a nutshell, the "secret to survival" was an increased potential for innovation – and innovation diffusion – made possible by TSP-fueled increases in teamwork capabilities that enabled communities to grow in number and to achieve far more than what any individual or small group could hope to accomplish. This increase in population size in turn enabled cumulative cultural evolution to be more reliably sustained, thus insuring that important innovations did not have to be repeatedly rediscovered by subsequent generations. The demands associated with socially navigating these larger groups and engaging in cultural learning led to bigger and more powerful brains and a greater capacity to solve both interpersonal and ecological problems.

Setting the Stage for the Cooperation Divide: Life on the Savanna

What kinds of challenges did our hominid ancestors experience as they struggled to survive in their "environment of evolutionary adaptiveness" (EEA) – the habitat in which most human structures and functions evolved? For several million years, small hominid groups lived and evolved on the African savanna – an ecosystem dominated by open grasslands and adjacent wooded areas that afforded access to natural resources as well as some degree of shelter and security. The size of this population was surprisingly small, with one recent estimate (based on the composition of the human genome) placing the number of our ancestral breeding individuals 1.2 million years ago at about 18,500 (Stringer, 2012). Nor does it appear that any substantial growth in the size of this population occurred over the course of the next million years. Yet this was an important stage in the evolution of humanity, as many "preadaptations" (i.e., functional innovations that were created using existing or slightly modified structures) arose during this period. These preadaptations set the stage for the emergence of the egalitarian living patterns and cumulative cultural achievements associated with life on the other side of the Cooperation Divide.

What were the most important preadaptations in the evolving lives of our hominid ancestors? Frequently cited examples include large body size, bipedalism, "marathoner" characteristics (e.g., sweat glands; leg and foot tendons and ligaments), and structures enabling the manipulation and throwing of objects (e.g., hands with opposable thumbs; nails rather than claws). The emergence of language capabilities and the ability to control fire were also notable developments (Joyce, 2006), especially in light of their importance for enabling cooperative group endeavors. For example, the ability to control fire contributed to the development of multigenerational defensible campsites and the use of campfires to cook and share meat (E. O. Wilson, 2012). These were big changes compared to the daily lives of other primates. For example, it is estimated that calories originating from meat consumption increased by a factor of 10 (compared to chimpanzees) when it became possible to cook meat over a fire (i.e., 30 percent vs. 3 percent of calorie consumption; E. O. Wilson, 2012).

The emergence of these and other preadaptations illustrates how our physiology and psychology continued to evolve in a manner consistent with Damasio's (2003) survival with well-being framework. However, the adaptation that was most responsible for launching the period of transformational change that may have started as early as 1.7 million years ago (E. O. Wilson, 2012), and that accelerated at an increasingly faster pace during the past 700,000 years (Geary, 2005), was the emergence of "modern" (i.e., longer-term, relationship-oriented) social purpose goals as a central organizing force in everyday life. As noted earlier, we have adopted D. S. Wilson's (2007) concept of the *Cooperation Divide* to summarize the bifurcation between hierarchical, alpha male–dominated social organization and a new type of lifestyle in which SP goals took on a leadership role. This more egalitarian way of life initially emerged one tribe at a time, like flickering flames dotting the African savanna. Eventually, though, the benefits of a more cooperative lifestyle in somewhat larger, more diverse groups "caught on" and became more widespread, thus setting the stage for remarkable evolutionary and cultural advances.

This crossing of the Cooperation Divide altered the course of human history in dramatic ways. As teamwork-oriented solutions to environmental problems emerged – for example, cooperative problem solving and alloparenting (shared caregiving; Hrdy, 2009) – the locus of our ancestors' survival struggles shifted from primarily ecological selection pressures, such as obtaining food and shelter and avoiding predators, to *social selection* pressures – for example, maintaining a positive reputation, developing new relationships and tracking their status, and keeping pace with new knowledge and skills generated by group members. The obvious (life and death!) benefits of caregiving, collaborating, and avoiding group rejection accelerated the process of SP goals becoming selected and used in subsequent generations.

> The idea [of social selection] is that people who are able to partner up, and partner up well, will outreproduce those who fail to do so …. There are several ways that social preferences of humans can affect genetic outcomes. One is that as individuals people may choose others with good reputations as marriage partners or as partners in cooperation, which helps their fitness. The other is that entire groups may come down hard on disliked social deviants, which damages their fitness …. As the severity and cost of such punishment escalated, this created a selection pressure that favored individuals with better personal self-control …. As our gene pools changed as a result, an increasingly moral social life offered new evolutionary possibilities, which have been experienced by no other species …. The result was social selection of a very different type, that contributed significantly to our becoming a species noted for its altruism. (Boehm, 2012, pp. 63, 15, 149, 178)

Fast forwarding ahead to the increasingly widespread adaptations employed by early humans on the savanna, one can see how different life had become on the other side of the Cooperation Divide. The transformational change process, though not yet complete, was now in full bloom, with SP goals at the center of daily life.

> Our hominid predecessors spent most of their minutes alive in the presence of other group members, living in close proximity in thirty- to seventy-five person groups . . .. The social environment of the EEA [was] defined by an acute tendency to care, by highly coordinated, face-to-face social exchanges, by the need to reconcile and the flattening of social hierarchies, [and] by perpetually negotiated conflicts of interests. (Keltner, 2009, pp. 57, 67)

Consistent with the evolutionary strategy of "layering" new adaptations over those that have proven to be effective for other purposes, there was no reduction in the strength of personal goals reflecting self-interest (that is why conflicts of interest had to be "perpetually negotiated" – just as they are today in families, courtrooms, and the halls of Congress!). Rather, to accommodate the now omnipresent need to be able to effectively pursue SP goals, self-interest was coupled with evolved self-control mechanisms designed to encourage restraint in circumstances where it would be unwise to prioritize selfish interests (e.g., not sharing meat acquired in a community hunt). Survival and well-being thus became increasingly dependent on capabilities associated with emotional wisdom and the equipoised pursuit of self-enhancing and other-enhancing personal goals. That in turn intensified the impact of selection pressures favoring bigger brains that could handle the social-cognitive requirements associated with cooperation, mind reading, and reputation tracking. Bigger brains also enabled cultural learning to become more pervasive and enduring and to be reinforced as a new way of enhancing individual and group functioning. That in turn accelerated the transformational change process even further.

The social circumstances fueling these remarkable developments are summarized in Figure 6.1, which emphasizes the evolutionary and cultural significance of the movement away from alpha male–dominated hierarchical living (as is typical of extant great apes, for example) to a more egalitarian social configuration characterized by participatory decision-making and a collective concern with group cohesion. The role of SP goals is clearly suggested by the representation of group members around a circle, now in somewhat larger communities, figuratively (and literally!) looking at each

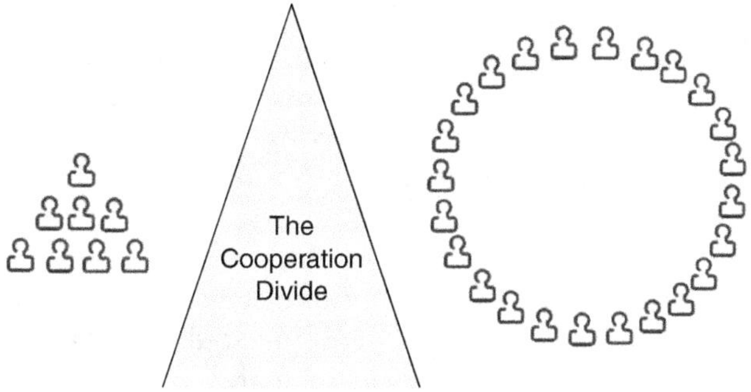

Figure 6.1 The Cooperation Divide.
Note: A conceptual diagram of the two types of hominid societies in the Middle Pleistocene –
relatively small hierarchical groups (e.g., as extant chimpanzees and apes live today) and much
larger egalitarian groups (e.g., as extant hunter-gatherer bands live) – and the cultural barrier
between them. When a critical mass of group members evolved modern TSP, they used their
TSP capabilities to "cross" the Cooperation Divide (D. S. Wilson, 2007) and form an egalitarian
culture. The "divide" metaphor illustrates how, once the divide had been crossed, these
hominids and their descendants were subject to very powerful group selection pressures leading
to rapid brain growth and cumulative cultural evolution throughout the Middle and Upper
Pleistocene.

other and sizing up the thoughts, feelings, and actions of group members as
they engage in cooperative caregiving activities, division of labor, and sharing
of resources.

Although the essential role of thriving motivational qualities in this
transformation may not be as apparent, they are deeply implicated in the
process of getting from one side of the divide to the other (as suggested by
the tall peak in the center part of the graphic). As Boehm (2012) explains,
"for today's definitive kind of egalitarianism to have flourished, it would
have been necessary for human social and political intelligence to become
powerful enough for subordinates to decisively curb the alphas in their
band" (p. 157). That is the kind of power that flows from the amplification
of the processes that compose human motivation – specifically, from an
active approach goal orientation that is strengthened and sustained by
personal optimism and *mindful tenacity* and guided every step of the way
by *emotional wisdom.*

Imagine the "guts" it must have taken for those embedded in
a hierarchical culture to stand up to an alpha male and then hold
the group together as they mentored group members who had never
experienced an egalitarian way of living. That must have required an
extraordinary willingness to take risks, to persist in the face of

daunting obstacles, and to manage fear and other volatile emotions. In addition, by amplifying growth-oriented motivation, thriving qualities also helped fuel and sustain the processes associated with cumulative cultural evolution – that is, the ratcheting up of a society's repertoire of K&S through activities such as innovation, teaching, and learning. As we explained in Chapter 2, motivation and creativity became inextricably linked when the human mind became capable of "virtual" operations such as self-awareness, mind reading, and mental time travel. When those capabilities were invested in shared goals and collective purposes, humanity began to soar.

How Our Social Purpose Goals Evolved

Caregiving and social bonding. A good place to start when searching for the evolutionary origins of SP goals is the relationship between mothers and their infant offspring. When mammals first emerged around 200 million years ago, babies began to be born in a vulnerable state, unable to feed themselves or to stay warm and safe without help from a caregiver. This meant that maternal helping behavior needed to be not only highly responsive but also highly reliable. As a result, a biologically based motivational system focused on this nurturing relationship evolved. As Hrdy (2009) explains,

> the first social bonds ever forged were between a mother and her offspring . . .. This requirement for mothers to bond with babies, and babies with mothers, meant that mammals' brains were designed for the formation of relationships in ways that the brains of other animals are not . . .. The neural and physiological underpinnings for helpful behaviors first evolved in the context of mother-infant relationships and subsequently became extended to others in groups of closely related animals. (pp. 41, 188)

These evolutionary developments created enormous selection pressures related to the strength and persistence of goals and emotions supporting effective caregiving.

Shared goals, collective activity, and group selection. In addition to the survival requirements associated with caregiving, our hominid ancestors were driven by environmental opportunities and threats to become increasingly reliant on collective activity for life-sustaining resources (e.g., sharing of limited food supplies; group hunting of large prey; shared strategies for detecting danger and avoiding predators). When those circumstances arose in our evolutionary history, conditions were ripe for the emergence of social purpose goals and the capabilities needed to pursue them.

It appears that, millions of years ago, a key adaptation occurred in early hominids that significantly accelerated the evolution of SP goals. The long-standing pattern of older children permanently leaving the group in which they were reared was suppressed, and small tribes of both related and unrelated multigenerational groups began to live together in defensible campsites (E. O. Wilson, 2012). From that point forward, group selection began playing an increasingly important role in the evolution of the species. While individual selection continued to shape each group member's fitness *within the group,* group selection shaped the fitness of the *group as a whole* in terms of how successful the collective was at obtaining food, defending their campsite, and rearing their young. Over time, these group selection mechanisms made it increasingly likely that those who survived would have strong SP goals (D. S. Wilson, 2007), while those with deficient SP goals would become extinct – along with their genes!

The idea that group selection played a significant role in shaping our motivational systems leads to the question of how selection pressures at the group level can work within individual organisms, where genes physically reside. Keep in mind that group selection presupposes that there are coherent collectives of individual organisms that function in a coordinated and unified way. Individuals cannot just be physically co-located; they must also function as an authentic group, as evidenced by a natural inclination to pursue shared goals. For many species this is an uncommon phenomenon, and individual selection is thus the dominant process governing their evolution.

Yet scientists have documented the existence of "social species" (i.e., species that often behave as collectives of organisms and that cannot survive on their own) throughout the animal kingdom. All such species have evolved genes and associated phenotypes designed to establish and maintain cooperative activity and group integrity. For example, a primitive yet highly effective group cohesion strategy (literally!) used by *mytillidae* marine mussels involves the secretion of a byssus substrate to physically and functionally attach themselves together on rocky shores, thus forming a vast cluster capable of efficiently capturing plankton (a feat that is typically beyond the capability of an individual mussel). Indeed, it may be that some sort of chemical bonding is involved in most highly social species (as suggested by the use of the term "attachment" to describe infant-caregiver bonding).

A very different group cohesion strategy can be seen in certain species of insects classified as "eusocial" (because they use collective action and division of labor to overcome ecological challenges) (E. O. Wilson, 2012). These insects have genetic preprogramming instructing them to "stick together" as they seek food and deal with predators (as illustrated by the metaphor of an "army" of ants). The remarkable effectiveness of this group cohesion strategy is evidenced by the fact that "this tiny minority of species dominate the rest of the insects in their numbers, weight, and their impact on the environment" (E. O. Wilson, 2012, pp. 110–111). However, this group cohesion strategy lacks flexibility as it relies so heavily on genetic relatedness.

Primates use yet another kind of group cohesion strategy – one that goes beyond the limitations associated with physical and genetic bonding. De Waal (1996) calls this motivation-based mechanism "community concern." The concept of community concern encompasses many of the themes, albeit in primitive form, that we include in our concept of "social purpose" – especially belongingness, a goal category focused on group cohesion. The range of cognitive and behavioral strategies that this motivational system supports is impressive both in terms of scope and variety.

> All primates have this tendency, and some even invest in the community as a whole. Instead of just focusing on their own position, they demonstrate group-oriented behavior. This is most evident in relation to social harmony .... In chimpanzees, both males and females actively broker community relations. In a large zoo colony that I studied, females would occasionally disarm males who were gearing up for a display .... [They would] go over to the angry male and pry open his hands to remove heavy branches and rocks. Remarkably, the males let them do so. Females also bring males together if they seem incapable of reconciling after a fight .... The males themselves also do a lot of conflict resolution. This is the task of top-ranking males, who will step in when disputes overheat. Most of the time a mere approach with an imposing posture calms things down, but if necessary, the male will literally beat the contestants apart ... In all of these cases, primates show *community concern*: They try to ameliorate the state of affairs in the group as a whole. (de Waal, 2009, pp. 34–35)

The emergence of group selection as an important mechanism in the evolution of humans was closely associated with rapid climate changes that created immense selection pressure for coordinated group efforts and sustained allegiance to a group (Richerson et al., 2005). As can be seen in many parts of our contemporary world, climates that are harsh and unpredictable can greatly increase the extent to which survival is an everyday struggle. During periods of scarce resources, the hominid groups that were more inclined to cooperate and more skilled at teamwork were able to reliably outcompete (and ultimately supplant) hominid groups that were less cohesive. In addition, individual selection for our prehuman ancestors increasingly became a matter of the individual's "social fitness" (i.e., how well they fit in within their group), as evidenced by qualities like cooperative teamwork, equitable resource distribution, and group loyalty.

The importance of group selection in the evolution of SP goals is clearly demonstrated by the remarkable ease with which the emotions activating goals related to in-group/out-group behaviors are triggered in humans. Most scholars agree that, when motivational systems are this strong and reliable, there must be a biological basis for their development and persistence.

> Behavioral scientists have been surprised to discover how little it takes for conflicts to arise between different groups. Evidence suggests that the mere existence of two groups is often all that's needed to create favoritism toward one's own group and animosity toward the other group . ... People display the in-group bias even if they have never met one another and don't know who the other members of their group are! (Leary, 2004, pp. 104–105)

As this quote suggests, there is a "dark side" to the group cohesion strategies that are so evident in our daily lives. Indeed, this is a prime example of how equipoise is so critical to the optimal functioning of motivational systems. Social purpose that is unchecked is just as dangerous as unrestrained self-interest – perhaps even more so given the potency of collective action (e.g., a hostile terrorist group can do far more damage than a hostile terrorist acting alone) (Koestler, 1978; D. S. Wilson, 2002). What has served our species well is the equipoised combination of self-enhancing and other-enhancing motivational systems. Each of these systems incorporates mechanisms that help us enjoy the "best of both worlds" – the advantages of *interdependence* without requiring us to give up our *independence*.

Gene–culture coevolution. The emergence of social purpose goals as a central organizing force in the evolution of humans was further strengthened by a phenomenon known as *gene–culture coevolution* (Richerson & Boyd, 2005; E. O. Wilson, 2012). Indeed, the emergence of culture itself can be seen as an example of gene-environment coevolution:

> the human cultural system arose as an adaptation because it can evolve fancy adaptations to changing environments rather more swiftly than is possible

> by genes alone. Culture would never have evolved unless it could do things genes can't! . . .. [Yet] culture is as much a part of human biology as walking upright . . .. Culture is taught by motivated human teachers, acquired by motivated learners, and stored and manipulated in human brains. Culture is an evolving product of populations of human brains, brains that have been shaped by natural selection to learn and manage culture. (Richerson & Boyd, 2005, p. 7)

Gene–culture coevolution arises when the long-term fitness of a particular genetic adaptation is enhanced through cultural changes, with both genetic and cultural diversity contributing to opportunities for such enhancements. Because culture enables humans to influence both their physical and social ecology to a far greater degree than any other species, examples of gene–culture coevolution are abundant. For example, meat-cooking traditions enabled by the controlled use of fire meant that less energy had to be expended on digesting food, thus leaving more in reserve to fuel energy-hungry brain growth (Joyce, 2006). The emergence of early language created selection pressures favoring tongue and throat characteristics that were capable of generating speech sounds with fidelity, as evidenced by a variety of distinctive features in anatomically modern humans (Lieberman, 2007). It is also apparent that the growing significance of language in cultural interactions encouraged brain-based biological adaptations that made it possible for young children to effortlessly learn the content and grammar of the ambient language (Hauser, 2006).

One of the most widely cited examples of gene–culture coevolution is the emergence of lactose tolerance, because it illustrates the speed with which innovations can spread, even in species with a relatively long lifespan. Although most adult humans lack the enzyme necessary to digest lactose (it normally stops functioning after an infant is weaned from its mother's milk), lactose tolerance emerged in areas of the world where dairy farming of domesticated animals became a tradition (Richerson & Boyd, 2005). As Wagner (2014) explains,

> if you are lucky enough to tolerate lactose, you have a mutation in the lactase control region, a stretch of DNA near the lactase gene that leaves the lactase gene turned on well into adulthood. Chances are that your distant ancestors were milk-drinking cattle farmers, because mutations that cause lactose tolerance first spread through pastoral populations, like those of East Africa and Scandinavia. And they spread blazingly fast, from zero to more than 90 percent of some populations, in a blip of time, the eight thousand or so years since humans first discovered the pastoral lifestyle. They are among

the strongest recent signatures that natural selection has left in our genomes. (p. 137)

We would argue, though, that the most consequential outcomes of gene–culture coevolution were those associated with the capacity for shared intentionality and the frequent activation of SP goal content. Ecological selection pressures were dominant in early hominid life (e.g., obtain food, avoid predators, find shelter), yet, as larger, multifamily tribes grew, and gene–culture coevolution took hold, it was mostly social selection pressures that shaped SP goals and supporting social intelligence capabilities. These social imperatives were the primary selection pressures that led to the Cooperation Divide and the subsequent upward spiral of growth in knowledge and skills and brain size (see Figure 6.1). As Richerson and Boyd (2005) explain,

> our ancestors six million years ago in the Miocene presumably cooperated in small groups mainly made up of relatives, as contemporary nonhuman primates do. There was no trade, little division of labor, and coalitions were limited to a small number of individuals . . .. Sometime between then and now, something happened that caused humans to cooperate in large, complex, symbolically marked groups. What caused this radical divergence from the behavior of other social mammals? We think that gene–culture coevolution provides the most likely solution to this puzzle . . .. Since larger, more-cooperative, and more-coherent groups should outcompete smaller, less cooperative groups, group selection could give rise to culturally transmitted cooperative, group-oriented norms, and systems of rewards and punishments to ensure that such norms are obeyed . . .. In culturally evolved social environments in which prosocial norms are enforced by systems of sanction and reward, individual selection will favor psychological predispositions that make individuals more likely to gain social rewards and avoid social sanctions. (pp. 195–196)

The individual and group fitness advantages of a social system organized around SP goal principles are clear and pervasive. We can easily see in our own lives how important teamwork is to accomplishing all but the simplest life tasks. We can immediately grasp how an authentic concern for the welfare of people beyond our own immediate family can elevate society as a whole. We can also readily imagine how an individual who lacks what we intuitively understand to be a "normal" sense of social purpose can cause so much misery for those around them. For example, many people have directly experienced how bullies, abusive family members, and tyrannical leaders can make it difficult to move forward in our personal and professional lives.

A Better Way of Life: Crossing the Cooperation Divide

To understand the journey to the other side of the Cooperation Divide, it is useful to start with a "before-and-after" picture of the two sets of social norms employed by our ancestors to achieve group cohesion. That contrast is a useful way to emphasize that the catalyst for far-reaching evolutionary change was *not* the emergence of group-oriented behavior. Humans descended from a long line of primates who lived (and continue to live) in interdependent groups (de Waal, 2009). Rather, the "essential ingredient" fueling this change was *cooperation*, which requires egalitarian social norms, core personal goals focused on equity, social responsibility, and resource provision, and an infrastructure of supporting social intelligence capabilities.

Alpha male dominance hierarchies. Our early (i.e., pre–Cooperation Divide) hominid ancestors lived in alpha male dominance hierarchies that effectively promoted group cohesion, but at a cost, as self-direction and innovation tend to be suppressed in groups where compliance with the social order is the primary requirement for survival. Such groups are held together by self-organizing (i.e., stability-maintaining) social forces that define each individual's status and permissible roles within a dominance hierarchy. Such definitions help make it clear what the "right" actions are in the context of the group, while also suggesting that alternative actions may result in severe penalties (thus creating a strong disincentive to do anything risky or out of the ordinary).

The social norms supporting alpha male dominance hierarchies are generally effective at promoting social order and keeping conflicts from becoming overly disruptive. In addition, "dominance has a positive face in that dominant creatures tend to provide solutions for the problems of a community" (Damasio, 2003, p. 164). Yet the ability of such hierarchies to provide solutions to *novel* ecological and social problems is very limited, as few in the group are empowered to participate in group problem solving, and even fewer are capable of generating innovative solutions (due to limited opportunities to become skilled problem solvers, reinforced by cultural norms that reward conformity and conventional solutions). Moreover, it is commonplace for dominant individuals and dominant coalitions to become increasingly oppressive – and even abusive – as they exercise the power and control afforded by their position at the top of the hierarchy.

Cooperative egalitarian life. Given the shortcomings described in the preceding paragraphs, it is easy to see how attractive the benefits of egalitarian living must have seemed to those groups fortunate enough to have leaders with the TSP qualities needed to supplant the dominant alpha males. What the group could hope to accomplish in terms of food, shelter, and personal well-being must have seemed far greater in a setting where group members were actively engaged in teamwork, teaching, and learning from those with the greatest expertise, with immediate rewards for those capable of high-fidelity imitation (Richerson & Boyd, 2005). The inclination to share knowledge and skills (rather than hoard informational and material resources) enabled a *collective intelligence* to arise within the group that was dynamic, open to innovative solutions, and able to support larger coalitions than those typically found in dominance hierarchies. In other words, cooperative social norms encouraged the development of larger, "smarter" groups capable of surviving ecological and social challenges that smaller, less flexible groups could not overcome. Cooperative social norms also encouraged more systematic alloparenting practices (i.e., the sharing of child rearing and child care among group members), which some have pointed to as an essential factor enabling the long maturation times required for the development of big brains (Hrdy, 2009).

These benefits reliably produced very high levels of group commitment, as group members were able to enjoy the rewards of cooperative living without sacrificing their fundamental sense of personal agency. Rather than undermining motivation (a common experience for those low in a dominance hierarchy), egalitarian ideas and modes of interaction helped promote a thriving orientation to problem solving. That in turn had reverberating consequences favorable to survival with well-being. Egalitarian social norms thus became a powerful mechanism for promoting group cohesion (Romano & Balliet, 2017).

> The biological reality of self-preservation leads to virtue because in our inalienable need to maintain ourselves we must, of necessity, help preserve other selves. If we fail to do so we perish . . .. We are in a bind, literally, in the good sense of the word. (Damasio, 2003, p. 171)

The binding effects of egalitarian social norms were strong and pervasive on the other side of the Cooperation Divide. For example, such norms encouraged the view that it is justifiable (or even "moral") to help group members in proportion to their needs rather than in relation to the personal gains that might result from that help (D. S. Wilson, 2002). The focus on teamwork and reciprocity also led to close monitoring of group members' conduct with respect to standards of fairness and social responsibility – a challenging task requiring additional brain power as groups increased in size to the neighborhood of 150 members (Dunbar, 1993). Those with the best reputations in terms of meeting these standards were the most likely to earn group rewards and benefits, while "free riders" were susceptible to group punishment and rejection. That in turn created social selection pressures favoring motivational mechanisms that could function as a social "leash" – mechanisms like shame, guilt, and internalized moral values that encourage self-restraint and contribute to the development of emotional wisdom. Consistent with that premise, even preschool children will punish free riders when it is contextually appropriate to do so (F. Yang et al., 2018).

Those with the social and self-regulatory skills necessary to maintain exemplary reputations for prosocial behavior were able to experience the full benefits of group membership. In contrast, those who failed to "get with the (cooperation) program" faced increasingly dire consequences. How dire? For our ancestors, rejection from the group was tantamount to a death sentence. Consequently, the mere anticipation of reputational damage was often sufficient to prevent transgressions and encourage cooperation. Where did the genes of those prone to violate social norms go? They went "nowhere fast," as offenders were culled out of the genetic pool, thus insuring that repeated norm violations would become increasingly rare. The only reliable way to survive and prosper in the face of this "selection by reputation" process was to modulate self-interest with self-restraint. As Boehm (2012) explains,

> over time, human individuals with strong free-riding tendencies – but who exercised really efficient self-control – would not have lost fitness because these predatory tendencies were so well inhibited. And if they expressed their aggression in socially acceptable ways, this in fact would have aided their fitness . . .. This keeps them alive and well because in effect they have been "defanged" – and therefore are not targets of social control even though by genetic metaphor their poison sacs remain intact. (pp. 310, 199)

Hawley (2015) has also emphasized the adaptive value of motivational patterns that combine, in an equipoised way, self-serving and prosocial goals and strategies. By diluting the impact of aggressive strategies for acquiring resources with prosocial strategies that respect the value of sharing, helping, and reciprocating, it is possible to be both socially attractive (a quality we earlier associated with emotional wisdom) and socially successful (e.g., in terms of social status and interpersonal intimacy).

It is important to emphasize that, while cooperative egalitarian life did yield huge improvements with respect to survival with well-being – both in the immediate time frame and in terms of our species' future growth potential – the egalitarian side of the Cooperation Divide was not some kind of Nirvana. There were still many stressors in everyday life, including some new ones related to the more fluid relationship dynamics associated with collaboration, division of labor, and reputation tracking. Moreover, humans remained quite proficient at exercising dominance and fear-based authority (as has been evident in the course of human history). That is consistent with the idea that evolution progresses in a "layered" manner, with new adaptations elaborating on rather than supplanting existing capabilities.

Nevertheless, for an increasingly large segment of humanity, participation in decision-making and conflict management was now more widely distributed. The quality of emotional life must have also been far more equipoised, with a diverse mix of positive and negative emotions promoting cooperation and group cohesion (as opposed to the pervasive atmosphere of fear often associated with a dominance hierarchy).

Preadaptations That Helped Make It Possible to Cross the Cooperation Divide

It is important to emphasize that both thriving and social purpose existed long before humans crossed the Cooperation Divide, at least in primitive forms. For example, innovative tool making presumably required thriving motivational qualities such as forethought, initiative, tenacity, and resilience. And as we have seen, primate groups depend on community concern as one mechanism for promoting group cohesion (de Waal, 2009). Yet, it was not until a confluence of key evolutionary preadaptations had developed that TSP began to emerge as a coherent, "game-changing" force in human development. Consistent with theories of transformational change in complex systems, it was the *combination* of these preadaptations – not just one or two elements among them – that ultimately created the threshold effect that led to one of the most important milestones in human history.

> As soon as egalitarianism became sufficiently established, genetic evolution
> started to reshape our minds and bodies to function as team players rather

than competing against members of our own groups. The rudiments of physical and mental cooperation were always there; it was just a matter of selecting for them rather than against them. (D. S. Wilson, 2007, p. 165)

What preadaptations were the most consequential with respect to the events leading up to the Cooperation Divide? At the risk of oversimplifying a bit, we have organized what we regard as the most important and influential preadaptations into four categories:

1. **Mind reading ("Theory of Mind") capabilities.** The ability to infer the goals, emotions, beliefs, and perspectives guiding others' behavior from observable manifestations of their behavior and appearance (e.g., their actions, facial expressions, body language, and behavior patterns over time) is an essential prerequisite for cooperative goal pursuit.

2. **Social emotions associated with upholding or failing to conform to cooperative social norms.** Egalitarian living is impossible to sustain if these emotions (e.g., shame, guilt, pride, compassion) are not reliably triggered by a wide range of emotionally competent stimuli representing help or harm to others.

3. **"Modern" SP goals that focus not just on the here and now, but also more broadly on desired future living conditions expected to promote survival with well-being for self and others.** Creating and maintaining cooperative egalitarianism as an ongoing lifestyle requires a longer time perspective (compared to dominance hierarchies) and the ability to think in more complex "systems" terms (e.g., how changes in one relationship might impact other relationships; how "special treatment" might be perceived by other group members).

4. **"Modern" levels of thriving fueled by an expanded time perspective that supports innovative thinking and a "continuous improvement" motivational orientation.** It takes imagination, persistence, and a motivational horizon beyond the next few hours or days to work and live effectively in cooperative social groups. Moreover, it takes emotional wisdom to effectively integrate – and appropriately utilize – information derived from mind-reading capabilities (a vital source of social understanding) and social emotions (a necessity for SP goal activation).

Mind reading (Theory of Mind) capabilities. Consider how difficult it would be to interact effectively with someone if you had no idea what they were thinking or feeling. If all we had to go on were the things that we could perceive directly, with no ability to infer what is "really going on" in someone's mind, our ability to engage in shared goal pursuits would be severely crippled. Fortunately, absent pathology, we all possess "Theory of Mind" capabilities that make such instances relatively rare. That is not to say that our social judgments are always accurate or complete. Far from it! Social psychologists have vividly demonstrated a variety of shortcomings in the way the human mind makes social inferences (Nisbett & Ross, 1980), in large part due to selection pressures that prioritized speed over certainty. Nevertheless, we almost always have at least some idea of what those around us are feeling and thinking (notwithstanding occasional episodes of "cluelessness"), and those inferences enable us to make decisions and manage relationships more effectively than if we had no such insight.

One of the most compelling sources of evidence linking preadaptations associated with mind reading with the transition to a more egalitarian lifestyle is what Tomasello (2009) calls the "cooperative eye hypothesis." This is an example of how gene–culture coevolution likely accelerated the development of enhanced Theory of Mind capabilities in humans, who

> have a physiological characteristic that is highly unusual . . . . All 200-plus species of nonhuman primates have basically dark eyes, with the sclera – commonly called the "white of the eye" – barely visible. The sclera of humans (i.e., the visible part) is about three times larger, making the direction of human gaze much more easily detectable by others . . . . Evolutionarily, you can readily imagine why it is beneficial for you to be able to follow my eye direction easily – to spy distant predators and food, for example . . . . [Yet] advertising my eye direction for all to see could only have evolved in a cooperative social environment in which others were not likely to exploit it to my detriment. Thus, one possibility is that eyes that facilitated others' tracking of one's gaze evolved in cooperative social groups in which monitoring one another's attentional focus was to everyone's benefit in completing joint tasks. (Tomasello, 2009, pp. 75–76)

Remarkably, infants as young as seven months old appear to respond differently to people based on the size and orientation of the whites of their eyes (Jessen & Grossmann, 2014). For example, the brain activity of an infant looking at images of wide-open eyes (as one might see in someone who is afraid or surprised) is quite different from that of an infant looking at images of narrowly opened eyes (as one might see when someone is smiling). Similarly, babies respond differently when viewing direct versus averted gazes. Such evidence strongly suggests an evolutionary basis for this unique adaptation.

Another rather simple but far-reaching preadaptation that effectively supports cooperative interaction, and evidently is unique to humans, is the ability to use pointing to communicate helpful information to others.

> What could be simpler and more natural than pointing at an object to draw attention to it? But this is so only if you are human. Evidently, there is not a single reliable observation of one ape pointing something out for another, using a raised arm or any other equivalent gesture, in captivity or in the wild . . .. What comes naturally to humans, even young infants, is a sharing of intentions, an implicit knowledge that we are engaged in a common activity and are supposed to help each other out, if only by calling each other's attention to relevant objects. Our ape relatives evidently lack this awareness, which prevents them from understanding the meaning of pointing no matter how smart they are in other respects. (D. S. Wilson, 2007, pp. 168–169)

The development of mind-reading capabilities was further facilitated by the evolution of characteristic facial expressions and bodily responses for each prototypical type of emotion that humans experience (see Chapter 4, Table 4.1, for a partial list of emotions commonly regarded as prototypical for our species). These emotional displays are quite informative, as they are

- hard to fake, at least for the first few seconds after an emotion has been triggered (recall that we only become aware of triggered emotions after they have already begun to have their physiological effects);
- generally similar across many members of the species, notwithstanding some notable cultural variations (Barrett et al., 2019; Cordaro et al., 2018; Ekman, 1972; Russell, 1991); and
- often diagnostic of what desires and concerns are in a person's thoughts (keeping in mind that personal goals are activated by triggered emotions).

Being able to "read" a person's emotions is thus a critical mechanism for detecting commitment (or lack of commitment) to a shared objective and, more generally, to the principles underlying cooperation and social responsibility (Keltner, 2009).

Of particular importance in this regard is the smile, which signals trust and benevolence (assuming it is authentic – see Ekman, 2004). As Keltner (2009) explains, "in evolution's toolbox of adaptations that promote cooperation, the smile is perhaps the most potent tool" (p. 99). Smiles reduce interpersonal stress and activate reward centers in the brain (for both the originator and perceiver of the smile). They suggest that is safe to initiate, explore, and take risks. They facilitate bonding and signal an intention to help (or at least not to harm). In short, smiling is an efficient and reliable way to show cooperative intent and to communicate that "the door is open" to opportunities to initiate or further strengthen cooperative goal pursuits.

> A happy face can preempt conflict at the distance of a javelin's throw or rapidly defuse a misunderstood word or gesture in the blink of an eye. And once in the information-processing stream, the happy face can rise above typical limitations of attention, causing individuating features of a face to linger in memory, where they can cement future coalitional potentials. A consilience of the benefits that accrue to both the signaler and the receiver has rendered the happy facial expression vivid across many levels of cognitive processing, underscoring the more positive and prosocial side of human nature. (Becker & Srinivasan, 2014)

Along these same lines, the development of advanced language capabilities no doubt facilitated the ability of humans to cross the Cooperation Divide, as words and symbols make it possible to affirm and elaborate on the meaning, depth, and generality of an individual's cooperative intentions. Language was also important in enabling large groups of people to cooperate even though they couldn't all interact with one another directly. As we will see later in this chapter, by engaging in gossip about which group members could be counted on to be loyal and responsible, and which ones were unlikely to "play by the rules," large groups could efficiently rely on reputational information to make sound judgments about who they could trust. Through such enhancements language strengthened the motivational qualities and social-cognitive skills needed to sustain long-term cooperative relationships (Joyce, 2006).

Finally, there was an overarching preadaptation that enabled each of the mind-reading mechanisms described in the preceding paragraphs to flourish – namely, the emergence of human self-awareness. Once members of our species could think consciously about their own motives and develop self-concepts about their actions and capabilities, it was only a small additional step to imagine what *other people* might be thinking and feeling along these same lines (including thoughts and feelings that others might have about the mind reader!). This capability in turn created selection pressures for mechanisms that would enable people to make "good guesses" about what was going on in other people's minds. As we have seen, these mechanisms help us figure out what people are paying attention to (e.g., from inferences about eye gazing and pointing), what emotions they are experiencing (e.g., from inferences about facial expressions, vocal tone, and body language), and what thoughts are likely guiding their actions (e.g., from inferences about what they say and do). Taken together, these mind-reading skills gave our ancestors a powerful set of tools for enjoying the fruits of cooperation while minimizing the risks associated with misplaced trust.

Social emotions. As explained in Chapter 4, we are capable of experiencing a remarkable array of social emotions – often after "catching" them from others through empathy-related processes such as those supported by mirror neurons and Theory of Mind capabilities. Yet, all of these emotions conferred a similar benefit, namely, to encourage interpersonal bonding and cooperative living. Moreover, for all but the most self-centered members of our species, these emotions tend to be among the most compelling in our entire motivational repertoire. That is because social purpose is so central to human nature. We are intrinsically designed to feel bad when we violate norms associated with group loyalty and fairness, and to keep feeling bad until we take corrective action (as illustrated by emotions such as guilt and shame). Nor are we inclined to tolerate such norm violations in others (as evidenced by emotions such as anger and contempt). Indeed, we often take pride in helping others learn from their self-centered mistakes, especially when those mistakes were a result of ignorance rather than willful malevolence (as when teaching young children moral lessons or helping new group members "learn the ropes"). We also tend to experience strong feelings of affection for those group members who are the most helpful and trustworthy in their relationships with us.

Without these kinds of social emotions there would never have been a Cooperation Divide. As Gintis (2001) explains, "we would all be sociopaths, and human society would not exist, however strong the institutions of contract, exchange, and reputation" (p. xvii). In other words, it is not enough to intellectually understand how cooperation can be beneficial. We have to genuinely *care* about the people we interact with (i.e., have strong SP goals) and *feel* – at a visceral level – the disruptive emotions (recall Damasio's "change and commotion" metaphor) that compel people to behave in virtuous ways. That is why physical metaphors such as "social glue" are often used to refer to these emotions. Among such metaphors we particularly like the image of a "social leash," as social emotions not only bind people together as cooperative partners in a larger enterprise, they also curb unrestrained self-interest.

Once these social emotions became part of the inherited repertoire of basic human emotion patterns, cooperative living became "second nature" to our ancestors. Although self-interest remained a powerful motivational force, it was now reasonable to assume that, with the exception of a few outliers (e.g., sociopaths unmoved by circumstances that would normally trigger guilt or compassion), group members would have a variety of built-in "self-policing" mechanisms that would reliably motivate them to avoid getting too far off the cooperative path. Conversely, before these mechanisms evolved there was limited basis for mutual trust. Exchange relationships prior to the crossing of the Cooperation Divide could only work if they were based on simple reciprocity between confederates (e.g., "you scratch my back and I'll scratch yours") or on status-based rules for social interaction (e.g., "do as I say and you won't be punished").

"Modern" SP goals. Our distinction between "primitive" and "modern" social purpose goals relates to our ancestors' increasing capabilities for thinking beyond short-term goals and for envisioning *patterns* of future social interactions (as opposed to simply reacting to isolated events). As we have emphasized all along, SP goals must have existed long before the Cooperation Divide. Yet it is not possible to organize group interactions around cooperative principles with only community concern focused on isolated social encounters. There has to be a capacity to generalize beyond specific instances of cooperation and helping and to think in terms of interpersonal *relationships*. Moreover, group members have to be capable of envisioning those relationships extending into the future – that is, they have to be able to think in terms of *trust-based relationships* that are contingent on how people interact with one another over time (as opposed to relationship parameters that are "set in stone" by status definitions). In addition, there has to be a capacity for abstracting *relationship principles* that can provide a basis for socializing group members (especially young people and those who are new to the group) and helping them develop the emotional wisdom necessary to function effectively within the group.

Without these capabilities, the challenges associated with maintaining a cooperative egalitarian lifestyle would have been unmanageable. Community-sized groups are simply too dynamic and too complex to regulate using only episode-specific motivational mechanisms, even if those mechanisms include (primitive) SP goals and the social emotions capable of activating them. Crossing the Cooperation Divide required something more expansive and future oriented – namely, an ability to think in a more systematic and sustained way about concerns related to

- *belongingness* (e.g., how to sustain group cohesion without a rigid hierarchy);
- *equity* (e.g., how to make cooperation and fairness the "new normal");
- *social responsibility* (e.g., how to ensure ongoing conformity to social norms without relying primarily on coercive, fear-based strategies); and
- *resource provision* (e.g., how to make helping and sharing a natural way of life).

That is the essence of what we have termed modern SP goals.

"Modern" levels of thriving. Our use of the term "modern" with regard to the motivational amplifiers we have collectively labeled *thriving* follows the same logic as that used for modern SP goals. Humans did not suddenly become capable of personal optimism or mindful tenacity as they approached the Cooperation Divide. Nor did they suddenly become capable of pursuing goals with an active approach goal orientation and emotional wisdom. These elements of the thriving motivational pattern were part of the human experience (at least in a primitive form) long before that point in our species' history. Yet as our ancestors became increasingly capable of thinking about longer-term goal pursuits, and increasingly proficient at imagining how their short-term accomplishments could lead to "bigger and better things," thriving motivational *states* expanded to become thriving motivational *patterns* capable of empowering goal pursuit over prolonged periods of time. In other words, the extra potency and effectiveness gained by amplifying basic motivational functions was no longer confined to a particular life episode (e.g., enhanced performance during a hunt for prey). Motivational amplification could now have a cascading impact on a sequence of life episodes, with an individual's thriving qualities having the potential to influence both self (e.g., inventing better tools for hunting) and others (e.g., teaching a group of talented novices how to hunt more efficiently).

One can easily imagine the increasing importance of being able to sustain an active approach goal orientation and persistently positive personal agency beliefs as the time gap between formulating and achieving a goal increased. Indeed, one of the primary factors in the success of the human species was the capacity to imagine outcomes in the (relatively) distant future that were better than current conditions, and then – using self-awareness and mental time travel capabilities – to see oneself progressing toward those desired outcomes. In systems terms, during this period in human history motivation was becoming (relatively) less dependent on *feedback* information (i.e., information about the actual results of goal-directed activity) and increasingly guided by *feedforward* information (i.e., information about the anticipated results of goal-directed activity).

Yet, of all the thriving components perhaps the most significant in the transition from "primitive" to modern thriving was emotional wisdom. Cooperative living requires constant and effective "cross talk" between our mind-reading capabilities and our social emotions. Even the most powerful of emotions will be of little use if they are not triggered by the emotionally competent stimuli that make sense in a specific group context (e.g., if you keep an unequal share of food you personally obtained for the tribe, should you feel guilty? And how unequal can your share be before you risk a punitive response?). It was thus essential that people be capable of quickly acquiring "local knowledge" with respect to the kinds of circumstances in which it made sense to feel embarrassed, or guilty, or compassionate toward another member of the group. Such learning, helped along by our evolutionary readiness to make certain kinds of emotional connections, is often effortless once we understand the impact of our actions on others.

In addition, to avoid constant disruptions to group functioning, it was essential that anticipated consequences (feedforward) – not just actual consequences (feedback) – be capable of triggering social emotions. If the guidance provided by social emotions with respect to following cultural norms was not available until after a transgression had already occurred, that would leave people constantly vulnerable to group rejection. So, once again we see the importance of self-awareness and mental time travel in the development of modern thriving. Just as they do for us today, social emotions helped our ancestors make wise decisions that kept them together and capable of maintaining cooperative relationships. Yet the mechanisms for triggering those emotions were as much thought based (e.g., via mind reading and self-reflection) as event based. That is why the phrase "social intelligence" (or alternatively, "emotional intelligence") is often used to refer to the cognitive capabilities that contribute to emotional wisdom – and more broadly, TSP (Bar-On, 2006; M. Ford, 1986b; M. Ford & Maher, 1998; Mayer & Salovey, 1997; Mayer et al., 2008; E. O. Wilson, 2012).

When modern SP goals were infused into modern Thriving motivational patterns – as became increasingly common as humans approached the Cooperation Divide – the result was modern TSP. And that is when humanity began to soar. Stagnant and inflexible alpha male dominance hierarchies became a target for group members who could visualize a "better way of life" (egalitarian living) and far more effective methods for overcoming ecological challenges (teamwork and division of labor).

Inspired by strong SP goals, group members with amplified leadership qualities (including thriving motivational patterns) formed like-minded coalitions to oust the alpha male leaders and build a new community organized around principles of cooperation. This was no easy task, as illustrated by evidence showing that capital punishment was a common response to the alpha bullies (Boehm, 2012). Stoning, which was made possible by preadaptations that enabled skillful throwing, exemplified the use of community action to put a definitive end to the leadership reign of an alpha male bully. The TSP qualities of the new leaders in turn inspired others to cross to the other side of the Cooperation Divide, where they could become a contributing part of the new egalitarian culture.

And that's not all. With a new openness to ideas from a broad range of group members, motivation to share information about effective tools and techniques and to collaborate on new innovations skyrocketed. And with evolving cognitive mechanisms such as self-awareness, the ability to conduct mental simulations, a longer time perspective for goal-setting and planning, and Theory of Mind capabilities, humans were now able to transform their cooperative intentions into enduring cultural advances. That is how TSP set the stage for cumulative cultural evolution, which in turn fueled accelerated growth in the size of human brains, the portfolio of human knowledge and skills, and the pace of innovations capable of enhancing survival with well-being on a widespread scale.

No Going Back: Key Mechanisms Sustaining an Egalitarian Way of Life

In the previous section we outlined the advances that facilitated humanity's move from one side of the Cooperation Divide to the other. In this section we provide an overview of the essential mechanisms required to make the new egalitarian way of living work on a daily basis. As we will see, social purpose is at the heart of virtually all of these mechanisms, along with the motivational qualities we refer to as thriving.

Dominance and bullying behavior must be effectively repudiated. In their efforts to survive and experience well-being in ecologically challenging conditions, our ancestors found it increasingly useful to "team up" as they hunted and gathered food, defended themselves against predators and the elements, and cared for their offspring back at the campsite. That led to selection pressures for a variety of capabilities needed to engage in the kinds of cooperative activities and egalitarian methods of social control that we associate with "human nature at its best." Eventually a sufficient number of group members became endowed (through gene–culture coevolution) with the phenotypes needed to function as effective cooperators – including the ability to sustain "enforced equality" within a group setting (D. S. Wilson, 2007, p. 164). That is when cultural power began to "flip" from the physically strong alpha males in the group to those with TSP qualities. These new group leaders, through the strength of their amplified motivational resources and cohesion-building social skills, were able to organize large coalitions of cooperators to overthrow the alpha male bullies and condemn them to deviant status within – or if necessary, outside – the group (Keltner, 2009).

As noted earlier, the evolution of SP goals did not expunge dominance motives and capabilities from the repertoire of modern humans. Rather, it became a new "layer" of functional possibilities. That created a somewhat paradoxical "motivational fusion" in which we tend to resent being dominated, yet we often feel compelled to try to control others' behavior. We can also appreciate the practical value of hierarchical power arrangements in certain circumstances (e.g., in military organizations). Indeed, as population size began to grow, it became necessary to utilize some of the characteristics of hierarchical social organization to govern large-scale communities and societies. Yet wherever people are free to choose their preferred way of interacting with one another in small, face-to-face groups, they virtually always embrace egalitarian arrangements over dominance hierarchies. Notably, that is the case in the few remaining hunter-gatherer tribes that dot the Earth (Boehm, 2012).

Social purpose goals must be personally compelling and interpersonally contagious. Given the already well-established potency of self-assertive and self-protective personal goals, it was essential that modern social purpose goals become a similarly influential part of our ancestors' motivational systems for an egalitarian-based lifestyle to have any chance of being sustainable. The emergence of enriched mind-reading capabilities and powerful social emotions helped ensure that SP goals would have both the strength and immediacy needed to play a reliable leadership role in motivational headquarters. Emotional wisdom also played a key role in ensuring that SP goals remained in the forefront of decision-making when, for example, temptations arose to act in a selfish or socially irresponsible manner. The ability to link social emotions to *imagined* events (not just observed events) significantly increased both the timeliness of SP goal activation and the range of circumstances under which SP goals were likely to be activated.

In addition, to maintain an egalitarian social structure it was essential that individuals throughout the group develop shared understandings about the "rules of the cooperative game" and become emotionally responsive to the same kinds of stimuli (e.g., expressions of kindness or greed). Attaining these group-enhancing outcomes on a consistent and enduring basis would have been impossible without evolved, natural predispositions to share emotions (e.g., through emotional contagion processes) and to quickly learn (or automatically know) "right" and "wrong" ways of interacting with others. It is through such mechanisms that SP goals provide the underpinnings of a cooperative culture.

Compassion must be a commonly experienced reaction to helpless or distressed group members. For egalitarian groups to survive and prosper, individual group members needed to have the capacity for experiencing compassion not just toward offspring and close kin, but toward virtually any group member in need of assistance or support. For example, the capacity to feel compassion for young children other than one's own offspring was a critical prerequisite for the development of successful alloparenting practices (such practices inspired the contemporary phrase "it takes a village" to raise a child). Alloparenting is widely credited with enabling the longer developmental period required for the maturation of "big brains" (Hrdy, 2009).

That is not to say that feelings of compassion must be experienced on an undifferentiated basis before group members can sustain an egalitarian way of life. Although a generalized "compassionate mindset" is a good starting point, the key is to be especially likely to feel compassion for group members with reputations for helping others when they in turn need help. That is what creates a growing web of caring, trust, and influence among the group members most capable of sustaining an egalitarian way of life. This dynamic network of mutual support and advocacy helps explain why maintaining a good reputation is so important to our success in group settings – and why worrying about our reputations is both necessary and productive for cooperative group living. Indeed, it is "basic human nature" to be deeply concerned about our reputations and the reputations of others, and to share reputational information about group members (e.g., through constructive forms of "gossip"). That is the motivational foundation for creating whole *communities* with a compassionate mindset.

Acts of compassion can also model the benefits of social purpose to other group members. For example, in early societies, just as today, compassion served as a mechanism for defusing episodes of intragroup conflict, thus helping to ensure that feelings of anger or resentment toward others did not escalate to the point where they would tear the group apart. It is hard to sustain strong antagonistic feelings when even a twinge of compassion for the target of that animosity is triggered. Moreover, recipients of compassion are in turn more likely to be compassionate toward others (i.e., compassion is highly contagious). That motivational dynamic compounds the impact of what might otherwise be an isolated instance of compassion by encouraging others to engage in altruistic acts on behalf of the group, thus creating an upward spiral in the development of interpersonal bonding and overall group cohesion.

The capacity for compassion was probably well developed by the time humans crossed the Cooperation Divide, thus helping to ensure the sustainability of egalitarian patterns of social organization. One frequently cited source of evidence for this view focuses on "Turkana Boy," a nearly complete skeleton of a hominid (within either the *Homo ergaster* or *Homo erectus* lineage) found in 1984 on the shores of Lake Turkana, Kenya. Scientists have concluded that Turkana Boy likely could not have survived past early childhood without the support of a social group that responded compassionately to his apparent physical limitations.

> Turkana Boy suffered from a condition that stunted the growth of the openings in his vertebrae, the so-called vertebral canals. The resulting compression of his spinal cord would have made it difficult for him to get around. That the Turkana Boy survived past childhood may indicate that members of his social group protected and provided for him. (Johanson & Wong, 2010, p. 207)

Group members must be deeply and persistently concerned about their reputation and how their actions will impact their reputation. Reputation is an evolved mechanism (a mechanism often referred to as "indirect reciprocity") that makes it possible for people to predict how others will respond to them in future interactions even when they have little or no personal basis for making such a prediction. But reputation cuts both ways. It also enables others to predict how *you* are likely to respond to them in future interactions. Are you generally regarded as a cooperative person who can be relied upon to act in a socially responsible way? Or are you viewed as someone who can't be trusted to follow the rules, do your share, or remain loyal to the group?

In the short run people with self-serving motives can often fool people into thinking they can be trusted by being friendly and charming. But that is a tough act to sustain over time when people are paying attention to reputational information (and they usually are! – either consciously or beneath awareness). Conversely, it may take a while for those who are inclined to be generous and helpful to be appreciated if their actions are viewed from a cynical perspective. But over time authentic social purpose builds goodwill and trust, and that "reputational news" spreads to others (e.g., via gossip).

Recent research suggests that this process of *selection by reputation* is the secret to achieving the highest levels of success in competitive business and educational settings.

> Studies show that on average, from sales teams to paper mill crews to restaurants, the more giving group members do, the higher the quantity and quality of their groups' products and services. But it's not just their groups that get rewarded . . .. Extensive research reveals that people who give their time and knowledge regularly to help their colleagues end up earning more raises and promotions in a wide range of settings. (Grant, 2013, p. 74)

Admittedly, the idea of being concerned about your reputation may sound more self-promoting than other-promoting. Consistent with that assessment, the goal category (from the Taxonomy of Human Goals) most closely associated with reputation management is resource acquisition (i.e., "obtaining approval, support, assistance, advice, or validation from others; avoiding social disapproval or rejection"). Yet for most people the goal themes of resource acquisition, resource provision, and belongingness all tend to blend together in close relationships and in egalitarian group settings (M. Ford & Nichols, 1991; Orehek & Forest, 2016). These goals are often jointly activated because close relationships and cooperative social interactions involve a combination of giving (resource provision) and receiving (resource acquisition), while also strengthening group cohesion (belongingness). As a result, reputational concerns are naturally embedded within our ongoing efforts to pursue social purpose goals. That is why, for example, Grant and Mayer (2009) found that the employees rated by their supervisors as being the most helpful and taking the most initiative were those who reported not only a strong concern for benefiting others, but also an interest in creating a positive image for themselves.

Of course, we all know people who are preoccupied with their reputations to the detriment of other important goals. Indeed, in the extreme case (e.g., someone who is pathologically narcissistic), helping others may never be anything more than a means for self-affirmation and self-promotion. Yet that simply illustrates how our motivational strengths can quickly become liabilities when equipoise is lost between self-assertive and integrative goal pursuits.

Why is reputation such an important factor in maintaining an egalitarian way of life? People who are unconcerned about their reputations (or who fail to activate such goals at the appropriate times) are much more likely to engage in selfish or disrespectful actions toward others than those who are motivated to maintain a positive reputation. They are also more likely to actually harm others and to undermine the shared assumptions that make cooperative group living possible. Conversely, those who are appropriately concerned about how others' perceive them are far more likely to exercise self-restraint and to show generosity toward others (Barclay, 2010; Boehm, 2012). And when people who are concerned about their reputations are accused of not living up to a group's expectations, they will generally go to great lengths to try to repair their damaged reputations, thus validating the group's shared assumptions about proper conduct. In short, reputational concerns help keep self-interest in check.

Fortunately, there are not many people in this world who are habitually unconcerned about their reputation. Like all of the group-sustaining motivational mechanisms described in this chapter, personal goals related to reputational concerns were already well entrenched as humanity approached the Cooperation Divide – and not just at the level of cultural values. As a result of hundreds of thousands of years of learning how to effectively use reputational information to predict behavior, such concerns are innately "hardwired" into the biological infrastructure of the human species. We care deeply about our reputations because our successful ancestors (i.e., the survivors) had good ones!

Indeed, you may be surprised to learn how powerful and ubiquitous reputation-related personal goals are in the scope of human activity. It has been estimated that 60–70 percent of all of our conversational energies are devoted in some manner to reputation management (Emler, 1990). Wanting to show the world that we are "appropriate" and trustworthy cooperators is so automatic that we even do things to protect our reputation when only strangers are involved, as illustrated by the consistency with which people engage in their normal levels of tipping whether in local or out-of-town restaurants (Keltner, 2009). Similarly, in most cultures "we do not cut into queues, because we care what other people – even strangers – think of us" (Ridley, 1996, p. 142).

Research on the development of altruism in young children documents how ready members of our species are to use reputational evidence in their social decision-making once they have developed the cognitive infrastructure necessary to make such judgments:

> children begin learning early in life who and who not to be nice to based on their own experiences with those people . . .. The other set of social influences on children involves the values and norms of the cultural group . . . . Children at some point become aware that they are the targets of the judgments of others who are using social norms as standards. So children attempt to influence these judgments – what the sociologist Erving Goffman called "impression management." Through this kind of vigilance is born the public self, whose reputation we all spend so much time and energy cultivating and defending. (Tomasello, 2009, pp. 30–31)

Group members must collectively take responsibility for detecting and sharing information about cheaters and social deviants. A cultural system that relies heavily on reputational information to guide social decision-making can only work if there is a strong collective commitment to engage in the actions required to verify who is failing to live up to the norms of the group, and to communicate relevant evidence and concerns to other group members. Having an alpha male in charge is like having a lone police officer monitoring group members' conduct. In contrast, the metaphor of a "neighborhood watch" group is more applicable to egalitarian living on the other side of the Cooperation Divide.

The concept of "strong reciprocation" has been used to characterize how this commitment goes beyond self-interest to focus on group integrity and the protection of other group members. Strong reciprocation is defined as "a predisposition to cooperate with others, and to altruistically punish (punish at a personal cost, if necessary) those who violate the norms of cooperation, even when it is implausible to expect that these costs will be recovered at a later date" (Gintis et al., 2005, p. 8). This predisposition helps create a widespread understanding that if you don't follow the rules, you are likely to suffer not only some form of short-term punishment, but also a longer-term problem – namely, a damaged reputation. This is an essential mechanism for maintaining an egalitarian culture, as punishment (which by definition is "after the fact") is generally far less effective in regulating social conduct than the ever-present desire to avoid a disgraced reputation (Wu et al., 2016). The effects of reputational damage may take much longer to wear off, and cause much more personal suffering (e.g., shame) than a punishment that is very unpleasant but confined to a limited time period.

As we saw with reputation management at a personal level, the process of protecting a group's interests by exposing and protecting others' reputations can become distorted if it is done in a non-equipoised way. For example, while gossip is an essential and productive activity in groups that rely heavily on reputational information, overzealous and exaggerated reporting of norm transgressions can cause far more harm than good (e.g., by unfairly damaging someone's reputation or causing people to reject someone who could be an important asset to the group). Conversely, protecting the reputation of a group member who has engaged in extraordinarily transgressive behavior can ultimately become highly destructive to the group's ability to maintain loyalty and trust (as illustrated by instances where sexual harassment is minimized by group leaders).

There is considerable evidence that "cheater detection" – that is, detection of unfair responses from nonreciprocating opportunists – is an innate capability of humans (and present to a lesser extent in some other primates; Brosnan & de Waal, 2003). For example, young children participate in the enforcement of social norms from a very early age, almost at the same point when they themselves begin to actively comply with social norms (Tomasello, 2009). Similarly, "when an experimental subject is told that his partner already has defected in a Prisoner's Dilemma defection is the almost universal response" (Frank, 2001, p. 73). The idea that there is a biological basis for cheater detection competencies is further supported by research on brain-damaged individuals. These studies "suggest that cheater detection is supported by a specialized neural system that requires the coordinated functioning of areas of the prefrontal cortex and the amygdala, among other regions" (Geary, 2005, p. 181).

Members of large groups must be able to track each other's conduct over time and coordinate their responses to deficient (as well as exemplary) behavior. The primary mechanism through which this essential function is carried out is through the sharing of reputational information, which is typically called "gossip." Gossip is a universal and very efficient method of learning "a great deal about the social minutiae of a great many individuals" when groups are too large to accomplish this goal through direct observation (Joyce, 2006, p. 90). (Imagine, for example, trying to choose a doctor or hire a plumber without first checking out what previous patients and customers had to say about their experience.) As D. S. Wilson (2007) explains,

> a small-scale society bristles with defenses against subversion from within.
> The first line of defense is gossip, which maintains a dossier of information
> on every member and quickly detects social failings . . .. The defense system
> provides a social environment in which genuine trustworthiness and altru-
> ism can thrive, precisely because the wolves of selfishness are being held at
> bay. (pp. 160–161)

Recent research by Feinberg et al. (2014) illustrates the efficiency through which gossip can have a positive impact on group functioning through the process of selection by reputation. Participants in this study played several rounds of a public-goods game in groups of four (each round with different players) in which they made decisions that benefited either the group or themselves. Different experimental conditions varied the degree to which there was an opportunity to clue in the participants in the next round about selfish players, and for the new players to ostracize targeted individuals. As the rounds continued,

> individuals readily communicated reputational information about others,
> and recipients used this information to selectively interact with cooperative
> individuals and ostracize those who had behaved selfishly, which enabled
> group members to contribute to the public good with reduced threat of
> exploitation. Additionally, ostracized individuals responded to exclusion by
> subsequently cooperating at levels comparable to those who were not
> ostracized. These results suggest that the spread of reputational information
> through gossip can mitigate egoistic behavior. (p. 656)

Some scholars have speculated that one of the key factors leading to the emergence of language capabilities was selection pressure to be able to quickly assess qualities such as reliability and integrity within a large social group. Known as the "gossip hypothesis" (Dunbar, 1993; Joyce, 2006), this intriguing idea is supported by evidence documenting a significant correla-tion between group size and neocortex ratio (i.e., the ratio of neocortex volume to the volume of the rest of the brain). As group size increased from several dozen to well over 100 in the course of human evolution:

> increasing pressure was developing in favor of there being some new and
> more efficient means for exchanging information about the behavior and
> relationships of one's interactants. The pressure was first upon *Homo habilis,*
> and subsequently became so acute that we can assume that some solution
> must have been struck upon. Language, it is argued, is that solution . . ..
> A language of gossip is a language of reciprocity. (Joyce, 2006, p. 90)

Given the key role that gossip plays not only in supporting egalitarian group living (Peters et al., 2017), but also in motivating self-improvement

(Martinescu et al., 2014), it is unfortunate that this term is so often used in a pejorative way. That reflects the potential for gossip to "backfire" when it is communicated in a non-equipoised way, with inadequate respect for people's privacy and an inclination to eagerly accept unreliable rumors and assumptions (e.g., "I saw it on the Internet so it must be true!"). Yet, it is precisely this potential for "drama" that makes gossip such a powerful mechanism for motivating people to think carefully *before* acting in an inappropriately self-serving or antisocial way. The "fear of gossip all by itself serves as a preemptive social deterrent because most people are so sensitive about their reputations" (Boehm, 2012, p. 197).

Gossip also ensures that group members cannot simply invent their own reputations by repeatedly exercising their powers of personal persuasion (e.g., to get votes, money, or sexual favors). When people freely share reputational information with each other, even the most skilled cheaters and free riders cannot avoid exposure for very long. Indeed, in a "connected" world where information can be shared with increasing speed across a wide range of potential social partners, the need to diligently safeguard one's reputation has escalated to new heights.

And what better way to ensure a "bulletproof" reputation than to actually behave in a fair and helpful manner on a consistent basis? As explained in Chapters 3 and 4, such consistencies are typically associated with virtuous terms like "integrity." Indeed, the most reliable pathway to a secure reputation is to routinely prioritize goals such as equity and resource provision across *all* social partners and circumstances, without having to engage in complex calculations about the degree of kinship or potential for reciprocity (as many mathematical models of prosocial behavior seem to require).

In short, gossip is not only a natural and enjoyable part of our daily social life, it is a civic-minded way (when practiced in an equipoised manner) of ensuring that group members respect the egalitarian "rules of the game." Talking about people in the social networks we care about is an automatic part of "basic human nature" because our hominid ancestors who crossed the Cooperation Divide found it increasingly useful to gossip, and only those groups who engaged in and paid attention to gossip were able to survive.

Group members must be willing to sanction cheaters and social deviants when reputational incentives are insufficient, even if it involves some personal cost. Although reputational concerns, fortified by gossip, provide a highly effective mechanism for preventing social norm violations, it is still just a "first line of defense." When gossip is not enough, group members must be prepared to punish transgressors despite social and even physical risks that are likely to escalate as the level of sanctioning increases. The initial punishment might simply involve giving someone a disapproving glare or a "cold shoulder." Punitive verbal responses might also be directed at the transgressor – for example, in the form of criticism, ridicule, or some sort of public censure. If, despite such sanctions, the offending conduct persists, more serious measures such as ostracism (Williams & Zadro, 2001) or even expulsion from the group might then need to be considered. In primitive human societies, expulsion was, in effect, a death sentence. Yet, when the transgressor's conduct was perceived as placing others in immediate danger, the punishment of choice was more likely to be a swifter and more public form of execution. Notably, execution by stoning is still carried out in extant hunter-gatherer tribes in extreme cases of social deviance (D. S. Wilson, 2007).

The evidence from evolutionary science clearly suggests that all of these punitive measures are hardwired responses to social deviance. Such evidence is consistent with the idea that the punishment of deviance directly reduces the genetic fitness of deviant conduct and increases the genetic fitness of those who are willing to engage in "altruistic punishment" (i.e., punishment that is personally costly or results in no personal gain). The fact that "cooperation flourishes if altruistic punishment is possible, and breaks down if it is ruled out" (Fehr & Gächter, 2002, p. 137), also helps explain how behaviors that have a potential personal cost can actually strengthen a group and the individuals within it. When social deviance consistently triggers emotions such as anger and contempt, thereby activating the SP goals necessary to motivate people to put aside self-interest, there is a collective effort to "right the wrongs" that threaten the group's organizing principles. Moreover, by reducing the reproductive attractiveness (and longevity!) of those who were least willing to conform to egalitarian norms, early societies were able to shape "basic human nature" over the thousands of generations in which our species evolved, thus yielding an increasingly egalitarian profile. That is one key pathway through which humans became "wired to cooperate."

Social Purpose Goes Viral!

It appears that the "slope" on the other side of the Cooperation Divide must have been pretty steep, as changes in the social, cognitive, and motivational functioning of humans became increasingly fast-paced after the divide was crossed. Not unlike today's internet-based social networks, a classic "tipping point" was evidently reached when the number of converted groups grew beyond a few isolated outposts, and egalitarian living became an increasingly visible phenomenon.

And the rest, as they say, was (pre)history!

As illustrated by the extraordinary outcomes associated with cumulative cultural evolution, the significance of this evolutionary bifurcation was monumental, with consequences that ultimately reached far beyond the obvious surface-level changes in social interaction patterns. As we have seen, when a tipping point is reached in a developmental progression, conditions are ripe for the emergence of upward spirals of innovation and accomplishment. In the early phase of this progression, change tends to be tentative and incremental. But after a tipping point is reached, changes become more interconnected and mutually reinforcing. That speeds up the developmental process and makes each subsequent change more impactful. Large-scale transformations that once seemed unthinkable suddenly become not only credible, but seemingly inevitable. Who would have thought, for example, that a 1970s computer that filled up a large room would evolve into a computer that is a thousand times more powerful and a million times less expensive – and that you could hold in the palm of your hand! And who would have imagined, even toward the end of the twentieth century, that it might soon be possible to talk credibly about "crazy ideas" like constructing a digital copy of our own personal genome, or inserting a robot into our body to repair damaged tissue?

In the early days of human life, gene–culture coevolutionary progressions with these upward spiral characteristics were playing out both within and across societies. Once a particular group reached a threshold level of cooperators, social selection pressures accelerated the push toward egalitarian norms throughout that group. As Richerson and Boyd (2005) explain,

> these cooperators would have discriminated against individuals who carried genes that made them too belligerent to conform to the new cooperative norms. Then the cultural rules could expand cooperation a bit further, generating selection for still more-docile genes. (p. 15)

This made it possible for a minority of strong reciprocators (i.e., TSP individuals functioning as group influencers) to expand their influence and ultimately reorganize the entire group around egalitarian rules and ideals.

One by one, prehistoric hunting bands implemented mini-rebellions that permanently abolished the alpha male role in favor of a more egalitarian social order. Over time, as more individuals and coalitions became aware of this "new way of life," another tipping point was reached *across* groups. Indeed,

> the human moral community might have arrived rather quickly . . . because a group's taking over power from an alpha male despot is something of an all-or-none enterprise . . .. Once humans had acquired a sophisticated system of communication, they were ready to start acting as a community-wide coalition with a political goal of living without domination . . .. It is easy to see how this institution would have spread, for its advantages were perceptually obvious. Members of bands would have visited with egalitarian groups, and they would have seen entire bands routinely keeping down their strongest individuals – with the rank and file enjoying personal autonomy previously inconceivable. This could have served as a stimulus to rapid cultural diffusion. (Boehm, 2000, pp. 97–98)

How the Evolution of Thriving with Social Purpose Led to the "Social Conquest of Earth"

E. O. Wilson chose to include the phrase "social conquest of earth" in the title of his 2012 book to emphasize the prosocial origins of humanity and the power of group selection in precipitating the events that led to our species becoming a dominant force across the globe. It is an apt phrase for capturing the dramatic reproductive success of those who engaged in the "new and improved" egalitarian methods of living and working together.

> A group with members who could read intentions and cooperate among themselves while predicting the actions of competing groups, would have an enormous advantage over others less gifted. There was undoubtedly competition among group members, leading to natural selection of traits that gave advantage of one individual over another. But more important for a species entering new environments and competing with powerful rivals were unity and cooperation within the group. Morality, conformity, religious fervor, and fighting ability combined with imagination and memory to produce the winner. (E. O. Wilson, 2012, p. 224)

TSP enabled complex division of labor arrangements to blossom. In a dominance hierarchy, group members generally do what they are told (or physically compelled!) to do by those above them in the hierarchy. That affords a high degree of control, but it also inhibits innovation and the nurturing of special talents. In contrast, in an egalitarian culture organized around principles of self-direction and reciprocity, it becomes possible for people to explore different roles (at least to a somewhat greater extent) and to autonomously invest themselves in goal pursuits that build expertise. Moreover, different people can focus their goal seeking on different kinds of specialties. Add in reciprocity, and the opportunities for bigger and better accomplishments skyrocket. People can team up with trusted partners to create new capabilities and alliances, thus enabling them to overcome obstacles, work more efficiently, and protect each other's interests. They can enhance resources for themselves while also benefiting others through bartering, exchanges, and agreements about how to share or trade resources.

Ridley (1996) even goes so far as to suggest that the primary advantages of group living are those associated with division of labor arrangements that encourage people with specialized skills to join forces, thus creating ubiquitous win-win scenarios across a wide range of human communities – for example, in adult couples, in extended families, in hunting groups, in apprenticeships, and in many other kinds of mutually beneficial relationships.

> It is this synergy between specialists that makes human societies tick, and it is this that distinguishes us from all other social creatures .... The great advantage of human society is the division of labour, and the "non-zero-sumness" it achieves .... But this still does not tell us how human society got started in the first place .... The strongest hypothesis is that it was reciprocity. (Ridley, 1996, pp. 41, 49–50)

TSP fueled upward spirals of cumulative cultural evolution. The concept of cumulative cultural evolution refers to the ratcheting up of a society's repertoire of K&S and new innovations through activities designed to ensure the transmission and preservation of valuable tools, ideas, and behavioral practices across generations. Such activities include systematic observational learning, intentional teaching and mentoring, and the creation of artifacts and guides designed for use by future generations. Because these distinctly human activities (Richerson & Boyd, 2005; Tomasello, 2009) are both socially and intellectually demanding, they required larger brains with greater functionality. In effect, as the "software" requirements (selection pressures) for group living increased, the "hardware" requirements (brain structures) evolved accordingly. Bigger brains enabled new mental capabilities to emerge and develop (e.g., advanced planning and mental simulation capabilities; sustained capacity for self-awareness and empathy), which in turn made it possible to innovate even further and to become increasingly effective at transmitting K&S to others.

The ascendance of SP goals played a critical and pivotal role in this autocatalytic K&S/brain size upward spiral. In addition to enabling humans to cross the Cooperation Divide and experience a vastly improved day-to-day social life, SP goals motivated people to become curious about what other group members were thinking and to engage in intellectually demanding teaching, learning, and teamwork activities. As a result, brain size increases started to accelerate rather dramatically after the crossing of the Cooperation Divide (Geary, 2005). This acceleration process was fueled by selection pressures that were becoming magnified by an "arms race" of continuous K&S innovation versus the mental resources needed to enable people to understand, imitate, and adopt those innovations and then pass them on to others. Indeed, "just storing the large cultural repertoires involved with complex, accumulated cultural adaptations may require considerable brain volume" (Richerson & Boyd, 2005, p. 132). A period of rapid brain (and brainpower) expansion ensued, ultimately resulting in the emergence of the Anatomically Modern Human (E. O. Wilson, 2012). Those bigger brains required rather massive caloric intake (relative to the smaller brains of early hominids), which was only possible because – you guessed it – SP goals enabled egalitarian food sharing, especially in the context of large game hunting (Boehm, 2000).

Cumulative cultural evolution requires a society to have strong and pervasive capabilities for innovation, teaching, and learning. Yet, as anyone in the education profession can attest, many such activities require a great deal of effort, persistence, and patience – typically more than is required for familiar activities for which expertise has already been developed. Fortunately, our evolutionary heritage has given us powerful motivational predispositions to be inquisitive and to increase our competence (Elliot & Dweck, 2005, 2017; Harter, 1978; R. White, 1959). Yet, when the time requirements are extensive, and the rewards are more in the future than in the present (as is often the case), it is not easy to maintain the energy and mental focus needed to absorb new information, master new skills, and help others gain expertise. That is a key reason why the marriage of SP goals and thriving motivational qualities is such a potent combination. When the motivational forces that fuel initiative and persistence (thriving qualities) are infused with social purpose, learning and achievement efforts are amplified and increasingly self-sustaining (Wentzel, 1996; Wentzel & Wigfield, 1998).

TSP qualities became increasingly vital in maintaining an accelerated trajectory of innovation and adoption. Once cumulative cultural evolution started, it continuously accelerated, limited only by the innovative and imitative capacities of the adopters – which, as we have seen, are inextricably linked to TSP. Indeed, that exponentially accelerating trajectory continues today unabated. The growth of cumulative cultural evolution stands in sharp contrast to the patterns seen in genetic evolution, which are generally characterized by long periods of relative stability (notwithstanding some ongoing fine tuning), punctuated, on rare occasions, by episodes of rapid, transformational change (thus the use of the phrase "punctuated equilibrium" to describe such patterns; Gould & Eldredge, 1977).

TSP has been a powerful factor underlying the development of humankind's most important achievements because it accelerates both innovation *and* the cooperative activity required for innovation adoption (e.g., via direct and indirect methods of teaching and enculturation). Innovation frequency drives the cultural knowledge base, which in turn inspires the development of enhanced capabilities and resources, both within the individual (e.g., increased intelligence) and within the group (e.g., increased collective intelligence). Thus, in addition to its role as a "catalyst for humanity," TSP has played (and continues to play) an accelerator role in the cultural evolution of modern humans.

Why Knowing about Our SP Goals Is Important

We have invested substantial effort in this chapter to provide you with evidence that social purpose goals (i.e., belongingness, social responsibility, equity, and resource provision) are not only a natural and authentic part of human nature, but also at the heart of the dynamic circumstances that initiated human history and propelled it forward to unprecedented achievements. Yet understanding how our past shaped who we are today is not the only reason we have devoted so much time to these topics.

Whether we think of social purpose as a facade or as a motivationally irreducible part of human nature has a powerful impact on our future.

If you think that helping people and making socially responsible choices is "normal" and expected, that will lead you to make choices in which concern for others is often at the forefront of your thinking – consistent with the way we evolved as a species. Conversely, if you think that the smart and accepted way to interact with other people is to focus on maximizing personal gain, you are likely to view generosity and kindness as sentiments of people who are gullible or simple-minded, and act accordingly. Moreover, the cumulative effect of many people sharing this belief can be enormous. As Nesse (2001) warns, "individuals who believe that everyone is out for himself or herself are incapable of making subjective commitments; their social worlds are populated only by exchange partners whose motives are always suspect" (p. 19).

Now perhaps you are wondering, if our evolutionary heritage has shaped our species to be cooperative and egalitarian, won't those fundamental dispositions ultimately trump any effort to deny their existence? Unfortunately, things are not that simple. Humans are multifaceted – as we have emphasized all along, basic human nature includes both social purpose *and* self-interest. Indeed, optimal functioning requires the active, equipoised pursuit of both integrative and self-assertive personal goals (Koestler, 1967, 1978).

Nor does human development unfold along a fully predetermined trajectory. Our brains and our thoughts are "plastic" and constantly adapting to new information and new ideas as they are perceived and processed and combined with other cognitive constructions. This plasticity makes it possible for new stimuli to become emotionally competent and capable of activating core personal goals. Money is a good example of a learned emotionally competent stimulus that tends to suppress generosity and helpfulness, even in young children with limited understanding of how money works (Gasiorowska et al., 2016). At the same time, the potency of stimuli that might normally lead to the activation of social purpose goals (e.g., observing people who appear to be impoverished) can quickly fade if cultural support for that sentiment is lacking.

The power that money has to distort our evolved balance between self-interest and social purpose is illustrated by one of the most disheartening developments in modern human life – the tendency for economically privileged individuals to effectively use incorrect notions about basic human nature to justify excessive levels of greed and selfishness. Yet this is not how our hunter-gather ancestors in their "environment of evolutionary adaptiveness" (EEA; Bowlby, 1969) organized their daily lives. Wealth disparity is a relatively "recent" phenomenon ushered in with the domestication of flora and fauna. Non-equipoised patterns of wealth accumulation ignore the evolved tendency for people to prefer egalitarian forms of group functioning (as illustrated by the fact that when individuals are randomly assigned to a group, they almost always gravitate to a cooperative group structure). That is why wealth disparity can be such a demotivating influence in human development, even when (and perhaps especially when) the rhetoric of privileged leaders embraces social purpose themes like cooperation, helping, and social responsibility.

In short, the behaviors that flow from our thoughts and emotions are continually being shaped by what we observe and hear and experience. As a result, we all have a spectrum of "possible selves" (Markus & Nurius, 1986; Oyserman & Fryberg, 2006) that can range from reliably generous to persistently self-serving. Which possible selves are likely to emerge as "winners" over time? That depends largely on which ones we regard as genuine and comfortable. Frank (2001) observed, for example, that economics majors (whose curriculum champions the *homo economicus* assumption of rational self-interest) made almost twice as many uncooperative choices in the Prisoner's Dilemma game as non–economics majors. That suggests that our possible selves can develop in very different directions depending on cultural and contextual influences. For those socialized into believing that the rational thing to do is to prioritize your own interests, it will seem to make sense to try to "get as much as you can, whenever you can" from your social partners and collaborators. In contrast, for those who accept and appreciate the authenticity of social purpose goals, adopting such an exploitative mindset as a home page motivational orientation is likely to feel very uncomfortable, if not appalling.

The damage that can be done by erroneous beliefs about human nature grows exponentially when those beliefs become widespread within a particular subculture (Hamedani et al., 2013). As Grant (2013) explains,

> workplaces and schools are often designed to be zero-sum environments, with forced rankings and required grading curves that pit group members against one another in win-lose contests. In these settings, it's only natural to assume that peers will lean in the taker direction, so people hold back on giving. This reduces the actual amount of giving that occurs, leading people to underestimate the number of people who are interested in giving . . . . This is what happens in many businesses and universities: plenty of people hold giver values, but suppress or disguise them under the mistaken assumption that their peers don't share these values . . . . When people assume that others aren't givers, they act and speak in ways that discourage others from giving, creating a self-fulfilling prophecy. (pp. 241–243)

This self-fulfilling "prophecy of self-interest" can be seen all the way along the cultural continuum from very small groups (e.g., spouses or business partners who are constantly bickering about chores or resources rather than working together as a team), to the level of corporate and organizational cultures (e.g., firms focused solely on short-term profits rather than seeking win-win investments that benefit — and motivate – their customers or clients), to very large groups representing an entire state or nation (e.g., politicians who chronically refuse to engage in reasonable compromises with members of the opposition party). With regard to this latter example, it is revealing to see what emotions are typically activated in the general population by political subcultures that view cooperation and compromise as weaknesses to be avoided or, even worse, as conduct to be disparaged. Emotions such as disgust and disapproval are far more common in public opinion polls regarding such groups than feelings of pride or satisfaction. Yet politicians have become very skilled at convincing their constituents that, to preserve the voters' self-interest (because that is of course the only correct way to think about how to vote!), reelection is essential.

Consistent with these negative "gut reactions" to glaring instances of uncooperative behavior, there is clear scientific evidence to support the view that, rather than being naturally selfish when faced with opportunities to share and donate, our instinct is to be generous. It is only after we reflect on our choices that self-interest becomes a more salient consideration. For example, in the first of ten studies by Rand and his colleagues (Rand et al., 2012), they found that people who took a relatively long time to decide how much of a forty cent gift to donate to a communal pool donated the least. In a subsequent study, they controlled the amount of time participants had to make a donation decision (i.e., within ten seconds, not until after waiting ten seconds, or with no time constraint at all), and the same pattern emerged. Those required to make quick decisions donated the most, and those forced to wait at least ten seconds before making a decision donated the least. Additional research demonstrated that these patterns reliably occurred across different groups of people and across different kinds of tasks (including the Prisoner's Dilemma game).

Even more convincing with respect to the power of beliefs to promote or discourage generosity was a further experiment in this series of studies in which participants were primed to think about the relative efficacy of intuition versus careful reasoning. In one experimental condition people were asked to write an essay about a time in their life when their intuition led them in the right direction or when they were wrong despite careful reasoning. A second group was asked to write about a time in their life when careful reasoning led them in the right direction or their intuition led them astray. When each group was subsequently asked to donate money, donations were significantly higher for the group that was primed to value intuition over careful reasoning.

Such experiments help us understand the innate properties of our motivational systems and how they can be influenced. Apparently, our natural impulse is to be cooperative and helpful in settings where others are disadvantaged or in need. That is consistent with the premise that SP goals have ancient, deep-rooted origins, and thus are easily activated when we encounter a stimulus capable of triggering emotions like compassion, affection, or anticipatory guilt. And yet, when given time to question the wisdom of that impulse, there is a tendency for many of us to equivocate and become increasingly self-serving. Evidently the emotional impact of our generous and egalitarian instincts can quickly fade as we consciously reflect on the things our culture (or at least the *homo economicus* part of our culture) reinforces – and often celebrates – on a daily basis (e.g., self-gratification and the accumulation of material possessions).

In short, it seems evident that "selfish gene" (Dawkins, 1976) thinking causes us to behave selfishly, and to become more selfish versions of ourselves. In addition, it causes us to view other people with mistrust and suspicion, thus infusing negative context beliefs into our daily social interactions even when they are not accurate or appropriate (D. Miller & Ratner, 1998). That is clearly *not* a pathway to optimal functioning, either at the individual or societal level. For individuals, selfish gene thinking reduces access to social resources and deprives people of the motivational benefits associated with the pursuit of social purpose goals. And at a group level, belief systems that discount the authenticity of SP goals reduce the potential for constructing the collaborative partnerships that bring strength to organizations, communities, and nations.

Thriving with Social Purpose: Motivation at Its (Human) Best

When we started our quest to identify patterns of motivation that were consistently associated with optimal functioning, we had strong hypotheses about many of the aspects of motivation we have organized under the concept of *thriving*. After all, motivation scholars had been accumulating evidence for several decades linking school achievement, work productivity, and well-being with an active approach orientation to goal pursuit and with PAB patterns saturated with context-appropriate optimism and tenacity. (Work related to emotional wisdom was less plentiful but still sufficiently compelling to "point us in the right direction.") Yet we did not start with the idea that any particular kind of goal content would be uniquely important in the lives of humans (beyond the obvious subset of physiological goals necessary to maintain life). Indeed, like most scientists, we resisted the idea of making value judgments about what kinds of desired outcomes people should prioritize in their hierarchy of personal goals. The most important thing was for each person to have *something* in their goal profile that was personally engaging and meaningful, whatever that may be. "Different strokes for different folks" was our guiding principle when it came to goal content.

Yet, the more we learned about basic human nature – especially with respect to the motivational patterns that caused humanity to transcend the limitations of other species on the planet – the more we realized that a complete theory of motivation and optimal functioning must incorporate evidence regarding the unique role of integrative social relationship goals in human development. As we have seen, in a species as "ultrasocial" as humans, where very little can be accomplished without teamwork, cooperation, and sharing of material and informational resources, there is simply no substitute for strong, reliable social purpose goals. In contrast, plenty of people lead happy, productive lives despite only sporadic interest in goal categories like entertainment, bodily sensations, or transcendence. Many individuals find fulfilling life pathways even if they are not particularly concerned with, say, material gain, task creativity, or management goals. Yet, because SP goals are relevant in such a broad range of situations, it is virtually impossible to set them aside for very long. They don't always have to be the *most* important consideration, but if SP goals are not a routine part of what matters to you when you interact with other people, odds are that you won't get too far in your interpersonal relationships.

Fortunately, most people can accept some degree of self-centered behavior, as they are well aware that one aspect of human nature (including their own nature!) is to be selfish and irresponsible from time to time (especially when we think we're not being watched). But the consequences can be serious for those who ignore the interests of their social partners, or who lack either emotional wisdom or equipoise about when to exercise self-restraint. Imagine your reaction to someone who doesn't share when a situation clearly calls for equitable distribution of resources, or doesn't contribute anything to the group when a task requires cooperation and teamwork. You would likely be "turned off" by that blatant display of self-interest, and question the person's judgment and loyalty to the group. Even if you never directly witnessed any such episodes of social insensitivity, you might still be inclined to avoid that person if they had a reputation for being egocentric and self-serving. That is why people work so hard to try to maintain a positive reputation among those they depend on for resources, support, and validation.

It is important to reiterate that optimal functioning does not require that SP goals be at the forefront of your thinking in every situation. Sometimes SP goals are relevant more as a backdrop or boundary condition for an activity centered on self-enhancement. Indeed, we have repeatedly emphasized the importance of maintaining an equipoised balance between self-enhancing and other-enhancing goals. Nevertheless, even in the most self-focused goal pursuits we can imagine, maintaining progress and achieving long-term success virtually always requires a significant amount of teamwork and reliance on others. For example, elite athletes focused on individualistic accomplishments invariably depend on a strong and reliable network of supportive advocates and resource providers to help them achieve their competitive goals. Passionate artists and ivory tower scholars often rely on enabling cultural systems and the cumulative contributions of preceding generations of performers, scientists and technicians. Even the most reclusive members of our species must rely on – and therefore must "fit in" with – societal structures for acquiring desired information, food, and other life-sustaining materials.

In the next chapter, we focus on yet another body of scientific evidence that supports the notion that *Thriving with Social Purpose* is motivation at its (human) best. As it turns out, we not only evolved the multifaceted capabilities needed to enable TSP modes of goal pursuit, we also evolved the capacity to *sense* when we are functioning in an optimal way, through a unique – and uniquely powerful – type of feeling that tells us that *life is worth living*. These conscious feelings of *life meaning* encourage us to repeat and build upon the events that led to those feelings. That is an important way that TSP patterns of motivation are automatically sustained and strengthened within most members of our species.

CHAPTER 7

Life Meaning
Affirming the Role of TSP and Goal–Life Alignment in Optimal Human Functioning

> Man's search for meaning is the primary motivation in his life and not a "secondary rationalization" of instinctual drives . . .. The more one forgets himself – by giving himself to a cause to serve or another person to love – the more human he is.
> — Viktor Frankl, *Man's Search for Meaning*

> You're the meaning in my life, you're the inspiration
> You bring feeling to my life, you're the inspiration.
> — songwriters Peter Cetera and David Foster, "You're the Inspiration"

There are few experiences in life as motivationally powerful as those that generate deep feelings of life meaning – or conversely, that cause us to feel that life is meaningless. In this chapter we will use the *Thriving with Social Purpose* framework as a foundation for "demystifying" the concept of life meaning while also explaining how the pathways we follow and the connections we make in our goal pursuits can help make life feel personally meaningful.

Imagine, for example, looking into the eyes of your newborn baby or seeing your grandchild for the first time. Picture yourself becoming absorbed in an ambitious challenge or helping someone resolve a serious problem. Imagine reflecting on a life change you have made or a cause you have joined and thinking "now my life makes sense" or "I am making a positive difference in the world!" These are the kinds of experiences that stand out in a person's life journey and that are particularly informative in helping us understand the nature of motivation and optimal functioning. Notably, these experiences often involve the pursuit of social purpose goals – consistent with the evolutionary evidence we shared with you in Chapter 6.

Fortunately, there are reliable pathways to a more meaningful life for virtually everyone. The ability to experience life meaning is an intrinsic evolutionary adaptation, just like our capacity for experiencing many other kinds of feelings. As Klinger (1998) explains, "the search for meaning . . . is an inexorable result of the way the human brain is organized ... an inevitable outgrowth of human evolution" (p. 27).

Yet there is something very special about this particular adaptation when it comes to human motivation. As we will see, *life meaning is both a product of optimal functioning and a powerful motivational force that encourages optimal functioning.* That is why life meaning is such an effective tool for diagnosing the overall strength of motivational head-quarters and for "refueling" when we are feeling down or empty. Those who frequently experience feelings of life meaning are more positive, hopeful, and resilient, especially when "the going gets tough" (Brassai et al., 2011; Mascaro & Rosen, 2005; Owens et al., 2009; Steger, 2012; Zika & Chamberlain, 1992). They are also less likely to experience anxiety, depression, or physical deterioration following a serious illness (Chamberlain et al., 1992; Harlow et al., 1986; Krause, 2009). Life meaning is thus a powerful contributor to overall mental health as well as a vital protective factor in our ongoing struggle for survival (Czekierda et al., 2017; Hooker et al., 2018). As Hill and Turiano (2014) succinctly put it, "accruing evidence suggests that finding a purpose in life may add years to it" (p. 1482).

Overview of the Qualities Associated with Life Meaning

The topic of life meaning was a virtually unexplored area of human development until Viennese psychotherapist Viktor Frankl published his extraordinarily influential book, *Ein Psycholog erlebt das Konzentrationslager* (later retitled *Man's Search for Meaning*), in 1946 – four years after he and his wife, parents, and brother were arrested and taken to an Auschwitz concentration camp during World War II. Frankl was able to survive until the camp's liberation in 1945 in large part because he had a seemingly endless reserve of life meaning – meaning that flowed from a sense of deep responsibility both to his family and to the patients whose lives might be enhanced as a result of the ideas he had been working on (in a manuscript titled *The Doctor and the Soul* that was destroyed by his captors). After being liberated he was devastated to learn that he was the sole survivor among his imprisoned family. Yet he was able to press forward and complete the book he had been reconstructing on stolen slips of paper. Moreover, Frankl's experiences in captivity had given him insights about human nature that went well beyond that project. Those insights were so powerful that it reportedly took him only nine days to dictate, in vivid, memorable terms, a book about both his concentration camp experience and his ideas about life meaning, ultimately resulting in *Man's Search for Meaning* (Frankl, 1946/2006).

In this "introduction to logotherapy" (the book's subtitle), Frankl postulated that the will to pursue and experience meaning is the central dynamic in human motivation – the psychic fuel that empowers self-direction and enables our motivational systems to carry out their leadership functions. He further proposed that life meaning could only be experienced through *active goal striving* – with social purpose goals like responsibility and belongingness being particularly potent sources of meaning – and through *experiences of profound suffering* that test our will to live. Consistent with MST's emphasis on the value of increasing awareness of our core personal goals, Frankl believed that suffering had the potential to actually help people by revealing their natural capacity for resilience and by clarifying the things that make life worth living – for example, deep and enduring love for another person, being free to engage in work that is personally fulfilling, and understanding the central purpose of one's life.

Fortunately, few of us experience hardships of the kind faced by concentration camp prisoners. Yet victimization, abuse, and just plain "hard times" are far more commonplace than we would like to believe in people's everyday lives. Imagine, for example, being in a dismal marriage or a toxic work environment where you constantly feel belittled and oppressed. Or being burdened with family obligations you can't fulfill or mounting debts you can't repay. Under such conditions it may be difficult to maintain hope for a better future, especially if you feel trapped in your present circumstances. The motivation to try to repair or escape your adverse circumstances may slip away as a sense of futility permeates your daily life.

This "giving up" reaction is no evolutionary mistake. As explained in Chapter 4, feelings of helplessness and despair can be highly adaptive in situations where we need to retreat from unproductive goal-seeking efforts. Negative emotions and personal agency beliefs can also rally sympathy and support in others who may be able to help (e.g., by influencing the circumstances that are causing the negative feelings). Furthermore, these feelings steer us away from behaviors that may magnify feelings of failure and inefficacy. Indeed, as we explained earlier when emphasizing the need for *tenacity* to be *mindful*, knowing when to give up can be a critical skill in life (Ntoumanis & Sedikides, 2018).

However, like many evolutionary advances, the development of conscious mechanisms for recognizing when to give up also created a significant vulnerability. People often assume that they are somehow responsible for negative events outside their control (Leary, 2004). Under such conditions, helplessness can turn into hopelessness, and sorrow can descend into depression (as illustrated by the bottom row in Figure 4.6 in Chapter 4). Some may even contemplate suicide (Baumeister, 1990; Clark & Kissane, 2002). Nevertheless, many people survive and actually benefit from these feelings – for example, by making adaptive changes or by developing powerful coping skills. *The most salient characteristic of those able to move forward under adversity is the motivation to seek and experience life meaning* (Aspinwall & Staudinger, 2003; Frankl, 1946/2006; Steger, 2012).

In this chapter we will explain how the active, intentional pursuit of life meaning can help people turn hardship and unfavorable circumstances into opportunities for personal growth, and ordinary events into extraordinary experiences. In doing so we will consider a variety of pathways through which each of us can cultivate and enhance life meaning for self and others. As we will see, striving for life meaning can transform a defensive mindset of "just trying to survive" into a fulfilling quest for *survival with well-being* (Damasio, 2003). Indeed, the quest to feel life meaning is at the core of what it means to experience well-being (Markman et al., 2013; Wong & Fry, 1998). Life meaning is thus a biological imperative – an evolutionary adaptation that brings us comfort, contentment, and the motivation to take on challenges and opportunities in a world filled with uncertainty and danger. Frankl's insight was recognizing that circumstances that are filled with *dis*comfort and anguish are often the most revealing with respect to the power of life meaning to motivate us to overcome adversity.

Definition of Life Meaning

After careful consideration of the best thinking and scientific evidence available on this topic, we concluded that the best way to understand life meaning is to conceptualize it as a *conscious feeling* consistent with Damasio's (2003) definition of a feeling state, namely, "the perception of a certain state of the body along with the perception of a certain mode of thinking and of thoughts with certain themes" (p. 86). So when we say "life meaning," we are referring to an experience that we feel in our mind and body. Moreover, this feeling is linked to "certain themes" that reflect the design of our motivational systems, including coherence, purpose, and significance (George & Park, 2016; Heintzelman & King, 2014a; Martela & Steger, 2016).

Specifically, life meaning is defined in our TSP framework as follows:

Life meaning is a distinctive feeling that arises when a person believes that their life makes sense, has purpose, and is worthwhile.

This feeling includes compelling emotions and clarifying thoughts and perceptions that affirm two fundamental design principles of human functioning: *Organization* (i.e., the need to maintain a sense of system integrity and coherence) and *Goal–Life Alignment* (i.e., the need to experience a sense of fit between daily life activities and core personal goals) (Antonovsky, 1990; M. Ford, 1992; Klinger, 1998; Weinstein et al., 2013).

Notably, restoring a sense of organization (vs. disorganization) and facilitating goal–life alignment are major themes in therapeutic efforts seeking to facilitate the recovery of combat veterans, victims of abuse, and others who have experienced traumatic events that cause them to question whether their lives make sense, have purpose, and are worthwhile (Janoff-Bulman & McPherson Frantz, 1997).

Earlier (in Chapter 2) we explained that feelings strengthen motivation by amplifying the impact of emotions on motivational headquarters, thus enhancing the potency and effectiveness of our goal pursuits. Feelings of life meaning work in this same way. For example, they increase our awareness of the personal goals that are most important to us. They help us maintain a sense of comfort and stability when our lives are disrupted. Feelings of life meaning also provide a source of energy and wisdom when we are faced with major life dilemmas and decisions.

Life meaning can also become a desired outcome in and of itself, as feelings of life meaning reflect the highest levels of well-being that humans can experience in their quest for survival with well-being (Damasio, 2003). That proposition is consistent with the idea that feelings of life meaning arise when we experience a sense of system integrity and coherence (organization) and a sense of fit between daily life activities and core personal goals (goal–life alignment).

That is not to say that feelings of life meaning can only be experienced when functioning is optimal, or when we have adopted a TSP mindset. We can also draw upon our life meaning "reserves" when circumstances are far from optimal and we desperately need a source of vitality and courage. Life meaning is thus an evolved method for ensuring that people can survive and experience a sense of well-being even when their environment is unresponsive, their capabilities for coping with adverse circumstances are limited, and their will to keep striving toward core personal goals is weakened:

> Life satisfaction is associated with objective living conditions . . .. In contrast, our findings showed that meaning in life is not associated with objective living conditions. For instance, many residents of Niger, Sierra Leone, Togo, and Ethiopia live in difficult economic and political conditions . . .. Yet the overwhelming majority of residents in poor nations report having an important purpose or meaning in life . . .. It is noteworthy that meaning in life predicted the suicide rate, whereas life satisfaction did not. (Oishi & Diener, 2014, pp. 427–428)

In the pages that follow we will describe the essential nature of life meaning and how it can be acquired. In doing so we will attempt to clarify why life meaning is such an important element in our TSP theoretical framework and in efforts to motivate self and others.

Life Meaning Is Neither a Mystical Experience nor a Profound Secret

In this chapter we will not be seeking to answer the often posed question "What is the meaning of life?" That question implies that there is one simple, lucid answer that applies to everyone regardless of their personal goals or changing circumstances. As Baumeister (1991) has pointed out, "If such an answer were easily available, all we would have to do would be to know it" (p. 24). Rather, it is our intention to provide you with a conceptual framework that describes the various pathways through which each individual person seeks to find meaning *in* life. As we will see, there are common themes but also many personalized variations with respect to the specific experiences that generate feelings of life meaning.

It is also important to emphasize that we are not referring to life meaning as some kind of abstract experience only available to philosophers, scholars, and shamans. Nor is it a mystical experience that can only be achieved by transcending the boundaries of normal human existence. Rather, life meaning is simply an expression of our "basic human nature" that everyone can experience in their everyday lives. As King (2012) explains, "meaning is everywhere, widely available, and routinely accessed in an effortless fashion because it is inherent in human experience" (p. 129). For example, life meaning often flows from our interactions with the people we live and work with, from things we read and talk about throughout the course of a day, and from familiar routines that help structure our everyday lives.

Although intentional efforts to connect the past, present, and future are often involved when feelings of life meaning arise, many meaningful experiences are simple expressions of "here and now" emotions and bodily sensations that provide a physical marker for life meaning. In other words, we don't just make meaning; we also sense meaning (King, 2012). Consider, for example, simple "in-the-moment" perceptions like taking in the natural beauty of a meadow of wildflowers ("Wow – that is awesome!"), or listening to a stirring piece of music ("I get chills every time I hear that melody"), or observing a heartwarming act of generosity ("How wonderful was that?"). Such experiences may naturally trigger a rush of emotion or a warm glow that tells us we are part of something that is special and meaningful. The fact that these feelings tend to emerge spontaneously suggests that the neural and hormonal activity associated with life meaning can occur without prior analysis and reflection (Haidt, 2006). Such feelings and sensations cannot be forced; rather, they tend to flow automatically from goal pursuits with certain characteristics – including those that reflect the amplifying effects of thriving with social purpose motivational patterns.

Life Meaning Involves Both Cognition and Emotion

Feelings arise in our conscious minds when emotions are triggered and body maps are updated (Damasio, 2003). Yet, feelings are also infused with perceptions, memories, and anticipatory thoughts that help us interpret and understand the emotional responses we are experiencing. Feelings of life meaning are no different than other kinds of feelings in this regard. Yet when people are asked to describe the specific emotions they feel when they have experienced a particularly meaningful event, their interpretations suggest the presence of feelings that are deeper and more profound than one would ordinarily experience.

This sense of emotional depth fits well with the notion that our life experiences are especially likely to generate feelings of life meaning if they are connected in some way to our core personal goals (which helps explain our keen interest in the assessment of these meaning-rich goals, as discussed in Chapter 3). Indeed, the term "core" connotes a sense of something that is deep within us. Feelings of life meaning thus help us affirm that we are on track with respect to understanding and pursuing the goals that are the most important and rewarding to us.

The specific thoughts and perceptions that are associated with feelings of life meaning can be quite variable across individuals and cultures, and may even seem peculiar to those with different belief systems. Yet, consistent with the premise that life meaning is an evolved adaptation rather than a mere by-product of evolution, there are many commonalities among people's experiences of life meaning, and those commonalities are largely associated with the motivational elements we have highlighted in our *Thriving with Social Purpose Theory of Motivation and Optimal Functioning.* When we adopt TSP modes of functioning, the resulting feelings of life meaning enable us to experience a sense of coherence and personal integrity with respect to our choices and circumstances. Those feelings also help us combat feelings of personal disorganization and maintain a belief that *life is worth living.* In addition, life meaning that flows from TSP motivational patterns can also help us ward off the "curse of the self" – that is, the propensity to ruminate about our personal failings that emerged as a side effect of the evolution of self-awareness (Leary, 2004).

Distinguishing between the psychological experience of life meaning and the specific ideas and interpretations that may contribute to life meaning is useful because, whereas the capacity to experience life meaning is innate, discovering the specific pathways that are most likely to lead to those feelings is an acquired process. In that sense life meaning is indeed something that we create, not just something that is given to us. It is thus each person's responsibility to construct meaning in their lives, not only by drawing upon their individual and cultural experiences, but by actively investing in activities and relationships that are aligned with their core personal goals.

Life Meaning Is Derived from Goal–Life Alignment

Not all meaning-making efforts are reliable sources of life meaning. The specific ideas, activities, and experiences we find meaningful – and that in turn yield feelings of life meaning – tend to be those that flow from the *connections* we make as we invest ourselves in engaging work and recreational activities, as we pursue significant social relationship goals, and as we explore and affirm values and beliefs about who we are and what we want to become (Baumeister, 1991; Heine et al., 2006). Some degree of life meaning can be derived from "low-level" connections, such as those we experience in our everyday routines and through the repetition of familiar habits. Indeed, this is where people who are experiencing sorrow or despair often escape to find meaning (Baumeister, 1990). Yet, as we shall see, "high-level" connections that pertain to the top levels of our personal goal hierarchy (see Figure 3.1 in Chapter 3) are the ones most likely to yield deep feelings of hopefulness and fulfillment. That is the focus of those studying the development of *life purpose,* which Damon et al. (2003) define as "a stable and generalized intention to accomplish something that is at once meaningful to the self and of consequence to the world beyond the self" (p. 121).

What exactly do we mean by "connection" with respect to this process of pursuing personal goals at different levels? That is a reference to the concept of *goal–life alignment* that we have emphasized throughout this book as one of the keys to optimal functioning. Life meaning is derived from successful efforts to connect our daily activities and experiences to proximal subgoals that advance, or are somehow linked to, our core personal goals – the superordinate themes at the top of our goal network that bring coherence and stability to our lives and serve as our most reliable sources of life satisfaction.

As we explained in Chapter 3, people can find meaning from goal strivings associated with any of the twenty-four categories in the *Taxonomy of Human Goals.* Yet it appears that, for many people, themes associated with social purpose goals (e.g., being part of a family or valued group; caring for people who depend on you; helping others fulfill their hopes and dreams) are particularly potent sources of life meaning. That is consistent with the evidence we reviewed in Chapter 6 about the centrality of social purpose in the evolution of human motivational systems. Indeed, MacKenzie and Baumeister (2014) have emphasized that the most reliable sources of meaning are those that are inherently social or cultural. "Beyond the self" has also been a major theme in research on the development of life purpose in adolescence and young adults (Bronk, 2014; Damon et al., 2003).

Life Meaning Is Derived from Interpretations That Provide Clarity and Direction

As we will see, life meaning can be derived from many sources. We have observed, however, a common theme in many of these life-affirming pathways. It seems that we are particularly likely to find life meaning in activities and experiences that reduce feelings of disorganization and provide guidance about goal options (Heintzelman & King, 2014a; Proulx et al., 2013). For example, interpretations that enable us to better understand our "place in the world" and the circumstances we find ourselves in often yield abundant feelings of life meaning (e.g., "This is what I was meant to be"; "Now I understand why these things are happening to me"). Similarly, life meaning often flows from knowledge and beliefs that help resolve ambiguity and confusion about what choices we should make, both on a daily basis (e.g., "What should my number one priority be today?"; "What is the right thing to do in this situation?") and on a larger scale (e.g., "Is this the kind of work I want to be doing five years from now?"; "Am I better off with him or without him?").

Consistent with the idea that clarity is a source of meaning and comfort, our natural tendency in times of suffering is to generate explanations that help us cope with events that are frightening or painful (Silver & Updegraff, 2013). "People deal with misfortune and suffering by creating interpretations . . .. Simply having some explanation for one's woe makes it more bearable" (Baumeister, 1991, p. 247). Explanations that provide not only clarity but also direction are particularly effective when it comes to helping us find meaning in adverse circumstances (e.g., "I was put on this Earth to make sure no one else has to suffer like I did"; "We have a responsibility to keep on going, that's what she would have wanted").

It is noteworthy that explanations do not need to be verifiable or even sensible from an outsider's perspective to be meaningful. As long as the explanations feel comfortable and authentic to the individual striving for answers, they can help produce the desired clarity and guidance needed to generate powerful feelings of life meaning. That is why familiar beliefs and assumptions are so resistant to rejection even when the evidence suggests they are fallible, and why superstitions and conspiracy theories are so pervasive and persistent. We embrace explanations that help us make sense of the world and deal with adversity, even when it means accepting explanations that we suspect are flawed or that cannot be validated through experience or logic. We can live with explanations that are imperfect, but we cannot tolerate chronic feelings of emptiness or bewilderment. Meaning is not an optional "luxury" in the lives of humans.

Life Meaning Protects People from Downward Spirals of Mental and Physical Health

The essence of life meaning is a deep sense of purpose, coherence, and connection to people, activities, and events outside oneself (Baumeister & Vohs, 2002). "Lives may be experienced as meaningful when they are felt to have significance beyond the trivial or momentary, to have purpose, or to have a coherence that transcends chaos" (King et al., 2006, p. 180). Such feelings provide a strong antidote to psychologically disorganizing experiences such as rejection, abuse, and failure (Wong & Fry, 1998). Indeed, memorable experiences that tell us *life is meaningful* can override weeks, months, or even years of prolonged hardship. They can make long, grueling ordeals seem "worth it" even when the outcome is not everything we had hoped for. They can transform powerful negative emotions like helplessness and grief into tolerable life conditions. Life meaning is so powerful that it can prevent us from losing our will to live even in the most horrible conditions imaginable (Frankl, 1946/2006).

> There is growing evidence that a strong sense of meaning and purpose – which we regard as a paradigm instance of robust future orientation – is highly protective against psychopathology . . .. In one dramatic example, 84 soldiers who committed suicide had all taken the same test of strengths and weaknesses months before; those soldiers in the very lowest percentage of meaning (strongly disagreeing with "my life has meaning") were at extreme risk for suicide . . .. This suggests that building a foundation of meaning and purpose in life should be a major focus of therapy. (Seligman et al., 2013, p. 135)

Although the evolutionary value of life meaning is most evident under conditions of extraordinary challenge, the impact of life meaning on day-to-day mental and physical well-being is also quite pervasive and far-reaching (Heintzelman & King, 2014b; King, 2012; Markman et al., 2013; McKnight & Kashdan, 2009; Reker et al., 1987; Routledge et al., 2013; Steger, 2012; Windsor et al., 2015). Even when there is no immediate danger or vulnerability, meaningful life experiences can strengthen our biological, cognitive, and emotional resources, thus making us more resilient in the face of anticipated or future adversity. For example, life meaning can help us cope with chronic stress and recover from disease and trauma more readily by strengthening our affective "reserve capacity" (Gallo & Matthews, 2003).

The idea that we build up a reserve of motivational strengths is consistent with Fredrickson's (2003, 2009) *broaden-and-build* theory of positive emotions as well as theories that focus on the long-term impact of positive personal agency beliefs (e.g., Dweck, 2006; M. Ford, 1992; Ryan & Deci, 2018; Seligman, 1991). Being able to draw upon an underlying reserve of motivational resources seems to help people avoid demoralizing and health-depleting patterns such as those associated with chronic depression, anxiety, hostility, and hopelessness (Clark & Kissane, 2002; Gallo et al., 2009). Reserve capacity also seems to provide significant protection against the progressive decline associated with life-shortening diseases (e.g., Stern, 2006).

Ryff and Singer (1998) have constructed a framework that identifies several physiological mechanisms through which feelings of life meaning can influence physical health.

> To advance a perspective that is truly about optimal functioning of the mind and body, the study of the "physiological substrates of flourishing" is needed – that is, the biological underpinnings of wellness of mind, such as having a sense of purpose, meaning, and personal growth . . .. Included in this biological framework is *optimal allostasis*, which delineates multiple markers for tracking successful physiological adaptation to stress or life challenges; *immune competence*, which monitors immunity or resistance to infectious disease; and *cerebral activation asymmetry*, which describes patterns of brain activation associated with positive affective experiences . . .. Prior research on stress and health documents numerous instances of negative mind/body spirals . . . that is, how stressful conditions and depressive outlooks activate physiological processes that undermine the integrity of organ systems and the body's capacity to protect itself. In contrast, interest here is in advancing understanding of the dynamic unfolding of *positive mind/body spirals*. (pp. 213–214, 218, 223)

In earlier chapters we provided evidence that TSP patterns of functioning are associated with upward spirals of optimal functioning – not only with respect to performance accomplishments but also with respect to mental and physical well-being. In this chapter we will explain how feelings of life meaning are reliably and naturally produced when we pursue our core personal goals (especially social purpose goals) with an active approach orientation, personal optimism, mindful tenacity, and emotional wisdom. Life meaning is not the only pathway through which TSP facilitates positive human health, but it is undoubtedly one of the most powerful. TSP motivational patterns also enrich experiences of life meaning derived from our personal reflections and cultural interpretations.

How Life Meaning Is Acquired

Life meaning is an evolved adaptation that has been helping humans survive and experience well-being ever since our earliest ancestors first developed the capacity for self-awareness. Life meaning not only made it possible for our ancestors to better cope with adversity and uncertainty, it also provided a mechanism for amplifying all of the components of motivational headquarters, thus promoting the thriving motivational pattern that has helped enable and empower our species' greatest accomplishments. Striving for life meaning is thus an integral and universal property of "basic human nature."

From this perspective, the problem is not how to acquire the *capacity* for constructing meaningful thoughts or for experiencing feelings of life meaning. These capabilities, and the motivation to use them, are an innate part of our heritage as a self-directed, self-aware species. Rather, the challenge is how to find meaningful *content* – the content that is right for *you* – for the "life story" you are authoring. What kind of settings and plot lines would make the lead character in your story (you!) "come alive"? How can you make your life story as engaging and fulfilling as possible given your strivings, achievements, and aspirations? How can you contain the impact of traumatic events and life crises to specific chapters so that they do not become the headline or overall title of your life story? And how can you create an overall coherence to your multifaceted story – the good, the bad, the turning points, and the triumphs – that leaves you with the feeling that your life journey has been meaningful and worthwhile?

This autobiographical process involves far more than seeking out an occasional peak experience or pleasant diversion. As Frankl has taught us, the quest for life meaning can be a matter of life or death – it is not just something that is "nice to have." Without meaning, the motivation to pursue goals that can sustain personal health and vital social relationships can decline precipitously – especially for young people who have not yet developed enduring sources of life meaning they can draw upon, and for older adults who have suffered devastating losses to their "portfolio" of meaningful life experiences. As Wong (1998) explains, "frustration of the will to meaning leads to an 'existential vacuum'" characterized by feelings of emptiness, apathy, and indifference (p. 369). In contrast, feelings of life meaning help "fill up" that empty space inside of us. Such feelings tell us that life is precious and thus well worth the effort needed to sustain it and make it better. Life meaning is thus an intrinsic part of nature's overarching design principle, *survival with well-being* (Damasio, 2003).

To Acquire Meaning, One Must Make Connections

As Baumeister (1991) famously remarked, "meaning cannot be easily defined, perhaps because to define meaning is already to use meaning" (p. 15). Yet Baumeister helped steer his readers in a productive direction by emphasizing the centrality of *connections* as a defining feature of the concept of meaning. Earlier we focused on the connections involved in creating goal–life alignment, which results when there are direct linkages between our core personal goals and many of our daily life activities. One manifestation of this kind of connection is illustrated in our goal network diagram (Figure 3.1, Chapter 3). When there are rich connections between lower level subgoals and the superordinate (core) personal goals at the top of the hierarchy, life meaning can be derived from even the simplest of daily activities (e.g., reading a bedtime story to a young child; planting new seeds in a vegetable garden; hitting a golf shot that feels powerful yet effortless).

At an even more fundamental level, the process of simply *conceptualizing a goal* can be seen as a type of connection – namely, a temporal connection, a way of connecting our current circumstances with possible future circumstances (Heine et al., 2006; Waytz et al., 2015). We can also make temporal connections in the other direction by recalling meaningful past experiences that resonate with our core personal goals, as when we think nostalgically (Sedikides & Wildschut, 2018). Moreover, the process of *pursuing a goal* also involves making connections – for example, by identifying relevant information and connecting it to the mental "schema" that is guiding our progress toward a preferred state (Van Tongeren et al., 2018). In other words, *things become comprehensible when we can connect them to our personal goals.* In that sense meaning can be seen as the most basic requirement for human goal striving. As Klinger (1998) explains,

> the disposition to seek meaning stems straightforwardly from the evolution of purposiveness together with human intellect …. The human brain cannot sustain purposeless living. It was not designed for that. Its systems are designed for purposive action, and when that is blocked, they deteriorate, and the emotional feedback from idling those systems signals extreme discomfort and motivates the search for renewed purpose and hence meaning. (pp. 30, 33)

Kaufman (2018) also focuses on temporal variations in sources of life meaning in his essay on finding meaning through creative activity:

> a natural connection is how creativity can enhance life's meaning …. The past pathway of creativity helps someone make sense of one's past. It encourages a deeper understanding of one's life. The present pathway of creativity engages one in life, offering reminders of enjoyment and connections with others. The future pathway of creativity speaks to people's desire to live on after death, suggesting ways to connect with future generations. (pp. 734, 743–744).

Acquiring "Proximate" Meaning Is Just as Effective as Acquiring "Ultimate" Meaning

It is common for scholars and philosophers to make a distinction between two types of life meaning as they relate to the content of our ideas and interpretations (e.g., Wong, 1998). *Ultimate meaning* reflects our efforts to achieve clarity and guidance with respect to the "big" questions about life and death that transcend any particular individual (e.g., "Why are we here?"; "What happens to people after they die?"). *Proximate meaning,* on the other hand, is what we seek when we need clarity and guidance with respect to our own particular life story as it unfolds over time (e.g., "Who am I?"; "What is my purpose?" "What are my core personal goals?"). Yet, because the *feelings* of life meaning that may be generated are essentially the same for ultimate and proximate meaning, it is quite possible for people to experience abundant life meaning without ever asking (or answering) questions about ultimate meaning. Indeed, for most people proximate meaning is the more prevalent source of life meaning in their everyday lives.

This is an important observation because it helps explain how people with very different levels of curiosity about philosophical and spiritual questions, and very different levels of investment in organized religion, can nevertheless experience similar outcomes with respect to life meaning. That is not to say that philosophical, spiritual, and religious pathways to life meaning are unreliable or deficient. Both the ubiquity and strength of these phenomena throughout the course of human history make it obvious that these are uniquely potent and compelling pathways through which life meaning can be experienced (Emmons, 2005; Steger, 2012). Yet it is encouraging to realize that proximate pathways to meaning can generate feelings of life meaning of similar depth and intensity. In other words, we can experience the many benefits associated with life meaning by simply immersing ourselves in fulfilling vocational, educational, recreational, and social activities, and by helping others make progress toward the goals that are meaningful to them. As Halusic and King (2013) explain,

> if MIL [meaning in life] is, indeed, critical to survival, it ought not to be widely unavailable or attained only in the presence of particular or unusual psychological states (e.g., religious ecstasy). Perhaps it has become part of the mystique of MIL that it is portrayed, at times, as nearly unattainable, as if the meaningful life is a commodity earned only by a few rare and lucky

souls. Such a conceptualization of MIL would seem to be at odds with the notion of the role of MIL in general human functioning. It is simply untenable that a resource that is necessary for survival should be impossible or even difficult to attain . . .. If the experience of MIL is truly an adaptive experience, it must be embedded in the quotidian circumstances of our existence. (p. 458)

Overview of How Life Meaning Is Acquired

The *TSP Theory of Life Meaning* is intended to be a comprehensive (though not necessarily all-inclusive) framework for understanding the processes and pathways through which people acquire life meaning. There are three major avenues through which people strive for life meaning: existential interpretations, cultural interpretations, and goal–life alignment. We have placed goal–life alignment in the first row of Table 7.1 because self-directed goal pursuit (which may encompass efforts to derive meaning from personal and cultural experiences) is, for many of us, the key to experiencing life meaning on an everyday basis. TSP, in turn, is the key mechanism for amplifying feelings of life meaning that flow from existential interpretations, cultural interpretations, and goal–life alignment.

Striving for life meaning is an ongoing, continuous process. This process has both conscious and nonconscious manifestations. For example, we may not be aware as we are being acculturated that certain ideas and beliefs are taking hold as sources of life meaning. Yet at the same time we may deliberately engage in extensive reading and conversation on topics related to identity, ideology, and spirituality in an effort to construct meaning. We may have an acute awareness of the feelings of life meaning (or meaninglessness) resulting from alignment (or misalignment) between core personal goals and everyday experiences, but lack conscious insight about the specific reasons for those feelings (e.g., "I didn't expect to be so into this"; "I wish I knew why I feel so empty inside – I thought this was what I wanted").

The TSP Theory of Life Meaning outlines a variety of *capabilities* and *pathways* through which people acquire life meaning. This theory thus provides a thematic framework for understanding how and where humans are most likely to find life meaning. However, the actual experience of life meaning must be acquired at an individualized level through an active self-construction process. This process is dynamic, and thus what is meaningful to any particular person will inevitably change over the course of the life cycle. While many episodes in our "life story" will renew and reinforce

Table 7.1 *Summary of the Thriving with Social Purpose Theory of Life Meaning*

Column 1	Column 2	Column 3	Column 4
How people strive for life meaning:	What produces feelings of life meaning:	How *Thriving* can increase feelings of life meaning:	How *Social Purpose* can increase feelings of life meaning:
Goal–life alignment	Connections between daily activities and core personal goals	Engagement	Belongingness
Existential interpretations	Personal identity Spirituality Uplifting experiences	Goal progress Lasting contributions	Resource provision Equity
Cultural interpretations	Values/ethical principles Religiousness Ideology/philosophy	Affirmation	Social responsibility
People strive for life meaning by pursuing core personal goals and by seeking clarifying and comforting interpretations of life experiences.	*Feelings of life meaning can be reliably produced by following these potentially inspiring and enlightening pathways.*	*Thriving helps people strive for life meaning by amplifying the motivational impact of pathways that are capable of producing feelings of life meaning.*	*Social Purpose helps people strive for life meaning by amplifying the salience of personal goals focused on human connections.*

Note: Life meaning is a distinctive feeling that arises when a person believes that their life makes sense, has purpose, and is worthwhile. This figure displays three fundamental ways that humans strive for life meaning (column 1), with some corresponding pathways through which feelings of life meaning can be experienced (column 2). These pathways represent important domains of human endeavor that have endured over time as potent sources of life meaning. Thriving and Social Purpose contribute to life meaning by amplifying the motivational impact of those pathways (columns 3 and 4, respectively). Note that the boundaries between these life meaning pathways are "porous" – that is, efforts to seek life meaning through one set of pathways can influence other pathways and become integrated components of an individual's personality (e.g., as when religious beliefs become a central part of a person's identity or cultural values become connected to an individual's core personal goals). Similarly, the impact of Thriving motivational patterns and SP goal content can reverberate across different life meaning pathways.

what is meaningful to us, others will lead to significant revisions and new discoveries.

It is also important to understand that the outcome of this self-construction process is typically *not* some sort of unified life story.

Feelings of life meaning can be strengthened when we feel that there is some degree of coherence among our diverse story elements, yet "there is no reason that all the details of a life must fit into one single meaning" (Baumeister, 1991, p. 11). We have many possible selves (Markus & Nurius, 1986), each of which can yield feelings of life meaning in their own (potentially disparate) ways. For example, the meaning associated with an individual's identity as a worker may have little to do with the meaning that flows from their role as a parent or someone's life partner. The feelings of life meaning derived from a passionate investment in a recreational pursuit may be quite independent of the meaning acquired from a religious or spiritual commitment.

Existential interpretations. Humans are innately motivated to make sense of their experiences, especially as they relate to the outcomes they desire (i.e., their personal goals) and the outcomes they expect (as represented, for example, by their capability and context beliefs). Feedback that affirms our goals and expectations can help us define who we are and who we want to become (e.g., "Now this feels like the real me!"). Conversely, feedback that contradicts our expectations can force us to reconsider fundamental aspects of our developing identity ("Maybe I'm just not cut out for this line of work"). Aligning ideas about who we *think* we are with our ongoing experiences is a central theme in our efforts to construct existential interpretations (Rosso et al., 2010; Vondracek & Porfeli, 2011).

We also seek explanations for unexpected and unintended events in an effort to maintain a sense of psychological integrity. This aversion to "mental chaos" is consistent with the ideas presented in Chapter 4 about how living systems maintain coherent and effective functioning, as summarized by the terms *organization* and *equipoise*. Novelty and unpredictability can be engaging up to a point, yet we are motivated to avoid the disorganizing influences of uncertainty and confusion, even if it means accepting explanations that are simplistic or extreme. Moreover, there are limits to the pace of change we can tolerate, and some changes are simply unwelcome at any level. We need to be able to assimilate new information and experiences into our existing self-concepts in a harmonious way while also somehow accommodating things that don't fit within our current thinking. The feelings of life meaning that result from these kinds of existential interpretations tell us that we are effectively accomplishing these essential functions.

The TSP Theory of Life Meaning specifies three different pathways within the existential interpretation domain that reliably produce feelings of life meaning. *Personal identity* refers to the process of constructing self-concepts and autobiographical themes that feel natural, authentic, and worthy of a strong emotional commitment (e.g., "What kind of person am I?" "Who do I want to become?" "How do I want to be remembered?"). Challenges associated with identity development may be manifested in many different life domains – for example, career development, sexual orientation, ethnic identity, and family and gender roles (Marcia, 1987). For many, the development of a vocational identity is particularly consequential, as we spend so much of our lives in work-related roles and settings (Porfeli et al., 2013; Vondracek et al., 2014; Vondracek & Porfeli, 2011).

Spirituality refers to efforts to define ourselves as a part of humanity. What does it mean to be a member of the human race, living on the planet Earth in a vast universe we know relatively little about? Why are we here? What is our destiny? How should we live our lives? How are we going to survive in a world where resources are rapidly being depleted? What happens to us when we die? Oftentimes people look to religious beliefs and doctrines to provide meaningful answers to these questions. Yet we can also rely on interpretations and insights derived from less formal sources to help us understand what is "right" for us. In addition, many people are drawn to scientific and professional experts as a source of wisdom and inspiration. Notably, these different sources of life meaning are not mutually exclusive, nor can they be easily ranked in terms of their capacity to generate feelings of life meaning. Indeed, it seems evident that many people rely on all of these sources of guidance from time to time as they seek answers to their spiritual questions.

In addition, people can derive life meaning from *uplifting experiences* that are particularly memorable due to the magnitude and elevating quality of the emotions associated with those unique life episodes. Of course, experiences that are routine can also become "memorable" (in the sense of being easy to remember) if they are repeated sufficiently (e.g., we can picture the events that typically unfold at a wedding after seeing enough of them in person or on TV). Nevertheless, those memories tend to be generic and nondescript, like looking at a crowd of people from a distance. In contrast, when people describe an experience as special and meaningful (e.g., recalling your own wedding), it is because it feels like a unique or climactic moment in their *own* life story.

Cultural interpretations. Humans are also intrinsically motivated to interpret the customs, viewpoints, and ideals that they assimilate in a (mostly) automatic manner from their culture. Such interpretations help us navigate social life and fulfill our SP goal aspirations (e.g., by feeling connected to people who are important to us). As with existential interpretations, we use naturally occurring feedback from cultural sources to help us define who we are and who we want to become (e.g., in terms of the social roles we fill), and to help us explain things that are puzzling or disturbing. However, when we engage in cultural interpretations it is less likely to feel like a journey of self-construction than a process of trying to figure out where we fit in (e.g., "Is this a way of thinking that I am comfortable with?" "Am I like the people who share these beliefs and values?").

The TSP Theory of Life Meaning specifies three different pathways within the cultural interpretation domain that reliably produce feelings of life meaning. *Religiousness* is a pathway through which people invest themselves in organized belief systems about God, divine universal powers, and how the way we live our lives is related to those transcendent influences. For example, Frankl looked for a "hint from heaven" when, in 1941, he was torn between a desire to take advantage of his newly granted visa to America or stay in Austria and try to help his parents, who were among those about to be rounded up by the Nazis and taken to concentration camps. A marble fragment from the rubble of a nearby synagogue demolished by the Nazis gave him the guidance he was looking for, as that fragment had a part of the Fifth Commandment written upon it ("honor your mother and father") (Redsand, 2006). He chose to remain in Austria and, as a result, was later imprisoned.

Religiousness also suggests conformity to religious practices that demonstrate an individual's faith in those beliefs. For highly religious people, participation in those practices is a dependable and often profound source of life meaning (as illustrated by words like "sacred" and "reverence").

Another pathway to life meaning is one in which we invest ourselves in a cultural *ideology* or *philosophy* that feels intellectually authentic and emotionally satisfying. These belief systems provide us with explanations for how society should naturally or ideally operate, usually with strong economic, political, and lifestyle implications. For example, "conservatives" and "liberals" typically have very different views about a wide range of issues, such as how people should be governed, how resources should be distributed, and what kinds of societal practices should be permitted. Alternatively, people may become invested in ideologies and philosophies that are organized around a particular issue or theme (e.g., feminism, sustainability, libertarianism) that has broad implications for economic, political, and cultural institutions.

People can also find life meaning through culturally defined *values* and *ethical principles* that offer motivational clarity and energy because of their alignment with an individual's core personal goals. Embracing such ideals can be a source of security and inspiration, as illustrated by people who devote their lives to pursuing social justice or striving for excellence in a culturally valued arena (e.g., by entering the teaching or medical profession).

Goal–life alignment. In Table 7.1 we have intentionally used dotted lines to separate each row to suggest overlap and an open flow of influence among each of these pathways to life meaning. We have also placed goal–life alignment above the existential and cultural interpretation pathways to emphasize that, when it comes to life meaning, it is of paramount importance to have an ongoing stream of daily activity in which life circumstances facilitate (rather than constrain) efforts to prioritize and pursue your core personal goals. Without goal–life alignment it is very difficult to maintain an overall sense that life is meaningful. Life meaning that flows from existential and cultural interpretations can provide some protection against the demoralizing consequences of goal–life misalignment by enabling people to maintain hope that the future can be better than the present (e.g., "I've strayed from what I know is the real me and need to get back on the right path"; "God has a plan for me so I just need to keep the faith"). Yet when people are experiencing relentless hardship or chronic distress it may be difficult to avoid succumbing to chronic feelings of meaninglessness without a refocusing of attention on core personal goals and avenues for pursuing them that are capable of replenishing life meaning. That is why Frankl (1946/2006) wrote:

> A man who becomes conscious of the responsibility he bears toward a human being who affectionately waits for him, or to an unfinished work, will never be able to throw away his life. He knows the "why" for his existence, and will be able to bear almost any "how." (p. 80)

That is not to say that goal–life alignment is, by itself, the most reliable or potent pathway to life meaning. As implied by the dotted lines in Table 7.1, infusing meaning derived from existential and cultural interpretations can greatly enrich everyday goal pursuits and create upward spirals of motivation and well-being, consistent with the evolved role of life meaning as a mechanism for amplifying the overall functioning of motivational headquarters. Yet it is evident that many people can experience abundant feelings of life meaning without spending a lot of time struggling over big philosophical and spiritual questions. That suggests that meaning derived from goal–life alignment may also naturally produce positive, reverberating consequences in the existential and cultural domains. For example, finding a great new job that feels like an ideal fit can help answer existential questions about personal identity. Similarly, the everyday process of seeking out and cultivating relationships that feel comfortable and meaningful may also help you clarify your religious or ideological beliefs.

Thriving with social purpose. TSP plays a special role in our pursuit of life meaning by amplifying the motivational impact of pathways that are capable of producing feelings of life meaning, and by highlighting goal themes that are among the most reliable sources of life meaning for members of our (very social!) species. In Table 7.1 we have outlined the various ways that TSP helps people strive for life meaning while also amplifying the resulting feelings of life meaning.

The entries in the Thriving column (each of which applies to the entire spectrum of life meaning pathways) represent different ways that Thriving motivational patterns can impact life meaning. Recall that such patterns encompass an *active approach* orientation to goal seeking that is energized and strengthened by *emotional wisdom* and by "home page" capability and context beliefs characterized by *personal optimism* and *mindful tenacity*. When these elements are in place, life meaning naturally flows from the ongoing process of self-directed goal striving (engagement), especially when goal pursuit yields favorable results (goal progress, lasting contributions) and those results are acknowledged by others as being worthy and consequential (affirmation). In other words:

Feelings of life meaning are closely tied to the experience of feeling self-directed.

The entries in the Social Purpose column reflect the four different types of integrative social relationship goal content included in the Taxonomy of Human Goals (see Chapter 3) – namely, belongingness, resource provision, equity, and social responsibility (M. Ford & Nichols, 1987/2019, 1991). The first entry reflects the fact that, for most people, close relationships are an indispensable source of life meaning. Similarly – and often to the surprise of those socialized in cultures that celebrate self-interest and the "pursuit of (individual) happiness" – experiences involving helping, sharing, and self-sacrifice can also yield extraordinarily powerful feelings of life meaning. And yet that is exactly what one would expect if humans were designed with social purpose goals as an "essential ingredient" in optimal functioning (as explained in Chapter 6), with feelings of life meaning serving as motivation to continue doing what they were naturally designed to do.

Happiness and Life Meaning

Before proceeding to a more extended discussion of the elements included in our TSP Theory of Life Meaning, it is worth mentioning a related concept that is omitted from that framework – namely, happiness. Scholars in the field of positive psychology have invested a great deal of effort in recent years trying to better understand the nature and origins of happiness (e.g., Lyubomirsky, 2008; Seligman, 2002) and "subjective well-being" (e.g., Diener, 2009). In doing so, some researchers have made a distinction between *hedonic well-being*, which is evidenced by pleasant feelings and pain avoidance, and *eudaimonic well-being*, which is associated with feelings of virtue, personal growth, and life meaning (Ryan & Deci, 2001; Ryff & Singer, 2008; Waterman, 1993). As an offshoot of this effort, recent theoretical and empirical work has focused on the question of whether "meaningfulness" (eudaimonic well-being) is simply a manifestation of happiness (hedonic well-being). The answer is a resounding "No!" as illustrated by research conducted by Baumeister et al. (2013). They found that:

> Meaningfulness and happiness are positively correlated, so they have much in common. Many factors, such as feeling connected to others, feeling productive, and not being alone or bored contribute similarly to both . . . . [Yet] the two [are] distinct . . . . Our findings suggest that happiness is mainly about getting what one wants and needs, including from other people or even just by using money. In contrast, meaningfulness was linked to doing things that express and reflect the self and in particular to doing positive things for others . . . . Happiness went with being a taker more than a giver, while meaningfulness was associated with being a giver more than a taker. Whereas happiness was focused on feeling good in the present, meaningfulness integrated past, present, and future, and it sometimes meant feeling bad. Past misfortunes reduce present happiness, but they are linked to higher meaningfulness – perhaps because people cope with them by finding meaning. (p. 515)

Ample research has documented the expected association between happiness and many good outcomes – for example, stronger and more satisfying relationships, better sleep and energy levels, improved creativity – and yes, more life meaning (Baumeister et al., 2013; Halusic & King, 2013; Lyubomirsky, 2008; Lyubomirsky et al., 2005). Yet the impact of the kind of happiness that does not encompass feelings of life meaning may be rather superficial and fleeting. Enjoying the present and avoiding unhappy emotional states is surely part of the "good life." But from a motivational (i.e., future-oriented) perspective, it is not the most important part. That is why we agree with Kashdan (2009), who has eloquently argued that:

> We have been sold on the idea that being happy is the only or most important goal in life . . .. I believe that all the time and energy spent looking at and trying to move the happiness gauge a notch higher can be used much more effectively. Instead of constantly trying to be happy, we should focus on building a rich, meaningful life, guided by our core values and interests. (p. 2)

It is this perspective that has led us to focus less on happiness and more on feelings of life meaning as the primary manifestation of the "well-being" part of Damasio's concept of *survival with well-being*. Because happiness is generally a short-term experience associated with "here and now" circumstances, it is difficult to sustain for very long without constantly renewing the kinds of conditions that triggered the happy emotions. Yet, is it realistic to aspire to a life that is just one happy occasion after another? Life is full of challenges and obstacles even for those who are not facing chronically adverse or impoverished circumstances. The more authentic and reliable pathway to well-being, then, is the sustainable strength that comes from ongoing goal pursuits and interpretations that connect our past, present, and future selves, thereby giving us a rich portfolio of emotional experiences (Gruber et al., 2011) along with an underlying sense of coherence and enduring purpose (and, ideally, abundant opportunities to experience happiness!). The resulting feelings of life meaning help create a reservoir of positive energy that can keep the well-being "flywheel" spinning, even in the face of life's inevitable heartaches and hardships. That sturdiness under duress is an important element in maintaining upward spirals of motivation and optimal functioning, through good times and bad.

Focusing on happiness rather than life meaning can also create significant vulnerabilities when unpleasant circumstances persist and the next happy episode seems distant and uncertain. Life may seem just fine for those who are indifferent about anything beyond day-to-day gratifications when the "pursuit of happiness" is flowing along unimpeded by health challenges, opportunity constraints, or resource limitations. Yet when the going gets tough, there may be little in the way of inner strength and courage that one can draw upon. In contrast, for those who understand the motivational power of life meaning, such hardships can be seen as an opportunity for self-construction and personal growth and for focusing with greater clarity on "the things that really matter in life." That is why, for example, life meaning has been linked to successful aging (Freund & Baltes, 1998; Vaillant, 2002; Wong, 1998). Consistent with that assertion, Fredrickson et al. (2013) found that, in a comparison focused on the kind of cellular inflammation associated with many diseases (e.g., cancer), people who were happy because they lived a life full of purpose and meaning (aka eudaimonic well-being) manifested a very different profile than people who were happy because they lived "the good life" (aka hedonic well-being). Whereas the former group generally had low inflammation levels, those who were happy but deficient in life meaning had escalated inflammation levels similar to those of people experiencing chronic adversity.

In short, without life meaning, an extended "happiness dry spell" can put not only well-being at risk, but also survival. Life is hard when ongoing events seem relentlessly negative, but it is unbearable when life feels hopeless and meaningless. The natural inclination for those experiencing emotions and PABs associated with hopelessness (the most motivationally debilitating pattern depicted in Figure 4.6 in Chapter 4) is to try to find some way to escape those intolerable conditions. For many, that urgent motive leads to self-destructive patterns such as substance abuse, stepping outside of the subjective self and treating it as an unworthy object (e.g., as is sometimes the case in sexual and eating disorders), or seriously contemplating suicide (Baumeister, 1990, 1991).

Acquiring Life Meaning through Existential and Cultural Interpretations

Now I see myself as I am, feeling very free. Life is everything it's meant to be.
When my days have come to an end, I will understand what I've left behind – part of me.
I've been searching so long to find an answer. Now I know my life has meaning . . ..
It's only natural, good things in life take a long time.
          – songwriter James Pankow, "(I've Been) Searchin' So Long"

Throughout this book we have emphasized the fundamental idea that efforts to motivate self and others are facilitated when those efforts respect and capitalize on basic human nature. That is why we have devoted a full chapter to the topic of life meaning. One of the most unique and powerful evolved features of human motivational systems is the propensity to seek meaningful interpretations of our personal and cultural experiences – not only through conscious reflection, but also by making nonconscious choices to engage in activities that strengthen the ideas and predispositions that are most comfortable to us. Such interpretations are not just satisfying in an intellectual way; they are also fulfilling in an emotional way. Indeed, it is difficult to underestimate the motivational power that can be generated by the affirming feelings of life meaning that flow from our existential and cultural interpretations.

> Individuals are motivated to seek and construct meaning. This quest takes on two forms: (a) They actively seek to make sense of things that happen to them. When bad things happen to them, they automatically ask, "Why me? Why this?" (b) And, people constantly want to find a higher purpose to endow their lives with significance and meaning. The former may represent the reactive search for coherence and understanding, whereas the latter is the proactive search for purpose and significance. (Wong, 1998, p. 409)

The main criterion for assessing the effectiveness of our existential and cultural interpretations is not "accuracy" or "truth" in some objective, verifiable sense. Rather, we are seeking what might be called *authenticity* (Rosso et al., 2010) or *personal validity*. From a motivational perspective what matters most is that we have internalized the beliefs and explanations we derive from our life experiences and feel enlightened and comforted by those interpretations. That is what makes them meaningful for a particular individual in a particular set of circumstances.

Now, admittedly, it may be challenging to hold on to self-concepts and belief systems that people in your surrounding culture – and especially those you are close to – do not share. Imagine, for example, having political views that are in stark contrast to the people you live and work with. Or moving to a new country where people routinely dismiss aspects of your cultural heritage that are important to you. Or consider what it would be like to grow up in a family where your parents persistently reject your emerging career-related interests because your "destiny" (as they see it) is to enact their aspirations. Indeed, one of the most interesting dimensions on which cultures and families vary is the extent to which they view life meaning as something that people construct through a personal journey (the pathway we have labeled *existential interpretations*) or as something that we learn from the "tried-and-true" belief systems and traditions of our elders (the pathway we have labeled *cultural interpretations*). And yet, there is no "correct" answer to this choice either, as both pathways can (and often do!) lead to life-affirming motivational outcomes. Indeed, because the most comfortable interpretations tend to be those that have both personal and cultural validity, people generally rely on a mix of the two pathways.

Personal Identity and Values/Ethical Principles

Erikson's (1959, 1968) well-known model of the prototypical challenges associated with different developmental phases across the life-span highlights the search for life meaning in two different developmental periods. One is during adolescence, when *identity* versus *role confusion* moves to the forefront as a developmental imperative. During childhood, as the cognitive infrastructure for constructing personal and cultural belief systems is developing, challenges associated with trust, autonomy, self-direction, and competence development are confronted and (to a greater or lesser extent) mastered. A new challenge naturally emerges, however, as the mental capabilities for connecting past, present, and future expand exponentially in adolescence. The ability to think about one's life trajectory on a larger scale, and to speculate on what it would be like to follow different developmental pathways, fuels a more active and intensive search for life meaning, with meaning flowing from both the search process and the resulting achievements (Negru-Subtirica et al., 2016). This search process also has many practical consequences as adolescents begin to imagine themselves transitioning into adult roles and responsibilities in various arenas, including career development, ethnic and gender identity, religious and political beliefs, and intimate relationships. While the focus of those studying and seeking to enhance this exploration process has traditionally been rather self-oriented, identity development can also be facilitated by fostering social purpose goals, e.g., by creating opportunities for young people to contribute to their families, schools, and communities in consequential ways (Fuligni, 2019).

Marcia (1966, 1987) elaborated on Erikson's thinking in a way that emphasized the motivational processes involved in seeking life meaning through the identity development pathway. He suggested that young people can be classified with respect to their identity status in a particular domain by understanding the extent to which they had engaged in *exploration* of alternative values and choices and had made a *commitment* to a particular belief system or developmental pathway. This idea logically led to four distinct identity status groupings:

1. *Foreclosure* represents an identity status in which commitments to value systems and self-concepts are made without exploring alternatives, often as a result of strong parental socialization toward specific developmental outcomes (e.g., a particular career choice or set of religious beliefs).

2. *Moratorium* is the term Marcia used to describe individuals who were actively (often intensively) exploring alternative belief systems, career options, or lifestyle choices, but had not yet made any clear commitment to a particular alternative. The phrase "identity crisis" emerged as a way of characterizing the psychological struggle that individuals in this identity status may experience as they search for values and self-concepts that feel personally meaningful.

3. *Identity achievement* is the status that reflects successful self-construction of life-defining commitments after a period of exploration, although such achievements are not necessarily permanent (as suggested by the idea of a "mid-life crisis" in which previously accepted values and self-concepts no longer feel comfortable or authentic, or different ones emerge as a higher priority).

4. *Identity diffusion* reflects a status in which individuals are neither committed to identity-defining choices nor do they seem concerned about the need to explore alternatives along these lines. Although this identity status is commonplace among preadolescents who have not yet developed the capacity for thinking along expansive time frames, it is regarded as a significant source of developmental vulnerability among older adolescents and young adults, as identity diffusion can eventually lead to a generalized sense of meaninglessness.

The commitments that young people make to their careers, belief systems, and social relationships create developmental pathways into adulthood through which life meaning can be acquired and continually renewed. Marriage, parenting, career advancement, and community involvement are all venues in which feedback about existential questions like "Who am I?" and "What can I become?" tend to flow naturally and spontaneously, even if such questions are not pondered and analyzed in an intellectualized way.

Ultimately, though, as older adults near the end of their careers and enter their retirement years, a second developmental challenge focused specifically on life meaning tends to come to the forefront – one that is more intrinsically reflective in nature. Specifically, can these "life veterans" look back with satisfaction at the choices they have made and, despite some inevitable mistakes and disappointments, feel a general sense of contentment and fulfillment about what they have accomplished – an achievement Erikson calls *ego integrity*? Or will personal failures and lost opportunities lead to an overall sense of *despair* characterized by frequent regrets and a lack of self-respect? As we grow old, it is increasingly important to be able to look backward (in addition to looking forward) when assessing goal progress. Our twilight years can be an ordeal with little solace, or they can be saturated with feelings of life meaning that help us cope with the aches and pains and challenges associated with the aging process. Without a sense of ego integrity, it is difficult to maintain a sense that your life is – and has been – a meaningful journey. As you look back at your life and reflect on your choices and accomplishments, the sense of having been "true to yourself" can serve as an extraordinarily powerful antidote to the feelings of vulnerability that are naturally associated with the aging process. That is why it is so important to try to live your life from the perspective of an older, wiser version of yourself who routinely asks, "Is this (choice) consistent with who I am/who I want to be?" It is often easy to justify questionable decisions in the here and now ("I was really busy"; "Everybody does it"), but is that how you want to remember yourself when you are looking back at the choices you made? Is that how you would want others to remember you? Living your life from the perspective of your future self can help ensure that this vital source of life meaning is flourishing when you need it the most.

In Chapter 3 we also linked the process of seeking knowledge of your core personal goals with the concept of "possible selves" (Markus & Nurius, 1986), which can be seen as a more personalized version of the exploration and commitment concepts popularized by Marcia.

> Possible selves are the selves we imagine ourselves becoming in the future, the selves we hope to become, the selves we are afraid we may become, and the selves we fully expect we will become . . .. The source of these selves is varied. Possible selves can be rooted in one's own experience and past behavior or accomplishments . . .. Possible selves can be rooted in what

important others believe one should become. They can also be rooted in one's own values, ideals and aspirations. (Oyserman & Fryberg, 2006, p. 19)

This explanation of the concept of possible selves suggests that when feelings of life meaning arise from the values and self-concepts we personally embrace, they will naturally tend to flow along the pathways we have identified in the TSP Theory of Life Meaning. The notion that possible selves can emerge from "experience and past behavior or accomplishments" is consistent with the goal–life alignment pathway, in which meaning is derived by connecting daily activities with core personal goals. Recognition that possible selves can be derived from "what important others believe one should become" is closely associated with the cultural interpretation pathways (assuming, of course, that those beliefs are internalized as one's own). Similarly, the existential interpretation pathways are implicated in the suggestion that possible selves can emanate from "one's own values, ideals and aspirations."

Spirituality and Religiousness

Many people consider spirituality and religiousness to be synonymous. And indeed, both pathways to life meaning focus on similar topics (e.g., virtuous ways of life; connecting to something larger than yourself) and are capable of generating profoundly strong feelings of life meaning, especially when people are facing life-and-death circumstances. Yet the sources of meaning are quite distinctive. Religiousness represents the degree to which an individual has accepted and acts in accordance with culturally defined beliefs organized around the worship of a divine figure. The concept of spirituality, on the other hand, centers on an individual's private search for ways to connect with a divine figure (or some other life-giving force) and to learn more about themselves through this relationship. Spirituality may emerge through the foundation provided by religiousness; however, it may also flow from life experiences that have nothing to do with organized religion (Critcher & Lee, 2018).

Spirituality and religion address concerns that are, for most people, among the most emotionally challenging and complex they will ever face. Many of these concerns focus directly on (ultimate) life meaning. Why are we here? How can we know if we are living a life that is worthwhile? What happens to us when we die? The difficulty of addressing such questions solely on the basis of personal life experience helps explain why people often turn to religion (and other cultural belief systems). How in the world can we expect to answer questions about "the breath of life" (the meaning of the Latin root word *spiritus*) without help from those who came before us?

> All religions seek to help people to grapple with core existential concerns (i.e., questions of purpose and meaning) and posit rules and values that guide individuals' relationships, as well as their efforts to cope with the travails of life . . .. [Religions provide] beliefs and practices that are grounded in the conviction that there is a transcendent (non-physical) dimension of life. These beliefs are persuasive, pervasive, and stable. They inform the kinds of attributions that people make, the meanings they construct, and the ways they conduct relationships. (Peterson & Seligman, 2004, pp. 600–601)

Although a significant portion of humanity can be described as "devout" when it comes to the role of religion in their everyday life, for many people spirituality and religion are sources of life meaning that remain in the background until some sort of tragedy or hardship occurs that is outside their personal control. As we learned from Frankl (1946/2006), that is when it becomes essential to find some kind of meaning to hang on to, so that helpless experiences in the present do not deteriorate into hopeless feelings about the future. So, while life meaning may come to us through many pathways, there are certain kinds of circumstances that are so traumatic (e.g., a devastating injury; severe or repeated victimization; loss of a child or lifelong partner) that it may be extremely difficult to find meaning without connecting in some fashion to a larger force that is capable of explaining our misfortune and offering hope for the future. In such circumstances, those without some source of spiritual strength may find it hard to avoid a downward spiral into despair and depression.

From this perspective, spirituality and religion are particularly helpful sources of what motivation scholars have called *secondary control* (Morling & Evered, 2006; Rothbaum et al., 1982). As we explained in Chapter 3, humans are self-directed living systems who seek to control the thoughts, perceptions, and feelings that they experience as they pursue personal goals that are important and meaningful to them. That is how we are naturally designed – and why it can be so distressing to experience a loss of control over life events that directly impact our core personal goals. Imagine, for example, being told by a knowledgeable expert that it is no longer safe to engage in an activity that used to be at the center of your life. Or that you simply do not have (or never will have!) the skills required to achieve a lifelong goal. Or that you have a debilitating disease and no one can do anything about it. What protects people from going into an emotional freefall when this sort of "worst case scenario" happens?

In such circumstances efforts to exercise *primary control* strategies (e.g., taking constructive action, seeking practical help) may backfire by reinforcing the futility of trying to regain what has been lost. And yet there is another alternative to feeling completely "out of control" – one for which spiritual and religious beliefs are particularly well suited. Specifically, instead of trying to change circumstances that are intrinsically uncontrollable, people can exercise *secondary control* strategies that seek to adjust our goals, emotions, and personal agency beliefs in ways that help us accept or adapt to circumstances as they are.

Such acceptance may be facilitated, for example, by identifying with powerful, even superhuman forces that *are* capable of controlling those circumstances, thus injecting some degree of meaning into an otherwise inexplicable situation and making the bad outcomes seem less arbitrary and unfair ("This is my destiny" or "This must be God's plan"). In addition, people can find meaning in misfortune and tragedy by seeking *predictive control*, thus enabling them to better anticipate and prepare for future outcomes. Some degree of comfort can also be attained by seeking to better understand "why bad things are happening to me" – a coping mechanism that Rothbaum et al. (1982) called *interpretive control*. Religious and spiritual beliefs that help us see senseless outcomes in a more understandable – and thus more meaningful – light can help people maintain hope and courage even when things seem at their worst (e.g., This is God's way of testing me"; "Everyone experiences tragedy at some point in their lives").

The preceding discussion clarifies why spirituality and religiousness have been such powerful forces in human history for both individuals and cultural groups. As we have seen, life meaning is an evolved adaptation that is essential for survival with well-being. Natural selection was especially cruel to those who could not sustain feelings of life meaning. That is because *life meaning is not just "something nice" that happens when things are going well; it is a fundamental source of motivational strength and vitality.* Without an ongoing flow of feelings of life meaning, motivational headquarters can quickly become demoralized and disempowered. Meaninglessness is so aversive that it can cause people to lose the will to do the things they need to do to stay alive. It is therefore logical that mechanisms for avoiding this descent into despair would also evolve as the capacity for self-awareness developed and life meaning became an increasingly important element in our motivational systems.

Spirituality and religiousness are clearly among the most effective of these mechanisms (Emmons, 2005; Fry, 2000; Kashdan & Nezlek, 2012; C. Park, 2005; Steger & Frazier, 2005). Indeed, in a worldwide survey of 132 nations, Oishi and Diener (2014) concluded that a primary reason that residents of poor nations generally have a greater sense of meaning in life than residents of wealthy nations is because people in poorer nations are, at a collective level, more religious. Moreover, nations higher in life meaning had lower suicide rates. This correlation, which directly links well-being to survival, suggests that spirituality and religiousness should be central themes in any accounting of the evolutionary success of *Homo sapiens*. As D. S. Wilson (2002) explains,

> people who stand outside of religion often regard its seemingly irrational nature as more interesting and important to explain than its communal nature. Rational thought is treated as the gold standard against which religious belief is found so wanting that it becomes well-nigh inexplicable. Evolution causes us to think about the subject in a completely different way. Adaptation becomes the gold standard against which rational thought must be measured alongside other modes of thought. In a single stroke, rational thought becomes necessary but not sufficient to explain the length and breadth of human mentality, and the so-called irrational features of religion can be studied respectfully as potential adaptations in their own right. (pp. 122–123)

Ideology and Philosophy

Life meaning can also flow from emotionally compelling beliefs about what is valid and virtuous in domains other than spirituality and religion. The terms *ideology* and *philosophy* are often used in this context to refer to fundamental beliefs about human nature and how people should relate to each other and to their physical and cultural environments. Such beliefs may focus, for example, on economic concerns (e.g., how to distribute resources in a fair and equitable manner), political concerns (e.g., how much influence local and national governments should have on people's lives), ecological concerns (e.g., how to educate citizens about the long-term consequences of global warming), or group identity concerns (e.g., those pertaining to patriotism and citizenship). Scientific knowledge and ways of thinking can also serve as the basis for beliefs about human nature that seem valid and virtuous.

For some people, ideological and philosophical beliefs are useful in a pragmatic sense but rarely serve as a deep or robust source of life meaning.

For example, you might weakly identify with a political party based on a tendency to favor their general approach to social and economic policies. Or you might be ecologically minded in terms of certain day-to-day habits (e.g., recycling, using public transportation) but not give much thought to broader concerns about the future of the planet. Yet, for others, ideological and philosophical beliefs about society and nature can become heartfelt ideals that lead them to invest their time, energy, and money in causes for which they feel a great deal of passion and commitment. Over time such causes can become inextricably woven into our identity and values, thus amplifying the resulting feelings of life meaning. When we make progress toward the ideals that guide our cherished causes, it feels like a personal victory. Conversely, when those ideals are disrespected it feels like a personal attack. It is more than a metaphor to say that having something to fight for is having something to live for.

Some belief systems that provide us with life meaning are focused more on personal insight and understanding than on social change and public policy. The term *philosophy* is typically used for this psychologically oriented source of life meaning, whereas *ideology* is the more common choice when the ideas are intrinsically social and action oriented. Yet the origins of philosophical belief systems are mainly cultural, just as ideological belief systems are derived primarily from our cultural experiences. Individuals do not invent entire belief systems; rather, they are passed on and elaborated through education and socialization, where they can evolve at a collective level over time (as illustrated by cultural changes in attitudes toward equality and access to public resources). What makes this process personalized is when we try out particular viewpoints (the idea of exploring possible selves) and then adopt some of them as our own, perhaps with some "tweaking" to enhance personal comfort (e.g., advocating for a political or religious ideology but not applying its doctrines to circumstances that strike you as harsh or inflexible). This wedding together of cultural and existential interpretations is what leads us to internalize cultural belief systems as part of our identity, values, and ethical principles.

Uplifting Experiences

Up to now we have been focused primarily on informational sources of life meaning. As illustrated by terms like identity and ideology, our personalized network of values, beliefs, and self-concepts can be a strong and reliable wellspring when it comes to feelings of life meaning. Yet, life meaning can also be derived from experiences that are more visceral than reflective, and more perceptual than idea-driven. Emotion labels like awe, wonder, and "elevation" (see Chapter 4, Table 4.1) exemplify efforts to try to capture the inspirational qualities and unique bodily and emotional sensations associated with special experiences of this kind.

What are the defining qualities of these extraordinary experiences that help us feel that "life is worth living"? Citing Irish philosopher Edmund Burke, Keltner (2009) has suggested that there are two essential ingredients. One is the sense of being a part of something that is much larger than the self or well beyond our personal capabilities. Imagine, for example, being part of a powerful orchestra or choir. Or becoming immersed in an inspiring political campaign. Or fulfilling a key role on a crisis response team. Experiencing the "power of the collective" from the perspective of an active participant can help us better appreciate the amazing impact we can have when we join forces with others (as nature intended!).

The second element that often triggers uplifting emotions is a sense that we are experiencing something that is truly amazing and perhaps even difficult to comprehend. Awe-inspiring experiences (including those that arise from collective action) are not just unique; they are astonishing and hard to assimilate into our current understandings and interpretations. That is why such experiences often have life-changing effects – as illustrated by the "overview effect" that astronauts report when they look back at our beautiful but fragile planet from a cosmic perspective (F. White, 1987). This experience is both uplifting and sobering, as it clarifies how dependent the human race is on forces that transcend our individual lives, and how interdependent we all are with respect to the need to preserve and protect those life-sustaining qualities.

Keltner and Haidt (2003) conducted an analysis of the kinds of circumstances that trigger emotions like awe and elevation and organized the results into three categories: social elicitors, physical elicitors, and cognitive elicitors. Social elicitors involved personal or vicarious encounters with a powerful individual (e.g., God or an inspirational leader) as well as encounters with people of great skill or virtue ("Did you see that? That was incredible/beautiful!"). Physical elicitors included triggers that were extraordinarily fearsome (e.g., a tornado or earthquake) or unusually pleasing to the senses (e.g., awe-inspiring art or music; a grand vista such as those found in a national park or oceanfront setting). Finally, cognitive elicitors were exemplified by experiences of sudden or deep insight that caused people to feel overwhelmed by the power of an idea or some "truth" that had been revealed (e.g., a parent experiencing the unparalleled wonder of a newborn son or daughter for the first time).

In each of these cases, the importance of *connection* as a meaning-generating phenomenon is apparent – although in a unique way that transcends the goal strivings and ongoing relationships that fill our daily lives. As Keltner (2009) explains,

> the experience of awe is about finding your place in the larger scheme of things. It is about quieting the press of self-interest. It is about folding into social collectives. It is about feeling reverential toward participating in some expansive process that unites us all and that ennobles our life's endeavors. (p. 268)

It is these kinds of experiences that help us see life as a special gift that is worthwhile despite the inevitable challenges and hardships that come our way.

Acquiring Life Meaning through Goal–Life Alignment

Dream as if you'll live forever, live as if you'll die today.

– actor James Dean

As we have seen, we can derive life meaning from our efforts to answer fundamental questions about who we are and how we fit in to the world around us. Analogous to the process of building a home, we seek out raw materials (things we can believe in) and construct a framework for which we can feel "pride of ownership." This framework of ideas and ideals provides us with a sense of structure and integrity while also fulfilling our needs for security and comfort. It is a safe place we can return to after venturing out into the world and experiencing conflict and hypocrisy. It is source of warmth and reassurance that can give us strength when we are suffering or feeling discouraged.

Yet, with few exceptions, we spend most of our lives living in our homes, not building (or remodeling) them. While existential and cultural sources of life meaning may be at the center of our lives during certain developmental periods (as Erikson suggested), or while we are struggling with emotional turmoil (e.g., from a devastating loss or traumatic experience), the primary source of life meaning in our everyday activities is what we have been calling *goal–life alignment*. When our daily lives at work, with our family and friends, and in our leisure time provide us with ample opportunities and encouragement to pursue our core personal goals, we feel self-directed yet also in harmony with the world around us. Life seems worthwhile and fulfilling. We have a clear sense that "this is what I was meant to do." And in a very fundamental way, that feeling is right on target. As the ancient Greek philosopher Aristotle said, "Man is a goal-seeking animal – his life only has meaning if he is reaching out and striving for his goals."

Core Personal Goals and Life Meaning

As we explained in Chapter 3, the first step in achieving goal–life alignment as an everyday source of life meaning is to ensure that you have a clear understanding of your core personal goals and your overall goal profile. You may recall that this is the objective for which the *Assessment of Personal Goals* (M. Ford & Nichols, 2005) and the *APG Personal Application Guide* (M. Ford & Smith, 2013) were designed (both available at https://apg.gmu.edu). When you know what kinds of goal pursuits are most likely (and least likely!) to yield feelings of life meaning, you can identify sources of satisfaction and dissatisfaction in your daily life and make wise choices about how to invest your time and energy. Importantly, such wisdom is as much about what to say "no" to as what to say "go" to. In addition, goal awareness can help you make plans for the future that can transform the "possible selves" that seem most meaningful to you into a reality. In contrast, when we are unable to anticipate what kinds of activities or relationships or career pathways are likely to feel meaningful, life can deteriorate into a rudderless journey filled with worry, self-doubt, and downward spirals of self-absorbed negativity (T. D. Wilson, 2009).

Recognizing that feelings of meaninglessness may be resolvable through deliberate efforts to create goal–life alignment can be a joyful and rejuvenating experience for those who feel "stuck" in an unfulfilling job or relationship. Although the process of getting "unstuck" may be emotionally and financially challenging, the consequences of doing nothing may be far more costly in the long run. Nor is it always necessary to take drastic actions to set one's life course on a more fulfilling pathway. Sometimes all it takes is a few knowledgeable adjustments, analogous to a wheel alignment that makes it easier for us to steer straight ahead as we travel down the "highway of life."

When we see ourselves achieving or making progress toward our core personal goals on a daily basis, feelings of life meaning will naturally flow from those outcomes. Yet life meaning can also be derived from merely thinking about our core personal goals in ways that prepare us for future goal pursuits. For example, the process of identifying and reflecting on core goal themes can be inspiring and affirming (as illustrated by feedback we have received from people who have taken the APG). In addition, we can generate feelings of life meaning by translating our high-level goal thoughts (e.g., "I am highly motivated by opportunities to be intellectually creative") into concrete representations of those goal themes, thus revealing new "possible selves" (e.g., "Perhaps I would enjoy being a graphic designer . . . or an aspiring author . . . or a professional chef").

Along these same lines, life meaning is a common by-product when people assess the extent to which the specific activities they are currently invested in relate to their core personal goals (a goal–life alignment exercise included, among others, in the *APG Personal Application Guide*). Feelings of life meaning can also flow from efforts to seek feedback on how we are progressing toward our core personal goals. We can even acquire life meaning by trying to "retro-fit" aspects of our life history to broad purposes we may not have been aware of at the time (Klinger, 1998).

An important premise of Motivational Systems Theory is that life meaning can be derived from all types of goal striving, including goal pursuits in every one of the twenty-four goal categories included in the *Taxonomy of Human Goals*. And yet, for any given individual it is likely that there will only be a handful of goal themes that are consistently powerful and reliable when it comes to generating feelings of life meaning (Nichols, 1994). Indeed, it is fascinating to see how remarkably different people can be when it comes to the kinds of goal pursuits they find most meaningful, even when raised in similar circumstances or when sharing a substantial percentage of genetic material. That is one of the reasons we have highlighted the guiding principle that efforts to motivate self and others require an understanding of our basic nature *as a unique individual*. What works for a person with one set of core personal goals may not be effective for people with very different goal profiles. That motivational "fact of life" is a central challenge for educators and helping professionals, and for people who have chosen to live their lives together as partners or as a family.

Yet we have also emphasized that "basic human nature" involves species-wide commonalities in our motivational makeup. For example, absent severe pathology, we are all designed to be self-directed. We all have the capacity for mental time travel and thus the ability to formulate thoughts and experience feelings about desired future outcomes and how to progress toward those outcomes. That is an underlying theme in our concept of *thriving*. In addition, despite vast individual differences with regard to the strength of our self-assertive and integrative tendencies

(M. Ford & Nichols, 1991; Koestler, 1978), we are all designed to be a connected part of intimate social groups and broader social networks. As we explained in Chapter 6, that part of our evolutionary history has created a unique role for the four categories of goal content we have labeled *social purpose* goals (i.e., belongingness, equity, social responsibility, and resource provision). Consistent with the notion that meaning is derived from various kinds of connections that we formulate and experience, social purpose goals appear to be among the strongest of all sources of life meaning. That suggests that, for most people, goal–life alignment will be very hard to achieve in the absence of meaningful interpersonal relationships.

Obstacles to Goal–Life Alignment

Misguided beliefs about sources of life meaning. As we have seen, when people lack self-awareness of their core personal goals, that can create major barriers to achieving the benefits associated with goal–life alignment. One such barrier is the tendency to fill that knowledge void with misguided beliefs about the goal pursuits that are most likely to generate enduring feelings of life meaning – for example, those high-lighted by the popular culture. Media portrayals of success suggest that the most important achievements in life are things like good looks, fun times, and lots of material possessions. Why? Because those who are primarily concerned with selling us things have learned that the most effective way to influence buying decisions is to influence how our unconscious "like-o-meter" responds to their products. As a result of such emotionally provocative influences, people often lose equipoise with respect to balancing short-term pleasures with longer-term sources of life meaning.

Individuals and institutions trying to influence our beliefs and buying decisions have also found that a surprisingly wide range of people are eager to embrace "creative" explanations for things that are mysterious, disturb-ing, or hard to grasp through direct perception, even when those explana-tions seem implausible or absurd from an evidence-based perspective. Such explanations include astrology, witchcraft, conspiracy theories, and mythology about death and dying (e.g., ghosts, reincarnation). If you are like most people, you have probably been at least a little intrigued by one or more of these methods of explaining "the mysteries of life." Yet, even for those who are attracted to such ideas, it is hard to derive the level of informational clarity and coherence needed to reliably generate feelings of life meaning from these "otherworldly" explanations of life events.

Failure to connect current actions with meaningful purposes. Another obstacle to experiencing the feelings of life meaning associated with goal–life alignment is the tendency to lose track of the connections between our everyday objectives and the broader purposes they are intended to serve. As we explained in Chapter 3, focusing attention on "what I have to do today" is a great way to ensure that you will follow through on your intentions and make steady progress toward your goals. As the old saying goes, "if you take care of the little things, the big things will take care of themselves." Yet when it comes to life meaning, what matters most is how the "little things" are connected to the "big things." In other words, it's not just *what you have accomplished*, but also *why that is valuable*. The need to keep connections between actions and purposes firmly in mind is why some control systems theorists (e.g., Powers, 1973) have emphasized the importance of being able to focus attention on the right level of meaning at the right time. That is how life can become "not a series of accidents, but a work of art" (Gallagher, 2009, p. 2).

Hermans's (1998) version of the well-known bricklayer metaphor illustrates how making connections between "big things and little things" can transform a laborious chore into a personally meaningful project.

> Three bricklayers are at work. A passerby asks the first one: "Why are you picking up that brick?" He answers: "To take it upstairs to the other bricks." When asked the same question, the second man says "I am building a wall." The third man, in his turn, explains: "I am building a school." (p. 317)

Too many or too few goals. One of the most common obstacles to goal–life alignment is loss of equipoise with respect to the number of goals being actively pursued within a given time period. Too few goals can leave us feeling bored and disengaged, while too many goals can cause disorganizing feelings of stress and self-doubt. As we saw in Chapter 4, motivating self and others requires a sense of being *optimally challenged*, with conditions that spark our interest and test our skills and resources without undermining our capability and context beliefs. Under such conditions we experience vitality and fulfillment and are more likely to experience *flow*, the central concept in Csikszentmihalyi's (1991, 2003) theory of optimal experience.

In contrast, when challenges are not optimal, things can become quite demotivating. Too few goals can lead to a dreary sense of emptiness or discontent, while too many goals can make it hard to keep up with the commitments we have made to ourselves and others. The need to "right-size" goal pursuits is of particular concern at the level of core personal goals, where feelings of life meaning are most likely to arise. For example, people who are consumed by a single purpose may feel devastated if they suddenly find themselves unable to pursue their cherished goals (as when a star athlete's career is ended by a sudden injury, or a devoted caregiver's loved one passes away).

People who are invested in an excessive number of core personal goals may also be vulnerable to experiencing emotional disorganization, as illustrated by individuals whose APG goal profiles are heavily weighted toward very high scores. When there are too many goals "clogging up" motivational headquarters, the results can be just as toxic with respect to feelings of life meaning as when there are too few goals to keep motivational headquarters energized. Instead of anticipating and then experiencing the warm glow of fulfillment as we pursue the goals that are most important to us, life can end up feeling more like a series of emergencies, with lots of vexing choices. The only way to keep up when so many things are capturing our attention is to run around with the metaphorical equivalent of a fire extinguisher as we try to keep up with the flames (activated core personal goals) that keep flaring up all around us. Yet when it comes to life meaning, passion is no substitute for purpose. Without the clarity offered by a manageable set of priorities, we are left with "chronic inflammation" that undermines our capability and context beliefs and leaves us feeling emotionally drained.

Inflexible standards for goal attainment. Life is like a flowing stream that is constantly changing its shape and depth and composition as it zigzags toward its destinations (D. Ford, 1987/2019). It is therefore impossible to maintain goal–life alignment without making adjustments designed to ensure that our standards for goal attainment will continue to fit our changing circumstances. For example, when we encounter some rough patches (e.g., a bad economy or a hostile work environment), we may need to find life meaning in smaller achievements and not be so hard on ourselves when things don't go our way. Conversely, when life's routines begin to feel stale or irritating we may need to challenge ourselves and venture beyond our current "comfort zone" to find new sources of life meaning. Although we are creatures of habit, we are also a restless species that is naturally inclined to seek out new challenges, both large and small. Indeed, most of us find it easier to *raise* the bar than to lower it when adjusting standards to changing circumstances. And yet sometimes lowering the bar is the only way to "keep it real" with respect to how we set our goal-striving expectations.

Our natural inclination to elevate standards for goal attainment as we learn more and improve our skills is generally a good thing, as suggested by research that links *accelerating standards* to high levels of aspiration and achievement (e.g., Masters et al., 1977). Yet inflexible standards can also produce demotivating results when we are unable to find satisfaction in anything less than a perfectionistic result. That is why an equipoised approach to defining "progress" and "success" is so important. Some of the biggest achievements in life are those that simply help us regain some sense of equilibrium when life "throws us a curve." Indeed, many goal pursuits generate *more* life meaning when there is some adversity along the way and we are nevertheless able to "make the most of it" rather than becoming discouraged and giving up.

Preoccupation with avoidance goals. Experiences that generate feelings of life meaning are generally growth oriented. This is not surprising given the very different emotional outcomes associated with approach and avoidance goal orientations (see Chapter 4, Figure 4.4). Avoidance goals breed caution and apprehension. Approach goals, on the other hand, promote positivity and self-improvement (assuming that realistic standards are maintained). They expand our understanding of ourselves and the world around us. They strengthen our beliefs about what we are capable of doing. They add depth to the relationships that matter most to us. In short, they cause us to feel that life is worthwhile – and that the future could be even better.

In contrast, when we spend most of our time trying to protect ourselves from bad outcomes, we limit our opportunities for experiencing feelings of life meaning (Roskes et al., 2014). That is why equipoise with respect to approach and avoidance goals is so important to goal–life alignment. As illustrated by Halvorson and Higgins's (2013) research on when it is appropriate to have a *prevention* focus or a *promotion* focus in the pursuit of daily life goals, playing "defense" is certainly appropriate when there are clear threats and vulnerabilities. Yet if we don't balance that orientation with opportunities to explore and learn and improve (i.e., actively pursue approach goals), we may inadvertently shut off our primary sources of life meaning.

TSP and Life Meaning

> When we are motivated by goals that have deep meaning, by dreams that need completion, by pure love that needs expressing, then we truly live life.
>
> – author Greg Anderson

Throughout this book we have used the concept of *amplification* to explain how thriving and social purpose impact our basic motivational functions (i.e., our personal goals, emotions, and personal agency beliefs). In a nutshell, TSP transforms ordinary patterns of functioning into more optimal patterns of functioning by strengthening our personal and inter-personal leadership capabilities.

Along these same lines, TSP motivational patterns also contribute to our experiences of life meaning by invigorating the pathways through which life meaning can be acquired, and by amplifying the resulting feelings of life meaning. As illustrated in Table 7.1, the "meaningfulness" of our existential and cultural interpretations and our efforts to align daily activities with core personal goals can be greatly enhanced when they are energized by thriving motivational processes and infused with SP goal content. Indeed, after reviewing the work of the world's leading scholars on the topic of life meaning, we have concluded that the very best predictors of where and when life meaning is likely to be experienced are those associated with TSP motivational patterns (e.g., Baumeister, 1991; Csikszentmihalyi, 2003; Emmons, 2003; D. Feldman & Snyder, 2005; Frankl, 1946/2006; Keltner, 2009; Markman et al., 2013; Steger, 2012; Wong & Fry, 1998).

Consistent with our emphasis on self-direction as an overarching design feature of human motivational systems, some of the most dependable predictors of life meaning are focused on experiences associated with *purposeful goal striving*. The more important the goal, and the greater the investment in its pursuit, the more likely it is that life meaning will flow from that experience. For example, achieving your personal best at your favorite sport is likely to feel much more meaningful than an adequate performance in a sport that you dabble in from time to time. Successfully completing a complex project that few could have accomplished will predictably yield a greater sense of life meaning than completing a routine project that most anyone could do.

The integrative concept of *thriving* provides a useful way to summarize the predictors of life meaning associated with self-directed goal pursuit.

Thriving qualities not only help us strive for life meaning, they amplify the effect that meaningful experiences have on human motivation. In addition to the immediate, "in-the-moment" motivational boost that such experiences can provide, thriving adds to our residual capacity to adaptively deal with life's inevitable obstacles and setbacks (Scarmeas & Stern, 2003).

Humans evolved as social creatures whose survival depended on interpersonal bonding, cooperative group living, and supportive actions on behalf of vulnerable members of the species. Although the feeling that "life is worth living" may be associated with goals of all types, it is particularly likely to emerge in the context of goals related to this evolutionary mandate. That is because, as we saw in Chapter 6, *social purpose* provides the motivational "glue" that binds people together.

Our emphasis on social purpose should not be construed as negating or diminishing the importance of self-enhancing motives and accomplishments. Thriving without social purpose in the pursuit of self-enhancing goals may yield abundant feelings of life meaning. However, it does not appear that a surplus of thriving can compensate for deficits in social purpose – at least not for very long. Most people have a difficult time maintaining a sense that life is meaningful in the absence of enduring social bonds and clearly articulated social roles and responsibilities. Solitary confinement, for example, is considered among the harshest of all punishments. There is also substantial evidence linking social isolation and low levels of social support to negative health consequences and reduced longevity (Hawkley & Cacioppo, 2010; Kok et al., 2013; Ryff & Singer, 2001).

How Thriving Helps People Strive for and Amplify Their Feelings of Life Meaning

Based on a review of the relevant science and the core elements in our TSP Theory of Motivation and Optimal Functioning, we have identified four different predictors of life meaning associated with self-directed goal striving, each of which can be amplified by motivational patterns that incorporate an active approach goal orientation, personal optimism, mindful tenacity, and emotional wisdom.

Engagement. The process of *engagement* is arguably the most fundamental predictor of life meaning because it reflects the fact that trying to attain a goal can be meaningful even when outcomes are uncertain or things do not turn out quite the way we had envisioned. The fact that engagement occurs *during* goal pursuit and is not dependent on a successful outcome is a critically important feature of the evolved capacity for experiencing life meaning, as the pursuit of our most important goals (e.g., advancing toward a career goal, raising a child, creating new ideas and products) may involve many years of effort and commitment before the hoped-for results are evident. As Baumeister (1991) explains,

> the vital thing is to interpret one's current activities in relation to future or possible states. The purposes do not ever have to be realized or achieved in actual fact. It is quite possible to live a very meaningful life in pursuit of goals that are never reached during one's lifetime. (p. 32)

There is also ample evidence that the neural and biochemical processes associated with engagement facilitate good mental and physical health independent of the outcomes that may result (Ryff & Singer, 1998). For these reasons, engagement has emerged as one of the central themes in the scientific discipline of positive psychology (e.g., Schueller & Seligman, 2006). This theme is exemplified by Csikszentmihalyi's (1991, 2003) extensive work on *flow* experiences, during which high challenge is met with high skill and thriving motivational qualities naturally emerge. Such experiences combine the cognitive and neurochemical benefits of alertness and focused attention with the emotional and physical benefits associated with the activation of compelling goals and robust personal agency beliefs (Begley, 2007; Csikszentmihalyi, 1991).

Engagement has also become a major organizing concept in the management literature, especially as it relates to "positive organizational behavior" (Bakker & Schaufeli, 2008) and the management of human resources. Although life meaning is usually not the main focus in descriptions of employee engagement interventions – increased productivity from motivationally absorbed workers has been the big "selling point" – it is clearly an important and reliable outcome:

> the focus in modern organizations is on the management of *human capital.* Currently, organizations expect their employees to be proactive and show initiative, collaborate smoothly with others, take responsibility for their own professional development, and to be committed to high quality performance standards. Thus employees are needed who feel energetic and dedicated, and who are absorbed by their work. In other words, organizations need engaged workers. (Bakker & Schaufeli, 2008, p. 147)

Goal progress. Engagement is not the whole story, however, when it comes to predicting the benefits associated with a thriving motivational orientation. Results can also play a significant role in sustaining and enhancing life meaning. For example, feedback indicating that *goal progress* is being made can amplify the feeling that engaging in the pursuit of an important goal is meaningful (Diener & Fujita, 1995). Imagine, for example, starting a small business and seeing the first significant revenues roll in. Or imagine a team of scientists seeing the first signs of progress in combating a deadly disease after months of unsupported hypothesis testing. As a natural consequence of how our motivational systems are designed, such events can unleash a flood of thoughts and emotions confirming that *it was all worth it*.

Lasting contributions. As we've seen, life meaning can accumulate even in the absence of ultimate goal fulfillment ("it's the journey, not the destination"). Nevertheless, there's nothing quite like success! That is particularly true for efforts that result in *lasting contributions* to significant people in your life, to important community and societal institutions, or to the cultural and physical environments in which you live (Rosso et al., 2010). "Legacy" is a term that is sometimes used for this predictor of life meaning. How have you contributed to making the world a better place, as a parent, as a worker, as a citizen, as a leader? A telling (and potentially unsettling!) exercise is to ask yourself, "What will my obituary say?" Life meaning is closely associated with a perception that *I am making a difference*.

Affirmation. Because most of our goal pursuits occur in a social context, it is often difficult to assess progress or to appreciate the importance of your contributions without some feedback from personally or professionally significant people in your life. That is why *affirmation* is also an important predictor of life meaning. Imagine investing weeks preparing a eulogy or an important speech and then doing a great job when the time came to stand up in front of the assembled group. What if no one said much about it afterward? It might be hard to maintain a sense that you had accomplished something meaningful, even if it felt that way when you were actually speaking to the group. Now imagine that some people came up to you afterward and said that you had deeply touched their emotions or caused them to think differently about something important in their lives. With this kind of affirmation, you are likely to feel that your efforts were not just capable; they were also meaningful in a broader and more enduring way.

In sum, it is evident that a "sense that one's life is meaningful ... [is] closely related to having a range of satisfying personal goals and making reasonable progress toward attaining them," especially when those goals correspond to "individual core values" (Klinger & Cox, 2004, p. 20).

Thriving motivational patterns amplify feelings of life meaning by facilitating the effective pursuit of such goals.

How Social Purpose Helps People Strive for and Amplify Their Feelings of Life Meaning

As outlined in previous chapters, there are four major themes within the domain of social purpose, all of which appear to be robust predictors of life meaning. For consistency, the labels we have chosen for these themes are those used in the *Taxonomy of Human Goals* for integrative social relationship goals (see Table 3.1, Chapter 3).

Belongingness. Consistent with Baumeister's (1991) emphasis on how meaning flows from connections, perhaps the most fundamental theme linking social purpose and life meaning is *relationships*, or social bonding with others (Baumeister & Leary, 1995; Rosso et al., 2010). The greater the number of authentic connections you have with a person or group, the more likely it is that feelings of life meaning will emanate from those relationships. Those feelings in turn are likely to cause others to see you as more socially appealing.

Imagine, for example, a boss who not only assigns tasks and evaluates performance, but who is also your career mentor and family friend. Or a neighbor who is also your confidante and reliable informant with respect to newsworthy events in your community. Forming and maintaining relationships with these enriched and enriching kinds of qualities is important not only for our emotional well-being, but also for our physical health and longevity (Krause, 2009). As Heintzelman and King (2014b) conclude:

> Social relationships are a foundational source of meaning in life ....
> Individuals who are lonely, socially excluded, ignored, or ostracized are
> worse off on a number of psychological outcomes .... Even very superficial
> laboratory manipulations affect the experience of meaning in life .... When
> we are socially excluded, life feels less meaningful. When we are socially
> connected, life feels more meaningful. (pp. 562–563)

Strong bonds with family members and close friends are often the most reliable and durable predictors of life meaning. However, meaningful connections can be made not only with other individuals, but also with social groups with whom you feel a sense of belonging (Hirsch & Clark, 2019). For example, wise employers work hard to try to facilitate feelings of organizational identity and loyalty among their employees. You might also feel a strong connection to a political party, sports team, ethnic group, religious community, or your alma mater. It is important to recognize, however, that social connections can mutate into burdensome relationships if they become more a source of life stress than a source of life meaning. It is definitely possible to have too much of a good thing. This "double-edged sword" phenomenon further illustrates the important of maintaining equipoise in our relationships with others, both individually and collectively.

Resource provision. This predictor of life meaning is commonly referred to as *altruism*. With rare exceptions such as sociopaths (Boehm, 2012), we seem to be hardwired to care about those with whom we feel closely connected (Brown & Brown, 2006) and to feel that we are doing something meaningful when we help them. Because altruism generally flows from social bonds, altruistic motivation is selective. How selective? That depends on the network of connections you have constructed in your interpersonal relationships and group affiliations. If you have an expansive network or feel an affinity toward a large subset of humanity, altruism may be a common response. Conversely, if your social network is more circumscribed, you may only feel altruistic urges around a few people you are particularly close to.

Not that there's necessarily anything wrong with that! We have evolved to be selective in our giving so as to maximize the impact of our altruistic actions (Brown & Brown, 2006). In other words, while "universal altruism" may sound nice, it doesn't make biological sense. For example, while it is critical that parents altruistically invest in their children to ensure their survival and well-being, it would generally be considered inappropriate and unwise (especially if resources were limited) for parents to be similarly invested in children outside their immediate or extended family. Imagine an ancestral hunter charitably donating his day's bounty to some random family in another tribe while his genetically related offspring (and fellow tribe mates who helped produce the bounty) starved. Traits motivating indiscriminate altruism presumably would not have reproduced as efficiently as traits motivating a more selective kind of altruism.

The basic logic connecting altruism and life meaning is simple. Some mechanism was needed to ensure that parents, caregivers, and coalition members would be motivated to make "costly" long-term interpersonal investments, while also retaining sufficient personal resources to care for themselves (as illustrated by the equipoised preflight instruction to put on your own oxygen mask before helping a child seated next to you in the event of a loss of cabin pressure). Social bonding – an integrative process that organizes goals, emotions, memories, and neurohormonal processes around interactions with key people in your life – became the mechanism for accomplishing this evolutionary crucial purpose. "Social bonds evolved because they promoted giving away (as opposed to getting) valuable resources" (Brown & Brown, 2006, p. 1). This mechanism works largely because altruism reliably produces feelings of life meaning in the individual providing resources (assuming the giver does not feel overburdened). And, because those feelings are powerful and special, life meaning in turn motivates people to keep on giving. Indeed, "giving may be a more important determinant of well-being than receiving" (Brown et al., 2007, p. 308).

The positive impact of altruism on the giver can be seen in the emotional reactions that often accompany generosity and compassion. As noted in Chapter 3 (Table 3.1), Haidt (2006) uses an "uplifting" label for the emotional experience associated with enacting or observing good deeds, namely, *elevation*. Elevation appears to be associated with the release of oxytocin, which facilitates bonding and receptivity to new relationships. Both the experience of elevation and the connections they inspire can, in turn, broaden the range of individuals and circumstances that will trigger altruistic motives and resultant feelings of life meaning. As Haidt (2006) explains,

> people really do respond emotionally to acts of moral beauty, and these emotional reactions involve warm or pleasant feelings in the chest and conscious desires to help others or become a better person oneself. (p. 196)

The elevating impact of authentic social purpose can be seen in the way that we naturally respond to those who would seek to influence our behavior. For example, young people become emotionally engaged – and thus more motivationally receptive – when parents, teachers, and mentors display "heartwarming" qualities like empathy and genuine concern for the individual's welfare (M. Ford & Smith, 2011). Academic, business, and political leaders inspire their followers not so much through displays of power or technical expertise, but by doing and saying things that convey an authentic desire to serve others and a passion for doing so (Avolio et al., 2004).

Equity. We can also derive life meaning from efforts to promote *fairness* in the lives of people with whom we feel some kind of connection. Equity evolved as a powerful social organizing principle because the pursuit of this goal enhanced the effective functioning of social groups and the survival of the individuals within those groups (Joyce, 2006). As we saw in the previous chapter, groups that promoted fairness generally fared better than those that did not prioritize that value (Sober & Wilson, 1998; Stringer, 2012). In addition, social selection pressures *within* groups created significant fitness vulnerabilities for those who were unable to develop harmonious working and living relationships (Boehm, 2012). Even today one of the most effective ways to turn a group against you is to become a "free rider" and ignore norms and expectations with respect to fairness and reciprocity. Although people with good social manipulation skills may be able to get away with selfish behavior for a while, it generally doesn't take long for group members to recognize and punish those who are not pulling their own weight (Grant, 2013). As a result, most people are closely attuned not only to how resources are distributed and how others are treated, but also to the equity-related reputational implications of their own behavior.

Fairness concerns are often wedded together with altruistic motivation in ways that can amplify the amount of life meaning derived from addressing those concerns. For example, many people feel "elevated" when they act on behalf of people who have been unfairly victimized, whether at the interpersonal level (e.g., in response to someone being unfairly criticized or sanctioned) or at the societal level (e.g., in response to concerns about social justice for disadvantaged groups). Fairness is a particularly important and challenging issue for leaders, as they must focus not only on getting things done, but also on followers' expectations for equitable and unbiased treatment. Such expectations are more likely to be met — and life meaning is more likely to result — if social purpose is a core priority in the leader's hierarchy of personal goals.

Social responsibility. Last — but certainly not least — among our major predictors of life meaning is *responsibility to others*. As we pointed out at the beginning of this chapter, a compelling case for the link between responsibility and life meaning can be found in Frankl's (1946/2006) extraordinary book *Man's Search for Meaning*. Frankl, who was a professor of neurology and psychiatry at the University of Vienna and a survivor of four Nazi concentration camps, conceptualized responsibility as a felt obligation to contribute something important to an individual, group, or society. When confronted with a patient struggling with the meaning of their life, Frankl would ask them, "What does life demand of you at this moment?" In conversations with suicidal patients, Frankl would try to get them to realize that their life's work was unfinished — someone was counting on them to be a part of their life or to act on their behalf, or some future project needed to be completed to fulfill society's expectation that they do something meaningful with their life.

Admittedly, responsibility is a double-edged sword with respect to its motivational consequences. Responsibilities can become overwhelming if you think about all of the things your family, your job, and society expects of you. But there are also some beneficial side effects, which may explain why thriving, productive people seem to embrace responsibility. Sure, they have to work hard, but the work is meaningful in their way of thinking, and that makes it all worthwhile. The "trick" is to connect short-term actions with long-term purposes, as reflected in the roles and obligations that define who you are and what others expect of you. When current responsibilities are seen as purposeful (as opposed to meaningless), they become less burdensome. Stress becomes more manageable because there is a conviction that, at least in some small way, you are working toward a better future. You are a committed part of something larger than yourself, which is the essence of social purpose.

Life Meaning: The Ultimate Payoff

We started this book by suggesting that there is a substantial payoff awaiting those who make a serious investment in learning the fundamental scientific principles underlying motivation and optimal functioning and how those principles operate in the context of your own personal goals and life circumstances. Essentially, our "big bet" is that by making this investment you can gain the insights and analytic tools needed to increase your capacity for self-direction as well as your ability to lead – and to help others lead – a more successful and meaningful life. While this "payoff" may take a variety of different forms, the ultimate payoff is *life meaning* – the highest form of well-being that we can experience in our quest for *survival with well-being*. Life meaning not only tells us that "life is good," it fills us with vitality and strength that we can draw upon time and time again, in good times and bad. It is nature's way of helping us appreciate what is important in life not only for humanity in general, but also for our own personal destiny – a destiny that we can shape and control in powerful ways through our capacity for self-direction.

Life meaning can not only help make your life *better*, it can also help you live *longer* – consistent with the idea that well-being is itself a survival mechanism (Boyle et al., 2009; Hill & Turiano, 2014; Krause, 2009;

Windsor et al., 2015). That is why finding purpose in life is such an important developmental task throughout our adult years.

In this chapter we used a variety of motivational concepts and principles to explain how you can increase the fullness and frequency with which you experience the "distinctive feeling that arises when a person believes that their life makes sense, has purpose, and is worthwhile." We started by clarifying that meaning-making is a natural process that is inherent in the design of the human brain. The need to feel that life is sensible and purposeful arose from the evolved mechanisms that we have discussed throughout this book – for example, the emergence of self-awareness, the capacity for mental time travel (and thus awareness that our lives will someday come to an end), and the rapid ascent of social purpose in early human life. Yet there is no guarantee that these mechanisms will result in strong or abundant feelings of life meaning. That requires that our search for meaning be guided by the rudder of our *core personal goals*. Life meaning will flow more naturally when we understand how our strongest sources of motivation are linked not only to our daily life activities (what we have been calling *goal–life alignment*), but also to the guiding principles that bring coherence and comfort to our lives. For example, such principles may be reflected in our moral and ethical values, in our spiritual and religious beliefs, in our personal ideologies and philosophies, or in our enduring self-concepts.

The resulting feelings of life meaning can then be amplified by seeking meaning in ways that are consistent with the *thriving with social purpose* motivational pattern that, as we have seen, is reliably associated with optimal human functioning. Regardless of the direction or target, goal seeking feels particularly meaningful when we actively and confidently pursue our hopes and dreams and then see those efforts paying off. And as social beings we naturally experience "extra special" feelings of life meaning when we provide support and care to others and bond with people that are important to us.

In short, the key to experiencing greater life meaning is to take personal control over the motivational mechanisms through which life meaning arises. Among those mechanisms is the motivational upward spiral that naturally occurs when TSP qualities amplify our efforts to seek out meaningful ideas and engage in meaningful activities. That is the pathway through which you can experience a life that feels consequential and worthwhile – and through which you can help others find meaning in their own lives.

CHAPTER 8

Guiding Principles for Motivating Self and Others
Pathways to Optimal Human Functioning

> Human life is a voyage on a sea of meaning, not a net of information.
> — author Gregory Benford, *Foundation's Fear*

> Motivation is the art of getting people to do what you want them to
> do because they want to do it.
> — US president Dwight D. Eisenhower

The approach we have taken in *Motivating Self and Others* reflects our firm belief that the most powerful strategy for creating successful and meaningful lives is to become familiar with the design features that all humans share, while also appreciating the motivational qualities that make each of us a unique individual. To accomplish these objectives, we must

- better understand the fundamental developmental principles underlying motivation and optimal functioning and
- learn how those principles operate in the context of a particular individual's personal goals and life circumstances.

That is the "big bet" that motivated us to write this book, consistent with the very first quote appearing in this book:

> *There's so much to discover about being human. The more we know, the better equipped we are to build the lives we want. (Fredrickson, 2009, p. 18)*

In this chapter we summarize seven multifaceted principles that have guided our thinking about how best to motivate self and others, especially over the long haul. Each of these principles is an integral part of our fundamental premise regarding "basic human nature" that we identified at the beginning of Chapter 1:

> *Humans evolved to formulate and selectively pursue goals that, when accomplished, would enhance their survival and well-being, both individually and collectively.*

Note that this "meta-principle" focuses not only on our natural inclination to engage in goal-directed activity, but also on the broader developmental and social impact of human goal striving. That is why we have characterized our *Thriving with Social Purpose* (TSP) framework as not just a theory of motivation, but as a theory about motivation *and optimal functioning*. Whether we look at motivation in terms of the integrated functioning and combined strength of its component processes (Chapter 5), or in terms of the evolved capabilities that enabled human achievements to soar to unprecedented heights (Chapter 6), or in terms of the qualities that most reliably generate feelings of life meaning (Chapter 7), it is clear that *TSP is motivation at its (human) best.*

Functioning at our best of course involves more than just motivation. Yet motivation is the part of the overall person-system that has primary responsibility for directing, organizing, energizing, and regulating everything that we do. It is no wonder, then, that amplifying these self-leadership processes is such an effective pathway for enhancing human accomplishment and fulfillment.

Why You Need to Make the Big Bet

The *Thriving with Social Purpose Theory of Motivation and Optimal Functioning* celebrates the uniqueness of each individual through its emphasis on the motivational processes that enable humans to be *self-directed* and thus capable of improving both their own lives and the lives of those around them. These processes encourage self-discovery and creativity – for example, through the formulation of personalized goal images and ideas, the construction of networks and hierarchies of personal goals, the development of context-sensitive beliefs about personal agency, and the acquisition of learned emotional associations that are closely linked to an individual's unique life experiences. In addition, many distinctive personality characteristics are associated with the degree to which the "amplifiers" identified in the TSP framework – an *active approach* goal orientation, capability beliefs infused with *personal optimism*, context beliefs that encourage *mindful tenacity*, and emotion-related capabilities that promote *emotional wisdom* – are persistently influencing a particular individual's motivational states and patterns.

Yet, absent severe pathology, each of us is subject to the same basic design features and constraints that govern all members of our species. Our motivational systems all have the same essential components: personal goals, emotions, and personal agency beliefs (PABs). Despite many contextual nuances, there is a finite range of personal goal themes governing human activity (as detailed in the Ford and Nichols *Taxonomy of Human Goals* in Chapter 3). There are also a limited number of PAB and emotion patterns regulating our goal pursuits (see Figure 4.6 and Table 4.1, respectively, in Chapter 4). Moreover, the mechanisms through which motivational systems operate and impact other parts of the person-system are essentially the same in all humans (as described in Chapter 2 in our discussion of how motivational systems evolved, and in Chapters 3 and 4 in our presentation of *Motivational Systems Theory*).

The fact that we all share the same basic design elements makes it possible for each and every one of us to use the science of human motivation to better understand and more effectively approach life opportunities and challenges. Analogous to expert physicians who can reliably diagnose and remedy problems in patients they have never seen before, people equipped with an understanding of the fundamental architecture governing human motivation can quickly generate hypotheses about how to facilitate progress toward desired outcomes, even in new circumstances and with unfamiliar people. Of course, the diagnostic process can be significantly enhanced with "local knowledge" of a particular individual's motivational dispositions and habits, just as a doctor can proceed more efficiently with knowledge about the lifestyle and medical history of a specific patient. That is why our "big bet" recognizes the added value of understanding the core personal goals and learned motivational patterns that each individual brings to a particular situation. Yet the only way personalized information can provide any added value is if you know what that information means in the context of human functioning in general.

It is also important to recognize that knowledge of the basic principles governing human motivation is not just a "nice thing to have." When people have misconceptions about the way motivational systems work, the results can be devastating. Imagine having some frightening physical symptoms and trying to resolve them without the benefit of sound medical information. Both your uninformed self-treatment and the delay in seeking appropriate care could result in lasting damage. The same is true when motivational concerns are misunderstood or ignored.

Not having sound motivational information can also have a negative impact on your day-to-day quality of life. How can you, for example, get out of a self-defeating rut, or overcome demotivating obstacles to goal progress, or build a life filled with purpose and meaning if you do not understand how your essential self-leadership functions operate? Or the importance of your core personal goals to your overall well-being? Or how your decision-making can be undermined by unrealistic capability and context beliefs or a lack of emotional awareness? Our intuitions about motivational influences can provide some guidance, but without a deeper understanding, the best that most people experiencing these difficulties can hope for is to muddle through life's challenges and opportunities, with occasional successes but also much vulnerability.

This same concern applies to efforts to influence other people's thoughts and actions. We are designed as "control systems" (see Chapter 3), yet trying to control other people without respecting the fact that they too are self-directed can be highly demotivating – not only for those you are trying to control but for you as well. In contrast, when you understand that others' motivation is not governed by the outcomes *you* want, but by the goals, emotions, and personal agency beliefs in *their* "motivational head-quarters," you can take the more effective approach of trying to establish a partnership that strives for goal alignment. That is why

> *facilitation, not control, should be the guiding idea in attempts to motivate others.*

The need to acquire reliable information about how motivation works is particularly important when you have a responsibility for the development and welfare of others. For example, it is evident that, despite their good intentions, many parents and teachers are unable to anticipate how their actions and relationship styles may inadvertently produce motivational damage that is difficult to reverse. They may not realize, for example, that harsh punishment can leave permanent emotional scars through the power of "amplified" emotional learning. They may not understand how helping can backfire when it deprives young people of essential opportunities to become more self-directed and self-regulated. They may be acutely aware that they personally do not like being pressured or micromanaged, yet still rely on overbearing control tactics that discourage curiosity and initiative. Or they may not realize that when corrective feedback persistently "accentuates the negative," it is likely to fuel the development of personal agency belief patterns filled with self-doubt and mistrust.

Many organizational leaders are also at risk of unwittingly engaging in "motivational mismanagement" because they have been socialized to believe that human behavior is controlled primarily through external forces. It may be particularly difficult for people in positions of recognized power and authority to resist the urge to use coercive tactics. Yet, while it may be empowering for a leader to believe that people will automatically follow their directives, with no need to consider how those directives align with the personal goals of those being told what to do, that approach to motivating others is unlikely to inspire loyalty or to sustain motivation after "the pressure is off" (Cameron et al., 2003; Csikszentmihalyi, 2003).

Our "Principled" Approach to Helping You Make the Most Out of the Big Bet

We wrote *Motivating Self and Others* with the hope that it would help people learn how to experience (and create!) success and meaning in their lives, while also minimizing their vulnerability to life's inevitable setbacks and disappointments. The first step in this learning process is to understand the phenomena you wish to change or improve. That requires a *living systems* perspective that takes into account many processes and variables, just as an engineer building a bridge must take into account information that goes beyond the physical design and structure of the bridge (e.g., economic and regulatory limitations, geological and weather-related factors, anticipated traffic patterns and safety concerns).

Yet we recognize that understanding, by itself, may be insufficient to enable people to effectively motivate themselves and others. We also need to be able to get a sense of that understanding "in action," just as engineers need to be able to put their formulas and designs to the test under authentic conditions. That is why the remainder of this book will focus primarily on the challenge of *applying* the concepts and conclusions that were described in previous chapters. However, our approach in this regard is not to "drill down" to the level of specific motivational tactics and techniques. That is not a productive way to approach motivational challenges, as there are typically many different methods that can be used to facilitate progress toward a particular goal (in systems jargon this is known as the "equifinality principle"; Simon, 1967). Nor will the same method always work even with the same person in the same kind of situation. The elements involved in motivating self and others are simply too dynamic. Nevertheless, the underlying principles governing the success or failure of any particular technique in a specific set of circumstances will generally be the same across many different scenarios.

Our focus on motivational principles is analogous to the approach that savvy chess players and football coaches take when they prepare for a competition and respond to their opponent's schemes. Although they may begin with a "script" to get things started, most of their subsequent decision-making is guided by broad principles that can help them maintain a strong position in the game (e.g., maintaining good protection around the king or the quarterback; balancing offensive attacks with prudent defensive maneuvers). The key is to be able to make flexible selections from a versatile range of possible "game plans" rather than relying on the mechanical implementation of a few prepackaged formulas. Indeed, the essence of our big bet is that if you understand the basic principles governing motivation and optimal functioning, and supplement that with "local knowledge" of the person (or persons) you are trying to motivate, you should be well prepared to identify specific tactics that make sense in a particular situation.

Is the Payoff Worth It?

Perhaps you are wondering given our use of metaphors about physicians, engineers, and football coaches – professions that require many years of study and apprenticeship – whether the payoff from the big bet is worth the effort required to achieve the anticipated benefits. That, of course, is a question that only you can answer. Yet, thoughts and feelings about what we care about, how we judge ourselves, and how we react to the world around us are things that naturally capture the attention of each and every one of us as our life journey unfolds. The requirements of everyday living also give us many opportunities to make educated guesses about other people's goals, emotions, and personal agency beliefs. So it is not as if the subject matter is unfamiliar or only accessible to those with special training.

That is not to say that those with special training should be ignored in your efforts to motivate self and others. You may find it useful to seek help from professionals (e.g., counselors and organizational consultants) for particularly challenging motivational problems, or to simply help you get "unstuck" when you find it hard to change dysfunctional habits or relationship patterns.

Yet learning about guiding principles for motivating self and others can empower even those without special training to explore and learn and grow in ways that help them become increasingly capable of sizing up motivational problems and addressing them in creative and versatile ways. Indeed, like many skills, the greatest room for improvement for many people will be in the early part of the "learning curve." In that spirit, consider how much progress you may be able to make by starting with just a few simple steps. For example, you can take the online *Assessment of Personal Goals* (at https://apg.gmu.edu) and use the resulting profile to begin thinking about the goal themes that are most important to you and whether they are aligned with your current life circumstances. At that same website you can take the *Assessment of Personal Agency Belief Patterns* and discover the combination of capability and context beliefs that best represents your "home page" PAB pattern. You can also use the exercises in the *APG Personal Application Guide* to

- explore how your core personal goals align with the ways you actually spend your time;
- identify goal conflicts and unresponsive environmental circumstances that are inhibiting your ability to progress toward your most important goals; and then
- create a personalized, context-specific mapping of actions likely to increase your goal–life alignment.

Analogous to the charts of the human body and its various functional systems that you might see in a doctor's office, we have also tried to provide readers with a variety of useful tools that can help you "frame the problem" and "get the big picture" when engaging in efforts to diagnose and resolve motivation-related challenges. In that spirit, we encourage you to highlight the segments of this book that seem most useful to you, and to add them to your expanding motivational toolbox. To give you a head start on this process, we have collected together all of the key figures, formulas, and frameworks included in *Motivating Self and Others* in a concise final chapter. You can also utilize the extensive reference list provided at the end of this book to learn more about any specific concept or approach that you find particularly helpful or intriguing.

Before long, you will find yourself being able to identify with greater clarity the kind of goals that regularly compete for your attention and those that seem to have the greatest motivational force. That clarity, in turn, will help you recognize when you are achieving goal–life alignment and when you may need to make some life changes to avoid misalignment. In addition, you will better appreciate the mechanisms and pathways through which your emotions and personal agency beliefs influence the decisions you make, and be more capable of assessing whether the guidance provided by those motivational advisors is sound. And you will begin to gain a greater appreciation for how powerful motivation can be when it is amplified, as that is when we are most likely to feel like we are mentally and physically thriving and doing things that are meaningful and fulfilling.

Over time, as you become more deliberate about aligning your life choices and circumstances with your core personal goals, and better able to pursue those goals with a thriving motivational orientation that is infused with social purpose, it will become increasingly evident, we believe, that the payoff from the big bet was well worth it. And when you begin to see how you can use the *Thriving with Social Purpose* framework to enhance not only your own life, but also the lives of your children, your students, the people you work with, and friends and family members who depend on you, your appreciation for the power and utility of these motivational principles will escalate even further. That is because:

TSP is a natural way of being. We are born with a natural desire to explore, learn, and bond with others. But life experiences can inhibit or push aside those fundamental human motives. Learning how to encourage and restore TSP motivational patterns can help people progress effectively toward the goals that matter most, to themselves and to humanity.

TSP enables imagination and creativity to flourish. When we actively pursue the goals that capture our attention and imagination with confidence, tenacity, and productive energy, and we do so with a focus that extends beyond ourselves, our thinking is more open-minded and innovative.

TSP contributes to health, well-being, and longevity. Adopting habits of living and working that are aligned with what made our species naturally successful is a winning strategy when it comes to long-term health and survival.

Life meaning flows naturally from TSP experiences. *TSP* contributes to a feeling that "life is worth living." Such feelings are difficult to engineer, and yet they are a natural consequence of TSP modes of functioning.

Followers respond best to leaders with TSP qualities. People are naturally inclined to respond cooperatively and enthusiastically to people who have the following qualities:

- strong, clear goals pursued with an active approach orientation;
- optimism about personal capabilities paired with tenacity in the face of obstacles;
- positivity and emotional maturity, especially in interactions with others;
- authentic concern for the interests and well-being of followers; and
- equipoised expression of each of the above qualities.

Evidence supporting this theory-based list can be seen in extensive interviews conducted by Csikszentmihalyi (2003) with a wide range of visionary business leaders. Note how closely his conclusions about the qualities of effective leaders map onto the elements in the thriving with social purpose motivational pattern listed above:

- continuous curiosity and desire to learn;
- optimism and positivity about the future;
- ambition coupled with perseverance;
- empathy for others and a sense of mutual respect; and
- a sense of calling to accomplish something meaningful beyond themselves.

Similarly, when Collins (2001) identified eleven companies that went from "good to great" (operationally defined as fifteen years of adequate but below-average performance in their business sector followed by fifteen years of sustained above-average performance), he concluded that the distinguishing feature was the arrival of a new CEO who was focused primarily on others (social purpose) and who had an unusually strong profile of thriving motivational qualities (along with a strong foundation of relevant K&S, such as domain-specific expertise and the ability to make timely decisions). As we have seen, these are the elements that are most predictive of optimal functioning in general, and especially in a leadership role. Hogan and Kaiser (2005) were particularly struck by two recurring themes in the descriptions of the eleven CEOs who were the catalysts for transforming mediocre companies into great organizations.

> First, they were modest and humble, as opposed to self-dramatizing and self-promoting. Second, they were phenomenally, almost preternaturally, persistent. These findings were a jolt to the business literature (which had been promoting the cult of the charismatic CEO), but we think they make sense in terms of the data provided by ethnographic studies of leadership. (p. 174)

The Qualities Associated with Motivation and Optimal Functioning Are Malleable

If you are one of those people whose philosophy of life is to simply let life happen – "because, after all, there's really not much you can do to change things" – then perhaps the big bet is not for you. Yet our evolutionary heritage as self-directed creatures capable of adaptive behavior change suggests that a very different philosophy is likely to produce better outcomes for you and the people you care about:

"Life Happens," so try to make it happen the way you want (by applying MST/ TSP principles).

Our life outcomes are *not* predetermined. If that were the case, there would be no need for humans to have awareness of their personal goals, the capacity for emotional learning, or the ability to formulate beliefs about possible goal pursuits. Indeed, the reason we evolved these elaborate motivational systems is so we could imagine *alternative* future outcomes and then decide which outcomes we would like to pursue.

Nor are we stuck with the outcomes that have transpired in our lives thus far. We cannot rewrite history, but that does not mean that we have to keep reliving past life episodes that we regret or that we wish had turned out differently. Indeed, the core dynamic in human motivation is a *focus on the future* (Seligman et al., 2013). Learn from the past but don't dwell on it. Instead, imagine how you would like future episodes to unfold *moving forward*. Within each and every one of us is the power to improve – or even transform – our own lives and the lives of those around us. We can alter developmental trajectories that are dormant, stagnant, or perilous by amplifying

- our *motivational systems* (through the development of TSP qualities);
- our *knowledge and skill processes* (through the application of goal-striving skills);
- our *biological functions* (through increases in personal health responsibility); and
- our *environments* (through efforts to seek out or create more responsive environments).

There is of course no guarantee that even well-conceived efforts to change for the better will automatically or quickly produce the desired results. Others may be unsupportive or even resistant to your change efforts. Old habits may be surprisingly comfortable even when you know they aren't optimal. Sometimes it takes a lot of patience and persistence to create the neural equivalent of fresh tracks in the snow and then make that your natural way of functioning – especially when you already have well-worn tracks that you have been sledding on for a long time! Yet the main function of the human brain is to cause behaviors to occur that will help us maintain *survival with well-being* (Damasio, 2003) – the "prime directive" around which all goal pursuit is organized. So while there are *self-organizing* biases built into our brains to help us maintain coherence and stability, the brain is also designed to be *self-constructing* (D. Ford, 1987/2019), as evidenced by the remarkable degree of malleability (often called "plasticity") that can be seen in both brain and behavioral functioning and development (Begley, 2007; Doidge, 2007).

Brain plasticity is a natural and necessary part of the human capacity for directing our own thoughts and actions. The brain's dynamic properties make it possible for us to imagine new possibilities, to choose alternative destinations, and to be flexible and versatile in our pursuit of the goals we have envisioned. We have the capacity to take charge of our lives and to create not only new opportunities, but also new capabilities.

Motivation is of course not the only pathway to self-improvement or for helping others with their goal pursuits. However, because motivation plays a special leadership role in directing, organizing and regulating goal-directed activity, it is often the most powerful and efficient pathway for developing human potential. Even when obstacles to goal attainment are primarily nonmotivational in nature, motivation is often the key to encouraging us to do the things we need to make progress – like taking the steps necessary to develop new skills, to improve our health habits, or to seek out more responsive environments. Motivation focuses our attention, energizes our thoughts and actions, and keeps us going in the face of uncertainties and setbacks. Simply put, if motivation is sufficiently robust and durable, it can transform the entire system. That is why this book focuses on the challenge of motivating self and others. Motivation is the key to making your life a *better* life – a life filled with purpose, fulfillment, and meaning.

Seven Guiding Principles for Motivating Self and Others

In the remainder of this chapter we will focus on applications and implications of the seven motivational principles outlined in Table 8.1. In this table we provide a succinct, one-sentence definition for each principle (in italics) along with a summary description designed to clarify the meaning and importance of each principle. In doing so we recognize that each principle covers a lot of territory, with a wide variety of propositions and possible applications following from each one. Yet we also wanted to try to organize the core ideas of our TSP framework into the most concise form possible, so that it could serve as a useful resource for future reference.

Table 8.1 *Seven guiding principles for motivating self and others derived from the Thriving with Social Purpose Theory of Motivation and Optimal Functioning*

Principle		Definition
1.	The Principle of Evolved Human Nature	*Efforts to motivate self and others can best succeed if they are consistent with basic human nature.* People are more likely to respond favorably when efforts to strengthen motivation respect the fact that humans are self-directed yet highly interdependent; are creatures of habit yet capable of creative thought and action; and are influenced by context and culture yet led by motivational systems comprising personal goals, emotions, and personal agency beliefs. In contrast, efforts to motivate self and others are likely to fail if you assume that significant change is impossible; or that you don't need to consider others' personal goals and life circumstances; or that everyone will respond in the same way to a motivational incentive or contingency; or that people are only motivated by self-interest.
2.	The Principle of Goal–Life Alignment	*Motivation is enriched when daily life activities and important social relationships afford the attainment of core personal goals, and when self-awareness of such goals empowers you to make wise choices about future opportunities.* The sense of clarity and integrity that flows from this alignment between core personal goals and consequential decisions and actions enables people to be more productive and to experience more abundant feelings of life meaning. Goal–life alignment is facilitated by an active approach goal orientation that promotes exploration, openness to change, and personal growth and by contexts that afford the pursuit of multiple goal opportunities.
3.	The Principle of Accurate and Hopeful Personal Agency Beliefs	*To develop and sustain strong motivational patterns, you must have a fundamental belief that the future can be better than the present but also perceptions about current circumstances that are accurate and realistic.* Hope requires faith in yourself (capability beliefs) as well as faith in the people and resources you depend upon (context beliefs). Motivation is enhanced by welcoming feedback (both affirming and corrective) that can improve knowledge and skills, the accuracy of perceptions, and expectations about goal progress. The key is to maintain a generally optimistic but also experientially grounded view of future possibilities.

Table 8.1 *(cont.)*

Principle		Definition
4.	*The Principle of Emotional Wisdom*	*Your emotions can help you make wise choices and manage challenging situations, but only if you can assess whether they make sense given your current circumstances and then use those insights to make appropriate adjustments.* The self-oriented part of emotional wisdom requires authentic *self-awareness* and fluent emotional understanding as well as the ability to ratchet emotions up and down to meet situational demands and opportunities (*emotional self-regulation*). The social part of emotional wisdom involves the (mostly automatic) detection and triggering of the emotions that others are experiencing (*empathy*) at an amplitude that is motivationally impactful, and then acting on those emotions in contextually appropriate ways (*social-emotional competence*).
5.	*The Principle of Equipoised Social Purpose*	*Motivation is enhanced when people seek to accomplish things that are larger than themselves and of benefit to others, assuming they do not neglect their own needs.* Humans are "wired" to cooperate and to help others, especially those with whom they share social bonds. Concern for others must be properly balanced with concern for self, however. This equipoised form of social purpose is a powerful and reliable source of energy and life meaning, especially when combined with a thriving motivational orientation.
6.	*The Principle of Unitary System Functioning*	*Efforts to motivate self and others will be more effective if they are framed within a "big picture" developmental perspective that encompasses not only goals, emotions, and personal agency beliefs but also knowledge and skills, biological functions, and environmental circumstances.* A person *always* functions as an integrated unit, with dynamic interconnections that are both abundant and powerful. Consistent with that premise, there are many pathways through which motivation can be facilitated, including pathways that do not attempt to influence motivational processes directly – for example, those that rely on efforts to strengthen goal-striving skills, personal health responsibility, or environmental responsiveness.
7.	*The Principle of TSP Leadership*	*People respond favorably to leaders who pursue goals with an active approach orientation, personal optimism, mindful tenacity, and emotional wisdom (the thriving motivational pattern) and are guided by an authentic concern for the welfare of others (social purpose).* When someone in a leadership role is thriving with social

Table 8.1 *(cont.)*

Principle	Definition
	purpose, people intuitively sense the leader's positive energy and genuine desire to help and are naturally drawn to those qualities. Compared to the kind of leadership associated with dominance hierarchies (which remains a salient part of our evolutionary heritage and is potentially adaptive in special circumstances), TSP leadership is much more likely to promote long-term trust, commitment, and effective teamwork.

Principle 1: The Principle of Evolved Human Nature

Efforts to motivate self and others can best succeed if they are consistent with basic human nature.

QUESTION: This idea sounds simple on paper, but how can I tell if a particular motivational strategy is going to play out in a way that is "inconsistent" with basic human nature? Are there some guidelines or telltale clues that I should be looking for?

ANSWER: Indeed there are. Let's start with the powerful concept of *self-direction*. As we have seen, motivation comes from within. It is not something that happens outside the person. Consequently, any strategy that relies solely on external control is likely to be at odds with "basic human nature."

In some cases, this may be immediately evident, as people are often resistant to power-oriented tactics that are insensitive to their feelings and concerns (e.g., "You can't just order me around"; "All you care about is what you want"). Yet in many instances it may take a while to realize that you are on the wrong track. After all, most people are respectful of those in positions of authority. Moreover, it is often rather easy to change behavior in the short run using coercive techniques like threats, bribes, and intimidation. And if the short run is the only thing you are concerned about (e.g., because you really need someone to change their behavior *right now* to avoid disaster), that may be fine. But don't expect the short-term results those tactics are able to produce to result in any lasting change. And don't be surprised if your "quick fix" tactics produce some unintended side effects, like anxiety, resentment, and mistrust (not to mention decreased performance!).

Consider, for example, the common scenario in which well-intentioned parents implement what they assume will be a memorable punishment after their teenager commits a significant transgression. The savvy teenager expresses appropriate regret and what seems to be a sincere intention to "never do that again." Yet later the parents find out that not only was their harsh punishment ineffective, it may have backfired, as it inflamed antagonistic feelings about being controlled and disrespected.

Of course, teenagers are notorious for having particularly strong independence goals (e.g., they score significantly higher in self-determination on the *Assessment of Personal Goals* than any other age group). Yet even people who are quite willing to accept direction from others can quickly become discouraged and demoralized when they are not "treated like a person" (translation: like a *self-directed* person). Just ask anyone who has had to live in an impersonal institution or suffer under a tyrannical boss for an extended period.

Bottom line. To motivate people in ways that are consistent with evolved human nature, it is necessary to "get under the hood" and work with the underlying motivational "engine." You have to respect how that human engine was designed as well as the need to make timely adjustments when it's not running smoothly or seems to be losing power.

> *To create new behavior patterns with staying power, motivation must be facilitated "from the inside out."*

QUESTION: OK, I think I've got it – motivation comes from within the person, so if I want to have more than a superficial or short-term effect, I've got to somehow influence the decision-making team in "motivational headquarters." And they are ... umm ... give me a second ... there are three of them, right?

ANSWER: To help people remember what it is they actually need to change or influence when trying to motivate self or others, we have developed a simple formula that summarizes the "essential ingredients" in any motivational pattern:

Motivation (M) = Personal Goals (G) × Personal Agency Beliefs (PAB) × Emotions (E)

As we explained in Chapters 3 and 4:

Personal goals are thoughts about desired (and undesired) future outcomes. When particular goal thoughts are in a priority position relative to other activated goals, those ideas and images become the outcomes that the human "control system" is trying to control (e.g., outcomes like completing an assignment, feeling safe, or being accepted by a group).

Personal agency beliefs are thoughts about the anticipated consequences of pursuing a particular goal or a related set of goals. PABs provide advice about whether we "have what it takes" to successfully pursue a goal (*capability beliefs*) and whether the environment will be "with us or against us" in doing so (*context beliefs*).

Emotions prepare our mind and body for action and cause us to experience conscious feelings about the possible consequences of goal pursuit. Like PABs, they provide advice about what goals to pursue at what level of vigor and persistence. Yet they do so not only by influencing decisions about personal goals that are actively under consideration, but also by activating new goal thoughts.

From this motivational systems perspective, what comes naturally to us is to *think about the future*. We evolved to be *goal directed* – that is, to think about outcomes that are different than the ones we are experiencing right now, to assess how important and achievable those outcomes are, and to pursue the ones that emerge as our most compelling options at any given moment. Astonishingly, most of these processes take place beneath awareness, with little or no conscious effort required.

That is not to say that our motivational systems are always efficient or effective. Just as our biological systems may not always be at their best, our motivational systems can sometimes struggle to maintain optimal functioning. Yet the processes underlying human motivation are as natural as taking a breath or listening to the sounds around us. Life's ongoing stream of external and mental events constantly trigger emotions (analogous to sparks), some of which activate goals that we think about pursuing (analogous to flickering flames), with a few of those goals then becoming the intentions that guide our daily activity, at varying levels of commitment (analogous to an actual fire, the strength of which may vary from a raging inferno to a glowing ember).

Bottom line. Our motivational systems are designed to lead us toward outcomes that we imagine will be favorable and away from outcomes that we imagine will be unfavorable. If you have no idea what kind of outcomes a particular person naturally thinks about (e.g., their core personal goals), or how that person thinks and feels about those outcomes in a particular context, it will be difficult to identify methods that will reliably capture their attention and inspire action. Conversely, if you have some awareness of what an individual really cares about, and some creative ideas about what kinds of "emotionally competent stimuli" (Damasio, 2003) are likely to be associated with those goals, you may be able to connect the outcomes *you* desire with ideas and images that are emotionally compelling to the person you are trying to motivate.

Moreover, these same concepts are applicable to the challenge of motivating self. You can make a lot of good things happen if you have a clear idea of what personal goals are "core" for you and what kinds of circumstances are likely to activate and support those goals.

QUESTION: I can see that I won't get very far unless I can somehow get inside "motivational headquarters" and understand things from that perspective. But how do I do that, especially when people may not even be all that aware themselves of the things that motivate them?

ANSWER: It can be really hard to help people make wise choices or to guide them toward new opportunities (e.g., better career or relationship options) when you can only make "uneducated" guesses about what naturally motivates them. Similarly, it can be very difficult to facilitate change when you don't understand what's motivating an apathetic response or an emotionally volatile behavior pattern, and the person you are trying to influence can't do much to help you achieve that understanding (as any parent trying to figure out how to calm down a crying baby can tell you!).

Yet, in many cases you can learn a lot by simply asking the person to talk about what's important to them, what they are trying to accomplish, what they are trying to avoid, or how they feel about a particular situation. Then you can go to the next step and watch for observable indicators of their goals, emotions, and personal agency beliefs as they pursue a particular course of action and make decisions about how to invest their time. In particular, you can look for emotional "sparks" that may yield clues about what is motivating their behavior and the choices they make (keeping in mind the fact that strong emotions often suggest the presence of a core personal goal). Focusing on emotions and the conscious feelings that arise from those emotions can be particularly helpful when surface issues that seem blown out of proportion are obscuring "what is really going on" in motivational headquarters.

That is not to say that all you need to do to motivate others effectively is to become a skilled observer who knows the right questions to ask (using MST as your "road map"). Motivating others is also very much about the *relationship* you develop with the person whose motivation you are trying to enhance. Indeed, even if you have no idea what a person is thinking or feeling, you can create a favorable motivational climate for progressing in the right direction by developing a relationship that "opens doors" rather than "puts up walls" as you seek to learn more about the person and what strategies might work in a particular set of circumstances. The key is to adopt a motivational mindset that embraces two fundamental themes: *respect* ("You are important to me and I genuinely want to help you") and *collaboration* ("I am sure that I can help you if we work together as a team").

Respect for others is a natural by-product of *social purpose* – which, as we have seen, is a vital part of evolved human nature. If you are authentically concerned about a person's well-being, and can effectively communicate that interest, you may be able to create an emotional connection and a sense of trust that predisposes them to "follow your lead" even when they feel apprehensive.

Respect creates an *openness to change*. Combine that with a collaborative mindset grounded in relevant expertise, and you now have an approach that can *empower change*. A collaborative mindset conveys the idea that "we're in this together" (win-win approach), which is an effective way to activate the cooperative goals that are a natural part of our evolutionary heritage. Authentic collaboration acknowledges the intrinsic validity of another person's goals, emotions, and personal agency beliefs, and uses those as a starting point rather than egocentrically assuming that "I know what's best for you."

How can you tell if someone seeking to motivate you has adopted an authentically respectful, collaborative mindset? Perhaps the most telling indicator is whether that person asks for your input and then listens, with genuine interest, to what you have to say.

Bottom line. People are thinking, feeling, goal-directed individuals and not simply bodies in a classroom or boxes on an organizational chart or objects to be manipulated. That means that, with few exceptions (e.g., combat; high-stakes emergencies), the most effective motivational approach is to think about how to facilitate change through a *partnership* with a self-directed person whose existing behavior patterns may reflect personal goals and motivational habits that have been "years in the making." That is how you can best tap into the natural, evolved qualities that are distinctively human.

A useful thought experiment is to consider how you would like the people you live and work with to motivate *you*. Wouldn't you be more open to someone who focuses on what *you* care about rather than only thinking about what they want? Wouldn't you prefer a collaborative approach to one that felt coercive or manipulative? And wouldn't you be more receptive to someone who, instead of demanding immediate results or belittling your slow progress, showed some empathy and respect for your circumstances?

QUESTION: I certainly would! I especially like the idea of a "partnership." It drives me crazy when someone comes in and demands that I do what THEY want without any consideration for my goals and priorities. That is so demotivating! Why do so many people take that approach?

ANSWER: Keep in mind that our species never lost its propensity for using power-oriented motivational tactics (such as those characteristic of dominance hierarchies) when we evolved new "layers" of capabilities and preferences for cooperative group living. Control-oriented tactics are generally less effective than techniques that seek to facilitate motivation; however, they often take less time to implement and are less cognitively demanding.

So, what does it take to adopt an authentic facilitation mindset? In contrast to "fast and easy" tactics that rely on coercion and intimidation (e.g., "Just do it – or else"; "Because I said so!"), motivational facilitation is a more personalized approach that requires being *other-focused* rather than egocentrically focusing on your own viewpoint. That is challenging for people who lack the patience needed to learn about others' perspectives, or who find it hard to shift their attention from their own immediate feelings and desires. Even people who are normally caring and considerate can be demanding and controlling when they feel pressured by time constraints and external demands (as many parents and teachers can attest).

Motivational facilitation also requires more versatility than an approach that is power-oriented. Rather than relying on a few favored methods for "getting things done," you will need to take people's concerns, feelings, and expectations into account and tailor your methods accordingly. For those who are inexperienced or lack emotional wisdom, this can be quite a challenge. Even if you start with a facilitation mindset, your ability to make flexible adjustments may be limited if most of your own experiences have been with people who have relied primarily on coercive tactics. Indeed, people who engage in such tactics are often aware that their approach is not ideal, but don't know what else to do ("I swore I would never act that way with my own children!").

Bottom line. Power-oriented methods are often influential sources of behavior change at the point in time that external force is applied. And because such methods are a primordial part of our evolutionary heritage, it is relatively easy to learn how to use these methods and often easier to implement them compared to more collaborative alternatives. That is why external control tactics are so commonplace. Yet when it comes to *enduring* change, the real source of control is *motivational headquarters* – the goals, emotions, and personal agency beliefs that govern an individual's decisions and actions. External control methods may look effective as they are being imposed, but beware: they can narrow people's focus of attention, severely inhibit their creativity, and cause them to spend more time worrying than working. And unless there are internal changes in motivational headquarters, old habits are likely to reemerge as soon as the pressure is off. Indeed, coercive tactics are notoriously ineffective at controlling human behavior for more than a temporary period unless they are unrelenting or extraordinarily frightening.

QUESTION: So, are you saying that all those behaviorist types who talked about "engineering" behavior using rewards and punishments were wrong? I thought that was the scientific foundation for anyone trying to learn how to motivate self and others.

ANSWER: Behaviorists weren't too far off when they proposed that we do things because environmental consequences are controlling our actions. They just got it backward. *We do things because we are trying to control the consequences that we get from our environment.* Starting with that design principle is the key to understanding why facilitation rather than (external) control is the most natural and effective method for motivating self and others. Many behaviorists have viewed motivation as an engineering challenge in a linear, mechanistic sense. However, as we have seen, motivation is in fact a psychological challenge organized around the human capacity for self-direction and shared intentionality.

People of course do react (in wonderfully distinctive ways) to efforts to manipulate their behavior. But rather than waiting for a consequence to be imposed upon us, the natural design of our motivational systems is to start with *an idea about the future* – that is, an outcome that we want to attain, or avoid, or that we prefer to our current circumstances. In other words, motivation is primarily about *what might be,* not what is. That is why, to motivate self and others, one must "begin with the end in mind" (Covey, 1989).

Bottom line. It is hard to motivate yourself if you don't have a clear idea of what consequences are truly rewarding and emotionally satisfying for you. And it is hard to motivate others if you only focus on the consequences *you* desire, with no consideration or respect given to the personal goals of those you are seeking to influence. That is why concepts like *teamwork* and *goal alignment* are a better fit to "evolved human nature" than concepts like power and external control.

QUESTION: Let's get back to the problem of trying to get inside motivational headquarters. You sort of sidestepped the problem when you started talking about "respectful collaboration" as a way to open people up. But how am I supposed to tell if someone is genuinely interested in collaborating with me? How can I tell if any real change is happening? After all, we can't literally see a person's goal thoughts, or inner feelings, or personal agency beliefs.

ANSWER: Great question! Compared to other species, humans may be the experts at mind reading (see Chapter 6), but we are also pretty adept at hiding our thoughts and feelings (e.g., to protect our reputations or to avoid hurting other people). Nor are we always fully aware of all the motivational elements influencing our actions and decisions. So your best bet is to try to tap into motivational headquarters from a variety of different angles.

Our experience leads us to suggest that you focus on three different sets of indicators when trying to "get inside" motivational headquarters. As a first step, you can simply ask someone to talk about their goals. What's important to them? What kinds of concerns do they have? What kind of choices would feel natural or energizing? What would they like to happen next, or soon? The answers to these kinds of questions can be enormously clarifying, as personal goal thoughts are the motivational leaders that direct and organize our behavior.

Nevertheless, it is unwise to rely solely on what people say about their personal goals when trying to diagnose the contents of motivational headquarters. Even when we want to reveal as much as we can about our innermost thoughts and feelings (e.g., to encourage social bonding or help from others), we often struggle to make sense of our inner motives and to put those ideas and emotions into words that others can understand.

So, as a second step, a good strategy for trying to diagnose what is "really going on" in motivational headquarters is to pay attention to the emotions that a person displays (verbally and nonverbally). Emotions and feelings provide a window into motivational headquarters through their impact on what people attend to, their facial expressions, and their observable actions. People rarely get emotional about things they don't care about. Conversely, you can be pretty sure that if someone is expressing strong emotions, there must be a strong personal goal in play. Strong emotions also provide clues about the personal agency belief patterns that are influencing a person's behavior.

Yet it is also unwise to rely solely on a person's immediate emotional reactions, as emotions can ebb and flow rather quickly as circumstances change. For example, an enthusiastic response does not guarantee that the initial flow of energy will be sustained after the emotional "flywheel" has stopped spinning. Conversely, an initially wary response does not necessarily mean that progress will be difficult. It may simply mean that a trusting relationship needs to be developed before the collaborative process can proceed effectively.

These examples illustrate why the best source of evidence for identifying "what makes a person tick" is what they actually choose to do over the course of a variety of relevant situations. What people say and the emotions they express can help you judge if they have the right motivational mindset for making progress toward a particular goal and if they have formulated appropriate *intentions* with respect to that goal. But keep in mind that human motivation did not evolve simply to make sure everyone had "good intentions." Our motivational systems evolved to help us make decisions about what *actions* to take in complex environments that pose many challenges and afford many opportunities (e.g., Should I approach or avoid? Act now or wait until later? Keep trying or give up?). That means that your best bet when looking for indicators of meaningful change is to focus on *self-directed behavior over time.* What choices do people make in the absence of external pressures? Are their efforts vigorous or halfhearted? Do they persist when the going gets tough? Do they fall back into their old habits after the initial emotional energy has worn off?

Bottom line. While "mind reading" and verbal discussion about thoughts and feelings can provide valuable clues, the most trustworthy indicators of success in motivating self and others are *actions* that provide evidence of "reliability" (consistency over time and across situations) and "validity" (an authentic commitment has been made and it has staying power). Such actions suggest the presence of a self-directed motivational pattern that can be dependably mobilized over and over again by naturally occurring circumstances (i.e., without any special intervention or application of external force).

QUESTION: In Chapter 5 you said that you wanted to give people a framework for understanding not just motivation, but motivation *and optimal functioning*. And then you gave us the *Thriving with Social Purpose* framework to serve that purpose. So, is optimal functioning also a part of "evolved human nature"? Or is it just the basic motivational processes that are natural, and TSP qualities have to somehow be built on top of that evolutionary foundation?

ANSWER: You are now getting right to the heart of what *Motivating Self and Others* is all about. Perhaps the single most important take-home message of this book is that *we are wired for TSP*. That means that each and every one of us has the inherent capacity to thrive and to make the world a better place for the people we care about.

Now, this does not mean that we are always "at our best" or that TSP functioning is effortless. Consider, for example, the fact that humans have the capacity to do amazing things like sing a song (or play one on a keyboard), cook a meal (and then present it on a plate in an enticing way), or throw a ball (something no other species can do!). Yet to effectively translate our aptitudes into proficient actions, we need experience, practice, and informative feedback. Similarly, while the capacity for TSP functioning is an intrinsic part of how our species evolved, that potential can only be realized through a combination of life experience, intentional learning and practice, and environmental support and encouragement.

Bottom line. Within each and every one of us are natural mechanisms designed to *amplify* the potency and effectiveness of our motivational functions. These mechanisms make it possible for us to not only survive, but to thrive, and to help others thrive as well. The more you learn about and actively seek to cultivate these innate amplifying mechanisms, the better equipped you will be to use them to enhance both your own and others' ability to lead a successful and meaningful life.

Principle 2: The Principle of Goal–Life Alignment

Motivation is enriched when daily life activities and important social relation-ships afford the attainment of core personal goals, and when self-awareness of such goals empowers you to make wise choices about future opportunities.

QUESTION: The word "alignment" makes me think of trying to steer a car that would likely drift off the road or into oncoming traffic if I didn't keep pulling it back. Is this what you mean by alignment? Is that what "goal–life misalignment" feels like?

ANSWER: Yes, that metaphor does vividly illustrate one aspect of how it feels to be "motivationally misaligned" with respect to your everyday activities and relationships. Instead of life's journey feeling natural and enjoyable (notwithstanding an occasional bump in the road!), it feels more like a constant struggle. Moreover, the misalignment makes it hard to steer toward where you'd like to go.

Misalignment can also be a source of chronic annoyance and distress. Imagine having a dental procedure that leaves your "bite" just a little bit out of position. The nagging feeling that things are not quite right can be very distracting and persistently uncomfortable. Or consider a golf swing that gets into a "groove" that is slightly out of alignment. Watching your seemingly well-hit shots fly into trees and sand traps rather than fairways and greens can be extremely demotivating.

Bottom line. Although goal–life misalignment won't stop you from functioning, it will prevent you from achieving anything close to *optimal* functioning.

QUESTION: I am starting to see why you have placed so much emphasis on this motivational principle. But is it realistic to think that goal–life alignment can be an everyday thing? It seems like there's an awful lot of life that can get in the way of things we would really like to be doing.

ANSWER: Of course, no one can pursue their most compelling personal goals all the time, or magically ensure that everything is perfectly in synch with those goal pursuits. Yet, if you feel like you rarely have an opportunity to spend time doing the things that really matter to you, and that enable you to experience memorable feelings of satisfaction, or pride, or contentment, you may be a good candi-date for an "alignment analysis."

QUESTION: Hmmm . . . so what would that entail?

ANSWER: Analyzing goal–life alignment is a multifaceted process. Yet it is very clear where the process should start. The essential first step is to become more aware of your *core personal goals* – that is, the goals that will reliably provide you with the greatest emotional rewards when you pursue and attain them.

Admittedly this process of seeking out your motivational "heart and soul" can be a rather new kind of challenge for those who are just beginning to learn how motivation works. Our conscious goal thoughts tend to focus on *what* we have to do – our "low-level" objectives – rather than on *why* we are doing those things – our "high-level" purposes. That is why we constructed the online *Assessment of Personal Goals* (APG; M. Ford & Nichols, 2005) and the accompanying *APG Personal Application Guide* (M. Ford & Smith, 2013; both available at https://apg.gmu.edu). The APG was designed to help people improve their lives by providing a method for identifying deeply felt motives within a standardized but versatile framework (i.e., the *Taxonomy of Human Goals,* as detailed in Chapter 3). Using the common vocabulary of the *Taxonomy* makes it possible for people to share thoughts and feelings about the personal goal themes that matter most to them.

QUESTION: At work I've taken the Myers-Briggs test as well as the Clifton "StrengthsFinder" assessment. What can the APG tell me that I don't already know from these other online measures?

ANSWER: The Myers-Briggs test (MBTI) is theory based but it is not a goal assessment. In fact, it isn't even focused on motivation, nor can you get any result beyond the sixteen "types" specified in the theory. So while the MBTI may be useful for aligning or integrating certain kinds of personality types (e.g., in a work group), it has no direct relevance to the process of aligning core personal goals with daily life activities or using such information to help make consequential life decisions.

The StrengthsFinder assessment allows for a broader range of results, but the list of strengths is an eclectic array of human "talents" with no theoretical framework to organize them (other than a general "positive psychology" orientation). As a result, it offers no process model for explaining how various strengths might promote optimal functioning. Some of the strengths involve motivational qualities, but many do not. And of those that are relevant to motivation, many are focused on emotional strengths or personal agency belief patterns rather than on personal goal themes. So, while an assessment of "strengths" can help set the stage for an alignment analysis, it is no substitute for a theory-based goal assessment that specifically targets the underlying motivational mechanisms that can fuel the development of human potential. Understanding your core personal goals and their leadership role in motivational headquarters is the key to learning how to strengthen existing talents and develop new capabilities in ways that will be "self-propelled" and self-sustaining.

Bottom line. To identify your core personal goals with clarity and fidelity, you need tools that directly target these powerful sources of motivation and life meaning.

QUESTION: OK, so I just took your *Assessment of Personal Goals*. The goal themes in my "highly compelling" and "very important" ranges do seem like a good fit (including a couple of surprises!). But, with all due respect: Now what? It is interesting to see a description of the kinds of things that are my "most reliable sources of satisfaction and life meaning," but how do I go about actually using my goal profile to increase my effectiveness and get more meaning out of life?

ANSWER: Great question! Even when we know something is important – like reducing stress, or learning new health habits, or spending time with loved ones – we often put those high-priority goals "on the shelf" when there is no pressing need to do anything about them today ... or tomorrow ... or on any particular schedule. That is how our most *fulfilling* goals can be overpowered by *time-filling* goals that may be enticing at a surface level, but ultimately are not very impactful in terms of emotional satisfaction and life meaning.

So yes, goal–life alignment requires more than simply being aware of the goal themes that are most compelling and meaningful for you. You must also have strategies for keeping your core personal goals at the forefront of your thinking when you are setting priorities and making consequential decisions about jobs, relationships, living circumstances, and how to spend your time. In addition, you need to be able to analyze the "life" side of the goal–life alignment equation with that same kind of clarity. This might entail, for example, sizing up your work environment in terms of whether it affords frequent opportunities to pursue personal goals that really matter to you, and whether it *feels* like a good fit on a day-to-day basis. Or looking at your close relationships in terms of whether the occasional disagreements and disappointments are "small stuff" episodes that can be tolerated, or more serious "core goal violations" that need to be resolved.

For example, in our *APG Personal Application Guide,* we include exercises designed to help you sort out where you are spending too much time on unfulfilling goals and where you are missing out on the "best things in life" (for you). We also help you map out goal conflicts that may be keeping you from investing properly in your core goals. The end result is a personalized, context-specific "translation" designed to ensure that the knowledge you have gained about your core personal goals can be put to practical use and can continue to serve as a "guiding light" as you encounter interesting opportunities and tough choices moving forward.

Finding the right "lanes" to travel in as your life journey unfolds is not easy. And that brings us to an essential additional step in the process of seeking to improve goal–life alignment, namely, adopting an *active approach* goal orientation. You can't expect the world to just fall in line with your wishes and preferences without purposeful steering and sustained effort on your part. You need to take the natural capabilities for self-direction that we have described throughout this book and use them to actively seek out and cultivate goal–life alignment. Explore. Experiment. Learn about yourself. Learn something new – perhaps by enrolling in classes or seeking a credential that will expand your horizons. Meet new people. Focus on what feels meaningful – and *why.* Don't just settle. Keep moving forward – even if it means taking a step back and then trying again, or trying something else. Have the courage to make changes if the people and circumstances in your personal or professional life are violating your core personal goals or not providing you with opportunities to pursue those goals.

Bottom line. Along with TSP, goal–life alignment is the *sine qua non* of optimal functioning. Others can help you achieve it, or maintain it, but fundamentally goal–life alignment is *your* responsibility, as it requires self-awareness of your core personal goals and proactive efforts to find ways to pursue those goals on a daily basis. When you make choices that place you in environments that are responsive to your hopes and dreams and core personal goals, you will experience abundant life meaning along with a generalized sense of harmony and well-being.

QUESTION: The idea of harmony reminds me of stuff I've read about the experience of "flow" – which always seemed a bit mysterious (like trying to get "in the zone"), but now I'm wondering if it's basically just an example of what you are calling goal–life alignment.

ANSWER: Indeed it is! Although we have tended to focus on goal–life alignment in a broad sense, it is also possible to study what goal–life alignment looks like at the level of a specific "behavior episode" (D. Ford, 1987/2019) or across a series of connected episodes. Flow experiences tend to emerge at work, for example, when there are "clear goals that can be adapted to meet changing conditions" [thus ensuring continuing alignment between goals and contexts]; "immediate feedback to one's actions" [which helps ensure that things don't get misaligned]; "and a matching of the challenges of the job with the worker's skills" [which helps keep things aligned by ensuring that positive emotions and personal agency beliefs are maintained] (Csikszentmihalyi, 2003, p. 203).

Bottom line. The Principle of Goal–Life Alignment applies to all levels of your goal network, from the big, high-level goals that organize your self-directed goal pursuits to the interconnected lower level goals that make up your everyday life activities.

Principle 3: The Principle of Accurate and Hopeful Personal Agency Beliefs

> *To develop and sustain strong motivational patterns, you must have a fundamental belief that the future can be better than the present but also perceptions about current circumstances that are accurate and realistic.*

QUESTION: I can certainly understand how demotivating it can be to feel hopeless about the future. But isn't it also motivationally self-defeating to be an "eternal optimist"? I find that if I maintain a generally pessimistic outlook on life I'm rarely disappointed.

ANSWER: This is an intriguing question because, yes, there are many circumstances where positive outcomes are unlikely, and some degree of pessimism is both realistic and adaptive (e.g., expecting to lose money at a casino; expecting a newborn infant to disrupt your sleep). Nor does the phrase "eternal optimist" sound like an approach that balances hopeful thinking with realistic thinking!

Yet, just think for a moment about the motivational consequences of being "generally pessimistic." That PAB mindset is associated with a cautious, coping-oriented approach to life rather than a thriving motivational pattern. "Playing it safe" may be a great strategy for avoiding disappointment and protecting against losses, but in the broader scheme of human development not going backward isn't how most people would define optimal functioning. That is why we have combined the concepts of accuracy and hope into one principle. That mindset will enable you to maintain awareness of your vulnerabilities while also encouraging you to "go for it" when promising opportunities arise.

It may be foolish, for example, to try to hit a golf shot through a cluster of trees or over a lake that extends beyond your reach. But at the end of the day will it be the safe shots you remember, or the bold ones that left you feeling empowered and joyous? Will you want to tell your golfing buddies about the great round you had "with no double bogeys" or would you rather swap stories about the time you made an improbable par or a magnificent birdie?

Bottom line. There is no doubt that unrealistically optimistic thinking can lead to disappointment and regret. And it is easy to understand why so many people adopt a "better safe than sorry" approach to life, as this mindset is consistent with the way our earliest emotion-based motivational systems evolved. But success in life requires both caution and courage. That is why PAB patterns that combine accurate assessments of current circumstances with hopeful visions of the future are the ones most likely to fuel and support optimal growth and development. To achieve that equipoised mind-set, it is particularly important that you be able to see perceived risks and opportunities in a realistic light.

QUESTION: I hear what you're saying, but it seems like a lot of basically well-functioning people are cynical about their government leaders, pessimistic about the prospects for change, and worried about the future of humanity. Doesn't that contradict the idea that being hopeful about the future is a prerequisite for optimal functioning?

ANSWER: No, not at all. Keep in mind that not all beliefs are personal agency beliefs. Only those beliefs that are directly connected to your own day-to-day goal pursuits and life circumstances are likely to have any significant or enduring motivational impact. If you think the world is generally filled with corruption and incompetence, but things are basically fine when it comes to your own situation, what will win the day, motivationally speaking, is your positive profile of *personal* agency beliefs. Conversely, if you think that most people are happy, but your own life involves a lot of hardships and misfortune, those barriers to goal fulfillment are likely to be far more motivation-ally impactful than your global beliefs about "people in general." That is why we carefully chose the labels of *personal optimism* and *mindful* *tenacity* to refer to amplified capability and context beliefs, respectively.

Bottom line. It may be just fine to be a pessimist or a cynic when the topics are things that are at least a step or two removed from your daily goal pursuits. But if you lose faith in your ability to progress toward the things that are most important to you personally, watch out! That can put you on a downward motivational spiral that may be hard to stop.

QUESTION: I can definitely resonate to the idea of a downward spiral. That image helps me understand the surprisingly strong feelings of anxiety and dread that I sometimes have in situations where I feel really vulnerable. How can I increase my confidence and be more courageous in those kinds of situations?

ANSWER: The first thing to keep in mind is that *these feelings are normal.* As "living control systems," we are designed to try to exercise control over the outcomes that matter most to us, such as those related to our health and well-being, our close relationships, and our reputation in social groups. When we anticipate being able to control these outcomes, we feel confident and relaxed. But when we feel powerless to control, for example, what a doctor will say, or how an audience will react, or whether a spouse will be faithful, our motivational systems are designed to respond with emotions (like fear or anger) that will help us take the actions needed to regain some degree of control over those circumstances.

What kind of actions? When you have negative capability and context beliefs, and those beliefs are fundamentally accurate, the most effective actions are generally those that actually improve your capabilities (e.g., by diligently preparing for and practicing an upcoming speech), or that place you in environments that are directly responsiveness to your concerns (e.g., by seeking advice and expertise on how to handle a frightening health challenge). Yet, sometimes the root of the problem is the belief system itself. Suppose, for example, that you are panicking over a big test you have to take the next morning. If, in reality, you have not yet learned what you are about to be tested on, it would make perfect sense to gear up for an all-nighter to see if you can quickly raise your capabilities to the required level. But if you have in fact mastered that material, pulling an all-nighter because you lack confidence in your well-developed capabilities might be the absolute *worst* action you could take, as lack of sleep may leave you with insufficient energy and mental focus to perform at your best.

Similarly, your best course of action might be drastically different if persistent suspicions about a partner's trustworthiness are completely valid or "just in your head." If a spouse or business partner is actually behaving badly in ways that jeopardize the pursuit of your core personal goals, you should take the initiative to try to change or separate yourself from that toxic environment. But if your partner is in fact consistently acting in your best interest, the most constructive response would be to question your inaccurate context beliefs and make an authentic effort to see things in a more accurate and hopeful light. Otherwise you might drive away the very people who are most likely to help you achieve the things that are most important to you.

Bottom line. Strong feelings of vulnerability are a normal part of everyday life and closely linked to your capability and context beliefs. Yet these beliefs may or may not reflect "things as they really are." So when you experience these feelings, start by trying to understand their origins. When vulnerabilities arise from actual capability deficits or from authentically unresponsive elements of the environment, an active approach orientation (as opposed to an internally focused "state" orientation) is ideal, as that will motivate you to try to change the circumstances that are causing your distress. An active approach mindset can also help you take the steps needed to correct inaccurate beliefs that may be undermining your goal progress. Even small steps forward can make a world of difference, motivationally speaking. An injection of just a little bit of positivity and perceived control can help prevent a downward emotional spiral and establish a new, more hopeful motivational trajectory.

QUESTION: These are great suggestions that help me understand the root causes of self-doubt and mistrust. But let's be realistic – it takes time to increase capabilities, modify environments, and change belief systems. In the meantime, what can I do to manage the immediate feelings of distress? It's hard to focus on doing anything constructive when feelings of anxiety and distress are flooding my "motivational systems."

ANSWER: Recall that emotions tend to naturally dissipate if they are not continuously retriggered (like a flywheel that needs an occasional push to keep spinning). So, when emotions triggered by self-doubt and mistrust persist to the point of being overwhelming rather than informative, the key is to try to alter the thoughts and events that are sustaining the unproductive emotions.

The most common triggers sustaining persistently aversive emotions are what might be thought of as "mental tapes" that keep playing over and over again inside your head. These tapes typically highlight either distressing memories (e.g., from a frightening or embarrassing experience) or future scenarios filled with negative PABs and bad outcomes (e.g., imagining yourself being rejected by a hostile audience or humiliated by a display of incompetence).

When these mental tapes get stuck in your head, your efforts to replace them with more positive thoughts should be guided by the Principle of Accurate and Hopeful PABs. Optimal functioning is facilitated when you acknowledge past setbacks and current limitations, but also maintain a firm belief that better outcomes are possible in the future. To do that, however, you will need to make a conscious, deliberate effort to control what you pay attention to.

For example, if you are selectively focusing your attention on one "epic failure" (like a speech you had trouble delivering or a dentist visit that went poorly), and ignoring many past successes (all the speeches and dentist visits that went just fine), you should consciously seek to recall the good memories and include them in your thoughts as well. Imagining yourself experiencing good outcomes is an effective way to help "cool down" strong emotions that threaten to flood your motivational systems.

You might also focus your attention on the *aftermath* of an unpleasant episode that keeps intruding on your thoughts, and question "how bad was it, really?" in the long run. We all experience frightening and painful episodes from time to time, but usually their impact fades rather quickly and we move on. Sometimes adversity can even make us stronger. A little perspective and self-compassion can help us see life's challenges in a more realistic light and blunt the tendency to exaggerate the impact of distressing events based on selective recall of moments of peak emotion.

This same idea applies to the future scenarios that you imagine happening to yourself. The worst possible outcome is usually far less likely than many other more positive outcomes. As part of your *control of attention* strategy, you should make a deliberate effort to picture (yes, literally picture in your mind) those alternative outcomes as well. It's like mentally inserting a favorite song into your consciousness when you have an annoying one stuck in your head. That "change the mental tape" tactic is a tried-and-true way to disrupt the relentlessly negative emotions and insecurities that can make life so miserable.

Bottom line. The ability to control the memories, images, and interpretations you attend to can play a huge role in helping you maintain emotional balance and perspective. Otherwise you may find it hard to "tone down" powerful feelings that can turn self-doubt into panic and mistrust into paranoia. Equally important is maintaining an active approach goal orientation and a growth mindset (i.e., a belief in your ability to move forward and improve your capabilities and life circumstances). Taken together, these are among the fundamental ingredients of a *thriving* motivational pattern capable of fostering hope and resilience under stress.

Principle 4: The Principle of Emotional Wisdom

Your emotions can help you make wise choices and manage challenging situations, but only if you can assess whether they make sense given your current circumstances and can then use those insights to make appropriate adjustments.

QUESTION: I am going to need some help getting the gist of what this multifaceted principle is all about. What exactly does it mean to be "emotionally wise?"

ANSWER: Emotions evolved to help motivate us to act in ways that would enhance survival and well-being – both for ourselves and others we care about. These motivational effects are automatic and do not require "wisdom" in the usual sense of the word. Yet, for emotions to function optimally in support of your goal pursuits, you need to be *aware* of what emotions you are feeling, *understand* why you have these emotions, and *assess* whether they are the "right" or "best" continuing responses for the circumstances you are in and the goals you are seeking to accomplish. That is how you maximize the informational value of emotions. But then you also need to be able to effectively utilize those emotional insights by adjusting the *amplitude* of your emotional responses (up or down) to an optimal level. You may also need to adjust the *content* of your emotions if the ones you are experiencing are providing you with unsound advice (e.g., rejecting a fear response that is unrealistic or an anger response that is self-defeating).

And that is only the "self" (i.e., *self-awareness* and *self-regulation*) part of emotional wisdom! Now consider these same processes in the context of interacting with others who are also experiencing their own emotions. To effectively help, cooperate, or "fit in," you need to be *aware* of what emotions others are feeling, *understand* why they are experiencing those emotions, and be able to *assess* what would be the "right" or "best" interpersonal responses for the circumstances you are in and the goals you are seeking to accomplish. And then you also need to be able to effectively utilize these emotional insights to influence others and guide your own actions toward desired interpersonal outcomes. The concepts of *empathy* and *social-emotional competence* are typically used to refer to this type of emotional wisdom.

Bottom line. Emotions evolved as powerful motivational tools long before the capacity for "wisdom" developed. But in modern human life it is common for triggered emotions to send mixed signals or to be less than a perfect fit to the social, ecological, and technological circumstances for which we need motivational guidance. Emotional wisdom helps us make the adjustments needed to stay in touch with our feelings, in control of our emotional responses, and in synch with our social partners.

QUESTION: So, emotional wisdom involves sizing things up and making adjustments – kind of like a dimmer switch, or a thermostat?

ANSWER: You are on the right track – energy regulation (up and down) is definitely part of the concept (imagine using a dimmer switch to "set the mood" or brighten up a room). But a more complete metaphor would also need to encompass mechanisms for changing the *content* of the emotions that get triggered and expressed. Earlier we used the metaphor of a TV remote control for this purpose. With a device like this, you can not only adjust the "volume" of an emotion; you can also change "emotion channels" when your feelings are hindering rather than helping you progress toward your goals. For example, if fear of rejection is keeping you from pursuing a promising career option, it might help to consciously refocus your attention on features of this opportunity that cause you be excited about the future and proud of your past accomplishments. That will put you in a more balanced position to assess whether you have what it takes to succeed in a new role. Sometimes the best advice is indeed to wait until you are better prepared to pursue a goal. Yet sometimes putting yourself out there is the best way to learn about yourself and to gauge progress. The "wise" emotional mindset is thus one that motivates you to take "smart risks" when growth opportunities arise. That is a key way that emotional wisdom contributes to thriving motivational patterns.

Another reason we like the metaphor of a TV remote control is that, in addition to being able to change the "channel of the moment," you can also change the baseline settings for how you perceive things in general (via controls for brightness, hue, etc.). That is analogous to changing your emotional *mindset* so that you are inclined to have certain emotions triggered over others. For example, if you are "preprogrammed" to see variations from the status quo as interesting (rather than annoying or disturbing), you will be more open to exploring new ideas that may broaden your thinking and help you adjust to change. Similarly, if your settings predispose you to feel affection toward others (rather than resentment or mistrust), you will act with greater social purpose and be perceived as more socially competent (assuming that you are in fact not in a persistently hostile social environment). Seeking to control your general emotional mindset is consistent with Fredrickson's (2003, 2009) "broaden-and-build" theory of positive emotions, which highlights the far-reaching benefits of viewing the world through a filter that allows *positivity* to flourish while also limiting the flow of negative emotions to those that are truly informative and helpful.

Emotional wisdom also requires mind-reading capabilities that enable us to assess how *others* are feeling. The resulting insights, along with the empathic emotions those insights trigger, can then help us make appropriate adjustments to the ongoing emotional climate. Can the metaphor of a TV remote control capture those aspects of emotional wisdom as well? Perhaps, as these tools have been upgraded in recent years to include the ability to communicate with multiple devices and coordinate their functioning as they interact with one another. Consistent with the concept of "wisdom," these coordinating devices typically have the word "smart" attached to them in some fashion (as in smart TV, smartphone, etc.).

Bottom line. Emotional wisdom involves a variety of functions, analogous to what one might find on a universal remote control device. One set of functions helps you control the "volume" of your emotions so that they are loud enough to get their message across while not being so loud as to flood your motivational systems. Another set of functions helps you change "emotion channels" to those that are most appropriate and helpful for your current circumstances. You can also change your emotional "settings" so that you are predisposed to experience positive emotions as your baseline mode of functioning. Finally, there are functions that help us coordinate our interactions with others by sensing how others are feeling and making adjustments that maximize the clarity and power of the information and actions guiding shared goal pursuits.

QUESTION: It would be really cool if I could just "zap" to whatever emotion channel I wanted! But it doesn't seem like I have much actual control over the feelings I experience. I often wish I didn't feel anxious, or depressed, or resentful, but actually changing those feelings seems really hard. Is it realistic to think that we can control our emotions? It seems more like they are controlling me.

ANSWER: Whew, this is a tough one. Is it realistic to think that we can control our emotions? The honest answer would have to be NO. And YES! And part of emotional wisdom is appreciating how both of these answers can be correct.

Here's the "no" part of the answer. Recall that the process of triggering an emotion (as a result of perceiving or thinking about an "emotionally competent stimulus") is automatic and happens outside awareness. So, no, we are not designed to be able to fully control our feelings. Our emotion systems evolved as "first responders" that could act with extraordinary speed in an emergency – even faster than our conscious mind can keep up with (as illustrated by the classic case of swerving to avoid hitting a car that has veered into your path, and consciously feeling the flood of emotion *after* you have already taken action).

Understanding this design feature can help us understand why emotions often seem to have a "life of their own." If, for example, you have learned to evaluate a particular stimulus as scary (e.g., the image of speaking in front of an audience), or maddening (e.g., seeing someone jump ahead of you in a long line), or disgusting (e.g., seeing a hair in your food), you can't stop that emotion from being triggered. Nor is it easy to unlearn emotional connections that are strong and reinforced through repeated experience or through intrusive "mental simulations" (as illustrated by soldiers and assault victims with posttraumatic stress disorders).

Nevertheless, there are many things you can do to influence and manage the *aftermath* of the emotion-triggering process. And, with sufficient time and experience, it may even be possible to modify learned emotional connections that are disrupting your life. That is the "yes" part of our answer.

Indeed, it may be empowering simply to know that you are not *supposed* to be able to stop unwanted emotions from being triggered. After all, unpleasant emotions evolved to help us make wise choices in "alarming" circumstances (recall that such emotions are informative because they work like an alarm signal). It is thus normal to experience emotions other than those you prefer, and it is normal to not be able to effortlessly "zap" them away when they cause you to feel bad.

Yet that does not mean that you are helpless to control your emotions once they have been triggered. Recall that emotions evolved to serve an advisory role, not a directive role. As you experience the conscious feelings associated with a triggered emotion, you can question why you are feeling this way (i.e., what might have triggered the emotion) and whether it is actually useful to feel that way given the circumstances you are in and the outcomes you are concerned about. The key is to not let your emotions hijack the leadership team in motivational headquarters. If you focus your attention primarily on your emotions, you can become "out of control," like a rudderless sailboat that is blowing around in a shifting wind without direction. Keeping your goal and PAB thoughts "front and center" can help you see emotions for what they are – motivational advisors that are often helpful but sometimes misguided or even just plain wrong.

You can also try to gain control over your emotions by applying your knowledge of how emotions get triggered. The trick here is to shift your attention away from the perception or thought that triggered the distressing emotion, and focus instead on a different "emotionally competent stimulus." For example, instead of dreading the painful sensations associated with an upcoming dental procedure, you can try to anticipate how great it will feel when the procedure is over. You could even go one step further by trying to control attention at a moment-to-moment level, for example, by playing some of your favorite songs in your head while you use your fingers to tap on the arms of the chair like a drummer or piano player. Some people also find it helpful to "change the (emotion) channel" by redirecting their attention to pleasant images and experiences ("I'm going to close my eyes now and go to my happy place"). That strategy is particularly effective when you can imagine yourself actively pursuing a goal (mental simulation) rather than passively observing a setting that does not include you in it as an actor (e.g., singing along to a favorite song rather than just hearing it in your mind; walking along a familiar pathway and imagining what you would see rather than just visualizing a static image of a relaxing place). As we have noted from time to time throughout this book, the ability to control what you pay attention to is often the key to maintaining a positive motivational mindset and a general sense of well-being. This is so in large part because controlling your attentional focus is such an effective way to control your emotional experience.

Now, admittedly, sometimes emotions are so strong and intrusive that it is hard to set them aside, even for just a few minutes. Analogous to when we experience the feeling of having to go to the bathroom RIGHT NOW (!!!), it may be impossible to put emotions "in their place" using control of attention strategies when they become too overpowering. Under those circumstances there are two additional strategies that can help you gain control over strong, unwanted emotions. The first strategy capitalizes on the fact that emotions are biological as well as psychological phenomena, and are closely tied to the state of our physical body. The second strategy capitalizes on the fact that feelings are complex, personalized ideas that include thoughts and perceptions, not just emotions per se.

First, you can try to disrupt the triggering process or reduce its impact by taking medications (under the careful supervision of your doctor) that alter the biochemical context and/or affective experience of a particular emotion. That is what antidepressant and antianxiety medications are designed to do, for example. Many foods and natural supplements can also influence our emotional states. Keep in mind, however, that this kind of strategy is unlikely to change the underlying connection between an emotion trigger and emotional response. If that emotionally learned connection is intrinsically invalid (e.g., being persistently afraid of objectively harmless circumstances), or so strong that it impossible to manage with a straightforward (doctor-supervised) pharmaceutical intervention, psychotherapeutic strategies may also be necessary. Yet drug therapies have become extraordinarily popular because they are quite effective in helping people reduce the magnitude of unwanted emotions to a level that enables them to deal with those emotions using their own coping capabilities. Even when professional psychotherapy is necessary (D. Ford & Urban, 1998; Prochaska & Norcross, 2019), drug therapy can be a useful tool for subduing strong emotions sufficiently to allow for thoughtful application of other kinds of therapeutic strategies.

In that spirit, one can also try to get a handle on an individual's history of emotional learning in an effort to get to the root cause of the emotion-triggering process that is making it difficult for an individual to function in an optimal way. Consider, for example, individuals who are so frightened by social encounters or by imagined health problems that they feel chronically miserable and unable to function normally. The emotional experience may be similar in each case, but the thoughts and perceptions that trigger the unwanted emotions may be quite unique to each individual. Metaphorically speaking, it is like being on the "anxiety channel" with the volume turned way up, and what is being "broadcast" to you on that channel is not exactly the same "episode" that anyone else tuned to that channel would see. Rather, what you see are *personalized* episodes from your "emotional autobiography" – episodes that you may feel compelled to watch over and over again, especially if you find it hard to switch to another emotion channel. These episodes include perceptions, memories, beliefs, and interpretations that can help explain why you feel anxious, and why your feelings of anxiety have become so amplified.

Bottom line. The development of emotional wisdom is enhanced as we become more aware of what aspects of our emotional life are under our control, and as we learn strategies and tactics for exercising such control. *Control of attention* is at the heart of many of these techniques, as that can help us regulate strong emotions when they are causing "change and commotion" (Damasio, 2003) at a chaotic, disorganizing level. Biochemical and psychotherapeutic interventions implemented by trained professionals can also help when emotional distress remains at a very high level despite our best efforts.

QUESTION: I am starting to appreciate how understanding my basic motivational "design features" can really help me in my everyday life. But what about emotional wisdom as it applies to interacting with others? How can I become more insightful and effective in emotionally charged social situations?

ANSWER: This gets us back to the fundamental idea that, in most circumstances, the most effective way to motivate others is through a *motivational facilitation* approach that takes into account other people's interests, concerns, feelings, and expectations. Intrinsic to this approach is a mindset and strategy of "focusing on the other." In other words, *control of attention* is as central to social expressions of emotional wisdom as it is to self-oriented aspects of emotional wisdom. The difference is that you must now focus your attention on the goals, emotions, and personal agency beliefs that *other* people may be experiencing.

What does it mean to "focus on the other"? Perhaps a physical image will help you grasp this idea. Try putting your hands in front of your eyes, just an inch or two away from your face, and a pair of (disconnected) headphones over your ears. What can you perceive from that perspective? Not much in terms of the people around you. But you can still focus on your own mental activity, as that remains as accessible as ever, even with your vision blocked. And that is how people who lack emotional wisdom focus their attention. Whether due to immaturity, apathy, insecurity, or narcissism, they remain egocentrically preoccupied with their own concerns and can only "see" and "hear" things from their own perspective. They may be perfectly capable of being empathic and understanding in certain circumstances, as most people are (but watch out for those who lack the capacity for empathy, as they are a particularly dangerous breed – indeed, our prisons are full of them!). Yet, because of the persistently self-centered way their attentional resources are deployed, they are often unable to acquire enough social awareness and social under-standing to be emotionally appealing or to interact with others in a situationally appropriate and mutually satisfying way.

To make things even worse, if these *episodes* of social incompetence are sufficiently frequent, they can create lasting damage in your *relationships* with important people in your life – like your clients, colleagues, friends, and family. Keep in mind that your social partners and collaborators will be exercising their own emotional wisdom capabilities when they interact with you. If you are persistently self-focused in those interactions, they may quickly conclude that it is neither rewarding nor pleasant to interact with you ("You don't seem to be interested in what I think"; "All you care about is yourself").

Now take your hands away from your face and look *outward* into the social world around you. Pay close attention to what people are saying. Observe their facial expressions, their body language, and their actions. Don't assume that they have the same concerns and interests as you. Don't assume their viewpoint is the same as yours. Don't assume they are thinking what you want them to think (or what you fear they are thinking). Instead, try to use the clues available to you (including clues from previous interactions) to figure out what they are *actually* thinking and feeling. And in doing so pay particularly close attention to the interests and concerns of other people. That is what it means to "focus on the other" rather than focus on yourself.

In some circumstances a self-focused, egocentric orientation may simply result in inefficiency (due to communication and goal align-ment failures) or lost opportunities (as others seek to avoid you). Yet the consequences of not paying attention to others' authentic motivational experiences can be dire. Consider, for example, the clueless spouse who "never saw it coming" when the resentful partner, tired of being taken for granted, asked for a divorce. Or the arrogant politician who lost a winnable election after rejecting polling data in favor of "wishful thinking." Or the business owner who lost large sums of money after ignoring customer complaints about defective products.

As these examples illustrate, failure to pay attention to other people's perspectives is not just disrespectful. It limits your scope of vision and your ability to adapt to challenging circumstances. Interpersonal egocentrism is thus analogous to driving a car and looking at your smartphone rather than looking outward at the traffic around you. It may be tempting to give in to some immediate desire or concern that is capturing your attention, but at what price? The wise thing to do would be to look up, look around, and look out! ("Why are those brake lights going on in front of me?"; "That driver is texting, I need to get away from that car"). If you can maintain a focus on others' intentions and actions, you are much more likely to reach your "destination" without hurting other people or yourself ("I'll worry about what's going on at work after I'm safely parked").

Bottom line. The most effective way to become more emotionally wise in interpersonal and group settings is to adopt an outward focus of attention that seeks to understand what others are feeling, and why. It is particularly effective if you can apply this attentional focus to all three kinds of learning opportunities, namely, (a) learning from personal *experience* (as you interact with others), (b) learning from *observation* of others' expressions and actions (as you watch them interact with others), and (c) learning from what-if *simulations* that you preview in your mind before you say or do things that are likely to have an emotional impact. People often hide their "true feelings" to be polite or to avoid conflicts, so the more sources of information you can draw upon the better.

Earlier we noted that there is a close relationship between emotional wisdom and social purpose, and that this connection helps account for the amplifying effect that social purpose has on thriving motivational patterns. The way this connection works should now be clear. If you have strong social purpose goals (like cooperating, helping, or belonging), you will naturally be inclined to focus your attention on others' concerns. Conversely, if you lack social purpose, you may not care about what others are thinking and feeling, even if you are quite skilled at mind reading.

That concern brings us to our next guiding principle for motivating self and others.

Principle 5: The Principle of Equipoised Social Purpose

Motivation is enhanced when people seek to accomplish things that are larger than themselves and of benefit to others, assuming they do not neglect their own needs.

QUESTION: OK, let's start with the "equipoised" part of this principle. Is that a real word, or did you just make that up?

ANSWER: Yes, *equipoise* is a real word – though it took us a while to find it! When it became apparent to us that optimal functioning is more about versatility, timing, and flexibility than simply possessing the "right" attributes, we looked for a concept that captured the essence of that vital quality of overall system functioning. Concepts that emphasized an optimal state, like "homeostasis" and "equilibrium," were too narrow to capture the complex and creative nature of self-directed human activity. We also considered the concept of "dynamic equilibrium," as that emphasizes the need for continuous adjustments to maintain a stable outcome (as when a tightrope walker tries to avoid falling). Yet even that way of describing goal pursuit was too limiting, as it still associated optimal functioning with a relatively narrow range of "right answers."

What we needed was a more powerful (and more accurate) version of this concept that encompassed not only the *reactive* process of making adjustments to changing conditions, but also the *proactive* process of dynamically shifting and recalibrating personal goals and the flexible methods needed to attain those goals. As we explained in Chapter 4, optimal functioning requires effective balancing and counterbalancing of the *multiple* forces involved in goal pursuit, including all of the elements in the *Motivational Systems Theory* Formula for Human Functioning (i.e., motivation, knowledge and skills, biological functioning, and the environment).

While writing this book we asked scientists and educators in a variety of disciplines if they knew of any term that could effectively capture this essential property of effective system functioning. They appreciated the importance of the idea but could not pinpoint any words that fully captured its intended meaning. Then one day we came across the uncommon (but not obscure) word *equipoise*. This term was broader in scope than the alternatives we had rejected, and more consistent with the key ideas of versatility, timing, and flexibility. In particular, we liked the connotations associated with "poise," a concept that implies both smooth overall functioning and a capacity for resilience in the face of stress (as in "poise under pressure," a quality one might see in an NFL quarterback who is agile in the face of onrushing defensive linemen, or in an experienced salesperson who can remain calm and constructive while dealing with agitated customers). Poise also has another relevant meaning, namely, being prepared to take action "when the time is right" (as when an enterprise is poised to make a new product announcement but waits until market conditions are favorable).

Equipoise results when each element in a dynamic system functions in harmony toward a common purpose. And since we have many different purposes that guide our decisions and actions, equipoise requires effective balancing and counterbalancing of the multiple goals that are constantly competing for priority status in motivational headquarters. At a group level, equipoise can, for example, enable members of a team to put aside self-centered distractions and work together to achieve outcomes that greatly exceed what might be expected based on the individual talents of the team members. It can also empower individuals to juggle their relationship and task goals with a high degree of efficiency, effectiveness, and grace.

It is no wonder, then, that is so difficult to describe optimal functioning in terms of specific traits or behaviors. Just think, for example, of the wide variety of personalities and interaction styles you have observed in effective leaders. Perhaps you have even seen effective leaders become ineffective leaders when their goals or circumstances changed, and equipoise was lost as they failed to adapt to new challenges or they became preoccupied with maintaining power and resources.

Along these same lines, new parents often learn the hard way how unhelpful a formulaic approach to optimal functioning can be as they read contradictory advice about the "right" way to take care of their baby. And for those parents who think they have mastered the secrets to raising a perfect child, just wait fifteen years! – or at least until baby number two comes along, and much of what you thought you knew goes out the window. Although there are some critical boundary conditions for ensuring an infant's health and safety, and for nourishing the inborn motivational systems that support exploration, learning, and social-emotional development, there is no one parenting pathway that can ensure good outcomes. What works for one child may be far from optimal for another child. Strategies that work for one parent may not work at all for someone with a different profile of skills, experiences, and circumstances. And what works for a child at one point in time may not work at all even for the same child just a few months later.

That is why we need a concept like equipoise. Optimal functioning involves more than having the "right" elements in place. How those elements are configured and reconfigured over time is just as important.

Bottom line. When it comes to motivation, equipoise is more important than simply having a lot of some positive quality. Self-assurance is a powerful motivational asset, but untimely overconfidence can lead to very bad outcomes. Tenacity can overcome many obstacles, but it can also backfire if it becomes a mindless exercise in stubbornness. Emotions can be very informative up to a point, but beyond that threshold they can flood motivational headquarters and prevent the rational thought needed to move forward.

The same basic principle applies to social purpose goals. The *Principle of Equipoised Social Purpose* reminds us that optimal functioning is less about "how much" social purpose one possesses, and more about how and when social purpose goals are activated, prioritized, and pursued in relation to other goals.

QUESTION: Sorry to interrupt, but before you continue can you remind me, what exactly is "social purpose"?

ANSWER: Social purpose is a multifaceted type of goal content that reflects the fundamental human desire to be a part of – and to contribute to – something larger than your individual self. Social purpose may be expressed in your relationship with one other person, or arise in the context of a group you belong to, or be activated in reference to some larger social unit for which you feel a special affinity, like a community, country, culture, or work organization.

If you look back (in Chapter 3) to the Ford and Nichols Taxonomy of Human Goals, you will see that there are four different types of *integrative social relationship* (aka social purpose) goals: belongingness, social responsibility, equity, and resource provision. Like all twenty-four categories in the taxonomy, these are personal goal *themes* that capture the essence of the wide variety of outcomes that are in the thoughts, hopes, and concerns of people around the globe. Keep in mind that in addition to thematic content, our personal goals have experiential and context-specific properties that make them "our very own."

Social purpose goals stand in contrast to *self-assertive social relationship* goals – goals that also play out in social settings, but that focus on enhancing and promoting different aspects of the self. Self-assertive goals are not the "villains" to our social purpose "heroes"; indeed, both are essential for optimal functioning.

Specifically, whereas *belongingness* goals focus on "building or maintaining attachments, friendships, intimacy, or a sense of community," *individuality* goals strive to strengthen the identity of the self as a separate unit ("feeling unique, special, or different"). *Social responsibility* goals reflect a sense of social duty ("keeping interpersonal commitments, meeting social role obligations, and conforming to social and moral rules"), which contrasts with the central theme of *self-determination* goals, which is to be free of social expectations and constraints ("experiencing a sense of freedom to act or make choices"). *Equity* goals focus on an essential quality of cooperative group functioning ("promoting fairness, justice, or equality" in comparisons with others), whereas *superiority* goals emphasize a desire to "compare favorably to others in terms of winning, status, or success." Finally, *resource provision* and *resource acquisition* goals reflect two different sides of the "give and take" involved in social relationships (i.e., providing and acquiring "approval, support, assistance, advice or validation" when interacting with others).

As Koestler (1978) emphasized using the metaphor of the Roman god Janus (whose head has two faces looking in opposite directions), self-assertion and integration are two sides of a unified motivational system. When either of those two motivational tendencies becomes overly dominant (i.e., when equipoise is lost), bad outcomes are likely.

QUESTION: Like what? I can easily imagine really selfish people and how that can lead to social rejection and a terrible reputation. But what's wrong with being super responsible and fair and giving? Isn't that the ideal, and what we want our children to grow up to be?

ANSWER: Great question, as this helps explain why we don't have a separate principle of "equipoised self-interest." Just try walking out of a store without paying for your purchases, or grabbing someone's delicious-looking food without asking permission. Social reactions to unmitigated self-interest tend to be immediate and powerful, much like the pain that comes from touching a hot stove. Yet, because unmitigated social purpose is likely to benefit rather than harm others, feedback about the negative consequences of "ignoring the self" may be muted or indirect. For example, a desire to show allegiance to a group may yield immediate rewards in terms of feedback from group leaders, but what if those efforts turn into mindless obedience? Losing a sense of self may feel empowering as you join with a collective, but it can ultimately lead to very harmful consequences to self and others if equipoise is lost (as illustrated by cult members and religious zealots who are willing to sacrifice lives – perhaps even their own – to empower the group).

Similarly, a pattern of giving to others that ignores personal needs can be motivationally compelling in the short run but may be costly to your own well-being in the long run. Health care providers, for example, quickly learn that they will "burn out" if they do not find ways to regulate their feelings of caring and empathic concern for their patients. People who freely give their time and resources to others often learn the hard way that they must guard against "predators" if they want to prevent selfish people from taking advantage of them.

Bottom line. Social purpose goals are a uniquely important part of our motivational heritage. When our ancient ancestors began to think in terms of shared goals and collective purposes, humanity began to soar. Social purpose goals empower cooperation, teamwork, sharing of resources, and perhaps most important, a desire to engage in teaching and other activities that promote cumulative cultural evolution. Yet, this same "power of the collective" can undermine both well-being and survival if it is not integrated with motives to preserve and protect one's own identity, agency, and well-being.

QUESTION: So, we just need a balance between self-interest and social purpose, right? "Everything in moderation," as my grandmother used to say.

ANSWER: No, that is NOT the take-home message with respect to the Principle of Equipoised Social Purpose. Optimal functioning requires the frequent and timely activation of social purpose goals that are both compelling and authentic. That is why our theory of motivation and optimal functioning is called Thriving *with* Social Purpose. The idea of equipoised social purpose is not a message about needing to "moderate" the strength of goals that motivate us to help others, seek fairness, work as a team, and feel a sense of belonging. It is a message about needing to ensure that those goals do not operate in the absence of goals that help us maintain our own survival and well-being.

Adam Grant (2013) nails this idea in his revealing book *Give and Take*. He first establishes that the most favorable outcomes in work organizations, for both self and others, result from the actions of those who have strong, frequently activated social purpose goals.

> Studies show that on average, from sales teams to paper mill crews to restaurants, the more giving group members do, the higher the quantity and quality of their groups' products and services. But it's not just their groups that get rewarded .... Extensive research reveals that people who give their time and knowledge regularly to help their colleagues end up earning more raises and promotions in a wide range of settings. (Grant, 2013, p. 74)

But then Grant also documents the fact that the most giving employees are not only those most likely to generate the *best* outcomes, they are also overrepresented among those with the *worst* outcomes. How could that be? The clear answer is loss of equipoise. In other words, social purpose can only lead to effective outcomes if it is embedded in a motivational pattern Grant calls *otherish* giving, where "concern for others is coupled with a healthy dose of concern for the self" (in contrast to *selfless* giving).

This same finding pervades research in personality and social psychology. For example, in Chapter 6 we saw the Principle of Equipoised Social Purpose play out in the context of the popular "Prisoner's Dilemma" game, where the best long-term strategy for maximizing gains is to engage in mutual cooperation while remaining alert to instances of misplaced trust. The importance of having strong social purpose goals infused with a "healthy dose of concern for self" is also evident in research on stereotypically "masculine" and "feminine" personality attributes (which tend to emphasize self-assertive and integrative themes, respectively). This extensive body of research consistently shows that the most favorable personality pattern with respect to success and well-being is to have high levels of *both* sets of attributes (Spence & Helmreich, 1978; Wiggins & Holzmuller, 1978). That is the pattern associated with the greatest overall versatility and effectiveness (as opposed to having self-assertive and integrative qualities "in moderation").

Bottom line. Optimal functioning for both individuals and social groups is associated with robust social purpose goals that are frequently activated in context-appropriate ways. Social purpose not only leads to better outcomes, it is also a uniquely powerful and reliable source of life meaning. Yet the empowering effects of social purpose goals can be negated or corrupted if they are not integrated with goals that maintain your strength and integrity as an individual person. This *equipoised* version of social purpose is what reliably leads to the best outcomes.

Principle 6: The Principle of Unitary System Functioning

Efforts to motivate self and others will be more effective if they are framed within a "big picture" developmental perspective that encompasses not only goals, emotions, and personal agency beliefs but also knowledge and skills, biological functions, and environmental circumstances.

QUESTION: Doesn't this kind of go without saying? It seems pretty obvious that motivation won't get us very far if we don't have what it takes to progress toward a goal, or there are huge obstacles in the way.

ANSWER: Some folks may intuitively resonate to this "systems" way of thinking, yet when it comes to actually doing something to enhance motivation, people seem to get enamored by "one big idea" and not pay much attention to the fact that there are a lot of elements that need to work together to make that "big idea" viable. A simplified, linear approach may be appropriate for an academic researcher who is trying to figure out if some particular quality or process (like goal setting, or self-efficacy, or mindfulness) is influential by controlling for the effects of other variables. But that is not the way things work in the real world.

    Bottom line. We always function as a whole person-in-context. Moreover, both our personal qualities and our contexts are dynamically evolving, even when we might wish things would stay just as they are!

QUESTION: I get the basic concept, but is it realistic to say that we can't do much of anything unless we first think of everything? That requirement seems both intimidating and discouraging.

ANSWER: Well, when you put it that way, the principle does sound rather daunting. But that would be exaggerating the intended meaning of this "requirement." Think of it more like the old driver education adage to "get the big picture" by paying attention to your broader surroundings, as well as the dynamic changes in those surroundings. There may be times when it is all you can do to pay attention to just one thing (like the white stripe on the edge of the road when driving in a dense fog). But in general you will make better decisions and get to your destination more efficiently (and safely!) if you think about factors that go beyond your immediate visual focus – like what other drivers around you are doing, what the traffic looks like beyond the next few hundred feet, and what information your vehicle is providing you about its functioning.

Now, take this analogy and apply it to the task of motivating self and others. What factors do you need to think about to make sure you "get the big picture"? Start with the simple *Motivational Systems Theory* Formula for Human Functioning (introduced in Chapter 4). That formula states that the effective pursuit of personal goals (aka human functioning) requires four essential elements:

1. The person must have the *motivation* needed to initiate and maintain goal pursuit until the desired outcome is attained.
2. The person must have the *knowledge and skills* needed to construct and execute actions that will produce the desired outcomes.
3. The person's *biological structure and functioning* must be able to support the motivation and knowledge and skills elements required for successful goal pursuit.
4. The person's *environment* must facilitate, or at least not excessively impede, progress toward the desired outcome.

QUESTION: Simple enough, but these are pretty big categories. I assume that I may need some additional tools to figure out in a more precise way what needs to be done to effectively motivate someone.

ANSWER: That may indeed be the case – and yes, there are quite a few such tools in this book – but you don't have to start with a full-blown "wiring diagram" of the whole system. Indeed, simply being aware that there may be other things going on in a person's mind, body, and life beyond what is immediately evident can help you avoid oversimplified conclusions. That awareness can then lead you to more specific hypotheses about what else you might need to consider as you continue to try to size up how you might respond to a particular problem or opportunity.

Suppose, for example, that a student or employee is not meeting your performance standards. Your first thought might be that this individual is disinterested in the goals you want them to accomplish, or just plain lazy (i.e., the person is motivationally deficient). But before "jumping to conclusions" it might be wise to first consider a broader spectrum of possibilities. Perhaps your teenage student is coming to your 7:30 AM class each morning with insufficient sleep and no breakfast (biological functioning). Perhaps you have made some incorrect assumptions about an employee's prior training and experience (knowledge and skills). Perhaps there are some profoundly stressful life events that are making it difficult for the individual to focus on their daily assignments (environmental circumstances).

Another tool you can use to avoid superficial thinking is the *Motivational Systems Theory* Formula for Human Motivation, which "drills down" to the fundamental elements within the motivational systems component of human functioning. Motivation comprises *personal goals, emotions, capability beliefs,* and *context beliefs* (with the latter two paired together under the label *personal agency beliefs*). Because these processes work together in organized patterns (thus our metaphor of "motivational headquarters"), it is important to keep all of these elements in mind when trying to understand the choices people make and the feelings they experience. For example, someone under a lot of stress (like a novice classroom teacher) may experience it as "good stress" if they are engaged in the pursuit of a challenging goal and feel confident about their abilities and the support they can count on if they encounter difficulties. Conversely, if they are coping with unexpected challenges and feeling unprepared and alone, the stressful emotions they experience may feel overwhelming (Groundwater, 2006).

In this same spirit, we have provided readers (in Chapter 5) with tools to drill down to some of the fundamental elements within each of the other basic categories of human functioning – while also suggesting how each of those elements might be "amplified" to help facilitate optimal functioning via goal-striving skills, personal health responsibility, and efforts to increase environmental responsiveness. This is not what you would typically find in a book about human motivation. Yet that is the essence of what it means to think in a "systems-oriented" way. Motivation rests on a biological foundation influenced by nutrition, sleep, stress, and overall brain and body functioning. The "leaders" in motivational headquarters can issue directives all day long, but little will come of it if there are no "troops" that can translate those directives into concrete goal representations, context-appropriate strategies and plans, and deliberate action. And even the most robust motivational patterns can be thwarted if the opportunities and resources needed to support the envisioned outcomes are unavailable or deficient.

Nor is this systems perspective just a generic warning to not forget about the "supporting cast," like an Oscar-winning actor who (endlessly!) thanks everyone connected to their success. Our Principle of Unitary System Functioning goes beyond a simple recognition of the "obvious" fact that motivation is not the only pathway to self-improvement or for helping others with their goal pursuits. It also takes advantage of the essential property of *organization,* where changes in one part of a system can be expected to have at least some impact on other parts of the system. So, yes, it is of course important to keep in mind that optimal human functioning can be promoted not only by strengthening motivational processes, but also by developing knowledge and skills, by enhancing biological health and fitness, and by increasing available opportunities and resources. But the more fundamental idea when it comes to unitary system functioning is the insight that there are many pathways through which motivation can be facilitated, including pathways that do not attempt to influence motivational processes directly.

The best way to strengthen someone's capability beliefs, for example, may be to ignore those beliefs and instead work on developing the knowledge and skills the person needs to in fact be more capable. The best way to strengthen your trust in others (a type of context belief) may be to actually remove yourself from contexts that require you to interact with untrustworthy people. The best way to cultivate emotional "positivity" may be to take more time to improve your physical health (e.g., through regular exercise and improved nutrition and sleep habits) rather than trying to directly combat the negative emotions you are experiencing.

Bottom line. Motivation plays a special leadership role in directing, organizing, and regulating goal-directed activity, and is therefore a good starting point when it comes to addressing human problems and developing human potential. But motivational systems are not only complex units in their own right, they are highly dependent on biological fitness, knowledge and skills, and environmental circumstances. That means that, when trying to assess motivational problems, you cannot stop with the first plausible idea that pops into your head, or that you just read about on a cool psychology website. You need to "get the big picture" and thoughtfully consider other potentially important features of the person and environment.

This property of unitary functioning is both a constraint and an opportunity when it comes to motivating self and others. Although efforts to enhance motivation may be inhibited by limitations in other parts of the system, you can also count on those same linkages to provide you with opportunities to strengthen motivation even when you are not having much success doing so directly – for example, through efforts to improve goal-striving skills, personal health responsibility, or environmental responsiveness.

Principle 7: The Principle of TSP Leadership

People respond favorably to leaders who pursue goals with an active approach orientation, personal optimism, mindful tenacity, and emotional wisdom (the thriving motivational pattern) and are guided by an authentic concern for the welfare of others (social purpose).

QUESTION: Let's start with that age-old question about leadership: are some people just "born leaders," or is leadership something that has to be taught and cultivated?

ANSWER: Consistent with our metaphorical portrayal of personal goals as "the leaders within you," it is evident that we are *all* born with the capacity to lead. There are of course vast individual differences in the innate dispositions and skills that contribute to effective leadership, and those capabilities will only manifest themselves if they are cultivated through relevant life experiences – just like other complex human motives and abilities (e.g., those contributing to academic and practical intelligence). But just because some people have more highly developed leadership skills than their peers does not mean that they have some "inborn gift" that others are lacking. At least at a basic design level, all of us are "born leaders" as a direct outcome of our evolutionary heritage.

And doesn't that make sense given the universality of leadership roles like teaching and parenting?

QUESTION: So if we are all "born leaders" with (more or less) the same inherited potential to lead, why are there such vast differences in leadership styles?

ANSWER: Don't forget that our leadership capabilities come in two evolved layers: the hierarchical, power-oriented leadership style that dominated the lives of our ancient ancestors, and the cooperative egalitarian leadership style championed by the courageous pioneers who led their tribes – and ultimately the entire human species – across the Cooperation Divide (as explained in Chapter 6). The evolution of this newer TSP-oriented leadership style did not replace the older methods. Consistent with many of our other motivational characteristics, TSP leadership qualities were instead added as a new layer within our evolved repertoire of possible leadership adaptations.

Now, that is not to say that these different leadership styles are equally effective. Indeed, it is obvious that, with few exceptions, the post–Cooperation Divide leadership approach emphasizing equity and cooperation is our innately preferred way of being treated by leaders, and the style we gravitate to when given the freedom to create group leadership structures. Even for people who assume that power-oriented leadership is the norm, they still prefer to follow TSP leaders because, emotionally, that leadership style *feels* more natural, more respectful, and more motivating. Yet there is no doubt that our species never lost the capacity to function like the alpha male leaders of ancient times, and we intuitively understand that there are circumstances in which authoritarian control and enforced obedience can be adaptive (e.g., circumstances involving military combat; dealing with criminals and chronic "free riders"; or enforcing safety rules that, when ignored, may have deadly consequences).

Bottom line. It is no surprise that coercive leadership patterns are still a common part of the human experience, as that remains a salient part of our evolutionary heritage. Yet its adaptive value is quite limited. In most settings trying to control followers through dictatorial methods will undermine rather than fuel motivation, creativity, productivity, and the cooperative spirit needed to sustain loyalty and teamwork.

QUESTION: I appreciate the fact that there is a scientific basis for your ideas about leadership. I've read a lot of different books on leadership, but to be honest most of them don't seem very scientific. But I'm still having trouble wrapping my head around the idea that your TSP Theory of Motivation and Optimal Functioning can also serve as a theory of leadership. Can you help me better understand that connection?

ANSWER: Leadership is a complex concept, but at its core leadership is about identifying, communicating, and pursuing group goals. This requires an ability to envision alternative future outcomes and pathways based on experience or insight from self and/or others, to effectively share those future-oriented and "visionary" ideas with others, and to organize followers' thoughts, emotions, and actions around shared beliefs and objectives.

In Chapter 3 we described personal goals as "the leaders within you." Thus, in the context of self-direction, *leadership is fundamentally about motivating self*, especially as it relates to goal alignment and the pursuit of core personal goals. As we have seen, TSP modes of functioning are generally associated with goal progress and personal growth.

Similarly, in a group or dyad or organization, *leadership is fundamentally about motivating others*. Humans are social animals who have evolved to live and work in groups and in collaboration with other individuals. In many of these settings there is a need for designated people to carry out, at an interpersonal or collective level, the same leadership functions fulfilled by "motivational headquarters" at the individual level. TSP motivational patterns thus enhance the effectiveness of a leader's efforts to direct others in the same way that those motivational patterns enhance self-direction (i.e., by amplifying the impact of goals, emotions, and personal agency beliefs). And because group members intuitively associate TSP qualities with competence and trustworthiness, they resonate to leaders with these qualities and want to follow them. Indeed, we are hardwired to want to respond cooperatively and enthusiastically to people who are motivationally thriving and who manifest authentic social purpose.

That is not to say that TSP leaders have it easy. Often followers are more focused on their own individual goals than on group goals. Yet getting self-absorbed or disengaged followers to follow the group's agenda is precisely the kind of problem for which TSP leadership is particularly well suited. Take, for example, the challenge of persuading elite athletes who are used to receiving a lot of attention and adulation to develop a less egocentric style of play. For these athletes, appeals to authority and demands to "get with the program" are more likely to backfire than to yield the desired commitment. Yet TSP-oriented coaches who can convey an authentic intent to promote the athlete's interests by aligning those interests with the goals of the group are often able to "bring out the best" even in players that others regard as "uncoachable" (assuming, of course, that the coach is perceived as having the knowledge and skills needed for team success). When these athletes recognize that their coach's primary interest is to support their efforts to improve and succeed within a team concept (rather than to show them "who's the boss"), many are inspired by this leadership style and become loyal and passionate followers.

Bottom line. The best leaders are those who are effective in helping others progress toward optimal functioning in their own lives. And that happens, in large part, through motivational pathways.

QUESTION: So almost anyone could be an effective leader if they develop TSP qualities, right?

ANSWER: Anyone with TSP qualities has the *potential* to be an effective leader, so that should certainly be a primary focus of leadership selection, training and development initiatives. However, it is important that we not lose sight of the other elements required for optimal functioning. Specifically, to lead effectively, one must also be physically energetic and healthy (the biological component of human functioning), have the necessary content expertise to function optimally in a particular leadership role (the knowledge and skills component of optimal functioning), and have authentic opportunities to exercise one's leadership capabilities rather than being controlled by powerful others (the responsive environment component of optimal functioning). And yet, the reverse is also true: being in an empowered leadership role and being an energetic and capable content expert in that domain does not necessarily make you an effective leader. Without well-developed TSP qualities, you are unlikely to be seen as an effective leader by those you are trying to lead.

Bottom line. Effective leadership requires context-specific strength and versatility in all four elements of human functioning: motivation, knowledge and skills, biological functioning, and environmental opportunities and resources. So don't assume that aspiring leaders with TSP qualities are ready to take on leadership roles for which they are not yet well prepared from an experience and expertise perspective. Yet an even worse mistake is to hand over the leadership reins to people who look like they should be effective leaders "on paper" but who are sorely lacking in TSP qualities – and thus are very likely to consistently revert to hierarchical, power-oriented leadership tactics. Appointing (or electing) such people to leadership roles is a recipe for disappointment, if not disaster.

QUESTION: Defining leadership roles primarily in terms of "motivating others" seems pretty broad. What kind of roles are we talking about?

ANSWER: From our perspective, if you are in a role where you are responsible for influencing, guiding, or shaping other people's behavior, then, in the context of that role, you are responsible for carrying out leadership functions. That way of thinking about leadership encompasses stereotypical images like being a chief executive or military officer, but it also embraces much more common leadership roles like being a parent, teacher, or counselor. Or being a supervisor, coach, or manager.

From this perspective it is evident that each of us is sometimes in a leadership role, and sometimes in a follower role. So beware of falling into the trap of assuming that people in leadership roles are intrinsically better or more worthy than those who are being led. Or that you are entitled to preferential treatment if you are elevated into a leadership position. In some other context you might be the follower, and one of your followers might be the leader.

QUESTION: Are you saying that people shouldn't have any kind of special respect for their leaders?

ANSWER: Absolutely not! For families, communities, and organizations to function effectively, it is essential that followers be willing to align at least some of their personal goals with group interests and priorities. That requires respect for those who are in leadership positions as well as respect for the group's "rules and traditions."

Yet we do want to emphasize that the reverse principle is equally important:

It is essential that leaders respect the goals, emotions, beliefs, and circumstances of their followers.

This *principle of human respect* (M. Ford, 1992) – one of the core defining features of TSP leadership patterns – is not just some sort of philosophical stance about the value of an individual person. It is also a practical statement about what it takes to motivate others. Each follower is a self-directed individual with their own unique profile of personal goals, emotions, and personal agency beliefs. Leaders who ignore that fact are likely to demotivate their followers rather than inspire them. Indeed, when followers feel disrespected, the foundation of trust and collaboration that is required for effective leadership can rapidly break down.

The "accountability" movement in K-12 education illustrates how leaders' well-intentioned efforts to motivate their followers can backfire when those followers are treated like "standardized" employees and students rather than respected as self-directed individuals (Lambert & McCarthy, 2006). In this misguided enterprise policy makers have tried to motivate school administrators to produce improved educational outcomes by tying funding and accreditation to rising test scores. As a result, administrators are coerced into thinking of students as "today's numbers" rather than "tomorrow's citizens." The excessive emphasis on high-stakes testing has not only taken the humanity out of one of our species' most uniquely human activities (i.e., teaching and learning), it has also caused many school leaders to become risk averse and highly controlling when it comes to (dis)respecting teachers' motivation and capabilities for educating their students. Teachers soon find themselves struggling to find much of anything engaging in their day-to-day work ("teaching to the test" is *not* what they signed up for). To conform to their administrators' directives, their work is increasingly (mis)directed toward outcomes that are poorly aligned with their core personal goals, while also being limited to standardized content and procedures that stifle autonomy and creativity. Students in turn are demotivated by the emphasis on achievements that feel impersonal and disconnected from "me and my life and things that really matter."

QUESTION: I get it! It really makes me mad when someone acts like they just don't care about what's important to me, or what I can bring to the table. It's OK if you have a different priority or a different viewpoint, but please don't treat me like I'm not a person. Show a little respect!

Yet now you're making me wonder if I too might be doing things that inadvertently make my followers feel disrespected when I provide direction and feedback. How can I avoid that unintended result?

ANSWER: Great question! Indeed, just by asking this question you are showing the kind of self-awareness and "emotional wisdom" that helps make a leader effective.

Often the best way to show respect and motivate others is to closely observe the emotional responses of your followers, while also listening carefully to what they have to say about their feelings and concerns (perhaps in response to an open and genuine request for their opinions or feedback). If you ask questions and then listen attentively and authentically to their answers – especially statements about their goals, emotions, and personal agency beliefs – chances are they will feel that you are working with them rather than against them as you seek to offer guidance and direction. Even if you have no options to offer to them at that time, you can make the directives you need to deliver feel at least somewhat collaborative by showing that you are interested in their point of view and committed to trying to take their perspective into account.

And then, as you respond to what you are observing and hearing, keep firmly in mind the core idea that *facilitation, not control, is the key to motivating others* (M. Ford, 1992). Using authoritarian power and arbitrary bureaucratic rules to control followers creates resentment and discourages commitment. Successful leaders emphasize social purpose goals rather than personal or institutional power to motivate followers – for example, by affirming values and expectations related to teamwork, group loyalty, responsibility to peers, internal equity, and the specific ways that followers can contribute to the group.

Leaders also seek to inspire others by explicitly highlighting how contributing to the group's success will help followers attain their own core personal goals. This recognition and appreciation of the importance of *goal–life alignment* is an essential quality of effective leaders, and an effective way to show that you respect each of your followers. Indeed, in cases where there is serious motivational misalignment, the most respectful approach might be to try to find a new group for that particular follower – either within the same organization or, if necessary, outside the organization. Sometimes that is just what troubled followers need to resolve their own motivational predicament.

Now, admittedly, sometimes encouraging the reassignment or departure of a misaligned follower is not a realistic option. Suppose, for example, that you are an academic administrator and you want your tenured faculty to bring in more grant money. Perhaps the most common motivational tactic in this scenario is exhortation, followed closely by threats to penalize those who do not bring in significant external funding (e.g., by withholding support for academic tenure and promotion rewards). But why should the administration's desire for more grant money be a priority for a veteran faculty member? For scholars who do not feel a compelling need to seek grant funding to advance their *own* research agenda, the natural response to such motivational tactics is likely to be "That's your problem, not mine." They may reluctantly "go through the motions" to avoid punitive consequences, but that is not an effective strategy for building a self-sustaining culture of external funding. Other faculty might see the value in becoming more involved in grant-seeking efforts but feel incapable of doing so without more training or support. Exhortations and demands will just exacerbate the negative capability and context beliefs that are inhibiting such faculty. Still others might be quite willing to pursue more grant funding, but only "if you show a little respect and treat me like a person rather than a commodity."

A more productive approach in these common motivational scenarios is for leaders to engage in individual conversations with followers using a "motivational diagnostician" approach (as suggested in Chapter 4). What personal goals does a particular follower have that might be effectively aligned with the leader's organizational goal? Perhaps new policies need to be developed that make it clear how leaders will share the financial rewards with followers who contribute to the organization's objective. What emotions and PABs are inhibiting their inclination to pursue grants? Perhaps a mentoring approach would be helpful for those who feel insecure about their grant-writing capabilities (or who have actual knowledge and skill deficits that need to be addressed). Or perhaps the instructional and administrative support services provided to faculty need to be strengthened to address negative context beliefs. Without such support it is easy to conclude that seeking external funding is not worth the bureaucratic hassle. And for those faculty who remain unwilling to contribute to this particular organizational goal, the administrator can focus on alternative positive ways that the faculty member can contribute to the organization (e.g., by taking on additional high-value teaching or service roles) rather than making the person feel rejected and unwanted.

QUESTION: If power and control tactics are as ineffective as you say, why do so many leaders use them?

ANSWER: This would indeed seem to be a puzzlement, but don't forget that until our ancestors "crossed the Cooperation Divide," the alpha male power-based culture was the *only* leadership style known to our species. Even though our ancestors evolved a vastly more capable egalitarian leadership style, our species never lost its hierarchical power-based predecessor. And so, although we innately prefer TSP leadership, we also understand situations where power and control tactics may be necessary, and – as socially responsible members of the group – we (usually) tolerate and abide by those tactics (assuming they aren't too extreme).

Yet that is not an adequate justification for the use of such tactics as a general or preferred leadership style. TSP leadership is not just "a little bit better" than power-based leadership, or more effective "on average." It is *far* better over time, and clearly more effective across a very wide range of circumstances. So why are power and control tactics so widely used by group leaders?

One explanation is that people who are highly motivated by goals such as power and ego enhancement often seek out leadership positions so that they can satisfy those core personal goals. If that motivation is combined with strong social purpose goals, the result may still be favorable. But if a leader is both power-hungry and self-absorbed, watch out!

Another explanation for the prevalence of coercive motivational tactics is the durability of cultural beliefs about leadership that assume – or even celebrate – attributes associated with power and adulation. Even those who instinctively know that people don't like heavy-handed tactics or over-inflated egos may assume that leaders are naturally expected to behave that way.

But perhaps the simplest explanation for the prevalence of power-oriented motivational tactics is that they are expedient (in the short run), both with respect to time and effort. When you rely on power there is no need to understand your followers' motives or to get to know them as individuals. There is no need to listen to other people's views and concerns. And there is no need to do things differently depending on the target of your directives. You just focus on the outcome *you* want and order it (or otherwise force it) to happen.

A leader may also conclude from such efforts that power-oriented tactics are quite effective. Yet such a conclusion is only possible if the focus is narrowly and exclusively on the immediate outcomes being controlled. Beyond that the motivational consequences are usually negative, and may be disastrous. Motivation by fear not only breeds resentment and ill will, it also makes followers risk averse, thus paralyzing their ability to make consequential decisions and to exercise creativity. Followers focus on protecting themselves and "getting by" rather than being authentically engaged in meaningful work and learning activities designed to produce positive group outcomes.

QUESTION: I can picture exactly what you are saying – especially when I think about how different leaders responded to the deadly COVID-19 pandemic. I can also see how easy it can be even for well-intentioned leaders to get into an impatient mindset. But how do I stay in a "facilitative" mode rather than in a "controlling" mode when the heat is on, with time pressure, performance pressure, and interpersonal conflict pushing me toward power-oriented tactics? Can you give me a short, simple list of the key things I need to keep in mind to stay on a positive motivational track and avoid demotivating my followers?

ANSWER: Well, OK, but keep in mind that, like a chess game, your best course of action always depends to some extent on the specific circumstances that are in play at the time. To effectively lead, you must be both open-minded (i.e., *willing* to flexibly adjust to changing circumstances) and versatile (i.e., *able* to adjust to changing circumstances). That is why we have included the concept of *equipoise* in our *Thriving with Social Purpose* Formula for Optimal Functioning.

Having said that, there are some guiding principles that you can rely on over and over again as you engage in leadership initiatives and face leadership challenges.

1. Maintain a laser-like focus on helping goals. It's OK to be interested in leadership roles for self-enhancing reasons, but those motives should always be subordinate to social purpose goals. What does that mean? Leaders serve and promote the common good by strengthening the effectiveness and integrity of the group (belongingness), by encouraging people to "do the right thing" with respect to the interests of the group and its individual members (social responsibility), by promoting fairness and justice (equity), and by empowering people through the acquisition and allocation of material, informational, and social-emotional resources (resource provision). Those are the goals that need to be at the forefront of a leader's thoughts to be effective in motivating followers and facilitating successful group outcomes. That means that if your overall goal profile does not include social purpose goals as prominent themes, you should only take on leadership opportunities in specific contexts where SP goals are likely to "rise to the top" (as is typically the case, for example, for those in parenting roles). You should also try to size up the strength and authenticity of SP goals when you have an opportunity to assess candidates for leadership positions that will impact your goal pursuits and daily life experiences. Leaders who manifest thriving qualities like self-confidence and an active approach goal orientation, but who are deficient in SP goals, can create motivational havoc as they pursue their self-focused agenda.

Maintaining a laser-like focus on helping goals also means that, when serving in a leadership role, you must embrace the need to provide timely, personally relevant, context-appropriate feedback to those who are directly impacted by your vision, directives, priorities, and plans. Nor should this essential leadership responsibility be framed as a one-way communication function. Effective leaders develop helping-oriented *relationships* that are focused on what followers need to become successful contributors to the group. Feedback from the leader should naturally focus on the acquisition or improvement of knowledge and skills (K&S). However, this is also an opportunity for leaders to help their followers become more self-aware with regard to the importance of thriving motivational qualities in optimal performance, and the essential role that social purpose plays in group success.

Bottom line. When you interact with your followers you do not need to be their friend or their "pal." That can be artificial and could even be counterproductive if it caused followers to disregard or devalue your leadership authority. But you do need to communicate respect and an authentic intention to serve the interests of others. And then you actually need to support your followers by systematically providing effective, context-appropriate feedback that will help them learn and improve and succeed as contributing group members. If you are focused primarily on what's good for *you* rather than on what's good for others, then you are not leading.

2. Make it your mission to really understand your followers and treat them like persons, not objects. Recall our premise that leadership is primarily about motivating others – with each follower having their own unique profile of personal goals, emotions, and personal agency beliefs and their own unique history of experiences that have shaped their lives. From that perspective it is evident that you can't be an effective leader if you don't make meaningful efforts to understand your followers and to update that understanding frequently as your followers grow and change over time. In larger groups, where it may not be feasible to interact with all your followers on a regular basis, it is essential that your assistants, managers, and supervisors understand the need to "really get to know" the people they are directing, mentoring, and evaluating, and for you to take steps to understand, at a personal level, those who are helping you carry out your leadership functions.

How do you do this? Start with the MST formulas for human functioning and human motivation (as explained in Chapter 4), and use them as a "diagnostic map" that can help point you to the key elements that define each follower's motives, knowledge and skills, and biological and environmental strengths and constraints. The elements within motivational headquarters are particularly dynamic, as emotions and personal agency beliefs can be significantly influenced by daily interactions and events. Those motivational advisors can in turn significantly influence what goals followers prioritize, both on a day-to-day basis and in terms of their overall commitment to group goals.

Bottom line. Leaders inspire followers by helping them see how cooperation and group participation can help them attain their own personal goals and thus achieve the goal–life alignment that is such a reliable source of satisfaction and life meaning.

3. Develop and communicate a clear vision of the "better future" you are trying to help create and show both confidence and courage as you pursue those desired outcomes. When seeking to direct and guide others, leaders must effectively (and persistently) convey compelling ideas and images about what they want followers to do and where that will take them. Leaders can also inspire followers by encouraging them to believe that they have the ability and opportunity to be successful. And the best way to do that is to show them that *you* believe in them – and in yourself.

Bottom line. In many cases it appears that much of a leader's success is attributable to the infectious nature of the leader's own thriving motivational characteristics.

4. Contain negativity so that you don't inadvertently become an aversive emotional trigger for followers. There is no doubt that "motivation by fear" (e.g., through intimidation, threats, or coercive contingencies) can influence behavior in the moment. However, such tactics are notoriously ineffective in producing sustainable change. Indeed, they usually backfire by undermining trust and creating negative emotional associations with the leader. So don't inadvertently become a negative "emotionally competent stimulus" (Damasio, 2003) for your followers by trying to bully them into compliance. Instead, think of leadership as a partnership between you and your followers ("we are in this together – let's try to co-create a solution").

It is essential that leaders convey, in an equipoised manner, a steady stream of "positivity" by communicating with followers about successes, strengths, and opportunities. Leaders also need to show, in authentic and natural ways, appropriate gratitude and appreciation for the contributions of followers.

Bottom line. Try to create circumstances that are emotionally inviting and clearly aligned with the personal goals of the people you are trying to influence. If you want people to be motivated to follow you at a nonconscious emotional level, you must respect the fact that they are self-directed, with a mind of their own (just like you!), and are naturally attracted to people who manifest emotional positivity, both dispositionally and in their interactions with others.

QUESTION: Perfect – I can remember a 1, 2, 3, 4 list. And, if I understand TSP, #1 is focused on social purpose; #2 is goal–life alignment; #3 is actively defining goals and pursuing them with personal optimism and mindful tenacity; and #4 is emotional wisdom. Right?

ANSWER: You got it! Follow these four guidelines and you will experience what effective leadership is all about.

Bottom line. Humans have an innate urge to cooperate with and follow the lead of individuals who are authentically helpful – and who have a reputation for being helpful. We also resonate to people who can get things done (thriving) on our behalf (social purpose). Such people are particularly effective in leadership roles and more likely to be seen as "natural leaders" by others (M. Ford & Smith, 2011). As Hogan and Kaiser (2005) conclude, "who we are is how we lead – and this information can be used to select future leaders or improve the performance of current incumbents" (p. 169).

QUESTION: There's one more question on my mind, but I hesitate to ask it because it may sound, well, selfish. But if I'm being honest, I need to confess that sometimes I just don't know if being a leader is really worth it. Look at all the leadership roles you listed earlier. Being a parent is relentlessly challenging. Being a teacher is really hard work. Taking on a counseling role can be emotionally exhausting. And leadership roles in organizations seem to involve an awful lot of bureaucracy and antagonism. Why should I embrace leadership roles rather than avoid them?

ANSWER: If a particular leadership role pushes you away from TSP modes of functioning (as illustrated by motivational patterns such as antagonism, helplessness, or self-absorption), then perhaps you *should* avoid that role. Followers need and deserve to have leaders who are capable of maintaining a focus on others' welfare, and who have the personal strength needed to deal with adversity without losing their emotional control and stability.

And yet, there are *so* many ways that serving others can be a positive, life-sustaining force when the "burden" of leadership is embraced with a TSP mindset. When we focus on others and strive to make their lives better, our thinking is more open-minded and inspired. Our emotional experiences are enriched. We feel better about ourselves. And there is clear evidence that the pursuit of social purpose goals is good for our physical health and well-being.

TSP leadership also contributes to our sense that "life is worth living" in ways that are uniquely powerful, even profound. This psychological experience of *life meaning* is difficult to engineer, and yet it is a natural consequence of engaging in leadership roles like raising children, teaching and mentoring the next generation, and serving as a trusted source of inspiration, guidance, and wisdom in organizations and community settings. Indeed, when people immerse themselves in these kinds of roles, they often experience feelings of life meaning that are uniquely special and transformative.

Bottom line. Are the rigors and responsibilities associated with demanding, high-stress leadership roles "worth it"? For those guided by a TSP motivational orientation, the nearly universal response is "absolutely!" Indeed, many TSP leaders derive so much meaning and purpose from their leadership roles that those roles become a core part of their identity – a "calling" that is as fulfilling as anything they have ever experienced in their lives (Csikszentmihalyi, 2003). And those profound (and often unexpected) feelings of life meaning in turn help motivate people to take on leadership roles that are crucial for promoting the survival and well-being of humanity.

Motivating Self and Others: Final Thoughts

We started this book project with some rather lofty ideas about what we would ideally like to accomplish. We wanted to help people across a wide variety of disciplines, professions, and life circumstances understand how success and well-being naturally flow from goal–life alignment and the development of TSP motivational qualities. We wanted our message about the catalytic role of social purpose in human evolution and human development to be timely in a world that is challenged as never before by threats to survival and well-being. Indeed, it is hard to find a more compelling demonstration of how thriving and social purpose qualities reveal "human motivation at its best" than by looking at the TSP qualities of first responders, medical professionals, and research teams trying to find treatments and vaccines for the SARS-CoV-2 disease. Yet we also wanted this book to be timeless in the sense of providing information and guidance that could help fuel upward spirals of scientific research and practical know-how about human motivation for many years to come.

Our strategy was risky, as we chose to focus on motivation and optimal functioning in *Homo sapiens* rather than concentrating on a particular subgroup or professional context (e.g., education, business, counseling, health care, athletics). Yet that also made sense to us because motivation is at the core of *all* consequential human activity. It is the key to effective parenting. It is at the heart of the teaching and learning process. It is the central dynamic in organizational success. It is the essence of visionary leadership. It is an essential contributor to healing and well-being. In short, motivation is the force that keeps us growing and improving – which we intuitively know because of the way we feel when we are pursuing our core personal goals in alignment with our life circumstances, when we are thriving with social purpose in consequential activities and relationships, and when we are experiencing the abundant life meaning that naturally flows from these achievements.

That is how we are naturally designed. And that is why this book highlights opportunities for "motivating self and others" that are available to us on a daily basis. Within each and every one of us is the power to envision a better future for ourselves and others, and then to take steps to try to transform the things that we have imagined into reality.

CHAPTER 9

Your Toolbox for Motivating Self and Others
Figures, Formulas, and Frameworks You Can Use to Enhance Effectiveness, Well-Being, and Life Meaning in Self and Others

If the only tool you have is a hammer, you tend to see every problem as a nail.

> – Abraham Maslow, *The Psychology of Science: A Reconnaissance*

Life isn't about getting and having, it's about giving and being.

> – author Kevin Kruse

The Big Bet

Scientific understanding of what makes humans naturally successful, coupled with	+	*Self-understanding* of your core personal goals and learned motivational patterns, can provide you with	→	The insights and tools needed to increase your *effectiveness, well-being, and life meaning*

If you make an effort to learn the fundamental science underlying motivation and optimal functioning, and then apply that knowledge to your own personal goals and life circumstances, you will increase your capacity for self-direction as well as your ability to lead – and to help others lead – a more successful and meaningful life.

When people invest themselves in activities that are aligned with their core personal goals, and those goals are infused with *social purpose* and pursued with a *thriving* motivational orientation, they experience greater effectiveness, an enhanced sense of life meaning, and improved health outcomes.

> ## Efforts to Motivate Self and Others Are More Likely to Succeed If They Are Consistent with Basic Human Nature

The fundamental, overarching design principle that best describes "basic human nature" – and which must be respected to empower efforts to motivate self and others – can be summarized as follows:

> *Humans evolved to formulate and selectively pursue goals that, when accomplished, would enhance their survival and well-being, both individually and collectively.*

In other words, we are all designed to be *self-directed*. Within each and every one of us is the power to improve – or even transform – our own lives and the lives of those around us. Our minds and bodies evolved to enable us to engage in self-directed decision-making and action designed to produce desired consequences for self and others. That is why *collaborative facilitation* – not *coercive control* – must be the guiding idea in efforts to motivate self and others. When motivation is sparked, and shaped, and encouraged, it can grow and flourish. In contrast, when motivation is imposed, it tends to be unreliable and short-lived.

Motivational systems evolved first with *primordial goals* and sensors to activate them. Later, organisms became capable of *neuroimaged goals* that they constructed from their life experience. Finally, with the emergence of self-awareness, motivational systems led by self-constructed *personal goals* evolved. This made it possible to not only perceive and remember goal images and ideas, but also to invent and transform them. Ultimately, the escalation of *social purpose goals* in the personal goal hierarchies of our ancient ancestors – empowered by a *thriving* motivational orientation and advanced social-cognitive skills – set the stage for the evolution of our species' most remarkable and uniquely human qualities.

The Motivational Systems Theory (MST) Formula for Human Functioning

In a nutshell, the *effective pursuit of personal goals* (aka human functioning) requires four essential elements:

1. The person must have the *motivation* needed to initiate and maintain goal pursuit until the desired outcome is attained.
2. The person must have the *knowledge and skills* needed to construct and execute actions that will produce the desired outcomes.
3. The person's *biological structure and functioning* must be able to support the motivation and knowledge and skills elements required for successful goal pursuit.
4. The person's *environment* must facilitate, or at least not excessively impede, progress toward the desired outcome.

In MST these ideas are summarized using the formula in Figure 9.1 (see also Chapter 4, Figure 4.1).

$$\text{Human Functioning} = \frac{\text{M} \times \text{K\&S}}{1/\text{Biology}} \times \text{Env}$$

Figure 9.1 The *Motivational Systems Theory* Formula for Human Functioning.
Note: The large-scale components of human systems and the relationships among them can be represented using a heuristic formula that emphasizes the dynamic interactions among motivational processes (M), knowledge and skills (K&S), biological subsystems, and the environment (Env). The formula shows biology as a denominator to emphasize that its primary role is to support the M and K&S components. Biology is represented in reciprocal form since its role is to nourish and strengthen (rather than weaken) the impact of the other components on human functioning.

The Motivational Systems Theory (MST) Formula
for Human Motivation

In MST human motivation is defined as an organized system focused on self-direction. Specifically:

> *Motivation is the organized patterning of the mind's leadership and advising functions:*
> *personal goals* (directive thoughts about desired and undesired potential future states),
> *emotions* (mechanisms that activate goal thoughts and energize and regulate goal pursuit), and
> *personal agency beliefs* (thoughts about the anticipated consequences of pursuing a goal).

This conceptualization of human motivational systems can be summarized using the formula in Figure 9.2 (see also Chapter 4, Figure 4.2).

Motivation (M) = G X PAB X E

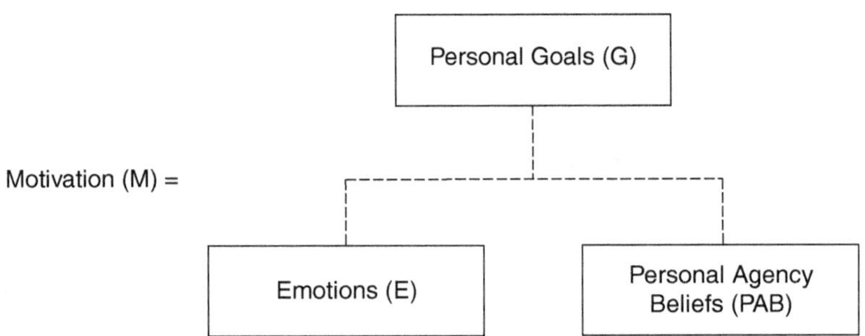

Figure 9.2 The *Motivational Systems Theory* Formula for Human Motivation with an associated diagram.
Note: The components of motivational systems and the relationships among them can be represented using a heuristic formula or a graphical representation. The formula emphasizes the dynamic interactions among personal goals, emotions, and personal agency beliefs. The diagram emphasizes the leadership role played by personal goals in motivational systems, with emotions and personal agency beliefs serving primarily in an advisory capacity.

How the Leadership Team in "Motivational Headquarters" Incorporates the Other Components of Human Functioning

As outlined in Figure 9.3, Motivational Systems Theory affirms that there are two distinct types of personal agency beliefs (see also Chapter 4, Figure 4.5). *Capability beliefs* reflect judgments about whether you have the knowledge, skills and biological capabilities needed to attain a goal. In contrast, *context beliefs* focus on whether the environment will support your efforts to pursue a goal. Personal agency beliefs (PABs) thus make it possible to bring all of the major components of human functioning into the decision-making process in motivational headquarters.

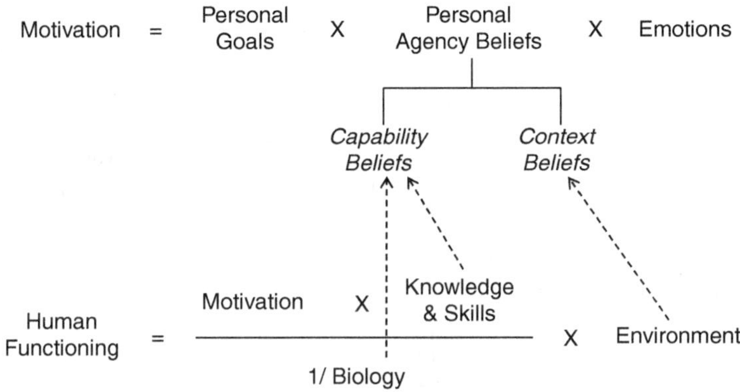

Figure 9.3 Illustration of how appraisals of biological functioning, knowledge and skills, and the environment are represented in "motivational headquarters."

Thoughts about Personal Goals Can Be Categorized into Twenty-Four Different Types of Goal Themes

To assess the strength of each of the twenty-four goal themes in the *Taxonomy of Human Goals*, as detailed in Table 9.1 (see also Chapter 3, Table 3.1), go to https://apg.gmu.edu and take the *Assessment of Personal Goals* (APG).

Table 9.1   *The Ford and Nichols Taxonomy of Human Goals*

Integrative social relationship goals	
Belongingness	Building or maintaining attachments, friendships, intimacy, or a sense of community; avoiding social isolation or separateness
Social responsibility	Keeping interpersonal commitments, meeting social role obligations, and conforming to social and moral rules; avoiding social transgressions and unethical or illegal conduct
Equity	Promoting fairness, justice, or equality; avoiding unfair actions
Resource provision	Giving approval, support, assistance, advice, or validation to others; avoiding selfish or uncaring behavior
Self-assertive social relationship goals	
Individuality	Being unique, special, or different; avoiding similarity or conformity
Self-determination	Being free to act or make choices; avoiding social pressure, constraints, or coercion
Superiority	Comparing favorably to others in terms of winning, status, or success; avoiding unfavorable comparisons with others
Resource acquisition	Obtaining approval, support, assistance, advice, or validation from others; avoiding social disapproval or rejection
Affective feeling goals	
Entertainment	Experiencing feelings of excitement or heightened arousal; avoiding boredom or stressful inactivity
Tranquility	Feeling relaxed and at ease; avoiding stressful overarousal
Happiness	Experiencing feelings of joy, satisfaction, or well-being; avoiding feelings of emotional distress or dissatisfaction

Table 9.1 *(cont.)*

Bodily sensations	Experiencing feelings of pleasure associated with physical sensations, physical movement, or bodily contact; avoiding unpleasant or uncomfortable bodily sensations
Physical well-being	Feeling healthy, energetic, or physically robust; avoiding feelings of lethargy, weakness, or ill health

Cognitive goals

Exploration	Satisfying one's curiosity about personally meaningful events; avoiding a sense of being uninformed or not knowing what's going on
Understanding	Gaining knowledge or making sense out of something; avoiding misconceptions, erroneous beliefs, or confusion
Intellectual creativity	Engaging in activities involving original thinking or novel or interesting ideas; avoiding mindless or familiar ways of thinking
Positive self-evaluations	Maintaining a sense of self-confidence, pride, or self-worth; avoiding a sense of failure, guilt, or incompetence

Task goals

Mastery	Meeting a challenging standard of achievement or improvement; avoiding incompetence, mediocrity, or decrements in performance
Task creativity	Engaging in activities involving artistic expression or creativity; avoiding tasks that do not provide opportunities for creative action
Management	Maintaining order, organization, or productivity in daily life tasks; avoiding sloppiness, inefficiency, or disorganization
Material gain	Increasing the amount of money or tangible goods one has; avoiding the loss of money or material possessions
Safety	Being unharmed, physically secure, and free from risk; avoiding threatening, depriving, or harmful circumstances

Subjective organization goals

Unity	Experiencing a profound or spiritual sense of connectedness, harmony, or oneness with people, nature, or a greater power; avoiding feelings of psychological disunity or disorganization
Transcendence	Experiencing optimal or extraordinary states of functioning; avoiding feeling trapped within the boundaries of ordinary experience

Personal Agency Belief (PAB) Patterns

To identify your "home page" motivational orientation with respect to PABs (see also Chapter 4, Figure 4.6), go to https://apg.gmu.edu and take the *Assessment of Personal Agency Belief Patterns* (APP).

	Strong	A1/A2 Antagonistic or Accepting	T Tenacious	R Robust
Capability Beliefs Expectations about your knowledge and skills and biological resources	*Moderate or Variable*	D Discouraged	C Cautious	E Encouraged
	Negative	H Hopeless	I Insecure	F Fragile
		Negative	*Moderate or Variable*	*Positive*

Context Beliefs

Expectations about the responsiveness of your environment

Figure 9.4 The *Motivational Systems Theory* taxonomy of personal agency belief patterns.

Emotions and Feelings – and How They Are Different

Emotions play out in the theatre of the body. Feelings play out in the theatre of the mind. (Damasio, 2003, p. 28)

Emotions are composed of three subcomponents integrated into a functional unit (D. Ford, 1987/2019). At the heart of each emotion pattern is a *biological* component that supports the energy production and action requirements associated with the pursuit of an activated goal in a particular set of circumstances (e.g., increased or decreased heart rate; accelerated breathing). Emotions also include an *expressive* element, as evidenced by the fact that there are characteristic facial and vocal expressions, gestures, and body language associated with different kinds of emotion patterns. These expressive features help communicate what is being felt to others, which is an important way that people influence how others respond to them. Each emotion pattern also includes an *affective* element. That is the conscious "feeling" part of the emotion that evolved to help sustain its motivational impact.

When emotions are triggered, the motivational response begins at a nonconscious, automatic level. *Feelings* are conscious perceptions that arise from the brain's mapping of the bodily changes caused by the triggering of an emotion (feelings can also arise from nonemotional changes in bodily states). Each feeling typically has a valence – some variation on pleasure or pain. That is why we tend to think of emotions as being "positive" or "negative" even though the feelings associated with each emotion pattern are qualitatively unique. At the core of each feeling is an "idea of the body being in a certain way." Specifically, a feeling is "the perception of a certain state of the body along with the perception of a certain mode of thinking and of thoughts with certain themes" (Damasio, 2003, pp. 85–86).

Some Common Emotions and Their Associated Motivational Functions

A representative list of some of the most commonly studied emotions is provided in Table 9.2. (See Chapter 4, Table 4.1, for an explanation of why a comprehensive emotion taxonomy is not feasible.)

Table 9.2 *The motivational functions of selected emotions*

Emotion pattern	Associated motivational function
Examples of emotions that evolved to facilitate the activation, continuation, or inhibition of behavior	
Happiness	Encourages continuation of effective/rewarding behavior *"YES, we're making progress. This is terrific! I'd like to try that again."*
Sadness	Encourages termination of ineffective/unrewarding behavior *"NO, this just isn't working out. It's bad and I can't do anything about it. I give up."*
Interest	Promotes exploration and information acquisition *"Hey, check this out. I may need to know this. I wonder what would happen if … ?"*
Boredom	Delays or terminates exploration and information acquisition *"This is so irrelevant. I'm just wasting my time. We've been over this a million times."*
Examples of emotions that evolved to help people cope with potentially disruptive or damaging circumstances	
Surprise	Interrupts and refocuses attention *"What's going on here? What in the world … ? You're kidding!"*
Anger	Urges surmounting or removing of obstacles or actions in response to perceived injustice, insult, or encroachment *"This has got to stop. I can't take this anymore! That is totally unfair!"*
Fear	Elicits caution or threat avoidance *"Something bad is about to happen to me. I've got to escape. I'm in danger!"*
Disgust	Urges avoidance of contaminated environments *"This is repulsive. I've never experienced anything so revolting. I can't stand it."*
Examples of emotions that evolved to help facilitate interpersonal bonding and promote cooperation	
Affection/love	Fosters caretaking and the development of committed relationships *"I care about you. We're all in this together. You're part of me."*

Table 9.2 (cont.)

Emotion pattern	Associated motivational function
Loneliness	Fosters social contact and reunion with significant others *"I miss him/her. I need someone to be with me. I feel alone and isolated."*
Shame/Guilt	Encourages conformity with social norms, values, and rules *"I feel so humiliated. I'll never do that again. I need to make amends."*
Contempt	Urges rejection of or efforts to influence transgressors *"You're not like us. You don't belong here. Shape up or ship out!"*
Elevation	Encourages virtuous conduct on behalf of others *"That is inspiring – humanity at its best. I want to follow that example."*

The Thriving with Social Purpose (TSP) Theory of Motivation and Optimal Functioning: Formula for Optimal Human Functioning

---

The primary – and primordial – function of motivation is to *cause us to take actions* that will enhance our *survival with well-being*, including efforts to strengthen and sustain our knowledge and skills, our physical health and capacity, and the responsiveness of the environments in which we pursue our personal goals. Motivation also plays a leadership role in promoting optimal functioning by orchestrating the dynamic changes required to maintain *equipoise* – that is, the effective, context-appropriate balancing and counterbalancing of the multiple forces involved in goal pursuit:

$$\text{Optimal Human Functioning} = \left[\frac{[\text{TSP}]\text{M} \times [\text{GSS}]\text{K\&S}}{1/\,[\text{PHR}]\text{Biology}} \times [\text{R}]\text{Env} \right] \text{Equipoise}$$

Key:

        M = Motivation
     TSP = Thriving with Social Purpose (amplified M infused with Social Purpose [SP] Goals)
     K&S = Knowledge and Skills
     GSS = Goal-Striving Skills (a set of K&S amplifiers)
  Biology = Biological Systems
     PHR = Personal Health Responsibility (a set of Biology amplifiers)
     Env = Environment
  [R]Env = Responsive Environment (amplification through contextual influences)
Equipoise = Dynamic, System–Wide Adaptation to Changing Conditions

---

Elements of a *Thriving* Motivational Pattern

Imagine each element in our motivational system operating at consistently high levels of potency and effectiveness. *Thriving* is the term we have selected to describe what happens when all of the elements in *motivational headquarters* are collectively amplified while also operating in an equipoised manner. When motivational systems are thriving, the personal goal leaders are dynamic and action oriented. The emotion advisors are savvy, insightful, and capable of providing disciplined guidance. The PAB advisors are generally confident and hopeful but also grounded in reality.

Thriving motivational patterns are composed of four different amplifying qualities. An *active approach goal orientation* is what results when the directive function of personal goals is amplified in such a way as to favor action over inaction, and movement toward positive outcomes rather than away from negative outcomes (in contrast to a passive/reactive/avoidant goal orientation). *Personal optimism* and *mindful tenacity* enable us to maintain effort and persistence under a wide array of circumstances, consistent with the Robust, Encouraged, and Tenacious PAB patterns (see Figure 9.4). Finally, *emotional wisdom* integrates the themes associated with an astute, trusted advisor, such as experience, social insight, and prudence:

Amplified Motivation (Thriving) = $[\,[AA]G \times [PO][MT]PAB \times [EW]E\,]$ Equipoise

Key:

$$
\begin{aligned}
G &= \text{Personal Goal} \\
AA &= \text{Active Approach (goal amplifier)} \\
PAB &= \text{Personal Agency Beliefs} \\
PO &= \text{Personal Optimism (capability belief amplifier)} \\
MT &= \text{Mindful Tenacity (context belief amplifier)} \\
E &= \text{Emotions} \\
EW &= \text{Emotional Wisdom (emotion amplifier)} \\
\end{aligned}
$$
Equipoise = Dynamic, System–Wide Adaptation to Changing Conditions

Active Approach: Amplifying Motivation through Strong Self-Leadership

Twenty years from now you will be more disappointed by the things you didn't do than by the ones you did do. So throw off the bowlines. Sail away from safe harbor. Catch the tradewinds in your sails. Explore, Dream, Discover.

– H. Jackson Brown Jr., P.S. I Love You

Personal Optimism: Amplifying Motivation through Confident Self-Assurance

Believe you can and you're halfway there.

          – US president Theodore Roosevelt

Mindful Tenacity: Amplifying Motivation through Creative Persistence

When we tackle obstacles, we find hidden reserves of courage and resilience we did not know we had.

          – Indian president A. P. J. Abdul Kalam

Emotional Wisdom: Amplifying Motivation through Attractive Adaptability

I've learned that people will forget what you said, people will forget what you did, but people will never forget how you made them feel.

          – author and poet Maya Angelou

Emotional wisdom involves several different themes, as summarized in Figure 9.5.

	Self	*Social*
Perception and understanding	Emotional Self-Awareness	Empathy
Control over actions and emotions	Emotional Self-Regulation	Social-Emotional Competence

Figure 9.5 Four facets of emotional wisdom.

Thriving with Social Purpose: Motivation at Its Best

Whereas the benefits of a thriving motivational pattern can be experienced whether people focus on self-enhancing or other-enhancing goal content, the best long-term outcomes for both individuals and groups seem to be associated with the adoption of a *thriving with social purpose* "home page" motivational orientation. TSP is "motivation at its best" because, quite simply, it is the quality of people's functioning that is the most human. Indeed, *TSP is what made us human.*

> *The essence of social purpose is the idea of seeking to accomplish something that is larger than yourself and of benefit to others.*

Some scholars and philosophers have concluded, based on the fact that social purpose originates in the (goal) thoughts of self-directed individuals, that all altruistic actions can be boiled down to self-interest, and social purpose is just some kind of facade. But that conclusion ignores the ways in which our motivational systems are designed. Saying that we only do good things for others because it makes us feel good puts the motivational cart before the horse, so to speak. *All* successful goal pursuit feels good "after the fact." That is our evolved mechanism for ensuring that we continue to take the steps necessary to progress toward important goals and repeat what made us successful in similar future episodes. But when it comes to motivation, what matters is what happens "before the fact" (i.e., before we engage in something that causes us to feel good).

> *Like all goals, social purpose goals are activated by evolved, hardwired emotions that are triggered by some sort of "emotionally competent stimulus."*

Motivation is, by design and by definition, *future oriented.* Social purpose thus reflects the way that we envision ourselves living our lives. It is a natural and authentic manifestation of the way our species evolved. And yet human behavior is malleable. That is why:

> *Whether we think of social purpose as a facade or as a motivationally irreducible part of human nature has a powerful impact on our future.*

This conceptualization of "motivation at its best" is displayed in Figure 9.6 (see also Chapter 5, Figure 5.4), which builds on the MST graphic by adding the four thriving amplifiers along with an "infusion" of SP goal content.

Thriving with Social Purpose (TSP) = [[SP] Thriving] Equipoise

Key:

          SP = Social Purpose (Integrative social relationship goal content)

 Thriving = [AA] G X [PO] [MT] PAB X [EW] E

           G = Personal Goal

        AA = Active Approach (goal amplifier)

     PAB = Personal Agency Beliefs

       PO = Personal Optimism (capability belief amplifier)

       MT = Mindful Tenacity (context belief amplifier)

         E = Emotions

       EW = Emotional Wisdom (emotion amplifier)

 Equipoise = Dynamic, System–Wide Adaptation to Changing Conditions

Thriving with Social Purpose (TSP) =

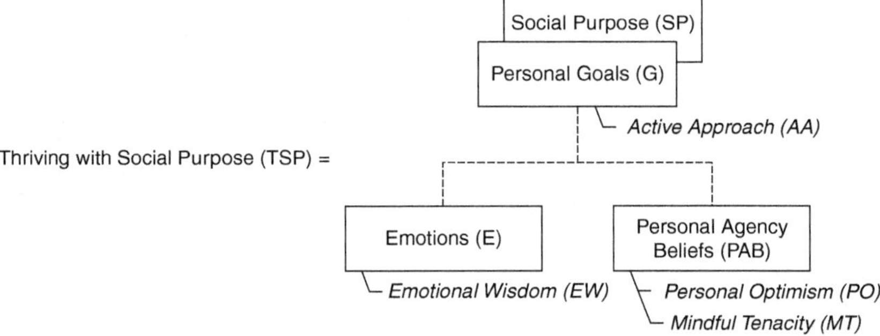

Figure 9.6 *Thriving with Social Purpose:* Formula for "motivation at its (human) best" with an associated diagram.

Note: The elements composing the motivational pattern that is most closely associated with optimal human functioning – Thriving with Social Purpose (TSP) – can be represented using a heuristic formula or diagram that encompasses the amplified motivational components constituting the Thriving pattern of human motivation along with infused Social Purpose goal content.

> ## The Thriving with Social Purpose Theory of Motivation and Optimal Functioning

See Table 9.3 for a unified listing of all the amplifiers that are highlighted in the expanded version of our *TSP Theory of Motivation and Optimal Functioning*. Collecting each of these contributors to optimal functioning together in one table is an effective way to highlight our essential premise that motivating self and others involves the whole person-in-context, not just the "featured cast members" in motivational headquarters.

Table 9.3 *Summary of the TSP Theory of Motivation and Optimal Functioning*

$$\text{Optimal Human Functioning} = \left[\frac{[\text{TSP}]\text{M}\times[\text{GSS}]\text{K\&S}}{1/[\text{PHR}]\text{Biology}} \times [\text{R}]\text{Env}\right]\text{Equipoise}$$

Thriving with Social Purpose (***TSP***)	Motivation (M) amplifiers: • Active Approach • Personal Optimism • Mindful Tenacity • Emotional Wisdom *TSP results when these motivational amplifiers are infused with Social Purpose (i.e., integrative social relationship goal content, including Belongingness, Social Responsibility, Equity, and Resource Provision)*
Goal-Striving Skills (***GSS***)	Knowledge and Skill (K&S) amplifiers: • Intentional Goal Setting • Creative Action Planning • Deliberate Practice and Simulation • Authentic Reflection
Personal Health Responsibility (***PHR***)	Biology amplifiers: • Equipoised Diet • Revitalizing Sleep • Exercise • Relaxation • Individualized Care
Responsive Environment ([***R***]Env)	Environment (Env) amplifiers: • Resource-Rich Physical Environment • High-Quality Tools and Materials • Informative Feedback and Abundant Learning Opportunities

Table 9.3 (*cont.*)

	• Nourishing Social-Emotional Resources • Person–Environment Goodness of Fit
Equipoise	Effective, context-appropriate balancing and counterbalancing of the multiple forces involved in goal pursuit

Note: This table (see also Chapter 5, Table 5.4) summarizes the expanded version of the Thriving with Social Purpose Theory of Motivation and Optimal Functioning. Each row represents one of the five major components of human functioning: (a) motivation, (b) knowledge and skills, (c) biology, (d) environment, and (e) equipoise (a property of the overall functioning of the person-system). Reliable mechanisms for "amplifying" (i.e., enhancing the effectiveness and potency of) human functioning are listed in the right-hand column. Each group of amplifier mechanisms is organized under the heading that appears in the corresponding left-hand column.

The Thriving with Social Purpose Theory of Life Meaning

Table 9.4 summarizes the processes and pathways through which people acquire life meaning.

Table 9.4 *Summary of the Thriving with Social Purpose Theory of Life Meaning*

Column 1	Column 2	Column 3	Column 4
How people strive for life meaning:	What produces feelings of life meaning:	How *Thriving* can increase feelings of life meaning:	How *Social Purpose* can increase feelings of life meaning:
Goal–life alignment	Connections between daily activities and core personal goals	Engagement	Belongingness
Existential interpretations	Personal identity Spirituality Uplifting experiences	Goal progress Lasting contributions	Resource provision Equity
Cultural interpretations	Values/ethical principles Religiousness Ideology/philosophy	Affirmation	Social responsibility
People strive for life meaning by pursuing core personal goals and by seeking clarifying and comforting interpretations of life experiences.	*Feelings of life meaning can be reliably produced by following these potentially inspiring and enlightening pathways.*	*Thriving helps people strive for life meaning by amplifying the motivational impact of pathways that are capable of producing feelings of life meaning.*	*Social Purpose helps people strive for life meaning by amplifying the salience of personal goals focused on human connections.*

Note: Life meaning is a distinctive feeling that arises when a person believes that their life makes sense, has purpose, and is worthwhile (see also Chapter 7, Table 7.1). This figure displays three fundamental ways that humans strive for life meaning (column 1), with some corresponding pathways through which feelings of life meaning can be experienced (column 2). These pathways represent important domains of human endeavor that have endured over time as potent sources of life meaning. Thriving and Social Purpose contribute to life meaning by amplifying the motivational impact of those pathways (columns 3 and 4, respectively). Note that the boundaries between these life meaning pathways are "porous" – that is, efforts to seek life meaning through one set of pathways can influence other pathways and become integrated components of an individual's personality (e.g., as when religious beliefs become a central part of a person's identity, or cultural values become connected to an individual's core personal goals). Similarly, the impact of Thriving motivational patterns and SP goal content can reverberate across different life meaning pathways.

Seven Guiding Principles for Motivating Self and Others

Table 9.5 summarizes the major themes involved in motivating self and others. Each guiding principle is outlined using a succinct, one-sentence definition along with a summary description designed to clarify the meaning and importance of each principle.

Table 9.5 *Seven guiding principles for motivating self and others derived from the Thriving with Social Purpose Theory of Motivation and Optimal Functioning*

Principle		Definition
1.	*The Principle of Evolved Human Nature*	*Efforts to motivate self and others can best succeed if they are consistent with basic human nature.* People are more likely to respond favorably when efforts to strengthen motivation respect the fact that humans are self-directed yet highly interdependent; are creatures of habit yet capable of creative thought and action; and are influenced by context and culture yet led by motivational systems comprising personal goals, emotions, and personal agency beliefs. In contrast, efforts to motivate self and others are likely to fail if you assume that significant change is impossible; or that you don't need to consider others' personal goals and life circumstances; or that everyone will respond in the same way to a motivational incentive or contingency; or that people are only motivated by self-interest.
2.	*The Principle of Goal–Life Alignment*	*Motivation is enriched when daily life activities and important social relationships afford the attainment of core personal goals, and when self-awareness of such goals empowers you to make wise choices about future opportunities.* The sense of clarity and integrity that flows from this alignment between core personal goals and consequential decisions and actions enables people to be more productive and to experience more abundant feelings of life meaning. Goal–life alignment is facilitated by an active approach goal orientation that promotes exploration, openness to change, and personal growth and by contexts that afford the pursuit of multiple goal opportunities.
3.	*The Principle of Accurate and Hopeful Personal Agency Beliefs*	*To develop and sustain strong motivational patterns, you must have a fundamental belief that the future can be better than the present but also perceptions about current circumstances that are accurate and realistic.* Hope requires faith in yourself (capability beliefs) as well as

Table 9.5 (*cont.*)

Principle	Definition
	faith in the people and resources you depend upon (context beliefs). Motivation is enhanced by welcoming feedback (both affirming and corrective) that can improve knowledge and skills, the accuracy of perceptions, and expectations about goal progress. The key is to maintain a generally optimistic but also experientially grounded view of future possibilities.
4. *The Principle of Emotional Wisdom*	*Your emotions can help you make wise choices and manage challenging situations, but only if you can assess whether they make sense given your current circumstances and then use those insights to make appropriate adjustments.* The self-oriented part of emotional wisdom requires authentic *self-awareness* and fluent emotional understanding as well as the ability to ratchet emotions up and down to meet situational demands and opportunities (*emotional self-regulation*). The social part of emotional wisdom involves the (mostly automatic) detection and triggering of the emotions that others are experiencing (*empathy*) at an amplitude that is motivationally impactful, and then acting on those emotions in contextually appropriate ways (*social-emotional competence*).
5. *The Principle of Equipoised Social Purpose*	*Motivation is enhanced when people seek to accomplish things that are larger than themselves and of benefit to others, assuming they do not neglect their own needs.* Humans are "wired" to cooperate and to help others, especially those with whom they share social bonds. Concern for others must be properly balanced with concern for self, however. This equipoised form of social purpose is a powerful and reliable source of energy and life meaning, especially when combined with a thriving motivational orientation.
6. *The Principle of Unitary System Functioning*	*Efforts to motivate self and others will be more effective if they are framed within a "big picture" developmental perspective that encompasses not only goals, emotions, and personal agency beliefs but also knowledge and skills, biological functions, and environmental circumstances.* A person *always* functions as an integrated unit, with dynamic interconnections that are both abundant and powerful. Consistent with that premise, there are many pathways through which motivation can be facilitated, including pathways that do not attempt to influence motivational processes directly – for example, those that rely on efforts to strengthen goal-striving skills, personal health responsibility, or environmental responsiveness.

Table 9.5 *(cont.)*

Principle	Definition
7. *The Principle of TSP Leadership*	*People respond favorably to leaders who pursue goals with an active approach orientation, personal optimism, mindful tenacity, and emotional wisdom (the thriving motivational pattern) and are guided by an authentic concern for the welfare of others (social purpose).* When someone in a leadership role is thriving with social purpose, people intuitively sense the leader's positive energy and genuine desire to help and are naturally drawn to those qualities. Compared to the kind of leadership associated with dominance hierarchies (which remains a salient part of our evolutionary heritage and is potentially adaptive in special circumstances), TSP leadership is much more likely to promote long-term trust, commitment, and effective teamwork.

References

Abramson, L. Y., Seligman, M. E. P., & Teasdale, J. D. (1978). Learned helplessness in humans: Critique and reformulation. *Journal of Abnormal Psychology*, *87*(1), 49–74. https://doi.org/10.1037/0021-843X.87.1.49

Agyeman, A. A., & Ofori-Asenso, R. (2015). Perspective: Does personalized medicine hold the future for medicine? *Journal of Pharmacy & BioAllied Sciences*, *7*(3), 239–244. https://doi.org/10.4103/0975–7406.160040

Ainsworth, M. D. S., Blehar, M. C., Waters, E., & Wall, S. (1978). *Patterns of attachment: A psychological study of the strange situation*. Hillsdale, NJ: Erlbaum.

Aknin, L. B., Barrington-Leigh, C. P., Dunn, E. W., Helliwell, J. F., Burns, J., Biswas-Diener, R., Kemeza, . . . Norton, M. I. (2013). Prosocial spending and well-being: Cross-cultural evidence for a psychological universal. *Journal of Personality and Social Psychology*, *104*(4), 635–652. https://doi.org/10.1037/a0031578

Aldwin, C. M. (2007). *Stress, coping, and development: An integrative perspective* (2nd ed.). New York: Guilford.

Algoe, S. B., & Haidt, J. (2009). Witnessing excellence in action: The "other-praising" emotions of elevation, gratitude, and admiration. *The Journal of Positive Psychology*, *4*(2), 105–127. https://doi.org/10.1080/17439760802650519

Amabile, T. M. (1996). *Creativity in context*. Boulder, CO: Westview.

Ames, C. (1992). Classrooms: Goals, structures, and student motivation. *Journal of Educational Psychology*, *84*(3), 261–271. https://doi.org/10.1037/0022-0663.84.3.261

Angier, N. (2009, December 22). Sorry vegans: Brussel sprouts like to live, too. *New York Times*, p. D2.

Antonovsky, A. (1990). Personality and health: Testing the sense of coherence model. In H. S. Friedman (Ed.), *Personality and disease* (pp. 155–177). New York: John Wiley.

Arend, R. A., Gove, F. L., & Sroufe, L. A. (1979). Continuity of individual adaptation from infancy to kindergarten: A predictive study of ego-resiliency and curiosity in preschoolers. *Child Development*, *50*(4), 950–959. https://doi.org/10.2307/1129319

Arsenio, W. F., & Ford, M. E. (1985). The role of affective information in social-cognitive development: Children's differentiation of moral and conventional events. *Merrill-Palmer Quarterly*, *31*(1), 1–17.

Ashmore, R. D., Jussim, L., & Wilder, D. (Eds.). (2001). *Social identity, intergroup conflict, and conflict reduction.* Oxford: Oxford University Press.

Aspinwall, L. G., & Staudinger, U. M. (Eds.). (2003). *A psychology of human strengths: Fundamental questions and future directions for a positive psychology.* Washington, DC: American Psychological Association. https://doi.org/10.1037/10566-000

Austin, J. T., & Vancouver, J. B. (1996). Goal constructs in psychology: Structure, process, and content. *Psychological Bulletin, 120*(3), 338–375. https://doi.org/10.1037/0033-2909.120.3.338

Avolio, B. J., Gardner, W. L., Walumbwa, F. O., Luthans, F., & May, D. R. (2004). Unlocking the mask: A look at the process by which authentic leaders impact follower attitudes and behaviors. *The Leadership Quarterly, 15*(6), 801–823. https://doi.org/10.1016/j.leaqua.2004.09.003

Bakan, D. (1966). *The duality of human existence.* Boston: Beacon Press.

Bakker, A. B., & Schaufeli, W. B. (2008). Positive organizational behavior: Engaged employees in flourishing organizations. *Journal of Organizational Behavior, 29*(2), 147–154. https://doi.org/10.1002/job.515

Balliet, D., & Van Lange, P. A. M. (2013). Trust, conflict, and cooperation: A meta-analysis. *Psychological Bulletin, 139*(5), 1090–1112. https://doi.org/10.1037/a0030939

Bandura, A. (1977). Self-efficacy: Toward a unifying theory of behavior change. *Psychological Review, 84*(2), 191–215. https://doi.org/10.1037/0033-295X.84.2.191

Bandura, A. (1982). Self-efficacy mechanism in human agency. *American Psychologist, 37*(2), 122–147. https://doi.org/10.1037/0003-066X.37.2.122

Bandura, A. (1986). *Social foundations of thought and action: A social cognitive theory.* Englewood Cliffs, NJ: Prentice Hall.

Bandura, A. (Ed.). (1995). *Self-efficacy in changing societies.* Cambridge: Cambridge University Press. https://doi.org/10.1017/cbo9780511527692

Bandura, A. (1997). *Self-efficacy: The exercise of control.* New York: Freeman.

Bandura A. (2005). The evolution of social cognitive theory. In K. G. Smith & M. A. Hitt (Eds.), *Great minds in management* (pp. 9–35). Oxford: Oxford University Press.

Bandura, A. (2019). Applying theory for human betterment. *Perspectives on Psychological Science, 14*(1), 12–15. https://doi.org/10.1177/1745691618815165

Bandura, A., & Cervone, D. (1986). Differential engagement of self-reactive influences in cognitive motivation. *Organizational Behavior and Human Decision Processes, 38*(1), 92–113. https://doi.org/10.1016/0749-5978(86)90028-2

Barclay, P. (2010). *Reputation and the evolution of generous behavior.* New York: Nova Science.

Barefoot, J. C., Maynard, K. E., Beckham, J. C., Brummett, B. H., Hooker, K., & Siegler, I. C. (1998). Trust, health, and longevity. *Journal of Behavioral Medicine, 21*(6), 517–526. https://doi.org/10.1023/A:1018792528008

Bargh, J. A. (2002). Losing consciousness: Automatic influences on consumer judgment, behavior, and motivation. *Journal of Consumer Research, 29*(2), 280–285. https://doi.org/10.1086/341577

Bargh, J. A. (2017). *Before you know it: The unconscious reasons we do what we do.* New York: Atria. https://doi.org/10.1080/00207411.2018.1439561

Bargh, J. A., & Barndollar, K. (1996). Automaticity in action: The unconscious as repository of chronic goals and motives. In P. M. Gollwitzer & J. A. Bargh (Eds.), *The psychology of action: Linking cognition and motivation to behavior* (pp. 457–481). New York: Guilford.

Barnes, C. M., & Drake, C. L. (2015). Prioritizing sleep health: Public health policy recommendations. *Perspectives on Psychological Science, 10*(6), 733–737. https://doi.org/10.1177/1745691615598509

Bar-On, R. (2006). The Bar-On model of emotional-social intelligence (ESI). *Psicothema, 18*, 13–25.

Barrett, L. F., Adolphs, R., Marsella, S., Martinez, A. M., & Pollak, S. (2019). Emotional expressions reconsidered: Challenges to inferring emotion from human facial movements. *Psychological Science in the Public Interest, 20*(1), 1–68. https://doi.org/10.1177/1529100619832930

Batson, C. D. (2011). *Altruism in humans.* Oxford: Oxford University Press.

Batson, C. D., Ahmad, N., Lishner, D. A., & Tsang, J. (2002). Empathy and altruism. In C. R. Snyder & S. J. Lopez (Eds.), *Handbook of positive psychology* (pp. 485–498). Oxford: Oxford University Press.

Baumeister, R. F. (1990). Suicide as escape from self. *Psychological Review, 97*(1), 90–113. https://doi.org/10.1037/0033-295X.97.1.90

Baumeister, R. F. (1991). *Meanings in life.* New York: Guilford.

Baumeister, R. F. (2016). Toward a general theory of motivation: Problems, challenges, opportunities, and the big picture. *Motivation and Emotion, 40*(1), 1–10. https://doi.org/10.1007/s11031-015–9521-y

Baumeister, R. F., & Leary, M. R. (1995). The need to belong: Desire for interpersonal attachments as a fundamental human motivation. *Psychological Bulletin, 117*(3), 497–529. https://doi.org/10.1037/0033-2909.117.3.497

Baumeister, R. F., & Tierney, J. (2011). *Willpower.* New York: Penguin.

Baumeister, R. F., & Vohs, K. D. (2002). The pursuit of meaningfulness in life. In C. R. Snyder & S. J. Lopez (Eds.), *Handbook of positive psychology* (pp. 608–618). Oxford: Oxford University Press.

Baumeister, R. F., Vohs, K. D., Aakerc, J. L., & Garbinsky, E. N. (2013). Some key differences between a happy life and a meaningful life. *The Journal of Positive Psychology, 8*(6), 505–516. https://doi.org/10.1080/17439760.2013.830764

Baumgartner, T., Heinrichs, M., Vonlanthen, A., Fischbacher, U., & Fehr, E. (2008). Oxytocin shapes the neural circuitry of trust and trust adaptation in humans. *Neuron, 58*(4), 639–650. https://doi.org/10.1016/j.neuron.2008.04.009

Baumrind, D. (1978). Parental disciplinary patterns and social competence in children. *Youth and Society, 9*(3), 239–276. https://doi.org/10.1177/0044118X7800900302

Becker, D. V., & Srinivasan, N. (2014). The vividness of the happy face. *Current Directions in Psychological Science, 23*(3), 189–194. https://doi.org/10.1177/0963721414533702

Begley, S. (2007). *Train your mind, change your brain: How a new science reveals our extraordinary potential to transform ourselves.* New York: Ballantine.

Bembenutty, H., Cleary, T. J., & Kitsantas, A. (Eds.). (2013). *Applications of self-regulated learning across diverse disciplines: A tribute to Barry J. Zimmerman.* Charlotte, NC: Information Age.

Bennett, G. G., Merritt, M. M., Sollers, J. J., & Edwards, C. (2004). Stress, coping, and health outcomes among African-Americans: A review of the John Henryism hypothesis. *Psychology and Health, 19*(3), 369–383. https://doi.org/10.1080/0887044042000193505

Benson, H. (1975). *The relaxation response.* New York: William Morrow.

Benton, D., & Young, H. A. (2017). Reducing caloric intake may not help you lose weight. *Perspectives on Psychological Science, 12*(5), 703–714. https://doi.org/10.1177/1745691617690878

Bergin, C. A. C. (2019). Prosocial development in toddlers: The patterning of mother-infant interaction. In M. E. Ford & D. H. Ford (Eds.), *Humans as self-constructing living systems: Putting the framework to work* (Routledge psychology library editions: Personality, pp. 121–143). New York: Routledge. (Original work published 1987) https://doi.org/10.4324/9780429025297-4

Bergin, D. A. (1989). Student goals for out-of-school learning activities. *Journal of Adolescent Research, 4*(1), 92–109. https://doi.org/10.1177/074355488941007

Berlyne, D. E. (1971). Arousal and reinforcement. In *Nebraska Symposium on Motivation* (Vol. 15, pp. 1–110). Lincoln: University of Nebraska Press.

Bernard, L. C., Mills, M., Swenson, L., & Walsh, R. P. (2005). An evolutionary theory of human motivation. *Genetic, Social, and General Psychology Monographs, 131*(2), 129–184. https://doi.org/10.3200/MONO.131.2.129–184

Berridge, K. C. (2003). Comparing the emotional brain of humans and other animals. In R. J. Davidson, H. H. Goldsmith, & K. Scherer (Eds.), *Handbook of affective sciences* (pp. 25–51). Oxford: Oxford University Press.

Block, J. H., & Block, J. (1980). The role of ego-resiliency and ego-control in the organization of behavior. In W. A. Collins (Ed.), *Minnesota symposia on child psychology* (Vol. 13, pp. 39–101). Hillsdale, NJ: Erlbaum.

Boehm, C. (2000). Conflict and the evolution of social control. *Journal of Consciousness Studies, 7*(1–2), 79–101.

Boehm, C. (2012). *Moral origins: The evolution of virtue, altruism, and shame.* New York: Basic Books.

Boekaerts, M., de Koning, E., & Vedder, P. (2006). Goal-directed behavior and contextual factors in the classroom: An innovative approach to the study of multiple goals. *Educational Psychologist, 41*(1), 33–51. https://doi.org/10.1207/s15326985ep4101_5

Boekaerts, M., Pintrich, P. R., & Zeidner, M. (Eds.). (2000). *Handbook of self-regulation: Theory, research and applications.* San Diego, CA: Academic Press.

Boekaerts, M., Smit, K., & Busing, F. (2012). Salient goals direct and energise students' actions in the classroom. *Applied Psychology, 61*(4), 520–539. https://doi.org/10.1111/j.1464-0597.2012.00504.x

Bonanno, G. A., & Burton, C. L. (2013). Regulatory flexibility: An individual differences perspective on coping and emotion regulation. *Perspectives on Psychological Science, 8*(6), 591–612. https://doi.org/10.1177/1745691613504116

Boothby, E. J., Clark, M. S., & Bargh, J. A. (2014). Shared experiences are amplified. *Psychological Science, 25*(12), 2209–2216. https://doi.org/10.1177/0956797614551162

Bower, G. H. (1981). Mood and memory. *American Psychologist, 36*(2), 129–148. https://doi.org/10.1037/0003-066X.36.2.129

Bowlby, J. (1969). *Attachment and loss: Vol. 1. Attachment.* New York: Basic Books.

Bowlby, J. (1973). *Attachment and loss: Vol. 2. Separation, anxiety, and anger.* New York: Basic Books.

Bowlby, J. (1988). Developmental psychiatry comes of age. *The American Journal of Psychiatry, 145*(1), 1–10. https://doi.org/10.1176/ajp.145.1.1

Boyle, P. A., Barnes, L. L., Buchman, A. S., & Bennett, D. A. (2009). Purpose in life is associated with mortality among community-dwelling older persons. *Psychosomatic Medicine, 71*(5), 574–579. https://doi.org/10.1097/PSY.0b013e3181a5a7c0

Brady, S. T., Reeves, S. L., Garcia, J., Purdie-Vaughns, V., Cook, J. E., Taborsky-Barba, S., . . . Cohen, G. L. (2016). The psychology of the affirmed learner: Spontaneous self-affirmation in the face of stress. *Journal of Educational Psychology, 108*(3), 353–373. https://doi.org/10.1037/edu0000091

Brassai, L., Piko, B. F., & Steger, M. F. (2011). Meaning in life: Is it a protective factor for adolescents' psychological health? *International Journal of Behavioral Medicine, 18*(1), 44–51. https://doi.org/10.1007/s12529-010-9089-6

Brehm, J. W. (1972). *Responses to loss of freedom: A theory of psychological reactance.* Morristown, NJ: General Learning Press.

Brewer, M. B. (2004). Taking the social origins of human nature seriously: Toward a more imperialist social psychology. *Personality and Social Psychology Review, 8*(2), 107–113. https://doi.org/10.1207/s15327957pspr0802_3

Brickman, P., & Campbell, D. T. (1971). Hedonic relativism and planning the good science. In M. H. Appley (Ed.), *Adaptation level theory: A symposium* (pp. 287–302). New York: Academic Press.

Bronk, K. C. (2014). *Purpose in life: A critical component of optimal youth development.* New York: Springer. https://doi.org/10.1007/978-94-007-7491-9

Brophy, J. (1981). Teacher praise: A functional analysis. *Review of Educational Research, 51*(1), 5–32. https://doi.org/10.3102/00346543051001005

Brosnan, S. F., & de Waal, F. B. M. (2003). Monkeys reject unequal pay. *Nature, 425*(6955), 297–299. https://doi.org/10.1038/nature01963

Brown, S. L., & Brown, R. M. (2006). Selective investment theory: Recasting the functional significance of close relationships. *Psychological Inquiry, 17*(1), 1–29. https://doi.org/10.1207/s15327965pli1701_01

Brown, S. L., Brown, R. M., Schiavone, A., & Smith, D. M. (2007). Close relationships and health through the lens of selective investment theory. In S. G. Post (Ed.), *Altruism and health: Perspectives from empirical research* (pp.

299–313). Oxford: Oxford University Press. https://doi.org/10.1093/acprof:oso/9780195182910.003.0020

Brown, S. L., Nesse, R. M., Vinokur, A. D., & Smith, D. M. (2003). Providing social support may be more beneficial than receiving it: Results from a prospective study of mortality. *Psychological Science, 14*(4), 320–327. https://doi.org/10.1111/1467-9280.14461

Brummelman, E., Nelemans, S. A., Thomaes, S., & de Castro, B. O. (2017). When parents' praise inflates, children's self-esteem deflates. *Child Development, 88*(6), 1799–1809. https://doi.org/10.1111/cdev.12936

Buckley, W. (1967). *Sociology and modern systems theory.* Englewood Cliffs, NJ: Prentice Hall.

Buckner, R. L., Andrews-Hanna, J. R., & Schacter, D. L. (2008). The brain's default network: Anatomy, function, and relevance to disease. *Annals of the New York Academy of Sciences, 1124*(1), 1–38. https://doi.org/10.1196/annals.1440.011

Buss, D. M. (1989). Sex differences in human mate preferences: Evolutionary hypotheses tested in 37 cultures. *Behavioral and Brain Sciences, 12*(1), 1–14. https://doi.org/10.1017/S0140525X00023992

Buysse, D. J. (2014). Sleep health: Can we define it? Does it matter? *Sleep, 37*(1), 9–17. https://doi.org/10.5665/sleep.3298

Cacioppo, J. T., Visser, P. S., & Pickett, C. L. (Eds.). (2006). *Social neuroscience: People thinking about people.* Cambridge, MA: MIT Press. https://doi.org/10.7551/mitpress/6304.001.0001

Cameron, K. S., Dutton, J. E., & Quinn, R. E. (Eds.). (2003). *Positive organizational scholarship.* San Francisco: Berrett-Koehler.

Campbell, A. (2010). Oxytocin and human social behavior. *Personality and Social Psychology Review, 14*(3), 281–295. https://doi.org/10.1177/1088868310363594

Cantor, N., & Fleeson, W. (1991). Life tasks and self-regulatory processes. In M. L. Maehr & P. R. Pintrich (Eds.), *Advances in motivation and achievement* (Vol. 7, pp. 327–369). Greenwich, CT: JAI.

Carlson, E. N. (2013). Overcoming the barriers to self-knowledge: Mindfulness as a path to seeing yourself as you really are. *Perspectives on Psychological Science, 8*(2), 173–186. https://doi.org/10.1177/1745691612462584

Carver, C. S. (2004). Self-regulation of action and affect. In R. F. Baumeister & K. D. Vohs (Eds.), *Handbook of self-regulation: Research, theory, and applications* (pp. 13–39). New York: Guilford.

Carver, C. S., & Scheier, M. F. (1981). *Attention and self-regulation: A control-theory approach to human behavior.* New York: Springer.

Carver, C. S., & Scheier, M. F. (1998). *On the self-regulation of behavior.* Cambridge: Cambridge University Press. https://doi.org/10.1017/cbo9781139174794

Carver, C. S., & Scheier, M. F. (2014). Dispositional optimism. *Trends in Cognitive Sciences, 18*(6), 293–299. https://doi.org/10.1016/j.tics.2014.02.003

Chamberlain, K., Petrie, K., & Azariah, R. (1992). The role of optimism and sense of coherence in predicting recovery following surgery. *Psychology and Health, 7*(4), 301–310. https://doi.org/10.1080/08870449208403159

Chevalier, N. (2015). Executive function development: Making sense of the environment to behave adaptively. *Current Directions in Psychological Science, 24*(5), 363–368. https://doi.org/10.1177/0963721415593724

Chida, Y., & Steptoe, A. (2008). Positive psychological well-being and mortality: A quantitative review of prospective observational studies. *Psychosomatic Medicine, 70*(7), 741–756. https://doi.org/10.1097/PSY.0b013e31818105ba

Christoff, K., Gordon, A. M., Smallwood, J., Smith, R., & Schooler, J. W. (2009). Experience sampling during fMRI reveals default network and executive system contributions to mind wandering. *Proceedings of the National Academy of Sciences of the USA, 106*(21), 8719–8724. https://doi.org/10.1073/pnas.0900234106

Chulef, A. S., Read, S. J., & Walsh, D. A. (2001). A hierarchical taxonomy of human goals. *Motivation and Emotion, 5*(3), 191–232. https://doi.org/10.1023/A:1012225223418

Clark, D. M., & Kissane, D. W. (2002). Demoralization: Its phenomenology and importance. *Australian and New Zealand Journal of Psychiatry, 36*(6), 733–742. https://doi.org/10.1046/j.1440-1614.2002.01086.x

Clift, J. (2003). The lab man: How experimental economics emerged from the shadows. *Finance and Development, 40*(1). Retrieved from www.imf.org/external/pubs/ft/fandd/2003/03/clif.htm

Cohen, S., & Wills, T. A. (1985). Stress, social support, and the buffering hypothesis. *Psychological Bulletin, 98*(2), 310–357. https://doi.org/10.1037/0033-2909.98.2.310

Colcombe, S., & Kramer, A. F. (2003). Fitness effects on the cognitive function of older adults: A meta-analytic study. *Psychological Science, 14*(2), 125–130. https://doi.org/10.1111/1467-9280.t01-1-01430

Collins, J. (2001). *From good to great.* New York: HarperBusiness.

Cordaro, D. T., Sun, R., Keltner, D., Kamble, S., Huddar, N., & McNeil, G. (2018). Universals and cultural variations in 22 emotional expressions across five cultures. *Emotion, 18*(1), 75–93. https://doi.org/10.1037/emo0000302

Correia, S. P. C., Dickinson, A., & Clayton, N. S. (2007). Western scrub-jays anticipate future needs independently of their current motivational state. *Current Biology, 17*(10), 856–861. https://doi.org/10.1016/j.cub.2007.03.063

Covey, S. R. (1989). *The 7 habits of highly effective people: Powerful lessons in personal change.* New York: Free Press.

Covington, M. V. (1992). *Emotion, motivation and cognition in school achievement.* New York: Cambridge University Press.

Cowan, N. (2001). The magical number 4 in short-term memory: A reconsideration of memory storage capacity. *Behavioral and Brain Sciences, 24*(1), 87–114. https://doi.org/10.1017/S0140525X01003922

Cowen, A. S., & Keltner, D. (2017). Self-report captures 27 distinct categories of emotion bridged by continuous gradients. *Proceedings of the National Academy of Sciences of the USA, 114*(38), E7900–E7909. https://doi.org/10.1073/pnas.1702247114

Cowen, A. S., Sauter, D., Tracy, J. L., & Keltner, D. (2019). Mapping the passions: Toward a high-dimensional taxonomy of emotional experience and expression. *Psychological Science in the Public Interest, 20*(1), 69–90. https://doi.org/10.1177/1529100619850176

Critcher, C. R., & Lee, C. J. (2018). Feeling is believing: Inspiration encourages belief in God. *Psychological Science, 29*(5), 723–737. https://doi.org/10.1177/0956797617743017

Csikszentmihalyi, M. (1975). *Beyond boredom and anxiety.* San Francisco: Jossey-Bass.

Csikszentmihalyi, M. (1991). *Flow: The psychology of optimal experience.* New York: HarperCollins.

Csikszentmihalyi, M. (2003). *Good business: Leadership, flow, and the making of meaning.* New York: Viking Penguin.

Czekierda, K., Banik, A., Park, C. L., & Luszczynska, A. (2017). Meaning in life and physical health: Systematic review and meta-analysis. *Health Psychology Review, 11*(4), 387–418. https://doi.org/10.1080/17437199.2017.1327325

Dai, H., Milkman, K. L., & Riis, J. (2015). Put your imperfections behind you: Temporal landmarks spur goal initiation when they signal new beginnings. *Psychological Science, 26*(12), 1927–1936. https://doi.org/10.1177/0956797615605818

Daly, M., Delaney, L., Egan, M., & Baumeister, R. F. (2015). Childhood self-control and unemployment throughout the life span: Evidence from two British cohort studies. *Psychological Science, 26*(6), 709–723. https://doi.org/10.1177/0956797615569001

Damasio, A. (1994). *Descartes' error: Emotion, reason, and the human brain.* New York: Grosset/Putnam.

Damasio, A. (2003). *Looking for Spinoza: Joy, sorrow, and the feeling brain.* Orlando, FL: Harcourt.

Damon, W. (2008). *The path to purpose: How young people find their calling in life.* New York: Free Press.

Damon, W., Menon, J., & Bronk, K. C. (2003). The development of purpose during adolescence. *Applied Developmental Science, 7*(3), 119–128. https://doi.org/10.1207/S1532480XADS0703_2

Davidson, R. J., Kabat-Zinn, J., Schumacher, J., Rosenkranz, M., Muller, D., Santorelli, S. F., . . . Sheridan, J. F. (2003). Alterations in brain and immune function produced by mindfulness meditation. *Psychosomatic Medicine, 65*(4), 564–570. https://doi.org/10.1097/01.PSY.0000077505.67574.E3

Dawkins, R. (1976). *The selfish gene.* Oxford: Oxford University Press.

Dean, L. G., Kendal, R. L., Schapiro, S. J., Thierry, B., & Laland, K. N. (2012). Identification of the social and cognitive processes underlying human cumulative culture. *Science, 335*(6072), 1114–1118. https://doi.org/10.1126/science.1213969

deCharms, R. (1968). *Personal causation.* New York: Academic Press.

Deci, E. L. (1980). *The psychology of self-determination.* Lexington, MA: Heath.

Deci, E. L., Koestner, R., & Ryan, R. M. (1999). A meta-analytic review of experiments examining the effects of extrinsic rewards on intrinsic motivation. *Psychological Bulletin, 125*(6), 627–668. https://doi.org/10.1037/00 33-2909.125.6.627

Deci, E. L., & Ryan, R. M. (1985). *Intrinsic motivation and self-determination in human behavior.* New York: Plenum. https://doi.org/10.1007/978-1-489 9-2271-7

DeLoache, J. S., Simcock, G., & Macari, S. (2007). Planes, trains, automobiles – and tea sets: Extremely intense interests in very young children. *Developmental Psychology, 43*(6), 1579–1586. https://doi.org/10.1037/0012-16 49.43.6.1579

Denton, D. (2005). *The primordial emotions: The dawning of consciousness.* Oxford: Oxford University Press. https://doi.org/10.1093/acprof:oso/9780199203147 .001.0001

de Quervain, D. J. F., Fischbacher, U., Treyer, V., Schellhammer, M., Schnyder, U., Buck, A., & Fehr, E. (2004). The neural basis of altruistic punishment. *Science, 305*(5688), 1254–1258. https://doi.org/10.1126/science .1100735

DeSteno, D., Breazeal, C., Frank, R. H., Pizarro, D., Baumann, J., Dickens, L., & Lee, J. J. (2012). Detecting the trustworthiness of novel partners in economic exchange. *Psychological Science, 23*(12), 1549–1556. https://doi.org/10.1177 /0956797612448793

de Vignemont, F., & Singer, T. (2006). The empathic brain: How, when and why? *Trends in Cognitive Sciences, 10*(10), 435–441. https://doi.org/10.1016/j .tics.2006.08.008

de Waal, F. B. M. (1996). *Good natured: The origins of right and wrong in humans and other animals.* Cambridge, MA: Harvard University Press.

de Waal, F. B. M. (2006). *Primates and philosophers: How morality evolved.* Princeton, NJ: Princeton University Press. https://doi.org/10.1515 /9781400830336

de Waal, F. B. M. (2009). *The age of empathy: Nature's lessons for a kinder society.* New York: Harmony Books.

Diener, E. (Ed.). (2009). *The science of well-being: The collected works of Ed Diener.* New York: Springer. https://doi.org/10.1007/978-90-481-2350-6

Diener, E., & Fujita, F. (1995). Resources, personal strivings, and subjective well-being: A nomothetic and idiographic approach. *Journal of Personality and Social Psychology, 68*(5), 926–935. https://doi.org/10.1037/0022-3514 .68.5.926

Diener, E., Lucas, R. E., & Scollon, C. N. (2006). Beyond the hedonic treadmill: Revising the adaptation theory of well-being. *American Psychologist, 61*(4), 305–314. https://doi.org/10.1037/0003-066x.61.4.305

Dijksterhuis, A., Smith, P. K., van Baaren, R. P., & Wigboldus, D. H. J. (2005). The unconscious consumer: Effects of environment on consumer behavior. *Journal of Consumer Psychology, 15*(3), 193–202. https://doi.org/10.1207 /s15327663jcp1503_3

Dindo, L., Brock, R. L., Aksan, N., Gamez, W., Kochanska, G., & Clark, L. A. (2017). Attachment and effortful control in toddlerhood predict academic achievement over a decade later. *Psychological Science, 28*(12), 1786–1795. https://doi.org/10.1177/0956797617721271

Doest, L., Maes, S., Gebhardt, W. A., & Koelewijn, H. (2006). Personal goal facilitation through work: Implications for employee satisfaction and well-being. *Applied Psychology, 55*(2), 192–219. https://doi.org/10.1111/j.1464-05 97.2006.00232.x

Doidge, N. (2007). *The brain that changes itself.* New York: Viking Penguin.

Domes, G., Heinrichs, M., Michel, A., Berger, C., & Herpertz, S. C. (2007). Oxytocin improves "mind-reading" in humans. *Biological Psychiatry, 61*(6), 731–733. https://doi.org/10.1016/j.biopsych.2006.07.015

Doran, G. T. (1981). There's a S.M.A.R.T. way to write management's goals and objectives. *Management Review, 70*(11), 35–36.

Drews, F. A., Pasupathi, M., & Strayer, D. L. (2008). Passenger and cell phone conversations in simulated driving. *Journal of Experimental Psychology: Applied, 14*(4), 392–400. https://doi.org/10.1037/a0013119

Duckworth, A. L., & Steinberg, L. (2015). Unpacking self-control. *Child Development Perspectives, 9*(1), 32–37. https://doi.org/10.1111/cdep.12107

Duckworth, A. L., White, R. E., Matteucci, A. J., Shearer, A., & Gross, J. J. (2016). A stitch in time: Strategic self-control in high school and college students. *Journal of Educational Psychology, 108*(3), 329–341. https://doi.org/10 .1037/edu0000062

Duffy, V. B., & Bartoshuk, L. M. (2000). Food acceptance and genetic variation in taste. *Journal of the American Dietetic Association, 100*(6), 647–655. https://doi .org/10.1016/S0002-8223(00)00191-7

Dunbar, R. I. M. (1993). Coevolution of neocortical size, group size and language in humans. *Behavioral and Brain Sciences, 16*(4), 681–694. https://doi.org/10 .1017/S0140525X00032325

Dunfield, K. A., & Kuhlmeier, V. A. (2010). Intention-mediated selective helping in infancy. *Psychological Science, 21*(4), 523–527. https://doi.org/10.1177 /0956797610364119

Dunn, E. W., Aknin, L. B., & Norton, M. I. (2008). Spending money on others promotes happiness. *Science, 319*(5870), 1687–1688. https://doi.org/10.1126/sci ence.1150952

Dunn, E. W., Aknin, L. B., & Norton, M. I. (2014). Prosocial spending and happiness: Using money to benefit others pays off. *Current Directions in Psychological Science, 23*(1), 41–47. https://doi.org/10.1177/0963721413512503

Dunning, D. (2016). Systems approaches to the treatment of motivation in human action: Three notes. *Motivation and Emotion, 40*(1), 27–30. https://doi.org/10 .1007/s11031-015-9533-7

Durlak, J., Domitrovich, C., Weissberg, R. P., & Gullotta, T. (Eds.). (2015). *Handbook of social and emotional learning: Research and practice.* New York: Guilford.

Dweck, C. S. (1986). Motivational processes affecting learning. *American Psychologist, 41*(10), 1040–1048. https://doi.org/10.1037/0003-066X.41.10.1040

Dweck, C. S. (2006). *Mindset: The new psychology of success.* New York: Random House.

Dweck, C. S. (2017). From needs to goals and representations: Foundations for a unified theory of motivation, personality, and development. *Psychological Review, 124*(6), 689–719. https://doi.org/10.1037/rev0000082

Dweck, C. S., & Leggett, E. L. (1988). A social-cognitive approach to motivation and personality. *Psychological Review, 95*(2), 256–273. https://doi.org/10.1037/0033-295X.95.2.256

Eakin, E. (2003, April 19). I feel therefore I am. Review of *Looking for Spinoza: Joy, sorrow, and the feeling brain* by Antonio Damasio. *New York Times.* Retrieved from www.nytimes.com/2003/04/19/books/i-feel-therefore-i-am.html

Eccles, J. S., Wigfield, A., & Schiefele, U. (1998). Motivation. In N. Eisenberg (Ed.), *Handbook of child psychology* (Vol. 3, 5th ed., pp. 1017–1095). New York: Wiley.

Ecker, Y., & Gilead, M. (2018). Goal-directed allostasis: The unique challenge of keeping things as they are and strategies to overcome it. *Perspectives on Psychological Science, 13*(5), 618–633. https://doi.org/10.1177/1745691618769847

Eisenberg, N., Losoya, S., & Spinrad, T. (2003). Affect and prosocial responding. In R. J. Davidson, K. R. Scherer, & H. H. Goldsmith (Eds.), *Handbook of affective sciences* (pp. 787–803). Oxford: Oxford University Press.

Ekman, P. (1972). Universals and cultural differences in facial expressions of emotion. In J. K. Cole (Ed.), *Nebraska symposium on motivation* (pp. 207–283). Lincoln: University of Nebraska Press.

Ekman, P. (2004). *Emotions revealed* (2nd ed.). New York: Times Books.

Elliot, A. J. (1999). Approach and avoidance motivation and achievement goals. *Educational Psychologist, 34*(3), 149–169. https://doi.org/10.1207/s15326985ep3403_3

Elliot, A. J., & Dweck, C. S. (Eds.). (2005). *Handbook of competence and motivation.* New York: Guilford.

Elliot, A. J., & Dweck, C. S. (Eds.). (2017). *Handbook of competence and motivation* (2nd ed.). New York: Guilford.

Ellis, S., Carette, B., Anseel, F., & Lievens, F. (2014). Systematic reflection: Implications for learning from failures and successes. *Current Directions in Psychological Science, 23*(1), 67–72. https://doi.org/10.1177/0963721413504106

Emler, N. (1990). A social psychology of reputations. *European Journal of Social Psychology, 1*(1), 171–193. https://doi.org/10.1080/14792779108401861

Emmons, R. A. (1986). Personal strivings: An approach to personality and subjective well-being. *Journal of Personality and Social Psychology, 51*(5), 1058–1068. https://doi.org/10.1037/0022-3514.51.5.1058

Emmons, R. A. (1989). The personal striving approach to personality. In L. Pervin (Ed.), *Goal concepts in personality and social psychology* (pp. 87–126). Hillsdale, NJ: Erlbaum.

Emmons, R. A. (2003). Personal goals, life meaning, and virtue: Wellsprings of a positive life. In C. L. M. Keyes & J. Haidt (Eds.), *Flourishing: Positive psychology and the life well-lived* (pp. 105–128). Washington, DC: American Psychological Association. https://doi.org/10.1037/10594-005

Emmons, R. A. (2005). Striving for the sacred: Personal goals, life meaning, and religion. *Journal of Social Issues, 61*(4), 731–745. https://doi.org/10.1111/j.1540-4560.2005.00429.x

Emmons, R. A., & King, L. A. (1988). Conflict among personal strivings: Immediate and long-term implications for psychological and physical well-being. *Journal of Personality and Social Psychology, 54*(6), 1040–1048. https://doi.org/10.1037/0022-3514.54.6.1040

Endsley, M. R. (1985). Toward a theory of situation awareness in dynamic systems. *Human Factors, 37*(1), 32–64. https://doi.org/10.1518/001872095779049543

Englund, M. M., Levy, A. K., Hyson, D. M., & Sroufe, L. A. (2000). Adolescent social competence: Effectiveness in a group setting. *Child Development, 71*(4), 1049–1060. https://doi.org/10.1111/1467-8624.00208

Erez, M. (1977). Feedback: A necessary condition for the goal setting-performance relationship. *Journal of Applied Psychology, 62*(5), 624–627. https://doi.org/10.1037/0021-9010.62.5.624

Erickson, K. I., Hillman, C. H., & Kramer, A. F. (2015). Physical activity, brain, and cognition. *Current Opinion in Behavioral Sciences, 4*, 27–32. https://doi.org/10.1016/j.cobeha.2015.01.005

Erikson, E. H. (1959). *Identity and the life cycle: Selected papers.* Oxford: International Universities Press.

Erikson, E. H. (1968). *Identity: Youth and crisis.* New York: W. W. Norton.

Farley, F. (1991). The Type-t personality. In L. P. Lipsin & L. L. Mitnick (Eds.), *Self-regulatory behavior and risk taking: Causes and consequences* (pp. 371–382). Norwood, NJ: Ablex.

Farnham, A. (1989). The trust gap. *Fortune, 120*(14), 56–78.

Fehr, E., & Gächter, S. (2002). Altruistic punishment in humans. *Nature, 415*(6868), 137–140. https://doi.org/10.1038/415137a

Fehr, E., & Schmidt, K. M. (1999). A theory of fairness, competition, and cooperation. *The Quarterly Journal of Economics, 114*(3), 817–868. https://doi.org/10.1162/003355399556151

Feinberg, M., Willer, R., & Schultz, M. (2014). Gossip and ostracism promote cooperation in groups. *Psychological Science, 25*(3), 656–664. https://doi.org/10.1177/0956797613510184

Feldman, D. B., & Snyder, C. R. (2005). Hope and the meaningful life: Theoretical and empirical associations between goal-directed thinking and life meaning. *Journal of Social and Clinical Psychology, 24*(3), 401–421. https://doi.org/10.1521/jscp.24.3.401.65616

Feldman, M. S., & Khademian, A. M. (2003). Empowerment and cascading vitality. In K. S. Cameron, J. E. Dutton, & R. E. Quinn (Eds.), *Positive organizational scholarship* (pp. 343–358). San Francisco: Berrett-Koehler.

Ferguson, M. J., & Zayas, V. (2009). Automatic evaluation. *Current Directions in Psychological Science, 18*(6), 362–366. https://doi.org/10.1111/j.1467-8721.2009.01668.x

Fitzsimons, G. M., & Finkel, E. J. (2018). Transactive-goal-dynamics theory: A discipline-wide perspective. *Current Directions in Psychological Science, 27*(5), 332–338. https://doi.org/10.1177/0963721417754199

Ford, C. M., & Gioia, D. A. (1995). Academic and practitioner conceptions of creativity in organizations. In C. M. Ford & D. A. Gioia (Eds.), *Creative actions in organizations: Ivory tower visions and real world voices* (pp. 3–11). Newbury Park, CA: Sage. https://doi.org/10.4135/9781452243535.n1

Ford, D. H. (2019). *Humans as self-constructing living systems: A developmental perspective on behavior and personality* (Routledge psychology library editions: Personality). New York: Routledge. (Original work published 1987) https://doi.org/10.4324/9780429025235

Ford, D. H. (2013). *Carol's Alzheimers journey: Treat them like a person, not a patient.* Morrisville, NC: Lulu.

Ford, D. H., & Ford, M. E. (2019). Humans as self-constructing living systems: An overview. In M. E. Ford & D. H. Ford (Eds.), *Humans as self-constructing living systems: Putting the framework to work* (Routledge psychology library editions: Personality, pp. 1–46). New York: Routledge. (Original work published 1987) https://doi.org/10.4324/9780429025297-1

Ford, D. H., & Lerner, R. M. (1992). *Developmental systems theory: An integrative approach.* Newbury Park, CA: Sage.

Ford, D. H., & Urban, H. B. (1963). *Systems of psychotherapy: A comparative study.* New York: Wiley. https://doi.org/10.1037/10782-000

Ford, D. H., & Urban, H. B. (1998). *Contemporary models of psychotherapy: A comparative analysis* (2nd ed.). New York: Wiley.

Ford, M. E. (1985). The concept of competence: Themes and variations. In H. A. Marlowe & R. B. Weinberg (Eds.), *Competence development* (pp. 3–49). Springfield, IL: Charles C. Thomas.

Ford, M. E. (1986a). For all practical purposes: Criteria for defining and evaluating practical intelligence. In R. J. Sternberg & R. K. Wagner (Eds.), *Practical intelligence: Origins of competence in the everyday world* (pp. 183–200). Cambridge: Cambridge University Press.

Ford, M. E. (1986b). A living systems conceptualization of social intelligence: Outcomes, processes, and developmental change. In R. J. Sternberg (Ed.), *Advances in the psychology of human intelligence* (Vol. 3, pp. 119–171). Hillsdale, NJ: Erlbaum.

Ford, M. E. (1992). *Motivating humans.* Newbury Park, CA: Sage. https://doi.org/10.4135/9781483325361

Ford, M. E. (1994). A living systems approach to the integration of personality and intelligence. In R. J. Sternberg & P. Ruzgis (Eds.), *Personality and intelligence* (pp. 188–217). New York: Cambridge University Press.

Ford, M. E. (1995). Advances in motivation theory and research: Implications for special education professionals. *Intervention in School and Clinic, 31*(2), 70–83. https://doi.org/10.1177/105345129503100203

Ford, M. E. (1996). Motivational opportunities and obstacles associated with social responsibility and caring behavior in school contexts. In J. Juvonen & K. Wentzel (Eds.), *Social motivation: Understanding children's school adjustment* (pp. 126–153). Cambridge: Cambridge University Press. https://doi.org/10.1017/CBO9780511571190.008

Ford, M. E., & Ford, D. H. (Eds.). (2019). *Humans as self-constructing living systems: Putting the framework to work* (Routledge psychology library editions: Personality). New York: Routledge. (Original work published 1987) https://doi.org/10.4324/9780429025297

Ford, M. E., & Maher, M. A. (1998). Self-awareness and social intelligence: Search engines, web pages, and navigational control. In M. Ferrari & R. Sternberg (Eds.), *Self-awareness: Its nature and development* (pp. 191–218). New York: Guilford.

Ford, M. E., & Nichols, C. W. (2019). A taxonomy of human goals and some possible applications. In M. E. Ford & D. H. Ford (Eds.), *Humans as self-constructing living systems: Putting the framework to work* (Routledge psychology library editions: Personality, pp. 289–311). New York: Routledge. (Original work published 1987) https://doi.org/10.4324/9780429025297-10

Ford, M. E., & Nichols, C. W. (1991). Using goal assessments to identify motivational patterns and facilitate behavioral regulation. In M. Maehr & P. Pintrich (Eds.), *Advances in motivation and achievement: Vol. 7. Goals and self-regulatory processes* (pp. 57–84). Greenwich, CT: JAI Press.

Ford, M. E., & Nichols, C. W. (2005). *Assessment of personal goals.* Retrieved from https://apg.gmu.edu

Ford, M. E., & Smith, P. R. (2007). Thriving with social purpose: An integrative approach to the development of optimal functioning. *Educational Psychologist, 42*(3), 152–171. https://doi.org/10.1080/00461520701416280

Ford, M. E., & Smith, P. R. (2010). *Assessment of personal agency belief patterns.* Retrieved from https://apg.gmu.edu

Ford, M. E., & Smith, P. R. (2011). Motivation. In B. B. Brown & M. J. Prinstein (Eds.), *Encyclopedia of adolescence* (Vol. 1, pp. 231–239). San Diego, CA: Academic Press. https://doi.org/10.1016/b978-0-12-373951-3.00028-4

Ford, M. E., & Smith, P. R. (2013). *The APG personal application guide.* Retrieved from https://apg.gmu.edu

Ford, M. E., & Thompson, R. A. (1985). Perceptions of personal agency and infant attachment: Toward a life-span perspective on competence development. *International Journal of Behavioral Development, 8*(4), 1–30. https://doi.org/10.1177/016502548500800402

Ford, M. E., Wentzel, K. R., Wood, D., Stevens, E., & Siesfeld, G. A. (1989). Processes associated with integrative social competence: Emotional and contextual influences on adolescent social responsibility. *Journal of Adolescent Research, 4*(4), 405–425. https://doi.org/10.1177/074355488944002

Fraley, R. C., & Roisman, G. I. (2019). The development of adult attachment styles: Four lessons. *Current Opinion in Psychology, 25,* 26–30. https://doi.org/10.1016/j.copsyc.2018.02.008

Frank, R. H. (2001). Cooperation through emotional commitment. In R. M. Nesse (Ed.), *Evolution and the capacity for commitment* (pp. 57–76). New York: Russell Sage Foundation.

Frankl, V. E. (2006). *Man's search for meaning* (5th ed.). Boston: Beacon Press. (Original work published in 1946)

Fredrickson, B. L. (2003). Positive emotions and upward spirals in organizations. In K. S. Cameron, J. E. Dutton, & R. E. Quinn (Eds.), *Positive organizational scholarship* (pp. 163–175). San Francisco: Berrett-Koehler.

Fredrickson, B. L. (2009). *Positivity.* New York: Crown.

Fredrickson, B. L., Grewen, K. M., Coffey, K. A., Algoe, S. B., Firestine, A. M., Arevalo, J. M. G., . . . Cole, S. W. (2013). A functional genomic perspective on human well-being. *Proceedings of the National Academy of Sciences of the USA, 110*(33), 13684–13689. https://doi.org/10.1073/pnas.1305419110

Freud, S. (1948). *Beyond the pleasure principle.* London: Hogarth. (Original work published 1920) https://doi.org/10.1037/11189-000

Freud, S. (1947). *The ego and the id.* London: Hogarth. (Original work published 1923)

Freund, A. M., & Baltes, P. B. (1998). Selection, optimization, and compensation as strategies of life management: Correlations with subjective indicators of successful aging. *Psychology and Aging, 13*(4), 531–543. https://doi.org/10.1037/0882-7974.13.4.531

Friedman, H. S. (Ed.). (1991). *Hostility, coping, and health.* Washington, DC: American Psychological Association. https://doi.org/10.1037/10105-000

Frijda, N. H. (1988). The laws of emotion. *American Psychologist, 43*(5), 349–358. https://doi.org/10.1037//0003-066x.43.5.349

Fry, P. S. (2000). Religious involvement, spirituality and personal meaning for life: Existential predictors of psychological wellbeing in community-residing and institutional care elders. *Aging and Mental Health, 4*(4), 375–387. https://doi.org/10.1080/713649965

Fuligni, A. J. (2019). The need to contribute during adolescence. *Perspectives on Psychological Science, 14*(3), 331–343. https://doi.org/10.1177/1745691618805437

Galak, J., & Redden, J. P. (2018). The properties and antecedents of hedonic decline. *Annual Review of Psychology, 69,* 1–25. https://doi.org/10.1146/annurev-psych-122216-011542

Gallagher, W. (2009). *Rapt: Attention and the focused life.* New York: Penguin.

Gallo, L. C., de los Monteros, K. E., & Shivpuri, S. (2009). Socioeconomic status and health: What is the role of reserve capacity? *Current Directions in Psychological Science, 18*(5), 269–274. https://doi.org/10.1111/j.1467-8721.2009.01650.x

Gallo, L. C., & Matthews, K. (2003). Understanding the association between socioeconomic status and physical health: Do negative emotions play a role? *Psychological Bulletin, 129*(1), 10–51. https://doi.org/10.1037/0033-2909.129.1.10

Gasiorowska, A., Chaplin, L. N., Zaleskiewicz, T., Wygrab, S., & Vohs, K. D. (2016). Money cues increase agency and decrease prosociality among children: Early signs of market-mode behaviors. *Psychological Science, 27*(3), 331–344. https://doi.org/10.1177/0956797615620378

Gawain, S. (2008). *Creative visualization: Use the power of your imagination to create what you want in life* (30th Anniversary ed.). Novato, CA: Nataraj.

Geary, D. C. (2005). *The origin of mind: Evolution of brain, cognition, and general intelligence.* Washington, DC: American Psychological Association. https://doi.org/10.1037/10871-000

Gehlbach, H., Brinkworth, M. E., King, A. M., Hsu, L. M., McIntyre, J., & Rogers, T. (2016). Creating birds of similar feathers: Leveraging similarity to improve teacher–student relationships and academic achievement. *Journal of Educational Psychology, 108*(3), 342–352. https://doi.org/10.1037/edu0000042

George, L. S., & Park, C. L. (2016). Meaning in life as comprehension, purpose, and mattering: Toward integration and new research questions. *Review of General Psychology, 20*(3), 205–220. https://doi.org/10.1037/gpr0000077

Gilbert, D. (2006). *Stumbling on happiness.* New York: Alfred A. Knopf.

Gintis, H. (2001). Beyond selfishness in modeling human behavior. In R. M. Nesse (Ed.), *Evolution and the capacity for commitment* (pp. xiii–xviii). New York: Russell Sage Foundation.

Gintis, H., Bowles, S., Boyd, R., & Fehr, E. (Eds.). (2005). *Moral sentiments and material interests: The foundations of cooperation in economic life.* Cambridge, MA: MIT Press. https://doi.org/10.7551/mitpress/4771.001.0001

Gittell, J. H. (2003). A theory of relational coordination. In K. S. Cameron, J. E. Dutton, & R. E. Quinn (Eds.), *Positive organizational scholarship* (pp. 279–295). San Francisco: Berrett-Koehler.

Goddard, R. D., Hoy, W. K., & Hoy, A. W. (2004). Collective efficacy beliefs: Theoretical developments, empirical evidence, and future directions. *Educational Researcher, 33*(3), 3–13. https://doi.org/10.3102/0013189X033003003

Goleman, D. (1995). *Emotional intelligence.* New York: Bantam.

Gollwitzer, P. M. (1999). Implementation intentions: Strong effects of simple plans. *American Psychologist, 54*(7), 493–503. https://doi.org/10.1037//0003-066x.54.7.493

Gollwitzer, P. M., Parks-Stamm, E. J., Jaudas, A., & Sheeran, P. (2008). Flexible tenacity in goal pursuit. In W. Gardner & J. Shah (Eds.), *Handbook of motivation science* (pp. 325–341). New York: Guilford.

Gollwitzer, P. M., & Sheeran, P. (2006). Implementation intentions and goal achievement: A meta-analysis of effects and processes. *Advances in Experimental Social Psychology, 38*, 69–119. https://doi.org/10.1016/S0065-2601(06)38002-1

Gordon, A. M., Mendes, W. B., & Prather, A. A. (2017). The social side of sleep: Elucidating the links between sleep and social processes. *Current Directions in Psychological Science, 26*(5), 470–475. https://doi.org/10.1177/0963721417712269

Gould, S. J., & Eldredge, N. (1977). Punctuated equilibria: The tempo and mode of evolution reconsidered. *Paleobiology, 3*(2), 115–151. https://doi.org/10.1017/S0094837300005224

Goyal, M., Singh, S., Sibinga, E. M. S., Gould, N. F., Rowland-Seymour, A., Sharma, R., . . . Haythornthwaite, J. A. (2014). Meditation programs for psychological stress and well-being: A systematic review and meta-analysis. *JAMA Internal Medicine*, *174*(3), 357–368. https://doi.org/10.1001/jamainternmed.2013.13018

Grant, A. M. (2008). The significance of task significance: Job performance effects, relational mechanisms, and boundary conditions. *Journal of Applied Psychology*, *93*(1), 108–124. https://doi.org/10.1037/0021-9010.93.1.108

Grant, A. M. (2013). *Give and take*. New York: Viking.

Grant, A. M. (2019). Writing a book for real people: On giving the psychology of giving away. *Perspectives on Psychological Science*, *14*(1), 91–95. https://doi.org/10.1177/1745691618808514

Grant, A. M., & Hofmann, D. A. (2011). It's not all about me: Motivating hospital hand hygiene by focusing on patients. *Psychological Science*, *22*(12), 1494–1499. https://doi.org/10.1177/0956797611419172

Grant, A. M., & Mayer, D. M. (2009). Good soldiers and good actors: Prosocial and impression management motives as interactive predictors of affiliative citizenship behaviors. *Journal of Applied Psychology*, *94*(4), 900–912. https://doi.org/10.1037/a0013770

Gross, J. J. (1998). The emerging field of emotion regulation: An integrative review. *Review of General Psychology*, *2*(3), 271–299. https://doi.org/10.1037/1089-2680.2.3.271

Gross, J. J. (2015). Emotion regulation: Current status and future prospects. *Psychological Inquiry*, *26*(1), 1–26. https://doi.org/10.1080/1047840X.2014.940781

Gross, J. J., & Jazaieri, H. (2014). Emotion, emotion regulation, and psychopathology: An affective science perspective. *Clinical Psychological Science*, *2*(4), 387–401. https://doi.org/10.1177/2167702614536164

Grossman, P., Niemann, L., Schmidt, S., & Walach, H. (2004). Mindfulness-based stress reduction and health benefits: A meta-analysis. *Journal of Psychosomatic Research*, *57*(1), 35–43. https://doi.org/10.1016/S0022-3999(03)00573-7

Groundwater, S. V. (2006). *Thriving with social purpose: A phenomenological investigation of resilience and the role of life meaning in a teacher's decision to remain in the teaching profession* (Unpublished doctoral dissertation). George Mason University, Fairfax, VA.

Gruber, J., Mauss, I. B., & Tamir, M. (2011). A dark side of happiness? How, when, and why happiness is not always good. *Perspectives on Psychological Science*, *6*(3), 222–233. https://doi.org/10.1177/1745691611406927

Guillot, A., & Collet, C. (Eds.). (2010). *The neurophysiological foundations of mental and motor imagery*. Oxford: Oxford University Press. https://doi.org/10.1093/acprof:oso/9780199546251.001.0001

Haidt, J. (2006). *The happiness hypothesis: Finding modern truth in ancient wisdom*. New York: Basic Books.

Halusic, M., & King, L. A. (2013). What makes life meaningful: Positive mood works in a pinch. In K. D. Markman, T. Proulx, & M. J. Lindberg (Eds.), *The psychology of meaning* (pp. 445–464). Washington, DC: American Psychological Association. https://doi.org/10.1037/14040-022

Halvorson, H. G., & Higgins, E. T. (2013). *Focus: Use different ways of seeing the world for success and influence*. New York: Penguin.

Hamedani, M. G., Markus, H. R., & Fu, A. S. (2013). In the land of the free, interdependent action undermines motivation. *Psychological Science*, *24*(2), 189–196. https://doi.org/10.1177/0956797612452864

Hamlin, J. K., Wynn, K., & Bloom, P. (2010). Three-month-olds show a negativity bias in their social evaluations. *Developmental Science*, *13*(6), 923–929. https://doi.org/10.1111/j.1467-7687.2010.00951.x

Harbaugh, W. T., Mayr, U., & Burghart, D. R. (2007). Neural responses to taxation and voluntary giving reveal motives for charitable donations. *Science*, *316*(5831), 1622–1625. https://doi.org/10.1126/science.1140738

Harley, J. M., Pekrun, R., Taxer, J. L., & Gross, J. J. (2019). Emotion regulation in achievement situations: An integrated model. *Educational Psychologist*, *54*(2), 106–126. https://doi.org/10.1080/00461520.2019.1587297

Harlow, L. L., Newcomb, M. D., & Bentler, P. M. (1986). Depression, self-derogation, substance use, and suicide ideation: Lack of purpose in life as a mediational factor. *Journal of Clinical Psychology*, *42*(1), 5–21. https://doi.org/10.1002/1097-4679(198601)42:1<5::AID-JCLP2270420102>3.0.CO;2-9

Harter, S. (1978). Effectance motivation reconsidered: Toward a developmental model. *Human Development*, *21*(1), 34–64. https://doi.org/10.1159/000271574

Harter, S. (1990). Causes, correlates, and the functional role of global self-worth: A life-span perspective. In R. J. Sternberg & J. Kolligian Jr. (Eds.), *Competence considered* (pp. 67–97). New Haven, CT: Yale University Press.

Hassin, R. R. (2013). Yes it can: On the functional abilities of the human unconscious. *Perspectives on Psychological Science*, *8*(2), 195–207. https://doi.org/10.1177/1745691612460684

Hatfield, E., Cacioppo, J. T., & Rapson, R. L. (1994). *Emotional contagion*. Cambridge: Cambridge University Press. https://doi.org/10.1017/cbo9781139174138

Hauser, M. D. (2006). *Moral minds: How nature designed our universal sense of right and wrong*. New York: HarperCollins.

Hawley, P. H. (2015). Social dominance in childhood and its evolutionary underpinnings: Why it matters and what we can do. *Pediatrics*, *135*(Suppl. 2), 531–538. https://doi.org/10.1542/peds.2014-3549D

Hawkley, L. C., & Cacioppo, J. T. (2010). Loneliness matters: A theoretical and empirical review of consequences and mechanisms. *Annals of Behavioral Medicine*, *40*(2), 218–227. https://doi.org/10.1007/s12160-010-9210-8

Hebb, D. O. (1949). *The organization of behavior*. New York: Wiley.

Heckhausen, H., & Kuhl, J. (1985). From wishes to action: The dead ends and short cuts on the long way to action. In M. Frese & J. Sabini (Eds.), *Goal-*

directed behavior: The concept of action in psychology (pp. 134–159). Hillsdale, NJ: Erlbaum.

Heine, S. J., Proulx, T., & Vohs, K. D. (2006). The meaning maintenance model: On the coherence of social motivations. *Personality and Social Psychology Review, 10*(2), 88–110. https://doi.org/10.1207/s15327957pspr1002_1

Heintzelman, S. J., & King, L. A. (2014a). (The feeling of) meaning-as-information. *Personality and Social Psychology Review, 18*(2), 153–167. https://doi.org/10.1177/1088868313518487

Heintzelman, S. J., & King, L. A. (2014b). Life is pretty meaningful. *American Psychologist, 69*(6), 561–574. https://doi.org/10.1037/a0035049

Henderson, S. J. (2009). Assessment of personal goals: An online tool for personal counseling, coaching, and business consulting. *Measurement and Evaluation in Counseling and Development, 41*(4), 244–249. https://doi.org/10.1080/07481756.2009.11909832

Hepach, R. (2016). Prosocial arousal in children. *Child Development Perspectives, 11*(1), 50–55. https://doi.org/10.1111/cdep.12209

Hepach, R., Vaish, A., & Tomasello, M. (2012). Young children are intrinsically motivated to see others helped. *Psychological Science, 23*(9), 967–972. https://doi.org/10.1177/0956797612440571

Hepach, R., Vaish, A., & Tomasello, M. (2017). The fulfillment of others' needs elevates children's body posture. *Developmental Psychology, 53*(1), 100–113. https://doi.org/10.1037/dev0000173

Hermans, H. J. M. (1998). Meaning as an organized process of valuation: A self-confrontational approach. In P. T. P. Wong & P. S. Fry (Eds.), *The human quest for meaning: A handbook of psychological research and clinical applications* (pp. 317–334). Mahwah, NJ: Erlbaum.

Hill, P. L., & Turiano, N. A. (2014). Purpose in life as a predictor of mortality across adulthood. *Psychological Science, 25*(7), 1482–1486. https://doi.org/10.1177/0956797614531799

Hilpert, J. C., & Marchand, G. C. (2018). Complex systems research in educational psychology: Aligning theory and method. *Educational Psychologist, 53*(3), 185–202. https://doi.org/10.1080/00461520.2018.1469411

Hirsch, J. L., & Clark, M. S. (2019). Multiple paths to belonging that we should study together. *Perspectives on Psychological Science, 14*(2), 238–255. https://doi.org/10.1177/1745691618803629

Hirschi, A. (2009). Career adaptability development in adolescence: Multiple predictors and effect on sense of power and life satisfaction. *Journal of Vocational Behavior, 74*(2), 145–155. https://doi.org/10.1016/j.jvb.2009.01.002

Hogan, R., & Kaiser, R. B. (2005). What we know about leadership. *Review of General Psychology, 9*(2), 169–180. https://doi.org/10.1037/1089-2680.9.2.169

Holbrook, T. L., Galarneau, M. R., Dye, J. L., Quinn, K., & Dougherty, A. L. (2010). Morphine use after combat injury in Iraq and post-traumatic stress disorder. *New England Journal of Medicine, 362*, 110–117. https://doi.org/10.1056/NEJMoa0903326

Holland, J. L. (1994). *The self-directed search* (4th ed.). Odessa, FL: Psychological Assessment Resources.

Holt-Lunstad, J., Robles, T. F., & Sbarra, D. A. (2017). Advancing social connection as a public health priority in the United States. *American Psychologist, 72* (6), 517–530. https://doi.org/10.1037/amp0000103

Holzel, B. K., Carmody, J., Vangel, M., Congleton, C., Yerramsetti, S. M., Gard, T., & Lazar, S. W. (2011a). Mindfulness practice leads to increases in regional brain gray matter density. *Psychiatric Research: Neuroimaging, 191*(1), 36–43. https://doi.org/10.1016/j.pscychresns.2010.08.006

Holzel, B. K., Lazar, S. W., Gard, T., Schuman-Olivier, Z., Vago, D. R., & Ott, U. (2011b). How does mindfulness meditation work? Proposing mechanisms of action from a conceptual and neural perspective. *Perspectives on Psychological Science, 6*(6), 537–559. https://doi.org/10.1177/1745691611419671

Hooker, S. A., Masters, K. S., & Park, C. L. (2018). A meaningful life is a healthy life: A conceptual model linking meaning and meaning salience to health. *Review of General Psychology, 22*(1), 11–24. https://doi.org/10.1037/gpr0000115

Hougaard, R., & Carter, J. (2018). *The mind of the leader: How to lead yourself, your people, and your organization for extraordinary results.* Boston: Harvard Business Review Press.

House, J. S., Landis, K. R., & Umberson, D. (1988). Social relationships and health. *Science, 241*(4865), 540–545. https://doi.org/10.1126/science.3399889

Howell, R. T., Kern, M. L., & Lyubomirsky, S. (2007). Health benefits: Meta-analytically determining the impact of well-being on objective health outcomes. *Health Psychology Review, 1*(1), 83–136. https://doi.org/10.1080/17437190701492486

Hrdy, S. B. (2009). *Mothers and others: The evolutionary origins of mutual understanding.* Cambridge, MA: Belknap Press.

Hull, C. L. (1943). *Principles of behavior.* New York: Appleton-Century-Crofts.

Iaffaldano, M. T., & Muchinsky, P. M. (1985). Job satisfaction and job performance: A meta-analysis. *Psychological Bulletin, 97*(2), 251–273. https://doi.org/10.1037/0033-2909.97.2.251

Immordino-Yang, M. H. (2016). *Emotions, learning, and the brain: Exploring the educational implications of affective neuroscience.* New York: W. W. Norton.

Immordino-Yang, M. H., & Damasio, A. (2007). We feel, therefore we learn: The relevance of affective and social neuroscience to education. *Mind, Brain, and Education, 1*(1), 3–10. https://doi.org/10.1111/j.1751-228X.2007.00004.x

Inzlicht, M., & Schmeichel, B. J. (2012). What is ego depletion? Toward a mechanistic revision of the resource model of self-control. *Perspectives on Psychological Science, 7*(5), 450–463. https://doi.org/10.1177/1745691612454134

Izard, C. E. (1977). *Human emotions.* New York: Plenum. https://doi.org/10.1007/978-1-4899-2209-0

Janoff-Bulman, R., & McPherson Frantz, C. (1997). The impact of trauma on meaning: From meaningless world to meaningful life. In M. J. Power & C. R. Brewin (Eds.), *The transformation of meaning in psychological therapies: Integrating theory and practice* (pp. 91–106). Hoboken, NJ: Wiley.

Jantsch, E. (1980). *The self-organizing universe*. Oxford: Pergamon.

Jessen, S., & Grossmann, T. (2014). Unconscious discrimination of social cues from eye whites in infants. *Proceedings of the National Academy of Sciences of the USA, 111*(45), 16208–16213. https://doi.org/10.1073/pnas.1411333111

Job, V., Dweck, C. S., & Walton, G. M. (2010). Ego depletion – Is it all in your head? Implicit theories about willpower affect self-regulation. *Psychological Science, 21*(11), 1686–1693. https://doi.org/10.1177/0956797610384745

Johanson, D. C., & Wong, K. (2010). *Lucy's legacy: The quest for human origins*. New York: Three Rivers Press.

Johnson, D. W., & Johnson, R. T. (1975). *Learning together and alone*. Englewood Cliffs, NJ: Prentice Hall.

Jones, G. R., & George, J. M. (1998). The experience and evolution of trust: Implications for cooperation and teamwork. *Academy of Management Review, 23* (3), 531–546. https://doi.org/10.5465/amr.1998.926625

Joyce, R. (2006). *The evolution of morality*. Cambridge, MA: MIT Press. https://doi.org/10.7551/mitpress/2880.001.0001

Judge, T. A., Thoresen, C. J., Bono, J. E., & Patton, G. K. (2001). The job satisfaction – job performance relationship: A qualitative and quantitative review. *Psychological Bulletin, 127*(3), 376–407. https://doi.org/10.1037/0033-2909.127.3.376

Kabat-Zinn, J. (1994). *Wherever you go, there you are: Mindfulness meditation in everyday life*. New York: Hyperion.

Kabat-Zinn, J. (2012). *Mindfulness for beginners: Reclaiming the present moment – and your life*. Boulder, CO: Sounds True.

Kaplan, A., & Garner, J. K. (2017). A complex dynamic systems perspective on identity and its development: The dynamic systems model of role identity. *Developmental Psychology, 53*(11), 2036–2051. https://doi.org/10.1037/dev0000339

Kaplan, A., Garner, J. K., & Brock, B. (2019). Identity and motivation in a changing world: A complex dynamic systems perspective. *Advances in Motivation and Achievement, 20*, 101–127. https://doi.org/10.1108/S0749-742320190000020006

Kaplan, U., & Tivnan, T. (2014). Moral motivational pluralism: Moral judgment as a function of the dynamic assembly of multiple developmental structures. *Journal of Adult Development, 21*(4), 193–206. https://doi.org/10.1007/s10804-014-9191-0

Kashdan, T. B. (2009). *Curious? Discover the missing ingredient to a fulfilling life*. New York: William Morrow.

Kashdan, T. B., Barrett, L. F., & McKnight, P. E. (2015). Unpacking emotion differentiation: Transforming unpleasant experience by perceiving distinctions in negativity. *Current Directions in Psychological Science, 24*(1), 10–16. https://doi.org/10.1177/0963721414550708

Kashdan, T. B., & Nezlek, J. B. (2012). Whether, when, and how is spirituality related to well-being? Moving beyond single occasion questionnaires to understanding daily process. *Personality and Social Psychology Bulletin, 38*(11), 1523–1535. https://doi.org/10.1177/0146167212454549

Kashdan, T. B., & Rottenberg, J. (2010). Psychological flexibility as a fundamental aspect of health. *Clinical Psychology Review, 30*(7), 865–878. https://doi.org/10.1016/j.cpr.2010.03.001

Kaufman, J. C. (2018). Finding meaning with creativity in the past, present, and future. *Perspectives on Psychological Science, 13*(6), 734–749. https://doi.org/10.1177/1745691618771981

Keltner, D. (2009). *Born to be good: The science of a meaningful life.* New York: W. W. Norton.

Keltner, D., & Haidt, J. (2003). Approaching awe, a moral, spiritual, and aesthetic emotion. *Cognition and Emotion, 17*(2), 297–314. https://doi.org/10.1080/02699930302297

Keltner, D., Marsh, J., & Smith, J. A. (Eds.). (2010). *The compassionate instinct.* New York: W. W. Norton.

Khoury, B., Sharma, M., Rush, S. E., & Fournier, C. (2015). Mindfulness-based stress reduction for healthy individuals: A meta-analysis. *Journal of Psychosomatic Research, 78*(6), 519–528. https://doi.org/10.1016/j.jpsychores.2015.03.009

King, L. A. (2012). Meaning: Ubiquitous and effortless. In P. R. Shaver & M. Mikulincer (Eds.), *Meaning, mortality, and choice: The social psychology of existential concerns* (pp. 129–144). Washington, DC: American Psychological Association. https://doi.org/10.1037/13748-007

King, L. A., Hicks, J. A., Krull, J. L., & Del Gaiso, A. K. (2006). Positive affect and the experience of meaning in life. *Journal of Personality and Social Psychology, 90*(1), 179–196. https://doi.org/10.1037/0022-3514.90.1.179

Kirsch, P., Esslinger, C., Chen, Q., Mier, D., Lis, S., Siddhanti, S., . . . Meyer-Lindenberg, A. (2005). Oxytocin modulates neural circuitry for social cognition and fear in humans. *The Journal of Neuroscience, 25*(49), 11489–11493. https://doi.org/10.1523/JNEUROSCI.3984-05.2005

Klinger, E. (1998). The search for meaning in evolutionary perspective and its clinical implications. In P. T. P. Wong & P. S. Fry (Eds.), *The human quest for meaning: A handbook of psychological research and clinical applications* (pp. 27–50). Mahwah, NJ: Erlbaum.

Klinger, E., & Cox, W. M. (2004). Motivation and the theory of current concerns. In W. M. Cox & E. Klinger (Eds.), *Handbook of motivational counseling* (pp. 3–27). New York: Wiley. https://doi.org/10.1002/9780470713129.ch1

Knauper, B., Roseman, M., Johnson, P. J., & Krantz, L. H. (2009). Using mental imagery to enhance the effectiveness of implementation intentions. *Current Psychology, 28*(3), 181–186. https://doi.org/10.1007/s12144-009-9055-0

Koch, C. (2004). *The quest for consciousness: A neurobiological approach.* Englewood, CO: Roberts.

Koestler, A. (1967). *The ghost in the machine.* New York: Macmillan.

Koestler, A. (1978). *Janus.* New York: Random House.

Kok, B. E., Coffey, K. A., Cohn, M. A., Catalino, L. I., Vacharkulksemsuk, T., Algoe, S. B., . . . Fredrickson, B. L. (2013). How position emotions build physical health: Perceived positive social connections account for the upward spiral between positive emotions and vagal tone. *Psychological Science, 24*(7), 1123–1132. https://doi.org/10.1177/0956797612470827

Koltko-Rivera, M. E. (2006). Rediscovering the later version of Maslow's hierarchy of needs: Self-transcendence and opportunities for theory, research, and unification. *Review of General Psychology, 10*(4), 302–317. https://doi.org/10.1037/1089-2680.10.4.302

Kosfeld, M., Heinrichs, M., Zak, P. J., Fischbacher, U., & Fehr, E. (2005). Oxytocin increases trust in humans. *Nature, 435*(7042), 673–676. https://doi.org/10.1038/nature03701

Koster, M., Ohmer, X., Nguyen, T. D., & Kartner, J. (2016). Infants understand others' needs. *Psychological Science, 27*(4), 542–548. https://doi.org/10.1177/0956797615627426

Krause, N. (2009). Meaning in life and mortality. *The Journals of Gerontology, 64B*(4), 517–527. https://doi.org/10.1093/geronb/gbp047

Kuhl, J., & Beckmann, J. (1994). *Volition and personality: Action and state orientation.* Toronto: Hogrefe & Huber.

Lakin, J. L., Jefferis, V. E., Cheng, C. M., & Chartrand, T. L. (2003). The chameleon effect as social glue: Evidence for the evolutionary significance of nonconscious mimicry. *Journal of Nonverbal Behavior, 27*(3), 145–162. https://doi.org/10.1023/A:1025389814290

Lambert, R., & McCarthy, C. (Eds.). (2006). *Understanding teacher stress in an age of accountability.* Greenwich, CT: Information Age.

Lancaster, T., Stead, L., Silagy, C., & Sowden, A. (2000). Effectiveness of interventions to help people stop smoking: Findings from the Cochrane Library. *BMJ, 321,* 355–358. https://doi.org/10.1136/bmj.321.7257.355

Landy, F. J., & Becker, L. J. (1987). Motivation theory reconsidered. *Research in Organizational Behavior, 9,* 1–38.

Langer, E. J. (1989). *Mindfulness.* Reading, MA: Addison-Wesley.

Langer, E. J. (2009). *Counter clockwise: Mindful health and the power of possibility.* New York: Ballantine.

Lazarus, R. S. (1991). Progress on a cognitive-motivational-relational theory of emotion. *American Psychologist, 46*(8), 819–834. https://doi.org/10.1037//0003-066x.46.8.819

Leary, M. R. (2004). *The curse of the self: Self-awareness, egotism, and the quality of human life.* Oxford: Oxford University Press. https://doi.org/10.1093/acprof:oso/9780195172423.001.0001

LeDoux, J. (1998). *The emotional brain: The mysterious underpinnings of emotional life.* New York: Simon & Schuster.

LeDoux, J. (2002). *Synaptic self: How our brains become who we are.* New York: Viking Penguin.

Legrand, E., Bieleke, M., Gollwitzer, P. M., & Mignon, A. (2017). Nothing will stop me? Flexibly tenacious goal striving with implementation intentions. *Motivation Science, 3*(2), 101–118. https://doi.org/10.1037/moto0000050

Lieberman, P. (2007). The evolution of human speech: Its anatomical and neural bases. *Current Anthropology, 48*(1), 39–66. https://doi.org/10.1086/509092

Little, B. R. (1983). Personal projects: A rationale and method for investigation. *Environment and Behavior, 15*(3), 273–309. https://doi.org/10.1177/0013916583153002

Locke, E. A. (2002). Setting goals for life and happiness. In C. R. Snyder & S. J. Lopez (Eds.), *Handbook of positive psychology* (pp. 299–312). Oxford: Oxford University Press.

Locke, E. A., & Latham, G. P. (1984). *Goal setting: A motivational technique that works.* Englewood Cliffs, NJ: Prentice Hall.

Locke, E. A., & Latham, G. P. (2019). The development of goal setting theory: A half century retrospective. *Motivation Science, 5*(2), 93–105. http://dx.doi.org/10.1037/moto0000127

Lopez, S. J. (2013). *Making hope happen: Create the future you want for yourself and others.* New York: Atria.

Lumsden, C. J., & Wilson, E. O. (1981). *Genes, mind and culture: The coevolutionary process.* Cambridge, MA: Harvard University Press. https://doi.org/10.1142/5786

Luthans, F., & Avolio, B. J. (2003). Authentic leadership development. In K. S. Cameron, J. E. Dutton, & R. E. Quinn (Eds.), *Positive organizational scholarship* (pp. 241–258). San Francisco: Berrett-Koehler.

Lyubomirsky, S. (2008). *The how of happiness: A scientific approach to getting the life you want.* New York: Penguin.

Lyubomirsky, S., King, L. A., & Diener, E. (2005). The benefits of frequent positive affect: Does happiness lead to success? *Psychological Bulletin, 131*(6), 803–855. https://doi.org/10.1037/0033-2909.131.6.803

MacCoon, D. G., Wallace, J. F., & Newman, J. P. (2004). Self-regulation: Context-appropriate balanced attention. In R. F. Baumeister & K. D. Vohs (Eds.), *Handbook of self-regulation: Research, theory, and applications* (pp. 422–444). New York: Guilford.

MacKenzie, M. J., & Baumeister, R. F. (2014). Meaning in life: Nature, needs, and myths. In A. Batthyany & P. Russo-Netzer (Eds.), *Meaning in positive and existential psychology* (pp. 25–37). New York: Springer. https://doi.org/10.1007/978-1-4939-0308-5_2

Macy, E., & Wilding-White, T. (2009). *Golfing with your eyes closed: Mastering visualization techniques for exceptional golf.* New York: McGraw-Hill.

Malone, T. W., Laubacher, R., & Dellarocas, C. (2010). The collective intelligence genome. *MIT Sloan Management Review, 51*, 21–31.

Mamede, S., Schmidt, H. G., Rikers, R. M. J. P., Custers, E. J. F. M., Splinter, T. A. W., & van Saase, J. L. C. M. (2010). Conscious thought beats deliberation without attention in diagnostic decision-making: At least when you are an expert. *Psychological Research, 74*(6), 586–592. https://doi.org/10.1007/s00426-010-0281-8

Mansfield, C., Wosnitza, M., & Beltman, S. (2012). Goals for teaching: Towards a framework for examining motivation of graduating teachers. *Australian Journal of Educational and Developmental Psychology, 12*, 21–34.

Manning, M. (1997). *Black liberation in conservative America.* Boston: South End Press.

Marcia, J. E. (1966). Development and validation of ego-identity status. *Journal of Personality and Social Psychology, 3*(5), 551–558. https://doi.org/10.1037/h0023281

Marcia, J. E. (1987). The identity status approach to the study of ego identity. In T. Honess & K. Yardley (Eds.), *Self and identity: Perspectives across the lifespan* (pp. 161–171). New York: Routledge & Kegan Paul.

Markman, K. D., Proulx, T., & Lindberg, M. J. (Eds.). (2013). *The psychology of meaning.* Washington, DC: American Psychological Association. https://doi.org/10.1037/14040-000

Markus, H., & Nurius, P. (1986). Possible selves. *American Psychologist, 41*(9), 954–969. https://doi.org/10.1037/0003-066X.41.9.954

Marsiske, M., Lang, F. B., Baltes, P. B., & Baltes, M. M. (1995). Selective optimization with compensation: Life-span perspectives on successful human development. In R. A. Dixon & L. Bäckman (Eds.), *Compensating for psychological deficits and declines: Managing losses and promoting gains* (pp. 35–79). Mahwah, NJ: Erlbaum.

Martela, F., & Steger, M. F. (2016). The three meanings of meaning in life: Distinguishing coherence, purpose, and significance. *Journal of Positive Psychology, 11*(5), 531–545. https://doi.org/10.1080/17439760.2015.1137623

Martin, K. A., Moritz, S. E., & Hall, C. R. (1999). Imagery use in sport: A literature review and applied model. *The Sports Psychologist, 13*(3), 245–268. https://doi.org/10.1123/tsp.13.3.245

Martinescu, E., Janssen, O., & Nijstad, B. A. (2014). Tell me the gossip: The self-evaluative function of receiving gossip about others. *Personality and Social Psychology Bulletin, 40*(12), 1668–1680. https://doi.org/10.1177/0146167214554916

Mascaro, N., & Rosen, D. H. (2005). Existential meaning's role in the enhancement of hope and prevention of depressive symptoms. *Journal of Personality, 73*(4), 985–1014. https://doi.org/10.1111/j.1467-6494.2005.00336.x

Maslow, A. H. (1943). A theory of human motivation. *Psychological Review, 50*(4), 370–396. https://doi.org/10.1037/h0054346

Maslow, A. H. (1954). *Motivation and personality.* New York: Harper and Row.

Maslow, A. H. (1962). *Towards a psychology of being.* Princeton, NJ: Van Nostrand. https://doi.org/10.1037/10793-000

Maslow, A. H. (1966). *The psychology of science: A reconnaissance.* Washington, DC: Gateway/Henry Regnery.

Maslow, A. H. (1969). Toward a humanistic biology. *American Psychologist, 24*(8), 724–735. https://doi.org/10.1037/h0027859

Mason, M. F., Norton, M. I., Van Horn, J. D., Wegner, D. M., Grafton, S. T., & Macrae, C. N. (2007). Wandering minds: The default network and stimulus-independent thought. *Science, 315*(5810), 393–395. https://doi.org/10 .1126/science.1131295

Masters, J. C., Furman, W., & Barden, R. C. (1977). Effects of achievement standards, tangible rewards, and self-dispensed achievement evaluation on children's task mastery. *Child Development, 48*(1), 217–224. https://doi.org/10 .2307/1128901

Matas, L., Arend, R. A., & Sroufe, L. A. (1978). Continuity of adaptation in the second year: The relationship between quality of attachment and later competence. *Child Development, 49*(3), 547–556. https://doi.org/10.2307 /1128221

Mayer, J.D., & Salovey, P. (1997). What is emotional intelligence? In P. Salovey & D. Sluyter (Eds.), *Emotional development and emotional intelligence: Implications for educators* (pp. 3–31). New York: Basic Books.

Mayer, J. D., Salovey, P., & Caruso, D. R. (2008). Emotional intelligence: New ability or eclectic traits? *American Psychologist, 63*(6), 503–517. https://doi.org/10 .1037/0003-066X.63.6.503

McClelland, D. C. (1985). *Human motivation*. Glenview, IL: Scott, Foresman.

McCombs, B. L. (1991). Motivation and lifelong learning. *Educational Psychologist, 26*(2), 117–127. https://doi.org/10.1207/s15326985ep2602_4

McDougall, W. (1933). *The energies of men*. New York: Scribner.

McKnight, P. E., & Kashdan, T. B. (2009). Purpose in life as a system that creates and sustains health and well-being: An integrative, testable theory. *Review of General Psychology, 13*(3), 242–251. https://doi.org/10.1037 /a0017152

McNulty, J. K., & Fincham, F. D. (2012). Beyond positive psychology? Toward a contextual view of psychological processes and well-being. *American Psychologist, 67*(2), 101–110. https://doi.org/10.1037/a0024572

Midgley, C., Kaplan, A., & Middleton, M. (2001). Performance-approach goals: Good for what, for whom, under what circumstances, and at what cost? *Journal of Educational Psychology, 93*(1), 77–86. https://doi.org/10.1037/0022-0663.93.1 .77

Miller, D. T., & Ratner, R. K. (1998). The disparity between the actual and assumed power of self-interest. *Journal of Personality and Social Psychology, 74*(1), 53–62. https://doi.org/10.1037/0022-3514.74.1.53

Miller, G. A. (1956). The magical number seven, plus or minus two: Some limits on our capacity for processing information. *Psychological Review, 63*(2), 81–97. https://doi.org/10.1037/0033-295X.101.2.343

Miller, G. A., Galanter, E., & Pribram, K. H. (1960). *Plans and the structure of behavior*. New York: Holt. https://doi.org/10.1037/10039-000

Miller, J. G. (1978). *Living systems*. New York: McGraw-Hill.

Miller, R. B., & Brickman, S. J. (2004). A model of future-oriented motivation and self-regulation. *Educational Psychology Review, 16*(1), 9–33. https://doi.org /10.1023/B:EDPR.0000012343.96370.39

Miller, R. B., DeBacker, T. K., & Greene, B. A. (1999). Perceived instrumentality and academics: The link to task valuing. *Journal of Instructional Psychology, 26* (4), 250–260.

Mischel, W., Shoda, Y., & Peake, P. K. (1988). The nature of adolescent competencies predicted by preschool delay of gratification. *Journal of Personality and Social Psychology, 54*(4), 687–696. https://doi.org/10.1037/002 2-3514.54.4.687

Miu, A. S., & Yeager, D. S. (2015). Preventing symptoms of depression by teaching adolescents that people can change: Effects of a brief incremental theory of personality intervention at 9-month follow-up. *Clinical Psychological Science, 3* (5), 726–743. https://doi.org/10.1177/2167702614548317

Moffitt, T. E., Arseneault, L., Belsky, D., Dickson, N., Hancox, R. J., Harrington, H., . . . Caspi, A. (2011). A gradient of self-control predicts health, wealth, and public safety. *Proceedings of the National Academy of Sciences of the USA, 108*(7), 2693–2698. https://doi.org/10.1073/pnas.1010076108

Moll, J., Krueger, F., Zahn, R., Pardini, M., de Oliveira-Souza, R., & Grafman, J. (2006). Human fronto-mesolimbic networks guide decisions about charitable donation. *Proceedings of the National Academy of Sciences of the USA, 103*(42), 15623–15628. https://doi.org/10.1073/pnas.0604475103

Morling, B., & Evered, S. (2006). Secondary control reviewed and defined. *Psychological Bulletin, 132*(2), 269–296. https://doi.org/10.1037/0033-2909 .132.2.269

Mulcahy, N. J., & Call, J. (2006). Apes save tools for future use. *Science, 312*(5776), 1038–1040. https://doi.org/10.1126/science.1125456

Muraven, M., & Baumeister, R. F. (2000). Self-regulation and depletion of limited resources: Does self-control resemble a muscle? *Psychological Review, 126*(2), 247–259. https://doi.org/10.1037//0033-2909.126.2.247

Murray, H. A. (1938). *Explorations in personality.* Oxford: Oxford University Press.

Negru-Subtirica, O., Pop, E. I., Luyckx, K., Dezutter, J., & Steger, M. F. (2016). The meaningful identity: A longitudinal look at the interplay between identity and meaning in life in adolescence. *Developmental Psychology, 52*(11), 1926–1936. https://doi.org/10.1037/dev0000176

Nesse, R. M. (2001). Natural selection and the capacity for subjective commitment. In R. M. Nesse (Ed.), *Evolution and the capacity for commitment* (pp. 1–44). New York: Russell Sage Foundation.

Nesse, R. M. (2006). Why a lot of people with selfish genes are pretty nice except for their hatred of *The Selfish Gene.* In A. Grafen & M. Ridley (Eds.), *Richard Dawkins: How a scientist changed the way we think* (pp. 203–212). Oxford: Oxford University Press.

Nichols, C. W. (1994). *Manual: Assessment of core goals.* Available from C. W. Nichols. nicknichols29@icloud.com

Nisbett, R. E., Aronson, J., Blair, C., Dickens, W., Flynn, J., Halpern, D. F., & Turkheimer, E. (2012). Intelligence: New findings and theoretical developments. *American Psychologist, 67*(2), 130–159. https://doi.org/10.1037 /a0027240

Nisbett, R. E., & Ross, L. D. (1980). *Human inference: Strategies and shortcomings of social judgment.* Englewood Cliffs, NJ: Prentice Hall. https://doi.org/10.2307/2184495

Ntoumanis, N., & Sedikides, C. (2018). Holding on to the goal or letting it go and moving on? A tripartite model of goal striving. *Current Directions in Psychological Science, 27*(5), 363–368. https://doi.org/10.1177/0963721418770455

O'Brien, E., & Kassirer, S. (2019). People are slow to adapt to the warm glow of giving. *Psychological Science, 30*(2), 193–204. https://doi.org/10.1177/0956797618814145

O'Dea, J. A. (2012). Body image and self-esteem. In T. F. Cash (Ed.), *Encyclopedia of body image and human appearance* (pp. 141–147). San Diego, CA: Elsevier. https://doi.org/10.1016/B978-0-12-384925-0.00021-3

Oishi, S., & Diener, E. (2014). Residents of poor nations have a greater sense of meaning in life than residents of wealthy nations. *Psychological Science, 25,* 422–430.

Orehek, E., & Forest, A. L. (2016). When people serve as means to goals: Implications of a motivational account of close relationships. *Current Directions in Psychological Science, 25*(2), 79–84. https://doi.org/10.1177/0956797613507286

Owens, G. P., Steger, M. F., Whitesell, A. A., & Herrera, C. J. (2009). Posttraumatic stress disorder, guilt, depression, and meaning in life among military veterans. *Journal of Traumatic Stress, 22*(6), 654–657. https://doi.org/10.1002/jts.20460

Oyserman, D., & Fryberg, S. (2006). The possible selves of diverse adolescents: Content and function across gender, race and national origin. In C. Dunkel & J. Kerpelman (Eds.), *Possible selves: Theory, research and applications* (pp. 17–39). New York: Nova Science.

Pajares, F., & Urdan, T. (Eds.). (2006). *Self-efficacy beliefs of adolescents.* Charlotte, NC: Information Age.

Park, C. L. (2005). Religion and meaning. In R. F. Paloutzian & C. L. Park (Eds.), *Handbook of the psychology of religion and spirituality* (2nd ed., pp. 357–379). New York: Guilford.

Park, D., Gunderson, E. A., Tsukayama, E., Levine, S. C., & Beilock, S. L. (2016). Young children's motivational frameworks and math achievement: Relation to teacher-reported instructional practices, but not teacher theory of intelligence. *Journal of Educational Psychology, 108*(3), 300–313. https://doi.org/10.1037/edu0000064

Parker, S. K., Bindl, U. K., & Strauss, K. (2010). Making things happen: A model of proactive motivation. *Journal of Management, 36*(4), 827–856. https://doi.org/10.1177/0149206310363732

Pekrun, R. (2018). Control-value theory: A social-cognitive approach to achievement emotions. In G. A. D. Liem & D. M. McInerney (Eds.), *Big theories revisited 2: A volume of research on sociocultural influences on motivation and learning* (pp. 162–190). Charlotte, NC: Information Age.

Pekrun, R., & Marsh, H. W. (2018). Weiner's attribution theory: Indispensable – but is it immune to crisis? *Motivation Science, 4*(1), 19–20. https://doi.org/10 .1037/mot0000096

Peters, K., Jetten, J., Radova, D., & Austin, K. (2017). Gossiping about deviance: Evidence that deviance spurs the gossip that builds bonds. *Psychological Science, 28*(11), 1610–1619. https://doi.org/10.1177/0956797617716918

Peterson, C., & Seligman, M. E. P. (2004). *Character strengths and virtues: A handbook and classification.* Oxford: Oxford University Press.

Pietromonaco, P. R., & Collins, N. L. (2017). Interpersonal mechanisms linking close relationships to health. *American Psychologist, 72*(6), 531–542. https://doi .org/10.1037/amp0000129

Pintrich, P. R. (1994). Continuities and discontinuities: Future directions for research in educational psychology. *Educational Psychologist, 29*(3), 137–148. https://doi.org/10.1207/s15326985ep2903_3

Pitman, R. K. (2011). Will reconsolidation blockade offer a novel treatment for posttraumatic stress disorder? *Frontiers of Behavioral Neuroscience, 5*(11), 1–2. https://doi.org/10.3389/fnbeh.2011.00011

Plutchik, R. (1980). *Emotion: A psychoevolutionary synthesis.* New York: Harper & Row.

Porfeli, E. J., Lee, B., & Vondracek, F. W. (2013). Identity development and careers in adolescents and emerging adults: Content, process, and structure. In M. L. Savickas & W. B. Walsh (Eds.), *Handbook of vocational psychology: Theory, research, and practice* (pp. 133–154). New York: Routledge.

Post, S. G. (2005). Altruism, happiness, and health: It's good to be good. *International Journal of Behavioral Medicine, 12*(2), 66–77. https://doi.org/10 .1207/s15327558ijbm1202_4

Post, S. G. (Ed.). (2007). *Altruism and health: Perspectives from empirical research.* Oxford: Oxford University Press. https://doi.org/10.1093/acprof:oso/97801951 82910.001.0001

Poulin, M. J., Holman, E. A., & Buffone, A. (2012). The neurogenetics of nice: Receptor genes for oxytocin and vasopressin interact with threat to predict prosocial behavior. *Psychological Science, 23*(5), 446–452. https://doi.org/10.1177 /0956797611428471

Powell, M. (2011, September 20). A knack for bashing orthodoxy. *New York Times,* p. D1.

Powers, W. T. (1973). *Behavior: The control of perception.* Chicago: Aldine.

Powers, W. T. (1989). *Living control systems.* Gravel Switch, KY: Control Systems Group.

Press, W. H., & Dyson, F. J. (2012). Iterated Prisoner's Dilemma contains strategies that dominate any evolutionary opponent. *Proceedings of the National Academy of Sciences of the USA, 109*(26), 10409–10413. https://doi.org /10.1073/pnas.1206569109

Prigogine, I., & Stengers, I. (1984). *Order out of chaos.* New York: Bantam.

Prochaska, J. O., & Norcross, J. C. (2019). *Systems of psychotherapy: A transtheoretical analysis* (9th ed.). Oxford: Oxford University Press.

Proulx, T., Markman, K. D., & Lindberg, M. J. (2013). Introduction: The new science of meaning. In K. D. Markman, T. Proulx, & M. J. Lindberg (Eds.), *The psychology of meaning* (pp. 3–14). Washington, DC: American Psychological Association.

Rabin, M., & Schrag, J. L. (1999). First impressions matter: A model of confirmatory bias. *The Quarterly Journal of Economics, 114*(1), 37–82. https://doi.org /10.1162/003355399555945

Raby, K. L., Lawler, J. M., Shlafer, R. J., Hesemeyer, P. S., Collins, W. A., & Sroufe, L. A. (2015). The interpersonal antecedents of supportive parenting: A prospective, longitudinal study from infancy to adulthood. *Developmental Psychology, 51*(1), 115–123. https://doi.org/10.1037/a0038336

Rand, D. G., Greene, J. D., & Nowak, M. A. (2012). Spontaneous giving and calculated greed. *Nature, 489,* 427–430. https://doi.org/10.1038/nature11467

Rattan, A., Savani, K., Chugh, D., & Dweck, C. S. (2015). Leveraging mindsets to promote academic achievement: Policy recommendations. *Perspectives on Psychological Science, 10*(6), 721–726. https://doi.org/10.1177/1745691615599383

Redsand, A. S. (2006). *Victor Frankl: A life worth living.* New York: Clarion.

Reker, G. T., Peacock, E. J., & Wong, P. T. P. (1987). Meaning and purpose in life and well-being: A life-span perspective. *Journal of Gerontology, 42*(1), 44–49. https://doi.org/10.1093/geronj/42.1.44

Reeve, J. (2013). How students create motivationally supportive learning environments for themselves: The concept of agentic engagement. *Journal of Educational Psychology, 105*(3), 579–595. https://doi.org/10.1037/a0032690

Richerson, P. J., Bettinger, R. L., & Boyd, R. (2005). Evolution on a restless planet: Were environmental variability and environmental change major drivers of human evolution? In F. M. Wuketits & F. J. Ayala (Eds.), *Handbook of evolution: Vol. 2. The evolution of living systems (including hominids).* New York: Wiley.

Richerson, P. J., & Boyd, R. (2005). *Not by genes alone: How culture transformed human evolution.* Chicago: University of Chicago Press. https://doi.org/10.7208 /chicago/9780226712130.001.0001

Ridley, M. (1996). *The origins of virtue: Human instincts and the evolution of cooperation.* New York: Penguin.

Rilling, J. K., Glenn, A. L., Jairam, M. R., Pagnoni, G., Goldsmith, D. R., Elfenbein, H. A., & Lilienfeld, S. O. (2007). Neural correlates of social cooperation and non-cooperation as a function of psychopathy. *Biological Psychiatry, 61*(11), 1260–1271. https://doi.org/10.1016/j.biopsych.2006.07.021

Rilling, J. K., Gutman, D. A., Zeh, T. R., Pagnoni, G., Berns, G. S., & Kilts, C. D. (2002). A neural basis for social cooperation. *Neuron, 35*(2), 395–405. https://doi.org/10.1016/S0896-6273(02)00755-9

Rilling, J. K., King-Casas, B., & Sanfey, A. G. (2008). The neurobiology of social decision-making. *Current Opinion in Neurobiology, 18*(2), 159–165. https://doi .org/10.1016/j.conb.2008.06.003

Rizzolatti, G., & Craighero, L. (2004). The mirror-neuron system. *Annual Review of Neuroscience, 27,* 169–192. https://doi.org/10.1146/annurev.neuro.27.070203.144230

Roberts, W. A. (2002). Are animals stuck in time? *Psychological Bulletin, 128*(3), 473–489. https://doi.org/10.1037/0033-2909.128.3.473

Rogers, C. R. (1961). *On becoming a person: A therapist's view of psychotherapy.* Boston: Houghton Mifflin.

Romano, A., & Balliet, D. (2017). Reciprocity outperforms conformity to promote cooperation. *Psychological Science, 28*(10), 1490–1502. https://doi.org/10.1177/0956797617714828

Roskes, M., Elliot, A. J., & De Dreu, C. K. W. (2014). Why is avoidance motivation problematic, and what can be done about it? *Current Directions in Psychological Science, 23*(2), 133–138. https://doi.org/10.1177/0963721414524224

Rosso, B. D., Dekas, K. H., & Wrzesniewski, A. (2010). On the meaning of work: A theoretical integration and review. *Research in Organizational Behavior, 30,* 91–127. https://doi.org/10.1016/j.riob.2010.09.001

Rotella, B. (1995). *Golf is not a game of perfect.* New York: Simon & Schuster.

Rothbaum, F., Weisz, J. R., & Snyder, S. S. (1982). Changing the world and changing the self: A two-process model of perceived control. *Journal of Personality and Social Psychology, 42*(1), 5–37. https://doi.org/10.1037/0022-3514.42.1.5

Rotter, J. B. (1966). Generalized expectancies for internal versus external control of reinforcement. *Psychological Monographs: General and Applied, 80*(1), 1–28. https://doi.org/10.1037/h0092976

Routledge, C., Sedikides, C., Wildschut, T., & Juhl, J. (2013). Finding meaning in one's past: Nostalgia as an existential resource. In K. D. Markman, T. Proulx, & M. J. Lindberg (Eds.), *The psychology of meaning* (pp. 297–316). Washington, DC: American Psychological Association. https://doi.org/10.1037/14040-015

Russell, J. A. (1991). Culture and the categorization of emotions. *Psychological Bulletin, 110*(3), 426–450. https://doi.org/10.1037/0033-2909.110.3.426

Ryan, R. M. (2012). (Ed.). *The Oxford handbook of human motivation.* Oxford: Oxford University Press. https://doi.org/10.1093/oxfordhb/9780195399820.001.0001

Ryan, R. M. (2019). (Ed.). *The Oxford handbook of human motivation* (2nd ed.). Oxford: Oxford University Press. https://doi.org/10.1093/oxfordhb/9780190666453.001.0001

Ryan, R. M., & Deci, E. L. (2001). On happiness and human potentials: A review of research on hedonic and eudaimonic well-being. *Annual Review of Psychology, 52,* 141–166. https://doi.org/10.1146/annurev.psych.52.1.141

Ryan, R. M., & Deci, E. L. (2018). *Self-determination theory: Basic psychological needs in motivation, development, and wellness.* New York: Guilford.

Ryff, C. D., & Singer, B. H. (1998). The role of purpose in life and personal growth in positive human health. In P. T. P. Wong & P. S. Fry (Eds.), *The human quest for meaning: A handbook of psychological research and clinical applications* (pp. 213–235). Mahwah, NJ: Erlbaum.

Ryff, C. D., & Singer, B. H. (Eds.). (2001). *Emotion, social relationships, and health*. Oxford: Oxford University Press. https://doi.org/10.1093/acprof:oso/9780195145410.001.0001

Ryff, C. D., & Singer, B. H. (2008). Know thyself and become what you are: A eudaimonic approach to psychological well-being. *Journal of Happiness Studies, 9*(1), 13–39. https://doi.org/10.1007/s10902-006-9019-0

Sanfey, A. G., Rilling, J. K., Aronson, J. A., Nystrom, L. E., & Cohen, J. D. (2003). The neural basis of economic decision-making in the ultimatum game. *Science, 300*(5626), 1755–1758. https://doi.org/10.1126/science.1082976

Saphire-Bernstein, S., Way, B. M., Kim, H. S., Sherman, D. K., & Taylor, S. E. (2011). Oxytocin receptor gene (OXTR) is related to psychological resources. *Proceedings of the National Academy of Sciences of the USA, 108*(37), 15118–15122. https://doi.org/10.1073/pnas.1113137108

Scarmeas, N., & Stern, Y. (2003). Cognitive reserve and lifestyle. *Journal of Clinical and Experimental Neuropsychology, 25*(5), 625–633. https://doi.org/10.1076/jcen.25.5.625.14576

Scheier, M. F., & Carver, C. S. (2018). Dispositional optimism and physical health: A long look back, a quick look forward. *American Psychologist, 73*(9), 1082–1094. https://doi.org/10.1037/amp0000384

Schetter, C. D. (2017). Moving research on health and close relationships forward – a challenge and an obligation: Introduction to the special issue. *American Psychologist, 72*(6), 511–516. https://doi.org/10.1037/amp0000158

Schork, N. J. (2015). Personalized medicine: Time for one-person trials. *Nature, 520*(7549), 609–611. https://doi.org/10.1038/520609a

Schueller, S. M., & Seligman, M. E. P. (2006). Pursuit of pleasure, engagement, and meaning: Relationships to subjective and objective measures of well-being. *Journal of Positive Psychology, 5*(4), 253–263. https://doi.org/10.1080/17439760003794130

Searle, J. R. (1981). The intentionality of intention and action. *Separata de Manuscrito, 4*, 77–101.

Sedikides, C., & Wildschut, T. (2018). Finding meaning in nostalgia. *Review of General Psychology, 22*(1), 48–61. https://doi.org/10.1037/gpr0000109

Seligman, M. E. P. (1975). *Helplessness: On depression, development, and death*. San Francisco: Freeman.

Seligman, M. E. P. (1991). *Learned optimism*. New York: Knopf.

Seligman, M. E. P. (2002). *Authentic happiness*. New York: Free Press.

Seligman, M. E. P., & Csikszentmihalyi, M. (2000). Positive psychology: An introduction. *American Psychologist, 55*(1), 5–14. https://doi.org/10.1037//0003-066x.55.1.5

Seligman, M. E. P., Railton, P., Baumeister, R. F., & Sripada, C. (2013). Navigating into the future or driven by the past. *Perspectives on Psychological Science, 8*(2), 119–141. https://doi.org/10.1177/1745691612474317

Semendeferi, K., & Damasio, H. (2000). The brain and its main anatomical subdivisions in living hominoids using magnetic resonance imaging. *Journal of Human Evolution, 38*(2), 317–332. https://doi.org/10.1006/jhev.1999.0381

Sherif, M., Harvey, O. J., White, B. J., Hood, W. R., & Sherif, C. W. (1988). *The Robbers Cave experiment: Intergroup conflict and cooperation*. Middletown, CT: Wesleyan University Press.

Shih, P. M. (2015). Photosynthesis and early Earth. *Current Biology*, *25*(19), R855–R859. https://doi.org/10.1016/j.cub.2015.04.046

Silk, J. S., Steinberg, L., & Morris, A. S. (2003). Adolescents' emotion regulation in daily life: Links to depressive symptoms and problem behavior. *Child Development*, *74*(6), 1869–1880. https://doi.org/10.1046/j.1467-8624.2003.00643.x

Silver, R. C., & Updegraff, J. A. (2013). Searching for and finding meaning following personal and collective traumas. In K. D. Markman, T. Proulx, & M. J. Lindberg (Eds.), *The psychology of meaning* (pp. 237–255). Washington, DC: American Psychological Association. https://doi.org/10.1037/14040-012

Silvers, J. A., & Haidt, J. (2008). Moral elevation can induce nursing. *Emotion*, *8*(2), 291–295. https://doi.org/10.1037/1528-3542.8.2.291

Simon, H. A. (1967). Motivational and emotional control of cognition. *Psychological Review*, *74*(1), 29–39. https://doi.org/10.1037/h0024127

Simpson, J. A. (2007). Psychological foundations of trust. *Current Directions in Psychological Science*, *16*(5), 264–268. https://doi.org/10.1111/j.1467-8721.2007.00517.x

Singer, T. (2006). The neuronal basis and ontogeny of empathy and mind reading: Review of literature and implications for future research. *Neuroscience and Biobehavioral Reviews*, *30*(6), 855–863. https://doi.org/10.1016/j.neubiorev.2006.06.011

Singer, T., & Lamm, C. (2009). The social neuroscience of empathy. *Annals of the New York Academy of Sciences*, *1156*, 81–96. https://doi.org/10.1111/j.1749-6632.2009.04418.x

Singer, T., Seymour, B., O'Doherty, J. P., Stephan, K. E., Dolan, R. J., & Frith, C. D. (2006). Empathic neural responses are modulated by the perceived fairness of others. *Nature*, *439*, 466–469. https://doi.org/10.1038/nature04271

Skinner, B. F. (1974). *About behaviorism*. New York: Knopf.

Skinner, E. A., Pitzer, J. R., & Steele, J. S. (2016). Can student engagement serve as a motivational resource for academic coping, persistence, and learning during late elementary and early middle school? *Developmental Psychology*, *52*(12), 2099–2117. https://doi.org/10.1037/dev0000232

Slavin, R. E. (1981). When does cooperative learning increase student achievement? *Psychological Bulletin*, *94*(3), 429–445. https://doi.org/10.1037/0033-2909.94.3.429

Slavin, R. E. (1987). Developmental and motivational perspectives on cooperative learning: A reconciliation. *Child Development*, *58*(5), 1161–1167. https://doi.org/10.2307/1130612

Snyder, C. R. (1994). *The psychology of hope: You can get there from here*. New York: Free Press.

Snyder, C. R., & Lopez, S. J. (Eds.). (2002). *Handbook of positive psychology*. Oxford: Oxford University Press.

Snyder, C. R., & Lopez, S. J. (Eds.). (2009). *Handbook of positive psychology* (2nd ed.). Oxford: Oxford University Press. https://doi.org/10.1093/oxfordhb/9780195187243.001.0001

Snyder, C. R., Rand, K. L., & Sigmon, D. R. (2002). Hope theory: A member of the positive psychology family. In C. R. Snyder & S. J. Lopez (Eds.), *Handbook of positive psychology* (pp. 257–276). Oxford: Oxford University Press.

Sober, E., & Wilson, D. S. (1998). *Unto others: The evolution and psychology of unselfish behavior*. Cambridge, MA: Harvard University Press.

Spence, J. T., & Helmreich, R. L. (1978). *Masculinity and femininity: Their psychological dimensions, correlates, and antecedents*. Austin: University of Texas Press.

Spivack, G., Platt, J. J., & Shure, M. B. (1976). *The problem-solving approach to adjustment*. San Francisco: Jossey-Bass.

Sroufe, L. A. (1983). Infant-caregiver attachment and patterns of adaptation in preschool: The roots of maladaptation and competence. In M. Perlmutter (Ed.), *Minnesota symposium on child psychology* (Vol. 16, pp. 41–83). Hillsdale, NJ: Erlbaum.

Sroufe, L. A. (2005). Attachment and development: A prospective, longitudinal study from birth to adulthood. *Attachment and Human Development, 7*(4), 349–367. https://doi.org/10.1080/14616730500365928

Sroufe, L. A., & Waters, E. (1977). Attachment as an organizational construct. *Child Development, 48*(4), 1184–1199. https://doi.org/10.2307/1128475

Steger, M. F. (2012). Making meaning in life. *Psychological Inquiry, 23*(4), 381–385. https://doi.org/10.1080/1047840X.2012.720832

Steger, M. F., & Frazier, P. (2005). Meaning in life: One link in the chain from religiousness to well-being. *Journal of Counseling Psychology, 52*(4), 574–582. https://doi.org/10.1037/0022-0167.52.4.574

Steinberg, A., & Ritzmann, R. F. (1990). A living systems approach to understanding the concept of stress. *Behavioral Science, 35*(2), 138–146. https://doi.org/10.1002/bs.3830350206

Steinberg, L. (2005). Cognitive and affective development in adolescence. *Trends in Cognitive Science, 9*(2), 69–74. https://doi.org/10.1016/j.tics.2004.12.005

Stellar, J. E., Gordon, A. M., Piff, P. K., Cordaro, D. T., Anderson, C. L., Bai, Y., . . .Keltner, D. (2017). Self-transcendent emotions and their social functions: Compassion, gratitude, and awe bind us to others through prosociality. *Emotion Review, 9*(3), 200–207. https://doi.org/10.1177/1754073916684557

Steptoe, A., Shankar, A., Demakakos, P., & Wardle, J. (2013). Social isolation, loneliness, and all-cause mortality in older men and women. *Proceedings of the National Academy of Sciences of the USA, 110*(15), 5797–5801. https://doi.org/10.1073/pnas.1219686110

Stern, Y. (2006). Cognitive reserve and Alzheimer disease. *Alzheimer Disease & Associated Disorders, 20*(3, Suppl. 2), S69–S74. https://doi.org/10.1097/00002093-200607001-00010

Sternberg, R. J. (Ed.). (2003). *Why smart people can be so stupid*. New Haven, CT: Yale University Press.

Sternberg, R. J., & Horvath, J. A. (1999). *Tacit knowledge in professional practice: Researcher and practitioner perspectives.* Hillsdale, NJ: Erlbaum. https://doi.org /10.4324/9781410603098

Sternberg, R. J., & Spear-Swerling, L. (1998). Personal navigation. In M. Ferrari & R. J. Sternberg (Eds.), *Self-awareness: Its nature and development* (pp. 219–245). New York: Guilford.

Stewart, A. J., & Plotkin, J. B. (2012). Extortion and cooperation in the Prisoner's Dilemma. *Proceedings of the National Academy of Sciences of the USA, 109*(26), 10134–10135. https://doi.org/10.1073/pnas.1208087109

Strathearn, L., Fonagy, P., Amico, J., & Montague, P. R. (2009). Adult attachment predicts maternal brain and oxytocin response to infant cues. *Neuropsychopharmacology, 34,* 2655–2666. https://doi.org/10.1038/npp.2009.103

Stringer, C. (2012). *Lone survivors: How we came to be the only humans on earth.* New York: Times Books.

Strohminger, N., Knobe, J., & Newman, G. (2017). The true self: A psychological concept distinct from the self. *Perspectives on Psychological Science, 12*(4), 551–560. https://doi.org/10.1177/1745691616689495

Suddendorf, T. (2006). Foresight and evolution of the human mind. *Science, 312* (5776), 1006–1007. https://doi.org/10.1126/science.1129217

Suddendorf, T., & Corballis, M. C. (1997). Mental time travel and the evolution of the human mind. *Genetic, Social, and General Psychology Monographs, 123*(2), 133–167.

Suddendorf, T., & Corballis, M. C. (2007). The evolution of foresight: What is mental time travel, and is it unique to humans? *Behavioral and Brain Sciences, 30* (3), 299–313. https://doi.org/10.1017/S0140525X07001975

Taylor, S. E., & Brown, J. D. (1994). Positive illusions and well-being revisited: Separating fact from fiction. *Psychological Bulletin, 116*(1), 21–27. https://doi.org /10.1037/0033-2909.116.1.21

Taylor, S. E., Dickerson, S. S., & Klein, L. C. (2002). Toward a biology of social support. In C. R. Snyder & S. J. Lopez (Eds.), *Handbook of positive psychology* (pp. 556–569). Oxford: Oxford University Press.

Tesser, A. (1986). Some effects of self-evaluation maintenance on cognition and action. In R. M. Sorrentino & E. T. Higgins (Eds.), *Handbook of motivation and cognition: Foundations of social behavior* (pp. 435–464). New York: Guilford.

Thaler, R. H., & Sunstein, C. R. (2008). *Nudge: Improving decisions about health, wealth, and happiness.* New Haven, CT: Yale University Press.

Thoits, P. A. (2010). Stress and health: Major findings and policy implications. *Journal of Health and Social Behavior, 51*(1, Suppl.), S41–S53. https://doi.org/10 .1177/0022146510383499

Thompson, R. A. (1991). Emotional regulation and emotional development. *Educational Psychology Review, 3*(4), 269–307. https://doi.org/10.1007 /BF01319934

Thompson, R. A. (2011). Emotion and emotion regulation: Two sides of the same coin. *Emotion Review, 3*(1), 53–61. https://doi.org/10.1177/1754073910380969

Thompson, R. A., Lewis, M. D., & Calkins, S. D. (2008). Reassessing emotion regulation. *Child Development Perspectives, 2*(3), 124–131. https://doi.org/10.1111/j.1750-8606.2008.00054.x

Tisak, M. S., & Ford, M. E. (1986). Children's conceptions of interpersonal events. *Merrill-Palmer Quarterly, 32*(3), 291–306.

Tomasello, M. (2009). *Why we cooperate*. Cambridge, MA: MIT Press. https://doi.org/10.7551/mitpress/8470.001.0001

Tulving, E. (1985). *Elements of episodic memory*. Oxford: Oxford University Press.

Vaillant, G. E. (2002). *Aging well: Surprising guideposts to a happier life from the landmark Harvard study of adult development*. New York: Little, Brown.

Van Lange, P. A. M. (2015). Generalized trust: Four lessons from genetics and culture. *Current Directions in Psychological Science, 24*(1), 71–76. https://doi.org/10.1177/0963721414552473

Van Tongeren, D. R., DeWall, C. N., Green, J. D., Cairo, A. H., Davis, D. E., & Hook, J. N. (2018). Self-regulation facilitates meaning in life. *Review of General Psychology, 22*(1), 95–106. https://doi.org/10.1037/gpr0000121

Vaux, A. (1988). *Social support: Theory, research, and intervention*. New York: Praeger.

Verduyn, P., & Lavrijsen, S. (2015). Which emotions last longest and why: The role of event importance and rumination. *Motivation and Emotion, 39*(1), 119–127. https://doi.org/10.1007/s11031-014-9445-y

Vohs, K. D., & Baumeister, R. F. (2016). *Handbook of self-regulation: Research, theory, and applications*. New York: Guilford.

von Bertalanffy, L. (1975). *Perspectives on general systems theory*. New York: George Braziller.

von Dawans, B., Fischbacher, U., Kirschbaum, C., Fehr, E., & Heinrichs, M. (2012). The social dimension of stress reactivity: Acute stress increases prosocial behavior in humans. *Psychological Science, 23*(6), 651–660. https://doi.org/10.1177/0956797611431576

Vondracek, F. W., Ferreira, J. A. G., & Santos, E. J. R. (2010). Vocational behavior and development in times of social change: New perspectives for theory and practice. *International Journal for Educational and Vocational Guidance, 10*(2), 125–138. https://doi.org/10.1007/s10775-010-9176-x

Vondracek, F. W., Ford, D. H., & Porfeli, E. J. (2014). *A living systems theory of vocational behavior and development*. Rotterdam, Netherlands: Sense. https://doi.org/10.1007/978-94-6209-662-2

Vondracek, F. W., & Porfeli, E. J. (2011). Fostering self-concept and identity constructs in developmental career psychology. In P. J. Hartung & L. M. Subich (Eds.), *Developing self in work and career: Concepts, cases, and contexts* (pp. 53–70). Washington, DC: American Psychological Association. https://doi.org/10.1037/12348-004

Wagner, A. (2014). *Arrival of the fittest: Solving evolution's greatest puzzle*. New York: Current.

Walsh, A., & Wu, H-H. (2008). Differentiating antisocial personality disorder, psychopathy, and sociopathy: Evolutionary, genetic, neurological, and sociological considerations. *Criminal Justice Studies, 21*(2), 135–152. https://doi .org/10.1080/14786010802159814

Walter, N. T., Markett, S. A., Montag, C., & Reuter, M. (2011). A genetic contribution to cooperation: Dopamine-relevant genes are associated with social facilitation. *Social Neuroscience, 6*(3), 289–301. https://doi.org/10.1080/17 470919.2010.527169

Warneken, F. (2015). Precocious prosociality: Why do young children help? *Child Development Perspectives, 9*(1), 1–6. https://doi.org/10.1111/cdep.12101

Warneken, F., & Tomasello, M. (2006). Altruistic helping in human infants and young chimpanzees. *Science, 311*(5765), 1301–1303. https://doi.org/10.1126/sci ence.1121448

Warneken, F., & Tomasello, M. (2013). Parental presence and encouragement do not influence helping in young children. *Infancy, 18*(3), 345–368. https://doi.org /10.1111/j.1532-7078.2012.00120.x

Waterman, A. S. (1993). Two conceptions of happiness: Contrasts of personal expressiveness (eudaimonia) and hedonic enjoyment. *Journal of Personality and Social Psychology, 64*(4), 678–691. https://doi.org/10.1037/0022–3514.64.4.678

Waters, E., Wippman, J., & Sroufe, L. A. (1979). Attachment, positive affect, and competence in the peer group: Two studies in construct validation. *Child Development, 50*(3), 821–829. https://doi.org/10.2307/1128949

Watson, C. B., Chemers, M. M., & Preiser, N. (2001). Collective efficacy: A multilevel analysis. *Personality and Social Psychology Bulletin, 27*(8), 1057–1068. https://doi.org/10.1177/0146167201278012

Watson, J. B. (1930). *Behaviorism.* New York: Norton.

Waytz, A., Hershfield, H. E., & Tamir, D. I. (2015). Mental simulation and meaning in life. *Journal of Personality and Social Psychology, 108*(2), 336–355. https://doi.org/10.1037/a0038322

Wegner, D. M. (2002). *The illusion of conscious will.* Cambridge, MA: MIT Press. https://doi.org/10.7551/mitpress/3650.001.0001

Weiner, B. (1986). *An attributional theory of motivation and emotion.* New York: Springer Verlag. https://doi.org/10.1007/978-1-4612-4948-1

Weinstein, N., Przybylski, A. K., & Ryan, R. M. (2013). The integrative process: New research and future directions. *Current Directions in Psychological Science, 22*(1), 69–74. https://doi.org/10.1177/0963721412468001

Weissberg, R. P. (2019). Promoting the social and emotional learning of millions of school children. *Perspectives on Psychological Science, 14*(1), 65–69. https://doi .org/10.1177/1745691618817756

Weisz, J. R., & Stipek, D. J. (1982). Competence, contingency, and the development of perceived control. *Human Development, 25*(4), 250–281. https://doi.org /10.1159/000272812

Wentzel, K. R. (1993). Does being good make the grade? Social behavior and academic competence in middle school. *Journal of Educational Psychology, 85*(2), 357–364. https://doi.org/10.1037/0022–0663.85.2.357

Wentzel, K. R. (1996). Social goals and social relationships as motivators of school adjustment. In J. Juvonen & K. R. Wentzel (Eds.), *Social motivation:*

Understanding children's school adjustment (pp. 226–247). Cambridge: Cambridge University Press. https://doi.org/10.1017/cbo9780511571190.012

Wentzel, K. R. (2019). Introduction to the special issue on social and emotional learning. *Educational Psychologist, 54*(3), 127–128. https://doi.org/10.1080/0046 1520.2019.1637739

Wentzel, K. R., & Wigfield, A. (1998). Academic and social motivational influences on students' academic performance. *Educational Psychology Review, 10*(2), 155–175. https://doi.org/10.1023/A:1022137619834

Wheatley, M. J. (1999). *Leadership and the new science: Discovering order in a chaotic world* (2nd ed.). San Francisco: Berrett-Koehler.

White, F. (1987). *The overview effect: Space exploration and human evolution.* Boston: Houghton Mifflin Harcourt.

White, R. W. (1959). Motivation reconsidered: The concept of competence. *Psychological Review, 66*(5), 297–333. https://doi.org/10.1037/h0040934

Wierzbicka, A. (1995). Emotion and facial expression: A semantic perspective. *Culture and Psychology, 1*(2), 227–258. https://doi.org/10.1177/1354067X9512005

Wiggins, J. S., & Holzmuller, A. (1978). Psychological androgyny and interpersonal behavior. *Journal of Consulting and Clinical Psychology, 46*(1), 40–52. https://doi.org/10.1037/0022-006X.46.1.40

Williams, K. D., & Zadro, L. (2001). Ostracism: On being ignored, excluded, and rejected. In M. R. Leary (Ed.), *Interpersonal rejection* (pp. 21–53). Oxford: Oxford University Press. https://doi.org/10.1093/acprof:oso/9780195130157 .003.0002

Wilson, D. S. (2002). *Darwin's cathedral: Evolution, religion, and the nature of society.* Chicago: University of Chicago Press. https://doi.org/10.7208/chicago/ 9780226901374.001.0001

Wilson, D. S. (2007). *Evolution for everyone: How Darwin's theory can change the way we think about our lives.* New York: Delacorte Press.

Wilson, E. O. (2012). *The social conquest of Earth.* New York: Liveright.

Wilson, T. D. (2002). *Strangers to ourselves: Discovering the adaptive unconscious.* Cambridge, MA: Belknap Press. https://doi.org/10.2307/j.ctvjghvsk

Wilson, T. D. (2009). Know thyself. *Perspectives on Psychological Science, 4*(4), 384–389. https://doi.org/10.1111/j.1745–6924.2009.01143.x

Windsor, T. D., Curtis, R. G., & Luszcz, M. A. (2015). Sense of purpose as a psychological resource for aging well. *Developmental Psychology, 51*(7), 975–986. https://doi.org/10.1037/dev0000023

Winell, M. (2019). Personal goals: The key to self-direction in adulthood. In M. E. Ford & D. H. Ford (Eds.,), *Humans as self-constructing living systems: Putting the framework to work* (Routledge psychology library editions: Personality, pp. 261–287). New York: Routledge. (Original work published 1987) https://doi .org/10.4324/9780429025297-9

Winerman, L. (September 2012). Changing our brains, changing ourselves. *APA Monitor, 43*(8), 30.

Witte, F., Goldschmidt, T., Wanink, J., van Oijen, M., Goudswaard, K., Witte-Maas, E., & Bouton, N. (1992). The destruction of an endemic species flock:

Quantitative data on the decline of the haplochromine cichlids of Lake Victoria. *Environmental Biology of Fishes 34*(1), 1–28. https://doi.org/10.1007/BF00004782

Wong, P. T. P. (1998). Spirituality, meaning, and successful aging. In P. T. P. Wong & P. S. Fry (Eds.), *The human quest for meaning: A handbook of psychological research and clinical applications* (pp. 359–394). Mahwah, NJ: Erlbaum.

Wong, P. T. P., & Fry, P. S. (Eds.). (1998). *The human quest for meaning: A handbook of psychological research and clinical applications.* Mahwah, NJ: Erlbaum. https://doi.org/10.4324/9780203146286

Wood R. M., Rilling, J. K., Sanfey, A. G., Bhadwagar, Z., & Rogers, R. D. (2006). Effects of tryptophan depletion on the performance of an iterated Prisoner's Dilemma game in healthy adults. *Neuropsychopharmacology, 31,* 1075–1084. https://doi.org/10/1038/sj.npp.1300932

Woolley, A., Chabris, C., Pentland, S., Hashmi, N., & Malone, T. W. (2010). Evidence for a collective intelligence factor in the performance of human groups. *Science, 330*(6004), 686–688. https://doi.org/10.1126/science.1193147

Wu, J., Balliet, D., & Van Lange, P. A. M. (2016). Gossip versus punishment: The efficiency of reputation to promote and maintain cooperation. *Science Reports, 6,* article no. 23919. https://doi.org/10.1038/srep23919

Wuchty, S., Jones, B. F., & Uzz, B. (2007). The increasing dominance of teams in production of knowledge. *Science, 316*(5827), 1036–1039. https://doi.org/10.1126/science.1136099

Wulfkuhle, J. D., Liotta, L. A., & Petricoin, E. F. (2003). Proteomic applications for the early detection of cancer. *Nature Reviews Cancer, 3,* 267–275. https://doi.org/10.1038/nrc1043

Wynn, K., Bloom, P., Jordan, A., Marshall, J., & Sheskin, M. (2018). Not noble savages after all: Limits to early altruism. *Current Directions in Psychological Science, 27*(1), 3–8. https://doi.org/10.1177/0963721417734875

Yang, F., Choi, Y., Misch, A., Yang, X., & Dunham, Y. (2018). In defense of the commons: Young children negatively evaluate and sanction free riders. *Psychological Science, 29*(10), 1598–1611. https://doi.org/10.1177/0956797618779061

Yang, Y., & Galak, J. (2015). Sentimental value and its influence on hedonic adaptation. *Journal of Personality and Social Psychology, 109*(5), 767–790. https://doi.org/10.1037/pspa0000036

Yeager, D. S., & Dweck, C. S. (2012). Mindsets that promote resilience: When students believe that personal characteristics can be developed. *Educational Psychologist, 47*(4), 302–314. https://doi.org/10.1080/00461520.2012.722805

Yerkes, R. M., & Dodson, J. D. (1908). The relation of strength of stimulus to rapidity of habit-formation. *Journal of Comparative Neurology and Psychology, 18*(5), 459–482. https://doi.org/10.1002/cne.920180503

Zahn-Waxler, C., Radke-Yarrow, M., Wagner, E., & Chapman, M. (1992). Development of concern for others. *Developmental Psychology, 28*(1), 126–136. https://doi.org/10.1037/0012-1649.28.1.126

Zainal, N. H., & Newman, M. G. (2019). Relation between cognitive and behavioral strategies and future change in common mental health problems across 18 years. *Journal of Abnormal Psychology, 128*(4), 295–304. http://doi.org/10.1037/abn0000428

Zak, P. J., Kurzban, R., & Matzner, W. T. (2005). Oxytocin is associated with human trustworthiness. *Hormones and Behavior, 48*(5), 522–527. https://doi.org/10.1016/j.yhbeh.2005.07.009

Zaki, J., & Mitchell, J. P. (2013). Intuitive prosociality. *Current Directions in Psychological Science, 22*(6), 466–470. https://doi.org/10.1177/0963721413492764

Zand, D. E. (1972). Trust and managerial problem solving. *Administrative Science Quarterly, 17*(2), 229–239. https://doi.org/10.2307/2393957

Zika, S., & Chamberlain, K. (1992). On the relation between meaning in life and psychological well-being. *British Journal of Psychology, 83*(1), 133–145. https://doi.org/10.1111/j.2044-8295.1992.tb02429.x

Index

CPSIA information can be obtained
at www.ICGtesting.com
Printed in the USA
LVHW081912161020
669014LV00006B/121